Microsoft® Office 2013 IN PRACTICE

excel COMPLETE

Kari Wood
BEMIDJI STATE UNIVERSITY

Randy Nordell
AMERICAN RIVER COLLEGE

McGraw Hill Education

Microsoft® Office

2013 IN PRACTICE

excel COMPLETE

Wood
Nordell

MICROSOFT OFFICE Excel 2013 Complete: IN PRACTICE
Published by McGraw-Hill/Irwin, a business unit of The McGraw-Hill Companies, Inc., 1221 Avenue of the
Americas, New York, NY, 10020. Copyright © 2014 by The McGraw-Hill Companies, Inc. All rights reserved.
Printed in the United States of America. No part of this publication may be reproduced or distributed in any
form or by any means, or stored in a database or retrieval system, without the prior written consent of The
McGraw-Hill Companies, Inc., including, but not limited to, in any network or other electronic storage or
transmission, or broadcast for distance learning.

Some ancillaries, including electronic and print components, may not be available to customers outside the
United States.

This book is printed on acid-free paper.

2 3 4 5 6 7 8 9 0 QVS/QVS 1 0 9 8 7 6 5 4

ISBN   978-0-07-748690-7
MHID   0-07-748690-0

Senior Vice President, Products & Markets: *Kurt L. Strand*
Vice President, Content Production & Technology Services: *Kimberly Meriwether David*
Director: *Scott Davidson*
Senior Brand Manager: *Wyatt Morris*
Executive Director of Development: *Ann Torbert*
Development Editor II: *Alan Palmer*
Freelance Development Editor: *Erin Mulligan*
Digital Development Editor II: *Kevin White*
Senior Marketing Manager: *Tiffany Russell*
Lead Project Manager: *Rick Hecker*
Buyer II: *Debra R. Sylvester*
Designer: *Jana Singer*
Interior Designer: *Jesi Lazar*
Cover Image: *Corbis Images*
Content Licensing Specialist: *Joanne Mennemeier*
Manager, Digital Production: *Janean A. Utley*
Media Project Manager: *Cathy L. Tepper*
Typeface: *11/13.2 Adobe Caslon Pro*
Compositor: *Laserwords Private Limited*
Printer: *Quad/Graphics*

Library of Congress Cataloging-in-Publication Data

Wood, Kari.
    Microsoft Office Excel 2013 complete: in practice / Kari Wood.
        pages cm
    Includes index.
    ISBN 978-0-07-748691-4 (alk. paper)—ISBN 0-07-748691-9 (alk. paper)
    1. Microsoft Excel (Computer file). 2. Microsoft Office. 3. Electronic spreadsheets—Computer
programs. 4. Business—Computer programs. I. Title.
    HF5548.4.M523W655 2014
    005.5—dc23
                                                                2013022292

The Internet addresses listed in the text were accurate at the time of publication. The inclusion of a website
does not indicate an endorsement by the authors or McGraw-Hill, and McGraw-Hill does not guarantee the
accuracy of the information presented at these sites.

dedication

To my amazing husband, Woody, and to my precious children, Sammie and JD, for their love, inspiration, and patience. Thank you for your encouragement and support through the countless hours I spent on this project.

—Kari Wood

To Kelly. Thank you for your love, support, and encouragement during the seemingly endless hours of writing and editing throughout this project. Your feedback on the content and proofreading were immensely valuable. I could not have done this without you! I'm looking forward to a summer with you without deadlines.

—Randy Nordell

brief contents

contents

CHAPTER 3: CREATING AND EDITING CHARTS   E3-133

CHAPTER 4: IMPORTING, CREATING TABLES, SORTING AND FILTERING, AND USING CONDITIONAL FORMATTING   E4-186

about the authors

KARI WOOD, Ph.D.

Kari Wood is a Professor of Business at Bemidji State University in Bemidji, Minnesota. She has been an educator for over 12 years at the university level and conducted industry software training prior to her professorship. She holds a bachelor's degree in Business Management from Bemidji State University; a master's degree in Business Administration from Minnesota State University, Moorhead; and a doctorate in Organizational Management, with an emphasis in Information Technology from Capella University, in Minneapolis, Minnesota. Kari is a Microsoft Certified Trainer (MCT). She holds Quality Matters (QM) certification as a peer reviewer for online course design and is also a Certified Computer Examiner (CCE). When she is not teaching, Kari enjoys spending time with her family, playing tennis, lifting, running, reading, and watching movies.

RANDY NORDELL, Ed.D.

Randy Nordell is a Professor of Business Technology at American River College in Sacramento, California. He has been an educator for over 20 years and has taught at the high school, community college, and university levels. He holds a bachelor's degree in Business Administration from California State University, Stanislaus; a single subject teaching credential from Fresno State University; a master's degree in Education from Fresno Pacific University; and a doctorate in Education from Argosy University. Randy is the author of *Microsoft Office 2013: In Practice* and *Microsoft Outlook 2010*, and he speaks regularly at conferences on the integration of technology into the curriculum. When he is not teaching, he enjoys spending time with his family, cycling, skiing, swimming, and enjoying the California weather and terrain.

preface

What We're About

We wrote *Microsoft Office Excel 2013 Complete: In Practice* to meet the diverse needs of both students and instructors. Our approach focuses on presenting Office topics in a logical and structured manner, teaching concepts in a way that reinforces learning with practice projects that are transferable, relevant, and engaging. Our pedagogy and content are based on the following beliefs.

Students Need to Learn and Practice Transferable Skills

Students must be able to transfer the concepts and skills learned in the text to a variety of projects, not simply follow steps in a textbook. Our material goes beyond the instruction of many texts. In our content, students practice the concepts in a variety of current and relevant projects *and* are able to transfer skills and concepts learned to different projects in the real world. To further increase the transferability of skills learned, this text is integrated with SIMnet so students also practice skills and complete projects in an online environment.

Your Curriculum Drives the Content

The curriculum in the classroom should drive the content of the text, not the other way around. This book is designed to allow instructors and students to cover all the material they need to in order to meet the curriculum requirements of their courses no matter how the courses are structured. *Microsoft Office Excel 2013 Complete: In Practice* teaches the marketable skills that are key to student success. McGraw-Hill's Custom Publishing site, **Create**, can further tailor the content material to meet the unique educational needs of any school.

Integrated with Technology

Our text provides a fresh and new approach to an Office applications course. Topics integrate seamlessly with SIMnet with 1:1 content to help students practice and master concepts and skills using SIMnet's interactive learning philosophy. Projects in SIMnet allow students to practice their skills and receive immediate feedback. This integration with SIMnet meets the diverse needs of students and accommodates individual learning styles. Additional textbook resources found on the text's Online Learning Center (**www.mhhe.com/office2013inpractice**) integrate with the learning management systems that are widely used in many online and onsite courses.

Reference Text

In addition to providing students with an abundance of real-life examples and practice projects, we designed this text to be used as a Microsoft Office 2013 reference source. The core material, uncluttered with exercises, focuses on real-world use and application. Our text provides clear step-by-step instructions on how readers can apply the various features available in Microsoft Office in a variety of contexts. At the same time, users have access to a variety of both online (SIMnet) and textbook practice projects to reinforce skills and concepts.

Textbook Learning Approach

Microsoft Office Excel 2013 Complete: In Practice uses the *T.I.P. approach:*

- **T**opic
- **I**nstruction
- **P**ractice

Topics

- Each Office application section begins with foundational skills and builds to more complex topics as the text progresses.
- Topics are logically sequenced and grouped by topics.
- Student Learning Outcomes (SLOs) are thoroughly integrated with and mapped to chapter content, projects, end-of-chapter review, and test banks.
- Reports are available within SIMnet for displaying how students have met these Student Learning Outcomes.

Instruction (How To)

- How To guided instructions about chapter topics provide transferable and adaptable instructions.
- Because How To instructions are not locked into single projects, this textbook functions as a reference text, not just a point-and-click textbook.
- Chapter content is aligned 1:1 with SIMnet.

Practice (Pause & Practice and End-of-Chapter Projects)

- Within each chapter, integrated Pause & Practice projects (three to five per chapter) reinforce learning and provide hands-on guided practice.
- In addition to Pause & Practice projects, each chapter has 10 comprehensive and practical practice projects: Guided Projects (three per chapter), Independent Projects (three per chapter), Improve It Project (one per chapter), and Challenge Projects (three per chapter). Additional projects can also be found on **www.mhhe.com/office2013inpractice**.
- Pause & Practice and end-of-chapter projects are complete content-rich projects, not small examples lacking context.
- Select auto-graded projects are available in SIMnet.

Chapter Features

All chapters follow a consistent theme and instructional methodology. Below is an example of chapter structure.

Main headings are organized according to the *Student Learning Outcomes (SLOs)*.

SLO 1.1 **Creating, Saving, and Opening Workbooks**

In Microsoft Excel, the file you create and edit is called a *workbook*. You c workbook from a blank workbook or from an existing, customizable Ex workbook file contains many *worksheets*, which are comparable to individu document. A worksheet is also referred to as a *spreadsheet* or a *sheet*, and terms interchangeably. This book also uses the terms "workbook" and "fil To create a new workbook, first open Excel on your computer.

CHAPTER 1

Creating and Editing Workbooks

CHAPTER OVERVIEW

Microsoft Excel (Excel) is a spreadsheet program you can use to create electronic to organize numerical data, perform calculations, and create charts. Using Excel, bo advanced users can create useful and powerful business spreadsheets. This chap the basics of creating and editing an Excel workbook.

STUDENT LEARNING OUTCOMES (SLOs)

After completing this chapter, you will be able to:

SLO 1.1 Create, save, and open an Excel workbook (p. E1-3).

SLO 1.2 Edit a workbook by entering and deleting text and numbers, using the *Fill Handle* to complete a series, and using the cut, copy, and paste features (p. E1-6).

SLO 1.3 Create a basic formula using *AutoSum* (p. E1-16).

SLO 1.4 Format a worksheet using different font attributes, borders, shading, c styles, themes, and the *Format Painter* (p. E1-19).

SLO 1.5 Resize, insert, delete, and hide and unhide columns and rows in a worksheet (p. E1-26).

SLO 1.6 Insert, delete, edit, format, and rearrange worksheets (p. E1-31).

SLO 1.7 Customize the Excel window by changing views, adjusting zoom level, freezing panes, and splitting a worksheet (p. E1-36).

SLO 1.8 Finalize a workbook by spell checking, adding document properties, applying page setup options, and printing (p. E1-41).

A list of Student Learning Outcomes begins each chapter. All chapter content, examples, and practice projects are organized according to the chapter SLOs.

CASE STUDY

Paradise Lakes Resort (PLR) is a vacation company with four resort chains located throughout northern Minnesota. PLR asks employees to use standard formats for spreadsheets to ensure consistency in spreadsheet appearance. In the Pause & Practice projects for Chapter 1, you create business workbooks for the Paradise Lakes Resort.

Pause & Practice 1-1: Create a business workbook.

Pause & Practice 1-2: Create basic formulas using *AutoSum* and format a workbook.

Pause & Practice 1-3: Customize cell contents and edit spreadsheet structure.

Pause & Practice 1-4: Customize the window and finalize the workbook.

The *Case Study* for each chapter is a scenario that establishes the theme for the entire chapter. Chapter content, examples, figures, Pause & Practice projects, SIMnet skills, and projects throughout the chapter are closely related to this case study content. The three to five Pause & Practice projects in each chapter build upon each other and address key case study themes.

How To instructions enhance transferability of skills with concise steps and screen shots.

HOW TO: Save a New Workbook

1. Click the **File** tab to display *Backstage* view.
2. Select **Save As** on the left to display the *Save As* area (see Figure 1-2).
   - You can also press **Ctrl+S** to open the *Save As* area on *Backstage* view when saving a workbook that has not yet been saved.
3. Select the location where you want to save your workbook.
   - You can save the workbook on your computer, in a *SkyDrive* folder, or on an external storage device.
   - If you click one of the *Recent Folders* options, the *Save As* dialog box opens.
4. Click the **Browse** button to open the *Save As* dialog box (Figure 1-3).
5. Select the location where you want to save the workbook in the left area of the *Save As* dialog box.
6. Type the name of the file in the *File name* area.
7. Click **Save** to close the *Save As* dialog box and save the file.

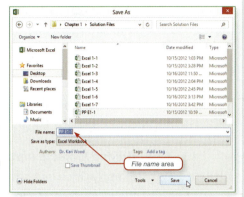

1-3 *Save As* dialog box

How To instructions are easy-to-follow, concise steps. Screen shots and other figures fully illustrate How To topics.

Students can complete hands-on exercises either in the Office application or in SIMnet.

Paradise Lakes Resort (PLR) is a vacation company with four resort chains located throughout northern Minnesota. PLR asks employees to use standard formats for spreadsheets to ensure consistency in spreadsheet appearance. In the Pause & Practice projects for Chapter 1, you create business workbooks for the Paradise Lakes Resort.

Pause & Practice 1-1: Create a business workbook.

Pause & Practice 1-2: Create basic formulas using *AutoSum* and format a workbook.

Pause & Practice 1-3: Customize cell contents and edit spreadsheet structure.

Pause & Practice 1-4: Customize the window and finalize the workbook.

Pause & Practice projects, which each cover two to three of the student learning outcomes in the chapter, provide students with the opportunity to review and practice skills and concepts. Every chapter contains three to five Pause & Practice projects.

> **MORE INFO**
>
> Click the **Alignment** launcher [*Home* tab, *Alignment* group] or press **Ctrl+1** to open the *Format Cells* dialog box, where you can further customize cell contents.

More Info provides readers with additional information about chapter content.

Another Way notations teach alternative methods of accomplishing the same task or feature such as keyboard shortcuts.

▶ **ANOTHER WAY**
Ctrl+F12 opens the *Open* dialog box.

Marginal notations present additional information and alternative methods.

End-of-Chapter Projects

Ten learning projects at the end of each chapter provide additional reinforcement and practice for students. Many of these projects are available in SIMnet for completion and automatic grading.

- ***Guided Projects (three per chapter):*** Guided Projects provide guided step-by-step instructions to apply Office features, skills, and concepts from the chapter. Screen shots guide students through the more challenging tasks. End-of-project screen shots provide a visual of the completed project.
- ***Independent Projects (three per chapter):*** Independent Projects provide students further opportunities to practice and apply skills, instructing them what to do, but not how to do it. These projects allow students to apply previously learned content in a different context.
- ***Improve It Project (one per chapter):*** In these projects, students apply their knowledge and skills to enhance and improve an existing document. Improve It projects are open-ended and allow students to use their critical thinking and creativity to produce attractive professional documents.
- ***Challenge Projects (three per chapter):*** Challenge Projects encourage creativity and critical thinking by integrating Office concepts and features into relevant and engaging projects.

Appendix

- ***Office 2013 Shortcuts:*** Appendix A covers the shortcuts available in Microsoft Office and within each of the specific Office applications. Information is in table format for easy access and reference.

Online Learning Center: www.mhhe.com/office2013inpractice

Students and instructors can find the following resources at the Online Learning Center:

www.mhhe.com/ office2013inpractice

Student Resources

- **Data Files:** Files contain start files for all Pause & Practice, Integration, and end-of-chapter projects.
- **SIMnet Resources:** Resources provide getting started and informational handouts for instructors and students.
- **Check for Understanding:** A combination of multiple choice, fill-in, matching, and short answer questions are available online to assist students in their review of the skills and concepts covered in the chapter.

Integration Projects

- **Integrating Applications:** Projects provide students with the opportunity to learn, practice, and transfer skills using multiple Office applications.
- **Integrating Skills:** Projects provide students with a comprehensive and integrated review of all the topics covered in each application (Word, Excel, Access, and PowerPoint). Available in individual application texts.

Appendices

- **SIMnet User Guide:** Appendix B introduces students to the SIMnet user interface; content demonstrates how to use SIMnet to complete lessons and projects, take quizzes, and search for specific topics as well as how to create practice exercises.
- **Office 2013 for Mac Users:** Appendix C presents instructions for Mac users on how to partition their computer drive to use the PC version of Microsoft Office 2013.
- **Business Document Formats:** Appendix D is a guide to regularly used business document formatting and includes numerous examples and detailed instructions.

Instructor Resources

- **Instructor's Manual:** An Instructor's Manual provides teaching tips and lecture notes aligned with the PowerPoint presentations for each chapter. The Manual also includes the solutions for online **Check for Understanding** questions.
- **Test Bank:** The extensive test bank integrates with learning management systems (LMSs) such as Blackboard, WebCT, Desire2Learn, and Moodle.
- **PowerPoint Presentations:** PowerPoint presentations for each chapter can be used in onsite course formats for lectures or can be uploaded to LMSs.
- **SIMnet Resources:** These resources provide getting started and informational handouts for instructors.
- **Solution Files:** Files contain solutions for all Pause & Practice, Integration, Check for Understanding, and End-of-Chapter projects.

acknowledgments

REVIEWERS

We would like to thank the following instructors, whose invaluable insights shaped the development of this series.

Frank Abnet
Baker College

Sven Aelterman
Troy University

Nisheeth Agrawal
Calhoun Community College

Jack Alanen
California State University

Doug Albert
Finger Lakes Community College

Lancie Anthony Alfonso
College of Charleston

Farha Ali
Lander University

Beverly Amer
Northern Arizona University

Penny Amici
Harrisburg Area Community College

Leon Amstutz
Taylor University

Chris Anderson
North Central Michigan College

Wilma Andrews
Virginia Commonwealth University

Mazhar Anik
Owens Community College

M. Hashem Anwari
Nova Community College

Ralph Argiento
Guilford Technical Community College

Karen M. Arlien
Bismarck State College

Gary Armstrong
Shippensburg University

Tom Ashby
Oklahoma City Community College

Laura Atkins
James Madison University

William Ayen
University of Colorado

Abida Awan
Savannah State University

Ijaz Awan
Savannah State University

Tahir Aziz
J. Sargeant Reynolds Community College

Mark Bagley
Northwestern Oklahoma State University

Greg Ballinger
Miami Dade College

David Barnes
Penn State Altoona

Emily Battaglia
United Education Institute

Terry Beachy
Garrett College

Michael Beard
Lamar University—Beaumont

Anita Beecroft
Kwantlen Polytechnic University

Julia Bell
Walters State Community College

Paula Bell
Lock Haven University of Pennsylvania

David Benjamin
Pace University

Shantanu Bhagoji
Monroe College

Sai Bhatia
Riverside City College

Cindy Hauki Blair
West Hills College

Scott Blanchard
Rockford Career College

Ann Blackman
Parkland College

Jessica Blackwelder
Wilmington University

James Boardman
Alfred State College

John Bodden
Trident Technical College

Gary Bond
New Mexico State University

Abigail Bornstein
City College of San Francisco

Gina Bowers
Harrisburg Area Community College

Craig Bradley
Shawnee Community College

Gerlinde Brady
Cabrillo College

Gerald Braun
Xavier University

Janet Bringhurst
Utah State University

Brenda Britt
Fayetteville Technical Community College

Annie Brown
Hawaii Community College

Judith Brown
University of Memphis

Menka Brown
Piedmont Technical College

Shawn Brown
Kentucky Community & Technical College

Sylvia Brown
Midland College

Cliff Brozo
Monroe College

Barbara Buckner
Lee University

Sheryl Starkey Bulloch
Columbia Southern University

Rebecca Bullough
College of Sequoias

Kate Burkes
Northwest Arkansas Community College

Sharon Buss
Hawkeye Community College

Angela Butler
Mississippi Gulf Coast Community College

Lynn Byrd
Delta State University

Carolyn Calicutt
Saint Louis Community College

Anthony Cameron
Fayetteville Technical Community College

Eric Cameron
Passaic County Community College

Michael Carrington
Nova Community College

Debby Carter
Los Angeles Pierce College

Cesar Augustus Casas
St. Thomas Aquinas College

Sharon Casseday
Weatherford College

Mary Ann Cassidy
Westchester Community College

Terri Castillo
New Mexico Military Institute

Diane Caudill
Kentucky Community & Technical College

Emre Celebi
Louisiana State University

Jim Chaffee
The University of Iowa Tippie College of Business

Jayalaxmi Chakravarthy
Monroe Community College

Bob Chambers
Endicott College

Debra Chapman
University of South Alabama

Marg Chauvin
Palm Beach Community College

Stephen Cheskiewicz
Keystone College

Mark Choman
Luzerne County Community College

Kungwen Chu
Purdue University

Carin Chuang
Purdue University—North Central

Tina Cipriano
Gateway Technical College

Angela Clark
University of South Alabama

James Clark
University of Tennessee

Steve Clements
Eastern Oregon University

Sandra Cobb
Kaplan University

Paulette Comet
Community College of Baltimore County

Marc Condos
American River College

Ronald Conway
Bowling Green State University

Margaret Cooksey
Tallahassee Community College

Lennie Cooper
Miami Dade College—North

Michael Copper
Palm Beach State College—Lake Worth

Terri Cossey
University of Arkansas

Shannon Cotnam
Pitt Community College

Missie Cotton
North Central Missouri College

Charles Cowell
Tyler Junior College

Elaine Crable
Xavier University

Grace Credico
Lethbridge Community College

Doug Cross
Clackamas Community College

Kelli Cross
Harrisburg Area Community College

Geoffrey Crosslin
Kalamazoo Valley Community College

Christy Culver
Marion Technical College

Urska Cvek
Louisiana State University

Penny Cypert
Tarrant County College

Janet Czarnecki
Brown Mackie College

Don Danner
San Francisco State University

Michael Danos
Central Virginia Community College

Louise Darcy
Texas A&M University

Tamara Dawson
Southern Nazarene University

JD Davis
Southwestern College

Elaine Day
Johnson & Wales University

Jennifer Day
Sinclair Community College

Ralph De Arazoza
Miami Dade College

Lucy Decaro
College of Sequoias

Chuck Decker
College of the Desert

Corey DeLaplain
Keiser University East Campus

Edward Delean
Nova Community College Alexandria

Darren Denenberg
University of Nevada—Las Vegas

Joy DePover
Minneapolis Community & Technical College

Charles DeSassure
Tarrant County Community College

John Detmer
Del Mar College

Michael Discello
Pittsburgh Technical College

Sallie Dodson
Radford University

Veronica Dooly
Asheville-Buncombe Technical Community College

Gretchen Douglas
State University of New York College—Cortland

Debra Duke
Cleveland State University

Michael Dumdei
Texarkana College

Michael Dunklebarger
Alamance Community College

Maureen Dunn
Penn State University

Robert Dusek
Nova Community College

Barbara Edington
St. Francis College

Margaret Edmunds
Mount Allison University

Annette Edwards
Tennessee Technology Center

Sue Ehrfurth
Aims Community College

Donna Ehrhart
Genesee Community College

Roland Eichelberger
Baylor University

Issam El-Achkar
Hudson County Community College

Glenda Elser
New Mexico State University

Emanuel Emanouilidis
Kean University

Bernice Eng
Brookdale Community College

Joanne Eskola
Brookdale Community College

Mohammed Eyadat
California State University—Dominguez Hills

Nancy Jo Evans
Indiana University—Purdue University Indianapolis

Phil Feinberg
Palomar College

Deb Fells
Mesa Community College

Patrick Fenton
West Valley College

Jean Finley
Asheville-Buncombe Technical Community College

George Fiori
Tri-County Technical College Pendleton

Richard Flores
Citrus College

Kent Foster
Winthrop University

Penny Foster
Anne Arundel Community College

Brian Fox
Santa Fe College

Deborah Franklin
Bryant & Stratton College

Judith Fredrickson
Truckee Meadows Community College

Dan Frise
East Los Angeles College

Michael Fujita
Leeward Community College

Susan Fuschetto
Cerritos College

Janos Fustos
Metropolitan State College—Denver

Samuel Gabay
Zarem Golde Ort Technical Institute

Brian Gall
Berks Technical Institute

Lois Galloway
Danville Community College

Saiid Ganjalizadeh
The Catholic University of America

Lynnette Garetz
Heald College Corporate Office

Kurt Garner
Pitt Community College

Randolph Garvin
Tyler Junior College

Deborah Gaspard
Southeast Community College

Marilyn Gastineau
University of Louisiana

Bob Gehling
Auburn University—Montgomery

Amy Giddens
Central Alabama Community College

Tim Gill
Tyler Junior College

Sheila Gionfriddo
Luzerne County Community College

Mostafa Golbaba
Langston University Tulsa

Kemit Grafton
Oklahoma State University—Oklahoma City

Deb Gross
Ohio State University

Judy Grotefendt
Kilgore College

Debra Giblin
Mitchell Technical Institute

Robin Greene
Walla Walla Community College

Nancy Gromen
Eastern Oregon University

Lewis Hall
Riverside City College

Linnea Hall
Northwest Mississippi Community College

Kevin Halvorson
Ridgewater College

Peggy Hammer
Chemeketa Community College
Patti Hammerle
Indiana University—Purdue University Indianapolis
Dr. Bill Hammerschlag
Brookhaven College
Danielle Hammoud
West Coast University Corporate Office
John Haney
Snead State Community College
Ashley Harrier
Hillsborough Community College
Ranida Harris
Indiana University Southeast
Dorothy Harman
Tarrant County College
Marie Hartlein
Montgomery County Community College
Shohreh Hashemi
University of Houston Downtown
Michael Haugrud
Minnesota State University
Rebecca Hayes
American River College
Terri Helfand
Chaffey College
Julie Heithecker
College of Southern Idaho
Gerry Hensel
University of Central Florida—Orlando
Cindy Herbert
Metropolitan Community College
Jenny Herron
Paris Junior College
Marilyn Hibbert
Salt Lake Community College
Will Hilliker
Monroe County Community College
Ray Hinds
Florida College
Rachel Hinton
Broome Community College
Emily Holliday
Campbell University
Mary-Carole Hollingsworth
Georgia Perimeter College
Terri Holly
Indian River State College
Timothy Holston
Mississippi Valley State University
David Hood
East Central College
Kim Hopkins
Weatherford College
Wayne Horn
Pensacola Junior College
Christine Hovey
Lincoln Land Community College
Derrick Huang
Florida Atlantic University
Susan Hudgins
East Central University
Jeff Huff
Missouri State University—West Plains
Debbie Huffman
North Central Texas College
Michelle Hulett
Missouri State University
Laura Hunt
Tulsa Community College
Bobbie Hyndman
Amarillo College
Jennifer Ivey
Central Carolina Community College
Bill Jaber
Lee University
Sherry Jacob
Jefferson Community College
Yelena Jaffe
Suffolk University
Rhoda James
Citrus Community College
Ted Janicki
Mount Olive College
Jon Jasperson
Texas A&M University
Denise Jefferson
Pitt Community College
John Jemison
Dallas Baptist University
Joe Jernigan
Tarrant County College—NE
Mary Johnson
Mt. San Antonio College
Mary Johnson
Lone Star College
Linda Johnsonius
Murray State University
Robert Johnston
Heald College
Irene Joos
La Roche College
Yih-Yaw Jou
University of Houston—Downtown

Jan Kamholtz
Bryant & Stratton College
Valerie Kasay
Georgia Southern University
James Kasum
University of Wisconsin
Nancy Keane
NHTI Concord Community College
Michael Keele
Three Rivers Community College
Debby Keen
University of Kentucky
Judith Keenan
Salve Regina University
Jan Kehm
Spartanburg Community College
Rick Kendrick
Antonelli College
Annette Kerwin
College of DuPage
Manzurul Khan
College of the Mainland
Julia Khan-Nomee
Pace University
Karen Kidder
Tri-State Business Institute
Hak Joon Kim
Southern Connecticut State University
James Kirby
Community College of Rhode Island
Chuck Kise
Brevard Community College
Paul Koester
Tarrant County College
Kurt Kominek
Northeast State Tech Community College
Diane Kosharek
Madison Area Technical College
Carolyn Kuehne
Utah Valley University
Ruth Kurlandsky
Cazenovia College
John Kurnik
Saint Petersburg College
Lana LaBruyere
Mineral Area College
Anita Laird
Schoolcraft College
Charles Lake
Faulkner State Community College
Marjean Lake
LDS Business College
Kin Lam
Medgar Evers College
Jeanette Landin
Empire College
Richard Lanigan
Centura College Online
Nanette Lareau
University of Arkansas Community College Morrilton
David Lee Largent
Ball State University
Linda Lannuzzo
LaGuardia Community College
Robert La Rocca
Keiser University
Dawn D. Laux
Purdue University
Deborah Layton
Eastern Oklahoma State College
Art Lee
Lord Fairfax Community College
Ingyu Lee
Troy University
Kevin Lee
Guilford Technical Community College
Leesa Lee
Western Wyoming College
Thomas Lee
University of Pennsylvania
Jamie Lemley
City College of San Francisco
Linda Lemley
Pensacola State College
Diane Lending
James Madison University
Sherry Lenhart
Terra Community College
Julie Lewis
Baker College—Flint
Sue Lewis
Tarleton State University
Jane Liefert
Middlesex Community College
Renee Lightner
Florida State College
Nancy Lilly
Central Alabama Community College
Mary Locke
Greenville Technical College
Maurie Lockley
University of North Carolina
Haibing Lu
San Diego Mesa College

Frank Lucente
Westmoreland County Community College
Clem Lundie
San Jose City College
Alicia Lundstrom
Drake College of Business
Linda Lynam
Central Missouri State University
Lynne Lyon
Durham Technical Community College
Matthew Macarty
University of New Hampshire
Sherri Mack
Butler County Community College
Heather Madden
Delaware Technical Community College
Susan Mahon
Collin College Plano
Nicki Maines
Mesa Community College
Lynn Mancini
Delaware Technical Community College
Amelia Maretka
Wharton County Junior College
Suzanne Marks
Bellevue Community College
Juan Marquez
Mesa Community College
Carlos Martinez
California State University—Dominguez Hills
Santiago Martinez
Fast Train College
Lindalee Massoud
Mott Community College
Joan Mast
John Wood Community College
Deborah Mathews
J. Sargeant Reynolds Community College
Becky McAfee
Hillsborough Community College
Roberta Mcclure
Lee College
Martha McCreery
Rend Lake College
Sue McCrory
Missouri State University
Brian Mcdaniel
Palo Alto College
Rosie Mcghee
Baton Rouge Community College
Jacob McGinnis
Park University
Mike Mcguire
Triton College
Bruce McLaren
Indiana State University
Bill McMillan
Madonna University
David Mcnair
Mount Wachusett Community College
Gloria Mcteer
Ozarks Technical Community College
Dawn Medlin
Appalachian State University
Peter Meggison
Massasoit Community College
Barbara Meguro
University of Hawaii
Linda Mehlinger
Morgan State University
Gabriele Meiselwitz
Towson University
Joni Meisner
Portland Community College
Dixie Mercer
Kirkwood Community College
Donna Meyer
Antelope Valley College
Mike Michaelson
Palomar College
Michael Mick
Purdue University
Debby Midkiff
Huntington Jr. College of Business
Jenna Miley
Bainbridge College
Dave Miller
Monroe County Community College
Pam Milstead
Bossier Parish Community College
Shayan Mirabi
American Intercontinental University
Johnette Moody
Arkansas Tech University
Christine Moore
College of Charleston
Carmen Morrison
North Central State College
Gary Mosley
Southern Wesleyan University
Tamar Mosley
Meridian Community College
Ed Mulhern
Southwestern College

Carol Mull
Greenville Technical College
Melissa Munoz
Dorsey Business School
Marianne Murphy
North Carolina Central University
Karen Musick
Indiana University—Purdue University Indianapolis
Warner Myntti
Ferris State University
Brent Nabors
Reedley College
Shirley Nagg
Everest Institute
Anozie Nebolisa
Shaw University
Barbara Neequaye
Central Piedmont Community College
Patrick Nedry
Monroe County Community College
Melissa Nemeth
Indiana University—Purdue University Indianapolis
Eloise Newsome
Northern Virginia Community College
Yu-Pa Ng
San Antonio College
Fidelis Ngang
Houston Community College
Doreen Nicholls
Mohawk Valley Community College
Brenda Nickel
Moraine Park Technical College
Brenda Nielsen
Mesa Community College
Phil Nielson
Salt Lake Community College
Suzanne Nordhaus
Lee College
Ronald Norman
Grossmont College
Karen Nunam
Northeast State Technical Community College
Mitchell Ober
Tulsa Community College
Teri Odegard
Edmonds Community College
Michael Brian Ogawa
University of Hawaii
Lois Ann O'Neal
Rogers State University
Stephanie Oprandi
Stark State College of Technology
Marianne Ostrowksky
Luzerne County Community College
Shelley Ota
Leeward Community College
Youcef Oubraham
Hudson County Community College
Paul Overstreet
University of South Alabama
John Panzica
Community College of Rhode Island
Donald Paquet
Community College of Rhode Island
Lucy Parker
California State University—Northridge
Patricia Partyka
Schoolcraft College
James Gordon Patterson
Paradise Valley Community College
Laurie Patterson
University of North Carolina
Joanne Patti
Community College of Philadelphia
Kevin Pauli
University of Nebraska
Kendall Payne
Coffeyville Community College
Deb Peairs
Clark State Community College
Charlene Perez
South Plains College
Lisa Perez
San Joaquin Delta College
Diane Perreault
Tusculum College
Michael Picerno
Baker College
Janet Pickard
Chattanooga State Technical Community College
Walter Pistone
Palomar College
Jeremy Pittman
Coahoma Community College
Morris Pondfield
Towson University
James Powers
University of Southern Indiana
Kathleen Proietti
Northern Essex Community College
Ram Raghuraman
Joliet Junior College
Patricia Rahmlow
Montgomery County Community College

Robert Renda
Fulton Montgomery Community College

Margaret Reynolds
Mississippi Valley State University

David Richwine
Indian River State College—Central

Terry Rigsby
Hill College

Laura Ringer
Piedmont Technical College

Gwen Rodgers
Southern Nazarene University

Stefan Robila
Montclair State University

Terry Rooker
Germanna Community College

Seyed Roosta
Albany State University

Sandra Roy
Mississippi Gulf Coast Community College—Gautier

Antoon Rufi
Ecpi College of Technology

Wendy Rader
Greenville Technical College

Harold Ramcharan
Shaw University

James Reneau
Shawnee State University

Robert Robertson
Southern Utah University

Cathy Rogers
Laramie County Community College

Harry Reif
James Madison University

Shaunda Roach
Oakwood University

Ruth Robbins
University of Houston—Downtown

Randy Rose
Pensacola State College

Kathy Ruggieri
Lansdale School of Business

Cynthia Rumney
Middle Georgia Technical College

Paige Rutner
Georgia Southern University

Candice Ryder
Colorado State University

Russell Sabadosa
Manchester Community College

Gloria Sabatelli
Butler County Community College

Glenn Sagers
Illinois State University

Phyllis Salsedo
Scottsdale Community College

Dolly Samson
Hawaii Pacific University

Yashu Sanghvi
Cape Fear Community College

Ramona Santamaria
Buffalo State College

Diane Santurri
Johnson & Wales University

Kellie Sartor
Lee College

Allyson Saunders
Weber State University

Theresa Savarese
San Diego City College

Cem Saydam
University of North Carolina

Jill Schaumloeffel
Garrett College

William Schlick
Schoolcraft College

Rory Schlueter
Glendale College

Art Schneider
Portland Community College

Helen Schneider
University of Findlay

Cheryl Schroeder-Thomas
Towson University

Paul Schwager
East Carolina University

Kay Scow
North Hennepin Community College

Karen Sarratt Scott
University of Texas—Arlington

Michael Scroggins
Missouri State University

Janet Sebesy
Cuyahoga Community College Western

Vicky Seehusen
Metropolitan State College Denver

Paul Seibert
North Greenville University

Pat Serrano
Scottsdale Community College

Patricia Sessions
Chemeketa Community College

Judy Settle
Central Georgia Technical College

Vivek Shah
Texas State University

Abul Sheikh
Abraham Baldwin Agricultural College

Lal Shimpi
Saint Augustine's College

Lana Shryock
Monroe County Community College

Joanne Shurbert
NHTI Concord Community College

Sheila Sicilia
Onondaga Community College

Pam Silvers
Asheville-Buncombe Technical Community College

Eithel Simpson
Southwestern Oklahoma State University

Beth Sindt
Hawkeye Community College

Mary Jo Slater
College of Beaver County

Diane Smith
Henry Ford College

Kristi Smith
Allegany College of Maryland

Nadine Smith
Keiser University

Thomas Michael Smith
Austin Community College

Anita Soliz
Palo Alto College

Don Southwell
Delta College

Mimi Spain
Southern Maine Community College

Sri' V. Sridharan
Clemson University

Diane Stark
Phoenix College

Jason Steagall
Bryant & Stratton College

Linda Stoudemayer
Lamar Institute of Technology

Nate Stout
University of Oklahoma

Lynne Stuhr
Trident Technical College

Song Su
East Los Angeles College

Bala Subramanian
Kean University

Liang Sui
Daytona State College

Denise Sullivan
Westchester Community College

Frank Sun
Lamar University

Beverly Swisshelm
Cumberland University

Cheryl Sypniewski
Macomb Community College

Martin Schedlbauer
Suffolk University

Lo-An Tabar-Gaul
Mesa Community College

Kathleen Tamerlano
Cuyahoga Community College

Margaret Taylor
College of Southern Nevada

Sandra Thomas
Troy University

Joyce Thompson
Lehigh Carbon Community College

Jay Tidwell
Blue Ridge Community and Technical College

Astrid Todd
Guilford Technical Community College

Byron Todd
Tallahassee Community College

Kim Tollett
Eastern Oklahoma State College

Joe Torok
Bryant & Stratton College

Tom Trevethan
Ecpi College of Technology

David Trimble
Park University

Charulata Trivedi
Quinsigamond Community College

Alicia Tyson-Sherwood
Post University

Angela Unruh
Central Washington University

Patricia Vacca
El Camino College

Sue van Boven
Paradise Valley Community College

Scott Van Selow
Edison College—Fort Myers

Linda Kavanaugh Varga
Robert Morris University

Kathleen Villarreal
Apollo University of Phoenix

Asteria Villegas
Monroe Community College

Michelle Vlaich-Lee
Greenville Technical College

Carol Walden
Mississippi Delta Community College

Dennis Walpole
University of South Florida

Merrill Warkentin
Mississippi State University

Jerry Waxman
The City University of New York, Queens College

Sharon Wavle
Tompkins Cortland Community College

Rebecca Webb
Northwest Arkansas Community College

Sandy Weber
Gateway Technical College

Robin Weitz
Ocean County College

Karen Welch
Tennessee Technology Center

Marcia Welch
Highline Community College

Lynne Weldon
Aiken Tech College

Jerry Wendling
Iowa Western Community College

Bradley West
Sinclair Community College

Stu Westin
University of Rhode Island

Billie Jo Whary
McCann School of Business & Technology

Charles Whealton
Delaware Technical Community College

Melinda White
Seminole State College

Reginald White
Black Hawk College

Lissa Whyte-Morazan
Brookline College

Sophia Wilberscheid
Indian River State College

Casey Wilhelm
North Idaho College

Amy Williams
Abraham Baldwin Agricultural College

Jackie Williams
University of North Alabama

Melanie Williamson
Bluegrass Community & Technical College

Jan Wilms
Union University

Rhonda Wilson
Connors State College

Diana Wolfe
Oklahoma State University—Oklahoma City

Veryl Wolfe
Clarion University of Pennsylvania

Paula Worthington
Northern Virginia Community College

Dezhi Wu
Southern Utah University

Judy Wynekoop
Florida Gulf Coast University

Kevin Wyzkiewicz
Delta College

Catherine Yager
Pima Community College

Paul Yaroslaski
Dodge City Community College

Annette Yauney
Herkimer County Community College

Yuqiu You
Morehead State University

Bahram Zartoshty
California State University—Northridge

Suzann Zeger
William Rainey Harper College

Steven Zeltmann
University of Central Arkansas

Cherie Zieleniewski
University of Cincinnati—Batavia

Mary Ann Zlotow
College of DuPage

Laurie Zouharis
Suffolk College

Matthew Zullo
Wake Technical Community College

TECHNICAL EDITORS

Chris Anderson
North Central Michigan College

Susan Fuschetto
Cerritos College

Mary Carole Hollingsworth
Georgia Perimeter College

Sandy Keeter
Seminole State College of Florida

Melinda White
Seminole State College of Florida

Thank you to the wonderful team at McGraw-Hill for your confidence in us and support on this first edition. Paul, Alan, Erin, Wyatt, Tiffany, Rick, and Julianna, we thoroughly enjoy working with you all! Thank you also to Debbie Hinkle, Michael-Brian Ogawa, Laurie Zouharis, Amie Mayhall, Sarah Clifford, Jeanne Reed, Lyn Belisle, and all of the reviewers and technical editors for your expertise and invaluable insight, which helped shape this book.

— Kari, Randy

CHAPTER

1

OFFICE 2013

Windows 8 and Office 2013 Overview

CHAPTER OVERVIEW

Microsoft Office 2013 and Windows 8 introduce many new features including cloud storage for your files, Office file sharing, and enhanced online content. The integration of Office 2013 and Windows 8 means that files are more portable and accessible than ever when you use *SkyDrive*, Microsoft's free online cloud storage. The new user interface on Office 2013 and Windows 8 allows you to work on tablet computers and smart phones in a working environment that resembles that of your desktop or laptop computer.

STUDENT LEARNING OUTCOMES (SLOs)

After completing this chapter, you will be able to:

SLO 1.1 Use the basic features of Windows 8 and Microsoft Office 2013 products (p. O1-2).

SLO 1.2 Create, save, close, and open Office files (p. O1-12).

SLO 1.3 Print, share, and customize Office files (p. O1-20).

SLO 1.4 Use the *Ribbon*, tabs, groups, dialog boxes, task panes, galleries, and the *Quick Access* toolbar (p. O1-23).

SLO 1.5 Use context menus, mini toolbars, and keyboard shortcuts in Office applications (p. O1-27).

SLO 1.6 Customize the view and display size in Office applications and work with multiple Office files (p. O1-31).

SLO 1.7 Organize and customize Office files and Windows folders (p. O1-34).

CASE STUDY

American River Cycling Club (ARCC) is a community cycling club that promotes fitness. ARCC members include recreational cyclists who enjoy the exercise and camaraderie and competitive cyclists who compete in road, mountain, and cyclocross races throughout the cycling season.

In the Pause & Practice projects, you incorporate many of the topics covered in the chapter to create, save, customize, and share Office 2013 files.

Pause & Practice 1-1: Log into Windows using your Microsoft account, customize the Windows *Start* page, open Office files, create a new file, open and rename an existing file, and share a file.

Pause & Practice 1-2: Modify an existing document, add document properties, customize the *Quick Access* toolbar, export a file as a PDF file, and share a document by sending a link.

Pause & Practice 1-3: Modify the working environment in Office and organize files and folders.

Using Windows 8 and Office 2013

Windows 8 is the *operating system* that makes your computer function and controls the working environment. The Office 2013 software provides you with common application programs such as Word, Excel, Access, and PowerPoint. These applications give you the ability to work with word processing documents, spreadsheets, presentations, and databases in your personal and business projects. Although the Windows 8 operating system and the Office software products work together, they have different functions on your computer.

Windows 8

The operating system on your computer makes all of the other software programs, including Office 2013, function. *Windows 8* has a new user interface—the new *Start page*—where you can select and open a program. Alternatively you can go to the *Windows desktop*, which has the familiar look of previous versions of Windows. You also have the option with Windows 8 to log in to your computer using a Windows account that synchronizes your Windows, Office, and *SkyDrive* cloud storage between computers.

Microsoft Account

In Windows 8 and Office 2013, your files and account settings are portable. In other words, your Office settings and files can travel with you and be accessed from different computers. You are not restricted to a single computer. When you create a free *Microsoft account* (Live, Hotmail, MSN, Messenger, or other Microsoft service account), you are given a free email account, a *SkyDrive* account, and access to Office Web Apps. If you do not yet have a Microsoft account, you can create one at www.live.com (Figure 1-1).

1-1 Create a Microsoft account

> ### MORE INFO
> You will use your Microsoft account for projects in this text.

When you sign in to your computer using Windows 8, you can log in with your Microsoft username and password. Windows uses this information to transfer your Office 2013 settings to the computer you are using and connects you to your *SkyDrive* folder.

Start Page

After logging in to Windows 8 using your Microsoft account (see *Pause & Practice: Office 1-1*, Step 1 on page O1–17), you are taken to the *Start page* (Figure 1-2), which is new to Windows 8. The *Start* page displays different *apps* (applications) as tiles (large and small buttons). Click an app tile to launch a program or task.

Windows 8 uses the term *apps* generically to refer to applications and programs. Apps include the Windows 8 Weather app, Microsoft Excel program, Control Panel, Google Chrome, or File Explorer.

When you start using Windows 8, you can customize your *Start* page. Include the apps you most regularly use, remove the apps you don't want displayed on the *Start* page, and rearrange apps tiles to your preference.

1-2 Windows *Start* page

HOW TO: Customize the Start Page

1. To move an app tile, click and drag the app tile to a new location on the *Start* page. The other app tiles shuffle to accommodate the placement of the app tile.

2. To remove an app tile from the *Start* page, right-click the app tile you want to remove to select it and display your options, and then select **Unpin from Start** (Figure 1-3).

   1-3 App options

   • When an app tile is selected, a check mark appears in the upper right corner.
   • The app tile is removed from the *Start* page, but the program or task is not removed from your computer.
   • Your options differ depending on the app tile you select.
   • You can right-click multiple app tiles, one after the other, to select and apply an option to all of them.

3. To add an app tile to the *Start* page, right-click a blank area of the *Start* page and click **All Apps** at the bottom right (Figure 1-4).

   1-4 Display all apps

4. Right-click the app you want to add to select it and click **Pin to Start** (Figure 1-5).

5. To resize an app tile, right-click the app tile to select it and click **Larger** or **Smaller**.

   • All options do not apply to all apps.

6. To uninstall an app, right-click the app you want to uninstall to select it and click **Uninstall**.

   1-5 Pin selected app to *Start* page

   • Unlike the unpin option, this option uninstalls the program from your computer, not just your *Start* page.

Windows 8 Navigation Options

You can access the Windows 8 options and navigate quickly to other areas from the *Start* page, the Windows desktop, or anywhere on your computer. The ***Windows 8 navigation area*** and options appear on the right side of your computer monitor when you place your pointer on the small horizontal line at the bottom right corner (Figure 1-6). The following list describes the different options available from the navigation area:

- **Search:** Displays all of the apps available on your computer and opens a search area at the right of your screen.
- **Share:** Displays options for sharing selected apps with other users.
- **Start:** Displays the *Start* page.
- **Devices:** Displays the devices available on your computer.
- **Settings:** Displays options for customizing computer settings; displays power options (Figure 1-7).

▶ **ANOTHER WAY**

Click the bottom left corner of your computer screen to toggle between the *Start* page and the desktop.

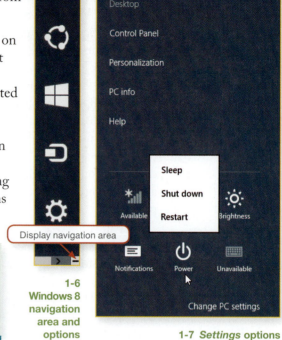

1-6 **Windows 8 navigation area and options**

1-7 *Settings* options

Desktop and Taskbar

The **Windows desktop** is the working area of Windows and is similar to previous versions of Windows. Click the **Desktop** app tile on the *Start* page to go to the desktop (Figure 1-8). When you install a program on your computer, typically a shortcut to the program is added to the desktop. When you open a program from the *Start* page, such as Microsoft Word, the desktop displays and the program opens.

The *Taskbar* displays at the bottom of the desktop. You can open programs and folders from the *Taskbar* by clicking on an icon on the *Taskbar* (Figure 1-9). You can pin programs and other Windows items, such as the Control Panel or File Explorer, to the *Taskbar*.

1-8 Windows *Desktop* tile on the *Start* page

1-9 *Taskbar* at the bottom of the desktop

HOW TO: Pin a Program to the Taskbar

1. Go to the *Start* page if it is not already displayed.
   - Put your pointer in the bottom right corner of your computer monitor and select **Start** in the navigation area.
   - If you are on the desktop, you can also click the **Start page** icon that appears when you place your pointer in the bottom left corner of your monitor.

2. Right-click a program or Windows item to select it (Figure 1-10).
   - A check appears in the upper right of a selected item.
   - Options display at the bottom of the *Start* page.
3. Click **Pin to taskbar**.

> **MORE INFO**
>
> You can drag items on the *Taskbar* to rearrange them.

1-10 Pin selected item to the *Taskbar*

File Explorer

The **File Explorer** is a window that opens on your desktop where you can browse for files stored on your computer (Figure 1-11). This window displays the libraries and folders on your computer on the left. When you select a library or folder on the left, the contents of the selection are displayed on the right. Double-click a file or folder on the right to open it.

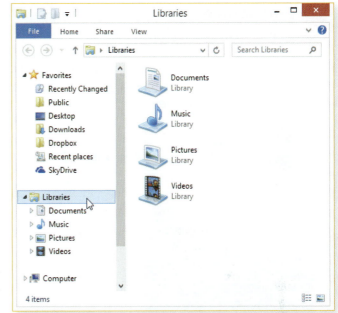

1-11 *File Explorer* window

SkyDrive

SkyDrive is a cloud storage area where you can store files in a private and secure online location that you can access from any computer. With cloud storage you don't have to be tied to one computer, and you don't have to carry your files with you on a portable storage device. When you store your files on *SkyDrive*, the files are actually saved on both your computer and on the cloud. *SkyDrive* synchronizes your files so when you change a file it is automatically updated on the *SkyDrive* cloud.

With Windows 8, the **Sky-Drive folder** is one of your storage location folder options, similar to your *Documents* or *Pictures* folders (Figure 1-12). You can

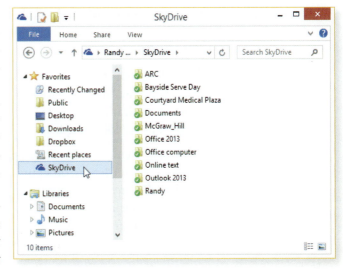

1-12 *SkyDrive* folder

save, open, and edit your *SkyDrive* files from a Windows folder. Your *SkyDrive* folder looks and functions similar to other Windows folders.

In addition to the *SkyDrive* folder on your computer, you can also access your *SkyDrive* files online using an Internet browser such as Internet Explorer, Google Chrome, or Mozilla Firefox. When you access *SkyDrive* online using a web browser, you can upload files, create folders, move and copy files and folders, and create Office files using Office Web Apps (see *Office Web Apps* later in this section).

HOW TO: Use SkyDrive Online

1. Open an Internet browser Window and navigate to the *SkyDrive* website (www.skydrive.com), which takes you to the *SkyDrive* sign in page (Figure 1-13).
   - You can use any Internet browser to access *SkyDrive* (e.g., Internet Explorer, Google Chrome, Mozilla Firefox).
2. Type in your Microsoft account email address and password.
   - If you are on your own computer, check the **Keep me signed in** box to stay signed in to *SkyDrive* when you return to the page.
3. Click the **Sign In** button to go to your *SkyDrive* web page.
   - The different areas of *SkyDrive* are listed under the *SkyDrive* heading on the left (Figure 1-14).
   - Click **Files** to display your folders and files in the folder area.
   - At the top of the page, there are buttons and drop-down menus that list the different actions you can perform on selected files and folders.

1-13 Log in to *SkyDrive* online

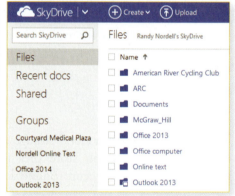

1-14 *SkyDrive* online

Office 2013

Microsoft Office 2013 is a suite of personal and business software applications. Microsoft Office comes in different packages and the applications included in each package vary. The common applications included in Microsoft Office and the primary purpose of each are described in the following list:

- *Microsoft Word:* Word processing software used to create, format, and edit documents such as reports, letters, brochures, and resumes.
- *Microsoft Excel:* Spreadsheet software used to perform calculations on numerical data such as financial statements, budgets, and expense reports.
- *Microsoft Access:* Database software used to store, organize, compile, and report information such as product information, sales data, client information, and employee records.
- *Microsoft PowerPoint:* Presentation software used to graphically present information in slides such as a presentation on a new product or sales trends.

- **Microsoft Outlook:** Email and personal management software used to create and send email and create and store calendar items, contacts, and tasks.
- **Microsoft OneNote:** Note-taking software used to take and organize notes, which can be shared with other Office applications.
- **Microsoft Publisher:** Desktop publishing software used to create professional-looking documents containing text, pictures, and graphics such as catalogs, brochures, and flyers.

Office Web Apps

Office Web Apps is free online software from Microsoft that works in conjunction with your online *SkyDrive* account (Figure 1-15). With Office Web Apps, you can work with Office files online, even on computers that do not have Office 2013 installed. This is a useful option when you use a computer at a computer lab or use a friend's computer that does not have Office 2013 installed.

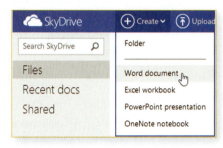

1-15 Office Web Apps

You can access Office Web Apps from your *Sky-Drive* web page and create and edit Word documents, Excel workbooks, PowerPoint presentations, and One-Note notebooks. Office Web Apps is a scaled-down version of Office 2013 and not as robust in terms of features, but you can use it to create, edit, print, share, and insert comments on files. If you need more advanced features, you can open Office Web Apps files in Office 2013.

In *SkyDrive,* you can share files with others. When you share files or folders with others, you establish the access they have to the items you share. You can choose whether other users can only view files or view and edit files. To share a file or folder in your *SkyDrive,* send an email with a link to the shared items or generate a hyperlink that gives access to the shared files to others.

HOW TO: Share an Office Web Apps File

1. Log in to your *SkyDrive* account.
2. Click an Office file to open the file in Office Web Apps.
3. In read-only mode, click the **Share** button above the file. A sharing window opens with different options (Figure 1-16).

   - You can also click the **File** tab and select **Share** on the left.

4. To send an email, click **Send email**, type the recipient's email address, and type a brief message.

1-16 Share an Office Web Apps file

   - Enter a space after typing an email address to add another recipient.
   - Alternatively, you can click **Get a link** to generate a link to send to recipients.

5. Check the **Recipients can edit** box if you want the recipient to be able to edit the file.

   - Deselect this check box if you want recipients to only view the file.
   - You can also require recipients to sign in to *SkyDrive* in order to view or edit the file by checking the **Require everyone who accesses this to sign in** box.

6. Click the **Send** button.

   - Recipients receive an email containing a link to the shared file or folder.
   - A window may open, prompting you to enter a displayed code to prevent unauthorized sharing. Enter the displayed code to return to the sharing window and click **Send**.

7. Click the **X** in the upper right corner or the browser window to exit *SkyDrive.*

Office Web Apps let you synchronously (i.e., at the same time) or asynchronously (i.e., not at the same time) collaborate on an Office file with others who have access to the shared file. If two or more users are working on the same file in Office Web Apps, collaboration information is displayed at the bottom of the Office Web Apps window (Figure 1-17). You are alerted to available updates and told how many people are editing the file.

1-17 Collaboration information displayed in the *Status* bar

Click **Updates Available** in the *Status* bar to apply updates to your file. Click **People Editing** to view the names of users who are currently editing the file.

▶ **MORE INFO**

The *Status* bar is displayed at the bottom of the application window and is available on all Office applications.

Open an Office Application

When using Windows 8, you click an app tile to open an Office application. If your *Start* page has the Office applications displayed, you can click the **Word 2013**, **Excel 2013**, **Access 2013**, or **PowerPoint 2013** tile to launch the application (Figure 1-18).

If the Office application apps are not on the *Start* page, you can search for the app.

1-18 Launch an Office 2013 application

HOW TO: Search for an App

1. Put your pointer at the bottom right corner of your computer screen to display the Windows 8 navigation options.
2. Click **Search** to display all apps and the *Search* pane on the right (Figure 1-19).
3. Type the name of the application to open (e.g., Access). Windows displays the apps matching the search text.
4. Click the app to launch it.
   - Alternatively, you can click a blank area away from the *Search* pane to close the *Search* pane, scroll through the available apps on your computer, and click an app to launch it.

1-19 Search for an app

▶ **MORE INFO**

Add commonly used apps to your Windows *Start* page to save you time.

Office Start Page

In addition to the new *Start* page in Windows 8, most of the Office applications (except Outlook and OneNote) have a new **Start page** that displays when you launch the application (Figure 1-20). From this *Start* page, you can create a new blank file (e.g., a Word document, an Excel workbook, an Access database, or a PowerPoint presentation), create a file from an online template, search for an online template, open a recently used file, or open another file. These options vary depending on the Office application.

1-20 Access *Start* page

Press the **Esc** key to exit the *Start* page and enter the program. In Access, you have to open an existing database or create a new one to enter the program.

Backstage View

Office 2013 incorporates the **Backstage view** into all Office applications. Click the **File** tab on the *Ribbon* to open the *Backstage* view (Figure 1-21). *Backstage* options vary depending on the Office application. The following list describes some of the common tasks you can perform from the *Backstage* view:

1-21 *Backstage* view in Excel

- *Info:* Displays document properties and other protection, inspection, and version options.
- *New:* Creates a new blank file or a new file from a template or theme.
- *Open:* Opens an existing file from a designated location or a recently opened file.
- *Save:* Saves a file. If the file has not been named, the *Save As* dialog box opens when you select this option.
- *Save As:* Opens the *Save As* dialog box.
- *Print:* Prints a file, displays a preview of the file, or displays print options.
- *Share:* Invites people to share a file or email a file.

- **Export:** Creates a PDF file from a file or saves as a different file type.
- **Close:** Closes an open file.
- **Account:** Displays your Microsoft account information.
- **Options:** Opens the *[Application] Options* dialog box (e.g., Excel Options).

Office 2013 Help

In each of the Office applications, a help feature is available where you can search for a topic and view help information related to that topic. Using the *[Application] Help* dialog box (e.g., *Access Help*), type in key words for your search. Links to online help resources display in the dialog box.

HOW TO: Use Office Help

1. Click the **Help** button (question mark) in the upper right corner of the Office application window (Figure 1-22). The *[Application] Help* dialog box opens (Figure 1-23).

1-22 **Help** button

2. In the *Search* text box, type in key words for your search and press **Enter** or click the **Search** button. A list of related articles appears in the dialog box (Figure 1-24).

- You can also click one of the links in the *Popular searches* and *Basics and beyond* areas to view related help articles.

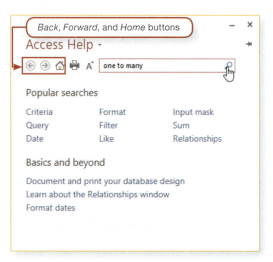

1-23 *Access Help* dialog box

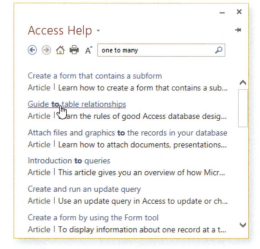

1-24 **Related articles displayed in the dialog box**

3. Click a link to display the article in the dialog box.

- You can use the *Back, Forward,* or *Home* buttons to navigate in the *Help* dialog box.
- Scroll down to the bottom of the list of articles to use the *Next* and *Previous* buttons to view more articles.

4. Click the **X** in the upper right corner to close the *Help* dialog box.

> ▶ **ANOTHER WAY**
>
> **F1** opens the *Help* dialog box.

Mouse and Pointers

If you are using Office on a desktop or laptop computer, use your mouse (or touch pad) to navigate around files, click tabs and buttons, select text and objects, move text and objects, and resize objects. The following table lists mouse and pointer terminology used in Office.

Mouse and Pointer Terminology

Term	Description
Pointer	When you move your mouse, the pointer moves on your screen. There are a variety of pointers that are used in different contexts in Office applications. The following pointers are available in most of the Office applications (the appearance of these pointers varies depending on the application and the context used): • *Selection pointer:* Select text or an object. • *Move pointer:* Move text or an object. • *Copy pointer:* Copy text or an object. • *Resize pointer:* Resize objects or table column or row. • *Crosshair:* Draw a shape.
Insertion point	The vertical flashing line where text is inserted in a file or text box. Click the left mouse button to position the insertion point.
Click	Click the left mouse button. Used to select an object or button or to place the insertion point in the selected location.
Double-click	Click the left mouse button twice. Used to select text.
Right-click	Click the right mouse button. Used to display the context menu and the mini toolbar.
Scroll	Use the scroll wheel on the mouse to scroll up and down through your file. You can also use the horizontal or vertical scroll bars at the bottom and right of an Office file window to move around in a file.

Office 2013 on a Tablet

The new user interface in Windows 8 and Office 2013 is designed to facilitate use of Windows and the Office applications on a tablet computer or smart phone. With tablets and smart phones, you use a touch screen rather than using a mouse, so the process of selecting text and objects and navigating around a file is different from when you select and navigate on a desktop or laptop computer. The following table lists some of the gestures used when working on a tablet or smart phone (some of these gestures vary depending on the application used and the context).

Tablet Gestures

Gesture	Used To	How To
Tap	Make a selection or place the insertion point. Double tap to edit text in an object or cell.	
Pinch	Zoom in or resize an object.	
Stretch	Zoom out or resize an object.	
Slide	Move an object or selected text.	
Swipe	Select text or multiple objects.	

Creating, Saving, Closing, and Opening Files

Creating, saving, and opening files is primarily done from the *Start* page or *Backstage* view. These areas provide you with many options and a central location to perform these tasks. You can also use shortcut commands to create, save, and open files.

Create a New File

When you create a new file in an Office application, you can create a new blank file or a new file based on a template (in PowerPoint, you can also create a presentation based on a theme). On the *Start* page, click **Blank [file type]** to create a new blank file in the application you are using (in Word, you begin with a blank document; in Excel, a blank workbook; in Access, a blank desktop database; and in PowerPoint, a blank presentation). From the *Backstage* view, the new file options are available in the *New* area.

HOW TO: Create a New File from the Start Page

1. Open the Office application you want to use. The *Start* page displays when the application opens.
2. From the *Start* page, click **Blank [file type]** or select a template or theme to use for your new blank file. A new file opens in the application you are using.
    - The new file is given a generic file name (e.g., *Document1*, *Book1*, or *Presentation1*). You can name and save this file later.
    - When creating a new Access database, you are prompted to name the new file when you create it.
    - Some templates and themes (in PowerPoint only) are displayed on the *Start* page, but you can search for other online templates and themes using the *Search* text box at the top of the *Start* page.

> **MORE INFO**
>
> **Esc** closes the *Start* page and takes you into the Office application (except in Access).

If you have been using an application already and want to create a new file, you create it from the *Backstage* view.

HOW TO: Create a New File from the Backstage View

1. Click the **File** tab to display the *Backstage* view.
2. Select **New** on the left to display the *New* area (Figure 1-25).
3. Click **Blank [file type]** or select a template or theme to use in your new blank file. A new file opens in the application.
    - The new file is given a generic file name (e.g., *Document1*, *Book1*, or *Presentation1*). You can name and save this file later.
    - When you are creating a new Access database, you are prompted to name the new file when you create it.
    - Some templates and themes (in PowerPoint only) are displayed on the *Start* page, but you can search for other online templates and themes using the *Search* text box at the top of the *Start* page.

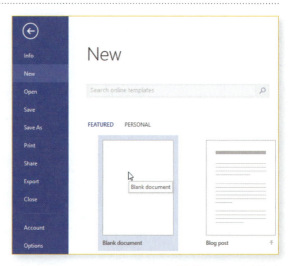

1-25 *New area in Word*

Save a File

In Access, you name a file as you create it, but in Word, Excel, and PowerPoint, you name a file after you have created it. When you save a file, you type a name for the file and select the location where the file is saved.

HOW TO: Save a File

1. Click the **File** tab to display the *Backstage* view.
2. Select **Save** or **Save As** on the left to display the *Save As* area (Figure 1-26).
   - If the file has not already been saved, clicking *Save* or *Save As* takes you to the *Save As* area on the *Backstage* view.
3. Select a place to save your file in the *Places* area.
4. On the right, click a folder in the *Recent Folders* area or click the **Browse** button to open the *Save As* dialog box (Figure 1-27).
5. In the *Folder* list on the left, select a location to save the file.
6. In the *File name* area, type a name for the file.
7. In the *Save as type*, select the file type to save.
   - By default, Office selects the file type, but you can change the file type in this area.
8. Click **Save** to close the dialog box and save the file.

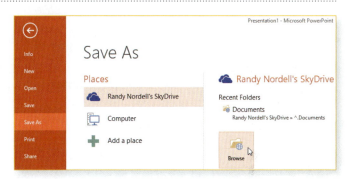

1-26 *Save As* area in PowerPoint

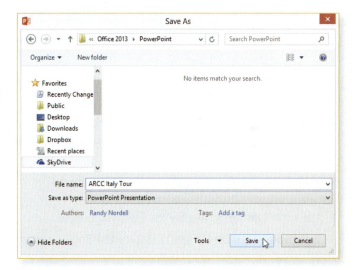

1-27 *Save As* dialog box

Create a Folder

When saving files, it is a good idea to create folders to organize your files. Organizing your files in folders makes it easier to find your files and saves you time when you are searching for a specific file (see *SLO 1.7: Organizing and Customizing Folders and Files* for more information on this topic). When you save an Office file, you can also create a folder in which to store that file.

HOW TO: Create a Folder

1. Click the **File** tab to display the *Backstage* view.
2. Select **Save As** on the left to display the *Save As* area.
3. Select a place to save your file in the *Places* area.
4. On the right, click a folder in the *Recent Folders* area or the **Browse** button to open the *Save As* dialog box.
5. In the *Folder* list at the left, select a location to save the file.
6. Click the **New Folder** button to create a new folder (Figure 1-28).
7. Type a name for the new folder and press **Enter**.

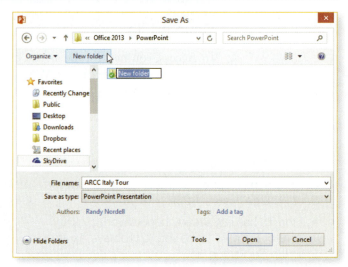

1-28 Create a new folder

> ### ANOTHER WAY
>
> **F12** opens the *Save As* dialog box (except in Access).

Save As a Different File Name

After you have saved a file, you can save it again with a different file name. If you do this, you have preserved the original file and you can continue to revise the second file for a different purpose. For example, you might want to save a different version of a file with a different file name.

HOW TO: Save As a Different File Name

1. Click the **File** tab to display the *Backstage* view.
2. Select **Save As** on the left to display the *Save As* area.
3. Select the location where you want to save your file in the *Places* area.
4. On the right, click a folder in the *Recent Folders* area or the **Browse** button to open the *Save As* dialog box.
5. In the *Folder* list on the left, select a location to save the file.
6. In the *File name* area, type a name for the file.
7. Click **Save** to close the dialog box and save the file.

Office 2013 File Types

When you save an Office file, by default Office saves the file in the most recent file format for that application. You also have the option of saving files in older versions of the Office

O1-14

application you are using. For example, you can save a Word document as an older version to share with or send to someone who uses an older version of Word. Each file has an extension at the end of the file name that determines the file type. The *file name extension* is automatically added to a file when you save it.

The following table lists some of the common file types used in the different Office applications.

Office File Types

File Type	Extension
Word Document	.docx
Word Template	.dotx
Word 97-2003 Document	.doc
Rich Text Format	.rtf
Excel Workbook	.xlsx
Excel Template	.xltx
Excel 97-2003 Workbook	.xls
Comma Separated Values (CSV)	.csv
Access Database	.accdb
Access Template	.accdt
Access Database (2000-2003 format)	.mdb
PowerPoint Presentation	.pptx
PowerPoint Template	.potx
PowerPoint 97-2003 Presentation	.ppt
Portable Document Format (PDF)	.pdf

Close a File

There are a few different methods you can use to close a file.

- Click the **File** tab and select **Close** on the left.
- Press **Ctrl+W**.
- Click the **X** in the upper right corner of the file window. This method closes the file and the program.

When you close a file, you are prompted to save the file if it has not been named or if changes were made after the file was last saved (Figure 1-29). Click **Save** to save and close the file or click **Don't Save** to close the file without saving. Click **Cancel** to return to the file.

1-29 Prompt to save a document before closing

Open an Existing File

You can open an existing file from the *Start* page when you open an Office application or you can open an existing file while you are working on another Office file.

HOW TO: Open a File from the Start Page

1. Open an Office application to display the *Start* page (Figure 1-30).
2. Select a file to open in the *Recent* area on the left.
   - If you select a file in the *Recent* area, the file must be located on the computer or an attached storage device in order to open. If the file has been renamed, moved, or on a storage device not connected to the computer, you received an error message.
3. Alternatively, click the **Open Other [file type]** (e.g., Documents, Workbooks, Files, or Presentations) link to open the *Open* area of the *Backstage* view (Figure 1-31).
4. Select a location in the *Places* area.
5. Select a folder in the *Recent Folders* area or click the **Browse** button to open the *Open* dialog box (Figure 1-32).
6. Select a location from the *Folder* list on the left.
7. Select the file to open and click the **Open** button.

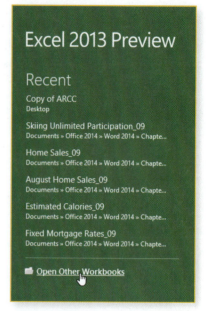

1-30 **Open a file from the *Start* page**

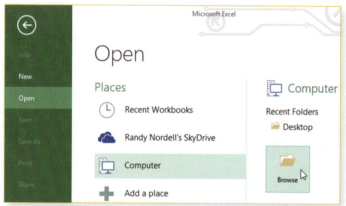

1-31 ***Open* area in the *Backstage* view**

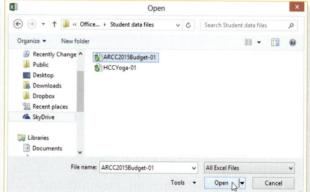

1-32 ***Open* dialog box**

To open a file from within an Office application, click the **File** tab to open the *Backstage* view and select **Open** on the left to display the *Open* area. Follow steps 4–7 above to open a file.

You can also open a file from a Windows folder. When you double-click a file in a Windows folder, the file opens in the appropriate Office application. Windows recognizes the file name extension and launches the correct program.

> ### ANOTHER WAY
> **Ctrl+F12** opens the *Open* dialog box when you are in the working area of an Office application (except in Access).

For this project, you log in to Windows using your Microsoft account, customize the Windows *Start* page, create and save a PowerPoint presentation, create a folder, open and rename an Excel workbook, use *Help*, and share a file in *SkyDrive*.

Note to Students and Instructor:

Students: *For this project, you share an Office Web App file with your instructor. You also create a Microsoft account if you don't already have one.*

Instructor: *In order to complete this project, your students need your Microsoft email address. You can create a new Live or Hotmail account for projects in this chapter.*

File Needed: **ARCC2015Budget-01.xlsx**
Completed Project File Names: **[your initials] PP O1-1a.pptx** and **[your initials] PP O1-1b.xlsx**

1. Log in to Windows using your Microsoft account if you are not already logged in.
    a. If you are not logged in to Windows using your Microsoft account, you might need to log out or restart to display the log in page. When Windows opens, type in your Windows account username and password.
    b. If you have not yet created a Microsoft account, open a browser Window and go to www.live.com and click the **Sign up now** link. Enter the required information to create your free Windows account.

2. After logging in to Windows, customize the *Start* page to include Office 2013 apps. If these apps tiles are already on the *Start* page, skip steps 2a–e.
    a. Right-click a blank area of the *Start* page.
    b. Click **All apps** on the bottom right to display the *Apps* area of Windows.
    c. Locate and right-click **Word 2013** to select it (Figure 1-33).
    d. Click **Pin to Start** on the bottom left to add this app to the *Start* page.
    e. Repeat steps 2a–d to pin *Excel 2013*, *Access 2013*, and *PowerPoint 2013* to the *Start* page.

1-33 Word 2013 selected

3. Return to the *Start* page and arrange apps.
    a. Place your pointer on the bottom right of your screen and select **Start** from the Windows navigation options.

 ANOTHER WAY

Click the bottom left corner of your screen to return to the *Start* page.

    b. Drag the app tiles you added to the *Start* page to your preferred locations.

4. Create a PowerPoint presentation and save in a new folder.
    a. Click the **PowerPoint 2013** app tile on your *Start* page to open the application.
    b. On the PowerPoint *Start* page, click **Blank presentation** to create a new blank presentation (Figure 1-34). A new blank presentation opens.

PowerPoint 2013 Preview

Search online templates and themes

Recent

CMP Staying Active_09
Documents » Office 2013 » Word 2013...

Cavalli Presentation_09
Documents » Office 2014 » Word 2014...

CMP Staying Active_09
Documents » Office 2014 » Word 2014...

Blank Presentation

Blank Presentation

1-34 Create a new blank PowerPoint presentation

c. Click in the **Click to add title** area and type American River Cycling Club.

d. Click the **File** tab to open the *Backstage* view and click **Save As** on the left to display the *Save As* area.

e. Click *[your name's]* **SkyDrive** in the *Places* area and click **Browse** to open the *Save As* dialog box (Figure 1-35).

f. Click the **New Folder** button to create a new folder in your *SkyDrive* folder.

g. Type American River Cycling Club and press **Enter**.

h. Double-click the folder you created to open it.

i. In the *File name* area, type [your initials] PP O1-1a (Figure 1-36).

j. Click **Save** to close the dialog box and save the presentation.

k. Click the **X** in the upper right corner of the window to close the file and PowerPoint.

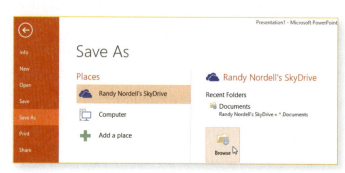

1-35 **Save the file in *SkyDrive***

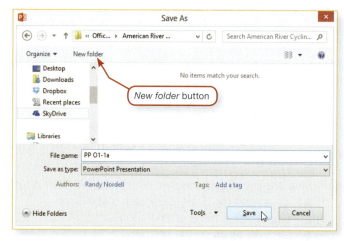

1-36 *Save As* dialog box

5. Open an Excel file and save as a different file name.

a. Return to the Windows *Start* page.

b. Click the **Excel 2013** app tile to open it.

c. From the Excel *Start* page, click the **Open Other Workbooks** link on the bottom left to display the *Open* area of the *Backstage* view.

d. Click **Computer** in the *Places* area and click **Browse** to open the *Open* dialog box (Figure 1-37).

e. Browse to your student data files and select the **ARCC2015Budget-01** file.

f. Click **Open** to open the workbook.

g. Press **F12** to open the *Save As* dialog box.

h. Click **SkyDrive** in the *Folder* list on the left.

i. Double-click the **American River Cycling Club** folder to open it.

j. In the *File name* area type [your initials] PP O1-1b.

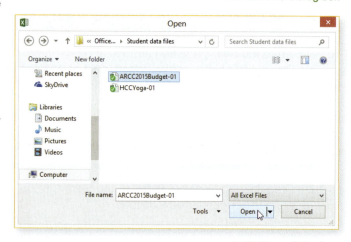

1-37 *Open* dialog box

k. Click **Save** to close the dialog box and save the workbook.

6. Use *Excel Help* to find articles about selected topics.

a. Click the **Help** button in the upper right corner of the Excel window. The *Excel Help* dialog box opens.

b. Type pivot table in the *Search* text box and press **Enter**.

c. Click one of the displayed articles and quickly read about pivot tables.

d. Click the **Home** button to return to the home page of Excel help.

e. Type sum function in the *Search* text box and press **Enter**.

f. Click one of the displayed articles and quickly read about sum functions.

g. Click the **X** in the upper right corner to close the *Excel Help* dialog box.

h. Press **Ctrl+W** to close the Excel workbook.

i. Click the **X** in the upper right corner of the Excel window to close Excel.

7. Share an Office Web Apps file on *SkyDrive* with your instructor.

a. Return to the Windows *Start* page.

b. Open an Internet browser window and go to the *SkyDrive* (www.skydrive.com) sign-in page (Figure 1-38).

c. Type in your Microsoft account email address and password and click the **Sign In** button to go to your *SkyDrive* web page.

d. Click the navigation button on the upper left and select **SkyDrive** (if your *SkyDrive* is not already displayed) (Figure 1-39).

e. Click the **American River Cycling Club** folder to open it.

f. Click the **PP O1-1b** Excel workbook to open it in Office Web Apps (Figure 1-40).

g. Click the **File** tab to open the *Backstage* view.

h. Click **Share** on the left and select **Share with People**. A sharing window opens with different options (Figure 1-41). Sharing requires the recipient to have a Microsoft account. Also, you might be directed to complete an online form for security purposes the first time you share a file.

i. Click **Send email**, type your instructor's email address, and type a brief message.

j. Check the **Recipients can edit** check box.

k. Click the **Share** button.

8. Select **[your name]** on the upper right of the *SkyDrive* window and select the **Sign out** from the *Account* drop-down list.

1-38 Log in to *SkyDrive* online

1-39 Go to your *SkyDrive*

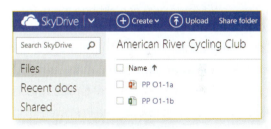

1-40 Open a file in Office Web Apps

1-41 Share an Office Web App file

Printing, Sharing, and Customizing Files

On the *Backstage* view of any of the Office applications, you can print a file and customize how a file is printed. You can also export an Office file as a PDF file in most of the Office applications. In addition, you can add and customize document properties for an Office file and share a file in a variety of formats.

Print a File

You can print an Office file if you need a paper copy of it. The *Print* area on the *Backstage* view displays a preview of the open file and many print options. For example, you can choose which page or pages to print and change the margins of the file in the *Print* area. Some of the print settings vary depending on the Office application you are using and what you are printing.

HOW TO: Print a File

1. Open the file you want to print from a Windows folder or within an Office program.
2. Click the **File** tab to open the *Backstage* view.
3. Click **Print** on the left to display the *Print* area (Figure 1-42).
   - A preview of the file displays on the right. Click the **Show Margins** button to adjust margins or **Zoom to Page** button to change the view in the *Preview* area. The *Show Margins* button is only available in Word and Excel.
   - On the left a variety of options are listed in the *Settings* area.
   - The *Settings* options vary depending on the Office application you are using and what you are printing.
4. In the *Copies* area, you can change the number of copies to print.
5. The default printer for your computer is displayed in the *Printer* drop-down list.
   - Click the **Printer** drop-down list to select a different printer.
6. In the *Settings* area, you can customize what is printed and how it is printed.
   - In the *Pages* area (*Slides* area in PowerPoint), you can select a page or range of pages (slides) to print.
   - By default all pages (slides) are printed when you print a file.
7. Click the **Print** button to print your file.

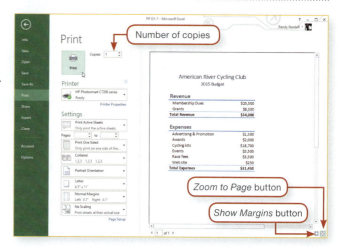

1-42 *Print* area on the *Backstage* view

ANOTHER WAY

Ctrl+P opens the *Print* area on the *Backstage* view.

Export as a PDF File

Portable document format, or **PDF**, is a specific file format that is often used to share files that are not to be changed or to post files on a web site. When you create a PDF file from an Office application file, you are actually exporting a static image of the original file, similar to taking a picture of the file.

The advantage of working with a PDF file is that the format of the file is retained no matter who opens the file. PDF files open in Adobe Reader, which is free software that is installed on most computers, or Adobe Acrobat, which is software users have to buy. Because a PDF file is a static image of a file, it is not easy for other people to edit your files. When you want people to be able to view a file but not make changes, PDF files are a good choice.

MORE INFO

Word 2013 allows you to open PDF files and edit the file as a Word document.

When you export an Office application file as a PDF file, Office creates a static image of your file and prompts you to save the file. The file is saved as a PDF file.

HOW TO: Export a File as a PDF File

1. Open the file you want to export to a PDF file.
2. Click the **File** tab and click **Export** to display the *Export* area on the Backstage view (Figure 1-43).
3. Select **Create PDF/XPS Document** and click the **Create PDF/XPS**. The *Publish as PDF or XPS* dialog box opens.
4. Select a location to save the file.
5. In the *File name* area, type a name for the file.
6. Click **Publish** to close the dialog box and save the PDF file.
   - A PDF version of your file may open. You can view the file and then close it.

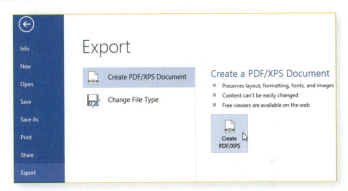

1-43 Export a file as a PDF file

Document Properties

Document properties are hidden codes in a file that contain identifying information about that file. Each piece of document property information is called a *field*. You can view and modify document properties in the *Info* area of the *Backstage* view.

Some document properties fields are automatically generated when you work on a file, such as *Size, Total Editing Time, Created,* and *Last Modified.* But you can modify other document properties fields, such as *Title, Comments, Subject, Company,* and *Author.* You can use document property fields in different ways such as inserting the *Company* field in a document footer.

HOW TO: View and Modify Document Properties

1. Click the **File** tab and click **Info**. The document properties display on the right (Figure 1-44).
2. Click in the text box area of a field that can be edited (e.g., *Add a title* or *Add a tag*) and type your custom document property information.
3. Click the **Show All Properties** link at the bottom to display additional document properties.
   - When all properties are displayed, click **Show Fewer Properties** to display fewer properties.
   - This link toggles between *Show All Properties* and *Show Fewer Properties.*
4. Click the **File** tab to return to the file.

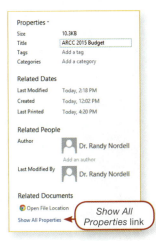

1-44 Document properties

Share a File

Windows 8 and Office 2013 have been developed to help you share and collaborate effectively. The *Share* area on the *Backstage* view provides different options for sharing files from within an Office application. When you save a file to your *SkyDrive*, Office gives you a variety of options to share your file (Figure 1-45). Your sharing options vary depending on the Office application you are using. The following list describes some common ways you can share files with others:

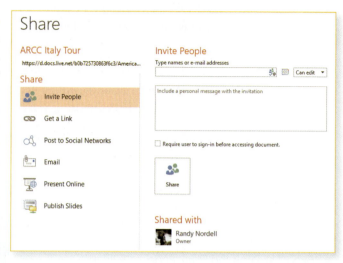

1-45 Share an Office file

- *Invite People* to view or edit your file.
- *Get a Link* to the online file that you can send to others or post online.
- *Post to Social Networks* such as LinkedIn or Facebook.
- *Email* the file as an attachment, link, or PDF file.

> **MORE INFO**
>
> There is not a *Sharing* area on the *Backstage* view in Access.

HOW TO: Share a File

1. Click the **File** tab and select **Share**.
   - If your file is not saved on *SkyDrive*, select **Invite People** and click **Save to Cloud** (Figure 1-46).
   - Save your file to your *SkyDrive* folder.
   - If your file is not saved to *SkyDrive*, you will not have all of the sharing options.
2. Select one of the *Share* options on the left. Additional information is displayed on the right (Figure 1-47).
   - In most of the *Share* options, you can set the permission level to **Can view** or **Can edit**, which controls what others can do with your file.
   - In order to post a file to a social network site, you must connect your social network site to your Microsoft account. Go to the *Account* area of the *Backstage* view to connect to social network sites.

1-46 Save a file to the cloud before sharing

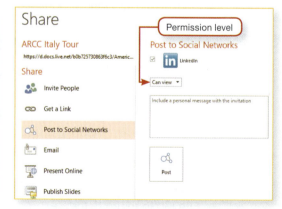

1-47 Share a file on a social network site

Program Options

Using the program options, you can make changes that apply globally to the Office program. For example, you can change the default save location to your *Sky-Drive* folder or you can turn off the *Start* page that opens when you open an Office application.

Click the **File** tab and select **Options** on the left to open the **[Program] Options** dialog box (e.g., Word Options, Excel Options, etc.) (Figure 1-48). Click one of the categories on the left to display the category options on the right. The categories and options vary depending on the Office application you are using.

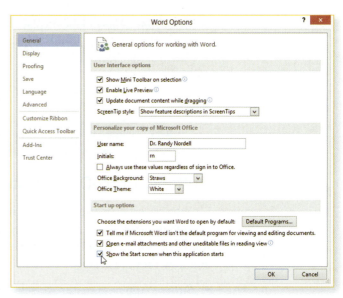

1-48 *Word Options* dialog box

SLO 1.4

Using the Ribbon, Tabs, and Quick Access Toolbar

You can use the *Ribbon*, tabs, groups, buttons, drop-down lists, dialog boxes, task panes, galleries, and the *Quick Access* toolbar to modify your Office files. This section describes the different tools you can use to customize your files.

The Ribbon, Tabs, and Groups

The **Ribbon**, which appears at the top of an Office file window, displays the many features available to use on your files. The *Ribbon* is a collection of **tabs**. On each tab are **groups** of features. The tabs and groups that are available on each Office application vary. Click a tab to display the groups and features available on that tab.

Some tabs are always displayed on the *Ribbon* (e.g., *File* tab and *Home* tab). Other tabs are **context-sensitive**, which means that they only appear on the *Ribbon* when a specific object is selected in your file. Figure 1-49 displays the context-sensitive *Table Tools Table* tab that displays in Access when you open a table.

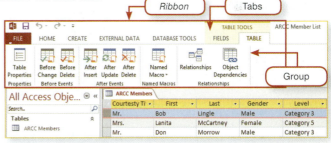

1-49 Context-sensitive *Table Tools Table* tab displayed

Ribbon Display Options

The *Ribbon* is by default displayed when an Office application is open, but you can customize how the *Ribbon* displays. The **Ribbon Display Options** button is in the upper right corner of an Office application window (Figure 1-50). Click the **Ribbon Display Options** button to select one of the three options.

1-50 *Ribbon Display Options*

- *Auto-Hide Ribbon:* Hides the *Ribbon.* Click at the top of the application to display the *Ribbon.*
- *Show Tabs: Ribbon* tabs display. Click a tab to open the *Ribbon* and display the tab.
- *Show Tabs and Commands:* Displays the *Ribbon* and tabs, which is the default setting in Office applications.

> **MORE INFO**
>
> **Ctrl+F1** collapses or expands the *Ribbon* to display only tabs.

Buttons, Drop-Down Lists, and Galleries

Groups on each of the tabs contain a variety of *buttons, drop-down lists,* and *galleries.* The following list describes each of these features and how they are used:

- *Button:* Applies a feature to selected text or object. Click a button to apply the feature (Figure 1-51).
- *Drop-Down List:* Displays the various options available for a feature. Some buttons are drop-down lists only, which means when you click one of these buttons the drop-down list of options appears (Figure 1-52). Other buttons are *split buttons,* which have both a button you click to apply a feature and an arrow you click to display a drop-down list of options (Figure 1-53).

1-51 *Bold* button in the *Font* group on the *Home* tab

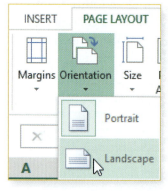

1-52 Drop-down list

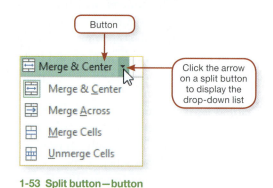

1-53 Split button—button and drop-down list

- *Gallery:* Displays a collection of option buttons. Click an option in a gallery to apply the feature. Figure 1-54 is the *Styles* gallery. You can click the **More** button to display the entire gallery of options or click the **Up** or **Down** arrow to display a different row of options.

1-54 *Styles* gallery in Word

Dialog Boxes, Task Panes,
and Launchers

Not all of the features that are available in an Office application are displayed in the groups on the tabs. Additional options for some groups are displayed in a *dialog box* or *task pane*. A *launcher*, which is a small square in the bottom right of some groups, opens a dialog box or displays a task pane when you click it (see Figure 1-56).

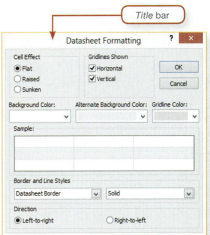

1-55 *Datasheet Formatting* dialog box

- *Dialog box:* A new window that opens to display additional features. You can move a dialog box by clicking and dragging on the title bar, which is the top of the dialog box where the title is displayed. Figure 1-55 is the *Datasheet Formatting* dialog box that opens when you click the *Text Formatting* launcher in Access.
- *Task pane:* Opens on the left or right of the Office application window. Figure 1-56 is the *Clipboard* pane, which is available in all Office applications. Task panes are named according to their feature (e.g., *Clipboard* pane or *Navigation* pane). You can resize a task pane by clicking and dragging on its left or right border. Click the **X** in the upper right corner to close a task pane.

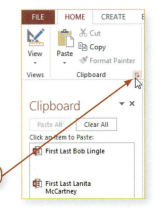

1-56 *Clipboard* pane

ScreenTips

ScreenTips display descriptive information about a button, drop-down list, launcher, or gallery selection in the groups on the *Ribbon*. When you put your pointer on an item on the *Ribbon*, a ScreenTip displays information about the selection (Figure 1-57). The ScreenTip appears temporarily and displays the command name, keyboard shortcut (if available), and a description of the command.

Radio Buttons, Check Boxes,
and Text Boxes

Within dialog boxes and task panes there are a variety of features you can apply using radio buttons, check boxes, text boxes, drop-down lists, and other buttons. A *radio button* is a round button that you click to select one option from a list of options. A selected radio button has a solid dot inside the round button. When you see a *check box*, you can use it to select one or more options. A check appears in a check box you have selected. A *text box* is an area where you can type text.

A task pane or dialog box may also include drop-down lists or other buttons that open additional dialog boxes. Figure 1-58 shows the *Page Setup* dialog box in Excel, which includes a variety of radio buttons, check boxes, text boxes, drop-down lists, and other buttons that open additional dialog boxes.

1-57 ScreenTip

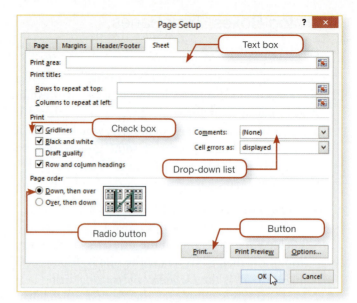

1-58 *Page Setup* dialog box in Excel

Quick Access Toolbar

The **Quick Access toolbar** is located above the *Ribbon* on the upper left of each Office application window. It contains buttons you can use to apply commonly used features such as *Save, Undo, Redo,* and *Open* (Figure 1-59). The *Undo* button is a split button. You can click the button to undo the last action performed or you can click the drop-down arrow to display and undo multiple previous actions.

1-59 *Quick Access* toolbar

Customize the Quick Access Toolbar

You can customize the *Quick Access* toolbar to include features you regularly use, such as *Quick Print, New,* and *Spelling & Grammar*. The following steps show how to customize the *Quick Access* toolbar in Word. The customization process is similar for the *Quick Access* toolbar in the other Office applications.

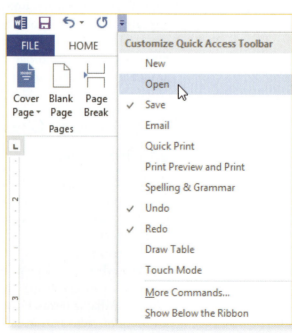

HOW TO: Customize the Quick Access Toolbar

1. Click the **Customize Quick Access Toolbar** drop-down list on the right edge of the *Quick Access* toolbar (Figure 1-60).
2. Select a command to add to the *Quick Access* toolbar. The command appears on the *Quick Access* toolbar.
   - Items on the *Customize Quick Access Toolbar* drop-down list with a check mark are displayed on the *Quick Access* toolbar.
   - Deselect a checked item to remove it from the *Quick Access* toolbar.
3. To add a command that is not listed on the *Customize Quick Access Toolbar,* click the **Customize Quick Access Toolbar** drop-down list and select **More Commands**.

1-60 Customize the *Quick Access* toolbar

The *Word Options* dialog box opens with the *Quick Access Toolbar* area displayed (Figure 1-61).

4. Click the **Customize Quick Access Toolbar** drop-down list on the right and select **For all documents** or the current document.

   - If you select *For all documents*, the change is made to the *Quick Access* toolbar for all documents you open in Word.
   - If you select the current document, the change is made to the *Quick Access* toolbar in that document only.

5. On the left, select the command you want to add.

   - If you can't find the command you're looking for, click the **Choose commands from** drop-down list and select **All Commands**.

6. Click the **Add** button and the command name appears in the list on the right.

7. Add other commands as desired.

8. To rearrange commands on the *Quick Access* toolbar, select the command to move and click the **Move Up** or **Move Down** button.

9. Click **OK** to close the *Word Options* dialog box.

1-61 Customize the *Quick Access* toolbar in the *Word Options* dialog box

---

> **MORE INFO**
>
> To remove an item from the *Quick Access* toolbar, right-click an item and select **Remove from Quick Access Toolbar**.

SLO 1.5

Using a Context Menu, Mini Toolbar, and Keyboard Shortcuts

Most of the formatting and other features you will want to apply to text are available in groups on the different tabs. But many of these features are also available using content menus, mini toolbars, and keyboard shortcuts. You can use these tools to quickly apply formatting or other options to text or objects.

Context Menu

A **context menu** is displayed when you right-click text, a cell, or an object such as a picture, drawing object, chart, or *SmartArt* (Figure 1-62). The context menu is a vertical rectangle menu that lists a variety of options. These options are context-sensitive, which means they vary depending on what you right-click.

1-62 Context menu

Some options on the context menu are buttons that perform an action (e.g., *Cut* or *Copy*), some are buttons that open a dialog box or task pane (e.g., *Save as Picture* or *Size and Position*), and some are selections that display a drop-down list of selections (e.g., *Bring to Front* or *Wrap Text*).

Mini Toolbar

The **mini toolbar** is another context menu that displays when you right-click text, a cell, or an object in your file (Figure 1-63). The mini toolbar is a horizontal rectangle menu that lists a variety of formatting options. These options vary depending on what you right-click. The mini toolbar contains a variety of buttons and drop-down lists. Some mini toolbars automatically display when you select text or an object, such as when you select a row of a table in Word or PowerPoint.

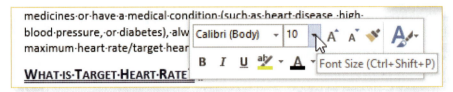

1-63 Mini toolbar

Keyboard Shortcuts

You can also use a **keyboard shortcut** to quickly apply formatting or perform actions. A keyboard shortcut is a keyboard key or combination of keyboard keys that you press at the same time. These can include the *Ctrl, Shift, Alt,* letter, number, and function keys (e.g., *F1* or *F7*). The following table lists some common Office keyboard shortcuts.

> **MORE INFO**
>
> See Appendix A for more Office 2013 keyboard shortcuts.

Common Office Keyboard Shortcuts

Keyboard Shortcut	Action or Displays	Keyboard Shortcut	Action or Displays
Ctrl+S	Save	Ctrl+Z	Undo
F12	*Save As* dialog box	Ctrl+Y	Redo or Repeat
Ctrl+O	*Open* area on the *Backstage* view	Ctrl+1	Single space
Shift+F12	*Open* dialog box	Ctrl+2	Double space
Ctrl+N	New blank file	Ctrl+L	Align left
Ctrl+P	*Print* area on the *Backstage* view	Ctrl+E	Align center
Ctrl+C	Copy	Ctrl+R	Align right
Ctrl+X	Cut	F1	*Help* dialog box
Ctrl+V	Paste	F7	*Spelling* pane
Ctrl+B	Bold	Ctrl+A	Select All
Ctrl+I	Italic	Ctrl+Home	Move to the beginning
Ctrl+U	Underline	Ctrl+End	Move to the end

For this project, you work with a document for the American River Cycling Club. You modify the existing document, add document properties, customize the *Quick Access* toolbar, export the document as a PDF file, and share a link to the document.

Note to Instructor:

Students: *For this project, you share an Office Web App file with your instructor.*
Instructor: *In order to complete this project, your students need your Microsoft email address. You can create a new Live or Hotmail account for projects in this chapter.*

File Needed: ***ARCCTraining-01.docx***
Completed Project File Names: ***[your initials] PP O1-2.docx*** and ***[your initials] PP O1-2.pdf***

1. Open Word 2013 and open the ***ARCCTraining-01*** file from your student data files.

2. Save this document as ***[your initials] PP O1-2*** in the *American River Cycling Club* folder in your *SkyDrive* folder.

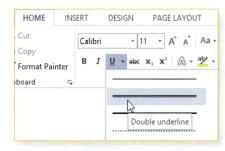

3. Use a button, drop-down list, and dialog box to modify the document.
   a. Select the first heading, "**What is Maximum Heart Rate?**"
   b. Click the **Bold** button [*Home* tab, *Font* group].
   c. Click the **Underline** drop-down arrow and select **Double underline** (Figure 1-64).

   1-64 Apply *Double underline* to selected text

   d. Click the **launcher** in the *Font* group [*Home* tab] to open the *Font* dialog box (Figure 1-65).
   e. In the *Size* area, select **12** from the list or type 12 in the text box.
   f. In the *Effects* area, click the **Small caps** check box to select it.
   g. Click **OK** to close the dialog box and apply the formatting changes.
   h. Select the next heading, "**What is Target Heart Rate?**"
   i. Repeat steps 3b–g to apply formatting to selected text.

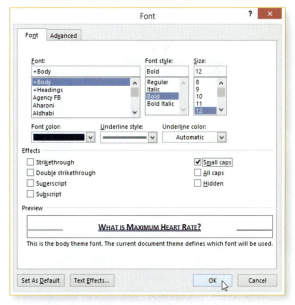

4. Add document properties.
   a. Click the **File** tab to display the *Backstage* view.
   b. Select **Info** on the left. The document properties are displayed on the right.
   c. Click in the **Add a title** text box and type ARCC Training.
   d. Click the **Show All Properties** link near the bottom to display more document properties.

   1-65 *Font* dialog box

   e. Click in the **Specify the subject** text box and type Heart rate training.
   f. Click in the **Specify the company** text box and type American River Cycling Club.
   g. Click the **Show Fewer Properties** link to display fewer document properties.
   h. Click the **Back** arrow on the upper left to close the *Backstage* view and return to the document.

5. Customize the *Quick Access* toolbar.
   a. Click the **Customize Quick Access Toolbar** drop-down arrow and select **Open** (Figure 1-66).
   b. Click the **Customize Quick Access Toolbar** drop-down arrow again and select **Spelling & Grammar**.
   c. Click the **Customize Quick Access Toolbar** drop-down arrow and select **More Commands**. The *Word Options* dialog box opens (Figure 1-67).
   d. Click the **Customize Quick Access Toolbar** drop-down list on the right and select **For all documents**.

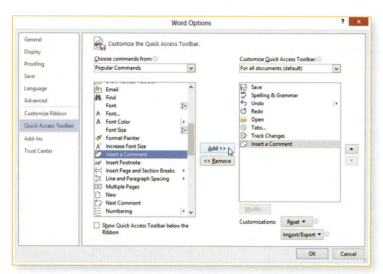

1-67 Customize the *Quick Access* toolbar in the *Word Options* dialog box

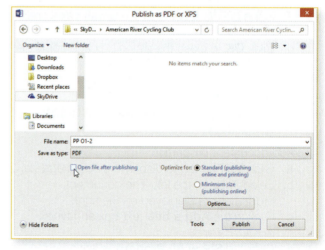

1-68 *Publish as PDF or XPS* dialog box

   e. In the list of commands at the left, click **Insert a Comment**.
   f. Click the **Add** button to add it to your *Quick Access* toolbar list on the right.
   g. Click **OK** to close the *Word Options* dialog box.
   h. Click the **Save** button on the *Quick Access* toolbar to save the document.

6. Export the file as a PDF file.
   a. Click the **File** tab to go to the *Backstage* view.
   b. Select **Export** on the left.
   c. Select **Create PDF/XPS Document** and click the **Create PDF/XPS** button. The *Publish as PDF or XPS* dialog box opens (Figure 1-68).
   d. Select the **American River Cycling Club** folder in your *SkyDrive* folder as the location to save the file.
   e. In the *File name* area, type [your initials] PP O1-2 if it is not already there.
   f. Deselect the **Open file after publishing** check box if it is checked.

g. Select the **Standard** (publishing online and printing) radio button.

h. Click **Publish** to close the dialog box and create a PDF version of your file.

7. Get a link to share a document with your instructor.

   a. Click the **File** tab to open the *Backstage* view.

   b. Select **Share** at the left. Your file is already saved to *SkyDrive* so all of the *Share* options are available.

   c. Select **Get a Sharing Link** on the left (Figure 1-69).

   d. In the *View Link* area, click the **Create Link** button. A link for the document is created and displayed on the right of the button.

   e. Select this link and press **Ctrl+C** to copy the link.

   f. Click the **Back** arrow to close the *Backstage* view and return to your document.

8. Save and close the document (Figure 1-70).

9. Email the sharing link to your instructor.

   a. Using your email account, create a new email to send to your instructor.

   b. Include an appropriate subject line and a brief message in the body.

   c. Press **Ctrl+V** to paste the link to your document in the body of the email.

   d. Send the email message.

1-69 *Get a Link* **to share a file**

1-70 **PP O1-2 completed**

Working with Files

When you work with Office files, there are a variety of views to display your file. You can change how a file is displayed, adjust the display size, work with multiple files, and arrange the windows to view multiple files. Because most people work with multiple files at the same time, Office makes it intuitive to move from one file to another or display multiple document windows at the same time.

File Views

Each of the different Office applications provides you with a variety of ways to view your document. In Word, Excel, and PowerPoint, the different views are available on the *View* tab

(Figure 1-71). You can also change views using the buttons on the right side of the *Status* bar at the bottom of the file window (Figure 1-72). In Access, the different views for each object are available in the *Views* group on the *Home* tab.

The following table lists the views that are available in each of the different Office applications.

1-71 *Workbook Views* group on the *View* tab in Excel

1-72 **PowerPoint views on the *Status* bar**

File Views

Office Application	Views	Office Application	Views
Word	Read Mode Print Layout Web Layout Outline Draft	**Access** *(Access views vary depending on active object)*	Layout View Design View Datasheet View Form View SQL View Report View Print Preview
Excel	Normal Page Break View Page Layout View Custom Views	**PowerPoint**	Normal Outline View Slide Sorter Notes Page Reading View Presenter View

Change Display Size

You can use the ***Zoom feature*** to increase or decrease the display size of your file. Using *Zoom* to change the display size does not change the actual size of text or objects in your file; it only changes the size of your display. For example, if you change the *Zoom* level to 120%, you increase the display of your file to 120% of its normal size (100%), but changing the display size does not affect the actual size of text and objects in your file. You could also decrease the *Zoom* level to 80% to display more of your file on the screen.

There are a few different ways you can increase or decrease the *Zoom* level on your file. Your *Zoom* options vary depending on the Office application you are using.

- ***Zoom level on the* Status *bar*** (Figure 1-73): Click the + or − buttons to increase or decrease *Zoom* level.

Zoom level buttons

Fit slide to current window button

1-73 *Zoom* level area on the *Status* bar in PowerPoint

- ***Zoom group on the View tab*** (Figure 1-74): There are a variety of *Zoom* options in the *Zoom* group. These vary depending on application.

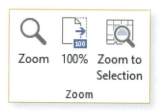

1-74 *Zoom* group in Excel

- **Zoom dialog box** (Figure 1-75): Click the **Zoom** button in the *Zoom* group on *View* tab or click **Zoom level** on the *Status* bar to open the *Zoom* dialog box.

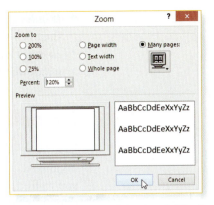

1-75 *Zoom* dialog box in Word

Manage Multiple Open Files and Windows

When you are working on multiple files in an Office application, each file is opened in a new window. You can **minimize** an open window to place the file on the Windows *Taskbar* (the bar at the bottom of the Windows desktop), **restore down** an open window so it does not fill the entire computer screen, or **maximize** a window so it fills the entire computer screen. The *Minimize, Restore Down/Maximize,* and *Close* buttons are in the upper right of a file window (Figure 1-76).

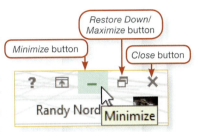

1-76 Window options buttons

- **Minimize:** Click the **Minimize** button to hide this window. When a document is minimized, it is not closed. It is collapsed so the window is not displayed on your screen. Click the application icon on the Windows *Taskbar* at the bottom to display thumbnails of open files. You can click an open file thumbnail to display the file (Figure 1-77).
- **Restore Down/Maximize:** Click the **Restore Down/Maximize** button to decrease the size of an open window or maximize the window to fill the entire screen. This button toggles between *Restore Down* and *Maximize.* When

1-77 Display open files on the Windows *Taskbar*

a window is restored down, you can change the size of a window by clicking and dragging on a border of the window. You can also move the window by clicking and dragging on the title bar at the top of the window.
- **Close:** Click the **Close** button to close the window. If there is only one open file, the Office application also closes when you click the *Close* button on the file.

You can switch between open files or arrange the open files to display more than one window at the same time. There are a few ways to do this.

- **Switch Windows button:** Click the **Switch Windows** button [*View* tab, *Window* group] (not available in Access) to display a drop-down list of open files. Click a file from the drop-down list to display the file.

- **Windows Taskbar:** Click an Office application icon on the Windows *Taskbar* to display the open files in that application. Click an open file to display it (see Figure 1-77).
- **Arrange All button:** Click the **Arrange All** button [*View* tab, *Window* group] to display all windows in an application. You can resize or move the open file windows.

Organizing and Customizing Folders and Files

The more you use your computer and create and use files, the more important it is to stay organized. You can do this by using folders to store related files, which makes it easier for you to find, edit, and share your files. For example, you can create a folder for the college you attend. Inside the college folder, you can create a folder for each of your courses. Inside each of the course folders you might create a folder for student data files, solution files, and group projects. Folders can store any type of files, and you are not limited to Office files.

Create a Folder

You can create folders inside of other folders. In *SLO 1.2: Creating, Saving, Closing, and Opening Files,* you learned how to create a new folder when saving an Office file in the *Save As* dialog box. You can also create a folder using a Windows folder.

HOW TO: Create a Windows Folder

1. Open a Windows folder.
   - From the Windows *Start* page, click **File Explorer**, **Computer**, or **Documents** to open a Windows window.
   - Your folders and computer locations are listed on the left.
2. Select the location where you want to create a new folder.
3. Click the **New folder** button on the top left of the window. A new folder is created in the folders area (Figure 1-78).
   - You can also click the **Home** tab and click the **New folder** button [*New* group].
4. Type the name of the new folder and press **Enter**.

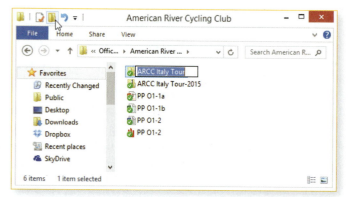

1-78 Create a new Windows folder

> ▶ **ANOTHER WAY**
> **Ctrl+Shift+N** creates a new folder in a Windows folder.

Move and Copy Files and Folders

You can move or copy files and folders using the *Move to* or *Copy to* buttons on the *Home* tab of a Windows folder. You can also use the move or copy keyboard shortcuts (**Ctrl+X**, **Ctrl+C**, **Ctrl+V**) or the drag and drop method. When you move a file or folder, you cut it from one location and paste it in another location. When you copy a file or folder, you create a copy of it and paste it in another location so the file or folder is in two or more locations. If there are files in a folder you move or copy, the files in the folder are moved or copied with the folder.

To move or copy multiple folders or files at the same time, press the **Ctrl** key and select multiple items to move or copy. Use the *Ctrl* key to select or deselect multiple non-adjacent files or folders. You can also use the *Shift* key to select a range of files or folders. Click the first file or folder in a range, press the **Shift** key, and select the last file or folder in the range to select all of the items in the range.

HOW TO: Move or Copy a File or Folder

1. In a Windows folder, select a file or folder to move or copy.
2. Click the **Home** tab to display the tab in the open window.
3. Click the **Move to** or **Copy to** button [*Organize* group] and select the location where you want to move or copy the file or folder (Figure 1-79).

1-79 Move or copy a selected file or folder

   • If the folder you want is not available, select **Choose location** to open the *Move Items* or *Copy Items* dialog box.
   • To use the keyboard shortcuts, press **Ctrl+X** to cut the file or folder or **Ctrl+C** to copy the file or folder from its original location, go to the desired new location, and press **Ctrl+V** to paste it.
   • To use the drag and drop method to move a file or folder, select the file or folder and drag and drop on the new location.
   • To use the drag and drop method to copy a file or folder, press the **Ctrl** key, select the file or folder, and drag and drop on the new location.

> **ANOTHER WAY**
>
> Right-click a file or folder to display the context menu where you can select **Cut, Copy,** or **Paste.**

Rename Files and Folders

When you need to change the name of a file or folder, you can rename these in a Windows folder.

HOW TO: Rename a File or Folder

1. In a Windows folder, select the file or folder you want to rename.
2. Click the **Rename** button [*Home* tab, *Organize* group].
3. Type the new name of the file or folder and press **Enter**.

> **ANOTHER WAY**
>
> Select a file or folder to rename, press **F2**, type the new name, and press **Enter.** You can also right-click a file or folder and select **Rename** from the context menu.

Delete Files and Folders

You can also easily delete files and folders. When you delete a file or folder, it is moved from its current location to the ***Recycle Bin*** on your computer, which is the location where deleted items are stored. If a file or folder is in the *Recycle Bin,* you can restore this item to its original location or move it to a different location. You also have the option to permanently delete a file or folder; the item is deleted and not moved to the *Recycle Bin*. If an item is permanently deleted, you do not have the restore option.

There are several ways to delete a file or folder. To ensure that you don't delete anything by mistake, when you delete a file or folder, a confirmation dialog box opens, prompting you to confirm whether or not you want to delete the selected file or folder.

HOW TO: Delete Files and Folders

1. Select the file or folder you want to delete.
   - You can select multiple files and folders to delete at the same time.
2. Click the **Delete** drop-down arrow [*Home* tab, *Organize* group] to display the list of delete options (Figure 1-80).
3. Click **Recycle** or **Permanently delete**. A confirmation dialog box opens.
   - *Recycle* deletes the selected item(s) and moves them to the *Recycle Bin*.
   - *Permanently delete* deletes the item(s) from your computer.
   - The default action when you click the *Delete* button (not the drop-down arrow) is *Recycle*.
4. Click **Yes** to delete.

1-80 Delete selected files and folders

> ### ANOTHER WAY
>
> Press **Ctrl+D** or the **Delete** key on your keyboard to recycle selected item(s).
> Press **Shift+Delete** to permanently delete selected item(s).

Compressed and Zipped Folders

If you want to share multiple files or a folder of files with classmates, coworkers, friends, or family, you can **zip** the files into a **zipped folder** (also called a **compressed folder**). For example, you can't attach an entire folder to an email message, but you can attach a zipped folder to an email message. Compressing files and folders decreases their size. You can zip a group of selected files, a folder, or a combination of files and folders, and then share the zipped folder with others through email or in a cloud storage location such as *SkyDrive*.

HOW TO: Create a Zipped Folder

1. Select the file(s) and/or folder(s) you want to compress and send.
2. Click the **Zip** button [*Share* tab, *Send* group] (Figure 1-81). A zipped folder is created.
   - The name of the zipped folder is the name of the first item you selected to zip. You can rename this folder.
   - The icon for a zipped folder looks similar to the icon for a folder except it has a vertical zipper down the middle of the folder.

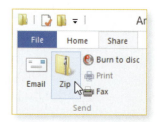

1-81 Create a zipped folder

If you receive a zipped folder from someone via email, save the zipped folder and then you can **extract** its contents. Extracting a zipped folder creates a regular Window folder from the zipped folder.

HOW TO: Extract a Zipped Folder

1. After saving the zipped folder to a location on your computer, select the folder (Figure 1-82).
2. Click the **Extract all** button [*Compress Folder Tools Extract* tab]. The *Extract Compressed (Zipped) Folders* dialog box opens (Figure 1-83).
3. Click **Extract** to extract the folder.
    *   Both the extracted folder and the zipped folder display in the folder where they are located.
    *   If you check the **Show extracted files when complete** check box, the extracted folder will open after extracting.

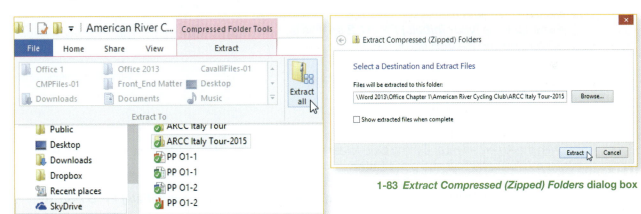

1-82 **Extract files from a zipped folder**

1-83 *Extract Compressed (Zipped) Folders* **dialog box**

For this project, you copy and rename files in your *SkyDrive* folder on your computer, create a folder, move and copy files, create a zipped folder, and rename a zipped folder.

Files Needed: *[your initials] PP O1-1a.pptx*, *[your initials] PP O1-1b.xlsx*, and *[your initials] PP O1-2.docx*
Completed Project File Names: *[your initials] PP O1-3a.pptx*, *[your initials] PP O1-3b.xlsx*, *[your initials] PP O1-3c.docx*, and **ARCC Italy Tour-[current year]** (zipped folder)

1. Open your *SkyDrive* folder.
    a. From the Windows *Start* page, click the **File Explorer** or **Computer** tile to open a Windows folder. If these options are not available on the *Start* page, use *Search* to find and open the *File Explorer* or *Computer* window.

b. Click the **SkyDrive** folder on the left to display the folders in your *SkyDrive* folder.

c. Double click the **American River Cycling Club** folder to open it.

2. Copy and rename files.

a. Select the ***[your initials] PP O1-1a*** file (this is a PowerPoint file).

b. Click the **Copy to** button [*Home* tab, *Organize* group] and select **Choose Location** to open the *Copy Items* dialog box (Figure 1-84).

c. Select the **American River Cycling Club** folder in your *SkyDrive* folder and click **Copy**.

d. Select the copy of the file (***[your initials] PP O1-1a – Copy***) and click the **Rename** button [*Home* tab, *Organize* group].

e. Type [your initials] PP O1-3a and press **Enter**.

f. Select the ***[your initials] PP O1-1b*** file (this is an Excel file).

g. Press **Ctrl+C** to copy the file and then press **Ctrl+V** to paste a copy of the file.

h. Rename this file [your initials] PP O1-3b.

i. Right-click the ***[your initials] PP O1-2*** file (this is a Word file and the third one in the list) and select **Copy** from the context menu.

j. Right-click a blank area of the open window and select **Paste** from the context menu.

k. Rename this file [your initials] PP O1-3c.

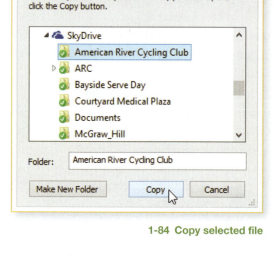

1-84 Copy selected file

3. Create a new folder and move files.

a. With the *American River Cycling Club* folder still open, click the **New folder** button on the upper left.

b. Type ARCC Italy Tour and press **Enter**.

c. Select the ***[your initials] PP O1-3a*** file.

d. Hold down the **Ctrl** key, select the ***[your initials] PP O1-3b*** and ***[your initials] PP O1-3c*** files.

e. Click the selected files and drag and drop on the *ARCC Italy Tour* folder (don't hold down the *Ctrl* key while dragging). The files are moved to the *ARCC Italy Tour* folder.

f. Double-click the **ARCC Italy Tour** folder to open it and confirm the files are moved.

g. Click the **Up** or **Back** arrow to return to the *American River Cycling Club* folder.

4. Create a zipped folder.

a. Select the **ARCC Italy Tour** folder.

b. Click the **Zip** button [*Share* tab, *Send* group]. A zipped (compressed) folder is created.

c. Right-click the zipped folder and select **Rename** from the context menu.

d. At the end of the folder name, type - (a hyphen), type the current year, and press **Enter** (Figure 1-85).

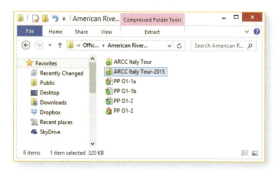

1-85 PP O1-3 completed

5. Email the zipped folder to your instructor.

a. Using your email account, create a new email to send to your instructor.

b. Include an appropriate subject line and a brief message in the body.

c. Attach the ***ARCC Italy Tour-[current year]*** zipped folder to the email message.

d. Send the email message.

Chapter Summary

1.1 Use the basic features of Windows 8 and Microsoft Office 2013 products (p. O1-2).

- **Windows 8** is the operating system on your computer.
- A **Microsoft account** is a free account you create. When you create a Microsoft account, you are given an email address, a **SkyDrive** account, and access to **Office Web Apps**.
- **SkyDrive** is the **cloud storage** area where you can store files in a private and secure online location.
- In Windows 8, the **SkyDrive folder** is one of your file storage location options.
- The **Start page** in Windows 8 is where you select what you want to do on your computer.
- The **Windows desktop** is the working area of Windows and the **Taskbar** is at the bottom of the desktop. You can pin applications to the Taskbar.
- The **File Explorer** is a window that displays libraries, files, and folders on your computer.
- You can access your *SkyDrive* folders and files using an Internet browser window.
- **Apps** are the applications or programs on your computer. App buttons are arranged in tiles on the Windows 8 *Start* page.
- You can customize the *Start* page to add, remove, or arrange apps.
- **Navigation options** display on the right side of your computer monitor when you put your pointer in the bottom right corner.
- **Office 2013** is application software that contains **Word**, **Excel**, **Access**, **PowerPoint**, **Outlook**, **OneNote**, and **Publisher**.
- **Office Web Apps** is free online software that works in conjunction with your online *SkyDrive* account.
- In *SkyDrive*, you can share Office files with others.
- When you open each of the Office applications, a **Start page** is displayed where you can open an existing file or create a new file.
- In the **Backstage view** in each of the Office applications, you can perform many common tasks such as saving, opening an existing file, creating a new file, printing, and sharing.
- **Office Help** contains searchable articles related to specific topics.

- Use the mouse (or touch pad) on your computer to navigate the pointer on your computer screen. Use the pointer or click buttons to select text or objects.
- When using Office 2013 on a tablet, use the touch screen to perform actions.

1.2 Create, save, close, and open Office files (p. O1-12).

- You can create a new Office file from the *Start* page or *Backstage* view of the Office application you are using.
- When you **save a file** for the first time, you give it a **file name**.
- You can create **folders** to organize saved files, and you can save a file as a different file name.
- A variety of different **file types** are used in each of the Office applications.
- You can close an Office file when you are finished working on it. If the file has not been saved or changes have been made to the file, you are prompted to save the file before closing.
- In each of the Office applications, you can open an existing file from the *Start* page or from the *Backstage* view.

1.3 Print, share, and customize Office files (p. O1-20).

- You can print a file in a variety of formats. The *Print* area on the *Backstage* view lists your print options and displays a preview of your file.
- You can export a file as a **PDF file** and save the PDF file to post to a web site or share with others.
- **Document properties** contain information about a file.
- You can **share** Office files in a variety of ways and allow others to view or edit shared files.
- **Program options** are available on the *Backstage* view. You can use the program options to make global changes to an Office application.

1.4 Use the Ribbon, tabs, groups, dialog boxes, task panes, galleries, and the Quick Access toolbar (p. O1-23).

- The **Ribbon** appears at the top of an Office window. It contains **tabs** and **groups** that allow you to access features you regularly use.

O1-39

- The **Ribbon Display Options** provides different ways the *Ribbon* can be displayed in Office applications.
- Within groups on each tab are a variety of **buttons**, **drop-down lists**, and **galleries**.
- **Dialog boxes** contain additional features not always displayed on the *Ribbon*.
- Click the **launcher** in the bottom right corner of some groups to open a dialog box for that group.
- A **ScreenTip** displays information about commands on the *Ribbon*.
- Dialog boxes contain **radio buttons**, **check boxes**, **drop-down lists**, and **text boxes** you can use to apply features.
- The **Quick Access toolbar**, which contains buttons that allow you to perform commands, is displayed in all Office applications on the upper left.
- You can add or remove commands on the *Quick Access* toolbar.

1.5 Use context menus, mini toolbars, and keyboard shortcuts in Office applications (p. O1-27).

- A **context menu** displays when you right-click text or an object. The context menu contains different features depending on what you right-click.
- The **mini toolbar** is another context menu that displays formatting options.
- You can use **keyboard shortcuts** to apply features or commands.

1.6 Customize the view and display size in Office applications and work with multiple Office files (p. O1-31).

- In each of the Office applications, there are a variety of **views**.
- The **Zoom feature** changes the display size of your file.
- You can work with multiple Office files at the same time and switch between open files.

1.7 Organize and customize Office files and Windows folders (p. O1-34).

- **Folders** store and organize your files.
- You can create, move, or copy files and folders. Files stored in a folder are moved or copied with that folder.
- You can rename a file to change the file name.
- When you delete a file or folder, it is moved to the **Recycle Bin** on your computer by default. Alternatively, you can permanently delete files and folders.
- A **zipped (compressed) folder** makes it easier and faster to email or share multiple files. You can zip files and/or folders into a zipped folder.
- When you receive a zipped folder, you can **extract** the zipped folder to create a regular Windows folder and access its contents.

Check for Understanding

In the **Online Learning Center** for this text (www.mhhe.com/office2013inpractice), there are a variety of resources that can be used to review the concepts covered in this chapter.

The following Online Learning Resources are available in the Online Learning Center:

- Multiple choice questions
- Short answer questions
- Matching exercises

In these projects, you use your *SkyDrive* to store files. If you don't have a Microsoft account, see *SLO 1.1: Using Windows 8 and Office 2013* for information about obtaining a free personal Microsoft account.

Guided Project 1-1

For this project, you organize and edit files for Emma Cavalli at Placer Hills Real Estate. You extract a zipped folder, rename files, manage multiple documents, and apply formatting.
[Student Learning Outcomes 1.1, 1.2, 1.4, 1.5, 1.6, 1.7]

Files Needed: **CavalliFiles-01** (zipped folder)
Completed Project File Names: *[your initials] Office 1-1a.docx*, *[your initials] Office 1-1b.docx*, *[your initials] Office 1-1c.xlsx*, and *[your initials] Office 1-1d.pptx*

Skills Covered in This Project

- Copy and paste a zipped folder.
- Create a new folder in your *SkyDrive* folder.
- Extract a zipped folder.
- Move a file.
- Rename a file.
- Open a Word document.
- Switch between two open Word documents.

- Save a Word document with a different file name.
- Change display size.
- Use a mini toolbar, keyboard shortcut, context menu, and dialog box to apply formatting to selected text.
- Close a Word document.

1. Copy a zipped folder and create a new *SkyDrive* folder.
   a. From the Windows *Start* page, click **File Explorer** or **Computer** to open a Windows folder. If these options are not available on the *Start* page, use *Search* to find and open a Windows folder.
   b. Browse to the location on your computer where you store your student data files.
   c. Select the **CavalliFiles-01** zipped folder and press **Ctrl+C** to copy the folder.
   d. Select your **SkyDrive** folder at the left and click the **New folder** button to create a new folder.
   e. Type PHRE and press **Enter**.
   f. Press **Enter** again to open the *PHRE* folder.
   g. Press **Ctrl+V** to paste the copied **CavalliFiles-01** zipped folder in the *PHRE* folder.

2. Extract a zipped folder.
   a. Select the **CavalliFiles-01** zipped folder.
   b. Click the **Compressed Folder Tools Extract** tab and click the **Extract all** button. The *Extract Compressed (Zipped) Folders* dialog box opens.
   c. Deselect the **Show extracted files when complete** check box.
   d. Click the **Extract** button. The zipped folder is extracted and there are now two *CavalliFiles-01* folders. One folder is zipped and the other is a regular folder.
   e. Select the zipped **CavalliFiles-01** folder and press **Delete** to delete the zipped folder.

3. Move and rename files.
   a. With the *PHRE* folder still open, double-click the **CavalliFiles-01** folder to open it.
   b. Click the first file, press and hold the **Shift** key, and click the last file to select all four files.
   c. Press **Ctr+X** to cut the files from the current location.

d. Click the **Up** button to move up to the *PHRE* folder (Figure 1-86).
e. Press **Ctrl+V** to paste and move the files.
f. Select the ***Cavalli files-01*** folder and press **Delete** to delete the folder.
g. Select the ***CavalliPHRE-01*** file, click the **File** tab, and click the **Rename** button [*Organize* group].
h. Type [your initials] Office 1-1a and press **Enter**.
i. Right-click the ***FixedMortgageRates-01*** file and select the **Rename** from the context menu.
j. Type [your initials] Office 1-1b and press **Enter**.

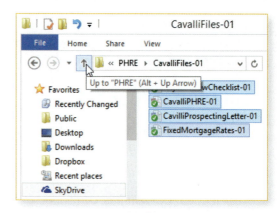
1-86 Go up to the *PHRE* folder

4. Open two Word documents and rename a Word document.
   a. Press the **Ctrl** key and click the ***BuyerEscrowChecklist-01*** and ***CavalliProspectingLetter-01*** files to select both files.
   b. Press the **Enter** key to open both files in Word.
   c. If the *BuyerEscrowChecklist-01* document is not displayed, click the **Switch Documents** button [*View* tab, *Window* group] and select ***BuyerEscrowChecklist-01***. You can also switch documents by selecting the document on the *Taskbar*.
   d. Click the **File** tab and select **Save As** at the left.
   e. Select **[your name's] SkyDrive** in the *Places* area and select the **PHRE** folder or click **Browse** and select the **PHRE** folder. The *Save As* dialog box opens.
   f. Type [your initials] Office 1-1c in the *File name* text box and click **Save**.
   g. Press **Ctrl+W** to close the document. The *Cavalli Prospecting Letter_01* remains open.

5. Change display size and edit and rename a Word document.
   a. Click the **Zoom In** or **Zoom Out** button at the bottom right of the document window to change the display size to 120% (Figure 1-87). This will vary depending on the current display size.

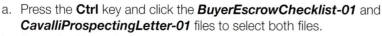
1-87 Use *Zoom* to increase or decrease the display size

   b. Select "**Placer Hills Real Estate**" in the first body paragraph of the letter and the mini toolbar is displayed (Figure 1-88).

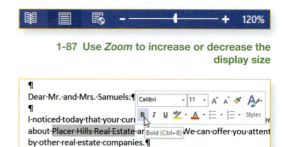
1-88 Use the mini toolbar to apply formatting

   c. Click the **Bold** button on the mini toolbar to apply bold formatting to the selected text.
   d. Select the first sentence in the second body paragraph ("**I am also a Whitney Hills . . .** ") and press **Ctrl+I** to apply italic formatting to the selected sentence.
   e. Select the text that reads "**Emma Cavalli**," below "Best regards."
   f. Right-click the selected text and select **Font** from the context menu to open the *Font* dialog box.
   g. Check the **Small Caps** check box in the *Effects* area and click **OK** to close the *Font* dialog box.
   h. With "**Emma Cavalli**" still selected, click the **Bold** button [*Home* tab, *Font* group].
   i. Press **F12** to open the *Save As* dialog box.
   j. Type [your initials] Office 1-1d in the *File name* text box and click **Save**.
   k. Click the **X** in the upper right corner of the document window to close the document and close Word.

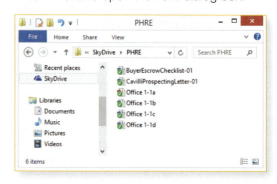
1-89 Office 1-1 completed

6. Your *PHRE* folder should contain the files shown in Figure 1-89.

Guided Project 1-2

For this project, you modify an Excel file for Hamilton Civic Center. You rename a file, add document properties, use *Help* to search a topic, share the file, and export a file as a PDF file.
[Student Learning Outcomes 1.1, 1.2, 1.3, 1.4]

Note to Students and Instructor:
Students: *For this project, you share an Office file with your instructor.*
Instructor: *In order to complete this project, your students need your Microsoft email address. You can create a new Live or Hotmail account for projects in this chapter.*

File Needed: ***HCCYoga-01.xlsx***
Completed Project File Names: ***[your initials] Office 1-2.xlsx*** and ***[your initials] Office 1-2.pdf***

Skills Covered in This Project

- Open Excel and an Excel workbook.
- Create a new *SkyDrive* folder.
- Save an Excel workbook with a different file name.
- Add document properties to a file.
- Use *Microsoft Excel Help* to search for a topic.
- Open a Word document.
- Share a file.
- Export a file as a PDF file.

1. Open Excel 2013 and open an Excel workbook.
   a. From the Windows *Start* page, click **Excel 2013** to open this application. If Excel 2013 is not available on the *Start* page, use *Search* to find and open it.
   b. From the Excel *Start* page, click **Open Other Workbooks** to display the *Open* area of the *Backstage* view.
   c. In the *Places* area, select where your student data files are stored and click the **Browse** button to open the *Open* dialog box.
   d. Browse to the location where your student data files are stored, select the ***HCCYoga-01*** file, and click **Open** to open the Excel workbook.

2. Save a file as a different file name in your *SkyDrive* folder.
   a. Click the **File** tab to open the *Backstage* view and select **Save As** at the left.
   b. In the *Places* area, select **[your name's] SkyDrive**.
   c. Click the **Browse** button to open the *Save As* dialog box.
   d. Select the **SkyDrive** folder on the left and click the **New folder** button to create a new folder.
   e. Type HCC and press **Enter**.
   f. Double-click the **HCC** folder to open it.
   g. In the *File name* area, type [your initials] Office 1-2 and click **Save** to close the dialog box and save the file.

3. Add document properties to the Excel workbook.
   a. Click the **File** button to open the *Backstage* view and select **Info** on the left. The document properties are displayed on the right.
   b. Put your insertion point in the *Title* text box ("Add a title") and type Yoga Classes.
   c. Click the **Show All Properties** link to display more properties.

d. Put your insertion point in the *Company* text box and type Hamilton Civic Center.

e. Click the **back arrow** in the upper left of the *Backstage* window to return to the Excel workbook.

4. Use *Help* to learn about a topic.

a. Click **Microsoft Excel Help** button (question mark) in the upper right corner of the Excel window or press **F1** to open the *Excel Help* dialog box.

b. Put your insertion point in the *Search help* text box, type AutoSum, and press **Enter**.

c. Click the first link and read about *AutoSum*.

d. Click the **Back** button to return to the search list of articles and click the second link.

e. Read about *AutoSum* and then click the **X** in the upper right corner to close the *Excel Help* dialog box.

5. Share an Excel workbook with your instructor.

a. Click the **File** tab and select **Share** at the left.

b. In the *Share* area, select **Invite People** (Figure 1-90).

c. Type your instructor's email address in the *Type names or email addresses* area.

d. In the drop-down list to the right of the email address, select **Can edit**.

e. In the body, type a brief message.

f. Click the **Share** button.

g. Click the **Save** button to save and return to the workbook.

1-90 Invite people to share a file

6. Export the Excel workbook as a PDF file.

a. Click the **File** button and select **Export** at the left.

b. In the *Export* area, select **Create PDF/XPS Document** and click the **Create PDF/XPS** button. The *Publish as PDF or XPS* dialog box opens.

c. Check the **Open file after publishing** check box. The publish location and file name are the same as the Excel file; don't change these.

d. Click **Publish** to create and open the PDF file (Figure 1-91). The PDF file opens in an Internet browser window in *SkyDrive*.

e. Close the Internet browser window.

7. Save and close the Excel file.

a. Click the **Excel** icon on the Windows *Taskbar* to display the Excel file.

b. Press **Ctrl+S** to save the file.

c. Click the **X** in the upper right corner of the Excel window to close the file and Excel.

1-91 PDF file displayed in *SkyDrive*

Independent Project 1-3

For this project, you organize and edit files for Courtyard Medical Plaza. You extract a zipped folder, rename files, export a file as a PDF file, and share a file in *SkyDrive*.
[Student Learning Outcomes 1.1, 1.3, 1.6, 1.7]

Note to Students and Instructor:

Students: *For this project, you share an* Office Web App *file with your instructor.*
Instructor: *In order to complete this project, your students need your Microsoft email address. You can create a new Live or Hotmail account for projects in this chapter.*

Files Needed: **CMPFiles-01** (zipped folder)
Completed Project File Names: **[your initials] Office 1-3a.pptx**, **[your initials] Office 1-3a-pdf.pdf**, **[your initials] Office 1-3b.accdb**, **[your initials] Office 1-3c.xlsx**, and **[your initials] Office 1-3d.docx**

Skills Covered in This Project

- Copy and paste a zipped folder.
- Create a new folder in your *SkyDrive* folder.
- Extract a zipped folder.
- Move a file.
- Rename a file.
- Open a PowerPoint presentation.
- Export a file as a PDF file.
- Use *SkyDrive* to share a file.

---

1. Copy a zipped folder and create a new *SkyDrive* folder.
   a. Using a Windows folder, browse to locate the **CMPFiles-01** zipped folder in your student data files and copy the zipped folder.
   b. Go to your *SkyDrive* folder and create a new folder named Courtyard Medical Plaza within the *SkyDrive* folder.

2. Copy and extract the zipped folder and move files.
   a. Paste the zipped folder in the *Courtyard Medical Plaza* folder.
   b. Extract the zipped folder and then delete the zipped folder.
   c. Open the **CMPFiles-01** folder and move all of the files to the *Courtyard Medical Plaza* folder.
   d. Delete the **CMPFiles-01** folder.

3. Rename files in the *Courtyard Medical Plaza* folder.
   a. Rename the **CMPStayingActive-01** PowerPoint file to [your initials] Office 1-3a.
   b. Rename the **CourtyardMedicalPlaza-01** Access file to [your initials] Office 1-3b.
   c. Rename the **EstimatedCalories-01** Excel file to [your initials] Office 1-3c.
   d. Rename the **StayingActive-01** Word file to [your initials] Office 1-3d.

4. Export a PowerPoint file as a PDF file.
   a. From the *Courtyard Medical Plaza* folder, open the **[your initials] Office 1-3a** file. The file opens in PowerPoint.
   b. Export this file as a PDF file. Don't have the PDF file open after publishing.
   c. Save the file as [your initials] Office 1-3a-pdf and save in the *Courtyard Medical Plaza* folder.
   d. Close the PowerPoint file and exit PowerPoint.

5. Use *SkyDrive* to share a file with your instructor.
   a. Open an Internet browser window and log in to your *SkyDrive* (www.skydrive.com) using your Microsoft account.
   b. Go to your *SkyDrive* files and open the **Courtyard Medical Plaza** folder.
   c. Open the ***[your initials] Office 1-3a*** file in PowerPoint Web App.
   d. Share this file with your instructor.
   e. Send an email to share the file and include your instructor's email address and a brief message. Allow your instructor to edit the file.
   f. Sign out of *SkyDrive*.

6. Close the Windows folder containing the files for this project (Figure 1-92).

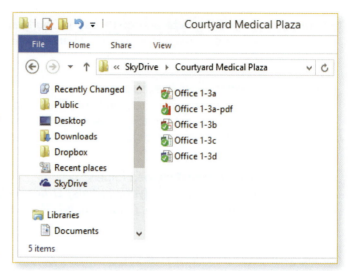

1-92 Office 1-3 completed

Independent Project 1-4

For this project, you modify a Word file for Life's Animal Shelter. You rename the document, add document properties, modify the document, share a link to the document, export a document as a PDF file, and create a zipped folder.
[Student Learning Outcomes 1.1, 1.2, 1.3, 1.4, 1.5, 1.6, 1.7]

Note to Students and Instructor:
Students: *For this project, you share an Office file with your instructor.*
Instructor: *In order to complete this project, your students need your Microsoft email address. You can create a new Live or Hotmail account for projects in this chapter.*

File Needed: ***LASSupportLetter-01.docx***
Completed Project File Names: ***[your initials] Office 1-4.docx***, ***[your initials] Office 1-4.pdf***, and ***LAS files*** (zipped folder)

Skills Covered in This Project

- Open Excel and an Excel file.
- Create a new *SkyDrive* folder.
- Save a file with a different file name.
- Apply formatting to selected text.
- Add document properties to the file.

- Use *Microsoft Excel Help* to search for a topic.
- Open a Word document.
- Share a file.
- Export a file as a PDF file.

1. Open Word 2013 and open a Word document.
   a. From the Windows *Start* page, open Word 2013.
   b. From the Word *Start* page, open the **LASSupportLetter-01** document from your student data files.

2. Create a new folder and save the document with a different file name.
   a. Open the **Save As** dialog box and create a new folder named LAS in your *SkyDrive* folder.
   b. Save this document as [your initials] Office 1-4.

3. Apply formatting changes to the document using a dialog box, keyboard shortcut, and mini toolbar.
   a. Select "**To**" and use the **launcher** to open the *Font* dialog box.
   b. Apply **Bold** and **All caps** to the selected text.
   c. Repeat the formatting on the other three memo guide words: "**From**," "**Date**," and "**Subject**."
   d. Select "**Life's Animal Shelter**" in the first sentence of the first body paragraph and use the keyboard shortcut to apply **bold** formatting.
   e. Select the first sentence in the second body paragraph ("**Would you again consider** . . . ") and use the mini toolbar to apply *italic* formatting.

4. Add the following document properties to the document:
   Title: Support Letter
   Company: Life's Animal Shelter

5. Get a link to share this document with your instructor.
   a. Create and copy an **Edit Link** you can email to your instructor.
   b. Create a new email to send to your professor using the email you use for this course.
   c. Include an appropriate subject line and a brief message in the body.
   d. Paste the link in the body of the email message and send the message.

6. Use the keyboard shortcut to **save** the file before continuing.

7. Export this document as a PDF file.
   a. Save the file in the same location and use the same file name.
   b. Close the PDF file if it opens after publishing.

8. Save and close the Word file and exit Word (Figure 1-93).

9. Create a zipped folder.
   a. Using a Windows folder, open the **LAS** folder in your *SkyDrive* folder.
   b. Select the two files and create a zipped folder.
   c. Rename the zipped folder LAS files (Figure 1-94).

10. Close the open Windows folder.

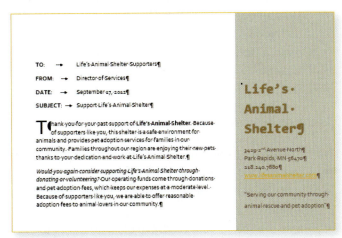

1-93 Office 1-4 completed

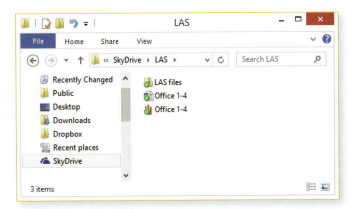

1-94 Office 1-4 completed

Challenge Project 1-5

For this project, you create folders to organize your files for this class and use *SkyDrive* to share a link with your professor.
[Student Learning Outcomes 1.1, 1.7]

Note to Students and Instructor:
Students: For this project, you share an Office file with your instructor.
Instructor: In order to complete this project, your students need your Microsoft email address.
You can create a new Live or Hotmail account for projects in this chapter.

File Needed: None
Completed Project File Name: Email link to shared folder to your instructor

Using a Windows folder, create *SkyDrive* folders to contain all of the files for this class. Organize your files and folders according to the following guidelines:

- Create a *SkyDrive* folder for this class.
- Create a *Student data files* folder inside the class folder.
- Extract student data files if you have not already done so. Make sure they are in the *Student data files* folder.
- Create a *Solution files* folder inside the class folder.
- Inside the *Solution files* folder, create a folder for each chapter.
- Create a folder to store miscellaneous class files such as the syllabus and other course handouts.

Using an Internet browser, log in to your *SkyDrive* and share your class folder with your instructor.

- In *SkyDrive*, select the check box to the right of your class folder and click the **Share** button.
- Create a link to *View only* the folder.
- Create an email to your professor and include an appropriate subject line and a brief message in the body.
- Paste the link to your *SkyDrive* class folder in the body of the email message and send the email.

Challenge Project 1-6

For this project, you save a file as a different file name, customize the *Quick Access* toolbar, share a file with your professor, and export a file as a PDF file.
[Student Learning Outcomes 1.1, 1.2, 1.3, 1.4]

Note to Students and Instructor:
Students: *For this project, you share an Office file with your instructor.*
Instructor: *In order to complete this project, your students need your Microsoft email address. You can create a new Live or Hotmail account for projects in this chapter.*

File Needed: Use an existing Office file
Completed Project File Name: *[your initials] Office 1-6*

Open an existing Word, Excel, or PowerPoint file. Save this file in a *SkyDrive* folder and name it *[your initials] Office 1-6*. If you don't have any of these files, use one from your Pause & Practice projects or select a file from your student data files.

With your file open, perform the following actions:

- Customize the *Quick Access* toolbar to add command buttons. Add commands such as *New*, *Open*, *Quick Print*, and *Spelling* that you use regularly in the Office application.
- Share your file with your instructor. Use *Invite People* and include your instructor's email, an appropriate subject line, and a brief message in the body. Allow your instructor to edit the file.
- Export the document as a PDF file. Use the same file name and save it in the same *SkyDrive* folder as your open file.

Microsoft® Office
IN PRACTICE

excel

CHAPTER 1

Creating and Editing Workbooks

CHAPTER OVERVIEW

Microsoft Excel (Excel) is a spreadsheet program you can use to create electronic workbooks to organize numerical data, perform calculations, and create charts. Using Excel, both new and advanced users can create useful and powerful business spreadsheets. This chapter covers the basics of creating and editing an Excel workbook.

STUDENT LEARNING OUTCOMES (SLOs)

After completing this chapter, you will be able to:

SLO 1.1 Create, save, and open an Excel workbook (p. E1-3).

SLO 1.2 Edit a workbook by entering and deleting text and numbers, using the *Fill Handle* to complete a series, and using the cut, copy, and paste features (p. E1-6).

SLO 1.3 Create a basic formula using *AutoSum* (p. E1-16).

SLO 1.4 Format a worksheet using different font attributes, borders, shading, cell styles, themes, and the *Format Painter* (p. E1-19).

SLO 1.5 Resize, insert, delete, and hide and unhide columns and rows in a worksheet (p. E1-26).

SLO 1.6 Insert, delete, edit, format, and rearrange worksheets (p. E1-31).

SLO 1.7 Customize the Excel window by changing views, adjusting zoom level, freezing panes, and splitting a worksheet (p. E1-36).

SLO 1.8 Finalize a workbook by spell checking, adding document properties, applying page setup options, and printing (p. E1-41).

CASE STUDY

Paradise Lakes Resort (PLR) is a vacation company with four resort chains located throughout northern Minnesota. PLR asks employees to use standard formats for spreadsheets to ensure consistency in spreadsheet appearance. In the Pause & Practice projects for Chapter 1, you create business workbooks for the Paradise Lakes Resort.

Pause & Practice 1-1: Create a business workbook.

Pause & Practice 1-2: Create basic formulas using *AutoSum* and format a workbook.

Pause & Practice 1-3: Customize cell contents and edit spreadsheet structure.

Pause & Practice 1-4: Customize the window and finalize the workbook.

EXCEL

Creating, Saving, and Opening Workbooks

In Microsoft Excel, the file you create and edit is called a ***workbook***. You can create an Excel workbook from a blank workbook or from an existing, customizable Excel template. Each workbook file contains many ***worksheets***, which are comparable to individual pages in a Word document. A worksheet is also referred to as a ***spreadsheet*** or a ***sheet***, and you can use these terms interchangeably. This book also uses the terms "workbook" and "file" interchangeably. To create a new workbook, first open Excel on your computer.

Create a New Workbook

By default, a workbook includes one worksheet, but a workbook can include multiple worksheets. The worksheet tab is located near the bottom left of the workbook window and is labeled *Sheet1*.

When you first open Excel, the ***Excel Start page*** displays. From the *Start* page, you can create a new blank workbook, open a previously saved workbook, or create a new workbook from an Excel template. Click **Blank workbook** to open a new blank workbook. Alternatively, you can create a new blank workbook from the *New* area on the ***Backstage view***.

> **ANOTHER WAY**
>
> Press **Esc** to leave the Excel *Start* page and open a blank workbook.

HOW TO: Create a New Workbook

1. Click the **File** tab to display the *Backstage* view.
2. Select **New** on the left to display the *New* area on the *Backstage* view (Figure 1-1).
3. Click **Blank workbook** to create a new blank workbook.

> **ANOTHER WAY**
>
> **Ctrl+N** opens a new blank workbook.

1-1 *Backstage* view for creating new workbooks

Save a Workbook

When you open a blank workbook, Excel automatically assigns a file name to the file, such as *Book1*. The first time you save a new workbook you must type a file name for the workbook into the *Save As* dialog box (see Figure 1-3).

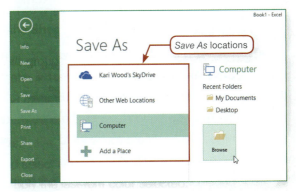

1-2 *Save As* locations

HOW TO: Save a New Workbook

1. Click the **File** tab to display *Backstage* view.
2. Select **Save As** on the left to display the *Save As* area (see Figure 1-2).
   - You can also press **Ctrl+S** to open the *Save As* area on *Backstage* view when saving a workbook that has not yet been saved.
3. Select the location where you want to save your document.
   - You can save the document on your computer, in a *SkyDrive* folder, or on an external storage device.
   - If you click one of the *Recent Folders* options, the *Save As* dialog box opens.
4. Click the **Browse** button to open the *Save As* dialog box (Figure 1-3).
5. Select the location where you want to save the workbook in the left area of the *Save As* dialog box.
6. Type the name of the file in the *File name* area.
7. Click **Save** to close the *Save As* dialog box and save the file.

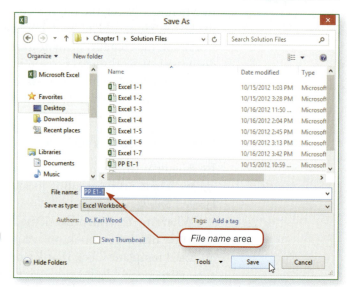

1-3 *Save As* dialog box

▶ ANOTHER WAY

Press **F12** to open the *Save As* dialog box.

Once a workbook has been saved, you can re-save it by pressing **Ctrl+S** or clicking the **Save** button on the *Quick Access* toolbar.

Save a Workbook with a Different File Name

You can save a workbook as a different name by opening the *Save As* dialog box and giving the workbook a different file name. This action does not remove the existing workbook but instead creates a copy of the file with a new name. For example, you might want to rename an existing expense report before updating it with current data. Saving a workbook with a different file name is similar to saving a new workbook.

HOW TO: Save As a Different File Name

1. Click the **File** tab to open *Backstage* view.
   - You can also press **F12** from the working area of Excel to open the *Save As* dialog box.
2. Click **Save As** to display the *Save As* area.
3. Select the location to save your document.
4. Click the **Browse** button to open the *Save As* dialog box (see Figure 1-3).
5. Select the location where you want to save the workbook in the left pane of the *Save As* dialog box.
6. Type the name of the file in the *File name* area.
7. Click **Save** to close the *Save As* dialog box and save the file.

Workbook File Formats

You can save an Excel workbook in a variety of formats. For example, you might want to save a workbook in an older Excel format to share with someone who uses an earlier version of Excel, or you may want to save a workbook in portable document format (.pdf) to create a static image of the file.

By default, Excel workbooks are saved as *.xlsx* files. To change the type of file format, select the format of your choice from the *Save as type* area of the *Save As* dialog box (Figure 1-4). The following table lists several common formats for saving an Excel workbook.

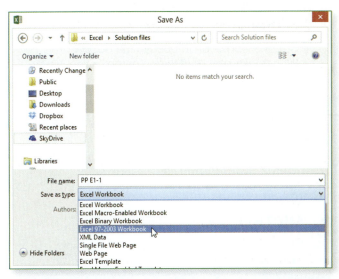

1-4 Workbook file formats

Save Formats

Type of Document	File Extension	Uses of This Format
Excel Macro-Enabled Workbook	.xlsm	Excel workbook with embedded macros
Excel 97-2003 Workbook	.xls	Excel workbook compatible with older versions of Microsoft Excel
Excel Template	.xltx	A new workbook based on a template
Excel Macro-Enabled Template	.xltm	A new workbook based on a template with embedded macros
Portable Document Format (PDF)	.pdf	A static image, similar to a picture, of a workbook; used to preserve the formatting of a file
Plain Text	.txt	Workbook can be opened with most spreadsheet applications and contains text only, with no special formatting.
Comma Separated Values (CSV)	.csv	A common file format that can be opened by most spreadsheet programs and is used to import and export data
Open Document Text	.ods	The spreadsheet software in the Open Office suite
Web Page	.htm, .html	A workbook that is formatted for web sites

Open a Workbook

You can open workbooks from your computer, USB drive, or *SkyDrive*. You can open a previously saved workbook from the *Start* page, *Open* area on the *Backstage* view, or *Open* dialog box.

HOW TO: Open a Workbook

1. Click the **File** tab to open *Backstage* view.
2. Click **Open** to display the *Open* area.
   - Select a workbook to open in the *Recent Workbooks* area or click one of the options in the *Open* area.
3. Select the location where the workbook is stored.
4. Click **Browse** or click a folder to display the *Open* dialog box.
5. Select the workbook and click **Open** (Figure 1-5).

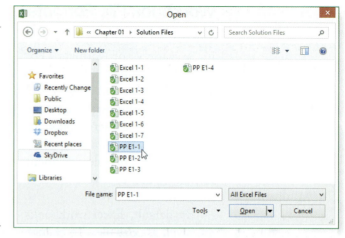

1-5 *Open* dialog box

> **ANOTHER WAY**
>
> **Ctrl+O** displays the *Open* area on the *Backstage* view.
> **Ctrl+F12** displays the *Open* dialog box.

SLO 1.2

Working with Text and Numbers

When you create or edit a workbook, you can type data, import data from another file, or copy data from a web page or another source. It is important to enter text and numbers correctly to create professional-looking workbooks. A *label* is text in a worksheet that identifies a title and subtitle, row and column headings, and other descriptive information. Labels are not included in calculations. A *value* is a number that you type in a cell. Use values for numbers, currency, dates, and percentages. Values are included in calculations. Occasionally you may need to enter a number as a label. To type a number as a label, click the cell, type an apostrophe ('), and type the number value.

A worksheet is arranged in **columns** (vertical) and **rows** (horizontal). Columns are labeled with letters and rows are labeled with numbers. You type text and numbers in a **cell**, which is the intersection of a column and a row. Each cell is identified with a **cell reference** (or **cell address**), which is the column letter and row number that represent the location of the cell. Cell A1 is the intersection of column A and row 1.

Before entering data in a worksheet, verify the workbook view settings. Click the **View** tab, and select the **Gridlines**, **Formula Bar**, and **Headings** options in the *Show* group. *Gridlines* display the cell boundaries, and the *Headings* option displays row and column headings. Use the *Formula bar* to insert formulas and to edit data.

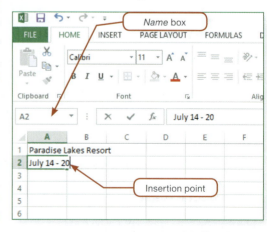

Enter Text and Numbers

To enter data into a spreadsheet, click the cell with your pointer to activate the cell. The **active cell** displays a solid border around the cell, and the reference for the active cell appears in the **Name box** (Figure 1-6).

1-6 Entering text

HOW TO: Enter Data into a Workbook

1. Select the cell and type the information.
   - The text appears inside the active cell with a blinking insertion point (see Figure 1-6).
2. Press **Enter** to accept the information you typed in the cell and to activate the cell below.
   - Press **Tab** to activate the cell to the right.
   - You can also use the arrow keys on your keyboard to activate a cell.

> **MORE INFO**
>
> When text is longer than the width of the cell, the text displays only if adjacent cells are empty. If the adjacent cells are not empty, the text appears cut off in the cell, but the *Formula bar* displays the entire entry. To display the entire entry, adjust the column width.

Edit Cell Contents

You can edit the content of the cell as you type or after the entry is complete. To edit text as you type (before you press *Enter*), use the **Backspace** key to delete characters to the left of the insertion point. Use arrow keys to move the insertion point, and use the **Delete** key to delete characters to the right of the insertion point. To edit a completed entry (after you press *Enter*), you must activate *edit mode* in the cell. To activate edit mode, double-click the cell or press **F2**. Either method displays an insertion point, and "EDIT" displays on the *Status bar*.

> **ANOTHER WAY**
>
> Click the **Enter** button on the *Formula bar* to complete an entry.

HOW TO: Edit Cell Contents (Completed Entry)

1. Activate edit mode by double-clicking the cell (Figure 1-7).
   - Another way to activate edit mode is to press **F2**.
2. Position the insertion point and edit the contents of the cell.
3. Press **Enter**.

Replace or Clear Cell Contents

To replace the contents of an existing cell, click to activate the cell, and type the new text. Press **Enter** or click the **Enter** button on the *Formula bar*. To remove the contents of the cell, select the cell and press **Delete** or click the **Clear** button [*Home* tab, *Editing* group]. When you click the *Clear* button, you can choose to *Clear All*, *Clear Formats*, or *Clear Contents*.

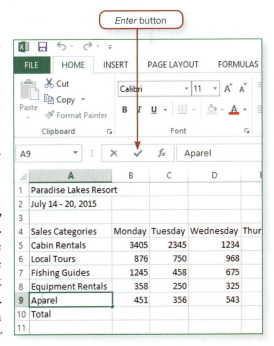

1-7 Activated cell for editing

HOW TO: Clear Cell Contents

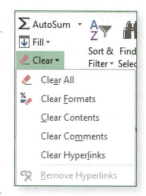

1. Select the cell or cells.
2. Click the **Clear** button [*Home* tab, *Editing* group].
   - Another way to remove cell contents is to press **Delete**.
3. Choose an option from the drop-down list (Figure 1-8).
   - *Clear All* removes formatting and content.
   - *Clear Formats* only clears formatting.
   - *Clear Contents* deletes content.

1-8 *Clear* options

Align and Indent Cell Contents

Excel recognizes any combination of letters, numbers, spaces, and other characters as text and aligns each entry in the bottom left corner of the cell. When you type only numbers into a cell, Excel recognizes your entry as numeric data (values). Excel aligns numeric entries in the bottom right corner of the cell.

You can change both the vertical and horizontal **alignment** of information in a cell. A number of horizontal and vertical alignment and indent options are available in the *Alignment* group on the *Home* tab (Figure 1-9). The vertical alignment options are *Top Align*, *Middle Align*, and *Bottom Align*. Horizontal alignment options are *Align Left*, *Center*, and *Align Right*.

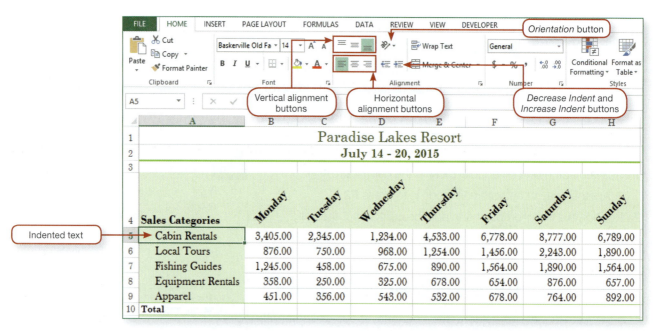

1-9 Alignment and indent options

You can also indent information in a cell. An **indent** increases the distance between the cell contents and the left boundary of the cell. It is common practice to indent row headings in a worksheet (see Figure 1-9). Use **Increase Indent** [*Home* tab, *Alignment* group] to indent cell contents to the right. Use **Decrease Indent** [*Home* tab, *Alignment* group] to remove a previously added indent and move cell contents to the left.

1. Select the cell.

2. Select a horizontal alignment option [*Home* tab, *Alignment* group].

   • *Align Left* aligns text on the left side of the cell.
   • *Center* centers text between the left and right sides of the cell.
   • *Right Align* aligns text on the right side of the cell.

3. Select a vertical alignment option [*Home* tab, *Alignment* group].

   • *Top Align* aligns text at the top of the cell.
   • *Middle Align* aligns text between the top and bottom of the cell.
   • *Bottom Align* aligns text at the bottom of the cell.

4. Select an indent option [*Home* tab, *Alignment* group].

   • *Increase Indent* moves text to the right of the left cell boundary.
   • *Decrease Indent* moves text toward the left cell boundary.

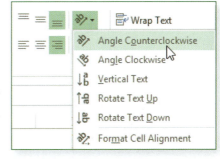

1-10 Text orientation options

By default, text and values are oriented horizontally from left to right, but you can change ***text orientation*** to display text vertically or at an angle. Click the **Orientation** button [*Home* tab, *Alignment* group] to select a text orientation from the drop-down list (Figure 1-10). Select the **Format Cell Alignment** option from the *Orientation* drop-down list to open the *Format Cells* dialog box and adjust the orientation to a specific degree.

> **MORE INFO**
>
> Click the **Alignment** launcher [*Home* tab, *Alignment* group] or press **Ctrl+1** to open the *Format Cells* dialog box, where you can further customize cell contents.

Select Cells

When you format or edit worksheets, the first step is to select a cell, ranges, columns, or rows. A group of cells is a ***range*** (or cell range). In a range of cells, a colon is used to represent "through" while a comma is used to represent "and." For example, (A1:A3) includes the cell A2 while (A1, A3) does not.

Excel uses multiple ***pointers*** to indicate various selecting, copying, and moving options within a worksheet. The following table describes the pointers in Excel.

Pointers

Pointer Icon	Pointer Use
	Selection pointer (block plus sign) selects a cell or ***cell range*** (group of cells); the selection pointer appears when you move your pointer over the center of a cell.
	Fill pointer (crosshair or thin black plus sign) copies cell contents, completes lists, and fills patterns of selected data; it appears when you place your pointer on the *Fill Handle* or black square in the bottom right corner of an active cell or cells.
	Move pointer (white pointer and four-pointed arrow) moves data; it appears when you place your pointer on the border of an active cell or cells.
	Resize pointer (two-pointed arrow) adjusts cell ranges in a formula and adjusts object sizes; it appears when you place your pointer on the selection handle in a range in a formula or on a sizing handle when an object is selected.

There are many different ways to select data in a worksheet (Figure 1-11). The following table lists the various selection methods.

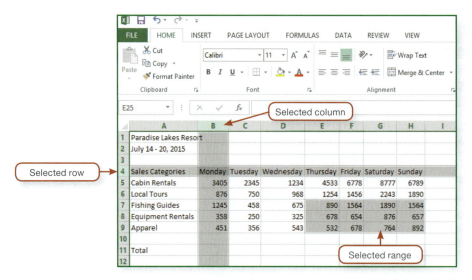

1-11 Selected text

Selection Methods

Name	Instructions
Select an Entire Column or Row	To select an entire column, point to and click a column heading. To select an entire row, point to and click a row heading.
Select the Worksheet	Press **Ctrl+A** or click the **Select All** button (above the row 1 heading and to the left of the column A heading) to select the entire sheet.
Select Adjacent Cells	To select groups of cells that are *adjacent* (next to each other), click and drag the selection pointer over the range of cells. Alternatively, you can select the first cell in the range, press **Shift**, and select the last cell in the range. You can also use the **arrow keys+Shift** to select adjacent cells.
Select Non-Adjacent Cells	To select groups of cells that are *non-adjacent* (not next to each other), use the selection pointer to select the first cell(s), hold down **Ctrl**, and select the next cell(s).
Use the *Name Box* to Select Cells	Type a cell reference or cell range in the *Name* box and press **Enter** to select cells. Type a colon (:) between cell references to select a range of cells.

> **MORE INFO**
>
> Selecting a *cell range* prior to entering data is a quick method for data entry in a defined area. Select the cell range, type the first entry, and press **Enter**. Continue typing and pressing **Enter** after each entry. When the last cell in the first column of the range is completed, the active cell automatically moves to the top of the second column.

Fill Handle

When you are typing data that is in a series, such as days of the week or months of the year, you can use the ***Fill Handle*** to complete the list. You can also use this tool to repeat numeric patterns, such as in a numbered list, or to copy cell contents to another location.

HOW TO: Use the Fill Handle to Create a Series

1. Type the first item in the series.

2. Press **Enter** and reselect the cell.

3. Place your pointer on the *Fill Handle* (small black square in the lower right corner of the cell) until a fill pointer (thin black plus sign) appears (Figure 1-12).

4. Click and drag the fill pointer through the last cell in the range. Release the pointer to complete the series.

   - The items in the series appear in the cell range.
   - The *Auto Fill Options* button displays and includes options to change the fill selection (Figure 1-13).

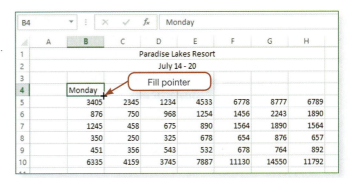

1-12 Use the *Fill Handle* to complete a series

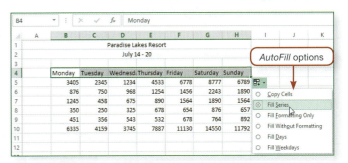

1-13 Completed series

Cut, Copy, and Paste Cell Contents

You can reorganize labels or numeric data quickly using *Cut, Copy,* and *Paste.* Use the *Cut* command to move cells or a cell range. The *Copy* command duplicates cell content from one cell or range to another location. When you cut or copy a cell or a range of cells, it is stored on the Windows *Clipboard.* When you use *Cut, Copy,* and *Paste* commands, the cell you cut or copy from is a **source cell** or cells and the cell you paste to is a **destination cell** or cells.

> ▶ **ANOTHER WAY**
> Use **Ctrl+C** to copy.
> Use **Ctrl+X** to cut.
> Use **Ctrl+V** to paste.

Move or Cut Cell Contents

You can move cell content using drag and drop, keyboard shortcuts, or *Cut* and *Paste* in the *Clipboard* group on the *Home* tab. When you use the drag and drop method, the selected cells are not placed on the clipboard.

HOW TO: Move Cell Contents Using Drag and Drop

1. Select the cell(s) you want to move.

2. Place your pointer on the border of the selection until the move pointer (white pointer and four-pointed arrow) appears.

3. Click and hold the move pointer on the border of the selected cell(s) (Figure 1-14).

4. Drag to the desired new location and release the pointer.

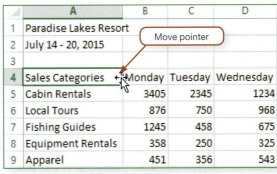

1-14 Move pointer

After you select and cut cells, the cells are placed on the *Clipboard*. To place the contents of the *Clipboard* in the spreadsheet, use the *Paste* command. There are three ways to move text using *Cut* and *Paste*.

- ***Ribbon buttons:*** **Cut** and **Paste** buttons [*Home* tab, *Clipboard* group]
- ***Shortcut commands:*** **Ctrl+X** to cut and **Ctrl+V** to paste
- ***Context menu:*** Right-click a cell or range of cells to display the context menu, and click **Cut**.

HOW TO: Move Cell Contents Using Cut and Paste

1. Select the cell or cell range you want to move.
2. Click **Cut** [*Home* tab, *Clipboard* group]. A moving border appears around the selected source cell or cell range (Figure 1-15).
   - If you choose not to move data, press **Esc** to remove the moving border.
3. Select the destination cell location.
   - Click the cell in the top left of the range where you want to paste.
4. Click **Paste** [*Home* tab, *Clipboard* group].
   - If the destination cell or cell range is not empty, pasted data overwrites existing data. To prevent loss of data, use **Insert Cut Cells** [*Home* tab, *Insert* group].
   - You can paste data that you cut only one time.

	A	B	C	D
1	Paradise Lakes Resort			
2	July 14 - 20, 2015			
3				
4	Sales Categories	Monday	Tuesday	Wednesday
5	Cabin Rentals	3405	2345	1234
6	Local Tours	876	750	968
7	Fishing Guides	1245	458	675
8	Equipment Rentals	358	250	325
9	Apparel	451	356	543
10				

1-15 *Moving cell contents using Cut and Paste*

> ### ANOTHER WAY
>
> Press **Ctrl+X** to cut or right-click the cell and select **Cut** from the context menu. Alternatively, you can press **Ctrl+V** to paste or right-click the destination cell and select **Paste** from the context menu.

Office Clipboard

The Office ***Clipboard*** stores cut or copied data from Excel or other Office applications, and the data stored on the *Clipboard* is available to Excel or to other applications such as Word and PowerPoint. The *Clipboard* can hold up to 24 items. Click the **Clipboard** launcher to open the *Clipboard* pane. Each time you cut or copy, the item appears at the top of the *Clipboard* pane. You can paste one item from the *Clipboard* or paste the entire contents of the *Clipboard*.

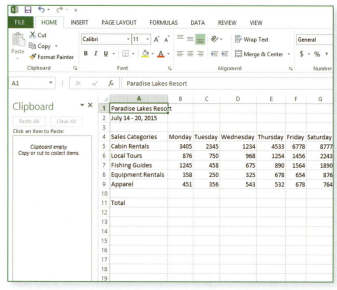

1-16 *Clipboard pane*

HOW TO: Use the Office Clipboard

1. Click the **Home** tab.
2. Click the **Clipboard** launcher to display the *Clipboard* pane (Figure 1-16).
3. Click **Clear All** to empty the *Clipboard*.

4. Cut or copy spreadsheet data to place data on the *Clipboard*. Each item you cut or copy is added to the top of the *Clipboard* pane.

5. Paste items from the *Clipboard* by clicking the item in the task pane. The data is pasted in the active cell.

6. Delete an item from the *Clipboard* by pointing to a *Clipboard* item and clicking the drop-down arrow that appears to the right of the item. Choose **Delete**.

7. Click **Close** to hide the *Clipboard*.

Copy Cell Contents

Copying a cell or a cell range places a duplicate of the selection on the *Clipboard*. The selected data remains in its original location, and a copy of the cell data is pasted in another location. You can copy text using the drag and drop method or *Copy* and *Paste* commands. Data that is copied can be pasted multiple times and in multiple locations.

HOW TO: Copy Using Drag and Drop

1. Select the cell(s) you want to copy.

2. Place your pointer over the border of the selection until the move pointer appears.

3. Press and hold **Ctrl** and click the border of the selected cell(s).
   - A small plus sign appears next to the pointer indicating the move pointer has changed to the copy pointer.

4. Drag the cell or cell range to the desired new location on the worksheet, release the pointer first, and then release **Ctrl** (Figure 1-17).

A4			f_x	Sales Categories	
	A	B	C	D	E	F

	A	B	C	D	E	F
1			Paradise Lakes Resort			
2			July 14 - 20			
3						
4	Sales Cate	Monday	Tuesday	Wednesd	Thursday	Friday
5		3405	2345	1234	4533	6778
6	A5	876	750	968	1254	1456
7		1245	458	675	890	1564
8		350	250	325	678	654

1-17 Copy data using drag and drop

Copying cells using the copy and paste method is similar to moving cells using the cut and paste method. The *Copy* command places the selection on the *Clipboard*, and the *Paste* command places the *Clipboard* contents in the worksheet.

- ***Ribbon buttons:*** **Copy** and **Paste** buttons [*Home* tab, *Clipboard* group]
- ***Shortcut commands:*** **Ctrl+C** to copy and **Ctrl+V** to paste
- ***Context menu:*** Right-click to display the menu, and click **Copy**.

Paste Cell Contents and Paste Options

When you are pasting cell data into a worksheet, you may want to paste plain text or cell formatting or formulas. Excel provides multiple paste options. After copying or cutting cells from your worksheet, click the bottom half of the **Paste** button in the *Clipboard* group on the *Home* tab to display the **Paste Options gallery** (Figure 1-18). The following groups are available in the *Paste Options* gallery:

- *Paste*
- *Paste Values*
- *Other Paste Options*

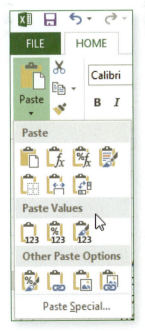

1-18 *Paste Options* gallery

Within these paste groups, there are many context-sensitive paste options. The following table describes each of these paste options.

Paste Options

Group	Paste Icon	Paste Option	Description
Paste		Paste	Copy contents and format of source cell(s); this is the default option.
		Formulas	Copy formulas from the source cell(s) but not contents or formats.
		Formulas & Number Formatting	Copy formulas and format for numbers and formulas of source area but not the contents.
		Keep Source Formatting	Copy contents, format, and styles of source cell.
		No Borders	Copy contents and format of source area but not borders.
		Keep Source Column Widths	Copy contents and format of source cell(s); change destination column widths to source column widths.
		Transpose	Copy the contents and format of the source cell(s), but transpose the rows and columns.
		Merge Conditional Formatting	Context-sensitive: Copy the contents, format, and *Conditional Formatting* rules of the source cell(s) to the destination cell(s).
Paste Values		Values	Copy contents of source cell(s) without formatting or formulas.
		Values & Number Formatting	Copy contents and formatting of source cell(s), but use the format of the destination area for labels.
		Values & Source Formatting	Copy contents and formatting of source cell(s) without formulas.
Other Paste Options		Formatting	Copy format of source cell(s) without the contents.
		Paste Link	Copy contents and format and link cells so that a change to the cells in the source area updates corresponding cells in the destination area.
		Picture	Copy an image of the source cell(s) as a picture.
		Linked Pictures	Copy an image of the source area as a picture so that a change to the cells in the source area updates the picture in the destination area.

> **MORE INFO**
>
> The default paste option is *Keep Source Formatting*. This option applies when you click the top half of the *Paste* button [*Home* tab, *Clipboard* group].

Businesses use spreadsheets to display data in a useful and meaningful manner. For this project, you create a business spreadsheet that displays one week's sales for Paradise Lakes Resort.

File Needed: None
Completed Project File Name: **[your initials] PP E1-1.xlsx**

1. Create a new workbook.
   a. Click the **File** tab.
   b. Click **New**.
   c. Click **Blank workbook** to open a new workbook.

2. Save the workbook.
   a. Press **F12** to open the *Save As* dialog box.
   b. Select a location to save the workbook (Figure 1-19).
   c. Name the file **[your initials] PP E1-1** in the *File name* area.
   d. Click **Save**. The *Save As* dialog box closes.

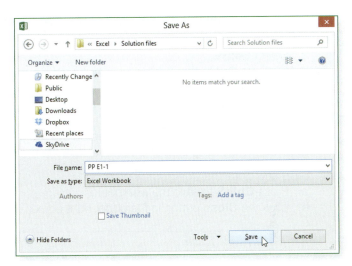

1-19 *Save As* dialog box

3. Enter data.
   a. Click to select cell **A1**, and type Paradise Lakes Resort.
   b. Press **Enter** and type July 14 – 20, 2015.
   c. Press **Enter** again.
   d. Type the remaining data in Figure 1-20. The data in the spreadsheet is displayed so that you can easily read the text for each column and row. You will learn the procedure to increase column width in SLO 1.5. To widen column A, drag the right column heading border to the right.

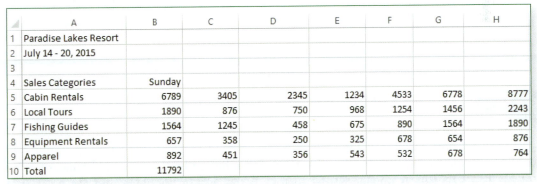

	A	B	C	D	E	F	G	H
1	Paradise Lakes Resort							
2	July 14 - 20, 2015							
3								
4	Sales Categories	Sunday						
5	Cabin Rentals	6789	3405	2345	1234	4533	6778	8777
6	Local Tours	1890	876	750	968	1254	1456	2243
7	Fishing Guides	1564	1245	458	675	890	1564	1890
8	Equipment Rentals	657	358	250	325	678	654	876
9	Apparel	892	451	356	543	532	678	764
10	Total	11792						

1-20 PP E1-1 data

4. Use the *Fill Handle* to create a series.
   a. Select **B4**.
   b. Place the pointer on the *Fill Handle* (small black square in the lower right corner of the cell) until a fill pointer appears.
   c. Click and drag to cell **H4**.
   d. Release the pointer.

5. Edit worksheet data.
   a. Select **B10**.
   b. Press **Delete** to remove the contents.
   c. Select **F5**.
   d. Type 4583 and press **Enter**.

6. Indent and align text.
   a. Select **A5:A9**.
   b. Click the **Increase Indent** button [*Home* tab, *Alignment* group].
   c. Select **B4:H4**.
   d. Click the **Align Right** button [*Home* tab, *Alignment* group].

7. Move text.
   a. Select **B4:B9**.
   b. Click the **Cut** button [*Home* tab, *Clipboard* group].
   c. Select **I4**.
   d. Click the **Paste** button [*Home* tab, *Clipboard* group].
   e. Select **C4:I9**.
   f. Point to the right border of the selected cell range.
   g. Drag the selected cells to **B4** and release the move pointer.

8. Save and close the workbook (Figure 1-21).
   a. Press **Ctrl+S** to save the workbook.
   b. Click the **Close** button in the upper right corner.

	A	B	C	D	E	F	G	H	I
1	Paradise Lakes Resort								
2	July 14 - 20, 2015								
3									
4	Sales Categories	Monday	Tuesday	Wednesday	Thursday	Friday	Saturday	Sunday	
5	Cabin Rentals	3405	2345	1234	4583	6778	8777	6789	
6	Local Tours	876	750	968	1254	1456	2243	1890	
7	Fishing Guides	1245	458	675	890	1564	1890	1564	
8	Equipment Rentals	358	250	325	678	654	876	657	
9	Apparel	451	356	543	532	678	764	892	
10	Total								
11									

1-21 PP E1-1 completed

SLO 1.3

Using the Sum Function

Sum is a built-in formula that adds the values in a selected range. To insert the *Sum* function, click the cell to make it active. When you click **AutoSum** [*Home* tab, *Editing* group], a formula (=SUM) displays in the cell followed by the suggested range of cells (for example, B5:B9). A moving border surrounds the cells in the range, and the function displays. Press **Enter** to complete the formula or adjust the cell range. The cell displays the result of the sum function, and the *Formula bar* displays the formula. Once a formula has been entered, it is automatically updated if the content of the worksheet is edited.

> **ANOTHER WAY**
>
> The *Function Library* group on the *Formulas* tab includes the *AutoSum* function.

HOW TO: Use the Sum Function

1. Click the cell where you want to display the calculation results.
2. Click the **AutoSum** button [*Home* tab, *Editing* group].
3. Press **Enter** to complete the formula (Figure 1-22).
   - You can double-click **AutoSum** to enter the formula. Click once to see the range and click a second time to complete the entry.

> ▶ **MORE INFO**
>
> To display formulas in the worksheet, click the **Formula** tab, and click **Show Formulas** or press **CTRL+`**.

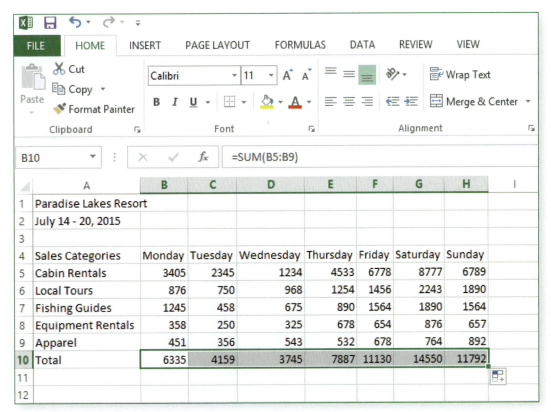

1-22 *AutoSum* function

Copy the Sum Function

The *Fill Handle* is a useful tool to copy functions and formulas, such as *Sum*, into adjacent cells. Notice that in Figure 1-23 each day of the week contains the same number of figures to total. The formula to sum the numbers in the "Tuesday" column is the same as the formula to add the numbers in the "Monday" column except for the cell references. When you drag the *Fill Handle,* Excel automatically adjusts cell references. The formula automatically changes relative to its location on the worksheet.

	A	B	C	D	E	F	G	H	I
		Monday	Tuesday	Wednesday	Thursday	Friday	Saturday	Sunday	
1	Paradise Lakes Resort								
2	July 14 - 20, 2015								
3									
4	Sales Categories	Monday	Tuesday	Wednesday	Thursday	Friday	Saturday	Sunday	
5	Cabin Rentals	3405	2345	1234	4533	6778	8777	6789	
6	Local Tours	876	750	968	1254	1456	2243	1890	
7	Fishing Guides	1245	458	675	890	1564	1890	1564	
8	Equipment Rentals	358	250	325	678	654	876	657	
9	Apparel	451	356	543	532	678	764	892	
10	Total	6335	4159	3745	7887	11130	14550	11792	
11									
12									

B10 — fx =SUM(B5:B9)

1-23 Using the *Fill Handle* to copy a formula

HOW TO: Use the Fill Handle to Copy Formulas

1. Click the cell containing the formula.
2. Point to the *Fill Handle* in the lower right corner of the cell.
3. Click and drag the fill pointer to the adjacent cells (see Figure 1-23).

Edit the Formula Cell Range

As you edit worksheet structure and contents, it may be necessary to adjust the cell range in a formula. You can edit the cell range using the *Formula bar* or by dragging the border that surrounds a range of cells. Remember that a cell displays the result of the formula and the **Formula bar** displays the formula.

You can also edit a cell reference or the cell range in a formula by dragging the border to reduce or expand the range. When dragging to include more or fewer cells, you will see a two-pointed arrow (resize pointer) when you point to a selection handle on the border.

HOW TO: Edit a Cell Reference Range Using the Formula Bar

1. Select the cell containing the formula.
2. Click the cell range displayed in the *Formula bar*. The range is highlighted, and a border displays around the cell range (Figure 1-24).
3. Edit the cell range.
4. Press **Enter**.

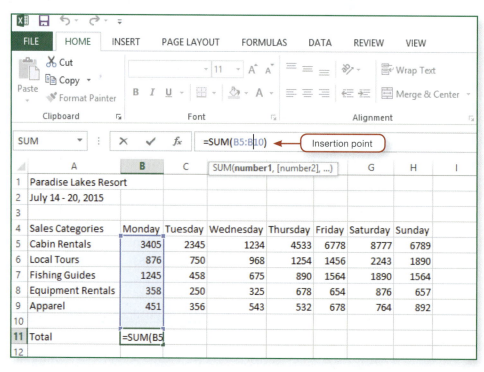

1-24 Editing the cell range in the *Formula bar*

HOW TO: Edit a Formula Cell Range by Dragging

1. Double-click the cell containing the formula.
2. Drag the border handle in the lower right corner to expand or contract the border (Figure 1-25).
3. Press **Enter** to complete the edit.
   - Click the **Enter** button on the *Formula bar* to complete an entry.

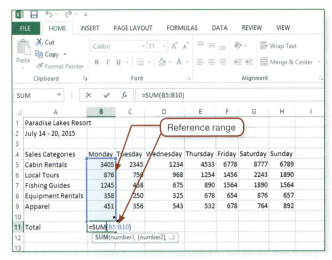

1-25 Edit a cell reference range by dragging

SLO 1.4 # Formatting a Worksheet

There are a variety of ways you can change the appearance of your worksheet. You can apply font attributes and add borders, or you can apply a format using *cell styles*. *Themes* provide consistency in format and help you create professional-looking workbooks.

Font Face, Size, Style, and Color

A font is a type design applied to an entire set of characters including the alphabet, numbers, punctuation marks, and other keyboard symbols. *Font size* describes the size of text and is measured in points. There are 72 points in one inch. *Font style* is the weight or angle of text, such as **bold**, underline, or *italic text*. *Font color* refers to the color of the characters. You can change the font attributes in a single cell, a group of cells, a worksheet, or an entire workbook.

The default font attributes for Excel 2013 workbooks are:

- *Font:* Calibri
- *Font Size:* 11 pt.
- *Font Color:* Black, Text 1

> **MORE INFO**
>
> The *Font* drop-down list has two sections: *Theme Fonts* and *All Fonts*.

HOW TO: Customize Font, Style, Font Size, and Font Color

1. Select the cell or range of cells to be formatted and choose an option from the *Font* group [*Home* tab] (Figure 1-26).
2. Click the **Font** drop-down list and select a font.
3. Click the **Font Size** drop-down list and select a font size or type a font size in the *Font Size* area.
   - You can also click the **Increase Font Size** or **Decrease Font Size** buttons to change the font size.
4. Click **Bold**, **Italic**, or **Underline** to apply one or more font styles.
5. Click the **Font Color** drop-down list [*Home* tab, *Font* group] and select a color.
   - Click the **Font Color** button (left of the drop-down arrow) to apply the last font color selected.

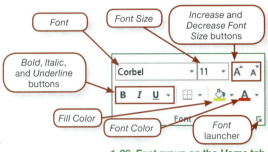

1-26 *Font* group on the *Home* tab

You can also apply font formats using one of the following methods:

1-27 Mini toolbar

- ***Mini toolbar:*** Right-click a cell or range of cells to display the mini toolbar (Figure 1-27).
- ***Format Cells dialog box:*** Click the **Font** launcher in the bottom right corner of the *Font* group on the *Home* tab or press **Ctrl+1** (Figure 1-28).
- ***Context menu:*** Right-click a cell or range of cells and select **Format Cells**.
- Keyboard shortcuts
  Bold: **Ctrl+B**
  Italic: **Ctrl+I**
  Underline: **Ctrl+U**

1-28 *Format Cells* dialog box

Format Painter

The ***Format Painter*** option allows you to copy formatting attributes and styles from one cell to another cell or group of cells. This method is a quick and easy way to apply a consistent look to worksheet data.

HOW TO: Use the Format Painter Button

1. Select the cell that contains the formatting you want to copy.
2. Click **Format Painter** [*Home* tab, *Clipboard* group].
3. Select the cell(s) where you want to apply the copied format (Figure 1-29).

   - The *Format Painter* automatically turns off after you apply the copied format one time.
   - To apply formatting to multiple areas, double-click **Format Painter**, apply the copied format to multiple areas, and click **Format Painter** again to turn off the option. You can also press **Esc** to cancel copying format.

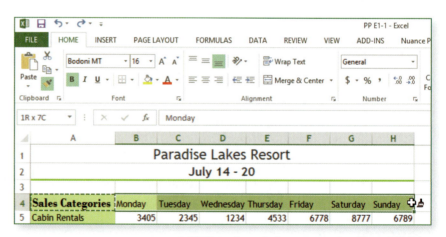

1-29 Copy formats to a range using *Format Painter*

Number Formats

In addition to text formatting, you can apply various number formats to cells so the numbers in your worksheet are clear and easy to understand. Common numeric formats used in worksheets include *Currency*, *Accounting*, and *Percentage*. You can also specify the number of decimal places a number displays by using the *Increase Decimal* or *Decrease Decimal* button. Open the *Format Cells* dialog box to customize number formatting. For example, the *Currency* format includes options to specify the number of decimal places, apply the $ symbol or no symbol, and control the appearance of negative numbers.

HOW TO: Format Numbers

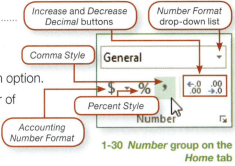

1-30 *Number* group on the *Home* tab

1. Select the cell range you want to format.
2. Click one of the numeric format buttons [*Home* tab, *Number* group] (Figure 1-30) or click the **Number Format** drop-down list and select an option.
3. Click **Increase Decimal** or **Decrease Decimal** to specify the number of decimal places after the whole number.
   - If pound signs (###) appear in any cell, it means your column is not wide enough to accommodate the entry. Adjusting column width is covered in *SLO 1.5: Editing Columns and Rows*.

> **MORE INFO**
>
> Click the **Number** launcher [*Home* tab, *Number* group] or press **Ctrl+1** to open the *Format Cells* dialog box where you can further customize a number format.

Borders and Shading

You can apply borders to a worksheet to place lines under headings, to show totals, or to group information. Use shading (or fill) to apply a background color or pattern to cells. You can use the *Ribbon* or *Format Cells* dialog box to apply a border or shading to selected cells.

HOW TO: Add Borders and Shading Using the Ribbon

1. Select the cell or range of cells to be formatted.
2. Click the arrow next to the *Borders* button [*Home* tab, *Font* group] and select a border option from the *Borders* drop-down list (Figure 1-31).
   - The *Borders* button displays the most recently used border style.
   - To remove a cell border, choose the **No Border** option from the *Borders* drop-down list.
3. Click the arrow next to the *Fill Color* button [*Home* tab, *Font* group] and select a background color (Figure 1-32).
   - Click **More Colors** to apply a custom color.
   - Click the **Fill Color** button to apply the most recently selected color.
   - To remove cell shading, click the arrow next to *Fill Color* and then select **No Fill**.

1-31 *Borders* drop-down list

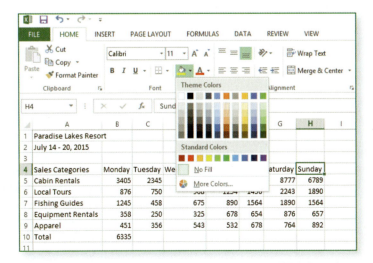

1-32 *Fill Color* palette

The *Format Cells* dialog box includes a tab for defining borders and applying a fill to selected cells. Each tab provides more borders and fill color choices than the *Ribbon* does. When creating a border design, select the border color and border line style before you apply the border to a preset or custom location. When selecting a solid or pattern fill, consider the content of the cell and whether readability will be affected.

HOW TO: Add Borders and Shading Using the Format Cells Dialog Box

1. Select the cell or range of cells to be formatted.
2. Click the **Font** launcher [*Home* tab, *Font* group] or press **Ctrl+1** to display the *Format Cells* dialog box.
3. Click the **Border** tab (Figure 1-33).
4. Select a line style in the *Style* area.
5. Choose a color from the *Color* drop-down list.
6. Click **Outline** in the *Presets* area to apply an outside border.
   - The *Preview* area displays the change.
7. Click **None** to remove the border.
8. Set individual borders by clicking a button in the *Border* area.
9. Click the **Fill** tab (Figure 1-34).
10. Select a color under *Background Color*.
    - To create a pattern with two colors, click a color in the *Pattern Color* box.
    - To create a gradient special effect, click **Fill Effects**, and select color and shading options.
11. Click a pattern style in the *Pattern Style* box.
12. Click **OK** to close the *Format Cells* dialog box.

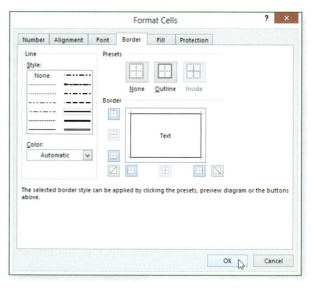

1-33 *Border* tab in the *Format Cells* dialog box

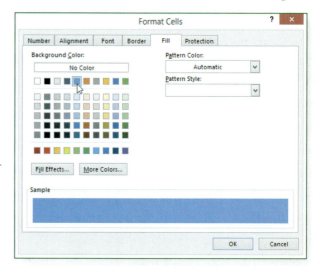

1-34 *Fill* tab in the *Format Cells* dialog box

Cell Styles

Cell Styles are a set of predefined formatting you can apply to titles, subtitles, column headings, row totals, and other areas of your worksheet. Styles apply formatting to the text, background, and border of a cell. You can also create your own cell styles to include specific character formatting, numeric formatting, borders, shading, or alignment. If you plan to use a *Cell Style*, apply the cell style before changing individual font attributes because the *Cell Style* overwrites other formats. Your screen may differ from the figures in this section. If you do not see a style gallery, click the **Cell Styles** button.

HOW TO: Apply Cell Styles to a Range of Cells

1. Select the cell or cell range where you want to apply a *Cell Style*.

2. Click the **More** button or the **Cell Styles** button [*Home* tab, *Styles* group] to display the *Cell Styles* gallery (Figure 1-35).

3. Select a style to apply to the selected cell(s) (Figure 1-36).

   • When you position your pointer on a *Cell Style* in the *Cell Styles* gallery, Excel provides a live preview of the style by temporarily applying the style to the selected cell(s).

1-35 *More* button

1-36 *Cell Styles* gallery

Workbook Themes

Applying a **theme** to a workbook formats a workbook quickly and applies a consistent design to the entire workbook. Themes include three combined elements: colors, fonts, and effects. The *Themes* gallery includes several themes to format a workbook; the default theme is called **Office**. Themes can be customized, and you can individually change **theme colors**, **theme fonts**, or **theme effects**. Additional themes are available online.

HOW TO: Apply Themes to a Workbook

1. Open the workbook.

2. Click the **Theme** button [*Page Layout* tab, *Themes* group] to display the *Themes* gallery (Figure 1-37).

   • Place your pointer on a theme to temporarily apply a live preview of the theme in your workbook.

3. Select a theme to apply to a workbook.

   • You can individually apply theme colors, theme fonts, or theme effects by clicking the **Colors**, **Fonts**, and **Effects** buttons [*Page Layout* tab, *Themes* group] and selecting from the drop-down lists.

> **MORE INFO**
>
> Themes change the colors that are available in a workbook. Place your pointer over each button in the *Themes* group on the *Page Layout* tab to view the current theme.

1-37 *Themes* gallery

For this project you continue working on the spreadsheet you created in *Pause & Practice Excel 1-1*. You add totals to the worksheet using *Sum* and copy formulas using *AutoFill*. You also format the spreadsheet. Formatting changes you apply in this exercise may cause the spreadsheet data to appear crowded or missing. You will adjust column width for the spreadsheet in Student Learning Objective 1.5.

File Needed: ***[your initials] PP E1-1.xlsx***
Completed Project File Name: ***[your initials] PP E1-2.xlsx***

1. Open the workbook and save it as a different name.
    a. Click the **File** tab and then click the **Open** button.
    b. Locate the folder where your files are saved.
    c. Open the workbook ***[your initials] PP E1-1***.
    d. Press **F12** to open the *Save As* dialog box.
    e. Locate the folder where your files are saved.
    f. Save the workbook as ***[your initials] PP E1-2***.

2. Calculate daily totals using *Sum*.
    a. Click cell **B10**.
    b. Click the **AutoSum** button [*Home* tab, *Editing* group].
    c. Press **Enter** to complete the formula.

3. Copy a formula across cells using the *Fill Handle*.
    a. Click cell **B10**.
    b. Point to the *Fill Handle* in the lower right corner of the cell.
    c. Click and drag to cell **H10** (Figure 1-38).

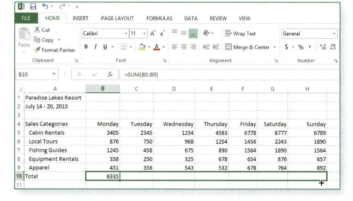

1-38 Copying a formula

4. Calculate sales category totals.
    a. Click cell **J5**.
    b. Double-click the **AutoSum** button [*Home* tab, *Editing* group].

5. Edit the cell reference range to remove the blank cell reference.
    a. Click cell **J5**.
    b. Click the cell range **B5:I5** in the *Formula bar* (Figure 1-39).

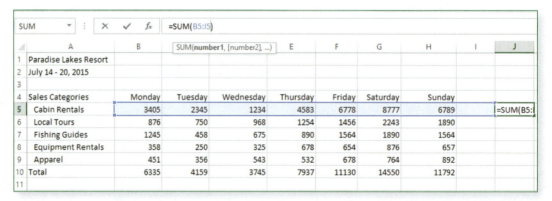

1-39 Edit cell reference in *Formula bar*

c. Change the cell range to **B5:H5**.
d. Press **Enter**.

6. Copy a formula down using the *Fill Handle*.
   a. Select **J5**.
   b. Point to the *Fill Handle* in the lower right corner of the cell.
   c. Click and drag to **J10**.

7. Apply *Cell Styles*.
   a. Select **A1** and then click the **More** button or the **Cell Styles** button [*Home* tab, *Styles* group] to display the *Styles* gallery (Figure 1-40).

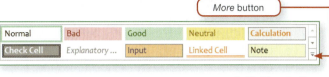

1-40 *More* button

   b. Locate the *Titles and Headings* category and select **Title**.
   c. Select **A2** and click the **More** button or the **Cell Styles** button [*Home* tab, *Styles* group].
   d. Locate the *Titles and Headings* category and select **Heading 2**.
   e. Drag to select **A10:H10** and then click the **More** button [*Home* tab, *Styles* group].
   f. Select **Total** in the *Titles and Headings* category.
   g. Select **A4:A9**, hold down and press **Ctrl**, and then select **B4:H4**.
   h. Click the **More** button [*Home* tab, *Styles* group].
   i. Select **20%**, **Accent 1** in the *Themed Cell Styles* category.

8. Apply themes.
   a. Click the **Themes** button [*Page Layout* tab, *Themes* group], and choose **Facet** from the gallery.
   b. Click the **Theme Fonts** button [*Page Layout* tab, *Themes* group] and select **Candara** from the gallery.

9. Apply font attributes to cell A4.
   a. Select **A4** and click the **Home** tab.
   b. Click the **Font** drop-down list [*Font* group], and select **Bodoni MT** in the *All Fonts* section.
   c. Click the **Font Size** drop-down list and select **16 pt**.
   d. Click the **Bold** button.
   e. Click the **Font Color** button and select **Blue-Grey**, **Text 2**, **Darker 50%** (fourth column, last row). Drag column heading border to widen if needed.

10. Apply font attributes to cells A1:A2.
    a. Select **A1:A2**.
    b. Click the **Font Color** button [*Home* tab, *Font* group].
    c. Select **Green**, **Accent 1**, **Darker 50%** (fifth column, last row in the *Theme Colors* category).

11. Apply font attributes to the cell range A5:H10.
    a. Select **A5:H10**.
    b. Change the font to **Arial Narrow** [*Home* tab, *Font* group, *Font*].
    c. Click the **Font Size** drop-down arrow and choose **12 pt**.

12. Use the *Format Painter* button to apply the formatting in A4 to the cell range B4:H4.
    a. Click **A4**.
    b. Double-click **Format Painter** [*Home* tab, *Clipboard* group] to turn on the option.
    c. Select the range **B4:H4** by clicking and dragging your pointer or select each cell in the range.
    d. Click **Format Painter** [*Home* tab, *Clipboard* group] to turn off the option.

13. Apply numeric formatting and align text.
    a. Select **B5:H9**.
    b. Click **Comma Style** [*Home* tab, *Number* group].
    c. Select **B10:H10**.
    d. Click the **Accounting Number Format** button [*Home* tab, *Number* group].

e. Select **B4:H4**.

f. Click **Align Right** [*Home* tab, *Alignment* group].

14. Delete text.

a. Select the cell range **J5:J10**.

b. Press **Delete**.

15. Add a bottom border and an outside border.

a. Select cells **A1:H10**.

b. Press **Ctrl+1** to display the *Format Cells* dialog box.

c. Click the **Border** tab.

d. Click a thick solid line style (second column, fifth style).

e. Click the **Color** drop-down list, and select **Black** (Automatic).

f. Click **Outline** in the *Presets* area.

g. Click **OK** to close the *Format Cells* dialog box.

h. Select **A4:H4**.

i. Click the **Border** button drop-down list [*Home* tab, *Font* group] (Figure 1-41).

j. Select **Bottom Border**.

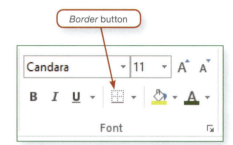

1-41 *Border* button

16. Press **Ctrl+S** to save the workbook (Figure 1-42). You can also save the workbook by clicking the **Save** button on the *Quick Access* toolbar or in *Backstage* view.

Paradise Lakes Resort
July 14 - 20, 2015

Sales Categories	Monday	Tuesday	Wednesday	Thursday	Friday	Saturday	Sunday
Cabin Rentals	3,405.00	2,345.00	1,234.00	4,583.00	6,778.00	8,777.00	6,789.00
Local Tours	876.00	750.00	968.00	1,254.00	1,456.00	2,243.00	1,890.00
Fishing Guides	1,245.00	458.00	675.00	890.00	1,564.00	1,890.00	1,564.00
Equipment Rentals	358.00	250.00	325.00	678.00	654.00	876.00	657.00
Apparel	451.00	356.00	543.00	532.00	678.00	764.00	892.00
Total	$ 6,335.00	$ 4,159.00	$ 3,745.00	$ 7,937.00	$ 11,130.00	$ 14,550.00	$ 11,792.00

1-42 *PP E1-2 completed*

17. Click the **File** tab and click **Close**, or press **Ctrl+W** to close the workbook.

SLO 1.5

Editing Columns and Rows

There are many ways to control the display of data within each column and row. Often the default column width and row height settings of Excel do not fit the requirements of the cell contents and require adjustment. You may also want to hide columns or rows containing sensitive data such as employee salaries. This section teaches you how to adjust column width and row height, as well as how to insert, delete, hide, and unhide columns and rows.

> ### MORE INFO
> Excel 2013 has 16,384 columns and 1,048,576 rows.

Adjust Column Width and Row Height

The default setting for each column is 8.43 characters. This number represents the number of characters that are viewable within the cell in the default font. You may change this width to any value between 0 and 255 characters. The default height of each row is 15 points. There are several ways to edit column width or row height, including dragging column or row heading borders, displaying the context menu, or selecting options from the *Format* drop-down list [*Home* tab, *Cells* group]. When you adjust column width or row height, the entire column or row changes.

HOW TO: Change Column Width or Row Height

1. Select a cell in the column or row you want to adjust.
   - To apply the same column width or row height to multiple columns or rows, select multiple columns or rows.
2. Click the **Format** button [*Home* tab, *Cells* group] and select **Row Height** or **Column Width** from the drop-down list to open the *Row Height* or *Column Width* dialog box (Figure 1-43).
3. Enter the desired height or width.
4. Click **OK** to close the dialog box.

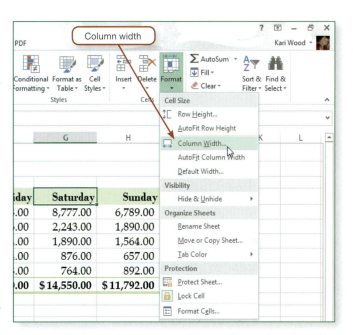

1-43 *Format* button drop-down list

> **ANOTHER WAY**
>
> To apply the same column width or row height to multiple columns or rows, select the columns or rows and right-click. Choose **Column Width** or **Row Height** from the context menu. Enter the new measurement and click **OK**.

> **MORE INFO**
>
> You can change the default sheet settings for column width by selecting the sheet tab or tabs, clicking **Format** [*Home* tab, *Cells* group], and selecting **Default Width** in the *Cell Size* category. Enter the new width for the selected sheets.

AutoFit Columns and Rows

The *AutoFit* feature resizes column width or row height to accommodate the width or height of the largest entry. You can use the *Format* button in the *Cells* group on the *Home* tab, or the context menu to *AutoFit* columns and rows. Another way to *AutoFit* a column is to double-click the right border of the column heading. When you point to the border, the pointer changes to a *sizing pointer* (Figure 1-44). To *AutoFit* a row, double-click the bottom border of the row heading.

HOW TO: Change Column Width or Row Height Using AutoFit

1. Select the columns or rows to adjust.
2. Click **Format** [*Home* tab, *Cells* group].
3. Click **AutoFit Column Width** or **AutoFit Row Height** (see Figure 1-44).

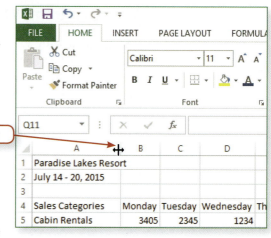

1-44 Double-click a column border to *AutoFit* column contents

Wrap Text and Merge Cells

The ***Wrap Text*** feature enables you to display the contents of a cell on multiple lines. You can format the cell to wrap text automatically, or you can enter a manual line break by pressing **Alt+Enter**. The cell contents wrap to fit the width of the column. If the text is not visible, it may be necessary to adjust the row height.

HOW TO: Wrap Text in a Cell

1. Select the cells to format.
2. Click the **Home** tab.
3. Click the **Wrap Text** button [*Alignment* group] (Figure 1-45).

1-45 *Wrap Text* button

> ### ANOTHER WAY
>
> Double-click a cell or press **F2** to activate edit mode in a cell and click to position the insertion point where you want to break the line. Press **Alt+Enter**.

The ***Merge & Center*** command combines two or more cells into one cell and centers the text. This feature is useful for centering worksheet titles over multiple columns. Before you merge cells, be sure the data appears in the upper-left cell. All data included in any other selected cell will be overwritten during the merge process.

HOW TO: Merge and Center

1. Select the cells you want to merge and center.
2. Click the **Home** tab.
3. Click the **Merge & Center** button [*Alignment* group] (Figure 1-46).

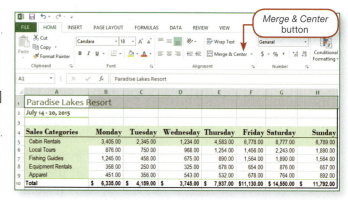

1-46 Select cells to merge and center

To merge cells without centering text, click the arrow next to *Merge & Center,* and choose **Merge Across** or **Merge Cells.** To unmerge cells, click the **Merge & Center** button or click the **Merge & Center** drop-down list and choose **Unmerge Cells.**

MORE INFO

Use the **Undo** button on the *Quick Access* toolbar or press **Ctrl+Z** to undo single or multiple actions.

Insert and Delete Columns and Rows

There are times when you need to insert or delete a row or column of information in your spreadsheet. For example, you can insert a row for an additional sales category or you might want to combine Saturday and Sunday sales figures into one column and delete the extra column. When you insert or delete columns and rows, Excel automatically shifts cells to make room for the new cells or fills the gap for deleted cells.

HOW TO: Insert Columns or Rows

1. Select a cell in the column that is to the right of where you want to insert a column, or click the row immediately below the row where you want to insert a new row.
2. Click the bottom half of the **Insert** button [*Home* tab, *Cells* group].
3. Select **Insert Sheet Rows** to add a row (Figure 1-47).
   • The new row appears directly above the originally selected row.

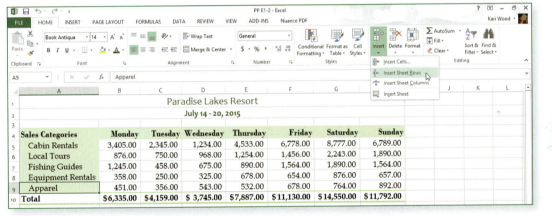

1-47 Insert a row

4. Select **Insert Sheet Columns** to add a column.
   • The new column appears directly to the left of the column you originally selected.
5. Select an individual cell and click the top half of the *Insert* button to insert a single cell rather than an entire row.
6. Select an entire column or row and click the top half of the *Insert* button to insert a column or row. To insert multiple columns or rows, select the number of columns or rows you want to insert.

ANOTHER WAY

To insert a column or row, select a column heading or row heading, right-click, and select **Insert** from the context menu. An alternative is to select column(s) or row(s), and press **Ctrl+plus sign (+)** on the numeric keypad.

When you delete a column or row, the contents in the cells of that column or row are deleted. Remaining columns and rows shift to the left or up after a deletion.

HOW TO: Delete Columns or Rows

1. Select a cell in the column or row you want to delete.
2. Click the bottom half of the **Delete** button [*Home* tab, *Cells* group].
3. Select **Delete Sheet Rows** to remove a row (Figure 1-48).
   - All the remaining rows below the deleted row shift up.

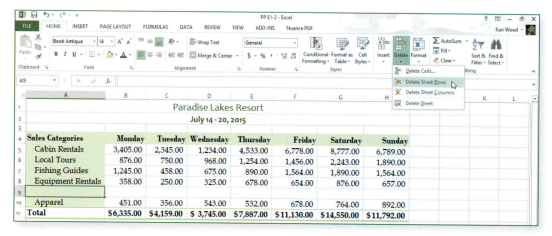

1-48 Delete a row

4. Select **Delete Sheet Columns** to remove a column.
   - All remaining columns to the right of the deleted column shift to the left.
5. Select an individual cell and click the top half of the *Delete* button to delete a cell rather than an entire row.
6. Select an entire column or row and click the top half of the *Delete* button to delete the column or row.

> **MORE INFO**
>
> Delete or insert single cells by choosing **Insert Cells** from the *Insert* drop-down list or **Delete Cells** from the *Delete* drop-down list [*Home* tab, *Cells* group].

Hide and Unhide Columns and Rows

If there is sensitive data in a worksheet, you may want to hide it before sharing the worksheet with others. Hiding a column or row does not delete the information in the worksheet nor does it affect the results of calculations. After hiding a column or row, you can unhide it so it again displays in the worksheet.

HOW TO: Hide and Unhide Columns or Rows

1. Select the column or row (or a cell in the column or row) you want to hide.
   - The hide feature applies to an entire column or row, not individual cells.
   - You can select multiple columns or rows to hide.
2. Click the **Format** button [*Home* tab, *Cells* group] and select **Hide & Unhide** in the *Visibility* category.

3. Select **Hide Columns** or **Hide Rows**.

- When a column or row is hidden, there is a small gap between the letters in column headings or numbers in row headings indicating that the column or row is hidden.
- Column or row headings are not lettered or numbered consecutively when a column or row is hidden.

4. To unhide a column or row, select the columns to the left and right of the hidden column or select the rows above and below the hidden row.

5. Click the **Format** button and select **Hide & Unhide** in the *Visibility* category (Figure 1-49).

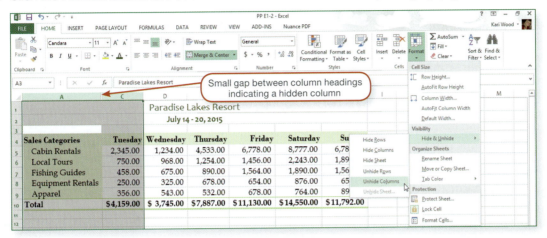

1-49 Unhide a column

6. Select **Unhide Columns** or **Unhide Rows** to display the hidden column or row.

> ### ANOTHER WAY
>
> **Ctrl+9** hides selected rows.
> **Ctrl+Shift+(** unhides hidden rows from a selection.
> **Ctrl+0** hides selected columns.

> ### MORE INFO
>
> To hide or unhide multiple columns or rows, select the columns or rows, right-click one of the selected columns or rows, and choose **Hide** or **Unhide** from the context menu.

SLO 1.6

Customizing Worksheets

An Excel workbook consists of one or more worksheets (or sheets), and each worksheet has a ***worksheet tab*** near the bottom left of the Excel window that displays the name of the worksheet.

The number of worksheets you can insert in a workbook is limited only by the amount of memory available on your computer. By default each workbook contains one sheet. Excel provides options to insert additional sheets, delete unwanted sheets, rename sheets, and change the tab color of sheets. Also, you may want to hide sheets if sensitive data should not be available to others. In this section, you learn to format, name, insert, delete, copy, rearrange, hide, and unhide worksheet tabs.

Insert and Delete Worksheets

There are times when you need to insert a worksheet to store additional information in your workbook. When there is more than one worksheet in a workbook, you select a worksheet by clicking the worksheet tab. There are multiple ways to both insert and delete worksheets. Inserted worksheets are automatically named.

> ### MORE INFO
>
> Press **Ctrl+Page Down** to move to the next worksheet. Press **Ctrl+Page Up** to move to the previous worksheet.

HOW TO: Insert and Delete Worksheets

1. Select a cell in the current worksheet.

2. To insert a worksheet, use one of the following methods:
   - Click the **New Sheet** button (plus sign) to the right of the existing worksheet tabs (Figure 1-50).
   - Click the bottom half of the **Insert** button [*Home* tab, *Cells* group] and select **Insert Sheet** (Figure 1-51).
   - Right-click a worksheet tab and select **Insert** from the context menu to open the *Insert* dialog box. Select **Worksheet** and click **OK**.

3. To delete a worksheet from a workbook, click the bottom half of the **Delete** button [*Home* tab, *Cells* group] and select **Delete Sheet** to remove the active worksheet.
   - Alternatively, you can right-click the worksheet tab and select **Delete** from the context menu.

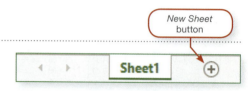

1-50 *New Sheet* button

1-51 *Insert* button: Adding a new worksheet

> ### ANOTHER WAY
>
> Press **Shift+F11** to insert a new worksheet.

> ### MORE INFO
>
> To delete or insert multiple worksheets, click the worksheet tabs while pressing **Ctrl**, right-click one of the selected worksheet tabs, and choose **Delete** or **Insert** from the context menu.

Rename Worksheets and Change Tab Color

The default names for the sheets within a workbook are *Sheet1*, *Sheet2*, and so on. After adding worksheets to a workbook, you might want to *rename* each worksheet with a more meaningful name. The size of the sheet tab adjusts to fit the name. You can also apply a *tab color* to further distinguish each worksheet. There is no default color for worksheet tabs.

HOW TO: Rename a Worksheet and Apply a Tab Color

1. Right-click the worksheet tab and choose **Rename** from the context menu (Figure 1-52).

2. Type the new name on the worksheet tab and press **Enter**.
   - You can also click the **Format** button [*Home* tab, *Cells* group] and select **Rename Sheet**.

3. Right-click the worksheet tab, choose **Tab Color** from the context menu, and select a color to apply to the background of the worksheet tab.
   - When a worksheet tab is active (selected), it displays as a light version of the tab color, and when a worksheet is not active, it displays the tab color (Figure 1-53).
   - You can also apply a tab color to the active worksheet by clicking the **Format** button, selecting **Tab Color**, and then choosing a color.

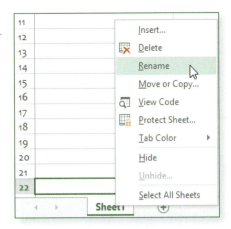

1-52 Rename a worksheet

1-53 Tab color applied to a worksheet

> **MORE INFO**
>
> To color multiple sheet tabs in a workbook the same color at the same time, select the sheet tabs you want to apply the color to, right-click one of the selected sheet tabs, and choose **Tab Color** from the context menu.

> **ANOTHER WAY**
>
> Rename a sheet tab by double-clicking the sheet tab name, typing the new name, and pressing **Enter**.

Move and Copy Worksheets

You can use the move feature to change the order of worksheets within a workbook or to move worksheets to a different workbook. The copy feature saves time by eliminating the need to reenter data. If you need to move or copy a worksheet a short distance, use the drag and drop method. Otherwise, use move, copy, and paste.

HOW TO: Move Worksheets

1. Right-click the worksheet tab you want to move.

2. Select **Move or Copy** from the context menu (Figure 1-54). The *Move or Copy* dialog box opens (Figure 1-55).
   - Alernatively, you can click the **Format** button [*Home* tab, *Cells* group] and select **Move or Copy Sheet**.
   - To move or copy the selected worksheet into a workbook other than the current one, select a different workbook from the *To book* drop-down list.
   - If you are moving a worksheet between workbooks, the destination workbook must be open prior to opening the *Move or Copy* dialog box.

3. Locate the *Before sheet* area, and select the worksheet that the active sheet will precede when it is moved.

4. Deselect the **Create a copy** check box if it is checked.

5. Click **OK** to close the dialog box.

1-54 Move or copy a worksheet

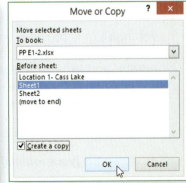

1-55 *Move or Copy* dialog box

When you move or copy worksheets, you can select multiple sheets to move or copy. Selecting multiple worksheets creates a group, and the title bar displays "[Group]" after the workbook name. To select multiple sheets, select a sheet tab, press **Shift**, and click another sheet tab. Once you have moved or copied the grouped worksheets, "[Group]" disappears from the title bar. To ungroup the sheets (prior to moving or copying), right-click a grouped tab, and choose **Ungroup**.

HOW TO: Copy Worksheets

1. Right-click the worksheet tab you want to copy and select **Move or Copy** from the context menu (see Figure 1-54). The *Move or Copy* dialog box opens (see Figure 1-55).
   - You can also click the **Format** button [*Home* tab, *Cells* group] and select **Move or Copy Sheet**.
   - To copy the selected worksheet into a workbook other than the current one, select a destination workbook from the *To book* drop-down list.
   - If you are copying a worksheet between workbooks, the destination workbook must be open prior to opening the *Move or Copy* dialog box.
2. Select the worksheet that the active sheet will precede when it is copied in the *Before sheet* area.
3. Check the **Create a copy** box in the bottom left corner of the dialog box.
4. Click **OK** to close the dialog box.
   - The copied sheet has the same name as the original worksheet with a (2) after it, as shown in Figure 1-56.

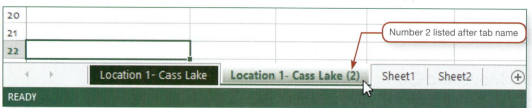

1-56 New worksheet copy

> **ANOTHER WAY**
>
> To move a worksheet, click the worksheet tab and drag to the left or right. To copy a worksheet, press and hold **Ctrl** while you drag the worksheet tab to the left or right.

PAUSE & PRACTICE: EXCEL 1-3

For this project, you open your previous Pause & Practice file (*[your initials] PP E1-2*) to adjust the column and row widths; insert a row for a new sales category; delete unwanted sheets; and copy, rename, and format a spreadsheet for another location of Paradise Lakes Resorts.

File Needed: *[your initials] PP E1-2.xlsx*
Completed Project File Name: *[your initials] PP E1-3.xlsx*

1. Open the *[your initials] PP E1-2* workbook.
2. Save the file as *[your initials] PP E1-3*.

3. Change the width of columns B through H.
   a. Click and drag column headings **B** through **H** to select the columns.
   b. Click the **Format** button [*Home* tab, *Cells* group].
   c. Select **Column Width** from the menu.
   d. Enter 20.0 characters as the new width.
   e. Click **OK**.

4. Apply new row heights to rows 4 and 10.
   a. Click row heading **4**, hold down **Ctrl**, and click row heading **10**.
   b. Right-click row heading **4**.
   c. Choose **Row Height** from the context menu.
   d. Enter 24.0 as the new height.
   e. Click **OK**.

5. Insert a new row and row label above row 9.
   a. Right-click row heading **9**.
   b. Choose **Insert** from the context menu to add a new row.
   c. The new row appears directly above the originally selected row.
   d. Select cell **A9** and type Food & Beverages.
   e. Press **Enter**.

6. Hide the newly inserted row 9.
   a. Click cell **A9**.
   b. Click the **Format** button [*Home* tab, *Cells* group].
   c. Select **Hide & Unhide** in the *Visibility* category.
   d. Select **Hide Rows**.

7. Merge and center the worksheet title and date.
   a. Select **A1:H1**.
   b. Click the **Merge & Center** button [*Home* tab, *Alignment* group].
   c. Select **A2:H2** and merge and center the cells.

8. Rename *Sheet1* and color the sheet tab.
   a. Double-click the **Sheet1** tab.
   b. Type the following new name for the sheet: Location 1- Cass Lake.
   c. Press **Enter**.
   d. Click the **Format** button [*Home* tab, *Cells* group].
   e. Select **Tab Color** in the *Organize Sheets* category.
   f. Select **Green Accent 1**, **Darker 50%** (last color in the fifth *Theme Color* column).

9. Insert a new sheet.
   a. Click the bottom half of the **Insert** button [*Home* tab, *Cells* group] and select **Insert Sheet**. The sheet appears to the left of the *Location 1- Cass Lake* sheet.
   b. Click the **New Sheet** button to insert another sheet.

10. Delete the extra blank sheets.
    a. Click the **Sheet2** tab, press and hold **Shift**, and click the **Sheet3** tab. Release **Shift** (both worksheet tabs are selected).
    b. Click the **Delete** button drop-down list [*Home* tab, *Cells* group].
    c. Select **Delete Sheet** to remove the selected worksheets.

11. Create a copy of the worksheet *Location 1- Cass Lake* and rename the new worksheet tab.
    a. Right-click the **Location 1- Cass Lake** tab.
    b. Choose **Move or Copy** from the context menu.
    c. The *Move or Copy* dialog box displays.
    d. Choose **(move to end)** in the *Before Sheet* box.
    e. Check the **Create a copy** box in the bottom left corner of the window.

f. Click **OK**. The new sheet is automatically named *Location 1- Cass Lake (2)*.
g. Double-click the new worksheet tab **Location 1- Cass Lake (2)**, and type the new sheet name: Location 2- Breezy Point.
h. Press **Enter**.
i. Color the tab **Orange**, **Accent 4**, **Darker 50%** (last color in the eighth *Theme Color* column).

12. Press **Ctrl+S** to save the workbook.

13. Click the **File** tab and click **Close** to close the workbook (Figure 1-57).

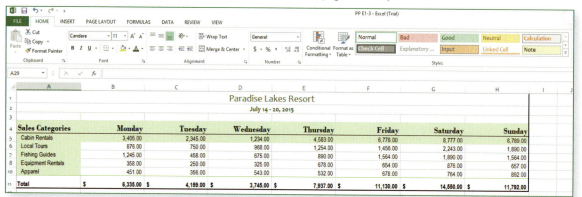

1-57 PP E1-3 completed worksheet with hidden row

SLO 1.7

Customizing the Window

In this section you explore several ways to customize the Excel window including changing workbook views, zooming options, freezing panes, splitting a worksheet into panes, and switching windows.

Workbook Views

Excel has three main views: ***Normal, Page Layout,*** and ***Page Break Preview.*** A fourth view, ***Full Screen*** view, displays a spreadsheet without screen elements so you can see more of the sheet. Each view in Excel has a specific purpose.

- *Normal* view is the default view. Use *Normal* view to create and modify spreadsheets.
- Use *Page Layout* view to apply headers and footers and to view the layout of the spreadsheet prior to distribution.
- Use *Page Break Preview* to adjust page breaks within your workbook using the drag and drop technique.
- Use *Full Screen* view to display worksheet data without the *Ribbon* and other screen elements.

The *Normal* view, *Page Layout* view, and *Page Break Preview* buttons are on the right side of the *Status bar*. You can also change views using *Normal, Page Layout,* and *Page Break Preview* buttons located on the *View* tab in the *Workbook Views* group (Figure 1-58).

1-58 *View* tab

HOW TO: Switch Workbook Views Using the Ribbon

1. Open a workbook. The *Normal* view displays by default.

2. Click the **View** tab.

3. Click the **Page Layout** button [*View* tab, *Workbook Views* group].

   - This view displays spreadsheet headers, footers, and page breaks (Figure 1-59).

4. Click **Page Break Preview** [*View* tab, *Workbook Views* group] to view page breaks.

   - Click and drag the dark blue page break lines to adjust page breaks (Figure 1-60).

5. Click **Normal** [*View* tab, *Workbook Views* group] to return to the default view.

6. Click **Ribbon Display Options** in the upper right corner of the Excel window and select **Auto-Hide Ribbon** to display *Full Screen* view (Figure 1-61).

   - *Full Screen* view increases the spreadsheet view by hiding the *Ribbon* and the *Status bar*.
   - The *Ribbon Display Options* menu includes three options: *Auto-Hide Ribbon*, *Show Tabs*, or *Show Tabs and Commands* (Figure 1-62). The entire *Ribbon* disappears from view when you select *Auto-Hide Ribbon*. *Show Tabs* displays *Ribbon* tabs only. Click a tab to display *Ribbon* commands. The *Show Tabs and Commands* option displays the *Ribbon* tabs and commands.

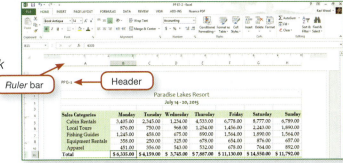

1-59 *Page Layout* view

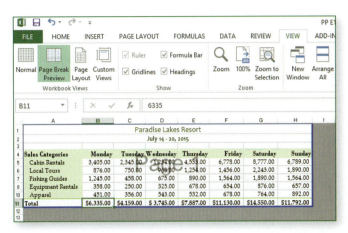

1-60 *Page Break Preview*

1-61 *Full Screen* view

1-62 *Ribbon Display Options*

7. Click **Ribbon Display Options** and choose **Show Tabs and Commands** to display the *Ribbon* and tab commands.

> ▶ **ANOTHER WAY**
>
> Use the *Status bar* buttons in the bottom right corner of the window to switch views.

Zoom Options

You can change a window's zoom level to see more of its content (zoom out) or to read the content more easily (zoom in). Zoom controls increase or decrease the magnification of the spreadsheet contents. You can increase or decrease the zoom level using *Zoom* in the *Zoom* group on the *View* tab (Figure 1-63) or the zoom controls on the *Status bar*.

HOW TO: Increase Zoom Using the Ribbon

1. Click the **Zoom** button [*View* tab, *Zoom* group].
   - The *Zoom* dialog box opens.
2. Click to select the radio button next to the desired *Magnification*.
   - Select **Fit selection** for a range of cells to fill the entire screen.
   - Choose **Custom** to enter an exact magnification (Figure 1-64).
3. Click **OK** to see the change in magnification in your workbook.

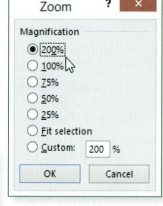

> **ANOTHER WAY**
>
> Other useful buttons are located in the *Zoom* group on the *View* tab: **100%** and **Zoom to Selection**. The *100%* option returns the magnification to the default. The *Zoom to Selection* option fills the entire screen with the range of cells selected in the worksheet.

Freeze Panes

When spreadsheets are magnified or contain multiple pages, it is difficult to see all of the information on the same screen. You can use scroll bars to move to those sections that are not immediately in view, but this process is tedious if you have to scroll repeatedly. You can also *Freeze Panes* so that column and row headings display whether you are at the top, bottom, left, or right of the spreadsheet. When you apply the freeze option, the Excel window is split into one or more panes, and displays multiple areas of a spreadsheet. A darker border displays when a row or column is frozen.

HOW TO: Freeze Panes Using the Ribbon

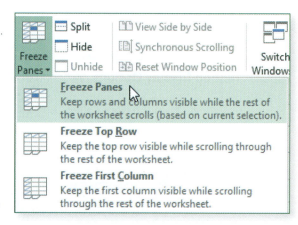

1. Select a cell in the worksheet that is located below the rows and to the right of the columns you want to freeze.
2. Click the **Freeze Panes** button [*View* tab, *Window* group].
   - Choose **Freeze Panes** to keep rows and columns visible.
   - Select **Freeze Top Row** to keep the top row visible.
   - Choose **Freeze First Column** to keep the first column visible.
3. Select **Freeze Panes** (Figure 1-65).
   - All rows above the active cell are frozen, and all columns to the left of the active cell are frozen.

4. Use the right horizontal scrolling arrow to view other columns of information.

   - Notice the row headings do not move (Figure 1-66).

5. Use the down vertical scrolling arrow to view the last row of data.

   - Notice the column headings remain constant.

6. Click the **Freeze Panes** button [*View* tab, *Window* group].

   - A new option, *Unfreeze Panes*, displays.

7. Select **Unfreeze Panes** to return the workbook to its original viewing state.

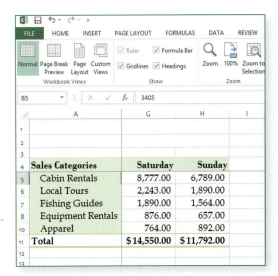

Sales Categories	Saturday	Sunday
Cabin Rentals	8,777.00	6,789.00
Local Tours	2,243.00	1,890.00
Fishing Guides	1,890.00	1,564.00
Equipment Rentals	876.00	657.00
Apparel	764.00	892.00
Total	$14,550.00	$11,792.00

1-66 *Freeze Panes* view results

Split a Worksheet into Panes

You can use the split feature to show different parts of the same spreadsheet in separate panes. The split feature can divide a worksheet into two or four scrollable windows (panes) that you can view simultaneously. You can scroll and edit each window independently and size the panes by dragging the *Splitter bar*.

HOW TO: Split a Worksheet into Panes

1. Select the row, column, or cell where you want to split a worksheet into panes.

   - Click a cell to split a worksheet into four panes.
   - Click the first cell in the row or column to split a worksheet into two panes.

2. Click the **Split** button [*View* tab, *Window* group].

3. Adjust the size of the panes by pointing to the *Splitter bar* and dragging to reposition the splitter bar (Figure 1-67).

4. Click the **Splitter** button [*View* tab, *Window* group] to remove the splitter bar.

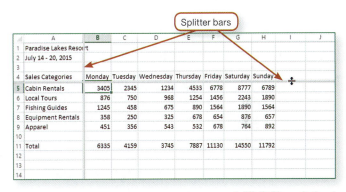

1-67 **Split worksheet**

> **ANOTHER WAY**
>
> Remove a window split by double-clicking the *Splitter bar*.

Hide or Unhide Worksheets

When worksheets contain confidential information, you can hide the sheets without affecting the worksheet data or calculations in the sheet. Hidden worksheets do not appear in a print-out. You can hide a worksheet using the *Ribbon* or by right-clicking a sheet tab. You cannot hide a sheet if there is only one sheet in the workbook.

HOW TO: Hide and Unhide Worksheets

1. Click the sheet tab you want to hide.
   - You can use the **Ctrl** key to select multiple sheets to hide.
2. Click the **Home** tab.
3. Click the **Format** button [*Cells* group] and choose **Hide & Unhide** in the *Visibility* group.
4. Select **Hide Sheet**. The worksheet tab does not display.
5. Click the **Format** button [*Cells* group] and choose **Hide & Unhide** in the *Visibility* group.
6. Click **Unhide Sheet** to open the *Unhide* dialog box (Figure 1-68).
7. Select the worksheet to unhide.
   - When multiple sheets are hidden, you must unhide each sheet individually.
8. Click **OK**.

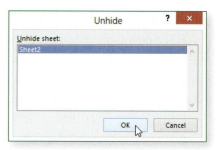

1-68 *Unhide* dialog box

> **ANOTHER WAY**
>
> To hide the worksheet, right-click the worksheet you want to hide and choose **Hide** from the context menu. To unhide the worksheet, right click a worksheet tab and choose **Unhide**. Select the worksheet to unhide.

You can hide an open workbook window by clicking the **View** tab and clicking the **Hide** button. To unhide a workbook, click the **View** tab and click the **Unhide** button.

Switch Windows Option

The **Switch Windows** feature is useful for viewing or editing multiple open workbooks.

HOW TO: Switch Windows Using the Ribbon

1. Verify that you have more than one workbook open.
2. Click the **Switch Windows** button [*View* tab, *Window* group].
   - A list of open workbooks displays.
3. Select the workbook you want to view.
   - You can view workbooks side-by-side by selecting **View Side by Side** [*View* tab, *Window* group] (Figure 1-69).
   - The *Synchronous Scrolling* option is available when viewing two workbooks side by side. *Synchronous Scrolling* scrolls both files in the same direction at the same time. It is useful for editing different versions of similar spreadsheets or sharing information between two different workbooks.
4. Click **Maximize** to restore a workbook to full size.

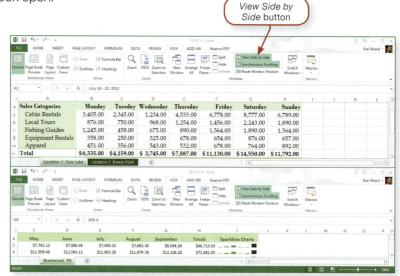

1-69 *View Side by Side*

View Multiple Worksheets at the Same Time

You can view multiple worksheets at the same time. Use the *New Window* feature to open a second window and to view different parts of the same worksheet. Use the *Arrange All* feature to position open windows. Click **Maximize** to restore a workbook to full size.

HOW TO: View Multiple Worksheets at the Same Time

1. Verify that you have more than one workbook open.
2. Click **Arrange All** [*View* tab, *Window* group] to open the *Arrange Windows* dialog box (Figure 1-70).
3. Choose an option to display more than one workbook: *Tiled, Horizontal, Vertical,* or *Cascade*.
4. Click **OK**.
5. Click **Maximize** to restore a workbook to full size.
6. Click the **View** tab, and click **New Window**.
   - A second window of the worksheet displays. Notice the change in the title bar. Each window displays a number after the name of the workbook.
7. Click **Arrange All** [*View* tab, *Window* group].
8. Choose **Vertical** in the *Arrange Windows* dialog box.
9. Select the **Windows of active workbook** check box.
10. Click **OK**.
11. Scroll the windows to display cells to edit.
12. **Close** the windows.

1-70 *Arrange Windows* dialog box

SLO 1.8

Finalizing a Workbook

After customizing your workbook content, structure, and format, Excel provides you with features to finalize your workbook. It's important to spell check a workbook for accuracy before printing or sending to others. You can also add document properties and a header and footer to your worksheet for document identification. If you are working with a large worksheet, you can customize page breaks and how your worksheet prints.

Check Spelling

The ***Spelling*** feature scans a worksheet and locates words that do not match entries in its main dictionary. You can add entries to the main dictionary such as proper names or technical terms. Duplicated words are also identified when you check spelling. You can check an entire worksheet or a selected range of cells. If you are not at the beginning of your worksheet, Excel starts spell checking at the active cell and checks to the end of the worksheet. When it reaches the end of the worksheet, a dialog box displays and asks if you want to continue checking at the beginning of the sheet. The *Spelling* dialog box displays several options when Excel finds an error. The following table describes each option.

Spelling Dialog Box Options

Option	Action
Ignore Once	Skips the word
Ignore All	Skips all occurrences of the word in the spreadsheet
Add to Dictionary	Adds the word to the default dictionary file. You can also create a custom dictionary.
Change	Changes the word to the entry you choose in the *Suggestions* box
Change All	Same as *Change*, but changes the word throughout the worksheet
Delete	Appears for duplicated words. Click to delete one occurrence of the word.
AutoCorrect	Adds the word to the list of corrections Excel makes automatically
Options	Changes the spelling options in Excel
Undo Last	Changes back to the most recent correction made
Cancel	Discontinues the checking operation

HOW TO: Spell Check a Worksheet

1. Press **Ctrl+Home** to move to the beginning of the worksheet.
2. Click the **Review** tab and click the **Spelling** button [*Proofing* group] (Figure 1-71).
3. Use the buttons on the right to change or ignore each identified error.
   - If a recommendation that is acceptable does not appear in the *Suggestions* box, edit the *Not in Dictionary* text box and click **Change**.

1-71 *Spelling* dialog box

Document Properties

Document Properties are details that you can add to any Office file. Document properties are also called *metadata*, and you can use them to organize or to gather basic information about workbooks. Several properties are created automatically by Excel including *Creation* date, *Modified* date, *Accessed* date, and file *Size*. You can edit other document properties, such as *Title, Author, Comments, Subject,* and *Company*. You can view or edit document properties using *Backstage* view, displaying the *Document Panel*, or opening the *Property* dialog box.

HOW TO: Add Document Properties

1. Click the **File** tab to display *Backstage* view.
2. Click **Info** if it is not already selected (Figure 1-72).
   - Document property field names are listed on the left and the property fields are listed on the right.
3. Click a field property and type or edit the entry.
4. Click the **Show All/Show Fewer Properties** link at the bottom to display more or fewer document property fields.

1-72 Workbook properties

Document Panel

You can view and edit document properties using the *Document* panel in *Normal, Page Layout,* or *Page Break Preview* views. The panel appears above the *Formula bar* and below the *Ribbon* (Figure 1-73). To display the *Document* panel, use the *Backstage* view. Close the *Document* panel by clicking the *Document* panel close button.

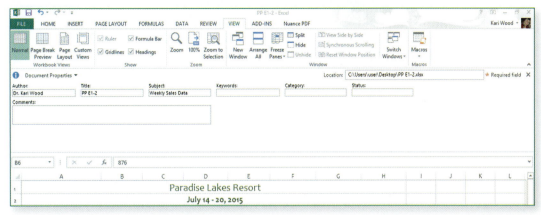

1-73 Document Properties panel

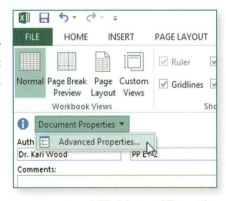

HOW TO: Display the Document Properties Panel

1. Click **File** to display *Backstage* view.
2. Click **Info** if it is not already selected.
3. Click the **Properties** drop-down list at the top of the *Properties* pane (Figure 1-74).
4. Select **Show Document Panel**.
   - The *Backstage* view closes and the *Document* panel displays above the *Formula bar* in the Excel window.
5. Edit or add text in the *Document Properties* fields.
6. Click **X** in the upper right corner of the *Document* panel to close the panel.

1-74 Show Document Panel

Advanced Properties

The ***Advanced Properties*** option displays the *Properties* dialog box. You can open the *Properties* dialog box using the *Backstage* view or the *Document* panel (Figure 1-75).

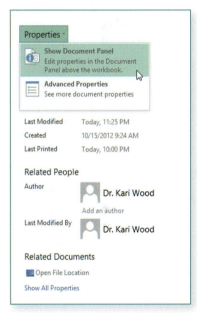

1-75 Advanced Properties

HOW TO: Open the Properties Dialog Box

1. Display the *Backstage* view and click **Info**.

2. Click the **Properties** button to display the drop-down list (see Figure 1-74).

3. Select **Advanced Properties**. The *Properties* dialog box opens (Figure 1-76).

    - The *General*, *Statistics*, and *Contents* tabs provide document properties that are automatically created by Excel.
    - The *Summary* and *Custom* tabs allow you to edit fields.
    - Use the *Custom* tab to add custom document property fields to your workbook.

1-76 *Properties* dialog box

Page Layout

The *Page Layout* tab includes options that allow you to control the appearance of your worksheet such as margins, page orientation, and paper size (Figure 1-77). You can also use the *Page Setup* dialog box to customize worksheet settings (Figure 1-78). To view page layout changes, you can preview or print the worksheet.

Open the *Page Setup* dialog box to change multiple page setup options at one time. Click the **Page Setup**, **Scale to Fit**, or **Sheet Options** launcher on the *Page Layout* tab to open the *Page Setup* dialog box (see Figure 1-78). The following table describes each of the tabs in the *Page Setup* dialog box.

1-77 Customize page setup and print options

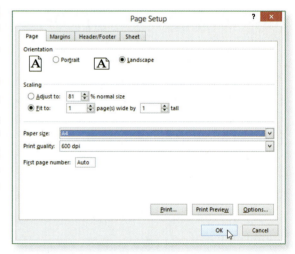

1-78 *Page* tab in the *Page Setup* dialog box

Page Setup Dialog Box Options

Tab	Tab Options
Page	Set the *Orientation* to *Portrait* or *Landscape*. *Scaling* adjusts the size of the printed worksheet as a percentage of the normal size, or you can use *Fit to* area to scale the worksheet to print on a specific number of pages. Use the *Paper size* drop-down list to select a paper size (see Figure 1-78).
Margins	Set the *Top*, *Bottom*, *Left*, and *Right* margins of the worksheet. You can also set the margins for the header and footer text in the worksheet. In the *Center on page* area, check the *Horizontally* and/or *Vertically* boxes to center the data in the worksheet on a printed page (see Figure 1-79).
Header/Footer	Add and customize headers and footers in the worksheet.
Sheet	Set the *Print area* by selecting a specified range of cells. In the *Print titles* area, you can designate certain rows or columns to repeat each time spreadsheet data spans more than one page. You can also specify printing options such as printing titles, gridlines, and row and column headings.

E1-44

Margins, Page Orientation, and Paper Size

The default settings for page layout for an Excel spreadsheet include the following:

- Top and bottom margins: 0.75
- Left and right margins: 0.7
- Header and footer margins: 0.3
- Portrait orientation
- Letter size paper

You can modify each of these settings for individual worksheets or multiple worksheets. To format multiple worksheets, select the worksheet tabs. Use **Shift** to select adjacent sheets. Use **Ctrl** to select non-adjacent sheets. Right-click a sheet tab and choose **Select All Sheets** to format an entire workbook. When changing margin settings, the top and bottom margin settings must be greater than the header and footer values or the worksheet data prints over the header and footer text.

HOW TO: Customize Margins, Page Orientation, and Paper Size

1. Click the **Margins** button [*Page Layout* tab, *Page Setup* group] and select a preset option from the drop-down list.
   - Select **Custom Margins** from the *Margins* drop-down list to open the *Page Setup* dialog box to enter a precise measurement (Figure 1-79).
   - Select the **Horizontally** and/or **Vertically** check boxes in the *Center on Page* area to center your worksheet [*Page Setup* dialog box, *Margins* tab]. *Horizontally* centers data between the left and right margins. *Vertically* centers data between the top and bottom margins.

2. Click the **Orientation** button [*Page Layout* tab, *Page Setup* group] and select **Portrait** or **Landscape** from the drop-down list.
   - When you select *Portrait*, the page is taller than it is wide; if you select *Landscape*, the page is wider than it is tall.
   - Use the *Page* tab in the *Page Setup* dialog box to change the page orientation.
   - You can also change orientation when you are ready to print. Select an option from the *Page Orientation* drop-down list in the *Print* area on the *Backstage* view.

3. Click the **Size** button [*Page Layout* tab, *Page Setup* group] and select a paper size from the drop-down list.
   - The default paper size is 8 ½"×11", which is called *Letter*.
   - Click **More Paper Sizes** to open the *Page Setup* dialog box.

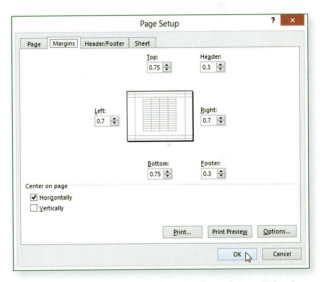

1-79 *Margins* tab in the *Page Setup* dialog box

Headers and Footers

Headers appear at the top of the worksheet in the *Header* area, while **footers** appear in the *Footer* area at the bottom of the worksheet. Each header and footer area has a left, middle, and right section where you can insert a page number, file name, date, or other information in text boxes.

Note that headers and footers appear on the worksheets only when you choose to add them. They do not appear on every sheet automatically. To add headers and footers to multiple worksheets at one time, select the worksheet tabs and open the *Page Setup* dialog box. Headers and footers do not display in *Normal* view. To view header and footer text, switch to *Print Layout* view or *Print Preview*.

HOW TO: Insert a Header and Footer Using the Ribbon

1. Select the worksheet.
2. Click the **Insert** tab.
3. Click the **Header & Footer** button [*Text* group].
   - The worksheet view changes to *Page Layout* view.
   - The header displays three text boxes. Information entered in the left text box is left aligned, text in the middle text box is centered, and text in the right text box is right aligned.
4. Click a text box in the header area.
   - Clicking a header or footer text box displays the *Header & Footer Tools Design* tab.
5. Click the **Design** tab to activate it (Figure 1-80).
6. Click an option in the *Header & Footer Elements* group [*Header & Footer Tools Design* tab].
   - A field is inserted with an ampersand (&) followed by the code enclosed in brackets.
   - If the header or footer contains text, you can edit or delete the contents.
   - To insert a pre-defined header or footer such as the page number or worksheet name, click the **Header** or **Footer** button [*Header & Footer Tools Design* tab, *Header & Footer* group].
7. Click **Go To Footer** [*Header & Footer Tools Design* tab, *Navigation* group].
8. Click one of the text boxes in the footer area.

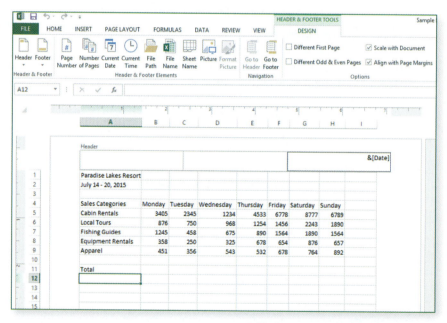

1-80 *Header* area in *Page Layout* view

9. Type text or click an element [*Header & Footer Elements* group].
   - If the text you type includes an ampersand (&), type two ampersands (&&) to distinguish text from the header or footer code. For example, you type "Research && Development" to display "Research & Development".
10. Scroll to the top of the worksheet and then click any cell to close the header and footer area.
    - The header and footer text displays in *Page Layout* view.
11. Switch to **Normal** view.
    - The header and footer are not visible in *Normal* view.

You can insert headers and footers using the *Page Setup* dialog box. One advantage of using the *Page Setup* dialog box to insert headers or footers is that this option allows you to add headers or footers to multiple sheets. The *Page Setup* dialog box includes preset header and footer fields located in the *Custom Header* or *Custom Footer* drop-down lists on the *Header/Footer* tab.

HOW TO: Insert Headers or Footers Using the Page Setup Dialog Box

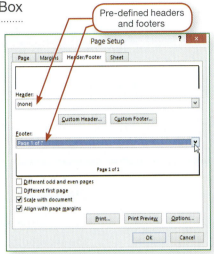

1. Click the worksheet tab (or tabs if applying the header or footer to multiple sheets).
   - To select two or more adjacent worksheets, use **Shift**.
   - To select two or more nonadjacent sheets, use **Ctrl**.
   - To select all worksheets in the workbook, right-click a tab and click **Select All Sheets**.
2. Click the **Page Layout** tab and then click the **Page Setup** launcher [*Page Setup* group].
   - The *Page Setup* dialog box displays.
3. Select the **Header/Footer** tab.
4. Click the drop-down arrow for the *Header* or *Footer* text box to see a list of predefined headers or footers (Figure 1-81).
   - Scroll to see additional options.
5. Choose **(none)** to create a new header or footer.

1-81 *Header/Footer* **tab in the** *Page Setup* **dialog box**

6. Click the **Custom Header** or **Custom Footer** button to open the *Header* or *Footer* dialog box (Figure 1-82).
7. Type text in the *Left* section, *Center* section, or *Right* section, or click a button to insert a field code.
   - Each button has a *ScreenTip* to identify the button (Figure 1-83).
8. Click **OK** to close the *Header or Footer* dialog box.
   - The information appears in the *Header or Footer* text box.
9. Click **OK** to close the *Page Setup* dialog box.

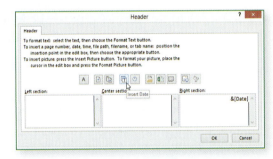

1-82 *Header* **dialog box**

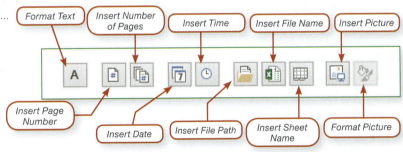

1-83 Buttons to insert header and footer content

Figure 1-83 displays the buttons available in the *Header* and *Footer* dialog boxes. When you click the *Format Text, Insert Picture,* or *Format Picture* button, another dialog box opens that provides you with additional options.

There are two ways to remove a header or footer. One method uses the *Page Setup* dialog box and the other uses the *Text* group on the *Insert* tab. Remember to use the *Page Setup* dialog box method to remove headers and footers from multiple sheets.

HOW TO: Remove Headers and Footers

1. Select the worksheet.
2. Click the **Page Layout** tab and click the **Page Setup** launcher.
3. Click the **Header/Footer** tab.
4. Click the **Header** or **Footer** drop-down list and select **(none)** (Figure 1-84).
5. Click **OK** to close the *Page Setup* dialog box.

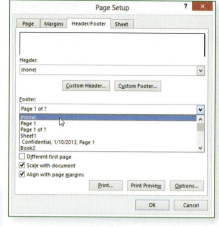

1-84 *Footer* drop-down list

> ### ANOTHER WAY
>
> To remove a header or footer, click the **Insert** tab and click **Header & Footer** [*Text* group]. Click the left, right, or center area, select the header or footer text, and press **Delete** or **Backspace**.

Page Breaks

When you complete a workbook you can preview the content before printing or distributing the workbook electronically. If the worksheet data is larger than one page, page breaks are inserted automatically. Paper size, margins, and scale options control the position of automatic page breaks. You can manually insert page breaks to change the number of rows or columns printed on the page. Use *Page Break Preview* to insert page breaks, move page breaks, or remove page breaks. Manual page breaks display as a solid line. Automatic page breaks display as a dotted or dashed line.

HOW TO: Insert a Page Break

1. Select the location to insert a page break.
   - Click the row below where you want to insert a horizontal page break.
   - Click the column to the right of where you want to insert a vertical page break.
   - Click the cell below and to the right of where you want to insert a horizontal and vertical page break.
2. Click the **Page Layout** tab.
3. Click the **Breaks** button (Figure 1-85).
4. Select **Insert Page Break**.
   - The page break displays as a solid line.

1-85 *Breaks* options

> ### ANOTHER WAY
>
> To insert a page break, right-click a row or column and choose **Insert Page Break** from the context menu.

Preview and Move a Page Break

In *Normal* view, you can use the *Breaks* command to insert, remove, and reset page breaks. You cannot drag page breaks to another location in *Normal* view. Use *Page Break Preview* to move a page break. Moving an automatic page break changes it to a manual page break.

HOW TO: Preview and Move a Page Break

1. Click the **View** tab.
2. Click the **Page Break Preview** button (Figure 1-86).
3. Drag the page break (solid line) to a new location.
   - The pointer changes to a resize pointer (two-pointed arrow) while dragging the page break.
4. Return to *Normal* view [*View* tab, *Workbook Views* group].

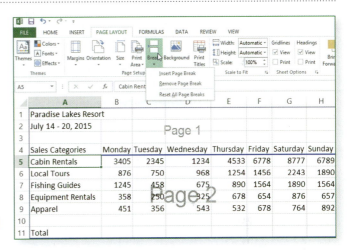

1-86 *Page Break Preview*

Remove a Manual Page Break

To remove a manual page break, use *Page Break Preview*. You cannot delete an automatic page break. You can, however, reposition an automatic page break by inserting or deleting columns and rows, changing page orientation, or adjusting column width and row height.

HOW TO: Remove a Manual Page Break

1. Switch to **Page Break Preview** [*View* tab, *Workbook Views* group].
2. Select the column or row next to the page break to be removed.
   - To delete a vertical page break, select the column to the right of the page break.
   - To delete a horizontal page break, select the row below the page break.
3. Click **Breaks** [*Page Layout* tab, *Page Setup* group] (Figure 1-87).
4. Click **Remove Page Break**.
   - To remove all manual page breaks, click **Reset All Page Breaks**.

1-87 *Remove page break*

Customize Worksheet Printing

You can print an entire workbook, a single worksheet, or a section of a worksheet. You can also control the appearance of the printout by displaying gridlines, printing column letters and row numbers, or including titles that repeat on each page.

HOW TO: Print Titles, Gridlines, Column Letters, and Row Numbers

1. Click the **Page Layout** tab and locate the *Sheet Options* group (Figure 1-88).

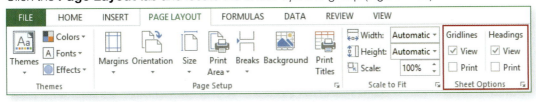

1-88 *Sheet Options*

2. Select the **Print** checkbox under *Gridlines*.

3. Select the **Print** checkbox under *Headings*.

   - Both *Gridlines* and *Row and column headings* are available in the *Print* area on the *Sheet* tab in the *Page Setup* dialog box.

4. Click the **Print Titles** button [*Page Layout* tab, *Page Setup* group] to open the *Page Setup* dialog box.

5. Click the **Rows to repeat at top** text box (Figure 1-89).

6. Drag to select the row or rows to repeat.

   - You can also type the reference of the row(s) that contains the column labels. For example, type $1:$1 to repeat the first row. Type $1:$2 to repeat the first two rows.

7. Click the **Columns to repeat at left** text box.

8. Click column **A** to select the column.

   - A second method is to type the reference of the column that contains the row labels. Type $A:$A to repeat the first column.

9. Click **OK**.

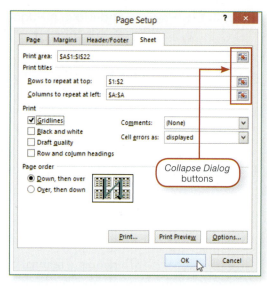

1-89 *Sheet* tab in the *Page Setup* dialog box

► **ANOTHER WAY**

Click the **Collapse Dialog** button on the right side of *Rows to repeat at top* or *Columns to repeat at left* and select the rows or columns to repeat. Click the **Collapse Dialog** button again to expand the *Page Setup* dialog box.

Scale to Fit

The **Scale to Fit** feature expands or reduces a worksheet to fit on a specific number of pages or a specific paper size. You can adjust the worksheet as a percentage of the normal size or change the height or width values.

HOW TO: Scale to Fit

1. Click the **Page Layout** tab.

2. Select a scaling option [*Scale to Fit* group] (Figure 1-90).

   - Click the **Width** drop-down list and select the number of pages.
   - Click the **Height** drop-down list and select the number of pages.
   - Click the **Scale** up and down arrows to scale the worksheet a percentage of the normal size (100%).
   - You can also click the **Scale to Fit** launcher to display the *Page* tab in the *Page Setup* dialog box where you can make adjustments in the *Scaling* area (Figure 1-91).

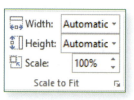

1-90 *Scale to Fit* options

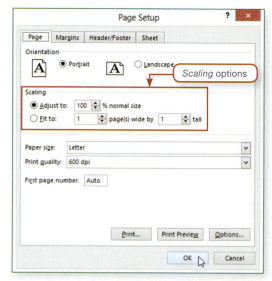

1-91 *Scaling* options in the *Page Setup* dialog box

Print Area

The *print area* is the section of the worksheet that prints. A print area consists of a single cell or a range of cells. You can add cells to a print area and you can clear the print area in order to print an entire worksheet.

HOW TO: Set and Clear Print Area

1. Select the cells to print.
   - Use **Ctrl** and drag to select multiple print areas.
2. Click the **Page Layout** tab.
3. Click the **Print Area** button [*Page Setup* group] (Figure 1-92).
4. Select **Set Print Area**.
   - Change the view to *Page Break Preview* to see the print area.
   - A print area is saved when the workbook is saved.
5. To enlarge the print area, select adjacent cells, click the **Print Area** button [*Page Layout* tab, *Page Setup* group], and then select **Add to Print Area**.
   - Switch to *Page Break Preview* to view the print area.
6. To clear the print area, click the **Print Area** button [*Page Layout* tab, *Page Setup* group] and select **Clear Print Area**.

1-92 *Print Area* options

> ▶ **ANOTHER WAY**
>
> You can print part of a worksheet using the *Page Setup* dialog box. Display the **Page Setup** dialog box and select the **Sheet** tab. Type the cell range to print in the *Print area* text box. Click **OK**.

Print a Worksheet or Workbook

Once you complete a worksheet, you can preview the worksheet to verify layout and formatting changes. There are two ways to preview a worksheet. One way is to click the **File** tab and then click **Print**. The other way is to open the *Page Setup* dialog box and click **Print Preview**.

HOW TO: Preview and Print a Worksheet

1. Click the **File** tab.
2. Click **Print** (Figure 1-93). A preview of your worksheet appears on the right.
   - If the workbook is more than one page, use the **Next Page** and **Previous Page** arrows to review each page.
   - Click **Show Margins** to manually adjust the header and page margins.
   - Click **Zoom to Page** to adjust the zoom level.
3. In the *Copies* area, set the number of copies to print.
4. Select an option to print the active sheet, print the entire workbook, or print a selection.
5. Specify the pages to print.
6. Verify orientation, paper size, and margin settings.
7. Click the **Page Setup** link to display the *Page Setup* dialog box and adjust settings.
8. Click **Print**.

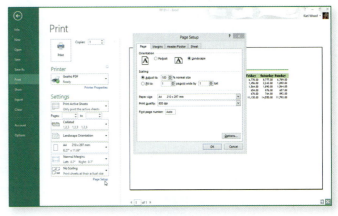

1-93 *Backstage* view: *Page Setup* dialog box

PAUSE & PRACTICE: EXCEL 1-4

For this project, you open your previous Pause & Practice file (*[your initials] PP E1-3.xlsx*) and change the display and view options, hide and unhide rows and worksheets, add document properties, and apply page setup formatting to finalize your Paradise Lakes Resorts workbook.

File Needed: *[your initials] PP E1-3.xlsx*
Completed Project File Name: *[your initials] PP E1-4.xlsx*

1. Open the *[your initials] PP E1-3* workbook.

2. Save the workbook as *[your initials] PP E1-4*.

3. Select the **Location 1 – Cass Lake worksheet**.

4. Unhide row 9 from the previous Pause & Practice (the "Food & Beverage" row).
   a. Drag to select row headings **8** and **10**.
   b. Right-click one of the selected row headings.
   c. Choose **Unhide** from the context menu. Row 9 appears between rows 8 and 10.

5. Enter the following "Food & Beverage" data in row 9 for the cell range **B9:H9**.

	B	C	D	E	F	G	H
9	254.00	209.00	198.00	402.00	519.00	677.00	399.00

6. Increase the zoom to 150%.
   a. Click the **Zoom** button [*View* tab, *Zoom* group].
   b. The *Zoom* dialog box opens.
   c. Select the **Custom** radio button and enter 150 for the magnification.
   d. Click **OK** to see the change in magnification in your workbook.

7. Use *Freeze Panes* in the worksheet.
   a. Select **B5** in the worksheet.
   b. Click the **Freeze Panes** button [*View* tab, *Window* group].
   c. Choose the **Freeze Panes** option.
   d. Use the right horizontal scrolling arrow to view the last two columns of information (Figure 1-94).

8. Hide a worksheet.
   a. Click the **View** tab and click the **100%** zoom button [*Zoom* group].
   b. Click the **Freeze Panes** button and select **Unfreeze Panes**.
   c. Right-click the **Location 2** worksheet tab.
   d. Select **Hide**.

	A	G	H
1			
2			
3			
4	**Sales Categories**	**Saturday**	**Sunday**
5	Cabin Rentals	8,777.00	6,789.00
6	Local Tours	2,243.00	1,890.00
7	Fishing Guides	1,890.00	1,564.00
8	Equipment Rentals	876.00	657.00
9	Food & Beverage	677.00	399.00
10	Apparel	764.00	892.00
11	**Total**	$ 15,227.00	$ 12,191.00

1-94 *Freeze Panes* view

9. Check the spelling of the worksheet.
   a. Click the **Spelling** button [*Review* tab, *Proofing* group].
   b. Correct any misspelled words in the worksheet.

10. Add document properties using the *Document Properties* panel.
    a. Click the **File** tab to display *Backstage* view.
    b. Click **Info** if it is not already selected.
    c. Click the **Properties** drop-down list at the top of the *Properties* pane and select **Show Document Panel**. The *Backstage* view closes and the *Document* Panel displays above the *Formula bar* in the Excel window.
    d. Add text in the following *Document Properties* fields (Figure 1-95):

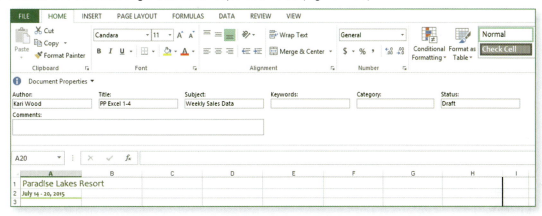

1-95 *Document* Panel

Title: PP Excel 1-4
Subject: Weekly Sales Data
Status: Draft

    f. Click the **X** in the upper right corner of the *Document* Panel to close the panel.

11. Change page setup options.
    a. Click the **Page Layout** tab.
    b. Click the **Orientation** button and select **Landscape**.
    c. Click the **Page Setup** launcher to display the *Page Setup* dialog box and select the **Margins** tab.
    d. Click the **Horizontally** check box in the *Center on page* area.
    e. Click **OK** to close the *Page Setup* dialog box.

12. Add a header and footer.
    a. Click the **Page Layout** tab.
    b. Open the *Page Setup* dialog box by clicking the **Page Setup** launcher.
    c. Click the **Header/Footer** tab.
    d. Click the **Header** drop-down list and select **[your initials] PP E1-4**. The name of the file displays in the header.
    e. Click the **Footer** drop-down list and select **Page 1** to insert a page number in the footer.
    f. Click **OK** to close the *Page Setup* dialog box.

13. Select the print area and preview the worksheet.
    a. Select the cell range **A1:H11**.
    b. Select the **Page Layout** tab.
    c. Click the **Print Area** button and select **Set Print Area**.
    d. Deselect the text.
    e. Click the **File** tab and select **Print**. The workbook *Print Preview* displays.

14. Save and close the workbook (Figure 1-96).

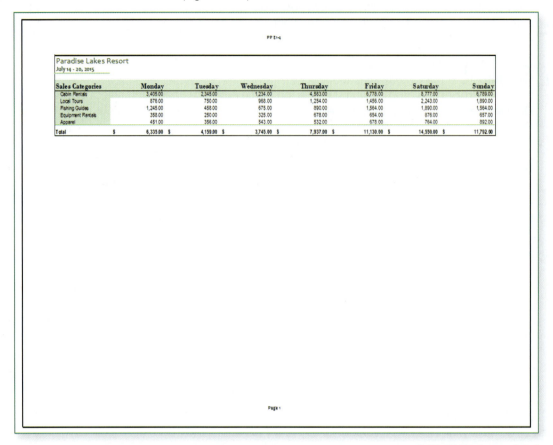

PP E1-4

Paradise Lakes Resort July 14 - 20, 2015							
Sales Categories	**Monday**	**Tuesday**	**Wednesday**	**Thursday**	**Friday**	**Saturday**	**Sunday**
Cabin Rentals	3,405.00	2,345.00	1,234.00	4,583.00	6,778.00	8,777.00	6,789.00
Local Tours	876.00	750.00	968.00	1,254.00	1,456.00	2,243.00	1,890.00
Fishing Guides	1,245.00	458.00	675.00	890.00	1,564.00	1,890.00	1,564.00
Equipment Rentals	358.00	250.00	325.00	678.00	654.00	876.00	657.00
Apparel	451.00	356.00	543.00	532.00	678.00	764.00	892.00
Total	$ 6,335.00	$ 4,159.00	$ 3,745.00	$ 7,937.00	$ 11,130.00	$ 14,550.00	$ 11,792.00

Page 1

1-96 PP E1-4 completed

Chapter Summary

1.1 Create, save, and open an Excel workbook (p. E1-3).

- When you create a blank workbook, Excel automatically assigns a file name to the file, such as *Book1*.
- You can save an Excel workbook in a variety of formats. By default, Excel workbooks are saved as *.xlsx* files.
- From the **Share** and **Export** areas of *Backstage* view, you have the option of saving in different online locations and saving a workbook as a PDF document.
- You can open workbooks from your computer, external storage device, or *SkyDrive*.

1.2 Edit a workbook by entering and deleting text, using the *Fill Handle* to complete a series, and using the cut, copy, and paste features (p. E1-6).

- When creating or editing a workbook, you can type data, import data from another file, or copy data from a web page or another source.
- Excel uses multiple pointers to indicate various selection, copying, resizing and moving options within a worksheet.
- Excel recognizes any combination of letters, numbers, spaces, and other characters as text and aligns each entry to the bottom left corner of the cell. Numeric entries align at the bottom right corner of the cell.
- Vertical alignment options include *Top Align, Middle Align,* and *Bottom Align*. Horizontal alignment options include *Align Left, Center,* and *Align Right*.
- Use the **Fill Handle** to complete lists, repeat numeric patterns, or copy cell contents to another location.
- Cut, copy, and paste data using the ***drag and drop*** method; **Cut**, **Copy**, and **Paste** buttons on the *Home* tab; the context menu; or shortcut keys on the keyboard.

1.3 Create a basic formula using *AutoSum* (p. E1-16).

- **AutoSum** is a button that automates the *Sum* function and other popular functions. *Sum* is used for adding values in a range.
- To adjust the cell range in a formula, use the *Formula bar* or drag the cell range border to reduce or expand the range.

1.4 Format a worksheet using different font attributes, borders, shading, cell styles, themes, and the *Format Painter* (p. E1-19).

- The default format for worksheet entries is 11 pt. Calibri.
- Customize font attributes using the *Font* group on the *Ribbon* or opening the *Format Cells* dialog box. You can change the **Font Face**, **Font Size**, **Font Style**, and **Font Type** in a single cell, a group of cells, a worksheet, or an entire workbook.
- Add borders, shading, and number formatting to a worksheet to improve readability and to add emphasis.
- The **Format Painter** option allows you to copy formatting attributes and styles from one cell to another.
- Use **Cell Styles** to format a worksheet attractively using predefined settings such as alignment, color, borders, and fill color.
- Apply **themes** to a workbook for consistency in color, font, and effects.

1.5 Resize, insert, delete, and hide and unhide columns and rows in a worksheet (p. E1-26).

- Control the display of data by adjusting column width or row height.
- Two methods you can use to insert or delete columns and rows are the context menu and the **Insert** or **Delete** button.
- Display multiple lines in a cell using **Wrap Text** or use **Merge & Center** to combine two or more cells.
- You can hide sensitive data in a column or incomplete information in a row using the context menu or the *Format* button.

1.6 Insert, delete, edit, format, and rearrange worksheets (p. E1-31).

- The number of worksheets contained in a workbook is limited only by the amount of your computer memory.
- The default names for the sheets within a workbook are *Sheet1, Sheet2,* and so on.
- The two methods you can use to insert or delete worksheets are the context menu and the **Insert** or **Delete** buttons.
- The context menu and the *Format* button include options to **Move** and **Copy** worksheets.

1.7 Customize the Excel window by changing views, adjusting zoom level, freezing panes, and splitting a worksheet (p. E1-36).

- Excel has three main views: **Normal**, **Page Layout**, and **Page Break Preview**.
- Display options such as **Zoom**, **Freeze Panes**, **Gridlines**, and **Headings** can help make larger spreadsheets easier to view.
- You can **Hide** and **Unhide** sheets if they include sensitive data.

1.8 Finalize a workbook by spell checking, adding document properties, applying page setup options, and printing (p. E1-41).

- Check spelling using the *Review* tab.
- Various **Document Properties** are created automatically. These include *Creation* date, *Modified* date, *Accessed* date, and file *Size*. You can add properties such as *Title*, *Author*, *Comments*, *Subject*, and *Company*.
- The *Document Information Panel* on the right side of *Backstage* view displays details that are available for update or change.
- The **Advanced Properties** option in the *Document Information* panel displays the *Properties* dialog box.
- Use *Page Setup* options to customize page layout settings and print preview to review worksheets.

Check for Understanding

In the **Online Learning Center** for this text (www.mhhe.com/office2013inpractice), there are a variety of resources that can be used to review the concepts covered in this chapter.

The following Online Learning Resources are available on the Online Learning Center:

- Multiple choice questions
- Short answer questions
- Matching exercises

Guided Project 1-1

Abdul Kohl has just been hired at Life's Animal Shelter and asked to track the organization's weekly expenses on a spreadsheet.
[Student Learning Outcomes 1.1, 1.2, 1.3, 1.4, 1.5, 1.6, 1.8]

File Needed: None
Completed Project File Name: *[your initials] Excel 1-1.xlsx*

Skills Covered in This Project

- Create and save a workbook.
- Enter text and numbers.
- Change font size and attributes.
- Create a formula using *AutoSum*.
- Use the *Fill Handle*.
- Apply *Cell Styles*.
- Apply a theme.
- Apply page layout options.

- Insert a row and adjust column width and row height.
- Rename and apply color to sheet tabs.
- Merge and center titles.
- Apply number formatting.
- Insert and delete sheets.
- Use spell check.

1. Open a new workbook.
   a. Click the **File** tab to open the *Backstage* view.
   b. Click **New** and then click **Blank workbook** to open a new blank workbook.

2. Save the workbook as *[your initials] Excel 1-1*.
   a. Press **F12** to open the *Save As* dialog box.
   b. Rename the file *[your initials] Excel 1-1* in the *File name* area.
   c. Select the folder or **Browse** to the location on your *SkyDrive*, computer, or storage device to save the workbook.
   d. Click **Save**.

3. Enter the data.
   a. Select **A1**, type Life's Animal Shelter, and then press **Enter**. Type September 1 – 7, 2015 and press **Enter**.
   b. Type the remaining data in Figure 1-97.

	A	B	C	D	E	F	G	H
1	Life's Animal Shelter							
2	September 1 - 7, 2015							
3								
4	Expense Categories	Monday						
5	Food	340.45	344.05	350.51	340.01	341.18	359.75	340.02
6	Medicine	525.33	529.31	535.25	524.59	527.99	543.39	540.01
7	Wages	675.21	580.91	575.88	579.55	680.81	750.05	565.9
8	Heat	25.75	26.01	28.05	25.03	25.99	31.04	24.99
9	Electricity	19.45	20.09	21.75	19.02	19.99	23.56	19.45
10	Total							

1-97 Excel 1-1 data

4. Use the *Fill Handle* to copy a series.
   a. Select **B4**.
   b. Place the pointer on the *Fill Handle* (small black square in the lower right corner of the cell) until the fill pointer (thin black plus sign) appears.
   c. Click and drag the fill pointer to **H4**.

E1-57

5. Apply *Merge & Center* to the title and subtitle of your worksheet.
   a. Select **A1:H1** and click the **Merge & Center** button [*Home* tab, *Alignment* group].
   b. Select **A2:H2** and click the **Merge & Center** button [*Home* tab, *Alignment* group].

6. Apply *Cell Styles*.
   a. Select **A1** and click the **More** button [*Home* tab, *Styles* group].
   b. Select **Title** in the *Titles and Headings* category.
   c. Select **A2** and click the **More** button [*Home* tab, *Styles* group].
   d. Select **Heading 2** in the *Titles and Headings* category.
   e. Select **A4:A9**, hold down **Ctrl**, and select **B4:H4**.
   f. Click the **More** button [*Home* tab, *Styles* group].
   g. Select **60%, Accent 1** in the *Themed Cell Styles* category.
   h. Select **A10:H10** and click the **More** button [*Home* tab, *Styles* group].
   i. Select **Total** in the *Titles and Headings* category.

7. Apply font attributes.
   a. Select **A4:A9**, hold down **Ctrl**, and then select **B4:H4**.
   b. Click the **Bold** button [*Home* tab, *Font* group].
   c. Select **A5:A9**, hold down **Ctrl**, and then select **B4:H4**.
   d. Click the **Increase Indent** button [*Home* tab, *Alignment* group] three times.
   e. Click the **Font Size** drop-down list [*Home* tab, *Font* group] and select **12 pt**.

8. Increase column width.
   a. Select **A4:H10**.
   b. Click the **Format** button [*Home* tab, *Cells* group].
   c. Select **AutoFit Column Width**. Deselect the cells.

9. Apply themes to the worksheet.
   a. Click the **Themes** button [*Page Layout* tab, *Themes* group] and choose **Integral** from the gallery (Figure 1-98).
   b. Click the **Theme Fonts** button [*Page Layout* tab, *Themes* group] and select **Franklin Gothic** from the gallery.

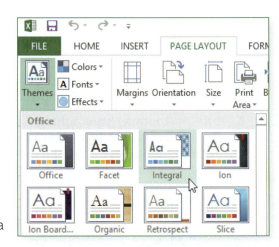

1-98 *Integral* theme button

10. Apply font attributes to the labels in the spreadsheet.
    a. Select **A4**.
    b. Click the **Font** drop-down list [*Home* tab, *Font* group] and select **Arial**.
    c. Click the **Font Size** drop-down list and select **14**.

11. Use *AutoSum* to calculate a total and copy the formula using the *Fill Handle*.
    a. Select **B10**.
    b. Click **AutoSum** [*Home* tab, *Editing* group] and press **Enter**.
    c. Select **B10** and place the pointer on the *Fill Handle* (small black square in the lower right corner of the cell) until the fill pointer (thin black plus sign) appears.
    d. Click and drag the fill pointer to cell **H10**.

12. Apply number formatting to the numeric data.
    a. Select **B5:H10**.
    b. Click the **Accounting Number Format** button [*Home* tab, *Number* group].

13. Adjust column width.
    a. Select **A4:H10**.
    b. Click the **Format** button [*Home* tab, *Cells* group].
    c. Select **AutoFit Column Width**.

14. Press **Ctrl+S** to save the workbook.

15. Change column width on a range of columns.
    a. Click and drag to select the column headings **B:H**.
    b. Click the **Format** button [*Home* tab, *Cells* group].
    c. Select **Column Width** from the menu.
    d. Enter 15.0 characters as the new width.
    e. Click **OK**.

16. Apply new row heights.
    a. Click row heading **4**, hold down **Ctrl**, and click row heading **10**.
    b. Right-click row heading **4**.
    c. Choose **Row Height** from the context menu.
    d. Enter 21.0 as the new height.
    e. Click **OK**.

17. Insert a new row and row heading.
    a. Right-click row heading **9**.
    b. Choose **Insert** from the context menu to add a new row. The new row appears directly above the originally selected row.
    c. Select cell **A9** and type: Cages & Equipment.

18. Increase the width of column A to **29.00**.

19. Enter the following information into the cell range **B9:H9**.

	B	C	D	E	F	G	H
9	199.03	209.25	198.90	229.05	245.09	351.98	205.55

20. Rename and color sheet tab.
    a. Double-click the **Sheet1** tab.
    b. Type the following name: Park Rapids, MN Location.
    c. Press **Enter**.
    d. Click the **Format** button [*Home* tab, *Cells* group].
    e. Select **Tab Color** in the *Organize Sheets* category to add a fill color to the background of the sheet tab.
    f. Select **Blue Accent 2**, **Darker 50%** (last color in the sixth *Theme Color* column) (Figure 1-99).

21. Insert a new sheet.
    a. Click the **Insert** button drop-down arrow [*Home* tab, *Cells* group] and select **Insert Sheet**. The new sheet named **Sheet2** appears to the left of the *Park Rapids* worksheet tab.
    b. Add another sheet to the workbook by clicking the **New Sheet** button.

22. Delete *Sheet2* and *Sheet3*.
    a. Click the **Sheet2** tab, press and hold **Shift**, click the **Sheet3** tab, and release **Shift**.
    b. Click the **Delete** button drop-down arrow [*Home* tab, *Cells* group] and select **Delete Sheet**.

23. Press **Ctrl+S** to save the workbook.

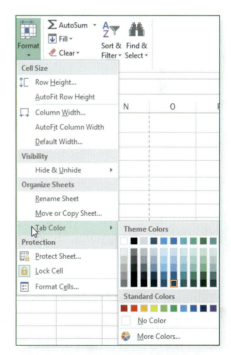

1-99 Worksheet *Tab Color* options

24. Change *Page Setup* options.
    a. Click the **Page Layout** tab and click the **Page Setup** launcher.
    b. Select the **Page** tab in the *Page Setup* dialog box.
    c. Click the **Landscape** radio button under *Orientation*.
    d. Click the **Fit to:** radio button under *Scaling* and enter 1 page wide by 1 tall.
    e. Click the **Header/Footer** tab.
    f. Click the **Header:** drop-down list and select *[your initials] Excel 1-1* from the list.
    g. Click the **Margins** tab.
    h. Click the **Horizontally** check box under *Center on page*.
    i. Click **OK**.

25. Spell check the worksheet.
    a. Press **Ctrl+Home** to go to cell **A1**.
    b. Click the **Spelling** button [*Review* tab, *Proofing* group].
    c. Correct any misspelled words.

26. Click the **File** tab and select **Print** to preview the workbook.

27. Save and close the workbook (Figure 1-100).

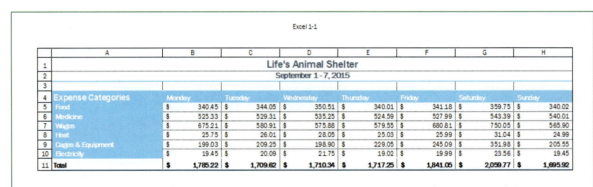

	A	B	C	D	E	F	G	H
				Excel 1-1				
1				Life's Animal Shelter				
2				September 1 - 7, 2015				
3								
4	Expense Categories	Monday	Tuesday	Wednesday	Thursday	Friday	Saturday	Sunday
5	Food	$ 340.45	$ 344.05	$ 350.51	$ 340.01	$ 341.18	$ 359.75	$ 340.02
6	Medicine	$ 525.33	$ 529.31	$ 535.25	$ 524.59	$ 527.99	$ 543.39	$ 540.01
7	Wages	$ 675.21	$ 580.91	$ 575.88	$ 579.55	$ 680.81	$ 750.05	$ 565.90
8	Heat	$ 25.75	$ 26.01	$ 28.05	$ 25.03	$ 25.99	$ 31.04	$ 24.99
9	Cages & Equipment	$ 199.03	$ 209.25	$ 198.90	$ 229.05	$ 245.09	$ 351.98	$ 205.55
10	Electricity	$ 19.45	$ 20.09	$ 21.75	$ 19.02	$ 19.99	$ 23.56	$ 19.45
11	Total	$ 1,785.22	$ 1,709.62	$ 1,710.34	$ 1,717.25	$ 1,841.05	$ 2,059.77	$ 1,695.92

1-100 Excel 1-1 completed

Guided Project 1-2

For this project, you edit and format a spreadsheet for a sales representative for Eller Software Services. The spreadsheet contains clients' personal information and a listing of their product purchases.
[Student Learning Outcomes 1.1, 1.2, 1.3, 1.4, 1.5, 1.6, 1.7, 1.8]

File Needed: *EllerSoftwareServices-1.xlsx*
Completed Project File Name: *[your initials] Excel 1-2.xlsx*

Skills Covered in This Project

- Open and save a workbook.
- Enter and format text and numbers.
- Copy text using the *Fill Handle*.
- Create a formula using *AutoSum*.
- Apply a theme and *Cell Styles*.
- Merge and center titles and subtitles.
- Change orientation.
- Apply font attributes.

- Apply numeric formatting.
- Apply date formatting.
- Apply a border.
- Change zoom level.
- Hide and insert a row and adjust column width.
- Rename and apply color to sheet tabs.
- Use spell check.
- Apply page layout options.

1. Open a workbook.
   a. Click the **File** tab and click **Open**.
   b. Locate the folder where your files are saved.
   c. Open the workbook ***EllerSoftwareServices-1.xlsx***.

2. Rename the workbook ***[your initials] Excel 1-2***.
   a. Press **F12** to open the *Save As* dialog box.
   b. Locate the folder where your files are located.
   c. Rename the file ***[your initials] Excel 1-2*** in the *File name* area.
   d. Click **Save**.

3. Apply a theme to the worksheet.
   a. Click the **Themes** button [*Page Layout* tab, *Themes* group].
   b. Choose **Retrospect** from the *Office* gallery.

4. Enter and format data.
   a. Select **E5**, type **MN**, and press **Enter**.
   b. Select **E5** and point to the *Fill Handle*.
   c. Click and drag the fill pointer to **E13**.
   d. Select **C5:C13**.
   e. Press **Ctrl+1** to open the *Format Cells* dialog box.
   f. Click the **Number** tab and click **Special** under *Category*.
   g. Select **Phone Number** and click **OK** to close the *Format Cells* dialog box.

5. Use *AutoSum* to calculate the total of gross sales and adjust the reference range.
   a. Type Total in **A15**.
   b. Select cell **I15**.
   c. Click **AutoSum** [*Home* tab, *Editing* group] and press **Enter**.
   d. Select **I15** and click the cell reference range in the *Formula bar*.
   e. Edit the cell range to **I13** and press **Enter**.

6. Apply *Merge & Center* to the title and subtitle of the worksheet.
   a. Select **A1:I1** and click the **Merge & Center** button [*Home* tab, *Alignment* group].
   b. Select **A2:I2** and click the **Merge & Center** button.

7. Apply *Cell Styles*.
   a. Select **A1** and click the **Cell Styles** button [*Home* tab, *Styles* group].
   b. Select **Title** in the *Titles and Headings* category.
   c. Select **A2** and click the **Cell Styles** button and select **Heading 2** in the *Titles and Headings* category.

    d. Select **A4:A15**, hold down **Ctrl**, and then select **B4:I4**.

    e. Click the **Cell Styles** button and select **40%- Accent 1** in the *Themed Cell Styles* category.

    f. Select **I15**, click the **Cell Styles** button, and then select **Total** in the *Titles and Headings* category.

8. Apply diagonal rotation to text.
   a. Select **A4:I4**.
   b. Click the **Orientation** button [*Home* tab, *Alignment* group].
   c. Select **Angle Counterclockwise**.

9. Apply font attributes.
   a. Select the cell range **A4:A15**, hold down **Ctrl**, and click and drag to select **B4:I4**.
   b. Click the **Font Size** drop-down list [*Home* tab, *Font* group] and select **12**.
   c. Click the **Font type** drop-down list [*Home* tab, *Font* group] and select **Verdana**.
   d. Click the **Bold** button [*Home* tab, *Font* group].
   e. Select the non-adjacent cell ranges **C5:C13** and **E5:F13**.
   f. Click **Center** [*Home* tab, *Alignment* group].
   g. Select **A1:A2** and click the **Increase Font Size** button [*Home* tab, *Font* group] two times.

10. Apply numeric formatting to your spreadsheet.
    a. Select **I5:I15**.
    b. Click **Comma Style** [*Home* tab, *Number* group].
    c. Select **I5**, press **Ctrl**, and select **I15**.
    d. Press **Ctrl+1** to open the *Format Cells* dialog box.
    e. Select the **Number** tab, if necessary, and select the **Accounting** category.
    f. Change the **Symbol** drop-down list to **$**.
    g. Click **OK** to close the *Format Cells* dialog box.

11. Apply date formatting to your spreadsheet.
    a. Select **H5:H13**.
    b. Click the **Short Date** format from the *Number Format* drop-down list [*Home* tab, *Number* group].

12. Increase the width of your columns.
    a. Select **A4:I15**.
    b. Click the **Format** button [*Home* tab, *Cells* group].
    c. Select **AutoFit Column Width**.

13. Press **Ctrl+S** to save the workbook.

14. Edit a cell.
    a. Double-click cell **G9** to activate edit mode.
    b. Delete the word **Software** from the cell contents and press **Enter**.

15. Change the width of a column.
    a. Click the column **G** heading to select the column.
    b. Click the **Format** button [*Home* tab, *Cells* group] and select **Column Width** from the menu.
    c. Enter 31.0 characters as the new width.
    d. Click **OK**.

16. Hide an existing row and insert a new row and row heading.
    a. Right-click row heading **10**.
    b. Choose **Hide** from the context menu.
    c. Right-click row heading **11**.
    d. Choose **Insert** from the context menu to add a new row. The new row appears directly above the originally selected row.
    e. Select cell **A11** and type Hilary Marschke.

Skills Covered in This Project

- Open and save a workbook.
- Enter and format text and numbers.
- Use the *Fill Handle* to copy a formula.
- Apply a theme and *Cell Styles*.
- Merge and center title and subtitle.
- Apply numeric formatting.
- Adjust column width and row height.

- Insert a column.
- Use *Page Layout* view to insert a footer.
- Move cell contents.
- Check spelling.
- Rename sheet tabs and apply color to sheet tabs.
- Apply page layout options.

---

1. Open and rename the workbook file.
   a. Press **Ctrl+O** to display the *Open* area.
   b. Locate the folder where your files are located.
   c. Open the workbook file ***WearEverShoes-1****.xlsx*.
   d. Press **F12** and locate the folder where your files are saved.
   e. Save the workbook as ***[your initials] Excel 1-3***.

2. Click the **Themes** button [*Page Layout* tab, *Themes* group] and choose **Ion** from the gallery.

3. Increase column width.
   a. Select **A4:I12**.
   b. Click the **Format** button [*Home* tab, *Cells* group].
   c. Select **AutoFit Column Width**.

4. Apply *Cell Styles*.
   a. Select **A1**, click the **More** button [*Home* tab, *Styles* group], and select **Title** in the *Titles and Headings* category.
   b. Select **A3**, click the **More** button, and select **Heading 2** in the *Titles and Headings* category.
   c. Select **A4:A12**, press **Ctrl**, and select **B4:I4**.
   d. Click the **More** button and select **40%- Accent 1** in the *Themed Cell Styles* category.
   e. Select **B5:I12**.
   f. Click the **More** button and select **20%- Accent 2** in the *Themed Cell Styles* category.

5. Apply *Merge & Center* to the title and subtitle of your worksheet.
   a. Select **A1:I1** and click **Merge & Center** [*Home* tab, *Alignment* group].
   b. Select **A3:I3** and click **Merge & Center**.

6. Apply formatting.
   a. Select the cell range **A4:A12**, press **Ctrl**, and select **B4:I4**.
   b. Click the **Font size** drop-down list [*Home* tab, *Font* group] and select **12 pt**.
   c. Click the **Font type** drop-down list [*Home* tab, *Font* group] and select **Trebuchet MS**.
   d. Select **A4:I4** and click the **Center** button [*Home* tab, *Alignment* group].
   e. Select **I5:I12** and click the **Center** button [*Home* tab, *Alignment* group].
   f. Select **E5:E12** and click the **Increase Indent** button [*Home* tab, *Alignment* group].

7. Use the *Fill Handle* to copy a formula.
   a. Click **H5**.
   b. Point to the *Fill Handle* in the lower right corner and drag the fill pointer to **H12**.

8. Apply numeric formatting and adjust column width.
   a. Select **F5:H12**.
   b. Click **Comma Style** [*Home* tab, *Number* group].

c. Select **A4:I12**.

  d. Click the **Format** button [*Home* tab, *Cells* group] and select **AutoFit Column Width**.

9. Save your workbook (Figure 1-104).

10. Edit a cell.

  a. Double-click cell **B7** to activate edit mode.

  b. Edit the cell's contents so it appears as Pink.

1-104 Formatted worksheet

11. Change the width of a column.

  a. Click column heading **A** to select the column.

  b. Click the **Format** button [*Home* tab, *Cells* group] and select **Column Width**.

  c. Enter 24.0 as the new width and click **OK**.

12. Apply a new row height.

  a. Right-click row heading **4**.

  b. Choose **Row Height** from the context menu.

  c. Enter 21.0 as the new height and click **OK**.

13. Insert a new column and type a column heading and data in the new column.

  a. Right-click column heading **D**.

  b. Choose **Insert** from the context menu to add a new column.

  c. Select cell **D4** and type: Discontinue.

  d. Increase the width of the new column if needed to automatically fit the contents of the column.

  e. Enter the following information into the cell range **D5:D12**:

	D
5	No
6	No
7	No
8	No
9	No
10	Yes
11	No
12	Yes

14. Rename and color the sheet tab.

  a. Double-click the **Sheet1** tab.

  b. Type the following name: Northern Warehouse and press **Enter**.

  c. Click the **Format** button [*Home* tab, *Cells* group].

  d. Select **Tab Color** in the *Organize Sheets* category to add a fill color to the background of the sheet tab.

  e. Select **Dark Red, Accent 1, Darker 50%** (last color in the fifth *Theme Color* column).

15. Click the **Save** button on the *Quick Access* toolbar to save the workbook changes.

16. Move cell contents and adjust column width.

  a. Select the cell range **D4:D12**.

  b. Click the **Cut** button [*Home* tab, *Clipboard* group].

c. Click cell **K4** and click the **Paste** button [*Home* tab, *Clipboard* group].

d. Select **E4:K12**.

e. Place the pointer on the right border of the selected cell range, drag the cell range to **D4**, and release the pointer.

f. Select **B4:J12**, click the **Format** button [*Home* tab, *Cells* group], and select **AutoFit Column Width**.

17. Click the **Spelling** button [*Review* tab, *Proofing* group] and correct any misspellings in the worksheet.

18. Use *Page Layout* view to insert a footer.

a. Click the **Insert** tab and click **Header & Footer**.

b. Click the **Header & Footer Tools Design** tab.

c. Click **Go to Footer** [*Header & Footer Tools Design* tab, *Navigation* group].

d. Click in the middle section of the footer area and select **File Name** in the *Header & Footer Elements* group. Click in the worksheet to see the file name.

e. Switch to *Normal* view.

19. Change the *Page Setup* options.

a. Click the **Page Layout** tab and click the **Page Setup** launcher.

b. Select the **Page** tab from the *Page Setup* dialog box and click the **Landscape** radio button under *Orientation*.

c. Click the **Fit to:** radio button and enter 1 page wide by 1 tall.

d. Click **OK**.

20. Save and close the workbook (Figure 1-105).

Wear-Ever Shoes

Outlet Product Inventory

Product	Color	Sizes	Quantity	Mens/Womens	Cost	Retail Price	Total Cost	Reorder	Discontinue
Rugged Hiking Boots	Brown and Black	W 5-11	45	Men	46.50	90.00	2,092.50	N	No
Comfy Walking Shoes	Brown and Black	R 5-12	52	Both	34.25	65.00	1,781.00	N	No
Lazy Flip-Flops	Pink and White	R 5-12	13	Both	7.50	14.00	97.50	Y	No
Seriously Tall Boots	Black	W 5-11	0	Women	42.50	80.00	-	Y	No
Glide Running Shoes	Green and Black	R 5-12	10	Both	36.50	75.00	365.00	Y	No
Classy Pumps	Navy Blue	R 5-12	40	Women	15.45	30.00	618.00	N	Yes
Chunky Heel Boots	Brown	W 5-11	10	Women	32.45	65.00	324.50	Y	No
Sassy Slip-Ons	Silver	R 5-12	25	Women	23.50	45.00	587.50	N	Yes

Excel 1-3

1-105 Excel 1-3 completed

Independent Project 1-4

You have just been hired as an administrative assistant at Blue Lake Sport Company. Your supervisor has asked you to convert her daily sales report into a spreadsheet that she can distribute at the department meeting.
[Student Learning Outcomes 1.1, 1.2, 1.3, 1.4, 1.5, 1.6, 1.7, 1.8]

File Needed: **BlueLakeSports-1.xlsx**
Completed Project File Name: **[your initials] Excel 1-4.xlsx**

Skills Covered in This Project

- Open and save a workbook.
- Enter and format text and numbers.
- Merge and center title and date.
- Use *AutoSum*.
- Create a formula and use the *Fill Handle*.
- Apply a theme and apply *Cell Styles*.

- Use *Page Layout* view to insert a header and footer.
- Apply page layout options.
- Adjust column width and row height.
- Rename and apply color to sheet tabs.

1. Open the workbook file **BlueLakeSport-1.xlsx**.

2. Save the presentation as **[your initials] Excel 1-4**.

3. Apply the **Slice** theme to the worksheet.

4. Edit worksheet data.
   a. Edit the title in **A1** so that the word "Sports" contains an apostrophe and appears as follows: Sport's.
   b. Edit the value in cell **B6** to 5102.

5. Merge and center the title in cell **A1** across the cell range **A1:H1**, and merge and center the date in cell **A2** across the cell range **A2:H2**.

6. Delete row **8**.

7. Use the *Fill Handle* to complete a series.
   a. Select **B4**.
   b. Use *Fill Handle* to add headings for columns **C:H**.

8. Apply *Cell Styles* to the labels in the spreadsheet.
   a. Apply the **Title Style** to **A1**.
   b. Apply the **Heading 1** style to the subtitle in **A2**.
   c. Apply the **20%- Accent 1** themed cell style to **B4:H4** and **A4:A8**.
   d. Apply the **20%- Accent 3** themed cell style to **B5:H8**.
   e. Select **A3:H3**, and apply the **Heading 1** style.

9. Format cell contents.
   a. Increase the font size of **A4:H8** to **12 pt**.
   b. Select **A5:A7** and click the **Increase Indent** button.
   c. Apply the **Comma** format to cells **B5:H8**.

10. Use *AutoSum* and the *Fill Handle* to calculate daily totals.
   a. Use *AutoSum* to create a *Sum* formula for **B8**.
   b. Use the *Fill Handle* to copy the formula in **B8** to cells **C8:H8**.

11. Apply additional formatting to the spreadsheet.
    a. Apply the **Total** cell style to cells **A8:H8**.
    b. Increase the font size to **12 pt.** in cells **B8:H8**.
    c. **Bold** all non-numeric entries in **A4:H8**.
    d. **Center** the days of the week.
    e. Select **B5:H7** and apply the *Comma Style* format.
    f. Select **B8:H8** and select **Accounting** from the *Number Format* drop-down list.

12. Adjust column width and row height.
    a. Change the width in column **A** to 22.0.
    b. Change the row height for rows **1:8** to 22.0.

13. Rename and color a sheet tab.
    a. Rename *Sheet1* Week 1 of May.
    b. Color the sheet tab **Dark Blue Accent 1**, **Darker 50%** (last color in the fifth *Theme Color* column).

14. Spell check the worksheet.

15. Apply page layout options.
    a. Change the page orientation to **Landscape**.
    b. Fit the spreadsheet to 1 page wide by 1 tall.
    c. Center the worksheet horizontally on the page.

16. Add a header and footer.
    a. Click the **Insert** tab and click **Header & Footer**.
    b. Click the left header section and add the **Sheet Name** field.
    c. Click **Go to Footer**, click the middle section, and add the **Page Number** field.
    d. Click a cell in the worksheet and switch to *Normal* view.

17. Preview the workbook.

18. Save and close the workbook (Figure 1-106).

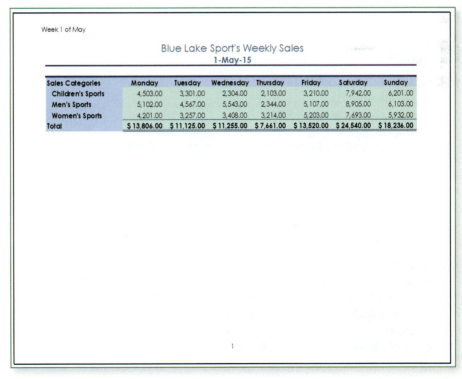

1-106 Excel 1-4 completed

Independent Project 1-5

Clemenson Imaging is a privately owned organization that employs certified staff to perform mobile medical imaging at many hospitals statewide. You have been hired as the scheduling dispatch coordinator. It is your job to schedule all the mobile technicians at various hospital locations every day. Your supervisor has requested that you convert your schedule to an Excel spreadsheet.
[Student Learning Outcomes 1.1, 1.2, 1.3, 1.4, 1.5, 1.6, 1.7]

File Needed: *ClemsonImaging-1.xlsx*
Completed Project File Name: *[your initials] Excel 1-5.xlsx*

Skills Covered in This Project

- Open and save a workbook.
- Enter and format text and numbers.
- Merge and center title and subtitle.
- Spell check.
- Add a border.
- Apply a theme and *Cell Styles*.
- Create a formula using *AutoSum*.
- Adjust column width and row height.
- Rename and apply color to sheet tabs.
- Apply *Freeze Panes*.
- Apply page layout options.

1. Open **ClemsonImaging-1.xlsx** and save it as *[your initials] Excel 1-5*.

2. Apply the **Ion Boardroom** theme to the worksheet.

3. Edit the title in **A1** so that "LLC" appears after the word "Imaging" and appears as Clemenson Imaging LLC.

4. Merge and center the title in cell **A1** across the cell range **A1:H1** and the subtitle in cell **A2** across the cell range **A2:H2**.

5. Edit the value in cell **E7** to 3.

6. Apply *Cell Styles*.
   a. Apply the **Title** style to **A1**.
   b. Apply the **Heading 1** style to the subtitle in **A2**.
   c. Apply the **40%- Accent 2** themed cell style to **A4:H4**.

7. Apply format changes.
   a. Increase the font size of **A4:H11** to **12 pt**.
   b. Increase the indent of cells **A5:A11**.

8. Add the title Total in cell **A13** and calculate the total number of patients in **E13** using *AutoSum*. Edit the formula cell range to **E11**.

9. Apply additional formatting to the spreadsheet.
   a. Apply the **Total Cell** style to **A13:H13**.
   b. Increase the font size to **12 pt.** in cells **A13:H13**.
   c. Select **A13** and **Decrease Indent**.
   d. **Bold** and center the data in **E5:E13** and **H5:H11**.
   e. Apply **bold** format to cells **A4:H4**.

10. Adjust column widths and row heights.
   a. Change the width in column **A** to 20.0.
   b. *AutoFit* the remaining columns (**B:H**).
   c. Change the row height for rows **4** and **13** to 21.00.
   d. Delete row **12**.

11. Apply **Freeze Panes** to cell **A5**.
   a. Click the **View** tab.
   b. Select **A5**.
   c. Click **Freeze Panes** and select **Freeze Panes**.

12. Rename *Sheet1* as 12-1-2015 and color the sheet tab **Plum Accent 1, Darker 50%**.

13. Select **A4:H4** and apply a thick bottom border using the **Plum, Accent 1, Darker 50%** color.

14. Spell check the worksheet.

15. Apply page layout options.
   a. Change the orientation to **Landscape** and fit the spreadsheet to one page.
   b. Center the worksheet horizontally on the page.
   c. Add the automatic footer **12-1-2015** to the worksheet using the *Footer* drop-down list.

16. Preview the spreadsheet.

17. Save and close the workbook (Figure 1-107).

Clemenson Imaging LLC
Technician Daily Schedule

Name	Hospital	Arrival Time	Departure Time	Patients	Image Type	Category	Priority
Bonna McFarland	East Memorial	8:00 AM	2:00 PM	4	Cardiac	Routine	2
Mary Anne Vonbank	Central Children's	9:00 AM	4:30 PM	5	General	Emergency	1
Jonathan Douglas	South Point	10:00 AM	12:30 PM	3	OB	Add on	3
Samantha Woods	Saint Josephs	8:00 AM	5:30 PM	6	General	Routine	2
Annie Olander	Haskins	7:30 AM	7:30 PM	8	Cardiac	Routine	2
Patti Lynn	North Lakes	11:00 AM	2:00 PM	3	OB	Add on	3
James Boyd	Western River	4:00 PM	9:00 PM	4	Cardiac	Emergency	1
Total				33			

12-1-2015

Independent Project 1-6

You have been hired as the accounts receivable clerk for a privately owned accounting company called Livingood Income Tax & Accounting. It is your job to track all the payments from clients every day. Your supervisor has requested that you convert your payment table to an Excel spreadsheet.
[Student Learning Outcomes 1.1, 1.2, 1.3, 1.4, 1.5, 1.6, 1.7, 1.8]

File Needed: None
Completed Project File Name: *[your initials] Excel 1-6.xlsx*

Skills Covered in This Project

- Create and save a workbook.
- Enter text and numbers.
- Change font size and attributes.
- Use *AutoSum*.
- Adjust column width and row height.
- Spell check.

- Apply *Freeze Panes*.
- Change zoom level.
- Apply a theme and *Cell Styles*.
- Apply page layout options.
- Hide a row.
- Rename and apply color to sheet tabs.

1. Start a new workbook and save it as *[your initials] Excel 1-6*.

2. Apply the **Organic** theme to the worksheet. Change the theme font to **Gill Sans MT**.

3. Select **A1** and type Livingood Income Tax and Accounting, press **Enter**, type Payment Schedule, and press **Enter** again.

4. Type in the remaining worksheet data from Figure 1-108.

5. Edit the title in **A1** to replace the word "and" with the symbol &.

6. Edit the value in cell **B5** to 451.25. Change "Over Due" in cell **F4** to Overdue.

7. Apply the **Title** style to **A1**.

8. Apply formatting to cell ranges.
   a. Increase the font size of **A4:G11** to **12 pt**.
   b. Select cells **B5:B11** and display the *Format Cells* dialog box. Select the **Accounting** format and change the *Symbol* to **None**.

	A	B	C	D	E	F	G
1	Livingood Income Tax and Accounting						
2	Payment Schedule						
3							
4	Invoice	Amount	Due Date	Paid	Payment Type	Over Due	Contact
5	4567	450.5	42278	Yes	Check 2005	No	No
6	3421	465.78	42248	No	Due	Yes	Letter
7	2456	250.25	42217	No	Due	Yes	Phone
8	4569	585.65	42278	Yes	Discover	No	No
9	4572	1245.89	42278	No	Due	No	No
10	1428	1245.67	42186	No	Due	Yes	Collections
11	2576	345.08	42217	Yes	Check 2345	No	No

1-108 Excel 1-6 data

9. Add the title Total in cell **A13** and calculate the total for **B13** using *AutoSum*. Adjust the cell range reference in the *Formula bar*.

10. Apply additional formatting.
    a. Apply the **Total** cell style to cells **A13:G13**.
    b. Select **A13:G13** and increase the font size to **12 pt**.
    c. **Bold** the entries in **A4:G4**.
    d. **Center** the data in **A4:G4, A5:A13, D5:D13**, and **F5:F13**.

e. Select **A4:G4** and open the *Format Cells* dialog box. Add a thick **Green, Accent 1, Darker 50%** bottom border and a **Green, Accent 1, Lighter 80%** fill color using the second color in the fifth column.

f. Select the cells in rows **6**, **8**, and **10** and apply the same fill color.

g. Use the **Border** button and apply a bottom border to cells **A2:G2**.

11. Adjust column width and row height.
    a. Change the width of columns **A:G** to 14.0.
    b. Change the row height for rows **4** and **13** to 19.50.

12. Hide row **12**.

13. Rename *Sheet1* 10-27-2015 and color the sheet tab **Green, Accent 1** (first color in the fifth *Theme Color* column).

14. Spell check the worksheet.

15. Apply *Freeze Panes* to **B5**.

16. Increase the magnification of the view to **125%**.

17. Apply page layout options.
    a. Change the orientation to **Landscape** and scale the page to fit on one page.
    b. Center the worksheet horizontally on the page.
    c. Click the **Custom Header** button and add the **Insert Sheet Name** field in the *Left Header* section. Click the **Format Text** button and apply the font color **Green, Accent 1, Darker 50%** to the header field.
    d. Add the page number to the right section of the footer.
    e. Select print preview in the *Page Setup* dialog box to view your settings.

18. Save and close the workbook (Figure 1-109).

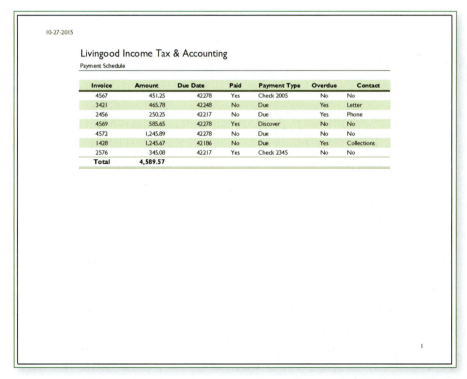

1-109 Excel 1-6 completed

Improve It Project 1-7

For this project, you create a flight schedule for the manager of Boyd Air. You edit and format the data in a spreadsheet and add page layout formatting.
[Student Learning Outcomes 1.1, 1.2, 1.3, 1.4, 1.5, 1.6, 1.7, 1.8]

File Needed: ***BoydAirFlightSchedule-1**.xlsx*
Completed Project File Name: ***[your initials] Excel 1-7.xlsx***

Skills Covered in This Project

- Open and save a workbook.
- Enter and format text and numbers.
- Merge and center title and subtitle.
- Format and delete rows and columns.
- Spell check.
- Use *AutoSum* to create a formula.

- Apply a theme and apply *Cell Styles*.
- Apply page layout options.
- Adjust column width and row height.
- Rename and apply color to sheet tabs.
- Freeze panes and change the zoom level.

1. Open the workbook ***BoydAirFlightSchedule-01.xlsx***.

2. Rename the workbook ***[your initials] Excel 1-7***.

3. Type Boyd Air in **A1** and type Flight Schedule in **A2**.

4. Merge and center the title in cell **A1** and the subtitle in cell **A2**.

5. Apply *Cell Styles* to the labels in the spreadsheet.
   a. Apply the **Title** style to **A1**.
   b. Apply the **Heading 1** style to the subtitle in **A2**.
   c. Apply the **Accent 1** cell style to **A4:F4**.
   d. Apply the **20%-Accent 1** cell style to **A5:F13**.

6. Apply formatting.
   a. Increase the font size of **A4:F4** to **14 pt**.
   b. Apply the **Total** cell style to cells **A13:F13**.
   c. **Bold** the entries in **A4:F4**.
   d. Select **A4**, **C4**, and **D4**, and click **Wrap Text** [*Home* tab, *Alignment* group].

7. Apply row and column formatting.
   a. Change the row height for row **4** to 38.00.
   b. Change the row height for row **13** to 21.00.
   c. Right align the text in **C4** and **D4**.

8. Delete row **12**.

9. Use *AutoSum* to calculate the total number of passengers.

10. Color the sheet tab **Dark Blue**, **Accent 1**, **Darker 50%** (last color in the fifth *Theme Color* column).

11. Edit the sheet tab name by deleting **Monday**.

12. *AutoFit* columns **A:F**.

13. Spell check the worksheet.

14. Apply *Freeze Panes* to **B5**.

15. Increase the magnification of the sheet to **150%**.

16. Apply page layout options.
    a. Change the orientation to **Landscape** and fit the spreadsheet to one page.
    b. Center the worksheet horizontally on the page.
    c. Add the **Insert File Name** field in the *Left Header* section and apply the font color **Dark Blue, Accent 1**.

17. Preview your settings.

18. Save and close the workbook (Figure 1-110).

Excel 1-7

Boyd Air
Flight Schedule

Flight Number	Destination	Arrival Time	Departure Time	Status	Passengers
BD 2345	Chicago, IL	8:00:00 AM	9:30:00 AM	On Time	90
BD 4567	Minneapolis, MN	9:00:00 PM	10:30:00 PM	On Time	75
BD 1234	Green Bay, WI	10:00:00 AM	12:30:00 PM	Delayed	80
BD 6578	St. Louis, MO	8:00:00 AM	9:30:00 AM	On Time	63
BD 2213	Orlando, FL	6:30:00 AM	7:00:00 AM	Delayed	90
BD 980	Fargo, ND	12:30:00 PM	2:00:00 PM	On Time	35
BD 1345	Houston, TX	4:45:00 PM	7:00:00 PM	On Time	90
Total					**523**

1-110 Excel 1-7 completed

Challenge Project 1-8

For this project, you create a spreadsheet that lists sales for a gourmet chocolate store. The sales report lists data for popular holidays within a calendar year.
[Student Learning Outcomes 1.1, 1.2, 1.3, 1.4, 1.5, 1.6, 1.7, 1.8]

File Needed: None
Completed Project File Name: *[your initials] Excel 1-8.xlsx*

Create a new workbook and save it as *[your initials] Excel 1-8*. Name the gourmet chocolate store and list five types of chocolate as row headings. For column headings, list four popular holidays for chocolate sales. Modify your workbook according to the following guidelines:

- Type sales data for each holiday.
- Include a date in the worksheet title area.
- Incorporate a theme, *Cell Styles,* and formatting.
- Use *AutoSum* to calculate totals.
- Insert header and footer text.
- Include document properties and spell check the workbook.

Challenge Project 1-9

For this project, you create a spreadsheet for a photography club. The photography club rents retail space for selling used photography equipment. The equipment available in the store includes camera bodies, lenses, tripods, and books. Each month a master list is created which includes the type of equipment for sale and current prices.
[Student Learning Outcomes 1.1, 1.2, 1.3, 1.4, 1.5, 1.6, 1.7, 1.8]

File Needed: None
Completed Project File Name: *[your initials] Excel 1-9.xlsx*

Create a new workbook and save it as *[your initials] Excel 1-9*. Modify your workbook according to the following guidelines:

- Name the photography club for the main title and create a subtitle to reflect the purpose of the spreadsheet.
- Create rows and columns of data for listing the photography equipment, price, and quantity available.
- Include other information that would be helpful to potential customers.
- Use *AutoSum* to calculate the value of the inventory.
- Incorporate a theme, *Cell Styles,* and other formatting to create a professional-looking spreadsheet.
- Include document properties and spell check the workbook.

Challenge Project 1-10

For this project, you create a spreadsheet that lists your monthly financial responsibilities. This spreadsheet is a valuable tool for money management.
[Student Learning Outcomes 1.1, 1.2, 1.3, 1.4, 1.5, 1.6, 1.7, 1.8]

File Needed: None
Completed Project File Name: *[your initials] Excel 1-10.xlsx*

Enter data for a monthly budget. Create a new workbook and save it as *[your initials] Excel 1-10*. Modify your workbook according to the following guidelines:

- Use blank rows to divide your worksheet into groups. For example, include a section for income and another section for expenses. You can create additional groups for expenses that occur monthly, quarterly, or annually.
- Insert worksheets for each month and name each sheet.
- Incorporate themes, *Cell Styles*, and formatting. (Remember that you can select multiple sheet tabs and apply Page Setup formatting to each sheet in a single step.)
- Use *AutoSum* to calculate total income and expenses.
- Include document properties and spell check the workbook.

Working with Formulas and Functions

CHAPTER OVERVIEW

Excel is a powerful tool for creating mathematical computations. You can use Excel to create a simple addition formula or a formula that includes complex calculations. When creating formulas, you can take advantage of Excel's error correcting techniques to ensure accuracy in your worksheets. This chapter introduces the basics of using formulas and functions in an Excel worksheet.

STUDENT LEARNING OUTCOMES (SLOs)

After completing this chapter, you will be able to:

SLO 2.1 Create and edit basic formulas (p. E2-79).

SLO 2.2 Use range names and relative, absolute, and mixed cell references in a formula (p. E2-83).

SLO 2.3 Apply mathematical order of operations when using parentheses, exponents, multiplication, division, addition, and subtraction (p. E2-88).

SLO 2.4 Use *AutoSum* and other common functions such as *AVERAGE, COUNT, MAX, MIN, TODAY*, and *NOW* (p. E2-93).

SLO 2.5 Apply financial, logical, and lookup functions such as *PMT, IF, VLOOKUP*, and *HLOOKUP* (p. E2-99).

SLO 2.6 Apply math and trigonometry functions such as *SUMIF, SUMPRODUCT*, and *ROUND* (p. E2-106).

CASE STUDY

In the Pause & Practice projects in this chapter, you create business workbooks related to a northern Minnesota resort business, Paradise Lakes Resort (PLR), which was introduced in Chapter 1. PLR is asking all managers to incorporate formulas into their monthly sales workbooks to determine future costs and net income projections. PLR is also considering several investment options and is using various formulas to examine and evaluate these opportunities.

Pause & Practice 2-1: Modify a workbook to include basic formulas.

Pause & Practice 2-2: Insert common functions into a workbook.

Pause & Practice 2-3: Apply financial, logical, lookup, math and trigonometry functions in a workbook.

EXCEL

Creating and Editing Basic Formulas

One reason why Excel is one of the most popular business software applications is because it gives users the ability to incorporate formulas into a workbook. A *formula* evaluates values and returns a result. Basic formula creation can involve adding weekly expenses, multiplying inventory by unit price to determine inventory value, or subtracting expenses from income. The formulas in Excel workbooks automatically update when cell values change.

Formula Syntax

The term *syntax* refers to the required parts of a formula and the rules controlling the order of the parts. As discussed in Chapter 1, the intersection of a column and row is a cell. Each cell has a *cell reference* (or cell address), which is the specific location of a cell within a worksheet. When you create formulas, you use cell references to identify cells rather than an actual number. For example, the formula to add the values in cells B5 and B6 is **=B5+B6**.

The equals sign [=] is always the first character you type when creating a formula. The equals sign alerts Excel that you are entering a formula and not text. The second component of the formula is the first cell reference (B5 in the example **=B5+B6**). The third component is the mathematical operator, which signifies the type of calculation. (In the example **=B5+B6**, the plus sign is the operator.) The final part of the sample formula is the last cell reference (B6 in the example **=B5+B6**).

Enter a Formula Using the Keyboard

There are two ways to enter cell references into a formula. You can type the formula manually using the keyboard or use the select method. Both methods require identifying the location of the formula, typing the equals sign, and then entering (by typing or selecting) the first cell reference, an arithmetic operator (+, -, *, or /), and the next cell reference. Formulas are not case sensitive, and Excel automatically changes cell references to uppercase. In both methods, you press **Enter** to complete the entry or click the **Enter** button (the check mark) on the *Formula bar*. To cancel a formula before it is complete, press **Esc**. Do not navigate using an arrow key while you are entering a formula. The cell you navigate to may accidentally be included in the formula.

HOW TO: Enter a Formula in a Cell Using the Keyboard

1. Click the cell where you want to create the formula (Figure 2-1).
2. Type = (equals sign) to begin the formula.
3. Type the first cell reference.
4. Enter the mathematical operator (+, -, *, or /).
5. Type the second cell reference.
   - Once a cell reference is entered using the keyboard, Excel color codes each cell reference.
6. Press **Enter**.
   - The result of the formula appears in the cell where the formula is located (Figure 2-2).
   - The *Formula bar* displays the formula.
   - You can use the **Enter** button (the check mark) on the *Formula bar* instead of pressing **Enter** on the keyboard (Figure 2-3). This button is only active when a cell is in *edit mode* (the insertion point is present within a cell).

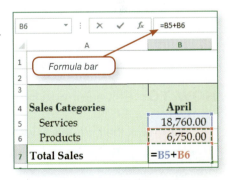

2-1 Formula syntax

2-2 Formula result

2-3 *Enter* button

Enter a Formula Using the Select Method

A popular and accurate technique of creating formulas is the *select method*. When creating a formula, you can select a cell with your pointer instead of manually typing the cell reference, which prevents typographical errors. When you click a cell or select a cell range, Excel automatically enters the cell addresses into the formula.

HOW TO: Enter a Formula in a Cell Using Selection

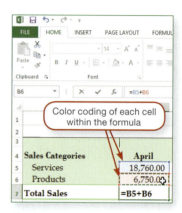

1. Click the cell where you want to create the formula (Figure 2-4).
2. Type = (equals sign).
3. Using your pointer, click the first cell you want to include in the formula.
4. Enter a mathematical operator.
5. Move the pointer to the next cell reference and select the cell.
6. Click the **Enter** button on the *Formula bar* to finalize the formula.
   - If you select a cell by mistake, press **Backspace**.
   - The result of the calculation appears in the cell where the formula is located.
   - Select the cell where the formula is located to display the formula in the *Formula bar*.

2-4 Formula syntax

Edit a Formula

There will be times when you make an error when creating a formula. You can edit a formula by double-clicking the cell where the formula is located and using edit mode to correct the formula. Another way to edit a formula is to use time-saving, color-coded editing options such as the *Range Finder* and *Formula Auditing* tools.

Range Finder

The *Range Finder* is a color-coded editing tool that applies different colors to each cell or cell range included within a formula. To activate the *Range Finder*, double-click the cell that contains the formula you want to edit or select the cell that contains the formula and click the *Formula bar*. The color-coded cells automatically appear and indicate each cell location within the formula.

HOW TO: Edit a Formula in a Cell Using the Range Finder

1. Double-click the formula you want to edit.
   - The *Range Finder* activates and the cell references appear color-coded.
   - The cell formula appears in the *Formula bar*.
2. Edit the formula.
   - Insert or delete text.
   - Drag a range finder border to move the frame to include the correct cells (Figure 2-5).
   - Drag a corner of the border to include additional cells or to reduce the number of cells.
3. Press **Enter** or click the **Enter** button on the *Formula bar* once your edit is complete.

2-5 Formula in edit mode using *Range Finder*

Formula Auditing

Formula Auditing refers to a group of editing options on the *Formulas* tab that you can use to review and correct errors in formulas. ***Trace Precedents*** and ***Trace Dependents*** are auditing tools that include a color-coded editing system. When you use these tools, different colors are applied to each cell or cell range and display arrows point to the cells and cell ranges included within a formula. *Trace Precedents* displays all cells referenced in a formula. *Trace Dependents* indicates which formulas reference a particular cell.

Evaluate Formula

Evaluate Formula is an additional auditing tool that is typically used for more complex formulas. Complex formulas may contain a syntax error. A syntax error occurs when a formula contains a typographical error, unnecessary or missing punctuation, incorrect order of arguments, or an incorrect cell reference. If your formula includes a syntax error, Excel displays an error message or returns an error code as the formula result. The *Evaluate Formula* tool reviews each part of a formula in sequence to determine where the error is.

To apply *Formula Auditing* options, display the *Formulas* tab, and choose an option in the *Formula Auditing* group (Figure 2-6). The following table describes the auditing options.

2-6 *Formula Auditing* options

Formula Auditing Tools

Button	Description
Trace Precedents	Displays arrows that point to the cells referenced in the selected formula
Trace Dependents	Displays arrows that point to the cells that contain a formula
Remove Arrows	Removes arrows for *Trace Precedents* or *Trace Dependents*
Show Formulas	Displays formulas instead of results
Error Checking	Checks for common errors
Evaluate Formula	Steps through each part of a formula
Watch Window	Adds cells to the *Watch Window*. Values are watched as the worksheet is updated.

HOW TO: Use Auditing Tools

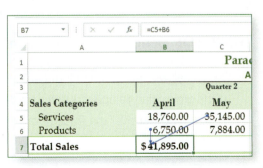

2-7 *Trace Precedents* arrows

1. Select the cell you want to edit (Figure 2-7).
2. Click the **Show Formulas** button [*Formulas* tab, *Formula Auditing* group].
   - The formula displays instead of the formula result. You may need to *AutoFit* the width of your columns to view the formula.
   - Press **Ctrl+`** to switch between formula and results views.
3. Select a cell containing a formula.

4. Click the **Trace Precedents** button [*Formulas* tab, *Formula Auditing* group].

- Arrows display indicating which cells in your workbook are included in the current cell's formula (see Figure 2-7).
- Blue arrows indicate cells with no errors.
- Red arrows indicate cells that cause errors.
- Black arrows point from the selected cell to a worksheet icon.

5. Click **Remove Arrows** [*Formulas* tab, *Formula Auditing* group] to remove the *Trace Precedents* arrows.

6. Click a cell that is included in a formula (not the formula cell).

7. Click **Trace Dependents**.

- An arrow displays leading from the selected cell to the formula cell.

8. Click **Remove Arrows** to remove the *Trace Dependents* arrows.

- Click the **Remove Arrows** drop-down list to specify the type of arrow to remove.

9. Click **Show Formulas** to display formula results.

> **MORE INFO**
>
> The *Error Checking* and *Evaluate Formulas* tools are helpful if a syntax error occurs. If the error occurs because you selected the incorrect cell, it may be more useful to use *Trace Precedents*.

> **MORE INFO**
>
> To print the formula view of a spreadsheet, click the **Show Formulas** button [*Formulas* tab, *Formula Auditing* group] prior to printing the worksheet.

Message Window

There are times when a typographical error may be the cause of your syntax error. After you complete a formula containing an error, a Microsoft Excel message window may display (Figure 2-8). The window indicates an error was found, and a corrected formula appears in the box. Click **Yes** to accept the correction or **No** to edit the formula manually.

2-8 **Microsoft Excel message window**

Trace Error

A green triangle in the top left corner of a cell indicates that the formula in the cell may contain an error. When you select a cell with the green triangle, the *Trace Error* button displays. You can point to the button to see a ScreenTip identifying the error. Click the drop-down arrow to view a list of options to ignore or repair the error.

HOW TO: Correct a Formula in a Cell Using the Trace Error Button

1. Click a cell with an incorrect formula (Figure 2-9).

- The green triangle appears in the top left corner of the cell.

2. Move the pointer over the *Trace Error* button that appears to the left of the selected cell.

- The *Trace Error* button looks like a yellow diamond with an exclamation mark (!).

2-9 *Trace Error* options

3. Click the **Trace Error** drop-down arrow.

4. Select an option from the *Trace Error* button list.

   - Select the **Ignore Error** option if the formula is correct.

Circular Reference

A *circular reference* occurs when a formula includes the cell address of the formula. For example, if the cell containing the formula is B7, and the syntax of the formula is =**B5+B7**, then you would have a circular reference because B7 is included in the calculation. When a circular reference occurs, a Microsoft Excel message appears (Figure 2-10). You can either click **OK** to accept the result or click **Help**.

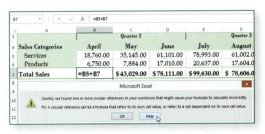

2-10 Circular reference and Microsoft Excel message window

Working with Cell References

There are three types of cell references you can use in a formula. The type of cell references included in a formula determines the result of a formula when it is copied. The three types of cell references are *relative*, *absolute*, and *mixed*.

- *Relative cell references* identify the location of a cell. When you are creating formulas, the default cell reference is *relative*. Column and row references automatically change when you copy a formula that contains a relative cell address. The cell address **B2** is an example of a relative cell reference.

- *Absolute cell reference* is the fixed location of a cell referenced in a formula or dialog box. Absolute cell addresses include a **$** (dollar sign) around both the column and row references. Cells that contain absolute references do not change when copied. The cell address **$B$2** is an absolute cell reference. You can quickly insert dollar signs around a cell reference in the *Formula bar* by pressing **F4**.

- *Mixed cell references* contain one relative reference (either the row number or column letter) and one absolute reference (the remaining row number or column letter). The cell address **$B2** refers to an absolute column address ($B) and a relative row address (2).

- *3D cell references* indicate cells in multiple workbooks or worksheets. To create a 3D cell reference, you include the name of the workbook (if referring to a different workbook), the name of the worksheet, and the cell reference. An example of a 3D cell reference is =**'[2016 Sales.xlsx]Sheet2'!B2**. Square brackets surround the workbook name ([2016 Sales]), and an exclamation point follows the sheet name (Sheet2!). If the name of the worksheet or workbook contains non-alphabetic characters, you need to enclose the name in single quotes. Excel automatically places absolute value symbols ($) around each cell reference if you select the cell from a different workbook or worksheet rather than type the reference.

The following table lists examples of cell reference types:

Cell Reference Examples

Cell Reference	Reference Type	Description
B2	Relative	The cell address changes when copied.
$B$2	Absolute	The cell address does not change when copied.

continued

Cell Reference Examples

Cell Reference	Reference Type	Description
$B2	*Mixed*	The column portion of the cell address is absolute; the row component changes when copied.
B$2	*Mixed*	The row portion of the cell address is absolute; the column component changes when copied.
Sheet2!B2	*3D Relative*	The cell address is located on a different worksheet and changes when copied.

Copy a Formula with a Relative Cell Reference

Relative cell references within a formula adjust automatically when you copy them. For example, if you create a formula that totals the sales for the month of January, you can copy that formula to calculate the totals for February and March. The cell references change automatically.

You can use the following methods to copy formulas:

- *Fill Handle*
- *Copy* and *Paste* buttons in the *Clipboard* group on the *Home* tab
- Shortcut commands **Ctrl+C** to copy and **Ctrl+V** to paste
- *Context-sensitive menu;* right-click to display the menu
- *Control* key combined with drag and drop

HOW TO: Copy a Formula with Relative Cell References

1. Select the cell that contains the formula you want to copy (Figure 2-11).
2. Click and drag the *Fill Handle* to the destination cell or range of cells.
3. Release the *Fill Handle.*
   - The formula in the destination cell adjusts to the corresponding relative cell references.
   - Click the **Show Formulas** and **Trace Precedents** buttons [*Formulas* tab, *Formula Auditing* group] to see how the formula's cell reference changes from the source cell to the destination cell during the copy process (Figure 2-12).

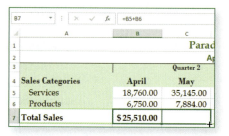

2-11 Using the *Fill Handle* to copy

2-12 *Trace Precedence* arrows

After you drag the *Fill Handle* over a range, the ***Auto Fill Options*** button displays. The drop-down list includes three options to control the fill data. Choose to *Copy Cells, Fill Formatting Only,* or *Fill Without Formatting.*

Copy a Formula with an Absolute Cell Reference

An absolute reference in a cell refers to a specific location, and it does not change when you copy or fill the formula. To change a relative cell reference to an absolute cell reference, type a **$** in front of the column letter and the row number of the cell address or select the cell address and press **F4** to insert the dollar signs quickly.

HOW TO: Copy a Formula with an Absolute Cell Reference

1. Select the cell that contains the formula you want to copy.
2. Click the *Formula bar* and click the cell reference you want to be absolute.
3. Press **F4** to change the cell address to an absolute cell reference.
4. Press **Enter** and re-select the cell to copy the formula.
5. Click and drag the *Fill Handle* to the destination cell.
6. Release the *Fill Handle.*

2-13 *Trace Precedence* arrows illustrate cell references

- The absolute cell reference remains constant when the formula is copied to the destination cell.
- Figure 2-13 displays *Trace Precedents* for the formulas with the correct formula syntax.

> ### MORE INFO
>
> **F4** is a four-way toggle key in the *Formula bar.* Press **F4** to toggle from absolute reference to mixed references to relative reference.

Range Names

You can use ***range names*** to navigate a worksheet or to identify a cell or group of cells (recall from Chapter 1 that a group of cells is called a ***range***). Range names describe the cell or purpose of a group of cells and make it easier to interpret a formula. For example, instead of referring to cell K4 in the formula **=K4*B7**, you can name cell K4 "Mortgage", and use the range name in the formula. The example formula would change to **=Mortgage*B7**.

When you name a cell or range, the name becomes an absolute reference. The first character of a name must be a letter, an underscore (_), or a backslash (\). Range names cannot contain spaces, special characters (#, $, &), or cell references. To signify a space between words, use the underscore (_) (e.g., "Mortgage_Payment" or "MortgagePayment"). You can create a range name using the *Name* box on the *Formula bar,* the *Create from Selection* button [*Formulas* tab, *Defined Names* group], or the *New Name* dialog box (Figure 2-14).

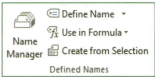

2-14 *Defined Names* group on the *Formulas* tab

To create range names using the *Name* box, select the cell or group of cells, and type the name of the range in the *Name* box.

HOW TO: Name a Cell and Use the Range Name in a Formula

1. Select the cell(s) you want to name.
2. Click the **Name** box beside the *Formula bar.*
3. Type a range name (e.g., "Tax_Rate") and press **Enter** (Figure 2-15).
4. Select the cell where you want the formula to appear and press = to begin the formula.
5. Type the beginning letters of the range name.
   - A list of names appears matching the letters typed.

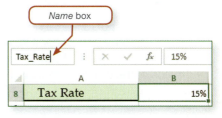

2-15 *Tax_Rate* range name

6. Double-click the range name from the list.
   - The drop-down list is known as *Formula AutoComplete*.
7. Type a mathematical operator.
8. Select the next cell reference or cell range (Figure 2-16).
9. Press **Enter**.

2-16 Formula with range name

> ## MORE INFO
>
> Manage range names by clicking the **Name Manager** button [*Formulas* tab, *Defined Names* group]. The *Name Manager* dialog box provides options for creating, editing, and deleting range names.

> ## ANOTHER WAY
>
> To insert a range name, press **F3** to display the *Paste Name* dialog box. Select a name and click **OK**.

A second method to name a range is to convert existing row and column labels to names. If a range in your worksheets contains column and or row headings, you can use these headings to name multiple cells simultaneously.

HOW TO: Name Multiple Cells Simultaneously Using the Ribbon

1. Select the range and include the row or column labels (Figure 2-17).
   - The cells and their labels must be adjacent to each other.
   - A range can consist of one cell, a range of cells, a formula, or a constant.
2. Click the **Create from Selection** button [*Formulas* tab, *Defined Names* group] to open the *Create Names from Selection* dialog box (see Figure 2-17).
3. Select the check box that best describes the label location in relation to the selected cells.
4. Click **OK**.
   - To view a list of range names, click the **Name** box arrow on the *Formula bar* (Figure 2-18).
   - The formula syntax shows the range name in place of the cell address (Figure 2-19).

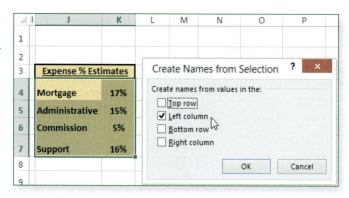

2-17 *Create Names from Selection* dialog box

2-18 *Name* box

2-19 Formula with range name

If you have already created formulas and are naming cells after copying formulas, select **Apply names** from the *Define Name* drop-down arrow [*Formulas* tab, *Defined Names* group] to open the *Apply Names* dialog box (Figure 2-20). Click **OK** to apply all newly created range names to existing formulas.

A third method to define range names is to use the *New Name* dialog box. The New Name dialog box includes an option to specify a range name for the entire workbook or an individual worksheet. After range names have been added to a worksheet, use the *Paste Name* dialog box to create a two-column list in a blank area of a worksheet to display defined names and their locations.

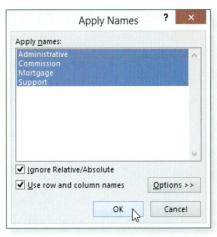

2-20 *Apply Names* dialog box

HOW TO: Use the New Name Dialog Box and the Paste Names Dialog Box

1. Select the cell range.
2. Click the **Define Name** button [*Formulas* tab, *Defined Names* group] to open the *New Name* dialog box (Figure 2-21).
3. Type the range name in the **Name** box.
4. Click the **Scope** drop-down arrow to select *Workbook* or *Worksheet.*
5. Click **OK**.
6. Click a cell in a blank area of the worksheet or a cell on a new sheet.
7. Click the **Use in Formula** button [*Formulas* tab, *Defined Names* group].
8. Select **Paste Names** to open the *Paste Name* dialog box.
9. Click **Paste List** to display the range names and their locations in the worksheet.

2-21 *New Name* dialog box

Copy a Formula with a Mixed Cell Reference

Mixed cell references are a combination of relative and absolute cell references within a single cell address. For example, you can copy a formula in a cell to another location and keep the column reference of the cell addresses constant but allow the row reference to be relative. The same rules that apply to mixed cell references apply to absolute cell references. Place a dollar sign before the part of the cell address that you want to remain absolute prior to copying.

HOW TO: Copy a Formula with a Mixed Cell Reference

1. Select the cell that contains the formula you want to copy.
2. Click the *Formula bar* and type a dollar sign next to the column letter or row number that you want to remain absolute (Figure 2-22).
3. Press **Enter**.
4. Select the cell you want to copy.
5. Click and drag the *Fill Handle* to the destination cell.
6. Release the *Fill Handle.*

2-22 **Formula with mixed cell reference**

Create a Formula with a 3D Reference

Sometimes data for your formula may be located in different worksheets. For example, sales for 2015 may be saved in a different worksheet than sales for 2016. To reference cells in both sheets within a formula, you can use *3D* references. The process of using cells in other workbooks is known as ***linking workbooks***.

A formula containing a *3D* cell reference follows the same rules and requirements of non-*3D* cell references with one exception. Because a *3D* cell reference is not physically located in the same sheet as the cell containing the formula, one extra step is required when using *3D* cell references. You must click the sheet tab that contains the cell you want to use in your formula before you select the cell. To select a cell in another sheet within a different workbook, select the open workbook from the *Excel* button on the *Taskbar* and then select the worksheet tab and cell within the tab.

Sample 3D References

Active Cell	Formula	Explanation
Sheet 1 – Cell B4	=Sheet2!B2+Sheet2!B3	Adds cells B2 and B3 on sheet 2.
Sheet 1 – Cell B4	=A4+February!D5+ '[Sales.xslx]10-27-2015'!$B$10+ '[Sales.xslx]10-27-2015'!$C$12	Adds cell A4 in current sheet, D5 on the February sheet in the current workbook, and cells B10 and C12 from the 10-27-2015 worksheet in the Sales workbook.

HOW TO: Create a Formula with a 3D Relative Cell Reference

1. Click the cell where you want to create the formula.
2. Type =.
3. Select the sheet tab of the first cell in the formula.
   - If copying a cell reference from another workbook, open that workbook before creating the formula.
4. Select the cell address of the first cell of the formula.
5. Type the mathematical operator.
6. Select the sheet tab of the next cell in the formula.
7. Select the cell address of the next cell in the calculation (Figure 2-23).
8. Press **Enter** or click the **Enter** button (check mark) on the *Formula bar*.
   - You can copy a *3D* formula using the *Fill Handle*.

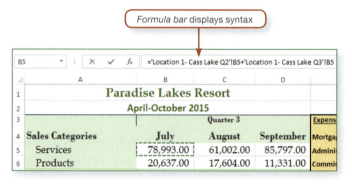

2-23 3D cell reference

Applying Mathematical Order of Operations

When you create formulas, arithmetic operators specify the type of calculation such as multiplication or addition. When more than one operator appears in a formula, it is important to understand the order in which Excel performs each operation (***mathematical order of operations***) so you create formulas that correctly calculate results.

The basic types of arithmetic operators in formulas are: addition, subtraction, multiplication, division, and exponentiation. Excel executes these operations in a specified order, but you can change the order by using parentheses.

You can use the following acronym to help remember the order: **P**lease **E**xcuse **M**y **D**ear **A**unt **S**ally. The first letter of each word in the acronym signifies an operator. The order of the words indicates which operator has precedence over another. In the event that two operators have the same level of precedence, Excel calculates the operations of the formula from left to right.

The following table describes the specific rules Excel follows in formulas with multiple operators.

Mathematical Order of Precedence in Formulas

Character	Operator Name	Order of Precedence	Acronym
()	*Parentheses*	First	Please
^	*Exponent*	Second	Excuse
*	*Multiplication*	Third	My
/	*Division*	Third	Dear
+	*Addition*	Fourth	Aunt
-	*Subtraction*	Fourth	Sally

Addition and Subtraction

Since addition and subtraction are on the same precedence level, Excel calculates from left to right if they are both included in a formula.

For example, consider the mathematical expression: **2+5-3**.
The addition operation (2+5) is completed first.
The result (7) is used in the subtraction operation (7-3).
The result is 4.

HOW TO: Use Addition and Subtraction in a Formula

1. Click the cell where you want to create the formula (Figure 2-24).
2. Type =.
3. Enter the cell address or select the first cell reference of the formula.
4. Type +.
5. Enter or select the next cell address of the calculation.
6. Type –.
7. Enter or select the last cell address of the formula.
8. Press **Enter**.

   • The result of the calculation appears in the cell containing the formula.
   • Use the *Formula bar* to view the syntax of the formula.

2-24 Formula with multiple operators

Multiplication and Division

Like subtraction and addition, multiplication and division are on the same precedence level. Excel calculates from left to right if multiplication and division appear in the same formula. If the syntax of the formula also includes addition or subtraction, the multiplying or dividing operators are computed before the addition or subtraction operators.

For example, consider the mathematical expression: **2+5*3**.
The multiplication operation (5*3) occurs first.
The result (15) is used in the addition operation (15+2).
The result is 17.

Conversely, consider the mathematical expression: **2*5+3**.
The multiplication operation (2*5) occurs first.
The result (10) is used in the addition operation (10+3).
The result is 13.

HOW TO: Use Multiplication and Addition in a Formula

1. Click the cell where you want to create the formula (Figure 2-25).

2. Type =.

3. Enter or select the first cell address of the formula.

4. Type +.

5. Enter or select the next cell address.

6. Type *.

7. Enter or select the last cell address of the formula.

8. Press **Enter**.

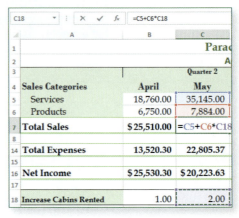

2-25 Addition and multiplication formula

Parentheses and Exponents

Excel calculates operations within parentheses before any other operation is performed. Within parentheses, Excel uses the order of operations to perform calculations.

For example, in the mathematical expression **4+(2+5)*3**.
The operation (2+5) in parentheses occurs first.
The result (7) is used in the multiplication operation (7*3).
The result (21) is used in the addition operation (21+4).
The result is 25.

HOW TO: Use Parentheses, Multiplication, Addition, and Subtraction in a Formula

1. Click the cell where you want to create the formula (Figure 2-26).

2. Type =.

3. Type ((open parenthesis).

4. Enter or select the first cell address of the formula.

5. Type +.

6. Select the next cell address and then type) (close parenthesis).

7. Type *.

8. Select the next cell address.

9. Type –.

10. Select the last cell address.

11. Press **Enter**.

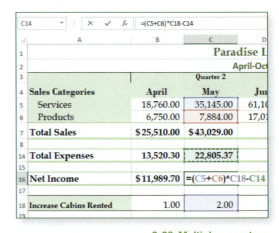

2-26 Multiple operators

Exponents raise a number to a power. Use the caret symbol (^) when writing a formula that includes an exponent. The formula **3^3** raises 3 to the power of 3 and produces the result of 27.

You can use the formulas in Excel to convey calculations in a time-saving and meaningful fashion. In this project, you add formulas to a business spreadsheet that displays two quarters of sales and expenses for Paradise Lakes Resort.

File Needed: **PLRSalesandExpenses-02.xlsx**
Completed Project File Name: **[your initials] PP E2-1.xlsx**

1. Open the **PLRSalesandExpenses-02.xlsx** workbook and save the workbook as **[your initials] PP E2-1**. (If you see a yellow bar at the top of the workbook entitled "Protected View," click **Enable Editing**.)

2. Enter an addition formula.
   a. Click cell **B7**.
   b. Type =.
   c. Select **B5**, the cell address of the first cell of the formula.
   d. Type +.
   e. Select **B6**, the next cell address of the formula.
   f. Press **Enter** or click the **Enter** button on the *Formula bar*. The syntax of the formula should read =B5+B6.

3. Copy the addition formula.
   a. Select cell **B7**.
   b. Place your pointer in the lower right corner of **B7**, click and drag the *Fill Handle* through the cell range **C7:G7**, and release the *Fill Handle* (Figure 2-27).

2-27 Using the *Fill Handle* to copy a formula

4. Create and copy the mortgage expense formula using absolute cell references.
   a. Select cell **B10**.
   b. Type the following formula to determine mortgage expenses: =K4*B7.
   c. Click to the left of the **K** column reference letter in the *Formula bar* and type $.
   d. Click to the left of the **4** row reference number and type $. You can also use **F4** to add the dollar signs in the cell reference (Figure 2-28). The formula should read: =$K$4*B7.

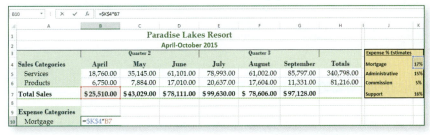

2-28 Mortgage expense formula

e. Press **Enter**.

f. Click and drag the *Fill Handle* on cell **B10** through the cell range **C10:G10**.

5. Create and copy expense formulas using multiplication and absolute cell references.

a. Enter the formulas listed in the table at right.

b. Select cells **B11:B14**.

c. Use the *Fill Handle* of cell **B14** to copy the formulas to **C11:G14**.

B11	=$K$5*B7
B12	=$K$6*B7
B13	=$K$7*B7
B14	=B10+B11+B12+B13

6. Create and copy a net income formula with a *3D* reference, multiple operators, and apply the mathematical order of precedence.

a. Click cell **B16** and type =(B5+.

b. Select cell **B6** and type).

c. Type -, select cell **B14**, and type -.

d. Click the **Cass Lake Tax** sheet tab.

e. Select **B5** on the *Cass Lake Tax* tab.

f. Press **Enter**.

g. Review the formula syntax. It should be =(B5+B6)-B14-'Cass Lake Tax'!B5.

h. Select cell **B16** and place your pointer over the *Fill Handle* of cell **B16**.

i. Use the *Fill Handle* to copy the formula to **C16:G16**.

j. Release the pointer.

7. Use auditing tools to review the formula in cell B16.

a. Select cell **B16**.

b. Click **Show Formulas** and **Trace Precedents** [*Formulas* tab, *Formula Auditing* group]. The black arrow indicates a cell reference on another worksheet.

c. Click **Remove Arrows** [*Formulas* tab, *Formula Auditing* group].

d. Click **Show Formulas** [*Formulas* tab, *Formula Auditing* group] to return to *Normal* view.

8. Copy and paste an existing formula without the formatting.

a. Select cell **H6** and use the *Fill Handle* to copy the formula to **H7:H16**.

b. Click the **Auto Fill Options** arrow button and select **Fill Without Formatting** to prevent overwriting existing cell formats.

c. Delete unnecessary formulas in cells **H8, H9**, and **H15**.

9. Save and close the workbook (Figure 2-29).

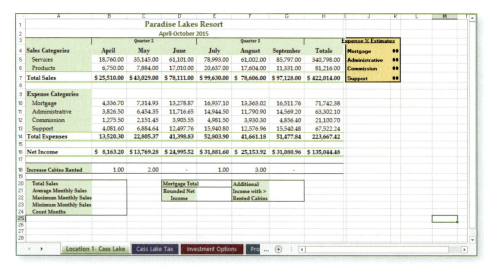

2-29 PP E2-1 completed

SLO 2.4

Working with Common Functions

Functions are pre-defined formulas and each function has a specific syntax pattern. Functions start with an equals sign (=) followed by the function name, an opening parenthesis, the arguments for the function separated by commas, and a closing parenthesis. ***Arguments*** are the pieces of information within parentheses that determine what value a function returns. For example, in the function =SUM(B2:B6), SUM is the function name and the cell range B2:B6 is the argument.

When you type a formula, ***Formula AutoComplete*** and ***Function Screen Tips*** appear to help you create and edit formulas. After you type an = and beginning letters of the function, *Formula AutoComplete* displays a list of functions and range names. Use the down arrow to move through the list or continue typing the function name. Press *Tab* or double-click the function name to insert it. A ScreenTip appears after you type the function name and an opening parenthesis. The ScreenTip includes the required syntax and arguments for the function. Click the ScreenTip function name to display the *Help* topic for the function.

In addition to the *AutoSum* function, which was introduced in Chapter 1 (see *SLO 1.3: Using the Sum Function*), there are other common functions that you can use to calculate values in a spreadsheet. Many times you may need to find an average or a minimum or maximum value in a range of numbers or you may want to count the numbers in a given range within a group of cells.

> **MORE INFO**
>
> Functions and formulas are similar but not exactly the same. All functions are also considered formulas, =SUM(B2:B6), but not all formulas are functions since they do not contain a function name, =B2+B3-B6.

AUTOSUM Function

As discussed in Chapter 1, the *AutoSum* button automates the insertion of the *SUM* function. Recall that when you use *AutoSum,* instead of typing a formula to add cell contents that separates each cell reference with a plus sign, you use the *SUM* function to add the cells. You can use *AutoSum* to insert the *SUM* function by clicking the *AutoSum* button in the *Function Library* group on the *Formulas* tab. In this chapter, we discuss the *AutoSum* function in more detail and explain how you can use the *AutoSum* drop-down list to insert other functions including *Average, Count Numbers, Max,* and *Min.*

HOW TO: Enter the SUM Function with AutoSum

1. Click the cell where you want to enter the function.
2. Click the **AutoSum** arrow [*Formulas* tab, *Function Library* group] (Figure 2-30).
   - When you click the upper half of **AutoSum**, the *SUM* function is inserted. Click the bottom half of **AutoSum** (the arrow) to display a list of functions.
3. Select **Sum** from the list.
   - The equals sign, function name, parentheses, and assumed cell range are entered automatically.
4. Select the cell range you wish to total if the range that Excel entered automatically is not correct.
   - The cell range appears between the parentheses in the function syntax (Figure 2-31).
5. Press **Enter**.

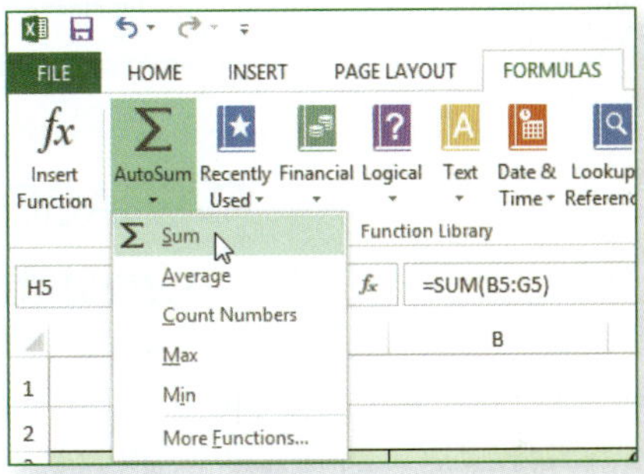

2-30 *AutoSum* function list

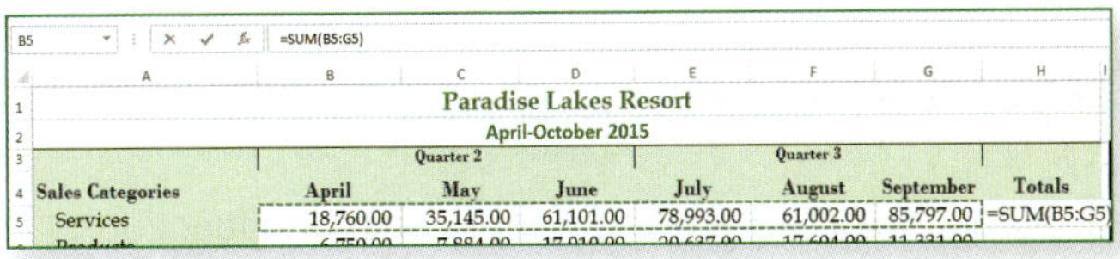

2-31 Selection of correct range

If you are entering multiple *AutoSum* functions in a worksheet, you can do this in one step rather than individually entering each *AutoSum* function.

HOW TO: Enter Multiple SUM Functions Simultaneously with AutoSum

1. Select the cells where you want to enter the functions (Figure 2-32).

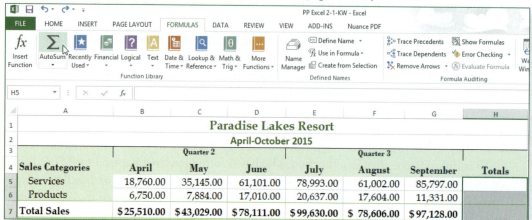

2-32 Selected cell range for simultaneous SUM function

2. Click the **AutoSum** arrow [*Formulas* tab, *Function Library group*].
3. Select **Sum** from the list.
   - It is not necessary to press **Enter**.
   - The results appear in the cells containing the formulas.

> **ANOTHER WAY**
>
> *AutoSum* is also located on the *Home* tab in the *Editing* group.
> Press **Alt+=** for the *SUM* function.

> **MORE INFO**
>
> The *AutoSum* button is also called the **Sigma** button.

AVERAGE Function

The **AVERAGE** function calculates an average by adding cell values together and dividing the total of the values by the number of values. The *AVERAGE* function performs the calculation quickly and eliminates the need to key cell addresses and mathematical operators manually. You can apply the *AVERAGE* function by using the *AutoSum* button in the *Function Library* group on the *Formulas* tab.

HOW TO: Enter the AVERAGE Function Using the AutoSum Button

1. Click the cell where you want to enter the function.
2. Click the **AutoSum** arrow [*Formulas* tab, *Function Library group*].

3. Select **Average**.

- The equals sign, function name, parentheses, and assumed cell range appear in the cell (Figure 2-33).

E5	▼ : ✕ ✓ *fx*	=AVERAGE(E5:G6)		*AVERAGE function range*		
	A	B	C	D	E	F	G

	A	B	C	D	E	F	G
3			Quarter 2			Quarter 3	
4	**Sales Categories**	**April**	**May**	**June**	**July**	**August**	**September**
5	Services	18,760.00	35,145.00	61,101.00	78,993.00	61,002.00	85,797.00
6	Products	6,750.00	7,884.00	17,010.00	20,637.00	17,604.00	11,331.00
7	**Total Sales**	$ 25,510.00	$43,029.00	$78,111.00	$99,630.00	$ 78,606.00	$97,128.00
19							
20	**Quarter 3 Total Sales**	$ 275,364.00		**Mortgage Total**		**Additional**	
21	**Average Sales**	=AVERAGE(E5:G6)		**Rounded Net**		**Income with >**	

AVERAGE function

2-33 AVERAGE function

4. Select a cell range if the range Excel automatically highlights is not correct.

- The cell range appears between the parentheses in the function syntax.

5. Press **Enter** or click the **Enter** button on the *Formula bar*.

COUNT Functions

Although you can manually count each number in a group of cells or each cell that contains descriptive labels, *COUNT* functions provide a more error-free method to accomplish this task. To add a *COUNT* function to the worksheet, use the *AutoSum* arrow in the *Function Library* group on the *Formulas* tab (Figure 2-34).

There are several *COUNT* functions. For example, you could use a *COUNTIF* function to insert a function that calculates all cells in a range that contain the product description label "Services." The following table lists several *COUNT* functions.

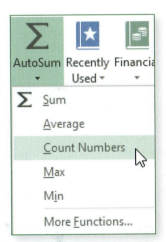

2-34 AutoSum function list

Common Count Functions

Count Functions	Description	Example Syntax
COUNT	Counts the number of cells in a range that contain numbers	=COUNT(A1:A15)
COUNTA	Counts the number of cells in a range that contain any data type, text, or numbers	=COUNTA(A1:A15)
COUNTBLANK	Counts the number of blank cells in a range	=COUNTBLANK(A1:A15)
COUNTIF	Counts the number of cells in a range based on specified criteria	=COUNTIF(A1:A15, "Services")
DCOUNT	Counts the amount of numbers in a database range that meet specified criteria	=DCOUNT(database, field, criteria)
DCOUNTA	Counts the amount of text entries in a database range that meet specified criteria	=DCOUNTA(database, field, criteria)

HOW TO: Enter the COUNT Function Using the AutoSum Button

1. Click the cell where you want to enter the function (Figure 2-35).

2. Click the **AutoSum** arrow [*Formulas* tab, *Function Library group*].

3. Select **Count Numbers** from the list to choose the *COUNT* function (see Figure 2-35).

   • The *COUNT* function counts the number of cells in a range that contain numbers.

4. Select a cell range if the range that Excel automatically highlights is not correct.

5. Press **Enter**.

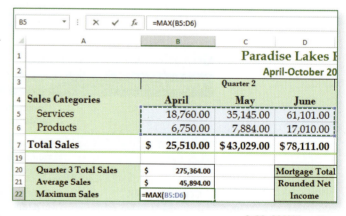

	B7	:	×	✓	fx	=COUNT(B7:D7)

	A	B	C	D
3			Quarter 2	
4	**Sales Categories**	**April**	**May**	**June**
5	Services	18,760.00	35,145.00	61,101.00
6	Products	6,750.00	7,884.00	17,010.00
7	**Total Sales**	$ 25,510.00	$43,029.00	$78,111.00
19				
20	Quarter 3 Total Sales	$ 275,364.00		Mortgage Total
21	Average Sales	$ 45,894.00		Rounded Net
22	Maximum Sales			Income
23	Minimum Monthly Sales			
24	Count Months	=COUNT(B7:D7)		

2-35 COUNT function

> ### MORE INFO
>
> You can use a "?" to take the place of one character in the *COUNT* function criteria. For example, the criteria "**Sal?**" finds results of 4-letter words beginning with *Sal* such as **Sale** or **Salt**. You can use an "*" to represent multiple characters in criteria. For example, the criteria "**Sal***" finds results such as **Salmon** or **Salt**.

MAX and MIN Functions

The *MAX* function finds the largest value in a cell range, and the *MIN* function finds the smallest value in a cell range. To apply the *MAX and MIN* functions use the *AutoSum* arrow in the *Function Library* group on the *Formulas* tab.

HOW TO: Enter the MAX or MIN Function Using the AutoSum Button

1. Click the cell where you want to enter the function.

2. Click the **AutoSum** arrow [*Formulas* tab, *Function Library group*].

3. Select the **MAX** or **MIN** function from the list (Figure 2-36).

4. Select a cell range if the range that Excel highlights is not correct.

5. Press **Enter**.

	B5	:	×	✓	fx	=MAX(B5:D6)

	A	B	C	D
1				**Paradise Lakes**
2				**April-October 20**
3			Quarter 2	
4	**Sales Categories**	**April**	**May**	**June**
5	Services	18,760.00	35,145.00	61,101.00
6	Products	6,750.00	7,884.00	17,010.00
7	**Total Sales**	$ 25,510.00	$43,029.00	$78,111.00
19				
20	Quarter 3 Total Sales	$ 275,364.00		Mortgage Total
21	Average Sales	$ 45,894.00		Rounded Net
22	Maximum Sales	=MAX(B5:D6)		Income

2-36 MAX function

AutoCalculate

AutoCalculate allows you to view totals, averages, or other statistical information without creating a formula. The *AutoCalculate* area is located on the *Status bar*. Right-click the *Status bar* to select *AutoCalculate* options. The *Average, Count,* and *Sum* options are selected by default. *AutoCalculate* results do not display in the spreadsheet.

HOW TO: Use AutoCalculate for a Range of Cells

1. Select the appropriate cell range.
2. Right-click the **Status bar** to display the *Customize Status Bar* menu (Figure 2-37).
3. Select the desired functions from the shortcut menu.
   - If a function has a checkmark to the left, it is already active.
4. View the *Status bar* to see the results of selected functions (Figure 2-38).

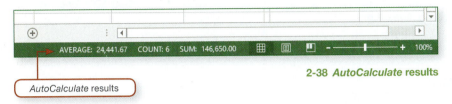

AVERAGE: 24,441.67   COUNT: 6   SUM: 146,650.00   100%

2-38 AutoCalculate results

AutoCalculate results

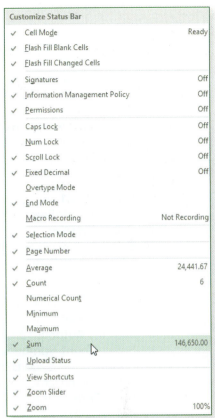

Customize Status Bar	
✓ Cell Mode	Ready
✓ Flash Fill Blank Cells	
✓ Flash Fill Changed Cells	
✓ Signatures	Off
✓ Information Management Policy	Off
✓ Permissions	Off
Caps Lock	Off
Num Lock	Off
✓ Scroll Lock	Off
✓ Fixed Decimal	Off
Overtype Mode	
✓ End Mode	
Macro Recording	Not Recording
✓ Selection Mode	
✓ Page Number	
✓ Average	24,441.67
✓ Count	6
Numerical Count	
Minimum	
Maximum	
✓ Sum	146,650.00
✓ Upload Status	
✓ View Shortcuts	
✓ Zoom Slider	
✓ Zoom	100%

2-37 Customize Status Bar menu

TODAY and NOW Functions

Excel has 24 date and time functions. *TODAY* and *NOW* are useful functions that are often included in spreadsheets to track the current date of reports. These functions reflect your computer's date and time stamp.

The *TODAY* function uses the syntax =TODAY() to automatically insert the current date. The TODAY() function does not have any arguments. The TODAY() function updates each time the spreadsheet is opened.

The *NOW* function uses the syntax =NOW() and is similar to the *TODAY* function. However, the *NOW* function includes the current time with the date. Like the *TODAY* function, the *NOW* function is updated each time the spreadsheet opens. Several formats are available for the date and time data. For example, if you prefer to view the date as 12/21/2015, you can choose the **Short Date** format from the *Number Format* drop-down list located in the *Number* group on the *Home* tab.

The *Function Library* group on the *Formulas* tab includes a **Date & Time** button. Click the **Date & Time** arrow to view the list of date and time functions.

PAUSE & PRACTICE: EXCEL 2-2

For this project, you open your previous Pause & Practice file and insert the *SUM, AVERAGE, COUNT, MIN,* and *MAX* functions to the Paradise Lakes Resort net income spreadsheet.

File Needed: *[your initials] PP E2-1.xlsx*
Completed Project File Name: *[your initials] PP E2-2.xlsx*

1. Open the workbook *[your initials] PP E2-1* and save the workbook as *[your initials] PP E2-2*.

2. Enter the *SUM* function using *AutoSum*.
   a. Click cell **B20**.
   b. Click the **AutoSum** arrow button [*Formulas* tab, *Function Library* group].
   c. Select **Sum**.
   d. Select the cell range **B7:G7**. Verify that the formula syntax is =SUM(B7:G7) (Figure 2-39).
   e. Press **Enter**.

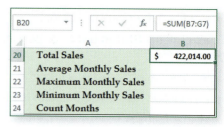

2-39 *SUM* function

3. Enter the *AVERAGE* function using *AutoSum*.
   a. Click cell **B21**.
   b. Click the **AutoSum** arrow button [*Formulas* tab, *Function Library* group].
   c. Select **Average**.
   d. Select the cell range **B7:G7**.
   e. Verify that the formula syntax is =AVERAGE(B7:G7).
   f. Press **Enter**.

4. Enter a *COUNT* function using *AutoSum*.
   a. Click cell **B24**.
   b. Click the **AutoSum** arrow button [*Formulas* tab, *Function Library* group].
   c. Select **Count Numbers**.
   d. Select the cell range **B7:G7**.
   e. Verify that the formula syntax is =COUNT(B7:G7).
   f. Press **Enter**. The formula's result should be 6.00 (Figure 2-40).

2-40 *COUNT* function

5. Enter the *MAX* function using *AutoSum*.
   a. Click cell **B22**.
   b. Click the **AutoSum** arrow [*Formulas* tab, *Function Library group*].
   c. Select **Max**.
   d. Select the cell range **B7:G7**.
   e. Verify that the formula syntax is =MAX(B7:G7).
   f. Press **Enter**.

6. Use auditing tools to review the formula in B22.
   a. Select **B22**.
   b. Click **Show Formulas** and **Trace Precedents** [*Formulas* tab, *Formula Auditing* group].
   c. Review the position of the arrows.
   d. Click **Remove Arrows** [*Formulas* tab, *Formula Auditing* group].
   e. Click **Show Formulas** [*Formulas* tab, *Formula Auditing* group] to return to *Normal* view.

7. Add absolute cell references to an existing formula.
   a. Select **B22**.
   b. Click the **Formula bar** and select the cell range **B7:G7** but not the parentheses.
   c. Press **F4** to add absolute references.
   d. Press **Enter**.
   e. Verify the formula syntax =MAX($B$7:$G$7).

8. Copy an existing formula and edit the function name.
   a. Select **B22** and use the *Fill Handle* to copy the formula to **B23**.
   b. Select cell **B23**.
   c. Click the **Formula bar** and replace the function name *MAX* with MIN.
   d. Press **Enter**.

9. Save and close the workbook (Figure 2-41).

	A	B	C	D	E	F	G	H	I	J	K
1				**Paradise Lakes Resort**							
2				April-October 2015							
3				Quarter 2			Quarter 3				Expense % Estimates
4	**Sales Categories**	**April**	**May**	**June**	**July**	**August**	**September**	**Totals**		Mortgage	17%
5	Services	18,760.00	35,145.00	61,101.00	78,993.00	61,002.00	85,797.00	340,798.00		Administrative	15%
6	Products	6,750.00	7,884.00	17,010.00	20,637.00	17,604.00	11,331.00	81,216.00		Commission	5%
7	**Total Sales**	**$ 25,510.00**	**$ 43,029.00**	**$ 78,111.00**	**$ 99,630.00**	**$ 78,606.00**	**$ 97,128.00**	**$ 422,014.00**		Support	16%
8											
9	**Expense Categories**										
10	Mortgage	4,336.70	7,314.93	13,278.87	16,937.10	13,363.02	16,511.76	71,742.38			
11	Administrative	3,826.50	6,454.35	11,716.65	14,944.50	11,790.90	14,569.20	63,302.10			
12	Commission	1,275.50	2,151.45	3,905.55	4,981.50	3,930.30	4,856.40	21,100.70			
13	Support	4,081.60	6,884.64	12,497.76	15,940.80	12,576.96	15,540.48	67,522.24			
14	**Total Expenses**	**13,520.30**	**22,805.37**	**41,398.83**	**52,803.90**	**41,661.18**	**51,477.84**	**223,667.42**			
15											
16	**Net Income**	**$ 8,163.20**	**$ 13,769.28**	**$ 24,995.52**	**$ 31,881.60**	**$ 25,153.92**	**$ 31,080.96**	**$ 135,044.48**			
17											
18	**Increase Cabins Rented**	1.00	2.00	-	1.00	3.00	-				
19											
20	Total Sales	$ 422,014.00		Mortgage Total		Additional					
21	Average Monthly Sales	$ 70,335.67		Rounded Net		Income with >					
22	Maximum Monthly Sales	$ 99,630.00		Income		Rented Cabins					
23	Minimum Monthly Sales	$ 25,510.00									
24	Count Months	6.00									
25											
26											

Location 1- Cass Lake | Cass Lake Tax | Investment Options | Product Cost

2-41 PP E2-2 completed

Working with Financial, Logical, and LOOKUP Functions

Excel's financial, logical, and lookup functions contain many advanced options. The *Insert Function* button automates hundreds of functions that are available in Excel. This section of the chapter focuses on using the *Insert Function* button to insert *PMT, IF, VLOOKUP,* and *HLOOKUP* functions.

The search feature within the **Insert Function dialog box** helps to quickly locate the function you need and tells you which arguments to include. Once the function is selected, you can complete most of the *arguments* (components or parts of the function) of the function by using point and click. This method can be very useful when you are not sure how to create the formula syntax or what the required arguments for a formula are. You can access the *Insert Function* button in the *Function Library* group on the *Formulas* tab (Figure 2-42) or click the f_x button located on the *Formula bar*.

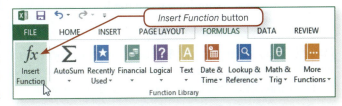

2-42 *Function Library* group

> ### ANOTHER WAY
> **Shift+F3** opens the *Insert Function* dialog box.

PMT Function

The *PMT* function calculates loan payment amounts. The *PMT* function assumes the borrower makes regular payments and the loan has a constant interest rate. The *PMT* function includes the principal (amount of money borrowed) and the interest rate when calculating the payment amount. It does not include other fees such as insurance costs or taxes.

The *PMT* function has five arguments, and the formula syntax for the function is:

$$=\textbf{PMT(rate, nper, pv, [fv], [type])}$$

- The *rate* argument is the interest rate per period for the loan; this argument is required.
- The *nper* argument is the total number of periods for repayment of the loan; this argument is required.
- The *pv* argument is the present value or the principal; this argument is required.
- The *fv* argument is the future value after you make the last payment; this argument is optional. If the fv argument is omitted, it is assumed the future value of the loan is zero.
- The *type* argument indicates when payments are due; this argument is optional. A zero or omitted argument indicates payments are due at the end of the period; this is the default setting. If the type argument is 1, payments are due at the beginning of the period.

Refer to Figure 2-43 to understand the following *PMT* function example:

The PMT function
=**PMT(C8/12,F4*12,C7)**

- **C8/12** is the *rate* argument and indicates an annual rate of 6.5% and that the borrower is making monthly payments (period is equal to one month), in other words 6.5% divided by 12.

	A	B	C	D	E	F	G
1							
2		Wilson Home Entertainment Systems					
3							
4		Item Description	Equipment		Loan Term	7	
5		Purchase Price	$ 45,000.00		Payment		
6		Down Payment	$ 10,000.00		Total Interest		
7		Loan Amount	$ 35,000.00		Total Principal		
8		Annual Percentage Rate	6.5%		Total Cost of the Loan		
9							

2-43 *PMT* function sample worksheet

- **F4*12** is the *nper* argument and indicates that the loan term is 7 years (cell F7) and there are 12 payments per year. (The total number of periods is 7 years times 12 periods per year.)
- **C7** is the *pv* argument (amount of the loan or the present value).

The result of this *PMT* function is ($519.73). The payment result is a negative number, which is indicated by the red color and the parentheses; the borrower is paying this amount and not receiving it.

HOW TO: Enter the PMT Function with the Insert Function Button

1. Click the cell where you want to enter the function.
2. Click the **Insert Function (f$_x$)** button to the left of the *Formula bar* to open the *Insert Function* dialog box (Figure 2-44).
3. Click the **Search for a function** box, type Payment, and click **Go**.
4. Select **PMT** from the function list and click **OK**. The *Function Arguments* dialog box opens (Figure 2-45).
5. Click the **Rate** argument text box and click the cell that contains the interest per period for the loan.
   - If the cell contains an APR (annual percentage rate), it must be converted to interest per period. Divide the interest rate by the number of payments that will be made in a year. For example, if the borrower is paying monthly, divide by 12; if the borrower is paying quarterly, divide by 4.

2-44 *Insert Function* dialog box

6. Click the **Nper** argument text box and click the cell that contains the term of the loan. The cell must contain the total number of periods for repayment of the loan.

- If the loan term is in years and payments are monthly, the total number of periods is the number of years * 12.
- If the loan term is in years and payments are quarterly, then the total number of periods is the number of years * 4.

7. Click the **Pv** argument text box and click the cell that contains the amount of the loan.

- You can omit the last two arguments because there will be a zero balance after the last payment is made, and payments will be made at the end of each period.

8. Click **OK** to close the dialog box and insert the function.

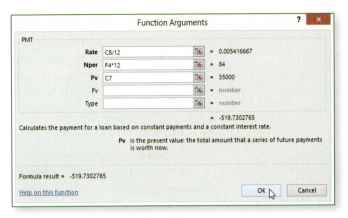

2-45 PMT Function Arguments dialog box

> **ANOTHER WAY**
>
> Use the **Financial** button [*Formulas* tab, *Function Library* group] to locate financial functions described in this section.

> **MORE INFO**
>
> To create an amortization schedule, you can use the *Loan Amortization Schedule* template in the *Templates* category from the *New* button [*File* tab]. Select the **Loan Amortization Schedule** from the *Business Schedules* subfolder located in the *Schedules* folder.

IF Function

The **IF** function evaluates a specified condition and returns one value if the condition is true and another value if the condition is false. For example, if you work for an organization that determines bonuses on the amount of sales revenue generated, you could use the *IF* function to determine if a sales goal was met and if a bonus should be paid and then calculate the amount of the bonus.

To evaluate the condition, you can use comparison operators. The table at the right lists comparison operators:

Comparison Operators

Operator	Description
=	Equal to
<>	Not equal to
>	Greater than
>=	Greater than or equal to
<	Less than
<=	Less than or equal to

The *IF* function has three arguments and the formula syntax for the function is:

=IF (logical_test, value_if_true, value_if_false)

- **The *logical_test*** argument is the value or expression to be evaluated as true or false; this argument is required. You can use any comparison operator in the logical test.

- The *value_if_true* argument is the value returned if the logical test argument is true. If the value returned is text, enclose the text in quotes.
- The *value_if_false* argument is the value returned if the logical test argument is false. If the value returned is text, enclose the text in quotes.

> ### MORE INFO
>
> Commas within a function indicate the start of a new argument, so it is a good idea to omit commas within a value argument. For example, type "5000," not "5,000," in a value argument.

Refer to Figure 2-46 to understand the following examples of using an *IF* function. The formula shown here determines if an item should be reordered:

	A	B	C	D	E	F
1			Product Catalog			
2						
3	Product #	Description	Qty on Hand	Unit Cost	Unit Price	Reorder?
4	101	T-Shirt	120	$ 4.00	$ 11.00	
5	102	Shorts	45	$ 2.50	$ 6.88	
6	103	Coffee Mug	25	$ 1.25	$ 3.44	
7	104	Pants	36	$ 7.25	$ 19.94	
8	105	Beach Towel	22	$ 3.50	$ 9.63	

2-46 *IF* function sample worksheet

=IF(C4<=100,"Yes","No")

- C4<=100 is the *logical_test* argument and determines whether *Qty on Hand* is less than or equal to 100.
- "Yes" is the *value_if_true* argument. "Yes" is the value returned if the quantity on hand is less than or equal to 100. A "Yes" response indicates that the quantity on hand is below the minimal amount required on hand and should be reordered. The logical test argument is true if this value is returned.
- "No" is the *value_if_false* argument. "No" is the value returned if the quantity on hand is greater than 100. A "No" response indicates that it is not necessary to reorder. The logical test argument is false if this value is returned.
- The value returned for this *IF* function is "No."

The following formula is based again on information in Figure 2-46 and determines how many items to order:

=IF(C5<50,50-C5,0)

- C5<50 is the *logical_test* argument.
- 50-C5 is the *value_if_true* argument. The result of 50-C5 is the value returned if the quantity on hand is less than 50. The amount to order is calculated. The logical test argument is true if this value is returned.
- 0 is the *value_if_false* argument. 0 is the value returned if the quantity on hand is greater than or equal to 50. Reordering is not necessary. The logical test argument is false if this value is returned.
- The value returned for this *IF* function is 5.

You can insert the *IF* function by typing the formula, using the *Insert Function* button on the *Formula bar*, or using the *Insert Function* button on the *Formulas* tab.

HOW TO: Enter the IF Function

1. Click the cell where you want to enter the function.
2. Click the **Insert Function** button [*Formulas* tab, *Function Library group*] to open the *Insert Function* dialog box.

3. Type IF in the **Search for a function** box and click **Go**.

4. Select **IF** from the function list and click **OK**. The *Function Arguments* dialog box opens (Figure 2-47).

5. Click the **Logical_test** argument text box, and select the cell that will be compared.

6. Type the comparison operator or operators.

7. Click the cell that contains the comparison amount or type the value.

   • Include absolute cell references if you plan to copy the formula to another location and are referencing a cell that must remain constant.

8. Click the **Value_if_true** argument text box and click the cell that contains the true value, type the true value, or type the argument text surrounded with quotation marks.

9. Click the **Value_if_false** argument text box and click the cell that contains the false value, type the false value, or type the argument text surrounded with quotation marks.

10. Click **OK** to close the dialog box and insert the function.

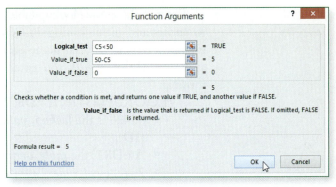

2-47 IF Function Arguments dialog box

> **MORE INFO**
>
> You can create nested *IF* functions that allow for more than one logical test.

LOOKUP Functions

LOOKUP functions retrieve a value from a range or table of cells located in another area of the worksheet or workbook. The two main types of *LOOKUP* functions are **VLOOKUP** (vertical lookup) and **HLOOKUP** (horizontal lookup). The *VLOOKUP* function finds a value in the first column of a range of cells and returns a value from any cell on the same row of the range. In order for the *VLOOKUP* function to work properly, the first column must be sorted in ascending order and each cell must contain a unique value.

The *VLOOKUP* function has four arguments and the formula syntax for the function is:

=VLOOKUP (lookup_value, table_array, col_index_num, [range_lookup])

   • The *lookup_value* argument is required and Excel searches for this value in the first column of the cell range or table. If the cells in the first column contain text, you must enclose the text in quotes when creating the formula. When searching for the lookup value in the first column of the range, Excel finds the largest value less than or equal to the value in the first column of the range.

   • The *table_array* argument is the range used for looking up data; this argument is required. You can enter a cell range or a range name. The data in the first column must be in ascending order.

   • The *col_index_num* argument is the column number of the cell range or table (counting from the left); this argument is required.

   • The *[range lookup]* argument is a logical value (True or False) that is used to find the nearest value (True) or an exact match (False); this argument is optional. The default value is "True."

Refer to the sample lookup table in Figure 2-48 to understand the following *VLOOKUP* function example. To find the last name of a student with a student ID of 33420, you enter the following formula:

=VLOOKUP(33420, A4:D8, 2)

- **33420** is the *lookup_value* argument (ID).
- **A4:D8** is the *table_array* argument (cell range).
- **2** is the *col_index_num* argument (the second column in the table which lists the last names of the students).
- The result of this *VLOOKUP* function is "Rosch."

	A	B	C	D
1	**Student Data Table**			
2				
3	**ID**	**Last Name**	**First Name**	**Degree**
4	11123	Boney	John	Business
5	22234	Eisenhauer	DeAnn	Education
6	33420	Rosch	Ariel	Psychology
7	42002	Bowman	Larry	Education
8	56009	Kranz	Sandra	Accounting

2-48 Lookup table

To find the degree of a student with an identification number of 33420, key the following formula:

=VLOOKUP(33420,A4:D8,4)

The result of this *VLOOKUP* function is "Psychology."

Apply the *VLOOKUP* and *HLOOKUP* functions by using the *Insert Function* button on the *Formula bar* or on the *Formulas* tab or by typing the function name into a cell.

HOW TO: Enter the VLOOKUP Function

1. Click the cell where you want to enter the function.

2. Click the **Insert Function** button [*Formulas* tab, *Function Library* group] to open the *Insert Function* dialog box (Figure 2-49).

3. Type VLOOKUP in the **Search for a function** text box and click **Go**.

4. Select **VLOOKUP** from the function list and click **OK** to open the *Function Arguments* dialog box (Figure 2-50).

5. Click the **Lookup_value** text box.

6. Click a cell in the first column of the cell range or table.

7. Click the **Table_array** argument text box and select the appropriate cell range.

   - When you drag to select, the *Function Arguments* dialog box collapses. The dialog box expands after the range is selected.
   - Apply absolute cell reference symbols to this range if you plan to copy the formula to another location.

8. Click the **Col_index_num** argument text box, and type the column number (count from the left).

   - Do not include the *Range_lookup* argument; it will default to *TRUE* and find the closest match instead of an exact match.

9. Click **OK** to close the *Functions Arguments* dialog box.

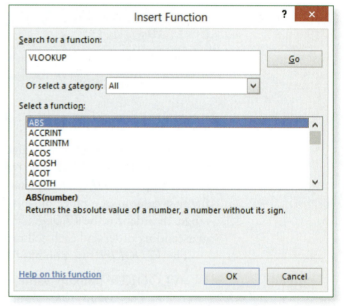

2-49 *Insert Function* dialog box

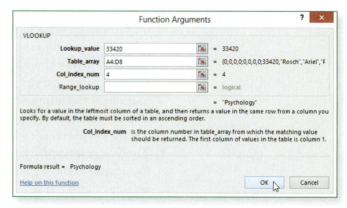

2-50 *VLOOKUP Function Arguments* dialog box

The *HLOOKUP* function is very similar to *VLOOKUP*. You can use *HLOOKUP* to find a value in the first row of a table or cell range and return a value from any cell in the same column of the range. Each entry in the first row must be a unique value.

The *HLOOKUP* function has four arguments, and the formula syntax for the function is:

=HLOOKUP (lookup_value, table_array, col_index_num, [range_lookup])

- The *lookup_value* argument is required and is the value Excel searches for in the first row of the cell range or table. If the cells in the first row contain text, you must enclose the text in quotes when creating the formula. When searching for the lookup value in the first row of the range, Excel finds the largest value less than or equal to the value in the first column of the range.
- The *table_array* argument is the range used for looking up data; this argument is required. You can enter a cell range or a range name. The data in the first row must be in ascending order from left to right if looking for an exact match.
- The *row_index_num* argument is the row number of the cell range or table (counting from the top); this argument is required.
- The *[range lookup]* argument is a logical value (True or False) that is used to find the nearest value (True) or an exact match (False); this argument is optional. The default value is "True."

Refer to the sample lookup table in Figure 2-51 to understand the following example:

=HLOOKUP("Last Name", A3:D8, 5)

- **Last Name** is the *lookup_value* argument found in the top row.
- **A3:D8** is the *table_array* argument (cell range).
- **5** is the *row_index_num* argument (the fifth row from the top of the cell range).
- The result of this *HLOOKUP* function is "Bowman".

	A	B	C	D
1	Student Data Table			
2				
3	ID	Last Name	First Name	Degree
4	11123	Boney	John	Business
5	22234	Esienhauer	DeAnn	Education
6	33420	Rosch	Aariel	Psychology
7	42002	Bowman	Larry	Education
8	56009	Dranz	Sandra	Accounting

2-51 Lookup table

HOW TO: Enter the HLOOKUP Function

1. Click the cell where you want to enter the function.
2. Click the **Insert Function** button [*Formulas* tab, *Function Library* group] to open the *Insert Function* dialog box.
3. Type HLOOKUP in the **Search for a function** box and click **Go**.
4. Select **HLOOKUP** and click **OK** to open the *Function Arguments* dialog box (Figure 2-52).

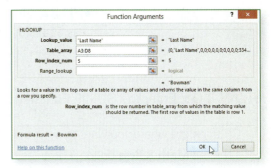

2-52 HLOOKUP Function Arguments dialog box

5. Click the **Lookup_value** argument text box and click a cell in the top row of the cell range or table.

6. Click the **Table_array** argument text box and select the cell range.

   • Be sure to apply absolute cell reference symbols to this range if you plan to copy the formula to another location.

7. Click the **Row_index_num** argument text box and type the row number (count from the top row).

   • Do not include the *Range_lookup* argument; it will default to *TRUE* and find the closest match instead of an exact match.

8. Click **OK** to close the dialog box and insert the function.

| SLO 2.6 | # Working with Math and Trigonometry Functions |

Excel includes many pre-defined math and trigonometry functions. In this section you learn to insert *SUMIF, SUMPRODUCT,* and *ROUND* functions in a spreadsheet.

SUMIF Function

The *SUMIF* function combines the *SUM* function with the logical criteria component of the *IF* function. The *SUMIF* includes cells in a calculation only if they meet a certain condition. For example, you may only want to add together cells that have values larger than 20.

The *SUMIF* function has three arguments and the formula syntax for the function is:

=SUMIF (range, criteria, [sum_range])
   • The **range** argument is the range of cells to be added; this argument is required.
   • The **criteria** argument defines which cells will be added (which condition must be met); this argument is required. Text criteria or logical or mathematical symbols must be enclosed in quotation marks (" ").
   • The **[sum_range]** argument is optional. It is used to add cells that are not included in the range argument.

Refer to Figure 2-53 for an example that adds values in a range if the "*Unit Price*" value is greater than 25.

=SUMIF(E4:E6,">25",F4:F6).
   • E4:E6 is the **range** argument (unit price).
   • >25 is the **criteria** argument (unit price greater than 25).
   • F4:F6 is the **sum_range** argument and adds the line total amounts.
   • The result of this *SUMIF* function is $147.26.

2-53 *SUMIF* function sample worksheet

HOW TO: Enter the SUMIF Function

1. Click the cell where you want to enter the function.

2. Click the **Math & Trig** button [*Formulas* tab, *Function Library* group] (Figure 2-54).

3. Scroll and select the **SUMIF** function. The *Function Arguments* dialog box opens (Figure 2-55).

E2-106

4. Click the **Range** argument text box if necessary.

5. Drag to select the cell range.

6. Click the **Criteria** argument text box and type the condition.

   - Enclose the argument in quotes.

7. Click the **Sum_range** argument text box and select a range.

   - The *sum_range* identifies the actual range of cells to add. If the text box is blank, the cells in the range argument are added.

8. Click **OK**.

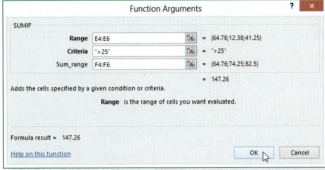

2-55 *SUMIF Function Arguments* dialog box

2-54 *Math & Trig* functions

> **ANOTHER WAY**
>
> Use *wild cards* (such as the asterisk [*]) in conjunction with criteria to sum all cells that meet corresponding criteria. For example, to sum all cells that have an associated criteria cell that begins with the letter A, type ("**A***") as the criteria.

SUMPRODUCT Function

The *SUMPRODUCT* function combines the *Sum* and *Product* mathematical operations. This function multiplies and then adds a series of arrays. An *array* is a range of cells in a row or column, such as A1:A4. An example of two arrays with the same dimension is A1:A5 and C1:C5. Two arrays with different dimensions are A1:A5 and C1:G1. The *SUMPRODUCT* is the sum of the products of several arrays. All arrays in a *SUMPRODUCT* function must have the same number of rows and columns.

The SUMPRODUCT function has the following arguments and the formula syntax is:

=SUMPRODUCT (array1, array2, [array_n], ...)

   - The *array1* argument is the argument that contains cells to multiply with the corresponding cells in the next array, and then those products are added together; this argument is required.
   - The *array2* argument must have the same number of cells and the same dimension as array1; this argument is required.

Refer to Figure 2-56 to understand the following example. The *SUMPRODUCT* function is:

=SUMPRODUCT (A4:A6,D4:D6)

	A	B	C	D	E
1					
2					
3	QTY	Item #	Description	Unit Price	Line Total
4	1	15	Snow Shoes	64.76	64.76
5	6	16	Hats	12.38	74.28
6	2	17	Ski Poles	41.25	82.50

2-56 *SUMPRODUCT* function sample worksheet

The function multiplies each specified cell in column A (quantity) times the specified cell in column D (unit price) and then adds the products.

QTY		Unit Price		Line Total
A4	*	D4	=	64.76
A5	*	D5	=	74.28
A6	*	D6	=	82.50
				221.54

The result of this *SUMPRODUCT* function is $221.54.

HOW TO: Enter the SUMPRODUCT Function

1. Click the cell where you want to enter the function.
2. Click the **Insert Function** button [*Formulas* tab, *Function Library* group] to open the *Insert Function* dialog box.
3. Type SUMPRODUCT in the **Search for a function** box and click **Go**.
4. Select **SUMPRODUCT** and click **OK** to open the *Function Arguments* dialog box (Figure 2-57).
5. Click the **Array1** argument text box and select a cell range.
6. Click the **Array2** argument text box and select a cell range.
   - Each selected array must contain the same number of cells and have the same dimensions.
7. Click **OK** to insert the function and close the dialog box.

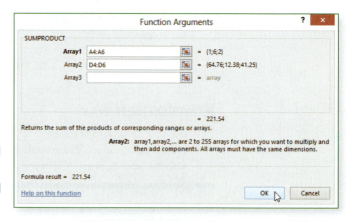

2-57 **SUMPRODUCT Function Arguments dialog box**

> **MORE INFO**
> Excel treats any empty cell in an array as if it has a value of 0.

ROUND Function

The *ROUND* function rounds a number to a specified number of decimal places. The *ROUND* function has two arguments and the formula syntax is:

=ROUND(number, num_digits)
- The *number* argument represents the number to round; this argument is required.
- The *num_digits* argument specifies the number of decimal places to round the number argument; this argument is required. If the *num_digits* argument is greater than zero, the number argument is rounded to the specified number of decimal places. If *num_digits* argument is zero, the number is rounded to the nearest whole number. If the *num_digits* argument is less than zero, the number is rounded to the left of the decimal point.

You can use the *ROUND* function to round the results of another formula. For example, if cell A1 contains the number 25.346, and you want to round the number to 1 decimal place, type the formula:

=ROUND(A1,1).

The result of this ROUND function is 25.3.

HOW TO: Enter the ROUND Function

1. Click the cell where you want to create the formula.
2. Click the **Insert Function** button [*Formulas* tab, *Function Library* group] to open the *Insert Function* dialog box.
3. Type ROUND in the **Search for a function** box and click **Go**.
4. Select the **ROUND** function and click **OK** to open the *Function Arguments* dialog box (Figure 2-58).
5. Click the **Number** argument text box and select a cell.
6. Click the **Num_digits** argument text box and type the number of digits you want to round the specified number.
7. Click **OK** to insert the function and close the dialog box.

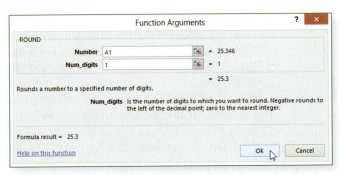

2-58 ROUND Function Arguments dialog box

> ## MORE INFO
>
> Excel also has a *ROUNDDOWN* function that always rounds a number down. The *ROUNDUP* function always rounds a number up.

PAUSE & PRACTICE: EXCEL 2-3

For this project, you open the previous Pause & Practice file and add the following kinds of functions: math and trigonometry, financial, logical, lookup, and date and time. These functions provide important financial information on sales and future investment opportunities to finalize the Paradise Lakes Resort workbook.

File Needed: *[your initials] PP E2-2.xlsx*
Completed Project File Name: *[your initials] PP E2-3.xlsx*

1. Open the *[your initials] PP E2-2* workbook, and save the workbook as *[your initials] PP E2-3*.
2. Enter the *SUMIF* function to determine the total mortgage.
   a. Click cell **E20**.
   b. Click the **Insert Function** button [*Formulas* tab, *Function Library* group] to open the *Insert Function* dialog box.
   c. Type SUMIF in the **Search for a function** box and click **Go**.

d. Select **SUMIF** from the function list and click **OK** to open the *Function Arguments* dialog box.

e. Click the **Range** argument text box and select the cell range A10:A13.

f. Click the **Criteria** argument text box and type "Mortgage".

g. Click the **Sum_range** argument and type H10:H13.

h. Verify that the formula syntax is =SUMIF(A10:A13,"Mortgage",H10:H13).

i. Click **OK**. The correct result for cell E20 is $71,742.38.

3. Enter a *SUMPRODUCT* function to determine additional income for extra rented cabins.
   a. Click cell **G20**.
   b. Click the **Insert Function** button [*Formulas* tab, *Function Library* group].
   c. Type SUMPRODUCT in the **Search for a function** box and click **Go**.
   d. Select **SUMPRODUCT** from the function list and click **OK** to open the *Function Arguments* dialog box.
   e. Click the **Array1** text box and select B16:H16.
   f. Click the **Array2** text box and select the cell range B18:H18.
   g. Verify that the formula syntax is =SUMPRODUCT(B16:H16,B18:H18).
   h. Click **OK**. The correct result for cell G20 is $143,045.12.

4. Enter a *ROUND* function to round the net income in the spreadsheet.
   a. Click cell **E21** and use the **Insert Function** button to insert the *ROUND* function.
   b. In the *Function Arguments* dialog box, type H16 in the *Number* argument text box.
   c. Type 1 in the *Num_digits* argument text box.
   d. Verify that the formula syntax is =ROUND(H16,1).
   e. Press **Enter**.
   The correct result for cell E21 is $135,044.50 (Figure 2-59).

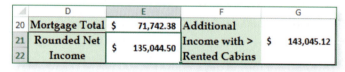

	D	E	F	G
20	Mortgage Total	$ 71,742.38	Additional	
21	Rounded Net	$ 135,044.50	Income with >	$ 143,045.12
22	Income		Rented Cabins	

2-59 *ROUND* function results

5. Enter a *PMT* function to determine payments if the organization were to purchase additional cabins.
   a. Click the **Investment Options** sheet tab.
   b. Click cell **B7** and use the **Insert Function** button to insert the *PMT* function.
   c. In the *Function Arguments* dialog box, click the **Rate** argument text box and click cell **B6**. Be sure to divide B6 by 12 (**B6/12**); the organization will be making monthly payments.
   d. Click the **Nper** argument text box and then click cell **B5**. Be sure to multiply B5 times 12 (**B5*12**); the organization will be making monthly payments.
   e. Click the **Pv** argument text box and then click cell **B4**.
   f. Omit the last two arguments because we want a zero balance after the last payment is made and payments will be made at the end of each period.
   g. Click **OK**.
   h. Verify that the formula syntax is =PMT(B6/12,B5*12,B4).
   i. Press **Enter**. The correct result for cell B7 is ($2,415.70) (a negative value).

6. Enter an *IF* function to determine if the organization should take out the loan for the investment. Compare the monthly payment to the lowest monthly sales total from the *Location 1- Cass Lake* sheet tab. If the monthly payment is lower, choose to make the investment.
   a. Click cell **B13** and use the **Insert Function** button to insert the *IF* function (Figure 2-60).

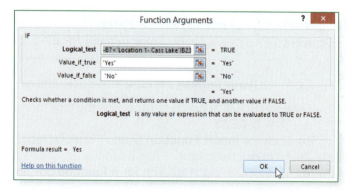

2-60 *IF Function Arguments* dialog box

b. In the *Function Arguments* dialog box, click the **Logical_test** argument box and then type -B7<, click the **Location 1- Cass Lake** sheet, and select **B23**.

c. Verify that the the **Logical_test** argument is -B7<'Location 1- Cass Lake'!B23.

d. Click the **Value_if_true** argument text box and type "Yes".

e. Click the **Value_if_false** argument text box and type "No".

f. Click **OK**. The result of the calculation appears in the cell containing the formula.

g. Verify that the formula syntax is =IF(-B7<'Location 1- Cass Lake'!B23,"Yes", "No").

h. Press **Enter**. The correct result for cell B13 is "Yes" (Figure 2-61).

7. Enter a *VLOOKUP* function to determine the cost of various products.

a. Select the **Product Cost** sheet tab.

b. Click cell **B4** and use the **Insert Function** button to insert the *VLOOKUP* function (Figure 2-62).

c. In the *Function Arguments* dialog box, click the **Lookup_value** argument text box and click **A4**.

d. Click the **Table_array** argument box and select the cell range **E4:G8**, and then apply absolute cell reference symbols by pressing **F4**.

e. Click the **Col_index_num** argument text box and type the column number 3.

f. Omit the **Range_lookup** argument; it will default to *TRUE* and find the closest match.

g. Click **OK**. The result of the calculation appears in B4.

h. Verify that the formula syntax is =VLOOKUP(A4,$E$4:$G$8,3).

i. Press **Enter**. The correct result in B4 is $25.50.

j. Copy the formula in **B4** to **B5:B6**. Apply **Accounting** formatting to **B4:B6**. Apply any borders needed to **A2:B6**.

8. Save and close the workbook (Figure 2-63).

	A	B
1	**New Purchase Monthly Payments**	
2		
3	Property	Cabins
4	Loan Amount	$ 450,000.00
5	Term in Years	30
6	Interest Rate	5%
7	**Payment**	($2,415.70)
8		
10		
11		
12	**Decision Table**	
13	Purchase New Property?	Yes

2-61 *PMT* function result

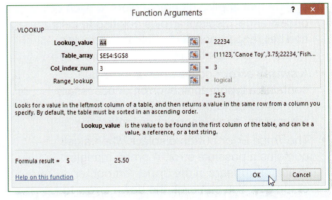

2-62 *VLOOKUP* Function Arguments dialog box

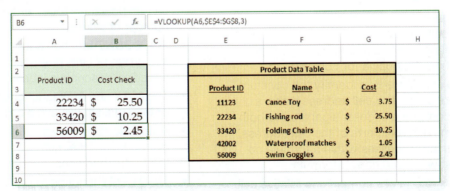

2-63 *VLOOKUP* function results after copying and formatting

Chapter Summary

2.1 Create and edit basic formulas (p. E2-79).

- The **syntax** of a formula refers to the required parts of the formula and the rules controlling the sequence of the parts.
- A popular and accurate technique for entering cells in formulas is the **select** method.
- Formulas calculate and update automatically when values in the worksheet change.
- Double-clicking a cell or pressing **F2** activates edit mode and allows you to modify a formula.
- The **Range Finder** is a color-coded editing tool that applies different colors to each cell or cell range within the formula syntax.
- **Formula Auditing** is a color-coded editing system that applies different colors to each cell or cell range, displays arrows pointing to cells and cell ranges included within the formula's syntax, and steps through syntax errors.
- A **syntax error** occurs when a formula contains a typographical error, unnecessary or missing punctuation, incorrect order of arguments, or an incorrect cell reference.
- The *Trace Error* button displays when a cell contains a possible error. A green triangle indicator appears in the upper left corner of the cell. You can click the down arrow to display a list of options to repair or ignore the error.
- A **circular reference** occurs when a formula includes the cell address of the formula.

2.2 Use range names and relative, absolute, and mixed cell references in a formula (p. E2-83).

- There are three basic types of cell references: **relative**, **absolute**, and **mixed**.
- Relative cell references identify the location of a cell. Relative cell addresses within a formula adjust when you copy a formula.
- Absolute cell references identify the constant location of a cell. The cell address within a formula contains a $ (dollar sign) around both the column and row parts of the cell address. Absolute cell addresses within a formula *do not* adjust when you copy a formula.
- Mixed cell references contain one relative cell address component (either the row number or column letter) and one absolute cell address component.

- **3D** cell references identify cells in worksheets other than where the formula resides. Using a *3D* cell reference in another workbook is called **linking workbooks**.
- You can apply a **range name** to a cell or groups of cells to describe the purpose of the group of cells and make it easier to interpret a formula. A range name is an absolute cell reference.
- The *Fill Handle* is a tool that allows you to copy formulas, lists, and numeric patterns.

2.3 Apply mathematical order of operations when using parentheses, exponents, multiplication, division, addition, and subtraction (p. E2-88).

- Excel follows a specified set of rules when it calculates a formula that has more than one operation.
- If the syntax of the formula includes parentheses, exponents, multiplication or division, and addition or subtraction, the operation within the parentheses is performed first, exponent operation is second, multiplying or dividing operators are computed third, and addition and subtraction are completed last.
- Use the following acronym to help remember the order of operations: **P**lease **E**xcuse **M**y **D**ear **A**unt **S**ally.

2.4 Use *AutoSum* and other common functions such as *AVERAGE, COUNT, MAX, MIN, TODAY*, and *NOW* (p. E2-93).

- Use the **AutoSum** button to insert frequently used functions.
- The **AVERAGE** function calculates an average by adding values together and dividing by the number of values.
- The **COUNT** function counts each number in a group of cells or each cell that contains specified descriptive labels.
- The **MAX** and **MIN** functions find the largest or the smallest value in a cell range.
- **AutoCalculate** allows you to view totals, averages, or other statistical information on the *Status bar* without creating any formulas.
- The **TODAY** function returns the current date each time a workbook is opened.
- The **NOW** function returns the current date and time each time a workbook is opened.

h. Select the **Auto Fill Options** button drop-down arrow and select **Fill Without Formatting** to ensure borders are not overwritten.

i. Release the pointer. The totals for F6 and F7 are $7,546.84 and $29,880.01, respectively.

5. Create a formula to calculate the rent expense (estimated to be 17% of total sales). Apply absolute cell references and copy the rent expense formula.

   a. Select **B10** (Figure 2-64).

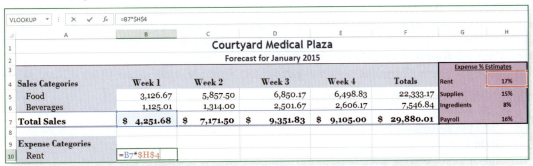

VLOOKUP	▾	:	×	✓	f_x	=B7*$H$4		

	A	B	C	D	E	F	G	H
1				Courtyard Medical Plaza				
2				Forecast for January 2015				
3								Expense % Estimates
4	Sales Categories	Week 1	Week 2	Week 3	Week 4	Totals	Rent	17%
5	Food	3,126.67	5,857.50	6,850.17	6,498.83	22,333.17	Supplies	15%
6	Beverages	1,125.01	1,314.00	2,501.67	2,606.17	7,546.84	Ingredients	8%
7	Total Sales	$ 4,251.68	$ 7,171.50	$ 9,351.83	$ 9,105.00	$ 29,880.01	Payroll	16%
8								
9	Expense Categories							
10	Rent	=B7*$H$4						

2-64 **Rent expense formula with an absolute reference**

   b. Type the following formula =B7*H4.
   c. Click the *Formula bar* to the left of the column letter **H** and then press **F4** to apply absolute cell references.
   d. Press **Enter**. Verify that the formula syntax is =B7*$H$4.
   e. Select **B10** and click and drag the fill pointer to cells **C10:F10**.

6. Name a cell to make it an absolute reference.
   a. Click **H7**.
   b. Click the **Name** box.
   c. Type Payroll in the *Name* box and press **Enter**.

7. Create and copy expense formulas for "Supplies", "Ingredients", and "Payroll". Use multiplication to calculate the expense and absolute cell references for the estimated percent of total sales.
   a. Enter the formulas in the table in the corresponding cells as shown in the following table.

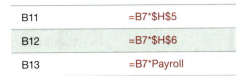

B11	=B7*$H$5
B12	=B7*$H$6
B13	=B7*Payroll

   b. Select cells **B11:B13**.
   c. Place your pointer over the *Fill Handle* of cell range **B11:B13**.
   d. Click and drag the fill pointer through cells **C11:F13**.

8. Create an addition formula to total the expenses for week 1 and copy the formula.
   a. Click **B14**.
   b. Type = (equals sign).
   c. Select **B10** and type +.
   d. Select **B11** and type +.
   e. Select **B12** and type +.
   f. Select **B13**.
   g. Press **Enter**.
   h. Verify that the syntax of the formula is =B10+B11+B12+B13. The result of the formula is $2,380.94.
   i. Select **B14** and click and drag the *Fill Handle* to cells **C14:F14**.

9. Create and copy a formula with multiple operators.
   a. Click **B16**.
   b. Type =(B5+B6)-B14.
   c. Press **Enter**. Verify the formula syntax is =(B5+B6)-B14.
   d. Select **B16** and click and drag the *Fill Handle* to cells **C16:F16**.

10. Use auditing tools to review a formula.
    a. Select cell **B16**.
    b. Click the **Show Formulas** button and the **Trace Precedents** button [*Formulas* tab, *Formula Auditing* group]. A blue dot appears in each cell referenced in the formula.
    c. Click the **Remove Arrows** button [*Formulas* tab, *Formula Auditing* group].
    d. Click the **Show Formulas** button [*Formulas* tab, *Formula Auditing* group] to return to results view.

11. Enter a *SUM* function to calculate monthly sales.
    a. Click cell **B20**.
    b. Click the **AutoSum** button drop-down arrow [*Formulas* tab, *Function Library* group] and select **SUM** from the drop-down list.
    c. Select the cell range **B7:E7**. Verify the formula syntax is =SUM(B7:E7).
    d. Press **Enter**. The formula result is $29,880.01.

12. Calculate average weekly sales by entering an *AVERAGE* function using the *AutoSum* button.
    a. Click cell **B21**.
    b. Click the **AutoSum** button drop-down arrow [*Formulas* tab, *Function Library* group] and select **Average** from the drop-down list.
    c. Select the cell range **B7:E7**.
    d. Press **Enter**. Verify the formula syntax =AVERAGE(B7:E7). The formula's result should be $7,470.00.

13. Calculate maximum weekly sales by entering a *MAX* function using the *AutoSum* button.
    a. Click cell **B22**.
    b. Click the **AutoSum** button drop-down arrow [*Formulas* tab, *Function Library* group] and select **Max** from the drop-down list.
    c. Select cell range **B7:E7**.
    d. Press **Enter**. Verify the formula syntax =MAX(B7:E7). The formula result is $9,351.83.

14. Use auditing tools to review a formula.
    a. Select cell **B22**.
    b. Click the **Show Formulas** button and the **Trace Precedents** button [*Formulas tab, Formula Auditing* group].
    c. Click the **Remove Arrows** button [*Formulas* tab, *Formula Auditing* group].
    d. Click the **Show Formulas** button [*Formulas* tab, *Formula Auditing* group] to return to results view.

15. Edit the maximum weekly sales formula to add absolute cell references.
    a. Select cell **B22**.
    b. Click the *Formula bar* and select the cell range **B7:E7**. Do not include the parentheses in your selection.
    c. Press **F4** key to add absolute reference symbols.
    d. Press **Enter**. The formula syntax should be =MAX($B$7:$G$7).

16. Copy an existing formula and edit the function name.
    a. Select cell **B22** and click and drag the *Fill Handle* to **B23**.
    b. Choose the **Auto Fill Options** button and select **Fill Without Formatting** to ensure your borders are not overwritten.

   c. Select cell **B23**.

   d. Click the *Formula bar*, delete the function name **MAX**, and type MIN.

   e. Press **Enter**. Verify the syntax of the formula is =MIN($B$7:$G$7). The formula result is $4,251.68.

17. Enter the *SUMIF* function to determine the rent total.

   a. Click cell **E20**.

   b. Click the **Insert Function** button [*Formulas* tab, *Function Library group*] to open the *Insert Function* dialog box.

   c. Type SUMIF in the **Search for a function** box and click **Go**.

   d. Select **SUMIF** from the function list and click **OK** to open the *Function Arguments* dialog box.

   e. Click the **Range** argument text box and select the cell range A10:A13.

   f. Click the **Criteria** argument text box and type "Rent".

   g. Click the **Sum_range** argument and type F10:F13.

   h. Verify that the formula syntax is =SUMIF(A10:A13,"Rent",F10:F13).

   i. Click **OK**. The correct result for cell E20 is $5,079.60.

18. Enter a *SUMPRODUCT* function to determine additional income for extra meal and beverage sales.

   a. Click cell **E24**.

   b. Click the **Insert Function** button [*Formulas* tab, *Function Library* group] to open the *Insert Function* dialog box.

   c. Type SUMPRODUCT in the **Search for a function** box and click **Go**.

   d. Select **SUMPRODUCT** and click **OK** to open the *Function Arguments* dialog box.

   e. Click the **Array1** argument text box and select the cell range **E22:F22**.

   f. Click the **Array2** argument text box and select the cell range **E23:F23**.

   g. Verify that the formula syntax is =SUMPRODUCT(E22:F22,E23:F23).

   h. Click **OK**. The correct result in E24 is $33.25. See Figure 2-65 for the complete *Restaurant* tab results.

2-65 Excel 2-1 *Restaurant* tab results

19. Enter a *PMT* function on the *Investment Options* sheet tab to calculate the payment amount if the organization purchased another restaurant.
    a. Click the *Investment Options* sheet tab and select cell **B7**.
    b. Click the **Insert Function** button [*Formulas* tab, *Function Library* group].
    c. Type Payment in the **Search for a function** box and click **Go**.
    d. Select **PMT** and click **OK** to open the *Function Arguments* dialog box.
    e. Click the **Rate** argument text box, click cell **B6** (the interest rate), and type /12 (B6/12) since the organization will be making monthly payments.
    f. Click the **Nper** argument text box, click cell **B5**, and type *12 (B5*12) since the organization will be making monthly payments.
    g. Click the **Pv** argument text box and click cell **B4**, which is the amount of the loan.
    h. Omit the last two arguments because a zero balance is desired after the last payment is made and payments will be made at the end of each period.
    i. Click **OK**. The formula syntax should be =PMT(B6/12,B5*12,B4).
    j. Press **Enter**. The correct result is ($2,952.52).

20. Enter the **TODAY** function to update the worksheet date every time you open the file.
    a. Click cell **G3**.
    b. Type =TODAY() and press **Enter**. The current date appears in cell G3.

21. Save and close the workbook (Figure 2-66).

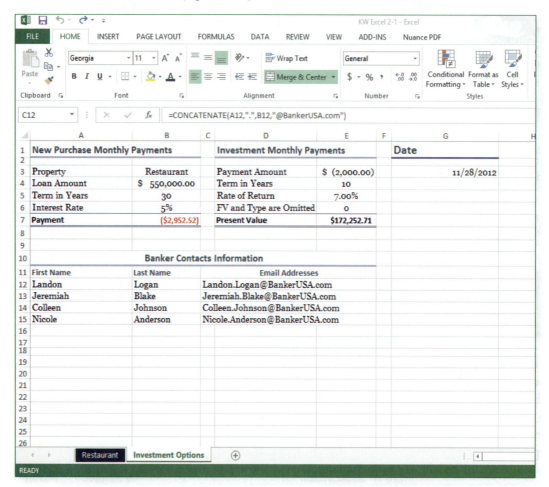

2-66 Excel 2-1 *Investment Options* tab results

Guided Project 2-2

Hamilton Civic Center (HCC) is a nonprofit community fitness center with an indoor pool, sauna, indoor track, project room, racquetball courts, meeting rooms, and a gift shop. HCC provides training and sponsors athletic and social events for adults and children. Tara Strachan is HCC's administrator for the gift shop. She has been asked to create an invoice template that links to the gift shop's product inventory spreadsheet.

[Student Learning Outcomes 2.1, 2.2, 2.3, 2.4, 2.5, 2.6]

File Needed: ***HCCInvoice-02.xlsx***
Completed Project File Name: ***[your initials] Excel 2-2.xlsx***

Skills Covered in This Project

- Create and copy basic formulas.
- Apply mathematical order of operations.
- Use relative, absolute, and mixed cell references.
- Apply the *VLOOKUP* function.
- Apply the *IF* function.
- Apply the *SUMIF* function.
- Apply the *TODAY* function.

1. Open the ***HCCInvoice-02.xlsx*** workbook from your student data files and save the workbook as ***[your initials] Excel 2-2.***

2. Enter a *VLOOKUP* function with *3D* references on the *Invoice* sheet tab.
   a. Click cell **C15** on the *Invoice* sheet tab.
   b. Click the **Insert Function** button [*Formulas* tab, *Function Library* group] to open the *Insert Function* dialog box.
   c. Type VLOOKUP in the **Search for a function** box and click **Go**.
   d. Select the **VLOOKUP** function from the list and click **OK** to open the *Function Arguments* dialog box (Figure 2-67).
   e. Click the **Lookup_value** argument text box and click cell **B15** (Item #).
   f. Click the **Table_array** argument text box and click the **Gift Shop Products** sheet tab.
   g. Select the cell range **A4:F18**.
   h. Press **F4** to apply absolute cell reference symbols to the A4:F18 range.
   i. Click the **Col_index_num** argument box and type 2, the column number.
   j. Omit the **Range_lookup** argument; if you include a *Range_lookup* argument, it will default to *TRUE* and find the closest match instead of the exact match you want to find.
   k. Click **OK**. The formula syntax should be =VLOOKUP(B15,'Gift Shop Products'!$A$4:$F$18,2). The result is "Shorts" and displays in C15 on the *Invoice* tab.

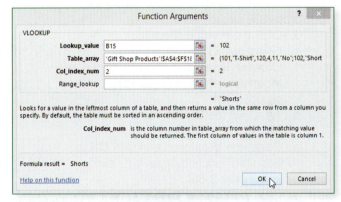

2-67 *VLOOKUP Function Arguments* dialog box

3. Copy the *VLOOKUP* formula.
   a. Select cell **C15**.
   b. Place your pointer over the *Fill Handle*.
   c. Click and drag the fill pointer through cells **C16:C17**.

4. Enter another *VLOOKUP* function with *3D* references on the *Invoice* sheet tab to insert unit price.
   a. Click cell **F15** on the *Invoice* sheet tab.
   b. Click the **Recently Used** button [*Formulas* tab, *Function Library* group].
   c. Select **VLOOKUP** to open the *Function Arguments* dialog box (Figure 2-68).
   d. Click the **Lookup_value** argument text box and click cell **B15**.
   e. Click the **Table_array** argument text box and click the *Gift Shop Products* sheet tab.
   f. Select the cell range **A4:F18** and press **F4** to apply absolute cell reference symbols to the range.
   g. Type 5 in the *Col_index_num* argument text box.
   h. Click **OK**. Verify that the formula syntax is =VLOOKUP(B15,'Gift Shop Products'!$A$4:$F$18,5). The result of the calculation is $6.88 and appears in cell F15 on the *Invoice* tab.

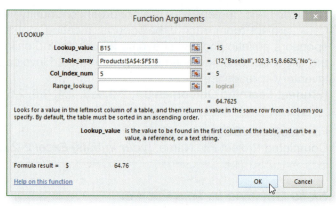

2-68 **VLOOKUP Function Arguments** dialog box

5. Copy the *VLOOKUP* formula.
   a. Select cell **F15**.
   b. Drag the *Fill Handle* through cells **F16:F17**.

6. Create an *IF* function to determine if the product is backordered.
   a. Click the **Invoice** sheet tab.
   b. Select cell **E15**.
   c. Click the **Insert Function** button [*Formulas* tab, *Function Library* group].
   d. Type IF in the **Search for a function** box and click **Go**.
   e. Select the **IF** function and click **OK** to open the *Function Arguments* dialog box (Figure 2-69).
   f. Click the **Logical_test** argument text box and click cell **A15**.
   g. Type <=.
   h. Click the **Gift Shop Products** sheet and select **C5**. The argument syntax is A15<='Gift Shop Products'!C5.
   i. Type "No" in the *Value_if_true* argument box.
   j. Type "Yes" in the *Value_if_false* argument box.
   k. Click **OK**. Verify that the formula syntax is =IF(A15<='Gift Shop Products'!C5,"No", "Yes"). The result of the calculation is "No" and displays in E15.
   l. Press **Enter**.
   m. Copy the formula in **E15** to **E16:E17**.

2-69 **IF Function Arguments** dialog box

7. Create a multiplication formula to calculate the sales total for shorts and use the *Fill Handle* to copy the formula.
   a. Click cell **G15**.
   b. Type =.

c. Select **A15**, type * (multiplication sign), and select **F15**.

d. Press **Enter**. Verify that the formula syntax is =A15*F15. The result should be $13.75.

e. Select cell **G15**.

f. Drag the *Fill Handle* through cells **G16:G17**. The totals for G16 and G17 should be $10.31 and $39.88.

g. Apply the **Accounting** numeric formatting to cells **F15:G17** if needed.

8. Create a *SUMIF* formula to total the line items that are not backordered.

a. Click cell **G31** and insert the **SUMIF** function.

b. Type E15:E17 in the *Range* argument box.

c. Type "No" in the *Criteria* argument box.

d. Click the **Sum_range** argument text box and select **G15:G17**.

e. Click **OK**. Verify that the formula syntax is =SUMIF(E15:E17,"No",G15:G17). The result in G31 should be $63.94.

f. Apply the **Accounting** formatting to **G31** if needed.

9. Create a formula with multiple operators and apply the mathematical order of precedence.

a. Click cell **G33**.

b. Type =G31+(G31*G32) and press **Enter**. Verify that the formula syntax is =G31+(G31*G32). The result in G33 should be $68.09.

c. Apply the **Accounting** formatting to **G33** if needed.

10. Use auditing tools to review a formula.

a. Select cell **G31**.

b. Click the **Show Formulas** button and the **Trace Precedents** button [*Formulas* tab, *Formula Auditing* group].

c. Review the formulas.

d. Click the **Remove Arrows** button [*Formulas* tab, *Formula Auditing* group].

e. Click the **Show Formulas** button [*Formulas* tab, *Formula Auditing* group] to return to results view.

11. Insert a date that will update every time you open the file.

a. Click cell **E5**.

b. Type =TODAY() and press **Enter**.

c. Format the date to **Short Date**.

12. Save and close the workbook (Figure 2-70).

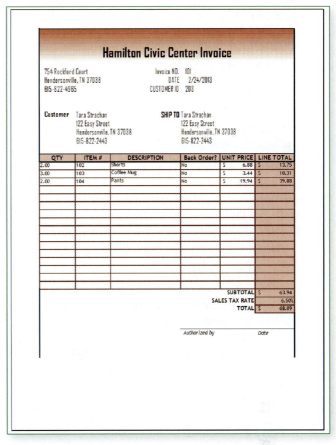

2-70 Excel 2-2 completed

Guided Project 2-3

Sierra Pacific Community College District (SPCCD) is a community college district composed of four individual community colleges. Ashlyn Varriano is the SPCCD administrator for the smallest of the four community colleges. She has been asked to explore an investment option and create an amortization schedule.
[Student Learning Outcomes 2.1, 2.2, 2.3, 2.5]

File Needed: **SPCCDInvestments-02.xlsx**
Completed Project File Name: **[your initials] Excel 2-3.xlsx**

Skills Covered in This Project

- Create and copy formulas.
- Apply mathematical order of operations.
- Use relative, absolute, and mixed cell references.
- Name cells and use the name range in a formula.
- Apply *PMT* function.

---

1. Open the **SPCCDInvestments-02.xlsx** workbook, and save the workbook as **[your initials] Excel 2-3**.
2. Apply range names.
   a. Select **C4:D8**.
   b. Click the **Create from Selection** button [*Formulas* tab, *Defined Names* group].
   c. Select the **Left Column** check box in the *Create Names from Selection* window. Deselect **Top row**.
   d. Click **OK**.
   e. Click the **Name** box drop-down arrow on the *Formula bar* to see a list of the new range names.
   f. Select **F4:G8**.
   g. Repeat steps 2b–d.
3. Enter the loan amount formula.
   a. Click **D7**.
   b. Type =.
   c. Select **D5** (*Purchase_Price*), press -, and select **D6** (*Down_Payment*).
   d. Press **Enter**. Verify that the formula syntax is =Purchase_Price − Down_Payment. The result of the formula should be $250,000.00.
4. Enter a *PMT* function.
   a. Click **G5**.
   b. Click the **Insert Function** button [*Formulas* tab, *Function Library* group] and insert the **PMT** function.
   c. Click the **Rate** argument box, click **D8** (named *Annual_Percentage_Rate*), and type /12 after D8 to divide it by 12 (*Annual_Percentage_Rate* /12) for monthly payments.
   d. Click the **Nper** argument box, click **G4** (*Term_of_the_Loan_in_Years*), and type *12 after G4 to multiply it by 12 (*Term_of_the_Loan_in_Years* *12) for monthly payments.
   e. Click **D7** (*Loan_Amount*) for the *Pv* argument.
   f. Click **OK**. Verify that the formula syntax is =PMT(Annual_Percentage_Rate/12,Term_of_the_Loan_in_Years*12,Loan_Amount). The correct result in G5 should be ($2,590.96).
   g. Edit the formula to create a positive number for the amortization schedule by typing a − (minus sign) in front of *Loan_Amount*. Verify that the formula syntax is =PMT(Annual_Percentage_Rate/12,Term_of_the_Loan_in_Years*12,-Loan_Amount).

5. Create a total interest formula.
   a. Click **G6** (*Total_Interest*).
   b. Type =.
   c. Select **G5** (*Payment*), type *, select **G4** (Term_of_the_Loan_in_Years), type *, type 12, type –, and select **D7** (*Loan_Amount*).
   d. Press **Enter**. Verify that the formula syntax is =Payment*Term_of_the_Loan_in_Years*12-Loan_ Amount. The result of the formula should be $60,915.23.

6. Create the total principal formula.
   a. Click **G7** (*Total_Principal*).
   b. Type =.
   c. Select **G5** (*Payment*), type *, select **G4** (Term_of_the_Loan_in_Years), type *, type 12, type –, and select **G6** (*Total_Interest*).
   d. Press **Enter**. Verify that the formula syntax is =Payment*Term_of_the_Loan_in_Years*12-Total_ Interest. The formula result should be $250,000.00.

7. Create an addition formula to calculate the cost of the loan.

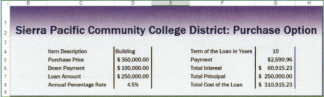

   a. Click **G8** (*Total_Cost_of_the_Loan*).
   b. Type =.
   c. Select **G6**, type +, and select **G7**.
   d. Press **Enter**. Verify that the formula syntax is =Total_Principal+Total_ Interest. The result of the formula should be $310,915.23 (Figure 2-71).

2-71 Formula results

8. Create and copy formulas for the amortization schedule.
   a. Create the formulas listed in the table at right.
   b. Select **C13** and double-click the *Fill Handle* to copy the contents through **C14:C131**.
   c. Select the range **D12:G12**, and double-click the *Fill Handle* to copy the contents through **D13:G131**. (The values in the columns will not be correct until the formulas in all columns have been copied.)

C12	=Total_Cost_of_the_Loan
C13	=G12
D12	=C12*(Annual_Percentage_Rate/12)
E12	=Payment-D12
F12	=D12+E12
G12	=C12-F12

9. Save and close the workbook (Figure 2-72).

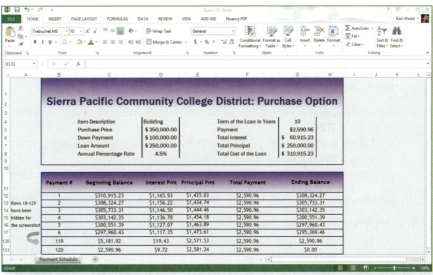

2-72 Excel 2-3 completed

Independent Project 2-4

Central Sierra Insurance (CSI) is a multi-office insurance company that handles all lines of commercial and personal insurance policies. CEO Eliana Lingle is planning to pay a bonus to employees calculated on each employee's base monthly salary. For this project, you create a spreadsheet for Ms. Lingle to summarize the bonus payments.
[Student Learning Outcomes 2.1, 2.2, 2.3, 2.4, 2.5, 2.6]

File Needed: *CentralSierra-02.xlsx*
Completed Project File Name: *[your initials] Excel 2-4.xlsx*

Skills Covered in This Project

- Create and copy formulas.
- Apply mathematical order of operations.
- Use relative, absolute, and mixed cell references.
- Use *AutoSum.*
- Apply the *VLOOKUP* function.
- Apply the *SUMIF* function.

1. Open the ***CentralSierra-02.xlsx*** workbook and save the workbook as *[your initials] Excel 2-4*.

2. Create a *VLOOKUP* function to calculate the bonus amount for each employee.
   a. Click the **Employees** sheet tab, and select **I4**.
   b. Type a formula to reference the *Base Monthly Salary* amount as the *lookup_value*.
   c. Click the **Bonus** sheet tab for the *table_array* argument.
   d. Use the second column of the table for the *col_index_num*.
   e. Verify that the formula syntax is =VLOOKUP(H4,Bonus!A4:B8,2).

3. Select the formula in **I4** and apply absolute values to the cell references.

4. Copy the formula in **I4** to **I5:I13**.

5. Type a formula in **J4** to calculate the total monthly salary.
   a. Use parentheses in the formula to calculate the amount of the bonus and then add the bonus to the *Base Monthly Salary*.
   b. Copy the formula in **J4** to **J5:J13**.

6. Select **J15** and use *AutoSum* to calculate a total for the *Total Monthly Salary* column.
   a. Edit the range.
   b. Apply the **Total** cell style to **J15**.

7. Create a *SUMIF* function to calculate the total monthly salary for each office.
   a. Select **B26**.
   b. Use the information in column **D** (Branch) for the range argument.
   c. Select **D4** (Cameron Park) for the criteria argument.
   d. Use the information in column **J** (Total Monthly Salary) for the sum_range argument.

8. Edit the formula in **B26** to include absolute cell references in all cell ranges.

9. Copy and edit a formula.
   a. Select the formula in **B26** and copy the formula through **B28**.
   b. Select **B27** and change the reference from Cameron Park (**D4**) to Folsom (**D8**).
   c. Select **B28** and change the reference from Cameron Park (**D4**) to Granite Bay (**D7**).

10. Select cell **B29** and create a formula to add the salary amounts for each branch.

11. Format the data in column **I** using the **Percent Style** button.

12. Format the salary amounts in columns **H** and **J** and the "Branch Totals" section to the **Accounting** style with no symbol.

13. Select the data from **A3:J30** and change the font to **Gill Sans MT** and the font size to **11 pt**.

14. Select **E26** and type Highest Salary.

15. Type Lowest Salary in **E27** and Average Salary in **E28**.

16. Select **F26** and type =ma. When you see *MAX*, double-click to insert the function. Drag to select **J4:J13**. Press **Enter** to complete the formula.

17. Select **F27** and use the **MIN** function to calculate the lowest salary.

18. Select **F28** and use the **AVERAGE** function to calculate the average salary.

19. Select **E25** and type Salary Summary.

20. Merge and center "Salary Summary" in cells **E25** and **F25**.

21. Format the "Salary Summary" section to match the "Branch Totals" section.
    a. Apply a fill color.
    b. Apply **All Borders** from the *Borders* button drop-down list.

22. Format the two total amounts (**B29** and **J15**) to include a dollar sign.

23. Adjust column widths if necessary.

24. Save and close the workbook (Figure 2-73).

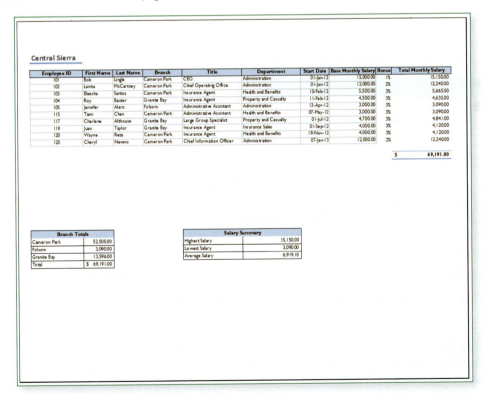

Central Sierra

Employee ID	First Name	Last Name	Branch	Title	Department	Start Date	Base Monthly Salary	Bonus	Total Monthly Salary
101	Bob	Lingle	Cameron Park	CEO	Administration	01-Jan-12	15,000.00	1%	15,150.00
102	Lanita	McCartney	Cameron Park	Chief Operating Office	Administration	01-Jan-12	12,000.00	2%	12,240.00
103	Beesha	Santos	Cameron Park	Insurance Agent	Health and Benefits	10-Feb-12	5,500.00	3%	5,665.00
104	Roy	Baxter	Granite Bay	Insurance Agent	Property and Casualty	11-Feb-12	4,500.00	3%	4,635.00
105	Jennifer	Alaro	Folsom	Administrative Assistant	Administration	13-Apr-12	3,000.00	3%	3,090.00
115	Tami	Chan	Cameron Park	Administrative Assistant	Health and Benefits	07-May-12	3,000.00	3%	3,090.00
117	Charlene	Althouse	Granite Bay	Large Group Specialist	Property and Casualty	01-Jul-12	4,700.00	3%	4,841.00
119	Juan	Taylor	Granite Bay	Insurance Agent	Insurance Sales	01-Sep-12	4,000.00	3%	4,120.00
120	Wayne	Reza	Cameron Park	Insurance Agent	Health and Benefits	19-Nov-12	4,000.00	3%	4,120.00
125	Cheryl	Nevens	Cameron Park	Chief Information Officer	Administration	07-Jan-13	12,000.00	2%	12,240.00

$ 69,191.00

Branch Totals	
Cameron Park	52,505.00
Folsom	3,090.00
Granite Bay	13,596.00
Total	$ 69,191.00

Salary Summary	
Highest Salary	15,150.00
Lowest Salary	3,090.00
Average Salary	6,919.10

2-73 Excel 2-4 completed

Independent Project 2-5

When San Diego Sailing received its end-of-year financial reports, its financial officers decided to evaluate the rental rates schedule for boats. You have been asked to create a spreadsheet to compare three different proposed rate changes that the group is considering implementing in the new year and to update information on the boat fleet.
[Student Learning Outcomes 2.1, 2.2, 2.3, 2.5]

File Needed: **SanDiego-02.xlsx**
Completed Project File Name: **[your initials] Excel 2-5.xlsx**

Skills Covered in This Project

- Create and copy formulas.
- Apply mathematical order of operations.
- Use relative, absolute, and mixed cell references.

- Apply the *IF* function.
- Name cells and use the name range in a formula.
- Apply the *TODAY* function.

1. Open the **SanDiego-02.xlsx** workbook and save the workbook as **[your initials] Excel 2-5**.

2. Select **H5** and create an *IF* function formula to determine which boats include a stove with the galley. Boats must be able to seat 8 or more people to have a stove in the galley.
   a. Use "Yes" for the *value_if_true* argument.
   b. Use "No" for the *value_if_false* argument.
   c. Copy the formula in **H5** to **H6:H19**.

3. Insert a worksheet and name the sheet Data.

4. Type the following information in the new worksheet:

	A	B
Row 3	Projected Increases	
Row 4	5% Increase	105%
Row 5	10% Increase	110%
Row 6	15% Increase	115%

5. Format the table text on the *Data* sheet.
   a. **Merge and Center** the text in **A3** over **A3:B3** and apply **bold** format.
   b. Apply **Accent 1** cell style to **A3**.
   c. Select **A3:B6** and apply the **All Borders** format.

6. Select **A4:B6** and assign range names using the **Create from Selection** button on the *Formulas* tab.

7. Select **J4** on the *Fleet* worksheet, and create a formula to calculate a 5% increase for the data in the "4 Hr. Rate" column using the range name assigned on the *Data* sheet.
   a. Type =.
   b. Select **F4** and type *.
   c. Press **F3** to open the *Paste Name* dialog box.
   d. Select **_5_Increase** and click **OK**.
   e. Press **Enter**.

8. Create formulas for **K4:O4** and copy the formulas to row 18.

9. Select the amounts in columns F, G, and J:O and apply **Currency** format with no symbol.

10. Select **A1** and type San Diego Sailing.

11. Format **A1** using the **Title** cell style and apply **bold** format. Adjust the column width.

12. Insert a row above the current row 2. Clear the formatting of the new row 2.

13. Insert the **TODAY()** function in **A2**. Format the date as **11 pt. bold** and align left.

14. Change the date format to display the month as a word followed by the day and year.

15. Apply the **All Borders** format to rows **4** through **19**.

16. Click the **Insert** tab and click the **Header & Footer** button.
    a. Switch to the *Footer* area.
    b. Click the right text box and type Page followed by a space.
    c. Click the **Page Number** button on the *Header & Footer Tools Design* tab.
    d. Click the worksheet and return to *Normal* view.

17. Paste range names in a worksheet.
    a. Click the **Data** sheet tab and select cell **A15**.
    b. Click the **Use in Formula** button [*Formulas* tab, *Defined Names* group].
    c. Click **Paste Names**.
    d. Click the **Paste List button** in the *Paste Name* dialog box.
    e. Click **OK**.

18. Save and close the workbook (Figure 2-74).

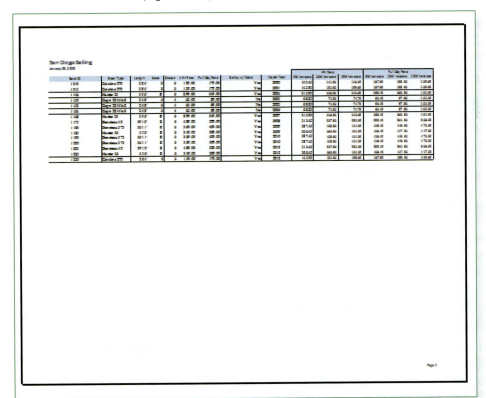

2-74 Excel 2-5 completed

Independent Project 2-6

Placer Hills Real Estate is a real estate company with regional offices throughout central California. In this project, you create a spreadsheet for the real estate company to provide summary information to its agents.
[Student Learning Outcomes 2.1, 2.2, 2.3, 2,4, 2.5]

File Needed: **PlacerHills-02.xlsx**
Completed Project File Name: **[your initials] Excel 2-6.xlsx**

Skills Covered in This Project

- Create and copy formulas.
- Apply mathematical order of operations.
- Use relative, absolute, and mixed cell references.
- Apply the AVERAGE, MAX, MIN, and COUNT functions.
- Apply the *VLOOKUP* function.

1. Open the **PlacerHills-02.xlsx** workbook and save the workbook as **[your initials] Excel 2-6**.

2. Type Placer Hills in cell **A1**, and apply the **Heading 1** style. Copy the contents of cell **A1** to the *Agent* worksheet cell **A1**.

3. Use the "SoldPrice" column data and the "ListPrice" column data on the *Listing* worksheet to calculate the percentage of list price.
   a. Select **O4**.
   b. Press = and click **N4**.
   c. Press / and click **C4**.

4. Copy the formula in **O4** to cells **O5:O12** and apply the **Percent Style** format to cells **O4:O12**.

5. Select **B20** and use the **Average** function to calculate the *Average List Price*.

6. Select **B21** and use the **Max** function to calculate the *Maximum List Price*.

7. Select **B22** and use the **Min** function to calculate the *Minimum List Price*.

8. Select **B23** and use the **Count** function to calculate the *Number of Listings*.

9. Calculate the number of brick homes by combining two functions.
   a. Select **B25**.
   b. Type =COUNTIF(
   c. Select **K4:K12**.
   d. Type ,"=Brick").
   e. Apply absolute cell references to the selected cell range.
   f. Press **Enter**.

10. Create individual formulas for **B26, B27, B29, B30, B31,** and **B32**, or copy the formula in **B25** and edit the formula.

11. Use the *VLOOKUP* function to insert the agent's last name in cells **E21:E26**.
    a. Use the agent number for the *lookup_value* argument.
    b. Use the table on the *Agent* sheet for the *table_array* argument.
    c. Use the *Last Name* column for the *col_index_num* argument.

d. Add absolute cell reference to the table_array argument.

e. Copy the formula in **B21** to **B22:B27**.

12. Select **D20:E26** and apply the **All Borders** format.

13. Format **D20:E20** with the **Accent 5** cell style and **bold** format.

14. Select **A3:O12** and apply the **All Borders** format.

15. Save and close the workbook (Figure 2-75).

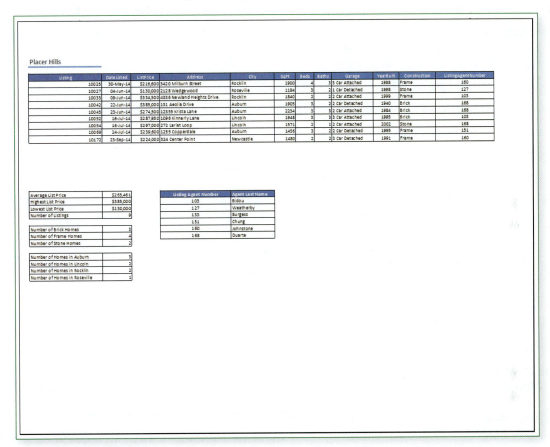

Improve It Project 2-7

Mary's Rentals serves the rental equipment needs of contractors and the general public. In this exercise you create formulas and format a spreadsheet for the rental company.
[Student Learning Outcomes 2.1, 2.2, 2.3, 2.4, 2.5, 2.6]

File Needed: *MarysRentals-02.xlsx*
Completed Project File Name: *[your initials] Excel 2-7.xlsx*

Skills Covered in This Project

- Create and copy formulas.
- Apply mathematical order of operations.
- Use relative, absolute, and mixed cell references.
- Edit formulas.
- Name cells and use range names in formulas.
- Apply the *SUM* function.
- Apply the *SUMPRODUCT* function.

---

1. Open the **MarysRentals-02.xlsx** workbook and save the workbook as **[your initials] Excel 2-7**.

2. Select **B20** and use the *SUMPRODUCT* function to create a formula to calculate income from daily rentals.
   a. Use **C5:C12** for the *array1* argument.
   b. Use **D5:D12** for the *array2* argument.

3. Create formulas for **B21** and **B22** using *SUMPRODUCT*.

4. Select **B23** and use **Sum** to calculate total rental income for the month of March.

5. Select **C5:C12** and name the range Daily.

6. Select **E5:E12** and name the range Weekly.

7. Select **G5:G12** and name the range Monthly.

8. Select **B26** and use the *Sum* function and the *Daily* range name to calculate the number of daily rentals.
   a. Type **=Su** to display a list of functions beginning with "SU."
   b. Double-click **SUM**.
   c. Type da to display a list of functions and range names.
   d. Double-click **Daily**.
   e. Press **Enter**.

9. Create formulas for **B27** and **B28** using *Sum* and range names.

10. Select **B29** and create a formula to add the **Daily**, **Weekly**, and **Monthly** range names together.

11. Change the theme to **Slice**.

12. Format **A1** and **A2**.
    a. **Merge & Center** the text in **A1** over **A1:H1**, and merge and center the text in **A2** over **A2:H2**.
    b. Edit **A2** to Month of March.
    c. Apply **Accent 1** cell style to **A1**.
    d. Apply **bold** formatting to **A1** and **A2**.
    e. Change the font size of **A1** to **18 pt**.

13. Format the column headings (**A4:H4**) with cell style **20% Accent 1**.

14. AutoFit column width and row height.

15. Format the numbers in columns **D, F**, and **H** using **Accounting** style with no symbol. Apply the **Accounting** style with no symbol format to cells **B20:B22**.

16. Apply **All Borders** to A4:H12, A20:B23, and **A26:B29**.

17. Change the orientation to **landscape**.

18. Save and close the workbook (Figure 2-76).

2-76 Excel 2-7 completed

Challenge Project 2-8

In this project, you create a spreadsheet to compare three purchase options you may be considering. Plan the spreadsheet layout so that a comparison of the three options is easy to read and understand.
[Student Learning Outcomes 2.1, 2.2, 2.3, 2.5]

File Needed: None
Completed Project File Name: *[your initials] Excel 2-8.xlsx*

Create and save a workbook as *[your initials] Excel 2-8*. Enter data in a spreadsheet that will be useful in planning a major purchase such as a car or home. Modify your workbook according to the following guidelines:

- Include headings to identify the cells. Headings may include "Description," "Loan Amount," "Term of the Loan," "Interest Rate," and "Payment." Assign range names to easily identify cell references in formulas.
- Create a *PMT* formula.
- Create a payment schedule with formulas.
- Add two sheets to your workbook. Create a second spreadsheet using the original parameters except change the interest rate. Calculate the amount of payment. Create a third spreadsheet using the original parameters except change the term of the loan. Calculate the amount of the payment.
- Add another sheet to the workbook to create a side-by-side comparison of the three loan scenarios.
- Include a date formula that automatically updates when you open the spreadsheet.
- Incorporate *Themes, Cell Styles,* and formatting.
- Include document properties and spell check your workbook.

Challenge Project 2-9

In this project, you create a spreadsheet to calculate your monthly expenditures and monthly income for one year. You also calculate the percentage of total expenses each of your individual expenses represents.
[Student Learning Outcomes 2.1, 2.2, 2.3, 2.4]

File Needed: None
Completed Project File Name: *[your initials] Excel 2-9.xlsx*

Create and save a blank workbook as *[your initials] Excel 2-9*. Plan the layout of the workbook to include one sheet for expenses and one sheet for income. You may want to plan a third sheet to compare expenses with income. Modify your workbook according to the following guidelines:

- On the income sheet, list all your sources of income including full-time and part-time employment. Arrange the data so that each column heading is a month of the year.
- On the expense sheet, place the months across the sheet and the expenses in the first column.
- Create a row of cells that lists the total expenses for each month. Consider grouping expenses by month, quarter, or year. Include subtotals for each section.
- Add a formula to calculate the percentage of your total expenses each expense represents. Use an absolute cell reference in the formula.
- Use formulas to calculate your net income, average income, and maximum income.
- Add a sheet to compare projected income and projected expenses for one month to actual income and actual expenses for one month.
- Incorporate *Themes, Cell Styles*, and formatting.
- Include document properties and spell check the workbook.

Challenge Project 2-10

In this project, you create a form for a store that sells and ships merchandise. You include a lookup table to calculate shipping costs and calculate the total cost of buying an item.
[Student Learning Outcomes 2.1, 2.2, 2.3, 2.4, 2.5, 2.6]

File Needed: None
Completed Project File Name: *[your initials] Excel 2-10.xlsx*

Create and save a blank workbook as *[your initials] Excel 2-10*. Modify your workbook according to the following guidelines:

- At the top of the spreadsheet, create a section to include the name of the store, address, telephone number, web site, and store hours.
- Include bill-to and ship-to sections. Arrange and format the data.
- Include a section below the bill-to and ship-to sections to include purchasing information such as "Item Number," "Quantity," "Item Description," "Price Subtotal," "Sales Tax," "Shipping," and "Total Cost."
- Name the worksheet tab and insert a second worksheet. Name the second sheet "Shipping Charges."
- On sheet 2 ("Shipping Charges"), create a *VLOOKUP* table for shipping charges. Use a price range to calculate charges. For example, for orders up to $50, the shipping cost is $6.95; for orders of $50.01 to $100.00, the shipping cost is $8.95; etc.
- Add borders and shading as well as cell styles and a theme to format the spreadsheets attractively.
- Use 6% as the sales tax rate.
- Add range names if appropriate.
- Add formulas to calculate the cost of buying an item including tax and shipping charges.
- Test the worksheet formulas.
- Include document properties and spell check the workbook.

Creating and Editing Charts

CHAPTER OVERVIEW

In addition to building formulas and functions in a worksheet, you can use Excel to graph or chart worksheet data. After selecting the correct data in a worksheet, you can quickly create a professional-looking chart with a few clicks of the mouse. This chapter introduces you to the basics of creating, editing, and formatting Excel charts.

STUDENT LEARNING OUTCOMES (SLOs)

After completing this chapter, you will be able to:

SLO 3.1 Create, size, and position an Excel chart object and create a chart sheet (p. E3-134).

SLO 3.2 Design a chart using *Quick Layouts* and chart styles (p. E3-137).

SLO 3.3 Switch row and column data, add or remove chart elements, change chart type, and edit source data (p. E3-141).

SLO 3.4 Format chart elements with shape styles, fill, outlines, and special effects (p. E3-148).

SLO 3.5 Use images, shapes, and *WordArt* in a chart (p. E3-152).

SLO 3.6 Create a pie chart and a combination chart (p. E3-157).

SLO 3.7 Insert and format sparklines in a worksheet (p. E3-161).

CASE STUDY

In the Pause & Practice projects in this chapter, you use Excel workbooks for the northern Minnesota resort business Paradise Lakes Resort (PLR). PLR has asked its managers to develop various charts for monthly sales data to better monitor the resort's business and to help formulate goals for next year.

Pause & Practice 3-1: Create and style charts in a workbook.

Pause & Practice 3-2: Edit and format charts in a workbook.

Pause & Practice 3-3: Create a combination chart and insert sparklines in a workbook.

Creating a Chart Object and a Chart Sheet

An Excel *chart* is a visual representation of numeric data in a worksheet. A chart helps you to easily identify trends, make comparisons, and recognize patterns in the numbers. Charts are dynamic and linked to the data, so if the numbers in your worksheet change, the chart is automatically redrawn.

There are different kinds of charts, and Excel can recommend the best chart type based on your selected data range or you can choose a chart type on your own. You can display a chart in the worksheet with the data or you can place a chart on its own sheet.

Create a Chart Object

A *chart object* is a selectable object surrounded by a square border that contains many customizable chart elements like data labels or a chart title. The chart elements are displayed as selectable components within the chart object. You can size and position a chart object on a worksheet.

Source data are the cells that contain values and labels to be graphed in the chart. In Figure 3-1, the source data includes the categories names, the month names, and four values for each of three months. Each of these values is a **data point**, a cell containing a

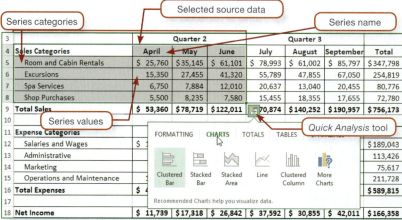

3-1 Source data and *Quick Analysis* suggestions

value. Each group of data points or values is a **data series**. In this example, Figure 3-1 sets up three data series for a clustered bar chart (the four items under each month). Each data series has a name (i.e., *April*, *May*, and *June*).

The text label that describes each data series is a **category label**. In Figure 3.1, the categories are the sales categories in column A (i.e., *Room and Cabin Rentals*, *Excursions*, *Spa Services*, and *Shop Purchases*).

> ### MORE INFO
> You can create a default chart object by selecting the appropriate data and pressing **Alt+F1**.

When you select source data that is adjacent (all the cells are next to each other), the **Quick Analysis** button appears at the lower right corner of the selection. The *Quick Analysis* tool lists tabs with the commands you are most likely to choose for your selected data, including *Charts*. After you click the *Charts* command, Excel displays recommended chart types. As you point to each chart type, you see a preview of the chart. This preview helps you to determine if you have selected the correct range. Click your preferred chart type to create a new chart object in the worksheet. The chart object is placed in the sheet next to the source data.

HOW TO: Create a Chart Object

1. Select the cell range that includes the data series and category labels you want to display in chart format.
2. Click the **Quick Analysis** button and select **Charts**.
3. Point at the preferred chart type and click to insert a chart (Figure 3-2).

> **MORE INFO**
>
> When the source data range is non-adjacent, the *Quick Analysis* tool does not display.

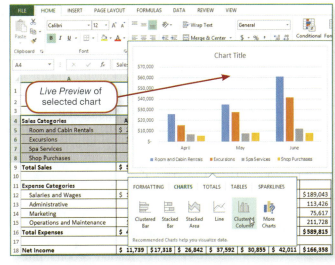

3-2 Chart object previewed

Excel Chart Types

Excel has many chart types that you can use to graph your data. Most chart types have several subtypes or variations. Excel recommends chart types based on your selected data, or you can choose the type of chart you want to use. The most common chart types are column or bar, line, and pie. Excel can also build powerful scientific and statistical charts when needed. The following table describes Excel chart types.

Excel Chart Types

Chart Type	Description	Category (Labels)	Values (Numbers)
Column	Illustrates data changes over a period of time or shows comparisons among items	Horizontal axis	Vertical axis
Bar	Displays comparisons among individual items or values at a specific period of time	Vertical axis	Horizontal axis
Pie	Uses one data series to display each value as a percentage of the whole		One data series shown by slice size
Line	Displays trends in data over time, emphasizing rate of change	Horizontal axis	Vertical axis
Area	Displays the magnitude of change over time and shows the rate of change	Horizontal axis	Vertical axis
XY (Scatter) or Bubble	Displays relationships among numeric values in two or more data series; these charts do not have a category	Horizontal axis (value 1-x)	Vertical axis (value 2-y)
Stock	Displays three series of data to show fluctuations in stock prices from high to low to close	Horizontal axis	Vertical axis
Surface	Displays optimum combinations of two sets of data on a surface	Horizontal axis (value 1-x)	Horizontal axis (value 1-x)
Radar	Displays the frequency of multiple data series relative to a center point. There is an axis for each category	NA	NA
Combo Chart	Uses two types of charts to graph values that are widely different	Either	Either

Size and Position a Chart Object

A chart object can be selected, sized, and positioned. When you select a chart object or it is active, it is surrounded by eight selection handles. A **selection handle** is a small round or rectangular shape on each corner and in the middle of each side. When you point at a selection handle, the pointer changes to a two-pointed arrow that you drag to make the chart smaller or larger. Drag a corner handle to size both height and width of the chart proportionally.

To move a chart object, point at the chart background to display a four-pointed move pointer. Then drag the chart to the desired location.

> ▶ **MORE INFO**
>
> When a chart object is selected, the *Chart Tools* tabs are visible in the *Ribbon* and three *Quick Chart Tools* are available at the top right corner of the object.

HOW TO: Move and Size a Chart Object

1. Select the chart object (Figure 3-3).
2. Place your pointer on the outside border of the chart to display a move pointer.
3. Drag the chart object to a new location and release.
4. Place your pointer on a selection handle to display a resize pointer.
5. Drag the pointer to resize the chart.

3-3 Selected chart object and move pointer

Creating a Chart Sheet

A *chart sheet* is an Excel chart that is displayed on its own sheet in the workbook. The chart sheet does not include rows, columns, and cells like a regular worksheet, but the chart is linked to its data on another worksheet.

When you create a chart from the *Quick Analysis* tool or from the *Insert* tab in the *Ribbon*, Excel creates a chart object. You can move any chart object that you have already created to its own sheet using the *Chart Tools Design* tab. When you do that, Excel moves the chart to a new sheet named *Chart1, Chart2*, and so on. You can type a new name for the chart sheet in the *Move Chart* dialog box. You can also create a new chart sheet from a new chart object.

From the *Charts* group on the *Insert* tab, you can click the **Recommended Charts** button or the specific chart type button to create the chart object.

HOW TO: Create a Chart Sheet

1. Select the cell range that includes the data series and category labels you want to display in chart format.
   - If the cell range is non-adjacent, hold down the **Ctrl** key to select each range (Figure 3-4).
2. Click the **Recommended Charts** button [*Insert* tab, *Charts* group].

3. Click the preferred chart type.

4. Click **OK**.

5. Click the **Move Chart** button [*Chart Tools Design* tab, *Location* group].

6. Click the **New sheet** radio button (Figure 3-5).

7. Type the name of the new sheet tab.

8. Click **OK**.

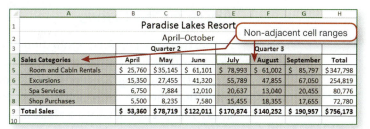

3-4 Source data ranges that are not next to each other

3-5 *Move Chart* dialog box

> **ANOTHER WAY**
>
> To move a chart object to its own sheet, right-click the chart object and choose **Move Chart**.

> **MORE INFO**
>
> You can create a default chart sheet for selected data by pressing **F11**.

SLO 3.2 **Designing a Chart with Quick Layouts and Styles**

Excel has many tools to help you develop consistent and appealing designs for your charts. From the *Chart Tools Design* tab, you can apply different chart layouts or choose from predefined styles. These choices affect the appearance of the entire chart.

Apply a Quick Layout

A **chart layout** is the complete set of elements that is displayed in the chart. These include parts of a chart such as the main title, axis titles, legend, and others. The *Quick Layout* command allows you to choose from 10 predefined layouts. After selecting a *Quick Layout*, you can add or remove individual chart elements, too.

To apply a *Quick Layout* use the **Quick Layout** button in the *Chart Layouts* group on the *Chart Tools Design* tab. As you point to each layout option, *Live Preview* redraws your chart so that you can decide if the layout is right for your needs.

HOW TO: Apply a Quick Layout to a Chart

1. Click the chart object or the chart sheet.

2. Click the **Quick Layout** button [*Chart Tools Design* tab, *Chart Layouts* group].

3. Point to a layout to preview its effect.

4. Click the preferred **Layout** (Figure 3-6).

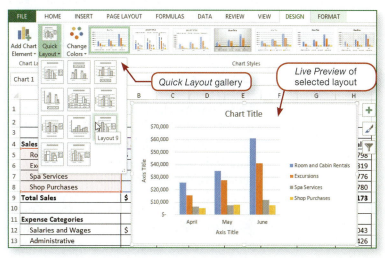

3-6 *Quick Layout* gallery

Apply a Chart Style

A **chart style** is a preset combination of colors and effects for a chart, its background, and its elements. The chart styles that are available for a chart are based on the current workbook theme. If you change the workbook theme, the chart style colors are updated, and your chart will reflect the new color palette. You can find chart styles in the *Chart Styles* group on the *Chart Tools Design* tab. Like a chart layout, you can preview the effects of a chart style as you point to each style in the gallery.

HOW TO: Apply a Chart Style

1. Select the chart object or the chart sheet.
2. Click the desired **Style** button [*Chart Tools Design* tab, *Chart Styles* group].
   - Click the **More** button [*Chart Tools Design* tab, *Chart Styles* group] to display the entire *Chart Styles* gallery (Figure 3-7).

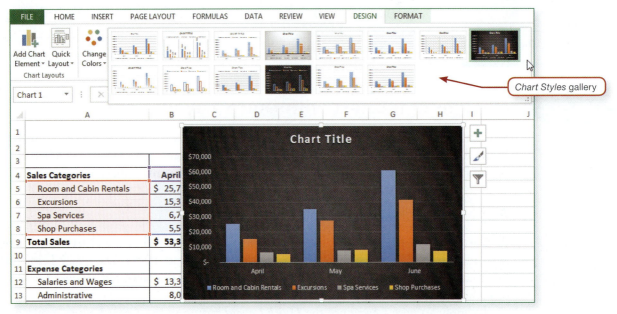

3-7 *Chart Styles* gallery and preview of selected style

> ▶ **MORE INFO**
> Chart styles may affect the current chart layout.

Print a Chart

You can print chart objects with the worksheet data or individually. When you want to print a worksheet with the chart object, you need to size and position the chart so that it fits on the page or scale the sheet to fit the complete worksheet contents. You can choose whether the data and chart should print in portrait or landscape orientation and you can insert headers or footers as well in a worksheet.

> ▶ **MORE INFO**
> Use the *Page Setup* dialog box or the *Insert* tab to insert a header or footer on a chart sheet.

You can print a chart sheet with a regular *Print* command. By default, a chart sheet prints in landscape orientation.

To print a chart object with its source data, click any cell in the worksheet. Then use the *Print* command from the *File* tab in the *Backstage* view and make your usual print choices. If you prefer to print a chart object on its own sheet, select the object first and then choose print.

HOW TO: Print a Chart with its Source Data

1. Click any cell in the worksheet.
   - To print a chart sheet, click the sheet tab.
2. Click the **File** tab to open the *Backstage* view (Figure 3-8).
3. Select **Print** at the left and set print options if necessary.
4. Click **Print**.

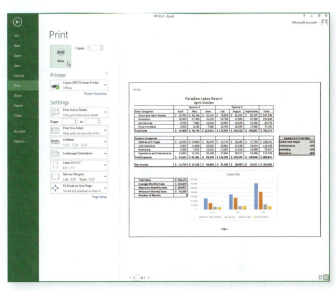

3-8 *Backstage* view, print options

PAUSE & PRACTICE: EXCEL 3-1

Charts illustrate worksheet data and make it clearer and easy to understand. For this project you insert a clustered column chart object in a worksheet that tracks sales and expenses for Paradise Lakes Resort. You also insert a clustered bar chart sheet to highlight second quarter results.

File Needed: **ParadiseLakes-03.xlsx**
Completed Project File Name: **[your initials] PP E3-1.xlsx**

1. Open the **ParadiseLakes-03** workbook.

2. Save this document as **[your initials] PP E3-1**.

3. Create a chart object.
   a. Select the cell range **A4:D8** for your chart.
   b. Click the **Quick Analysis** button and choose the **Charts** tab.
   c. Click **Clustered Column**.

4. Position and size the chart object.
   a. Click the chart object if it is not selected.
   b. Point at the chart area to display a move pointer.
   c. Drag the chart object so that its top left corner is at cell **C20**.

d. Point at the lower right selection handle to display a resize pointer.

e. Drag the pointer to reach cell **H35** as shown in Figure 3-9.

5. Apply a *Quick Layout*.
   a. Click the chart object if necessary.
   b. Click the **Quick Layout** button [*Chart Tools Design* tab, *Chart Layouts* group].
   c. Click **Layout 7**.

6. Create a chart sheet.
   a. Select the cell range **A4:A8**.
   b. Hold down **Ctrl** and select the cell range **E4:G8**.
   c. Click the **Recommended Charts** button [*Insert* tab, *Charts* group].
   d. Select **Clustered Bar**.
   e. Click **OK**.
   f. Click the **Move Chart** button [*Chart Tools Design* tab, *Location* group].
   g. Click the **New sheet** radio button.
   h. Type Quarter 3 as the new sheet name.
   i. Click **OK**.

7. Choose a chart style.
   a. Click the **Chart Styles** More button [*Chart Tools Design* tab, *Chart Styles* group] to display the gallery.
   b. Click **Style 10** (Figure 3-10).

8. Preview the charts.
   a. Select the **Quarter 3** sheet if necessary.
   b. Click the **File** tab to open the *Backstage* view.
   c. Click **Print** at the left to preview the chart sheet (see Figure 3-11).
   d. Click the **Back** button to return to the worksheet.
   e. Select the **Location 1 Cass Lake** sheet.
   f. Click cell **A1**.
   g. Click the **File** tab to open the *Backstage* view.
   h. Click **Print** to preview the worksheet and chart object.
   i. Click the **Back** button to return to the worksheet.

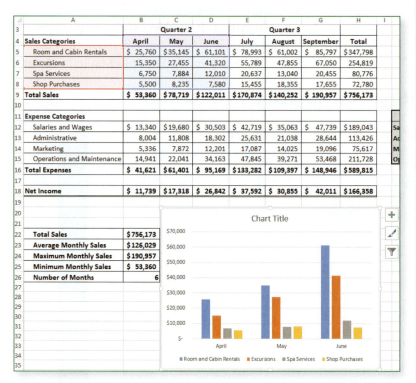

3-9 Chart object sized and positioned

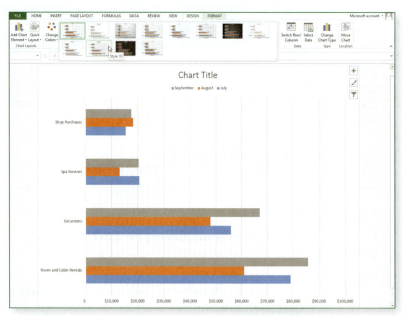

3-10 Chart sheet with new style

9. Save and close the workbook (Figure 3-11).

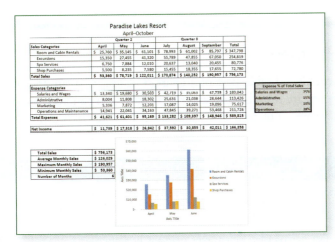
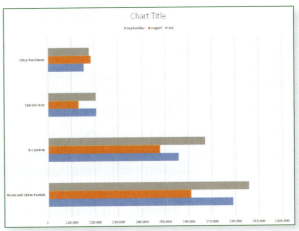

3-11 PP E3-1 completed chart object and chart sheet

SLO 3.3

Editing a Chart

You can edit a chart in many ways. For example, you will want to edit the contents of the placeholder text boxes that are inserted in your chart if you use a *Quick Layout*, or you might insert a legend to explain colors used for a data series. You can also add data labels that indicate the actual values on the chart, or you might decide to switch row and column data.

Switch Row and Column Data

When you choose a recommended chart, Excel plots the data series based on the number of rows and columns selected in the worksheet and the chart type. If you prefer, however, you can choose which data series is plotted on the X-axis and which is plotted on the Y-axis. In a column chart, by default, the X-axis is along the bottom of the chart; the y-axis is along the left.

HOW TO: Switch Row and Column Data

1. Click the chart object or chart sheet tab.
2. Click the **Switch Row/Column** button [*Chart Tools Design* tab, *Data* group] (Figure 3-12).
   - Click the **Switch Row/Column** button [*Chart Tools Design* tab, *Data* group] to toggle how the columns and rows are plotted.

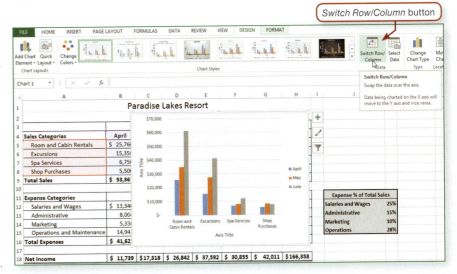

3-12 Column and row data switched

▶ ANOTHER WAY

Click the **Chart Filters** button in the top right corner of a selected chart and click **Select Data** at the bottom of the pane to switch the row and column data.

Add and Remove Chart Elements

A **chart element** is a separate, clickable, editable part of a chart. The chart layout and style that you choose affect which elements are initially displayed in a chart. You can add, remove, and format individual elements in a chart. The following table describes the chart elements.

Excel Chart Elements

Element	Description
Axis	Horizontal or vertical boundary that identifies what is plotted (the plural of axis is axes)
Axis title	Optional title for the categories or values
Chart area	Background for the chart; can be filled with a color, gradient, or pattern
Chart floor	Base or bottom for a 3-D chart
Chart title	Optional title or name for the chart
Chart wall	Vertical background or wall for a 3-D chart
Data label	Optional element that displays values with the marker for each data series
Data marker	Element that represents individual values. The marker is a bar, a column, a slice, or a point on a line
Data point	A single value or piece of data from a data series
Data series	Group of related values that are in the same column or row and translate into the columns, lines, pie slices, and other markers
Gridline	Horizontal or vertical line that extends across the plot area to help in identifying values
Horizontal (category) axis	Describes what is shown in the chart and is created from row or column headings. In a bar chart, the category axis is the vertical axis; the category axis is the horizontal axis in a column chart
Legend	Element that explains the symbols, textures, or colors used to differentiate data series
Plot area	Rectangular area bounded by the horizontal and vertical axes
Tick mark	Small line or marker on an axis to guide in reading values
Trendline	Displays averages in your data and can be used to forecast data by plotting future approximate averages
Vertical (value) axis	Shows the numbers on the chart. In a bar chart, the vertical axis is along the bottom; in a column chart, the vertical axis is along the side

You can show or remove chart elements by clicking the **Chart Elements** button to the right of the chart. When you click the button, the *Chart Elements* pane opens. In this pane, click the corresponding box to show or remove the element. To hide the pane, click the *Chart Elements* button again.

▶ ANOTHER WAY

Click the **Add Chart Elements** button [*Chart Tools Design* tab, *Chart Layouts* group] to add or remove a chart element.

When you point at a chart element, a ScreenTip describes the element. You can click the element to select it and make it active. When a chart element is active, it is surrounded by selection handles, as shown in Figure 3-13. The name of an active element also appears in the *Chart Elements* box on the *Chart Tools Format* tab.

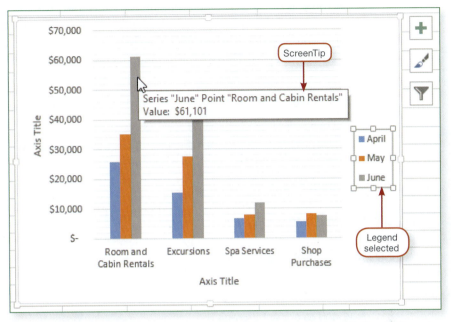

3-13 Selected legend and ScreenTip for a data series

Chart and Axes Titles

Some chart layouts include a placeholder or text box for a main chart title and axes titles. When a placeholder is shown, you need to edit the sample text to fit your data. When the layout does not include a placeholder title, you can add a placeholder or text box and then edit the text.

You can position a main chart title above the chart or within the chart area. Once you have created a text box, you can select it and move it anywhere on the chart. You can use an axis title to clarify what is represented by the categories or the values. However, keep in mind that many times an axis title is not required because the chart itself represents the data well.

HOW TO: Add a Chart Title

1. Click the chart object or chart sheet.
2. Click the **Chart Elements** button to the right of the chart.
3. Click to place a check mark next to **Chart Title** (Figure 3-14).
4. Click the menu arrow to choose a position for the title.
5. Type the title and press **Enter**.
   - To edit the chart title, triple-click the *Chart Title* placeholder, type the title, and click the chart background to deselect the element.

3-14 Chart title element added to chart object

In addition to adding and removing elements, you can edit placeholder text that is automatically placed in your chart when you select a chart layout or style. Select the element and type the new title. As you type a title, it appears in the *Formula bar*. It is placed in the chart when you press **Enter**.

If you select the placeholder element, you can triple-click the text to select all of it and display the mini toolbar. You can type new data and use the commands on the mini toolbar to reformat it. After you type the new text, click the chart background to deselect the element and complete your edit. If you press **Enter** while typing in a text box, you insert a second line for the title.

> **MORE INFO**
> Double-clicking a chart element opens its *Format* pane.

HOW TO: Edit Placeholder Text

1. Click the placeholder text box to display the selection handles.
2. Point at the label and triple-click to select all the text (Figure 3-15).
3. Type the new title.
4. Click the chart background to accept the edit.

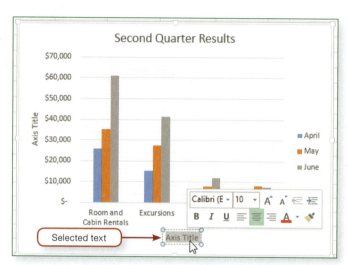

3-15 Placeholder text to be edited

You can delete chart elements when they are not necessary. For example, in a chart that illustrates dollar sales such as the one in Figure 3-15, the values on the vertical (y-axis) represent the amount of the sales. In a case like this, the vertical axis title is probably not necessary. To delete a chart element, click it to select it and press **Delete**. The chart may resize when certain elements are deleted.

Data Labels

Data labels display the value of a column, bar, pie slice, or other marker. Because the value axis uses a scale, it cannot show exact numbers, but a data label can.

HOW TO: Add Data Labels

1. Select the chart object or chart sheet.
2. Click the **Chart Elements** button to the right of the chart.
3. Click to place a check mark for **Data Labels**.
4. Click the menu arrow to choose a position for the labels (Figure 3-16).

3-16 Data labels shown outside bar markers

Data Table

A *data table* displays a table of the values of each data series based on your selected source data cells. You can add a data table to the bottom of your chart with or without legend markers (e.g., a mini legend to the left of the data table). By default, Excel does not include data tables with charts. To add a data table below your chart, use the *Data Table* button on the *Chart Tools Design* tab in the *Chart Layouts* group (Figure 3-17).

3-17 *Data Table* options

Trendlines

After adding chart elements, you may want to see any trends that occur. It is also useful to display trends in data to help predict future values. For example, a manager may need to forecast the next quarter's sales based on historical numbers. A *trendline* is a chart element that demonstrates averages in your data and that can be used to forecast data by plotting future approximate averages.

HOW TO: Add a Trendline to a Chart

1. Click the chart if it is not already selected.
2. Click the **Chart Elements** customization button in the top right corner of the chart.
3. Place your pointer over the *Trendline* check box until the arrow button appears and then click the **Trendline** arrow button.
4. Select the type of trendline you want to apply (Figure 3-18) to open the *Add Trendline* dialog box (Figure 3-19).
5. Select the data series you want to apply the *Trendline* to.
6. Click **OK** (Figure 3-20).

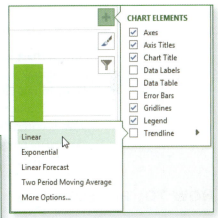

3-18 *Trendline* options

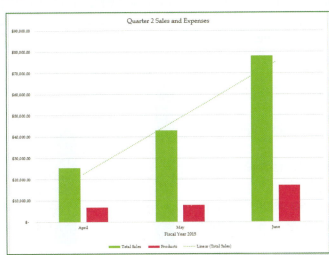

3-20 **2-D clustered column chart with "Total Sales" linear trendline**

3-19 *Add Trendline* dialog box

Change the Chart Type

It is possible to change the chart type. For example, you may decide to change some bar charts into column charts for consistency in a report to make it easier for your audience to quickly compare one chart to the next, or you might decide to use 3-D pie charts instead of 2-D.

> **MORE INFO**
>
> Excel 3-D charts add the perception of depth to a chart.

HOW TO: Change the Chart Type

1. Click the chart object or chart sheet.
2. Click the **Change Chart Type** button [*Chart Tools Design* tab, *Type* group].
3. Click the *Recommended Charts* tab.
4. Scroll the chart types in the left pane and click a tile to see a larger preview in the right pane.
5. Choose the preferred chart type and click **OK** (Figure 3-21).

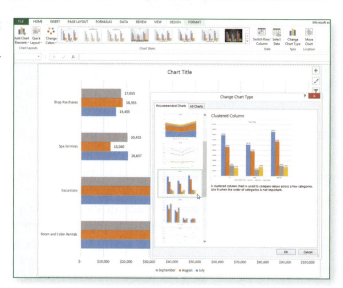

3-21 *Change Chart Type* options for selected chart sheet

Filter the Source Data

Once a chart is created, you can refine which data is displayed in the chart without changing the original source data range. This allows you to switch between several scenarios for your data without changing the underlying cell range.

You can accomplish this by applying a filter to either the values, the categories, or both. A *filter* is criteria that specifies which data is shown and which is hidden. Filters do not alter the source data range so you can return to the initial chart at any time.

HOW TO: Filter Source Data

1. Select the chart object or chart sheet.
2. Click the **Chart Filters** button in the top right corner of the chart.
   - The *Chart Filters* button is the bottom button and resembles a funnel-type filter.
3. Click to remove the check mark for the series or category you want to hide.
4. Click **Apply** (Figure 3-22).
5. Click the **Chart Filters** button to close the pane.

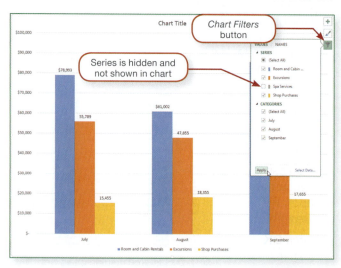

3-22 *Chart Filters* pane

Edit a Chart Data Source

In addition to filtering chart data, you can edit the existing chart data source or add a data series to a chart. In a column chart, adding a data series adds another column. To add a data series to a chart object, drag the sizing pointer in the lower right corner of the data range to expand or reduce the data range, as shown in Figure 3-23. Reducing the data range deletes the data series from the chart. To add a data series to a chart sheet, you use the *Select Data Source* dialog box.

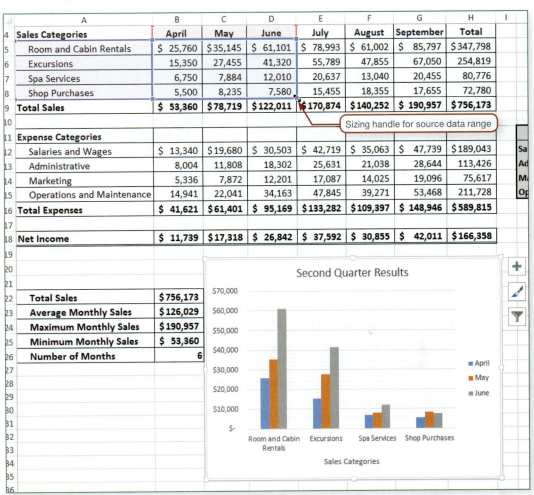

3-23 Chart object selected, sizing handle visible

While a chart filter does not change the source data range, editing the data source or adding a data series does change the source data range in the worksheet.

HOW TO: Add a Data Series in a Chart Sheet

1. Click the chart sheet.
2. Click the **Select Data** button [*Chart Tools Design* tab, *Data* group] to open the *Select Data Source* dialog box.
   - When the source data range is adjacent, you can click the **Collapse** button at the right of the *Chart data range* text box and drag to select a new range. Then click the **Expand** button and click **OK**.

3. Edit the cell references in the *Chart data range* text box to identify the new range (Figure 3-24).

4. Click **OK**.

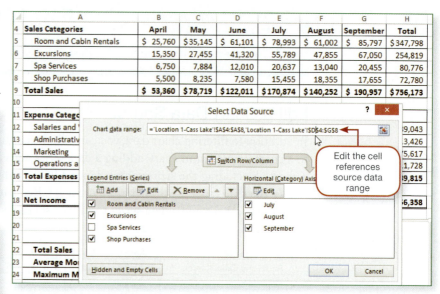

	A	B	C	D	E	F	G	H
4	Sales Categories	April	May	June	July	August	September	Total
5	Room and Cabin Rentals	$ 25,760	$35,145	$ 61,101	$ 78,993	$ 61,002	$ 85,797	$347,798
6	Excursions	15,350	27,455	41,320	55,789	47,855	67,050	254,819
7	Spa Services	6,750	7,884	12,010	20,637	13,040	20,455	80,776
8	Shop Purchases	5,500	8,235	7,580	15,455	18,355	17,655	72,780
9	Total Sales	$ 53,360	$78,719	$122,011	$170,874	$140,252	$ 190,957	$756,173

3-24 *Select Data Source* dialog box for a chart sheet

▶ **ANOTHER WAY**

You can open the *Select Data Source* dialog box by clicking **Select Data** in the *Chart Filters* pane.

▶ **MORE INFO**

You can apply or remove filters from the *Select Data Source* dialog box.

SLO 3.4

Formatting Chart Elements

In *SLO 3.2* and *SLO 3.3* you saw how you can quickly change the overall appearance and layout of a chart using *Quick Layouts* and *Chart Styles* and by adding or deleting chart elements. These commands are the first stages of designing a chart, but you will usually want to add your own format choices too.

Being able to personalize your charts is important. For example, your employer may have specific design requirements, or you may want to use colors and shapes from your organization or school in a chart. In either case, there are a variety of ways to enhance your charts to increase their readability.

▶ **MORE INFO**

Making your own format choices enables you to distinguish your charts from those of other Excel users.

You can format each element in a chart. Some chart elements consist of a group of related elements. A data series, for example, is the group of values for a particular item. Within each data series, there are several data points. You can format the entire data series or an individual data point.

When you select an individual chart element, certain options on the *Chart Tools Design* tab apply to only that element. For example, when the chart area (background) is selected, you can change its fill or border color.

Apply a Shape Style

A **Shape Style** is a predesigned set of borders, fill colors, and effects for a chart element. **Shape fill** is the background color for the element. **Shape outline** is the border around an element. **Shape effects** include shadows, glows, bevels, or soft edges.

You choose a shape style from the gallery. As soon as you click the style, it is applied to the selected element and you see the results. There is a *Live Preview* for chart elements, and you can click the **Undo** button to remove the style if you change your mind after selecting it.

HOW TO: Apply a Shape Style

1. Click the chart element to select it.
   - Select a chart element by name by clicking the **Chart Elements** drop-down arrow [*Chart Tools Format* tab, *Current Selection* group] and choosing the element.
   - If the *Format* pane for the chart element opens, close it.
2. Click the **More** button [*Chart Tools Format* tab, *Shape Styles* group] to open the *Shape Styles* gallery (Figure 3-25).
3. Click the selected style.

3-25 *Shape Style* gallery for the chart area

Apply Shape Fill, Outline, and Effects

Once you select a chart element, you can apply fill color, set outline width and color, or special effects. These three format options are available in the *Shape Styles* group on the *Chart Tools Format* tab. If a *Shape Style* has already been applied to the object, individual choices override the style.

When you set a fill color, you choose from the workbook theme colors shown in the gallery. In addition to theme colors, the standard colors are also available, or you can build a custom color. After you choose a color, you can refine it to use a ***gradient***, a variegated blend of the color.

Live Preview is available for shape fill so you can preview the results of your choice before committing to it. To preview, just point at a color tile in the gallery. When you find the color you want, click the color tile.

The *Shape Fill, Shape Outline,* and *Shape Effects* buttons apply the choice you made most recently when you click the icon. To make a choice from a gallery, click the drop-down arrow for the option.

HOW TO: Apply Gradient Fill to a Chart Element

1. Click the chart element.
2. Click the **Shape Fill** button drop-down arrow [*Chart Tools Format* tab, *Shape Styles* group].
   - Click the button icon to apply the most recently used color.
3. Select the desired color.
4. Click the **Shape Fill** drop-down arrow again.
5. Choose **Gradient** (Figure 3-26) to open the gallery.
6. Click the preferred gradient.

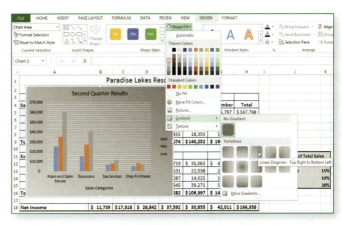

3-26 *Shape Fill* gallery and *Gradient* gallery

The outline for a shape is the border that surrounds or encircles the element. Not all chart elements are suited to an outline, but elements such as the chart or plot area often benefit from the use of an outline. When you add an outline to a chart element, you can select a weight or thickness for the line as well as a color. The thickness of an outline is measured in points, like fonts. Excel provides a gallery of weights to help you visualize the width. After you set an outline, it is easier to see the effect if you deselect the chart object.

HOW TO: Apply an Outline to a Chart Element

1. Click the chart element.
2. Click the **Shape Outline** button drop-down arrow [*Chart Tools Format* tab, *Shape Styles* group].
   • Click the button icon to apply the most recently used outline color and weight.
3. Click the desired color for the outline.
4. Click the **Shape Outline** drop-down arrow again.
5. Click **Weight**.
6. Choose a point size (Figure 3-27).

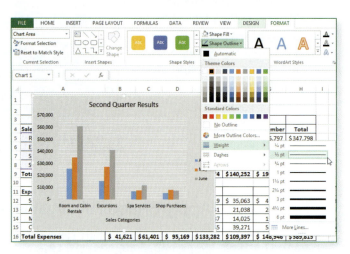

3-27 *Outline color* and *Weight* galleries

You can also apply special effects to a chart element. Popular effects include bevels and shadows, which give the element a realistic, three-dimensional look. These types of effects are best used on larger elements, such as the chart area, because they can overwhelm smaller elements.

HOW TO: Apply an Effect to a Chart Element

1. Click the chart element.
2. Click the **Shape Effects** button [*Chart Tools Format* tab, *Shape Styles* group].
3. Click the desired effect group for the object (Figure 3-28).
4. Choose the effect.

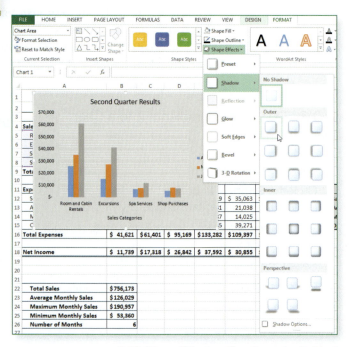

3-28 *Shape Effects* gallery for a chart object

To remove an effect, select the element and click the **Shape Effects** button drop-down arrow. Choose the type of effect and click the first option such as **No Shadow** or **No Bevel**.

The Format Task Pane

You can apply many format choices quickly from the *Chart Tools Format* tab. There are, however, several options for chart elements that are not available on the tab. Every chart element has a *Format* task pane that consolidates shape, fill, and color options and provides custom commands for the element (Figure 3-29).

To open the *Format* pane for a chart element, double-click the element or right-click it and choose *Format [Element Name]* from the menu. The *Format* pane opens to the right of the workbook window and automatically changes to reflect the selected element. For example, if you display the task pane for a data series and then select the chart title, the pane changes to the *Chart Title Format* pane.

3-29 *Format Data Series* pane

> **ANOTHER WAY**
>
> Open a *Format* task pane by clicking the **Format Selection** button [*Chart Tools Format* tab, *Selection* group].

> **MORE INFO**
>
> Expand or collapse a command group in the *Format* task pane by clicking the small triangle to the left of the group name.

Most *Format* task panes have three buttons at the top: *Fill & Line*, *Effects*, and *Options*. When you click a button, the pane displays the relevant commands. *Fill & Line* and *Effects* are similar for all chart elements. The *Options* panes are specific to the element.

HOW TO: Use the Format Task Pane to Change Shape Fill

1. Double-click the chart element.
   - Verify the name of the task pane. If the wrong task pane opens, click the element again.
   - You can also select an element from the **Chart Elements** button drop-down arrow [*Chart Tools Format* tab, *Current Selection* group].
2. Click the **Fill & Line** button in the *Format* task pane.
3. Click **Fill** to expand the group.
4. Click the **Fill Color** button to open the gallery.
5. Click the desired color (Figure 3-30).

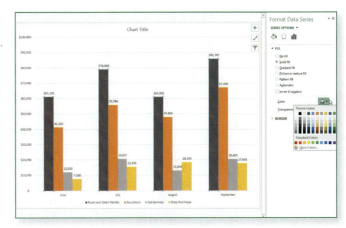

3-30 *Fill & Line* command in the *Format* task pane

There is an *Effects* command group in many *Format* task panes with the same options as the *Ribbon*. You can set shadows, bevels, glows, and more, depending on the selected element. Use these commands sparingly in most charts. Overuse of these commands can make the chart look too busy and overdesigned.

An *Options* group in a *Format* task pane is the command set that enables you to accomplish tasks that are specific to the type of element you select. For a data series in a column chart, for example, these commands determine whether numbers are shown on the right or left of the chart (secondary or primary axis), or you can choose to have the columns overlap. A pie chart, on the other hand, has series options that allow you to rotate the pie and explode the slices.

HOW TO: Use the Format Task Pane to Set Data Label Options

1. Double-click a data label element.
   - Right-click the element and choose **Format [Element Name]**.
   - If you have difficulty selecting the desired element, click the *Options* triangle next to the group name and choose the element from the drop-down list.
2. Click the **Label Options** button in the *Format* task pane.
3. Click **Label Options** or **Number** to expand the group.
4. Enter your format preferences in the task pane (Figure 3-31).

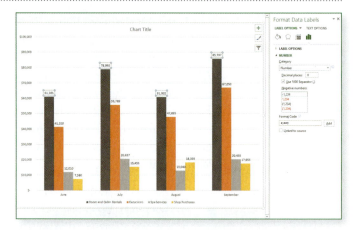

3-31 *Format Data Labels* pane

Using Images, Shapes, and WordArt in a Chart

A chart includes several selectable elements as part of its basic layout. You can add images, shapes, or *WordArt* in a chart to further personalize it. For example, a chart that illustrates the number of fish caught in a tournament could use a small image of a fish as fill for a data series rather than a fill color, or you might add a shape as a callout to a particular data point on a chart, such as a star to highlight the best sales record. You can also replace a chart title box with *WordArt* for a distinctive look.

Pictures, shapes, or *WordArt* are chart elements that you can size, position, and format.

Use a Picture as Shape Fill

In a chart, you can fill bars, columns, or pie slices with a picture that helps illustrate the data. To clarify, you might use a small stick-figure in a chart that graphs numbers of customers. You can use images that are filed on your computer or external storage device. You can search for and insert an online image, or you can copy an image from another application.

The size and design of an image are important. You cannot edit all images in Excel, so you may have to experiment with pictures to learn what works well in your charts. For example, you may not be able to change the color of a picture, or it may have a transparent background.

When you use a picture as a fill, you can use the ***Stretch*** option to stretch it across the data marker. This places a single copy of the image and stretches it to fill the shape. The ***Stack*** options resizes the picture to fit the width of the marker and repeats it to signify the values represented. There is also a ***Stack and Scale*** setting for more detailed sizing and placement of the picture.

HOW TO: Use a Picture as Fill

1. Select the data series and open its *Format* task pane.
2. Click the **Fill & Line** button in the *Format* task pane.
3. Click **Fill** to expand the group.
4. Click the **Picture or texture fill** button to open the gallery.
5. Click **Online** to search for an image or click **File** to choose a stored image.
6. Find and select the image you want to use as fill.
7. Click **Stack** to scale and repeat the image (Figure 3-32).

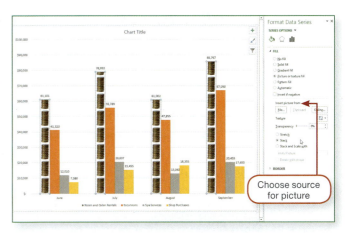

3-32 Online image used as fill for data series

Insert Shapes

Shapes such as arrows, circles, or callouts can be used to highlight important parts of a chart. For example, you can insert an arrow shape to emphasize the highest sales month or add a banner with text to congratulate the sales team.

The shapes that are available for use on a chart are the same shapes available in other Office applications. The *Shapes* gallery opens when you click the **More** button from the *Insert Shapes* group on the *Chart Tools Format* tab.

Once you place a shape in a chart, you can select it and format it from the *Picture Tools Format* tab.

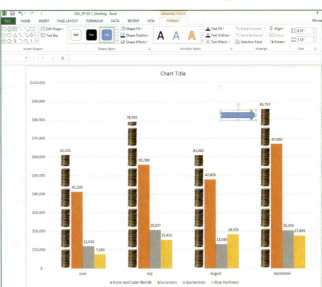

HOW TO: Insert a Shape in a Chart

1. Select the chart object or chart sheet.
2. Click the **More** button [*Chart Tools Format* tab, *Insert Shapes* group].
3. Select the shape.
4. Click and drag to draw the shape on the chart (Figure 3-33).
5. Format the shape as needed.
6. Add text to the shape by right-clicking and selecting **Edit Text** from the context-sensitive menu.

3-33 Shape inserted in chart

Use WordArt in a Chart

WordArt is a text box with preset font style, fill, and text effects. You might use *WordArt* in a chart in place of a regular chart title. You can apply a *WordArt* style to an existing chart title, or if a chart has no title, you can insert a *Text Box* shape and format it with a *WordArt* style.

HOW TO: Use WordArt in a Chart

1. Select the chart title or other chart element.
2. Click the **More** button to display *WordArt Styles* [*Chart Tools Format* tab, *WordArt Styles* group].
3. Click the preferred style (Figure 3-34).

3-34 *WordArt Style* gallery for selected chart title

PAUSE & PRACTICE: EXCEL 3-2

For this project, you open your first Pause & Practice file to edit and format the Paradise Lakes Resort charts. You switch row and column data and add and delete several chart elements. You also change the chart type so that the two charts in the workbook are consistent. Finally, you format the charts for easier reading.

File Needed: *[your initials] PP E3-1.xlsx*
Completed Project File Name: *[your initials] PP E3-2.xlsx*

1. Open the *[your initials] PP E3-1* workbook.
2. Save the workbook as *[your initials] PP E3-2*.
3. Switch the row and column data in the chart object.
   a. Click the **Location 1-Cass Lake** worksheet tab.
   b. Click the chart object.
   c. Click the **Switch/Row Column** button [*Chart Tools Design* tab, *Data* group].

4. Add and remove chart elements.
   a. Click the **Location 1-Cass Lake** worksheet tab and select the chart object if it is not already selected.
   b. Click the **Chart Elements** button to the right of the chart.
   c. Add a title by clicking the **Chart Title** check box.
   d. Click the **Chart Title** menu arrow and choose **Above Chart**.
   e. Point at the placeholder text and triple-click.
   f. Type Second Quarter Activity.
   g. Click the chart to deselect the title.
   h. Click the horizontal axis title placeholder.
   i. Press **Delete**.
   j. Delete the vertical axis title placeholder.
   k. Double-click the legend element at the right of the chart area to open its *Format* task pane.
   l. Click the **Legend Options** button if necessary (Figure 3-35).
   m. Click the **Bottom** radio button to reposition the legend.
   n. Close the *Format Legend* task pane.

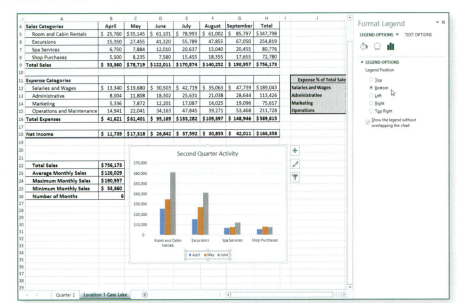

3-35 Chart in worksheet with elements added and removed

5. Change the chart type.
   a. Click the **Quarter 3** tab.
   b. Click the **Change Chart Type** button [*Chart Tools Design* tab, *Type* group] to open the *Change Chart Type* dialog box.
   c. Click the **Recommended Charts** tab.
   d. Find and select the first **Clustered Column** in the pane on the left.
   e. Click **OK**.

6. Filter the source data.
   a. Click the **Chart Filters** button in the top right corner of the chart.
   b. Click the **Excursions** check box to remove the check mark.
   c. Click **Apply**.
   d. Click the **Chart Filters** button to close the pane.

7. Apply shape styles and outlines to chart elements.
   a. Click the **Location 1-Cass Lake** tab.
   b. Click the chart object.
   c. Click the **Chart Elements** drop-down arrow [*Chart Tools Format* tab, *Current Selection* group].
   d. Choose **Plot Area** to select the plot area of the chart.
   e. Click the **More** button [*Chart Tools Format* tab, *Shape Styles* group].
   f. Click **Subtle Effect – Gold, Accent 4**.

g. Click the **Shape Outline** button drop-down arrow [*Chart Tools Format* tab, *Shape Styles* group].

h. Choose **Black, Text 1** in the top row of the *Theme Colors*.

i. Click the **Chart Elements** drop-down arrow [*Chart Tools Format* tab, *Current Selection* group].

j. Choose **Vertical (Value) Axis Major Gridlines** to select the major gridlines in the plot area.

k. Click the icon for the **Shape Outline** button [*Chart Tools Format* tab, *Shape Styles* group] to apply the last-used color (**Black, Text 1**).

l. Select the **Vertical (Value) Axis Minor Gridlines** and apply the same black outline color.

m. Click the chart area to see the change (Figure 3-36).

n. Click the **Chart Elements** drop-down arrow [*Chart Tools Format* tab, *Current Selection* group] and choose **Chart Area**.

o. Apply **Black, Text 1** for the outline.

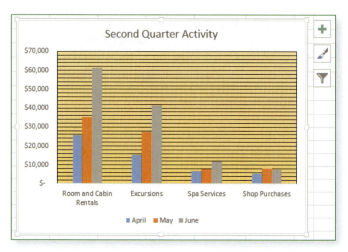

3-36 Plot area formatted

8. Use a picture as fill.

a. Click the **Quarter 3** tab.

b. Double-click one of the "Room and Cabin Rentals" columns to open the *Format Data Series* task pane.

c. Click the **Fill & Line** button.

d. Click **Fill** to expand the command group.

e. Click the **Picture or texture fill** button to open the gallery.

f. Click **Online**, type cabins in the *Office.com Clip Art* text box, and press **Enter** (Figure 3-37).

g. Choose an image and insert it.

h. Click **Stack** in the *Format Data Series* task pane.

i. Close the task pane.

3-37 Online search for a picture to use as fill

9. Use *WordArt* in a chart.

a. Triple-click the **Chart Title** placeholder to select the text.

b. Type Third Quarter Activity.

c. Click the chart area to deselect the title.

d. Triple-click the title text again.

e. From the mini toolbar, change the font size to **24 pt**.

f. Click the chart area to deselect the title.

g. Select the chart title to display the selection handles.

h. Click the **More** button [*Chart Tools Format* tab, *WordArt Style* group].

i. Choose **Fill – Black, Text 1, Shadow**.

10. Move the legend.
    a. Double-click the legend element below the chart title to open its *Format* task pane.
    b. Click the **Legend Options** button if necessary.
    c. Choose **Bottom** to reposition the legend.

11. Save and close the workbook (Figure 3-38).

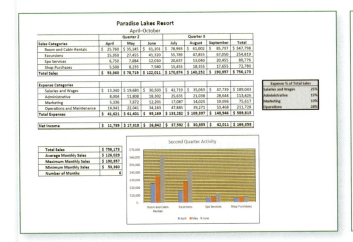

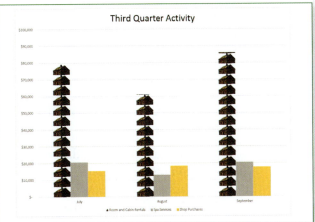

3-38 PP E3-2 completed worksheet and chart sheet

Creating and Editing a Pie Chart and a Combination Chart

When you use the *Quick Analysis* or *Recommended Charts* button, Excel chooses chart types that are suited to the data you have selected. As you develop your Excel skills and build more charts, you can choose your chart types directly from the *Charts* group on the *Insert* tab. With this method, when you click the specific chart type button, you see a small gallery with the available subtypes of the chart. As you point at each option, *Live Preview* previews the chart.

Charts created from a chart type button on the *Insert* tab are created as chart objects in the worksheet. Like any chart objects, you can move them to their own sheets.

Create a 3-D Pie Chart

A *pie chart* graphs one data series, one set of numbers. For most pie charts, you want to limit the number of categories to six or seven. A pie chart with many slices is difficult to interpret and often does not illustrate the relationship among the values. A pie chart illustrates how each number relates to the whole. In fact, you can set a value for the data series to show a percentage in the data label.

On the *Insert Pie or Doughnut Chart* button on the *Insert* tab, you can choose from a gallery of 2-D or 3-D pie types as well as a doughnut shape (see Figure 3-39). A doughnut chart is a pie chart with a hollow center. There are also two options for a pie chart with a bar or another pie chart.

HOW TO: Create a 3-D Pie Chart

1. Select the cell ranges that include the data series and the category labels.
2. Click the **Insert Pie or Doughnut Chart** button [*Insert* tab, *Charts* group] (Figure 3-39).
3. Choose **3-D Pie**.
   - Click the **Move Chart** button [*Chart Tools Design* tab, *Location* group] to move a pie chart to its own sheet.

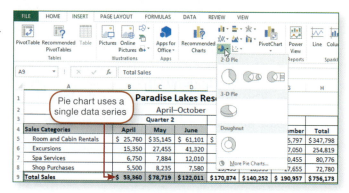

3-39 Selected data series and categories for a pie chart

Pie Chart Elements and Options

In a pie chart, the data series is represented by the whole pie. A data point is a slice of the pie. You can format the data series as a whole and you can format individual slices. It is important to note which element you have selected when you give a command. Remember the *Format* task pane. When you use it, it shows the name of the selected element. You can also view the element's name in the *Chart Elements* text box in the *Current Selection* group on the *Chart Tools Format* tab.

A pie chart can display a legend and a title. It does not, however, have axes and does not use axes titles. Data labels are often used instead of a legend for a pie chart because they show the same information. The chart area, as usual, is the background for the chart.

Pie charts do have *Quick Layouts* and *Quick Styles*. You can also set shape fill, color, and effects for the elements or objects, use a picture as fill, add an image, or insert *WordArt*.

Specialized commands for a pie chart are the angle of the first slice and the percent of explosion. The angle of the first slice allows you to rotate the pie. The first slice starts at the top of the chart at 0° (zero degrees). As you increase that value, the slice arcs to the right. *Live Preview* displays the results.

Exploding a pie slice emphasizes that slice because it moves the slice away from the rest of the pie. You set explosion as a percentage.

HOW TO: Rotate a Pie Chart and Explode a Slice

1. Double-click the pie chart to open the *Format Data Series* task pane.
   - You can also right-click the pie chart and choose **Format Data Series** to open the task pane.
2. Click the **Series Options** button to open the command group (Figure 3-40).
   - If the wrong *Format* task pane opens, click the arrow with **Series Options** and choose **Series 1**.
3. Set the angle for the first slice by dragging the slider control to the degree setting (see Figure 3-40).
   - You can also type the desired value in the text box or use the up or down spinner arrows to set a degree value.
4. Click the data point (slice) you want to explode.
   - Verify that the *Format Data Point* task pane is open.

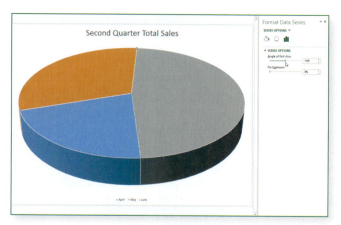

3-40 Angle of first slice adjusted

5. Set the percentage for the amount of explosion by dragging the slider control to the percent setting (Figure 3-41).
   - You can also type the new value in the text box or use the up or down spinner arrows to set a percent value.

3-41 Exploded pie slice

> **MORE INFO**
>
> You can explode all the slices in a pie chart by selecting the data series, not a data point.

Create a Combination Chart

A combination chart includes two chart types such as a line chart and a column chart. Paradise Lakes Resort can use a combination chart, for example, to compare revenue from cabin and room rentals to the operations and maintenance expense. These two values reflect different types of numbers, so showing one series as a line and the other as a column focuses the revenue/expense comparison (Figure 3-42).

The most common combination of chart types is line and column, but you can also use a line and area combination. Excel offers an option to create a custom combination, but it is best to use this only after you have experience charting your data.

	A	B	C	D	E
1			**Paradise Lakes Resort**		
2			April–October		
3				Quarter 2	
4	**Sales Categories**	April	May	June	July
5	Room and Cabin Rentals	$ 25,760	$35,145	$ 61,101	$ 78,993
6	Excursions	15,350	27,455	41,320	55,789
7	Spa Services	6,750	7,884	12,010	20,637
8	Shop Purchases	5,500	8,235	7,580	15,455
9	**Total Sales**	$ 53,360	$78,719	$122,011	$170,874
10					
11	**Expense Categories**				
12	Salaries and Wages	$ 13,340	$19,680	$ 30,503	$ 42,719
13	Administrative	8,004	11,808	18,302	25,631
14	Marketing	5,336	7,872	12,201	17,087
15	Operations and Maintenance	14,941	22,041	34,163	47,845
16	**Total Expenses**	$ 41,621	$61,401	$ 95,169	$133,282

3-42 Source data for a combo chart

> **MORE INFO**
>
> Some chart types cannot be combined. If you try to do so, Excel opens a message box to inform you.

In a combination chart, you can display two sets of values with two vertical axes. The axis on the left is the primary axis; the one on the right is secondary. This option is best when the values are very different such as when comparing the number of rooms booked to dollars earned.

You can create a combination chart from the *Charts* group on the *Insert* tab as well as from the *Recommended Charts* button in the same group.

HOW TO: Create a Combination Chart

1. Select the cell ranges to be charted.
2. Click the **Insert Combo Chart** button [*Insert* tab, *Charts* group].
3. Choose the subtype (Figure 3-43).
   - You can move a combination chart to its own sheet if desired.

> **ANOTHER WAY**
>
> Create a combination chart for selected data from the **Recommended Charts** button [*Insert* tab, *Charts* group] by clicking the *All Charts* tab.

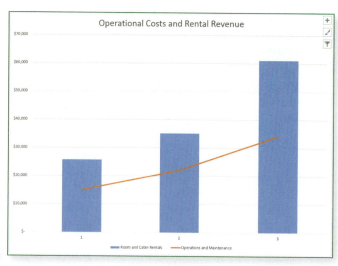

3-43 Line-Column combination chart

Combination Chart Elements and Options

A combination chart can have several data series, each shown in its own chart type. Keep this type of chart relatively simple, however, because its purpose is to compare unlike items.

A combination chart has most of the same elements as a regular column or line chart. You can apply chart styles and layouts, as well as shape fill, outline, effects, pictures, shapes, and *WordArt*, to a combination chart.

You can display or hide the secondary axis for a combination chart in the *Change Chart Type* dialog box. When you use a secondary axis, Excel builds the number scale based on the data. You can edit which data uses a line or a column from this dialog box as well (Figure 3-44).

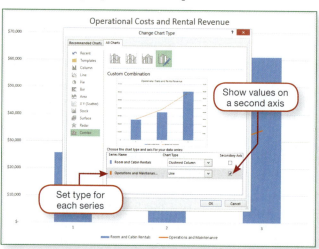

3-44 *Change Chart Type* dialog box for a combo chart

HOW TO: Display a Secondary Axis on a Combination Chart

1. Select the chart object.
2. Click the **Change Chart Type** button [*Chart Tools Design* tab, *Type* group].
3. Choose the chart type for each series if desired.
4. Click to place or remove a check mark for a secondary axis.
5. Click **OK** (Figure 3-45).

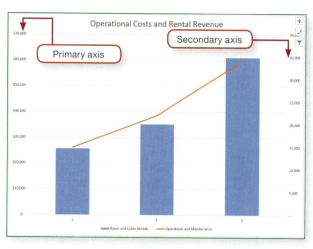

3-45 Secondary axis for a combo chart

SLO 3.7

Inserting Sparklines in a Worksheet

Sparklines are miniature charts displayed in a cell or cell range next to your data. They can be used to illustrate trends and patterns without adding a separate chart object or sheet.

Sparklines are created from a selected data range like a chart. You can place them in a location range, usually next to the worksheet data (Figure 3-46).

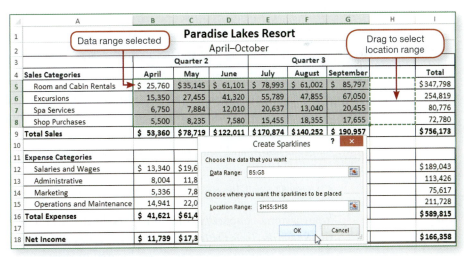

There are three sparkline types: **Line**, **Column**, and **Win/Loss**. The *Sparklines* command is located on the *Insert* tab for the worksheet. After you insert sparklines, they act like other objects in a worksheet. The **Sparkline Tools Design** tab opens when you click the sparkline object.

To insert sparklines, you may need to insert a column at the appropriate location in your data, or, if it is empty, you may be able to use the right-most column. Depending on the type of sparkline, you may also want to increase the row height or column width to better present the sparklines.

Insert Sparklines

To insert sparklines in a worksheet, decide where you want to place them and insert a column if necessary. Select the data range that includes the values to be illustrated. This range cannot include the range where the sparklines display.

The *Sparklines* group is on the *Insert* tab and in the *Type* group on the *Sparkline Tools Design* tab.

HOW TO: Insert Column Sparklines in a Worksheet

1. Select the cell range to be used for sparklines.
   - When you select the data range first, it is displayed in the *Data Range* box within the *Create Sparklines* dialog box.
2. Click the **Column Sparkline** button [*Insert* tab, *Sparklines* group].
3. Click in the **Location Range** box.
4. Click and drag in the worksheet to select the cell range for the sparklines (Figure 3-47).
5. Click **OK**.

3-47 Create Sparklines dialog box

> **ANOTHER WAY**
>
> Click the **Column Sparkline** button [*Insert* tab, *Sparklines* group] and select the *Data Range* and *Location Range* from the dialog box to insert sparklines.

Sparkline Design Tools

When sparklines are selected in a worksheet, the *Sparkline Tools Design* tab opens. This context-sensitive tab includes several choices for changing the appearance of your sparklines. There is a *Shape Style* option that changes the color of the sparkline group. You can also change the color with the *Sparkline Color* command. The *Marker Color* command enables you to choose a different color for identified values in the sparklines. A **marker** for a sparkline is the data point value. You can highlight a specific value or the high, low, first, or last value as well as negative values.

Other choices on the *Sparkline Tools Design* tab are in the *Type* and *Show* groups. For example, you can change a column sparkline to a line sparkline. The *Show* commands set the color of the identified values in the data range.

HOW TO: Format Sparklines

1. Click the sparkline group in the worksheet.
2. Click the *Sparkline Line Tools Design* tab if necessary.
3. Click the **High Point** check box in the *Show* group (Figure 3-48).
   - A default color is applied to the highest value in the sparklines for each row.
4. Click the **Marker Color** button [*Sparkline Tools Design* tab, *Style* group].
5. Choose **High Point** and select a color from the gallery.
6. Click the **Sparkline Color** button [*Sparkline Tools Design* tab, *Style* group].
7. Choose a color for the sparkline group that is different from the color you chose for the *High Point*.

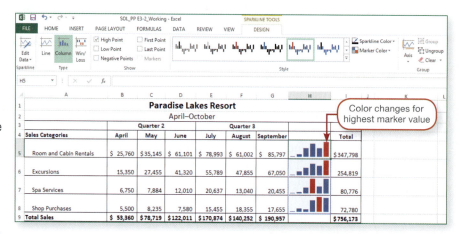

3-48 *High Point* marker selected for sparklines

Sparklines are inserted as a group in the location range. When you click any cell in the range with sparklines, the group is selected. Sparklines can be ungrouped if you need to make format choices for one sparkline cell or if you want to delete one sparkline in a range. The *Ungroup* command is in the *Group* group on the *Sparkline Tools Design* tab.

Clear Sparklines

You can remove sparklines from a worksheet with the *Clear* command in the *Group* group on the *Sparkline Tools Design* tab. After sparklines are cleared from a worksheet, you may need to delete the column where they were located or reset row heights and column widths.

HOW TO: Clear Sparklines

1. Select any cell in the sparklines range.
2. Click the **Clear Selected Sparklines** button [*Sparkline Tools Design* tab, *Group* group].
3. Choose **Clear Selected Sparklines Group**.

E3-162

For this project, you continue to build Paradise Lakes' sales report by inserting a pie chart that shows the proportion of each sales category in the organization's total sales. You also insert a combination chart sheet to compare rentals and maintenance expense. Finally, you insert sparklines in the worksheet.

File Needed: *[your initials] PP E3-2.xlsx*
Completed Project File Name: *[your initials] PP E3-3.xlsx*

1. Open the *[your initials] PP E3-2* workbook.

2. Save the workbook as *[your initials] PP E3-3*.

3. Create a pie chart for total sales revenue.
   a. Select the **Location 1– Cass Lake** tab.
   b. Select cells **A5:A8** as the category.
   c. Hold down **Ctrl** and select cells **H5:H8** as the data series.
   d. Click the **Insert Pie or Doughnut Chart** button [*Insert* tab, *Charts* group].
   e. Choose **3-D Pie** (Figure 3-49).
   f. Click the **Move Chart** button [*Chart Tools Design* tab, *Location* group].
   g. Click the **New sheet** button and type Pie Chart as the sheet name.
   h. Click **OK**.

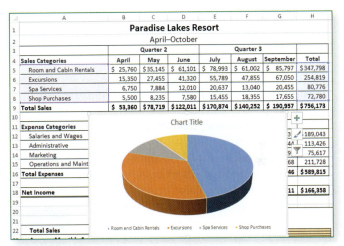

3-49 Pie chart object inserted

4. Format a pie chart.
   a. Select the **Pie Chart** tab.
   b. Click the **Chart Title** placeholder to select it and then triple-click the **Chart Title** placeholder text.
   c. Type Second and Third Quarters and press **Enter**.
   d. Type Sources of Revenue on the second line.
   e. Drag to select the first line of the title.
   f. From the mini toolbar, change the font size to **24 pt**.
   g. Drag to select the second line of the title.
   h. From the mini toolbar, change the font size to **18 pt**. (Figure 3-50).
   i. Click the chart area to deselect the title.
   j. Double-click the pie to open the *Format Data Series* task pane.
   k. Click the **Series Options** button in the *Format Data Series* task pane.
   l. Click the **Room and Cabin Rentals** slice to change to the *Format Data Point* task pane.

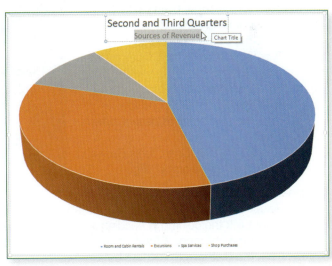

3-50 Chart titles typed and sized

m. Set the pie explosion percentage at **10%**.

n. Close the task pane.

o. Select the legend at the bottom of the chart to display selection handles.

p. Click the *Home* tab and change the font size to **12 pt**.

q. Point at the legend border (its edge) to display a move pointer.

r. Drag the legend object slightly closer to the chart (Figure 3-51).

s. Click the chart area to deselect the legend.

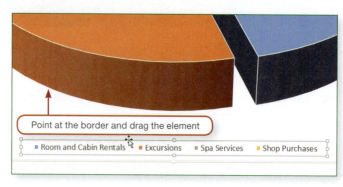

Point at the border and drag the element

3-51 Selected legend and move pointer

5. Create a combination chart for total sales revenue and room and cabin rentals.

a. Select the **Location 1– Cass Lake** tab.

b. Select cells **A4:G5** as one data series and category.

c. Hold down **Ctrl** and select cells **A9:G9** as another data series and category.

d. Click the **Insert Combo Chart** button [*Insert* tab, *Charts* group] (Figure 3-52).

e. Choose **Clustered Column – Line on Secondary Axis**.

f. Click the **Move Chart** button [*Chart Tools Design* tab, *Location* group].

g. Click the **New sheet** button and type Combo Chart as the sheet name.

h. Click **OK**.

3-52 *Insert Combo Chart* button

6. Format a combination chart.

a. Select the **Combo Chart** tab.

b. Click to select the **Chart Title** placeholder and then triple-click the **Chart Title** placeholder text.

c. Type Second and Third Quarters and press **Enter**.

d. Type Comparison of Rentals and Total Sales on the second line.

e. Click the chart area to deselect the chart title.

f. Choose **Style 6** [*Chart Tools Design* tab, *Chart Styles* group] (Figure 3-53).

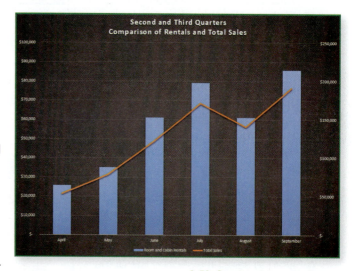

3-53 Combo chart with Style 6

7. Insert sparklines in a worksheet.

a. Select the **Location 1– Cass Lake** tab.

b. Right-click the column **H** heading and choose **Insert** to insert a new column.

c. Select the cell range **B5:G8** as the data to be charted with sparklines.

d. Click the **Column Sparkline** button [*Insert* tab, *Sparklines* group].

e. Click in the **Location Range** box.

f. Click and drag to select cells **H5:H8**.

g. Click **OK**.

8. Format sparklines.
   a. Click any cell in the sparkline group.
   b. Click the **Sparkline Color** button [*Sparkline Tools Design* tab, *Style* group] and select **Green, Accent 6, Darker 25%**.
   c. While the sparkline group is selected, click the **Format** button [*Home* tab, *Cells* group] and change the **Row Height** to **30 (40 pixels)**.
   d. Set column **H** to a width of **16.00 (117 pixels)**.
   e. Click **OK**.

9. Save and close the workbook (Figure 3-54).

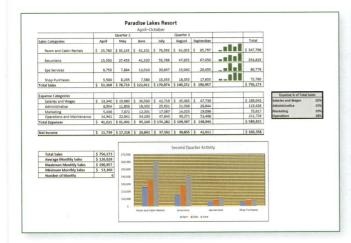

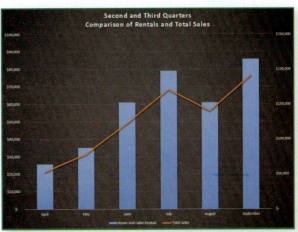

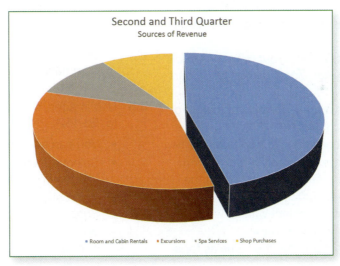

3-54 PP E3-3 completed worksheet and chart sheets

Chapter Summary

3.1 Create, size, and position an Excel chart object and create a chart sheet (p. E3-134).

- A **chart object** is a selectable object surrounded by a square border that contains many customizable chart elements like data labels or a chart title.
- Commonly used chart types are **Column**, **Line**, **Pie**, and **Bar**, but Excel can also create sophisticated statistical, financial, and scientific charts.
- The cells used to build a chart are its **source data**.
- You can size and position the chart object in a worksheet.
- A **chart sheet** is an Excel chart that is displayed on its own sheet tab in the workbook but is still linked to the source data.
- You can move a chart object to its own sheet by clicking the **Move Chart** button in the *Location* group on the *Chart Tools Design* tab.
- You can name a chart sheet tab to indicate the purpose or type of its chart.

3.2 Design a chart using *Quick Layouts* and chart styles (p. E3-137).

- A **chart layout** is a preset group of elements in a chart.
- You can apply a *Quick Layout* from the **Quick Layout** button [*Chart Tools Design* tab, *Chart Layouts* group].
- A **Chart Style** is a predefined combination of colors and effects for chart elements.
- Chart styles are based on the workbook theme.
- Apply a chart style by selecting a style from the gallery in the *Chart Styles* group on the *Chart Tools Design* tab.
- You can print a chart object with its worksheet data using the *Backstage* view.
- Print options for charts are the same as for a worksheet.
- A chart sheet prints on its own sheet in landscape orientation.

3.3 Switch row and column data, add or remove chart elements, change the chart type, and edit source data (p. E3-141).

- Excel plots source data based on the number of rows and columns selected; this determines what is shown on the horizontal or vertical axis.

- You can switch the row and column data when appropriate.
- A **chart element** is a selectable component that is part of the chart.
- Chart elements include chart and axes titles, data labels, legends, gridlines, and trendlines.
- You can change some chart types into another type. Use the **Change Chart Type** button on the *Chart Tools Design* tab.
- You can filter chart data to show or hide values or categories without changing the source data.
- Source data for a chart can be edited to add or delete a data series.

3.4 Format chart elements with shape styles, fill, outlines, and special effects (p. E3-148).

- Select a chart element with the pointer to format it or use the **Current Selection** group on the *Chart Tools Format* tab.
- A **Shape Style** is a predesigned combination of fill, borders, and effects.
- You can apply **Shape Fill**, **Shape Outline**, and **Shape Effects** separately from the *Chart Tools Format* tab.
- A chart element has its own *Format* task pane that includes fill, outline, and effects commands as well as specific options for the element.

3.5 Use images, shapes, and *WordArt* in a chart (p. E3-152).

- You can use a picture as fill for a shape.
- Select appropriately sized and designed images from your own or online sources.
- Insert shapes into a chart from the *Insert Shapes* group on the *Chart Tools Format* tab.
- You can apply **WordArt** to a chart title for special effect.
- Use the *Text Box* or *WordArt* buttons in the *Text* group on the *Insert* tab to add extra labels.

3.6 Create a pie chart and a combination chart (p. E3-157).

- A **pie chart** has one data series; it shows each data point as a part of the whole.
- Pie charts have many of the same elements as other charts, but they do not have axes.

- A *combination chart* uses two chart types to highlight differences in data or values.
- You can format a combination chart to show a secondary axis on the right side of the chart when values are widely different.

3.7 Insert and format sparklines in a worksheet (p. E3-161).

- A *sparkline* is a miniature chart in a cell or range of cells in the worksheet.
- Three sparkline types are available: *Line, Column*, and *Win/Loss*.

- Add sparklines to a worksheet from the *Sparklines* group on the *Insert* tab.
- Sparklines are grouped and can be formatted from the *Sparkline Tools Design* tab.
- Formatting options for sparklines include changing the color and identifying markers such as high and low values.
- Delete sparklines from a worksheet with the **Clear Selected Sparklines** button on the *Sparkline Tools Design* tab.

Check for Understanding

On the *Online Learning Center* for this text (www.mhhe.com/office2013inpractice), there are a variety of resources that can be used to review the concepts covered in this chapter.

The following Online Learning Resources are available on the Online Learning Center:

- Multiple choice questions
- Short answer questions
- Matching exercises

Guided Project 3-1

Life's Animal Shelter (LAS) is an animal care and adoption agency that accepts all unwanted or stray domestic animals. For this project, you create several expense charts and insert sparklines to help the agency track its expenses for the first six months of the year.
[Student Learning Outcomes 3.1, 3.2, 3.3, 3.4, 3.5, 3.6, 3.7]

File Needed: *LASExpenses-03.xlsx*
Completed Project File Name: *[your initials] Excel 3-1.xlsx*

Skills Covered in This Project

- Create a chart object.
- Create a chart sheet.
- Apply *Quick Layouts* and chart styles.
- Add and format chart elements.
- Change chart type.

- Filter the data series.
- Insert a shape in a chart.
- Create and format a combination chart.
- Insert and format sparklines in a sheet.

1. Open the *LASExpenses-03* workbook from your student data files folder.

2. Save the workbook as *[your initials] Excel 3-1*.

3. Create a pie chart object.
   a. Select cells **A4:A10**. Hold down **Ctrl** and select cells **I4:I10**.
   b. Click the **Insert Pie or Doughnut Chart** button [*Insert* tab, *Charts* group].
   c. Select the **2D-Pie** chart subtype.

4. Apply a chart style.
   a. Select the chart object.
   b. Click the **More** button [*Chart Tools Design* tab, *Chart Styles* group] and select **Style 12**.

5. Edit and format chart elements.
   a. Click the chart title.
   b. Place the insertion point in front of "Totals" in the title.
   c. Type Year-to-Date Expense and press the **spacebar** once.
   d. Click the chart area to deselect the title.
   e. Select the legend element.
   f. Click the **Font Size** arrow [*Home* tab, *Font* group] and change the size to **12 pt**. (Figure 3-55).
   g. Select the chart area.

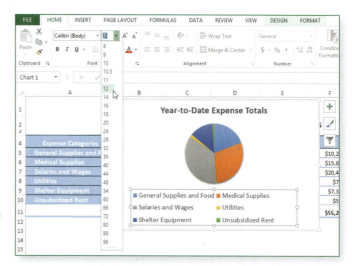

3-55 Legend selected for font size change

h. Click the **Shape Outline** button drop-down arrow [*Chart Tools Format* tab, *Shape Styles* group].
i. Choose **Black, Text 1** as the color.
j. Click the **Shape Outline** drop-down arrow again.
k. Choose **Weight** and **1 pt**.

6. Create a chart sheet.
   a. Click the pie chart object to select it.
   b. Click the **Move Chart** button [*Chart Tools Design* tab, *Location* group].
   c. Click the **New sheet** button.
   d. Type Pie Chart in the text box.
   e. Click **OK**.

7. Create a bar chart object.
   a. Click the **Half-Year Expenses** sheet tab.
   b. Select cells **A4:G10** as the source data range.
   c. Click the **Quick Analysis** button and select **Charts**.
   d. Select **Clustered Bar**.
   e. Point at the chart area to display a move pointer.
   f. Drag the chart object so its top left corner is at cell **B13**.
   g. Point at the bottom right selection handle to display a resize pointer.
   h. Drag the pointer to reach cell **G30** (Figure 3-56).

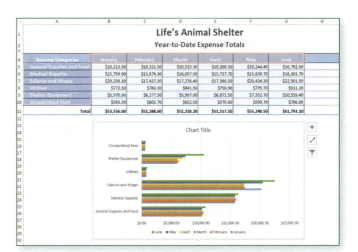

3-56 **Bar chart object sized and positioned**

8. Change the chart type.
   a. Click the chart object.
   b. Click the **Change Chart Type** button [*Chart Tools Design* tab, *Type* group].
   c. Click the **Recommended Charts** tab.
   d. Choose **Clustered Column** in the left pane.
   e. Click **OK**.

9. Filter the source data.
   a. Click the chart object.
   b. Click the **Chart Filters** button at the top right corner of the chart.
   c. Click to remove the check marks for **January**, **February**, and **March**.
   d. Click **Apply** in the *Chart Filters* pane (Figure 3-57).
   e. Click the **Chart Filters** button to close the pane.

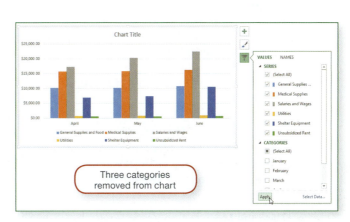

3-57 **Chart filter applied**

10. Edit and format chart elements.
    a. Click the chart title placeholder.
    b. Point at the text and triple-click or drag to select all the text.
    c. Type Second Quarter Expenses.
    d. Click the chart area to deselect the title.

e. Click to select the legend element.
f. Click the **Font Size** arrow [*Home* tab, *Font* group] and change the size to **8 pt**.
g. Click to select the chart area.
h. Click the **Shape Outline** button drop-down arrow [*Chart Tools Format* tab, *Shape Styles* group].
i. Choose **Black**, **Text 1** as the color.
j. Click the **Shape Outline** drop-down arrow again.
k. Choose **Weight** and **1 pt**.

11. Create a combination chart sheet.
    a. Select cells **A8:G8**. Hold down **Ctrl** and select cells **A11:G11**.
    b. Click the **Insert Combo Chart** button [*Insert* tab, *Charts* group].
    c. Select the **Clustered Column-Line** chart subtype.
    d. Click the combo chart object to select it.
    e. Click the **Move Chart** button [*Chart Tools Design* tab, *Location* group].
    f. Click the **New sheet** button.
    g. Type Combo Chart.
    h. Click **OK**.
    i. Click the **Change Chart Type** button [*Chart Tools Design* tab, *Type* group].
    j. Click the **Secondary Axis** check box for the line chart (Figure 3-58).
    k. Click **OK**.

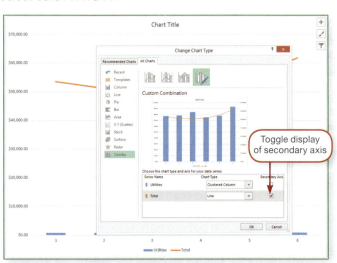

3-58 Combo chart and a secondary axis

12. Edit and format chart elements.
    a. Click the chart title placeholder.
    b. Point at the text and triple-click or drag to select all the text.
    c. Type Utilities Expense and Total Expenses.
    d. Click the chart area to deselect the title.
    e. Apply a **1 pt**. **black** outline to the chart area.

13. Insert sparklines in worksheet.
    a. Click the **Half-Year Expenses** sheet tab.
    b. Select cells **B5:G10** as the data range.
    c. Click the **Column Sparkline** button [*Insert* tab, *Sparklines* group].
    d. Click in the **Location Range** box.
    e. Click and drag to select cells **H5:H10**.
    f. Click **OK**.
    g. Click the **Format** button [*Home* tab, *Cells* group] and set the **Row Height** to **35**.
    h. Click the **Sparkline Color** button [*Sparkline Tools Design* tab, *Style* group] and select **White**, **Background 1**, **Darker 50%**.

14. Insert a shape in a chart.
    a. Click the **More** button [*Chart Tools Format* tab, *Insert Shapes* group].
    b. Select the text box shape.
    c. Draw a text box like the one shown in Figure 3-59.

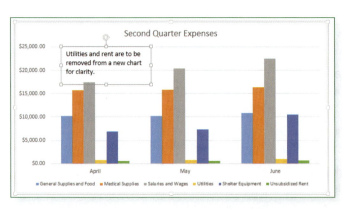

3-59 Text box shape inserted in chart

d. Type Utilities and rent are to be removed from a new chart for clarity.

e. Drag a selection handle to size the text box shape if necessary.

f. Point at an edge of the shape to display a four-pointed arrow and position it if needed.

15. Save and close the workbook (Figure 3-60).

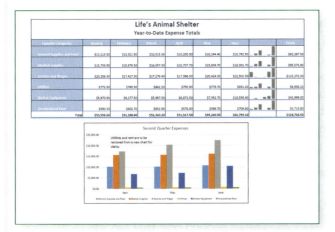

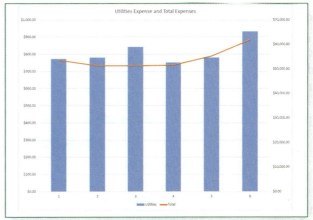

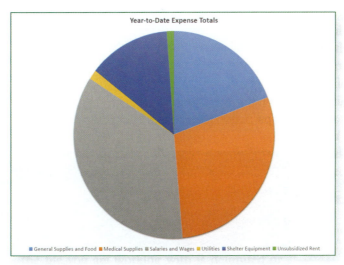

3-60 Excel 3-1 completed charts and worksheet

Guided Project 3-2

Wear-Ever Shoes is an shoe outlet with several locations. In a worksheet that tracks sales of popular items for the past six months, you create a bar chart to compare the number of pairs sold by style. You also create a combination chart to compare the number of pairs sold and the unit cost for each style.
[Student Learning Outcomes 3.1, 3.2, 3.3, 3.4, 3.5, 3.6]

File Needed: **WearEverSales-03.xlsx**
Completed Project File Name: **[your initials] Excel 3-2.xlsx**

Skills Covered in This Project

- Create a chart sheet.
- Change the chart type.
- Apply a chart style.
- Add and format chart elements.

- Use a picture as fill.
- Create and format a combination chart.
- Use *WordArt* in a chart.

1. Open the **WearEverSales-03** workbook from your student data files folder.

2. Save the workbook as **[your initials] Excel 3-2**.

3. Create a column chart sheet.
   a. Select cells **A5:B16**.
   b. Click the **Quick Analysis** button and choose **Charts**.
   c. Select **Clustered Column**.
   d. Click the chart object to select it.
   e. Click the **Move Chart** button [*Chart Tools Design* tab, *Location* group].
   f. Click the **New sheet** button.
   g. Type Sales Chart.
   h. Click **OK**.

4. Change the chart type.
   a. Click the **Sales Chart** sheet tab if necessary.
   b. Click the **Change Chart Type** button [*Chart Tools Design* tab, *Type* group].
   c. Click the **Recommended Charts** tab.
   d. Choose **Clustered Bar** in the left pane.
   e. Click **OK**.

5. Apply a chart style.
   a. Select the chart sheet if necessary.
   b. Click the **Chart Styles** button in the top right corner of the chart.
   c. Select **Style 7** (Figure 3-61).
   d. Click the **Chart Styles** button to close the pane.

6. Use a picture as fill for a data point.
   a. Select the chart sheet if necessary.

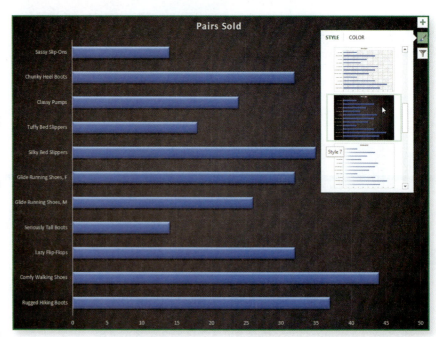

3-61 *Chart Styles* button and pane

b. Double-click any one of the bars to select the data series and open the *Format Data Series* task pane.

c. Point and click at the "Classy Pumps" bar to select it and display the *Format Data Point* task pane.

d. Click the **Fill & Line** button in the task pane.

e. Click **Fill** to expand the command group.

f. Click the **Picture or texture fill** button.

g. Click **Online** to open the *Insert Pictures* dialog box.

h. Type heels in the *Office.com Clip Art* search box and press **Enter** (Figure 3-62).

i. Select the image and click **Insert**.

j. Click **Stack** in the task pane.

k. Close the task pane and click the chart area.

Last used fill choice is applied

3-62 Online image search for fill in a data point

7. Create a combination chart sheet.
   a. Click the **Unit Sales** sheet tab.
   b. Select cells **A5:A16**. Hold down **Ctrl** and select cells **E5:F16**.
   c. Click the **Insert Combo Chart** button [*Insert* tab, *Charts* group].
   d. Select the **Clustered Column-Line on Secondary Axis** chart subtype.
   e. Select the combo chart object.
   f. Click the **Move Chart** button [*Chart Tools Design* tab, *Location* group].
   g. Click the **New sheet** button.
   h. Type Cost vs. Selling Price.
   i. Click **OK**.

8. Edit chart elements.
   a. Click the chart title placeholder.
   b. Select all the text in the placeholder.
   c. Type Cost and Selling Price Comparison.
   d. Select all the text in the chart title again.
   e. From the mini toolbar, change the font size to **20 pt**.
   f. Select the chart area.
   g. Apply a **1 pt**. **black** outline.

9. Use *WordArt* in a chart.
   a. Click the chart title.
   b. Click the **More** button [*Chart Tools Format* tab, *WordArt Style* group].
   c. Choose **Fill–Blue**, **Accent 1**, **Shadow**.
   d. Click the chart area to deselect the title.

10. Save and close the workbook (Figure 3-63).

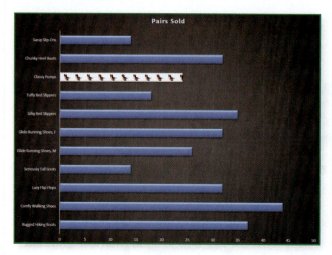

3-63 Excel 3-2 completed chart sheets

Guided Project 3-3

Blue Lake Sports has locations in several major cities and tracks sales by department in each store. For this project, you create a pie chart that shows each store's share of golf-related sales for the first quarter. You also create a line chart to illustrate week-to-week sales for specific departments in one of the stores and insert sparklines in the data.
[Student Learning Outcomes 3.1, 3.2, 3.3, 3.4, 3.6, 3.7]

File Needed: *BlueLakeSports-03.xlsx*
Completed Project File Name: *[your initials] Excel 3-3.xlsx*

Skills Covered in This Project

- Create, size, and position a pie chart object.
- Apply a chart style.
- Change chart type.
- Add and format chart elements in a pie chart.
- Create a line chart sheet.
- Apply a chart layout.
- Add and format chart elements in a line chart.
- Insert and format sparklines in a sheet.

1. Open the **BlueLakeSports-03** workbook from your student data files folder.
2. Save the workbook as **[your initials] Excel 3-3**.
3. Select the **Revenue by Department** tab.

4. Create a pie chart object.
   a. Select cells **A4:F4**, hold down **Ctrl**, and select cells **A13:F13**.
   b. Click the **Recommended Charts** button [*Insert* tab, *Charts* group].
   c. Choose **Pie** and click **OK**.

5. Apply a chart style.
   a. Select the chart object.
   b. Click the **More** button [*Chart Tools Design* tab, *Chart Styles* group].
   c. Select **Style 12**.

6. Size and position a chart object.
   a. Point at the chart area to display the move pointer.
   b. Drag the chart object so its top left corner is at cell **A21**.
   c. Point at the bottom right selection handle to display the resize pointer.
   d. Drag the pointer to cell **G36**.

7. Change the chart type.
   a. Click the pie chart object.
   b. Click the **Change Chart Type** button [*Chart Tools Design* tab, *Type* group].
   c. Click the **All Charts** tab.
   d. Choose **Pie** in the left pane.
   e. Choose **3-D Pie** and click **OK**.

8. Format pie chart elements.
   a. Double-click the pie to open the *Format Data Series* task pane.
   b. Click the **Atlanta** slice to update the pane to the *Format Data Point* task pane.
   c. Click the **Series Options** button in the *Format Data Series* task pane.
   d. Set the pie explosion percentage at **10%**.
   e. Close the task pane and click the chart area to deselect the **Atlanta** slice.

9. Add and format chart elements in a pie chart.
   a. Select the chart object if necessary.
   b. Click the **Chart Elements** button at the top right corner of the chart.
   c. Click the **Data Labels** check box (Figure 3-64).
   d. Display the submenu for **Data Labels** and choose **More Options**.
   e. In the *Format Data Point* task pane, click the **Label Options** button if necessary.

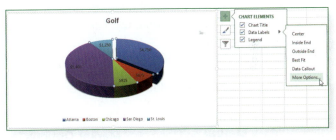

3-64 Data labels added to chart

   f. Click **Label Options** to expand the menu and click **Percentage** check box to show the percentage for each slice.
   g. Click to clear the **Value** check box and close the task pane.
   h. While the data labels are selected, press **Ctrl+B** to apply bold to the labels.
   i. While the data labels are selected, change the font size to **12 pt**. [*Home* tab, *Font* group].
   j. Click a worksheet cell to deselect the data labels and click the chart object to select it.
   k. Click the **Shape Outline** button drop-down arrow [*Chart Tools Format* tab, *Shape Styles* group] and choose **Purple**, **Accent 4**, **Darker 50%** as the color.
   l. Click the **Shape Outline** drop-down arrow again and choose **Weight** and **1 pt**.

10. Create a line chart sheet.
    a. Select the **Atlanta Revenue by Week** tab.
    b. Select cells **A4:E7**.

c. Click the **Quick Analysis** button and choose **Charts**.

d. Select **Line**.

e. Click the **Move Chart** button [*Chart Tools Design* tab, *Location* group].

f. Click the **New sheet** button.

g. Type Promo Depts.

h. Click **OK**.

11. Apply a chart layout.

a. Select the chart sheet if necessary.

b. Click the **Quick Layout** button [*Chart Tools Design* tab, *Chart Layouts* group].

c. Select **Layout 5** to add a data table to the chart sheet (Figure 3-65).

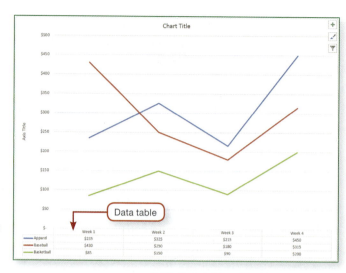

3-65 Data table added by chart layout

12. Change the chart type.

a. Right-click the **Promo Depts** chart and select **Change Chart Type**.

b. On the **All Charts** tab, choose **Line with Markers** in the **Line** category.

c. Click **OK**.

13. Edit chart elements in a line chart.

a. Click the chart title placeholder.

b. Type Sales for Promotion Departments and press **Enter**.

c. Click the vertical axis title placeholder.

d. Type Dollar Sales and press **Enter**.

e. Click the **Chart Elements** drop-down arrow [*Chart Tools Format* tab, *Current Selection* group].

f. Choose **Series "Apparel"** to select the line in the chart.

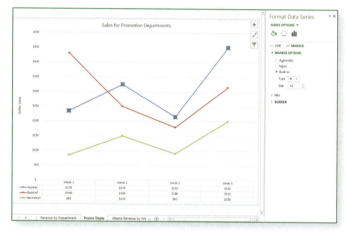

3-66 Marker options for the data series

g. Click the **Format Selection** button [*Chart Tools Format* tab, *Current Selection* group].

h. Click the **Fill & Line** button in the *Format Data Series* task pane.

i. Click **Marker** and then click **Marker Options** to expand the group (Figure 3-66).

j. Click **Built-in** and set a size of **10 pt**.

k. Click the **Series Options** triangle and choose **Series "Baseball"** to select that data series (Figure 3-67).

l. Make the same marker changes for the baseball series.

m. Select the basketball series and make the same marker changes.

n. Close the task pane and select the chart area.

14. Insert sparklines in worksheet.

a. Click the **Atlanta Revenue by Week** sheet tab.

b. Right-click the **column F** heading and choose **Insert** to insert a new column.

c. Select cells **B5:E18** as the data range.

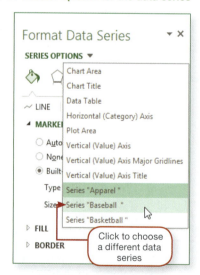

3-67 New data series selected

d. Click the **Line Sparkline** button [*Insert* tab, *Sparklines* group].

e. Click in the **Location Range** box.

f. Click and drag to select cells **F5:F18**.

g. Click **OK**.

15. Format sparklines in worksheet.

a. Click the **Format** button [*Home* tab, *Cells* group] and set the **Row Height** to **24**.

b. Click the **Format** button [*Home* tab, *Cells* group] and set the **Column Width** to **35**.

c. Click to place a check mark for **Markers** in the *Show* group in the *Sparkline Tools Design* tab.

d. Click the **Sparkline Color** button [*Sparkline Tools Design* tab, *Style* group].

e. Choose **Black, Text 1** for the line color.

16. Change the page orientation to landscape.

17. Save and close the workbook (Figure 3-68).

Blue Lake Sports
First Quarter Sales by City

Department	Atlanta	Boston	Chicago	San Diego	St. Louis	Total
Apparel	$ 2,600	$ 3,200	$ 3,800	$ 3,700	$ 3,200	$ 16,500
Baseball	$ 3,500	$ 1,200	$ 1,350	$ 2,100	$ 2,475	$ 10,625
Basketball	$ 1,800	$ 1,800	$ 2,250	$ 1,400	$ 1,750	$ 9,000
Bike & Skate	$ 1,500	$ 1,325	$ 1,225	$ 2,450	$ 1,650	$ 8,150
Exercise	$ 2,650	$ 2,875	$ 3,250	$ 3,775	$ 2,950	$ 15,500
Fishing	$ 2,350	$ 1,035	$ 1,250	$ 2,750	$ 1,450	$ 8,835
Footwear	$ 1,875	$ 2,675	$ 3,575	$ 3,250	$ 2,950	$ 14,325
Game Room	$ 1,300	$ 1,500	$ 1,900	$ 1,050	$ 1,275	$ 7,025
Golf	$ 4,750	$ 875	$ 925	$ 5,400	$ 1,250	$ 13,200
Hockey	$ 850	$ 1,875	$ 1,950	$ 750	$ 1,650	$ 7,075
Hunting	$ 2,000	$ 1,000	$ 650	$ 725	$ 950	$ 5,325
Lacrosse	$ 1,750	$ 1,800	$ 1,750	$ 1,375	$ 1,150	$ 7,825
Running	$ 1,925	$ 2,400	$ 2,800	$ 2,650	$ 2,000	$ 11,775
Winter Sports	$ 1,250	$ 34,350	$ 2,750	$ 550	$ 1,550	$ 40,450
Total	$ 30,100	$ 57,910	$ 29,425	$ 31,925	$ 26,250	$ 175,610

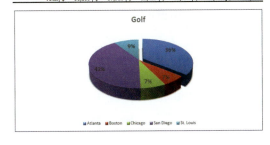

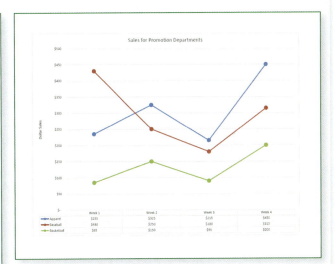

Blue Lake Sports
January Sales in Atlanta

Department	Week 1	Week 2	Week 3	Week 4		Total
Apparel	$ 235	$ 325	$ 215	$ 450		$ 1,225
Baseball	$ 430	$ 250	$ 180	$ 315		$ 1,175
Basketball	$ 85	$ 150	$ 90	$ 200		$ 525
Bike & Skate	$ 200	$ 325	$ 75	$ 175		$ 775
Exercise	$ 150	$ 160	$ 180	$ 170		$ 660
Fishing	$ 75	$ 150	$ 85	$ 200		$ 510
Footwear	$ 500	$ 350	$ 275	$ 330		$ 1,455
Game Room	$ 45	$ 75	$ 35	$ 15		$ 170
Golf	$ 175	$ 350	$ 580	$ 200		$ 1,305
Hockey	$ 85	$ 125	$ 50	$ 35		$ 295
Hunting	$ 125	$ 350	$ 475	$ 450		$ 1,400
Lacrosse	$ 200	$ 50	$ 65	$ 75		$ 390
Running	$ 165	$ 235	$ 325	$ 180		$ 905
Winter Sports	$ 75	$ 15	$ -	$ 15		$ 105
Total	$ 2,545	$ 2,910	$ 2,630	$ 2,810		$ 10,895

3-68 Excel 3-3 completed worksheet and charts

Independent Project 3-4

For this project, you create a column chart to illustrate April–September revenue for Classic Gardens and Landscapes. You also create a pie chart sheet to graph the proportion that each category contributes to total revenue.
[Student Learning Outcomes 3.1, 3.2, 3.3, 3.4, 3.5, 3.6]

File Needed: **ClassicGardensRevenue-03.xlsx**
Completed Project File Name: **[your initials] Excel 3-4.xlsx**

Skills Covered in This Project

- Create a chart object.
- Size and position a chart object.
- Edit and format chart elements.
- Edit the source data for a chart.
- Use the *SUM* function in a worksheet.
- Create a pie chart sheet.
- Use texture as fill.
- Add and format data labels in a chart.

1. Open the **ClassicGardensRevenue-03** workbook from your student data files folder.

2. Save the workbook as **[your initials] Excel 3-4**.

3. Create a *Clustered Column* chart object for cells **A4:G9**.

4. Move the chart object so that its top left corner is at cell **A12**. Size the bottom of the chart to reach cell **H30**.

5. Edit the chart title to display CGL Major Sales Revenue on one line and Second and Third Quarters on the second line.

6. Set the first line of the chart title to a font size of **20 pt**. Set the second title line to a size of **14 pt**.

7. Apply chart **Style 14** to the chart.

8. Apply a **½ point Black**, **Text 1** outline to the chart.

9. Remove the *Design Consulting* data series from the chart using the resizing pointer.

10. Enter *SUM* functions for the total column **H5:H9** and total row **B10:H10**.

11. Create a **3-D Pie** chart sheet named Revenue Breakdown for cells **A4:A9** and **H4:H9**.

12. Edit the chart title to display Revenue by Category. Set the font size to **32**.

13. Apply the **Oak** texture fill to the *Tree and Shrubbery* slice.

14. Add a data label in the center of each slice.
    a. Choose the **Accounting** format and set **0** decimal places (Figure 3-69).
    b. While the data labels are selected, set the font size to **14 pt**. and make them **bold** [*Home* tab, *Font* group].

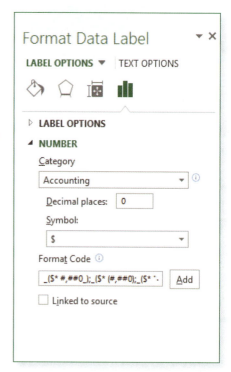

3-69 Data label options

15. Save and close the workbook (Figure 3-70).

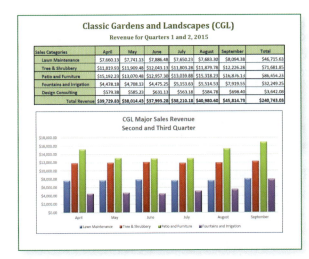
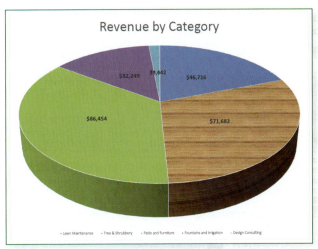

3-70 Excel 3-4 completed chart sheets

Independent Project 3-5

For this project, you create a stacked bar chart to illustrate projected tuition and fee amounts for Sierra Pacific Community College District (SPCCD). You also create a pie chart to show total projected revenue for the time period and add sparklines to the worksheet.
[Student Learning Outcomes 3.1, 3.2, 3.3, 3.4, 3.6, 3.7]

File Needed: *SierraPacificCC-03.xlsx*
Completed Project File Name: *[your initials] Excel 3-5.xlsx*

Skills Covered in This Project

- Create a chart object.
- Size and position a chart object.
- Apply a chart style.
- Switch row and column data.
- Edit chart source data.
- Create a pie chart sheet.
- Edit and format chart elements.
- Insert and format sparklines in a sheet.

1. Open the *SierraPacificCC-03* workbook from your student data files folder.

2. Save the workbook as *[your initials] Excel 3-5*.

3. Select cells **A3:E7** and create a stacked bar chart object.

4. Size and position the chart below the worksheet data in cells **A10:G28**.

5. Apply **Chart Style 6**.

6. Edit the chart title to display Tuition Revenue Projection.

7. Apply a dark blue ½ **pt**. outline to the chart object.

8. Switch the row and column data for the chart.

9. Edit the source data to remove the fees values from the chart.

10. Create a 3-D pie chart sheet for cells **A4:A7** and cells **G4:G7**. Move the chart to a new sheet named Total Revenue.

11. Apply **Chart Style 3** and a black ½ **pt**. outline.

12. Edit the chart title to Projected Revenue Sources.

13. Move the legend to the bottom and change its font size to **12 pt**.

14. Create column sparklines for cells **B4:E7** in the worksheet so that they appear in cells **F4:F7**.

15. Save and close the workbook (Figure 3-71).

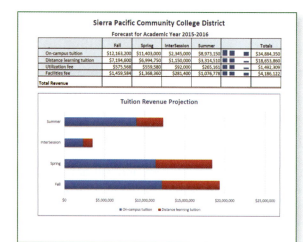
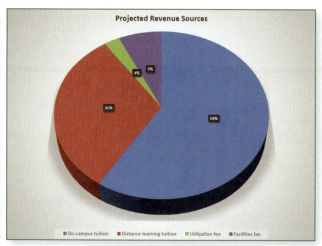

3-71 Excel 3-5 completed worksheet and chart

Independent Project 3-6

Courtyard Medical Plaza (CMP) is a full-service medical office complex providing customers with a variety of medical services in one location. For this project you create charts to illustrate data about the number of procedures performed at CMP as well as how patients come to the facility.
[Student Learning Outcomes 3.1, 3.2, 3.3, 3.4, 3.5]

File Needed: ***CourtyardMedical-03.xlsx***
Completed Project File Name: ***[your initials] Excel 3-6.xlsx***

Skills Covered in This Project

- *AutoFill* month names.
- Use the *SUM* function.
- Create a column chart sheet.
- Add and edit chart elements.

- Add and format a trendline in a chart.
- Insert a text box shape in a chart.
- Display gridlines in a chart.
- Use gradient fill for a chart object.

1. Open the **CourtyardMedical-03** workbook from your student data files folder.

2. Save the workbook as **[your initials] Excel 3-6**.

3. On the **Patient Count** worksheet, select cell **C5** and use the *Fill Handle* to complete the month names.

4. Complete the totals in **N6:N10** and **B10:M10** using the *SUM* function.
   a. Select all the values and apply **Comma Style** with no decimal places.
   b. *AutoFit* columns **B:N**.

5. Create a clustered column chart sheet named Immed Care for cells **A5:M5** and cells **A7:M7**.

6. Edit the chart title to display Immediate Care Patient Count.

7. Click the **Chart Elements** button and add a linear trendline to the chart.

8. Format the trendline.
   a. In the *Forecast* group, set the **Forward** value to **12**.
   b. Choose **Olive Green, Accent 3** for the line color.
   c. Set the **Width** of the trendline to **4 pt**.

9. Insert a text box in the chart. Draw a text box between the 300 and 400 gridlines and type The number of patients who come in for Immediate Care services will continue to grow. (Figure 3-72).

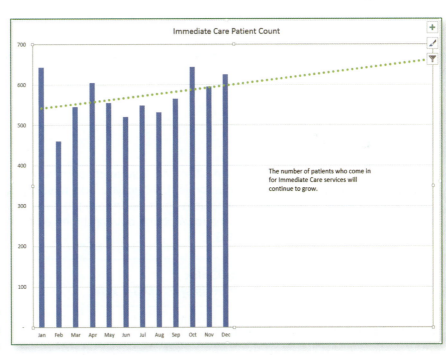

3-72 Text box shape in a chart

10. On the **Procedures Count** worksheet, select cells **A5:D16** and create a clustered column chart object. Move the chart to a new sheet named Procedures Chart.

11. Edit the chart title to display Number of Procedures on the first line and Three-Year Period on the second line.

12. Add **Primary Major Vertical** gridlines.

13. Format the plot area.
    a. Apply the fill **Tan, Background 2, Darker 10%**.
    b. Apply the **Gradient** shape fill. Choose **Linear Down**.

14. Save and close the workbook (Figure 3-73).

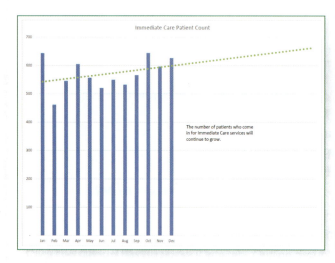
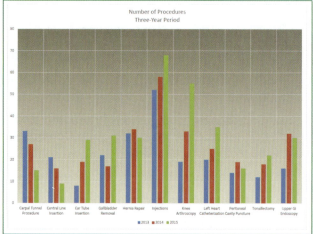

3-73 Excel 3-6 completed chart sheets

Improve It Project 3-7

Central Sierra Insurance (CSI) is a multi-office insurance company that handles commercial and personal insurance products. For this project, when you add missing data to a worksheet, the pie chart automatically updates, but the column chart incorrectly plots row and column data and does not update. To address this, you switch the row/column data and then edit the source data range.
[Student Learning Outcomes 3.2, 3.3, 3.4]

File Needed: *CentralSierraPolicies-03.xlsx*
Completed Project File Name: *[your initials] Excel 3-7.xlsx*

Skills Covered in This Project

- Insert a row within a chart source range.
- Switch row and column data.
- Apply a new color scheme to a chart and to a data series.
- Edit source data.

- Add and format elements in a 3-D chart.
- Use gradient fill for a chart object.
- Change chart type.
- Apply a chart style.
- Format chart elements.

1. Open the **CentralSierraPolicies-03** workbook from your student data files folder.

2. Save the workbook as **[your initials] Excel 3-7**.

3. Insert a new row at row 8.

4. In cell **A8,** type Motorcycle. In cells **B8:D8**, type these values: 15, 82, and 24.

5. Switch the row and column data for the column chart.

6. Edit the source data for the column chart to show cells **A5:D10**.

7. Change the chart color scheme to **Color 11** in the **Monochromatic** list.

8. Format chart elements.
   a. Apply the **Olive Green**, **Accent 3**, **Lighter 80%** shape fill to the **Side Wall** of the chart.
   b. Apply the **Linear Down** gradient for the shape fill.
   c. Apply the same fill and gradient to the **Walls** element.
   d. Apply the **Olive Green**, **Accent 3**, **Lighter 60%** with no gradient to the **Floor** element.

9. Change the pie chart to a **3-D Pie** and apply **Chart Style 3**.

10. Select the **Chart Area** of the pie chart and apply **Color 11** color scheme, **Olive Green**, **Accent 3**, **Lighter 80%** shape fill, and **Linear Down** gradient fill.

11. Apply a **½ pt**. **Olive Green**, **Accent 3**, **Darker 25%** outline to both chart objects.

12. Select the pie (**Series AJP**) and change the color to **Color 11** in the **Monochromatic** list.

13. Save and close the workbook (Figure 3-74).

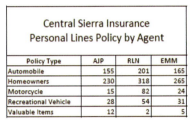

Policy Type	AJP	RLN	EMM
Automobile	155	201	165
Homeowners	230	318	265
Motorcycle	15	82	24
Recreational Vehicle	28	54	31
Valuable Items	12	2	5

Central Sierra Insurance
Personal Lines Policy by Agent

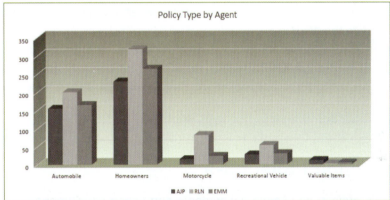

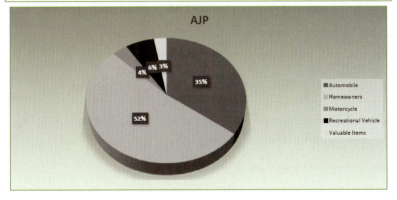

3-74 Excel 3-7 completed worksheet with charts

Challenge Project 3-8

For this project, you create a worksheet that outlines costs for trips to three of your favorite cities. From the data, you will create column or bar charts to compare the costs of the visits to each city.
[Student Learning Outcomes 3.1, 3.2, 3.3, 3.4, 3.5, 3.6]

File Needed: None
Completed Project File Name: *[your initials] Excel 3-8.xlsx*

Create a new workbook and save it as *[your initials] Excel 3-8*. Modify your workbook according to the following guidelines:

- As column headings, type the names of three cities that you would like to visit.
- As row headings, type five or six major expense categories for a trip. These might be labels such as "Air, Train, or Bus", "Hotel", "Entertainment", and similar expenses.
- Enter estimated costs for a five-day trip for each city using your own research about the city. Format your data as needed.
- Type a main and secondary title for your data.
- Create a column or bar chart sheet that compares the trips.
- Change the layout or apply a chart style.
- Use a picture as fill for one of the data series.
- Edit the chart title placeholder to display an appropriate title. Change the font size of the title to balance the chart.
- Format chart elements to create an attractive, easy-to-understand chart of your data.

Challenge Project 3-9

For this project, you create a worksheet and accompanying charts to track your daily usage of your smart phone.
[Student Learning Outcomes 3.1, 3.2, 3.3, 3.4, 3.5, 3.6]

File Needed: None
Completed Project File Name: *[your initials] Excel 3-9.xlsx*

Create a new workbook and save it as *[your initials] Excel 3-9*. Modify your workbook according to the following guidelines:

- Use the days of the week as the column headings.
- As row headings, type names of four or five tasks that you might do each day with your smart phone. You might use labels such as "Send text", "Receive phone call", "Use GPS", or similar tasks.
- Enter a value for the number of times you perform each task on each day.

- Type a main title for your data in row 1. Format your data.
- Create a column chart object that compares the number of times you did each task on Monday.
- Size and position the chart object below the worksheet data.
- Change the layout or apply a chart style.
- Edit the chart title placeholder to display an appropriate title.
- Format chart elements to create an attractive, easy-to-understand chart of your data.
- For the task with the greatest Monday value, create another column chart that displays the daily numbers for that one task.
- Size and position this chart object below the first chart.
- Format the second chart to complement the first chart.

Challenge Project 3-10

For this project, you create a worksheet and line chart that compares the temperature in your city or town at 12 noon for the past 10 days. You also insert a single sparkline in the data.
[Student Learning Outcomes 3.1, 3.2, 3.3, 3.4, 3.5, 3.6, 3.7]

File Needed: None
Completed Project File Name: *[your initials] Excel 3-10.xlsx*

Create a new workbook and save it as *[your initials] Excel 3-10*. Modify your workbook according to the following guidelines:

- In a worksheet, enter the dates for the last 10 days and enter a temperature in degrees for each date at 12 noon. Use a weather reference or your recollection of the day.
- Type a main title for your data (insert a row if necessary). Format your data.
- Create a line chart sheet that illustrates the daily temperature for 10 days.
- Change the layout or apply a chart style.
- Edit and format the chart elements as needed.
- In the worksheet, select the range of values and insert a line sparkline in the column to the right, in one cell, next to the first value.

CHAPTER 4

Importing, Creating Tables, Sorting and Filtering, and Using Conditional Formatting

CHAPTER OVERVIEW

Sharing data among software programs is essential in professional and personal work. Excel can both import data from several sources and export data in a number of formats. Because shared data is typically in the form of a list or table, Excel features a **Table** style with enhanced commands to help you manage list-type data. This chapter teaches you how to import data, create and format Excel tables, and protect your worksheets in an Excel workbook.

STUDENT LEARNING OUTCOMES (SLOs)

After completing this chapter, you will be able to:

SLO 4.1 Import data into Excel from a text file, database file, or a web site and use *Flash Fill* and data connections (p. E4-187).

SLO 4.2 Create and format an Excel table and a *PivotTable* and export data for use in other programs (p. E4-194).

SLO 4.3 Sort data by text, number, color, or icon (p. E4-205).

SLO 4.4 Apply an *AutoFilter* or an *Advanced Filter* to data (p. E4-209).

SLO 4.5 Use the *Subtotal* command and create groups and outlines (p. E4-212).

SLO 4.6 Apply and manage *Conditional Formatting* using cell rules, *Color Scales*, *Icon Sets*, and *Data Bars* (p. E4-218).

SLO 4.7 Use *Goal Seek* and protect a worksheet (p. E4-222).

CASE STUDY

For the Pause & Practice projects in this chapter, you create Excel workbooks for the northern Minnesota company, Paradise Lakes Resort (PLR), introduced in Chapters 1–3. In preparation for its annual department meetings, PLR is asking managers to import and sort data from external sources, format lists as tables and PivotTables, *and subtotal data for analysis.*

Pause & Practice 4-1: Import data for a workbook from text files and use *Flash Fill*.

Pause & Practice 4-2: Format an Excel list as a table, remove duplicate records, and create a *PivotTable*.

Pause & Practice 4-3: Sort and filter data in an Excel workbook and apply subtotals.

Pause & Practice 4-4: Use *Goal Seek*, apply conditional formatting, and protect a worksheet.

Importing Data

Data is available in many formats. A key Excel skill is knowing how to access and convert data for use in your Excel worksheets. *Importing* data refers to the task of obtaining data from another software program, another file format, or an Internet location. In many situations importing data saves time and increases accuracy. For example, at a retail business, you might import a supplier's catalog into a worksheet to help employees prepare routine orders. Or you might import calendar data from co-workers to build a daily schedule in a worksheet. Many companies buy customer or client lists and import the data from those lists into Excel to build prospect lists.

External data is data in a worksheet that originated in another program or format. You can import or copy external data into Excel from the *source*. The source can be a text file, a database, or a web location. If you import external data using the *Get External Data* group, you establish live connections that update the data in your worksheet if a change is made to the original data. If you simply copy data into a worksheet, you do not maintain a connection to the source. Data connections are discussed later in this section.

For most uses, it is best to import data in list format. List format features data organized in rows and columns with analogous information in the same column in each row.

Text Files

A *text file* is a document that includes basic data, no formatting, and commas or other characters to separate the data into columns and rows. Text files include *.txt* (text) documents such as those created in NotePad or WordPad. Another widely used format is *.csv* (comma separated values); you might see this type of file when you download a bank statement. Most software can save a *.prn* (printer) file, which is a simple text file that can be printed.

Text files separate data into columns, often called *fields,* in one of two ways. In one type of text file, a character, such as a comma or a tab, separates the fields. When a text file uses a special character, it is referred to as a *delimited* file (e.g., tab-delimited file). The *delimiter* in the file is the character used to separate the data.

The other text file type identifies fields or columns by a *fixed width.* Each field is a specified width, followed by a space. For example, if the first name field occupies 25 spaces and an individual's name is "Tom," it is imported as 3 characters followed by 22 empty spaces.

When you click the *From Text* button in the *Get External Data* group on the *Data* tab (Figure 4-1), the **Text Import Wizard** guides you through the data importing steps. The wizard usually is able to determine if the file you are working with is delimited or fixed width.

4-1 *Get External Data* group

> **MORE INFO**
>
> Many legacy or mainframe computer systems use fixed width files for data.

HOW TO: Import a Delimited Text File into a Worksheet

1. Select the cell where you want the imported data to start.
2. Click the **From Text** button [*Data* tab, *Get External Data* group].
3. Select the name of the text file in the *Import Text File* dialog box and click **Import** (Figure 4-2).
4. In the *Text Import Wizard – Step 1 of 3* window, click the **Delimited** radio button if necessary and click **Next** (Figure 4-3).

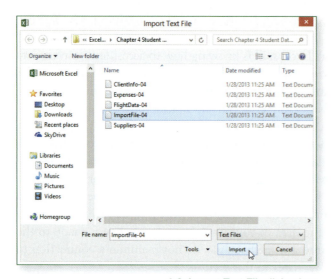

4-2 *Import Text File* dialog box

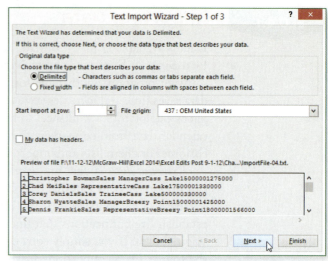

4-3 *Text Import Wizard – Step 1*

5. In the *Text Import Wizard – Step 2 of 3* window, check the **Tab** box if necessary and click **Next** (see Figure 4-4).

   - Look at the *Data preview* to determine if the correct delimiter is selected. You can try any of the listed delimiters or type a custom character.

6. Click **Finish** (Figure 4-5).

   - Select a column in the *Data preview* area and set its format in the *Column data format* group.
   - You can also format the data after it is imported.

7. Click **OK** in the *Import Data* dialog box (Figure 4-6).

   - Click **Properties** to open the *External Data Range Properties* dialog box. You can set options for imported data such as a *Refresh data* time or *Preserve cell formatting*. Click **OK** to close this dialog box.

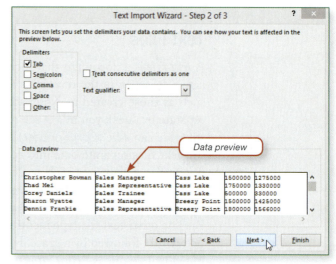

4-4 *Text Import Wizard – Step 2*

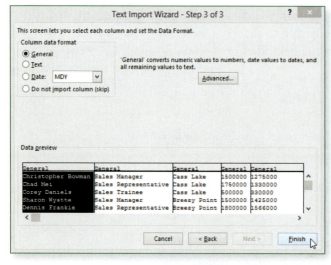

4-5 *Text Import Wizard – Step 3*

4-6 *Import Data* dialog box

You cannot directly import text from a Word document into Excel. However, you can copy and paste data from Word into an Excel worksheet. When you paste the data in Excel, you can retain the formatting used in the Word document, or you can choose the current format in the worksheet.

HOW TO: Copy Data from a Word Document

1. Select the cell in the worksheet where you want the imported data to start.
2. Open the Word document and select the table or list you want to import to Excel.
3. Click the **Copy** button [*Home* tab, *Clipboard* group].
4. Switch to the Excel worksheet.
5. Click the **Paste** button [*Home* tab, *Clipboard* group] or press **Ctrl+V**.
   - To retain the formatting from the Word document, click the arrow with the **Paste** drop-down button to choose the option to *Match Destination Formatting*.

> **ANOTHER WAY**
>
> Save a Word document as a Text file (*.txt*) and import the text file into Excel.

> **MORE INFO**
>
> To split data in a single column into separate columns, insert as many blank columns to the right as needed for the split data. Select the column to be split and click the **Text to Columns** button [*Data* tab, *Data Tools* group]. Complete the *Convert Text to Columns Wizard* to split the column.

Access Database Files

A *database* is a collection of related tables, queries, forms, and reports. *Microsoft Access* is a relational database management system that is part of the Office suite of products. Most companies, service organizations, schools, and other enterprises keep great amounts of data in databases, so it is quite common to import data from a database for use in Excel. For example, Access cannot illustrate data in a chart. If there is chartable sales data in a database table, you can import the relevant data from Access into Excel and build the chart.

You can import a table or a query from an Access database into an Excel worksheet. To do this, you import the data as an Excel table and then you convert a table into a normal data range (this topic is covered later in this chapter).

Access database files have an *.accdb* extension. When a database includes many tables and queries, the *Select Table* dialog box opens so that you can choose the table or query you want to import.

> **MORE INFO**
>
> If a database has a single table or query, it is automatically imported into Excel; the *Select Table* dialog box does not open.

HOW TO: Import an Access Table into a Worksheet

1. Select the worksheet cell where you want the imported data to start.

   - Because all Access tables or queries have column or field headings, you do not need column headings in the worksheet.

2. Click the **From Access** button [*Data* tab, *Get External Data* group].

3. Select the database name in the *Select Data Source* dialog box.

4. Click **Open** (Figure 4-7).

5. Select the name of the table or query you want to import in the *Select Table* dialog box (Figure 4-8).

6. Click **OK**.

7. In the *Import Data* dialog box, select **Table** and **Existing worksheet**.

   - You can choose a new worksheet for the imported data. If you do this, the data is imported starting at cell A1.
   - Click **Properties** to change options such as refresh timing.

8. Click **OK**.

   - An Excel table displays *AutoFilter* buttons with each column heading for sorting and filtering (Figure 4-9). Filters are covered in *SLO 4.4: Filtering Data*.

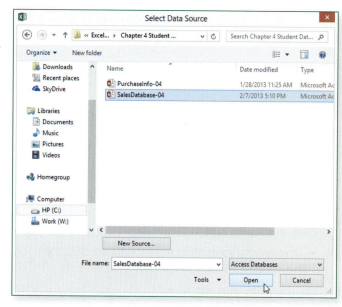

4-7 *Select Data Source* dialog box

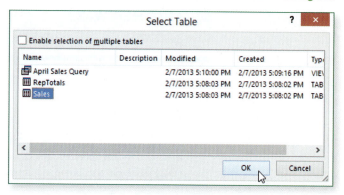

4-8 *Select Table* dialog box

> ### MORE INFO
>
> You can import tables and queries from relational databases such as SQL Server with the **From Other Sources** button [*Data* tab, *Get External Data* group].

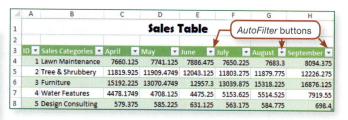

4-9 Imported Access table

Web Site Data

Many web sites include table-formatted data that you can import into a worksheet. For example, a company like Paradise Lakes Resort might import data from a web site about vacation spending so that company officers can project future rentals and purchases. Or they might import data from a weather site to build a chart about average temperatures and rainfall to plan marketing campaigns.

Web pages include a wealth of data, images, and sometimes even video. When you use the *From Web* command, data that you can import into Excel as a list or table is indicated on a web page with a small black arrow in a yellow box. This identifier enables you to easily locate which data you can import and format in columns and rows. When you click a yellow box with an arrow, the related table is selected, and the arrow changes to a green box with a check mark. The data is ready for importing.

Data that you import from a web page establishes a connection to the site that you can refresh whenever necessary.

HOW TO: Import Web Data into a Worksheet

1. Select the worksheet cell where you want the imported data to start.
   - Depending on how data is formatted on the web page, you may not need to insert column headings after importing.
2. Click the **From Web** button [*Data* tab, *Get External Data* group].
3. In the *New Web Query* dialog box, browse to locate the web site and data you want to import (Figure 4-10).
4. Click the **Click to select this table** arrow (yellow box with black arrow) next to the data you want to import.
   - Click the **Options** button to set options such as *Formatting* (Figure 4-11) and click **OK**.
5. Click the **Import** button in the *New Web Query* dialog box.
   - Click the **Properties** button to edit options such as *Refresh Control* or *Data Formatting and layout*. Click **OK** to save changes.
6. Click **OK** in the *Import Data* dialog box.
   - A message on screen may inform you that Excel is obtaining the data. When the import is complete, the data is displayed in the worksheet and looks similar to the example shown in Figure 4-12.

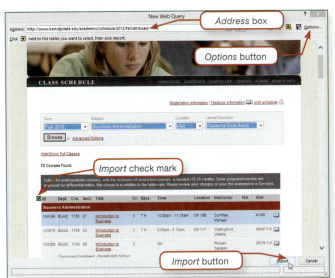

4-10 *New Web Query* window

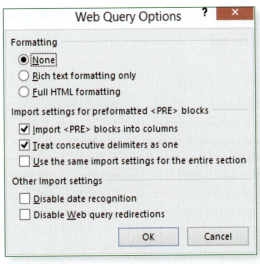

4-11 *Web Query Options* dialog box

4-12 Data imported from a web site

Flash Fill

Flash Fill is a new command in Excel 2013 that recognizes a pattern and duplicates it for matching cells. For example, imagine that in data that you import from a text file or a web site, individuals' first and last names are together in a single column. You want the first and last names to be in separate columns in your Excel document so in a new column in the first row, you type the first name of the first individual. When you enter the first name of the second person in the second row, *Flash Fill* completes the remaining cells in the column. The **Flash Fill Options** button appears after you press **Enter** so that you can undo the fill if necessary or accept all the suggestions.

HOW TO: Flash Fill Data in a Worksheet

1. Insert a new column to the right of the data you want to use in the *Flash Fill* column.

2. Click in the first cell in the new column for data.

3. Type the data you want to appear in the first cell in the column.

   - Figure 4-13 shows a pattern with the first and last name from the "Name" column with a period between names, followed by "@go.com."

4. Type data in the second cell following the same pattern.

   - If the *Flash Fill* suggestion list does not appear after the second item, type the third item.

5. Press **Enter** to complete the *Flash Fill*.

   - If the *Flash Fill* suggestion list does not appear, click the **Flash Fill** button [*Data* tab, *Data Tools* group] with the insertion point still in the column.

4-13 *Flash Fill* suggestion list

Data Connections

A *connection* is an identifier for data that originated outside the workbook. For any data that you import using a command in the *Get External Data* group on the *Data* tab, Excel establishes a connection that you can update, refresh, name, or remove. If you import the data from a text file or a database, you can refresh the data by importing it again. If you import the data as a web query, you can replace the data in your worksheet with current data on the web site.

A data connection to an Internet location is named *Connection*. You can access the properties for any connection and label it with a more recognizable name. A data connection to the file you import is named with the same file name as the imported file.

Depending upon your Excel options, you may see a security warning bar at the top of the worksheet when you open a workbook that has data connections. Click **Enable Editing** to work with the data.

HOW TO: Manage Data Connections

1. Click the **Connections** button [*Data* tab, *Connections* group] to open the *Workbook Connections* dialog box.

2. Select the name of the connection in the top pane (Figure 4-14).

3. Click **Refresh** to update the imported data.
   - The *Import Text File* dialog box opens if you have selected a connection for an imported text file.

4. Click the link **Click here to see where the selected connections are used** to identify where the data is located in the workbook.

5. Click **Properties** to open the *Connections Properties* dialog box.
   - You can set how the data is refreshed, change the connection name, or add a description.

6. Click **Close** to save changes.

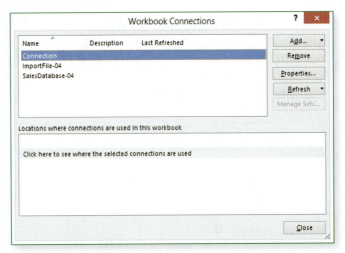

4-14 **Workbook Connections** dialog box

PAUSE & PRACTICE: EXCEL 4-1

For this project, you import data from a text file into an Excel worksheet, copy data from a Word document into the same worksheet, and use *Flash Fill* to build a worksheet for Paradise Lakes Resort.

Files Needed: **Sales-04.xlsx**, **ImportFile-04.txt**, and **ImportWord-04.docx**
Completed Project File Name: **[your initials] PP E4-1.xlsx**

1. Open the **Sales-04** workbook from the student data files folder. Click the **Enable Editing** button.

2. Save the workbook as **[your initials] PP E4-1**.

3. Import data from a text file.
   a. Select cell **A3**.
   b. Click the **From Text** button [*Data* tab, *Get External Data* group].
   c. Select the **ImportFile-04.txt** file in the *Import Text File* dialog box.
   d. Click **Import**.
   e. Select the **Delimited** button in the *Text Import Wizard – Step 1 of 3* dialog box.
   f. Click **Next**.
   g. Place a check mark for **Tab** in the *Text Import Wizard – Step 2 of 3* dialog box.
   h. Click **Next**.
   i. Click **Finish** in the last dialog box.
   j. Click **OK** in the *Import Data* dialog box.

4. Copy data from a Word document.
   a. Select cell **A17**.
   b. Open Microsoft Word and open the **ImportWord-04** Word document. Click the **Enable Editing** button.
   c. Select all the data and click the **Copy** button [*Home* tab, *Clipboard* group].

d. Switch to the Excel window.

e. Click the arrow with the **Paste** button [*Home* tab, *Clipboard* group] and choose **Match Destination Formatting** (Figure 4-15).

f. Select cells **D3:E26** and apply the **Currency** number format with zero decimals.

g. Adjust the widths of columns **C:E** to 15.00.

5. Create an email address column using *Flash Fill*.

a. Insert a new column between columns **A** and **B**.

b. Type Email Address in cell **B2**.

c. Increase the width of the "Email Address" column to 37.00.

d. Type Christopher.Bowman@ somewhere.com in **B3** and press **Enter**.

e. Type Chad.Mei@somewhere.com in **B4** and press **Enter** to complete the *Flash Fill* (Figure 4-16).

f. If the *Flash Fill* suggestion list does not appear, click the **Flash Fill** button [*Data* tab, *Data Tools* group].

6. Save and close the workbook. Close the Word document.

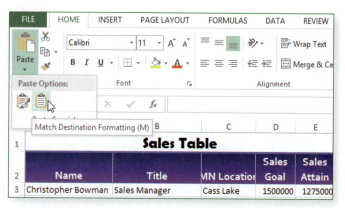

4-15 *Paste Options* for copied data

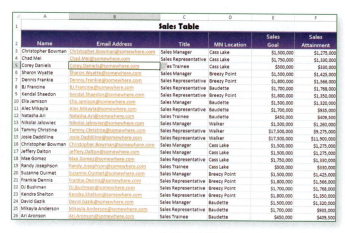

4-16 PP E4-1 completed worksheet

Creating Excel Tables

An Excel *table* is a list of related pieces of information that is formatted with a title row followed by rows of data. When your data is in table format, Excel commands allow you to organize, sort, filter, and calculate the data easily and quickly, much like a database.

The *header row* is the first row of the table with descriptive titles or labels. Each row of data is a *record* and each column is a *field*. The label in the header row is sometimes referred to as the *field name*. When you format your Excel data as a table, follow these guidelines to make your tables easier to use and navigate:

- Type descriptive labels in the first row and begin each label with a letter, not a number.
- Give each header a unique label; do not repeat any of the descriptive labels.
- Keep the same type of data within each column (e.g., text or values).
- Do not leave blank cells within the data.

Create an Excel Table

When data is arranged as a list and conforms to the guidelines just described, it is a straight-forward format command to create an Excel table. Select the data you want to include in the table and click the **Format as Table** button in the *Styles* group on the *Home* tab. There is also a **Table** button in the *Tables* group on the *Insert* tab.

After your data is formatted as a table, each label in the header row displays an *AutoFilter* button. Recall from Chapter 3 that a *filter* specifies which data is shown and which is hidden. In other words, a filter is a criterion or a specification that data must meet to be shown. The *AutoFilter* buttons allow you to quickly hide or display rows of data. For example, you might want to display only those persons from a particular location or only those who reached a certain level of sales. In *SLO 4.4: Filtering Data*, you learn how to create and customize filters.

The *Table Tools Design* tab appears when any cell is selected within a table.

HOW TO: Create an Excel Table

1. Select the cells that you want to include in a table, including the header row.
2. Click the **Format as Table** button [*Home* tab, *Styles* group].
3. Choose a **Table Style** from the *Style* gallery (Figure 4-17).
4. Verify the cell range in the *Format As Table* dialog box.
   - If the cell range for the table is incorrect, drag to reselect the correct cell range in the worksheet.
5. Verify that there is a check in the **My table has headers** box in the *Format As Table* dialog box.
   - If there is no header row in the cell range you select originally, Excel inserts a row above the data and names the columns *Column1*, *Column2*, and so on. You can edit these names.
6. Click **OK** to create the table (Figure 4-18).
   - When the selected range includes imported data, you will see a message box asking to remove the connection. Click **Yes** to create the table.

4-17 *Table Style* gallery

			Sales	Sales
Sales Table				
Name	Email Address	Title	MN Location	Goal	Attainment
Christopher Bowman	Christopher.Bowman@somewhere.com	Sales Manager	Cass Lake	$1,500,000	$1,275,000
Chad Mei	Chad.Mei@somewhere.com	Sales Representative	Cass Lake	$1,750,000	$1,330,000
Corey Daniels	Corey.Daniels@somewhere.com	Sales Trainee	Cass Lake	$500,000	$330,000
Sharon Wyatte	Sharon.Wyatte@somewhere.com	Sales Manager	Breezy Point	$1,500,000	$1,425,000
Dennis Frankie	Dennis.Frankie@somewhere.com	Sales Representative	Breezy Point	$1,800,000	$1,566,000
BJ Francine	BJ.Francine@somewhere.com	Sales Representative	Baudette	$1,700,000	$1,768,000
Kendal Shaedon	Kendal.Shaedon@somewhere.com	Sales Representative	Breezy Point	$1,800,000	$1,350,000
Ella Jamison	Ella.Jamison@somewhere.com	Sales Manager	Baudette	$1,500,000	$1,320,000
Alec Mikayla	Alec.Mikayla@somewhere.com	Sales Representative	Baudette	$1,700,000	$935,000
Natasha Ari	Natasha.Ari@somewhere.com	Sales Trainee	Baudette	$450,000	$409,500
Nikolai Jalowiec	Nikolai.Jalowiec@somewhere.com	Sales Manager	Walker	$1,500,000	$1,260,000
Tammy Christine	Tammy.Christine@somewhere.com	Sales Representative	Walker	$17,500,000	$9,275,000
Josie Daddiline	Josie.Daddiline@somewhere.com	Sales Representative	Walker	$17,500,000	$11,900,000
Christopher Bowman	Christopher.Bowman@somewhere.com	Sales Manager	Cass Lake	$1,500,000	$1,275,000

4-18 **Formatted Excel table**

Table Styles

A *table style* is a predesigned set of built-in format options such as borders, fill colors, and effects for a table. A table style includes a color scheme and may display alternating fill for the rows, vertical borders, and more. You select a style when you create a table, but you can apply a different style to a table once it exists to change the look of your data. Predefined table styles are classified as *Light*, *Medium*, and *Dark*.

HOW TO: Apply a Style to an Existing Table

1. Click any cell within the table to display the *Table Tools Design* tab.
2. Click the **More** button [*Table Tools Design* tab, *Table Styles* group] to open the *Table Styles* gallery.
3. Point at a style to see a *Live Preview* of its effect on the table.
4. Click to select and apply a style.

Table Style Options

The *Table Style Options* group on the *Table Tools Design* tab includes commands for showing or hiding various parts of the table. You can hide the header row or display a total row. You can choose banded columns or rows, which alternates shading on the rows or columns. You can also hide the *AutoFilter* buttons, if you like.

If you choose to show a total row, you can choose the calculation that is displayed in the row.

HOW TO: Display a Total Row in a Table

1. Click any cell within the table.
2. Click to check the **Total Row** box [*Table Tools Design* tab, *Table Style Options* group].
   - The total row displays after the last row in the table (Figure 4-19).

Save a New Table Style

You may have a preference for a particular table style, or your organization may have specific requirements. You can create and name custom table styles so that you can apply preferred format choices to tables you create with one click.

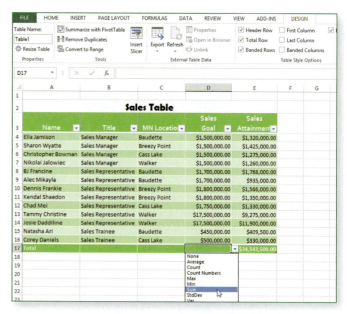

4-19 Table with total row

In the *New Table Style* dialog box, select an individual part of a table and specify how it should be formatted. For example, you can set the first column feature a different font color or bold italic font.

When you create your own table style, it is listed in a *Custom* group at the top of the *Table Styles* gallery.

HOW TO: Save a New Table Style

1. Click any cell within a table.
2. Click the **Table Styles** More button [*Table Tools Design* tab, *Table Styles* group].
3. Click the **New Table Style** button (Figure 4-20).
4. Type a style name in the *Name* box.
5. Select a *Table Element* and click **Format** to open the *Format Cells* dialog box.
   - Make format selections on the *Font*, *Border*, or *Fill* tabs in the dialog box and click **OK**.
6. Check or uncheck the set as default box to indicate if the new style should be the default for the current document.
7. Click **OK**.

4-20 *New Table Style* dialog box

The Table Tools Group

The ***Tools*** group on the *Table Tools Design* tab has four commands: *Summarize with PivotTable*, *Remove Duplicates*, *Convert to Range*, and *Insert Slicer* (Figure 4-21). *PivotTables* are covered later in this section. First, the other three commands are introduced.

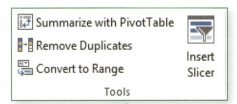

4-21 *Tools* group

A ***duplicate row*** is a row in a table that has exactly the same information in one or more columns. The *Remove Duplicates* command scans a table to locate and delete any rows with repeated data in the specified columns. In the *Remove Duplicates* dialog box, you specify which columns might have duplicate data.

HOW TO: Remove Duplicates

1. Click any cell within the table.
2. Click the **Remove Duplicates** button [*Table Tools Design* tab, *Tools* group] (Figure 4-22).
3. Place a check mark next to each column that you suspect may have duplicate data.
   - If you check all the columns, those rows containing the same data in every column are considered a duplicate and removed.
4. Click **OK**.
   - A message box indicates how many duplicate values were found and removed as well as how many unique values are still in the table (Figure 4-23).
   - This command does not preview which rows are deleted.
5. Click **OK** in the message box.

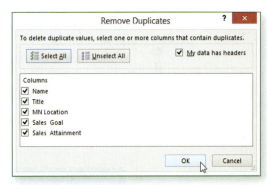

4-22 *Remove Duplicates* dialog box

4-23 *Duplicates Found* message box

In the *Tools* group, you can use the *Convert to Range* command to convert a table to a normal data in the worksheet. This removes all table formatting and the *AutoFilter* buttons.

HOW TO: Convert a Table to Range

1. Click any cell within the table.
2. Click the **Convert to Range** button [*Table Tools Design* tab, *Tools* group] (Figure 4-24).
3. Click **Yes** in the message box.

4-24 *Convert to Normal Range* dialog box

> **MORE INFO**
>
> You can show *AutoFilter* buttons in a normal data range by clicking the *Filter* button on the *Data* tab.

The *Insert Slicer* command opens a window where you can filter data to analyze smaller pieces of the whole. This command is also available for *PivotTables*, which are discussed later in this section.

Table Name and Structured References

By default, when you first create an Excel table, it is initially named *TableN* where *N* is a number. You can give an Excel table a more descriptive name using the *Table Tools Design* tab in the *Properties* group.

In an Excel table, each column is assigned a specific name based on the label in its header row. This name is known as a ***structured reference***. There is a structured reference for every column, and structured references are each preceded by the @ symbol. There are also several automatic structured references in a table. They include: #All, #Data, #Headers, #This Row, and #Totals.

You view these structured references when you build a formula by pointing to them (Figure 4-25). You can also refer to them elsewhere in the worksheet when creating a formula.

4-25 Structured references in a table

> **MORE INFO**
>
> To force your table formulas to use regular cell referencing in place of table headings, select **Options** from the *File* tab. Select **Formulas** on the left, navigate to the *Working with formulas* category, and remove the check next to *Use table names in formulas*.

PivotTables

A *PivotTable* is a summary report based on a list-type range of data in a worksheet. The list of data in a *PivotTable* is dynamic and contains movable field buttons and filter options; you can move and manipulate different components of a *PivotTable* for different analysis options.

In other words, a *PivotTable* is a separate worksheet in which you can sort, filter, and calculate large amounts of data. *PivotTables* are interactive, because you can rearrange parts of the report for analysis by clicking or dragging. Rearranging data is *pivoting* the data; pivoting allows you to look at data from a different perspective. A *PivotChart* can be built from a *PivotTable* and has similar features. It contains charted data that is dynamic (updates in real time) and contains the same movable field buttons and filter options that a *PivotTable* does. The *PivotChart* button is on the *PivotTable Tools Analyze* tab.

> **MORE INFO**
>
> If you create a *PivotChart* directly from list data in a worksheet, an underlying *PivotTable* is also automatically created.

PivotTables are sophisticated analysis tools. They enable you to "drill-down" into your data and assess various types of results or changes. For example, in a table or list with thousands of records, you can arrange a *PivotTable* to quickly show average sales by state, by city, or by other criteria, and, just as quickly, return to the entire list.

A *PivotTable* is based on a range of data, like a table, with a header row, although the data does not have to be formatted as an Excel table (Figure 4-26). Data for a *PivotTable* should follow the same guidelines as those recommended for an Excel table in the beginning of this section. A *PivotTable* is placed on its own sheet in the workbook.

The *Tables* group on the *Insert* tab includes the *PivotTable* button as well as the *Recommended PivotTables* button. When you are first learning about *PivotTables*, use the **Recommended PivotTables** button until you gain experience building these reports.

After you create a *PivotTable*, the *PivotTable Tools Analyze* and *Design* tabs are available for additional format choices and data commands.

	A	B	C
1			
2			
3	**Row Labels** ▼	**Sum of Sales Goal**	
4	⊟ **Baudette**	5350000	
5	Alec Mikayla	1700000	
6	BJ Francine	1700000	
7	Ella Jamison	1500000	
8	Natasha Ari	450000	
9	⊟ **Breezy Point**	5100000	
10	Dennis Frankie	1800000	
11	Kendal Shaedon	1800000	
12	Sharon Wyatte	1500000	
13	⊟ **Cass Lake**	3750000	
14	Chad Mei	1750000	
15	Christopher Bowman	1500000	
16	Corey Daniels	500000	
17	⊟ **Walker**	36500000	
18	Josie Daddiline	17500000	
19	Nikolai Jalowiec	1500000	
20	Tammy Christine	17500000	
21	**Grand Total**	50700000	
22			

4-26 An Excel *PivotTable*

> **MORE INFO**
>
> You must refresh a *PivotTable* after changes are made to the underlying worksheet data.

HOW TO: Create a PivotTable

1. Click anywhere within the data range.
   - The data range must have a header row.
   - You can select the entire range.

2. Click the **Recommended PivotTables** button [*Insert* tab, *Tables* group] (Figure 4-27).
   - A data range in the worksheet is assumed.
   - Click *Change Source Data* if the assumed range is incorrect.
   - You can create a blank *PivotTable* from this dialog box.
3. Click a preview tile and review the description of the proposed *PivotTable*.
4. Select the preferred *PivotTable* and click **OK**.

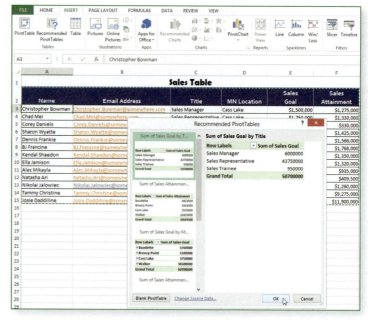

4-27 Recommended PivotTables for a data range

A *PivotTable* is created on a new sheet in the workbook and the *PivotTable Fields* pane opens at the right. From this pane, you can choose fields to be added to the report and hide or display other fields. You can drag field names into different areas in the pane to regroup how the data is organized.

> **MORE INFO**
>
> Delete the *PivotTable* layout by clicking the **Clear** button [*PivotTable Tools Analyze* tab, *Actions* group]. You can build a new *PivotTable* from the same data.

In the *PivotTable* report itself, each column label includes a filter arrow so that you can hide or display selected rows. Similarly, row labels may include collapse/expand buttons to hide or show data for that part of the report. In addition, you can add a report filter by dragging a field name into the *Filter* part of the *PivotTable Fields* pane.

It takes time and practice to create a useful *PivotTable* and to understand all its features. It is a good idea to experiment as you build *PivotTables* to develop skill in placing fields, and sorting and filtering data.

HOW TO: Add a PivotTable Report Filter and Pivot Fields

1. Click anywhere in the *PivotTable*.
2. Drag the field name into the *Filter* area and release the field (Figure 4-28).
   - Drag the field name from the *Choose fields to add to report* area or from another area in the *PivotTable Fields* pane.
   - The field is added with a filter button in row 1 of the *PivotTable*.

4-28 PivotTable Fields pane

3. Point and drag a field name from the *Choose fields to add to report* area into the *Values* area in the *PivotTable Fields* pane and release the field.

- A new column is added to the report (Figure 4-29).
- The calculation used for the *Values* fields is *Sum*. Change it by clicking in the column and selecting the **Field Settings** button [*PivotTable Tools Analyze* tab, *Active Field* group].

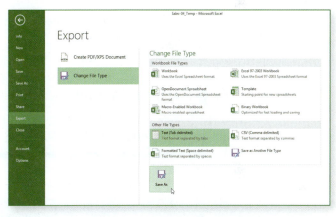

4-29 *PivotTable* **results**

Export Data

You have seen how you can import data from various sources for use in Excel. Similarly, you can export or save Excel data in a format that is usable in other programs and applications. For example, you can save an Excel table as a text file for use in any program that can read a text file. Since most software applications can read a text file, this is a common way to transfer or share data.

When you save worksheet data as a text file, Excel renames the sheet with the same file name that you type for the text file. You can save only one worksheet in a text file. If a workbook has multiple sheets, a message box will alert you that only the current sheet will be saved.

HOW TO: Save an Excel Table as a Text File

1. Save the workbook file you want to export.
2. Click the worksheet tab with the table or list you want to save and export.
3. Open the *Backstage* view and click **Export**.
4. Click the **Change File Type** button.
5. Select **Text (Tab delimited)** as the file type (Figure 4-30).
6. Click **Save As**.
7. Navigate to the location where you want the exported material to be saved and type the file name.
8. Click **Save**.

4-30 *Backstage* **view to export data**

A **SharePoint web server** is a server that runs *Microsoft SharePoint Services*, a network product that allows for collaboration and simultaneous work by groups of people via the Internet. You can export table data to a custom list on the server and make your data available for others with the *Export Table to SharePoint List Wizard*. A list on a SharePoint server stores and displays content that users can edit online. To work with the SharePoint server, you must have an Internet connection and permission from the network administrator.

HOW TO: Export an Excel Table to a SharePoint List

1. Click any cell within the table you wish to export.
2. Click the **Export** button [*Table Tools Design* tab, *External Table Data* group].
3. Select the *Export Table to SharePoint List* option.

4. Type the web address of the SharePoint site in the *Address* box (Figure 4-31).

- Check the **Create a read-only connection to the new SharePoint list** box if you do not want others to edit the data.
- Two columns are added to the table with a read-only connection. An *Item Type* column indicates whether a row represents a SharePoint list item or a folder. A *Path* column displays the folder path for a list item (mylist/foldername).

5. Type the *List* name and *Description* in the *Export Table to SharePoint List* dialog box.

- A list name is required and is displayed at the top of the list page.

6. Click **Next**.

7. Click **Finish** if the columns and data types are correct.

8. Click **OK**.

- Click the **Unlink** button [*Table Tools Design* tab, *External Table Data* group] to disconnect the Excel table from the SharePoint server.

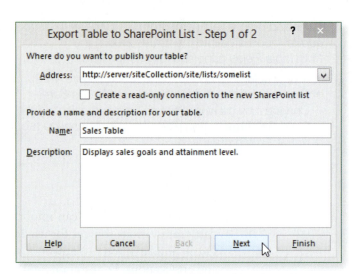

4-31 *Export Table to SharePoint List* wizard

> **MORE INFO**
>
> You can access and use SharePoint data in an Excel worksheet, or unlink the data to keep your own copy of the data separate.

> **ANOTHER WAY**
>
> View your SharePoint list by clicking the **Open in Browser** button [*Table Tools Design* tab, *External Table Data* group].

PAUSE & PRACTICE: EXCEL 4-2

For this project, you format data as an Excel table, add a total row, and remove duplicate records. Then you create a *PivotTable* for Paradise Lakes Resort using the Excel table as its source. Because the workbook has data connections, you will need to enable editing to work with it.

File Needed: ***[your initials] PP E4-1.xlsx***
Completed Project File Name: ***[your initials] PP E4-2.xlsx***

1. Open the ***[your initials] PP E4-1*** workbook. Click **Enable Editing**.

2. Save the workbook as ***[your initials] PP E4-2***.

3. Delete column **B**.

4. Select cells **A2:E2** and clear the formats.

5. Rename the sheet tab Sales Quota Data.

6. Format the data as an Excel table.
   a. Select cells **A2:E26**.
   b. Click the **Format as Table** button [*Home* tab, *Styles* group].
   c. Select **Table Style Medium 27** from the *Style* gallery.
   d. Verify that there is a check mark for **My table has headers** in the *Format As Table* dialog box.
   e. Click **OK**.
   f. Click **Yes** in the message box about external connections (Figure 4-32).

7. Add a total row to a table.
   a. Click a cell within the table.
   b. Click to place a check mark for **Total Row** [*Table Tools Design* tab, *Table Style Options* group].
   c. Click cell **D27** and choose **SUM** from the drop-down list.

8. Remove duplicate rows in a table.
   a. Click a cell within the table.
   b. Click the **Remove Duplicates** button [*Table Tools Design* tab, *Tools* group].
   c. Click **Unselect All** to remove all the check marks.
   d. Click **Name** to place a check mark (Figure 4-33). If you know that duplicate data is in a specific column, you can speed up the search by choosing only that column.
   e. Click **OK** in the *Remove Duplicates* dialog box.
   f. Click **OK** in the message box.

9. Create a *PivotTable*.
   a. Click cell **A3**.
   b. Click the **Recommended PivotTables** button [*Insert* tab, *Tables* group].
   c. Locate and click the **Sum of Sales Goal by MN Location (+)** preview tile.
   d. Click **OK**.
   e. Name the worksheet tab PivotTable.

10. Add a report filter in a *PivotTable*.
    a. Click a cell in the *PivotTable* to open the *PivotTable Fields* pane.
    b. Drag the **MN Location** field from the *Rows* group to the *Filters* group in the *PivotTable Fields* pane.
    c. Click the filter arrow in cell **B1** and click to place a check mark for **Select Multiple Items**.
    d. Click to remove the check marks for **Baudette** and **Breezy Point** (Figure 4-34).
    e. Click **OK**.

	A	B	C	D	E
1			Sales Table		
2	Name	Title	MN Location	Sales Goal	Sales Attainment
3	Christopher Bowman	Sales Manager	Cass Lake	$1,500,000	$1,275,000
4	Chad Mei	Sales Representative	Cass Lake	$1,750,000	$1,330,000
5	Corey Daniels	Sales Trainee	Cass Lake	$500,000	$330,000
6	Sharon Wyatte	Sales Manager	Breezy Point	$1,500,000	$1,425,000
7	Dennis Frankie	Sales Representative	Breezy Point	$1,800,000	$1,566,000
8	BJ Francine	Sales Representative	Baudette	$1,700,000	$1,768,000
9	Kendal Shaedon	Sales Representative	Breezy Point	$1,800,000	$1,350,000
10	Ella Jamison	Sales Manager	Baudette	$1,500,000	$1,320,000
11	Alec Mikayla	Sales Representative	Baudette	$1,700,000	$935,000
12	Natasha Ari	Sales Trainee	Baudette	$450,000	$409,500
13	Nikolai Jalowiec	Sales Manager	Walker	$1,500,000	$1,260,000
14	Tammy Christine	Sales Representative	Walker	$17,500,000	$9,275,000
15	Josie Daddiline	Sales Representative	Walker	$17,500,000	$11,900,000
16	Christopher Bowman	Sales Manager	Cass Lake	$1,500,000	$1,275,000
17	Jeffery Dalton	Sales Manager	Cass Lake	$1,500,000	$1,275,000
18	Mae Gomez	Sales Representative	Cass Lake	$1,750,000	$1,330,000
19	Randy Josephson	Sales Trainee	Cass Lake	$500,000	$330,000
20	Suzanne Ouimet	Sales Manager	Breezy Point	$1,500,000	$1,425,000
21	Frankie Dennis	Sales Representative	Breezy Point	$1,800,000	$1,566,000
22	DJ Bushman	Sales Representative	Breezy Point	$1,700,000	$1,768,000
23	Kendra Shelton	Sales Representative	Breezy Point	$1,800,000	$1,350,000
24	David Gazik	Sales Manager	Baudette	$1,500,000	$1,320,000
25	Mikayla Anderson	Sales Representative	Baudette	$1,700,000	$935,000
26	Ari Aronson	Sales Trainee	Baudette	$450,000	$409,500

4-32 Excel data formatted as a table

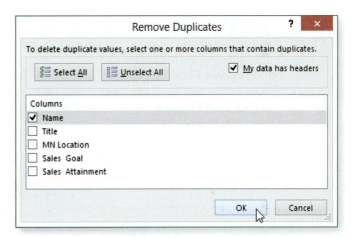

4-33 Duplicate record search in a single field

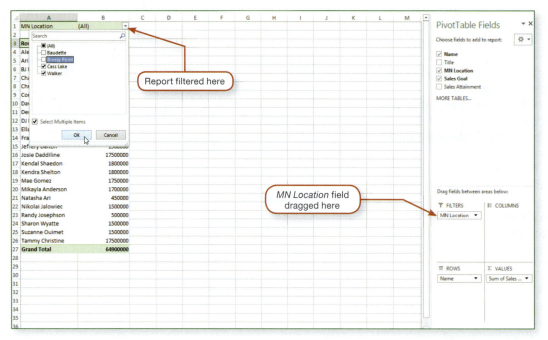

4-34 Report filter settings

11. Format data in a *PivotTable*.
    a. Right-click any cell in column B.
    b. Choose **Value Field Settings** (Figure 4-35).
    c. Click **Number Format** and set **Currency** format with no decimal places.
    d. Click **OK** to close each dialog box.

12. Save and close the workbook (Figure 4-36).

MN Location	(Multiple Items)
Row Labels	**Sum of Sales**
Chad Mei	$1,750,000
Christopher Bowman	$1,500,000
Corey Daniels	$500,000
Jeffery Dalton	$1,500,000
Josie Daddiline	$17,500,000
Mae Gomez	$1,750,000
Nikolai Jalowiec	$1,500,000
Randy Josephson	$500,000
Tammy Christine	$17,500,000
Grand Total	**$44,000,000**

4-36 PP E4-2 completed *PivotTable*

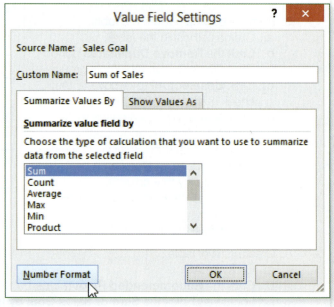

4-35 *Value Field Settings* dialog box

Sorting Data

Sorting is the process of arranging rows of data in an identified order. For Paradise Lakes Resort, for example, you may want to arrange the sales table by location to compare the sites. Or you may want to order the rows from best sales attainment to lowest.

You can sort data in ascending or descending order. *Ascending* order sorts data alphabetically from A to Z or numerically from smallest to largest value. In a *descending* sort, data are arranged alphabetically Z to A or numerically from largest to smallest value.

Sort Options

You can sort all Excel data that is organized in rows and columns. You can sort by one column or by multiple columns. In addition to normal text or number sorting, you can sort data by cell fill color, font color, or cell icons (from *Conditional Formatting*, covered later in this chapter in *SLO 4.6: Applying Conditional Formatting*).

The **Sort & Filter** button on the *Home* tab in the *Editing* group lists the *A to Z* sort, the *Z to A* sort, and the *Custom Sort* (multiple columns) commands. The same commands are available in the *Sort & Filter* group on the *Data* tab.

Sort Text Data

In a cell range that has a header row followed by rows of data, you can click any cell in the column you want to sort and click the appropriate button.

HOW TO: Sort Text Data by a Single Column

1. Select a cell in the column that contains the data you want to sort.
2. Click the **A to Z** button [*Data* tab, *Sort & Filter* group].
   - The records are arranged in alphabetical order based on the first character in the cell.
   - If the first character in a row is a value or special character, that record is sorted at the top.
   - Click the **Undo** button [*Home* tab, *Clipboard* group] to undo a sort.
3. Click the **Z to A** button [*Data* tab, *Sort & Filter* group].
   - The records are arranged in reverse alphabetical order based on the first character in the cell (Figure 4-37).
   - If the first character in a row is a value or special character, that record is sorted at the bottom.

	A	B	C	D	E
1			Sales Table		
2	Name	Title	MN Location	Sales Goal	Sales Attainment
3	Tammy Christine	Sales Representative	Walker	$17,500,000.00	$9,275,000.00
4	Sharon Wyatte	Sales Manager	Breezy Point	$1,500,000.00	$1,425,000.00
5	Nikolai Jalowiec	Sales Manager	Walker	$1,500,000.00	$1,260,000.00
6	Natasha Ari	Sales Trainee	Baudette	$450,000.00	$409,500.00
7	Kendal Shaedon	Sales Representative	Breezy Point	$1,800,000.00	$1,350,000.00
8	Josie Daddiline	Sales Representative	Walker	$17,500,000.00	$11,900,000.00
9	Ella Jamison	Sales Manager	Baudette	$1,500,000.00	$1,320,000.00
10	Dennis Frankie	Sales Representative	Breezy Point	$1,800,000.00	$1,566,000.00
11	Corey Daniels	Sales Trainee	Cass Lake	$500,000.00	$330,000.00
12	Christopher Bowman	Sales Manager	Cass Lake	$1,500,000.00	$1,275,000.00
13	Chad Mei	Sales Representative	Cass Lake	$1,750,000.00	$1,330,000.00
14	BJ Francine	Sales Representative	Baudette	$1,700,000.00	$1,768,000.00
15	Alec Mikayla	Sales Representative	Baudette	$1,700,000.00	$935,000.00

4-37 "Name" column sorted Z to A

> **MORE INFO**
>
> When you sort a cell range using the **A to Z** or **Z to A** buttons, complete rows of data are rearranged, not just the cells in the selected column.

To sort text data in more than one column or field, use the *Sort* dialog box. This dialog box opens when you click the **Sort** button [*Data* tab, *Sort & Filter* group] or when you choose **Custom Sort** from the **Sort & Filter** button options [*Home* tab, *Editing* group]. A common multiple column sort involves data that includes cities and states. You can first sort by state so that Alabama is before Arizona, and then within that sort, you can further sort by city. Another example of a common multiple column sort involves persons' names. When first and last names are listed in separate columns, you can sort by last name and then first name. If a list includes 15 people named "Smith," you can further sort them by first name.

The data in Figure 4-38 is sorted with a multiple sort.

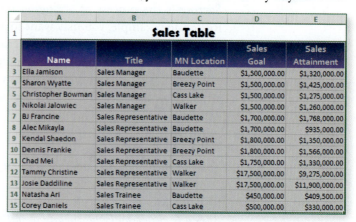

4-38 Data sorted first by "Title" and then by "MN Location"

HOW TO: Sort Text Data by Multiple Columns

1. Select a cell in the range of cells that you want to sort.
2. Click the **Sort** button [*Data* tab, *Sort & Filter* group].
3. Check the **My data has headers** box if your data has a header row.
4. Click the **Sort by** arrow and select the column heading for the first sort (Figure 4-39).
   - The *Sort On* option specifies *Values, Cell Color, Font Color,* or *Cell Icon.* Use *Values* for sorting text or numbers.
5. Click the **Order** arrow and choose a sort option.
6. Click **Add Level** to add a second sort column.
7. Click the **Then by** arrow and select the second column heading.
8. Click the **Order** arrow and choose a sort option.
   - Click the **Options** button in the *Sort* dialog box to specify case-sensitive sorting.
9. Click **OK**.

4-39 *Sort* dialog box

Sort Data with Values

To sort data that contains values, take the same steps you took to sort text data. A value sort can be smallest to largest or largest to smallest.

Dates are treated as values. When dates are sorted smallest to largest, the earliest dates are listed first. To show the most recent date at the top of a sort, sort largest to smallest.

HOW TO: Sort Values by a Single Column

1. Select a cell in the column you want to sort.
2. Click the **A to Z** button [*Data* tab, *Sort & Filter* group].
   - If some of the beginning characters are values and some are text, rows that begin with a value are sorted first.
3. Click the **Z to A** button [*Data* tab, *Sort & Filter* group].

In a multiple column sort, you can use both a value column and a text column if necessary. The same *Sort* dialog box is used, and the *Sort On* option is *Values* for both fields. The data in Figure 4-40 is sorted first by the "MN Location" column, a text sort, and then by the "Sales Attainment" column, a value sort.

Sales Table

	Name	Title	MN Location	Sales Goal	Sales Attainment
3	Natasha Ari	Sales Trainee	Baudette	$450,000.00	$409,500.00
4	Alec Mikayla	Sales Representative	Baudette	$1,700,000.00	$935,000.00
5	Ella Jamison	Sales Manager	Baudette	$1,500,000.00	$1,320,000.00
6	BJ Francine	Sales Representative	Baudette	$1,700,000.00	$1,768,000.00
7	Kendal Shaedon	Sales Representative	Breezy Point	$1,800,000.00	$1,350,000.00
8	Sharon Wyatte	Sales Manager	Breezy Point	$1,500,000.00	$1,425,000.00
9	Dennis Frankie	Sales Representative	Breezy Point	$1,800,000.00	$1,566,000.00
10	Corey Daniels	Sales Trainee	Cass Lake	$500,000.00	$330,000.00
11	Christopher Bowman	Sales Manager	Cass Lake	$1,500,000.00	$1,275,000.00
12	Chad Mei	Sales Representative	Cass Lake	$1,750,000.00	$1,330,000.00
13	Nikolai Jalowiec	Sales Manager	Walker	$1,500,000.00	$1,260,000.00
14	Tammy Christine	Sales Representative	Walker	$17,500,000.00	$9,275,000.00
15	Josie Daddiline	Sales Representative	Walker	$17,500,000.00	$11,900,000.00

4-40 Sorted data by "MN Location" and then by "Sales Attainment"

HOW TO: Sort Values and Text in Multiple Columns

1. Select a cell in the range you want to sort.
2. Click the **Sort** button [*Data* tab, *Sort & Filter* group].
3. Check the **My data has headers** box if your data has headers.
4. Click the **Sort by** arrow and select the column heading for the first sort.
5. Click the **Order** arrow and choose a sort option.
6. Click **Add Level** to add another column sort.
7. Click the **Then by** arrow and select the second column heading.
8. Click the **Order** arrow and choose a sort option.
9. Add more levels if necessary.
10. Click **OK**.

> **ANOTHER WAY**
>
> To sort data in a column, right-click a cell in the column to be sorted, choose **Sort**, and then choose the type of sort.

Sort by Font or Cell Color

In addition to basic sorting by the value or text content of data, you can sort data based on the font color or the cell fill color. For example, you might use color-coding in a large worksheet to identify cities, months, or individuals. You can use *Conditional Formatting* (discussed in detail later in this chapter in *SLO 4.6: Applying Conditional Formatting*) to apply fill or font color to cells. If font or fill color is used to classify data, you can group items with a sort command. In Figure 4-41 the cells with yellow fill are grouped at the top of the "Sales Attainment" column.

	A	B	C	D	E
1			**Sales Table**		
2	**Name**	**Title**	**MN Location**	**Sales Goal**	**Sales Attainment**
3	Natasha Ari	Sales Trainee	Baudette	$450,000.00	$409,500.00
4	Corey Daniels	Sales Trainee	Cass Lake	$500,000.00	$330,000.00
5	Tammy Christine	Sales Representative	Walker	$17,500,000.00	$9,275,000.00
6	Josie Daddiline	Sales Representative	Walker	$17,500,000.00	$11,900,000.00
7	Alec Mikayla	Sales Representative	Baudette	$1,700,000.00	$935,000.00
8	Ella Jamison	Sales Manager	Baudette	$1,500,000.00	$1,320,000.00
9	BJ Francine	Sales Representative	Baudette	$1,700,000.00	$1,768,000.00
10	Kendal Shaedon	Sales Representative	Breezy Point	$1,800,000.00	$1,350,000.00
11	Sharon Wyatte	Sales Manager	Breezy Point	$1,500,000.00	$1,425,000.00
12	Dennis Frankie	Sales Representative	Breezy Point	$1,800,000.00	$1,566,000.00
13	Christopher Bowman	Sales Manager	Cass Lake	$1,500,000.00	$1,275,000.00
14	Chad Mei	Sales Representative	Cass Lake	$1,750,000.00	$1,330,000.00
15	Nikolai Jalowiec	Sales Manager	Walker	$1,500,000.00	$1,260,000.00

4-41 Yellow fill sorted on top in "Sales Attainment" column

When you sort by color, there are two choices about the *Order* in the *Sort* dialog box. You set which color is to be first. Then you specify whether that color should sort to the top or the bottom. If you have three colors, you can indicate where each color should fall in the sort order.

HOW TO: Sort Data by Font or Cell Color

1. Select a cell in the column you want to sort.
2. Click the **Sort** button [*Data* tab, *Sort & Filter* group].
3. Check the **My data has headers** box if your data has headers.
4. Click the **Sort by** arrow and select the column heading for the first sort.
5. Click the **Sort On** arrow and choose **Cell Color** or **Font Color**.
6. Click the first **Order** arrow (on the left) and choose the first color (Figure 4-42).
7. Click the second **Order** arrow (on the right) and choose **On Top** or **On Bottom**.
8. Click the **Add Level** to add another column sort option as desired.
9. Click the **Then by** arrow and select the second column heading.
   - Add as many sort levels as there are colors to be sorted.
   - Choose the color and the sort position for each color.
10. Click **OK**.

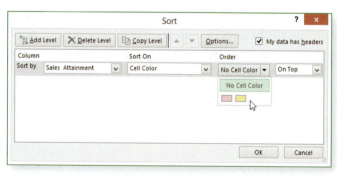

4-42 Cell color options in the *Sort* dialog box

Sort by Cell Icon

A cell icon is a small image that you can place in a cell with a *Conditional Formatting* command (see *SLO 4.6: Applying Conditional Formatting* in this chapter). You can apply icons in sets of three, four, or five, and you can sort by icon. The sorted data in Figure 4-43 has a two-set icon, sorted with the green icons on the top.

4-43 Data sorted by the cell icon in "Sales Attainment" column

HOW TO: Sort Data by Cell Icon

1. Select a cell with an icon in the column you want to sort.
2. Click the **Sort** button [*Data* tab, *Sort & Filter* group].
3. Check the **My data has headers** box if your data has headers.
4. Click the **Sort by** arrow and select the column heading for the first sort.
5. Click the **Sort On** arrow and choose **Cell Icon**.
6. Click the first **Order** arrow and select the first icon.
7. Click the second **Order** arrow (on the right) and choose **On Top** or **On Bottom** (Figure 4-44).
8. Click the **Add Level** button to add another sort option.
9. Click the **Then by** arrow and select the second column heading.
   - Add as many levels as there are icons.
   - Choose the sort order for each icon.
10. Click **OK**.

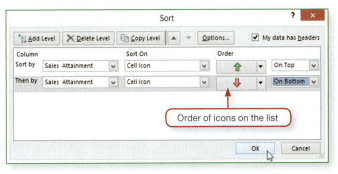

4-44 *Sort* dialog box

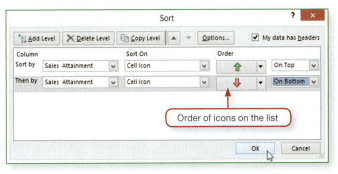

Filtering Data

When you work with large lists or tables, it is not practical to display thousands of rows of data on screen at once. It is easier to work with data if you filter the data to show the rows for the current month, the selected individual, or a specific product. Recall that a filter specifies which data is shown and which is hidden based on a specified criteria. When you filter data, information that doesn't meet the specified requirements is temporarily hidden.

The AutoFilter Command

Recall from earlier in the chapter that the *AutoFilter* button allows you to quickly hide or display rows of data. In list-type data or an Excel table, the **AutoFilter** command displays a filter arrow for each label in the header row. A table automatically shows *AutoFilter* arrows, but you need to activate them for a normal data range.

When you click an *AutoFilter* arrow for a header label, a pane displays sort options, filter types based on the data type, and check boxes for every piece of data. You can select check boxes to mark which records should be displayed or you can build a filter.

HOW TO: Use AutoFilters

1. Select a cell in the cell range to be filtered.
2. Click the **Filter** button [*Data* tab, *Sort & Filter* group].
3. Click the **AutoFilter** button so the column is filtered.
4. Click **(Select All)** to remove all check marks.
5. Check each record you want displayed (Figure 4-45).
6. Click **OK**.
   - Records that meet the criteria are visible with row headings in blue.
   - Records that do not meet the criteria and their row numbers are hidden.
   - A filter symbol appears with the column *AutoFilter* button (Figure 4-46).

4-45 *AutoFilter* for "MN Location"

Custom AutoFilter

From the *AutoFilter* button, you can build a custom *AutoFilter*, which is a dialog box where you build criteria. A custom *AutoFilter* gives you more options to specify how rows are displayed. You can build criteria to select ranges of data using relational operators *AND*, and *OR*. Relational operators are words like *Equals, Begins with,* or *Contains* (Figure 4-47).

The available filters depend on the type of data in the column. For example, if the column is text, *Text Filters* are available. There are also *Number Filters* and *Date Filters*.

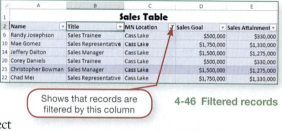

Shows that records are filtered by this column

4-46 **Filtered records**

> **ANOTHER WAY**
>
> To turn off an *AutoFilter*, click the **Filter** button [*Data* tab, *Sort & Filter* group].

To remove any filter and return to the complete list, click the **Clear** button in the *Sort & Filter* group on the *Data* tab. Alternatively, you can click the *AutoFilter* button for the column and choose **Clear Filter From (ColumnName)**.

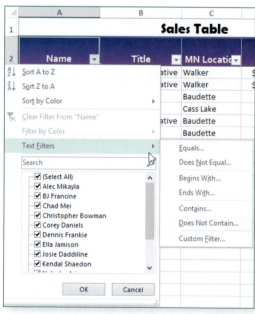

4-47 **Text filters for a custom** *AutoFilter*

HOW TO: Create a Custom Text AutoFilter

1. Select a cell in the cell range you want to filter.
2. Click the **Filter** button [*Data* tab, *Sort & Filter* group].
3. Click the **AutoFilter** button for the column you want to filter.
4. Select **Text Filters** and choose an operator.
5. Type the desired criteria in the *Custom AutoFilter* dialog box.
   - In Figure 4-48, the letter *B* is entered in the text box to filter for location names that contain the letter *B*.
6. Click **OK** in the *Custom AutoFilter* dialog box.
   - Rows that do not contain the letter *B* are hidden in Figure 4-49.

4-48 *Custom AutoFilter* dialog box

	A	B	C	D	E
1			**Sales Table**		
2	Name	Title	MN Location	Sales Goal	Sales Attainment
5	Natasha Ari	Sales Trainee	Baudette	$450,000.00	$409,500.00
7	Alec Mikayla	Sales Representative	Baudette	$1,700,000.00	$935,000.00
8	Ella Jamison	Sales Manager	Baudette	$1,500,000.00	$1,320,000.00
9	BJ Francine	Sales Representative	Baudette	$1,700,000.00	$1,768,000.00
10	Kendal Shaedon	Sales Representative	Breezy Point	$1,800,000.00	$1,350,000.00
11	Sharon Wyatte	Sales Manager	Breezy Point	$1,500,000.00	$1,425,000.00
12	Dennis Frankie	Sales Representative	Breezy Point	$1,800,000.00	$1,566,000.00

4-49 *AutoFilter* results for "MN Location" data containing the letter B

Advanced Filter

An *Advanced Filter* is similar to a query in a database. When you use an *Advanced Filter,* you build a criteria range separate from the actual data and type the criteria within that range. You can filter the data in the worksheet range or you can output data to another location on the sheet. Being able to output filter results allows you to create separate reports that include only filtered rows. An *Advanced Filter* requires more set-up work but allows you to apply more complex filters. You can even use a formula in your criteria.

To use an *Advanced Filter,* you need to create a **criteria range**. The criteria range must be at least two rows. The first row

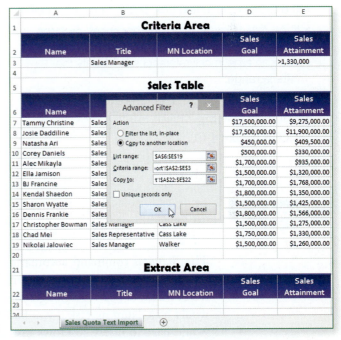

4-50 *Advanced Filter* set-up and dialog box

must use column names from the worksheet data but you need not use all of them. You type the actual criteria in the second row. You can create a criteria range in empty rows anywhere on the worksheet or on another sheet. In Figure 4-50, the criteria range is A2:E3.

You can use multiple rows after the header row in the criteria range to set *AND* or *OR* conditions. If you enter criteria on the same row, they are treated as *AND* conditions. This means both criteria must be met for the record to be displayed. In Figure 4-50, "Sales Manager" in cell B3 and ">1,330,000" in cell E3 are the criteria. This is an *AND* condition because both criteria are on the same row. For an *OR* condition, use a second (or third) row in the criteria range. An *OR* filter displays the record if any one of the requirements is met.

If you want to output filtered results to another location, you also create an *extract range*. You only need to specify one row for this range, and it should include the same column headings as the data. The filter results are copied to the area below these headings and take up as many rows as necessary. In Figure 4-50, the extract range is A22:E22. Filter results appear below the extract area header.

HOW TO: Create an Advanced Filter

1. Select the header row and copy the labels to a *Criteria* area on the same worksheet or to another sheet in the same workbook.

   - If you plan to use only one or two fields in the criteria, you only need to copy those labels to the criteria range.
   - If you place the criteria range above the data, leave at least one blank row between it and the data.

2. Select the header row and copy the labels to an *Extract* area in the same worksheet.

   - The output or extract area must be on the same sheet as the data you want to filter.
   - Leave enough blank rows below the labels for the filtered results.

3. Enter the criteria in the criteria range.

4. Click the **Advanced** button [*Data* tab, *Sort & Filter* group] to open the *Advanced Filter* dialog box (see Figure 4-50).

5. Select the **Copy to another location** button to display results in the extract area.

6. In the *List range* text box, verify or select the range (including the header row).

7. In the *Criteria range* text box, select the criteria cell range in the worksheet with its header row.

   - If the criteria range is on another sheet, click the worksheet tab and then select the range.
   - You can type in cell references to identify the criteria range.

8. In the *Copy to* text box, select the extract range in the worksheet.

9. Click **OK** (Figure 4-51).

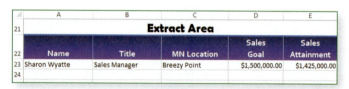

4-51 *Advanced Filter* **results for "Sales Managers" with a "Sales Attainment" greater than $1,330,000**

| SLO 4.5 | # Using the Subtotal Command and Creating Outlines and Groups |

The *Subtotal* command automatically inserts summary rows for data that are arranged in related groups. To obtain the summary amounts, you can use functions such as *SUM, AVERAGE, MAX,* or *MIN.* Although you can insert summary rows and formulas on your own, that would be a daunting task if you had 10,000 records sorted into 200 groups. For example, you would have to insert 200 rows in the correct location for each group and then copy the formula to each of those rows. The *Subtotal* command does this automatically.

Use the Subtotal Command with SUM

The *Subtotal* command is available for a normal range of cells. The command is not available when the range is formatted as an Excel table, because a table has its own total and sorting commands. If your data is formatted as a table, you must first convert it to a normal cell range before you can display subtotals.

For the *Subtotal* command to work properly, you must sort the rows by the main field (column) to be totaled. To display sales totals by city location, for example, sort the data by the city name. The *Subtotal* command groups the rows by this field.

The *Subtotal* command formats the list data as an **outline**. An **outline** is a summary that groups records so that they can be displayed or hidden from view. The *Subtotal* button is located in the *Outline* group on the *Data* tab.

HOW TO: Display Subtotals

1. Sort the data in the first column where you want to show subtotals.
   - Convert the data to a normal range if needed.
2. Select the cell range including the header row.
3. Click the **Subtotals** button [*Data* tab, *Outline* group].
4. Click the **At each change in** arrow and choose the column heading for the subtotals.
   - This is the same column you used to sort the data.
5. Click the **Use function** arrow and choose the function.
6. In the **Add subtotal to** list, check each field that should display a subtotal.
   - You can include a subtotal for other columns (fields).
7. Choose command options such as **Replace current subtotals** and **Summary below data** (Figure 4-52) as desired.
   - You can run the *Subtotal* command numerous times with different functions to analyze data by replacing any existing subtotals.
   - You can allow a group to split across pages.
   - The "Summary" row can be placed above the data if you prefer.
   - You can remove subtotals from this dialog box.
8. Click **OK** (Figure 4-53).
   - A subtotal row appears below each group.
   - A grand total appears after the last row of data.
   - Outline buttons appear to the left of the column and row headings.
   - The outline is expanded, showing all details.

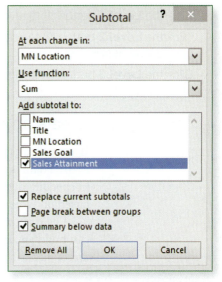

4-52 *Subtotal* dialog box

1 2 3		A	B	C	D	E
	1			**Sales Table**		
	2	**Name**	**Title**	**MN Location**	**Sales Goal**	**Sales Attainment**
	3	BJ Francine	Sales Representative	Baudette	$1,700,000.00	$1,768,000.00
	4	Alec Mikayla	Sales Representative	Baudette	$1,700,000.00	$935,000.00
	5	Ella Jamison	Sales Manager	Baudette	$1,500,000.00	$1,320,000.00
	6	Natasha Ari	Sales Trainee	Baudette	$450,000.00	$409,500.00
	7			**Baudette Total**		$4,432,500.00
	8	Dennis Frankie	Sales Representative	Breezy Point	$1,800,000.00	$1,566,000.00
	9	Kendal Shaedon	Sales Representative	Breezy Point	$1,800,000.00	$1,350,000.00
	10	Sharon Wyatte	Sales Manager	Breezy Point	$1,500,000.00	$1,425,000.00
	11			**Breezy Point Total**		$4,341,000.00
	12	Chad Mei	Sales Representative	Cass Lake	$1,750,000.00	$1,330,000.00
	13	Christopher Bowman	Sales Manager	Cass Lake	$1,500,000.00	$1,275,000.00
	14	Christopher Bowman	Sales Manager	Cass Lake	$1,500,000.00	$1,275,000.00
	15	Corey Daniels	Sales Trainee	Cass Lake	$500,000.00	$330,000.00
	16			**Cass Lake Total**		$4,210,000.00
	17	Tammy Christine	Sales Representative	Walker	$17,500,000.00	$9,275,000.00
	18	Josie Daddiline	Sales Representative	Walker	$17,500,000.00	$11,900,000.00
	19	Nikolai Jalowiec	Sales Manager	Walker	$1,500,000.00	$1,260,000.00
	20			**Walker Total**		$22,435,000.00
	21			**Grand Total**		$35,418,500.00

4-53 *Sales Attainment subtotals for each location*

> ### MORE INFO
>
> If you apply a filter to data with subtotals, you can hide the subtotal rows.

Outline Buttons

An **outline** groups and summarizes data. A worksheet can have only one outline; the outline can include all of the data on the sheet or a portion of it. Outlines have levels, indicated by the numbered buttons to the left of the column headings. Each of the *Outline Level* buttons shows increasing level of detail. The worksheet in Figure 4-53 has three levels. An outline can have up to eight levels.

Each level has an *Expand/Collapse* button. This button is a toggle and shows a minus sign (-) or a plus sign (+). When an individual group is collapsed, you do not see details for that group, only the subtotal.

HOW TO: Use Outline Buttons

1. Click a collapse button (-) to hide details for a row.
2. Click an expand button (+) to display details for a row.
3. Click the **Level 1** button (1) to reveal the grand total.
4. Click the **Level 2** button (2) to see the second outline level details (Figure 4-54).
5. Click the **Level 3** button (3) to display all details.

4-54 Level 2 outline results

Create an Auto Outline

If your data is consistently formatted, you can create an automatic outline. Consistently formatted data is grouped with related formulas in the same location. The formulas can be either in specific rows or columns, because an outline can use either. An *Auto Outline* inserts groups based on where the formulas are located in your data.

The data in Figure 4-55 is grouped and there is a *SUM* formula after each group. Excel can build an *Auto Outline* group from this type of data. If your data is not properly formatted, Excel displays a message that an *Auto Outline* cannot be created.

HOW TO: Apply an Auto Outline

1. Click a cell within the data range that you want to automatically outline.
2. Click the **Group** button arrow [*Data* tab, *Outline* group] and select **Auto Outline** (Figure 4-56).
   - Expand or collapse the outline to show or hide details.

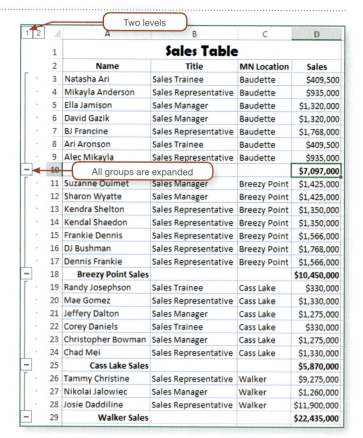

4-55 Data sorted by city with formulas after each city

4-56 *AutoOutline* with two levels

Define Groups

In addition to outlining data, you can create a group, by rows or columns, for data that does not have totals or formulas. To create a group, your data must be sorted or arranged so that you can select a range of cells to indicate the group, and you can insert a summary row either above or below the group (or a summary column to the left or right of the group). You can use these blank rows to enter subtitles for the data before or after grouping.

When you work with large numbers of records in a worksheet, you can use groups to hide data that is not needed at the moment. You can concentrate only on those groups that require editing or other work.

The data in Figure 4-57 is sorted by the "Title" column, so that groups can be created for each title. Note that a blank row has been inserted after each group.

4-57 Data sorted by Title; blank rows inserted after each title

HOW TO: Define a Group

1. Sort the data (or arrange columns) based on the preferred grouping.

2. Insert a blank row at the end of each sort group (or at the start of each group).
   - Include a blank row above the first group if you want to display a subtitle row for each group.
   - For column data, the summary column is usually to the right of the group.

3. Select a range of cells that includes each row (or column) of your first group.
   - Do not include the blank row or column.
   - You can select the entire range in the row or column.

4. Click the **Group** button [*Data* tab, *Outline* group].

5. Choose **Rows** or **Columns** (see Figure 4-57).
   - For example, you can create column groups for data that show 12 months in the header row to group them by quarters.

6. Click **OK**.

7. Repeat steps 1-6 for each group (Figure 4-58).

4-58 Defined groups

PAUSE & PRACTICE: EXCEL 4-3

For this project, you sort and filter data for Paradise Lakes Resort. You sort data according to location and sales values and use a *Number Filter* to display the best sales. You also build an advanced filter and include subtotals in your workbook. Because the workbook has data connections, you must enable editing.

File Needed: *[your initials] PP E4-2.xlsx*
Completed Project File Name: *[your initials] PP E4-3.xlsx*

1. Open the *[your initials] PP E4-2* workbook. Click **Enable Editing**.

2. Save the workbook as *[your initials] PP E4-3*.

3. Click the **Sales Quota Data** sheet tab.

4. Convert a table to a normal data range.
   a. Click any cell in the table.
   b. Click to remove the check mark for **Total Row** [*Table Tools Design* tab, *Table Style options* group].
   c. Click the **Convert to Range** button [*Table Tools Design* tab, *Tools* group].
   d. Click **Yes**.
   e. Select cells **A2:E25** and apply **No Fill** [*Home* tab, *Font* group].

5. Sort data in a worksheet.
   a. Click any cell in the data range.
   b. Click the **Sort** button [*Data* tab, *Sort & Filter* group].
   c. Click the **My data has headers** check box if necessary.
   d. Click the **Sort by** arrow and select **MN Location**.
   e. Choose **Values** for *Sort On* and **A to Z** for *Order*.
   f. Click the **Add Level** button.
   g. Click the **Then by** arrow and select **Sales Goal**.
   h. Choose **Values** for *Sort On* and **Largest to Smallest** for *Order* (Figure 4-59).
   i. Click **OK**. The data is sorted alphabetically first by "MN Location" and then by "Sales Goal" numbers in descending order.

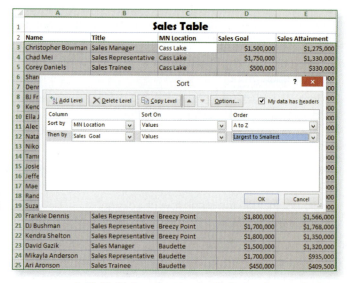

4-59 Multiple column sort with text and numeric data

6. Use a *Number AutoFilter*.
   a. Click any cell in the data range.
   b. Click the **Filter** button [*Data* tab, *Sort & Filter* group]. *AutoFilter* buttons appear with each label in the header row.
   c. Click the **AutoFilter** button for "Sales Attainment".
   d. Point at **Number Filters** and select **Greater Than Or Equal To**.
   e. In the **is greater than or equal to** text box, enter 1700000.
   f. Click **OK** (Figure 4-60).

	A	B	C	D	E
1			**Sales Table**		
2	**Name**	**Title**	**MN Location**	**Sales Goal**	**Sales Attainment**
3	BJ Francine	Sales Representative	Baudette	$1,700,000	$1,768,000
14	DJ Bushman	Sales Representative	Breezy Point	$1,700,000	$1,768,000
23	Tammy Christine	Sales Representative	Walker	$17,500,000	$9,275,000
24	Josie Daddiline	Sales Representative	Walker	$17,500,000	$11,900,000

4-60 *AutoFilter* results for Sales Attainment data greater than or equal to $1,700,000

7. Make a copy of the **Sales Quota Data** sheet to the right of the original.
   Hint: Right-click the worksheet tab.

8. Name the copied worksheet Advanced Filter.

9. Click the **Clear** button [*Data* tab, *Sort & Filter* group] to remove the filter.

10. Click the **Filter** button [*Data* tab, *Sort & Filter* group] to remove the *AutoFilter* buttons.

11. Create a criteria range and an extract range.
    a. Insert four rows above row 1.
    b. Select cells **A6:E6**. Copy and paste them in cells **A2:E2** and then in cells **A32:E32**.
    c. Type Criteria Area in cell **A1** and Extract Area in cell **A31**.
    d. Select **A5**, double-click the **Format Painter** button, and apply the formats to cells **A1** and **A31**. Click the **Format Painter** to turn it off.
    e. In cell **B3**, type Sales Trainee.
    f. In cell **E3**, type <400000.

12. Run an *Advanced Filter*.
    a. Click in **A7**.
    b. Click the **Advanced** button [*Data* tab, *Sort & Filter* group].
    c. Select the **Copy to another location** radio button.
    d. Verify that the correct data range is shown in the **List range** text box. If the data range is not correct, select cells **A6:E29**.
    e. Click in the **Criteria range** text box and select cells **A2:E3**.
    f. Click in the **Copy to** text box and select cells **A32:E32** (Figure 4-61).
    g. Click **OK**. Two records that meet the criteria, Corey Daniels and Randy Josephson, are displayed in rows 33:34.

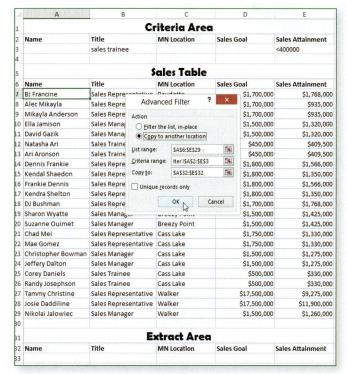

4-61 Criteria and extract ranges; *Advanced Filter* dialog box

13. Make a copy of the *Sales Quota Data* sheet to the right of the *Advanced Filter* sheet.

14. Name the copied worksheet Subtotals.

15. Click the **Clear** button [*Data* tab, *Sort & Filter* group] to remove the filter.

16. Click the **Filter** button [*Data* tab, *Sort & Filter* group] to remove the *AutoFilter* buttons.

17. Show subtotals in a list.
    a. Click a cell in the **Title** column and click the **Sort A to Z** button [*Data* tab, *Sort & Filter* group].
    b. Click the **Subtotal** button [*Data* tab, *Outline* group].
    c. Click the **At each change in** arrow and choose **Title**.
    d. Click the **Use function** arrow and choose **Average**.
    e. In the **Add subtotal to list** box, click to place check marks for **Sales Goal** and **Sales Attainment**.
    f. Click **OK** (Figure 4-62).

18. Save and close the workbook.

4-62 Completed PP E4-3 worksheet with subtotals

Applying Conditional Formatting

Conditional Formatting commands apply specified formats to cells only when the cells meet some criteria. You can use *Conditional Formatting* to highlight information in a worksheet by setting different fill colors or font styles for selected cells. For example, a sales manager might use *Conditional Formatting* to display sales amounts that are below a certain level in a bold red font.

Conditional Formatting is dynamic; the formatting adapts if the data changes. In our sales example, if sales values are updated and a particular person or department that was below the specified level has now met a goal, the bold red formatting is removed.

Basic *Conditional Formatting* commands are *Highlight Cells Rules* and *Top/Bottom Rules*. For these commands, you set the rule or criteria in a dialog box and choose the format. Another type of *Conditional Formatting* is **data visualization,** in which specified data is indicated with a fill color, a horizontal bar, or an icon within the cell. *Data visualization* commands include *Data Bars*, *Color Scales*, and *Icon Sets*.

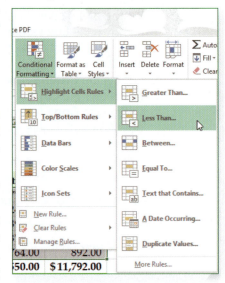

Cells Rules

Highlight Cells Rules uses relational or comparison operators to determine if the value or label in a cell should be formatted. *Highlight Cells Rules* includes common operators such as *Equal to* and *Greater Than*. You can also create your own rule using other operators or a formula.

You can access all of the conditional formatting options from the *Conditional Formatting* button in the *Styles* group on the *Home* tab (Figure 4-63). You can also choose a recommended conditional formatting style from the *Quick Analysis* tool options.

4-63 Highlight Cells Rules menu

HOW TO: Create a "Less Than" Highlight Cells Rule

1. Select the cell range to be formatted.
2. Click the **Conditional Formatting** button [*Home* tab, *Styles* group].
3. Click **Highlight Cells Rules** and select **Less Than**.
4. In the *Format cells that are LESS THAN* box, type a value. If the number in a cell is below this value, the cell will be conditionally formatted.

   • You can click a cell in the worksheet to enter a value.

5. Click the arrow in the *with* entry box and choose a preset option (Figure 4-64).

   • Alternatively, you can choose *Custom Format* to open the *Format Cells* dialog box and build a custom format.

6. Click **OK**.

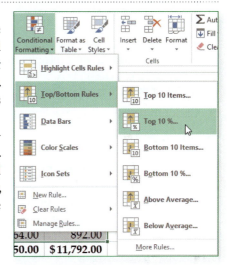

4-64 *Less Than* dialog box

Top/Bottom Rules use a ranking to format the highest (top) or lowest (bottom) items or a specified percentage of a list. You can also set a rule to format values that are above or below average (Figure 4-65). You are not limited to the percentages or numbers shown in the menu.

When you select a range of values, the *Quick Analysis* tool appears in the bottom right corner of the range. The *Totals* group typically provides likely conditional format choices. When you make your choice this way, the same dialog box opens so that you can build the format.

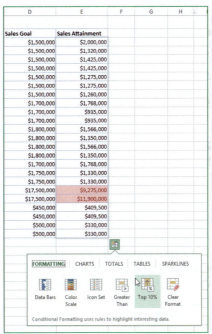

4-65 *Top/Bottom Rules*

HOW TO: Create a Top 10% Rule

1. Select the cell range you want to format.
2. Click the **Quick Analysis** button.
3. Click **Formatting** and choose **Top 10%** (Figure 4-66).
4. Click the arrow for the *with* box and choose **Custom Format**.
5. Click the appropriate tab to set a fill color, a font, or a border.
6. Click **OK** to close the *Format Cells* dialog box.
7. Click **OK** to close the *Top 10%* dialog box.

4-66 *Quick Analysis* options for conditional formatting

If you cannot find a *Highlight Cells* or *Top/Bottom* rule that fits your needs, create your own rule using operators, criteria, and formats in the *New Formatting Rule* dialog box. Options in this dialog box allow you to create a rule based on a formula as well. You can, for example, build a rule to format only cells that display a particular percentage of a specified value, such as sales that are 108% of the sales goal.

HOW TO: Create a New Conditional Formatting Rule

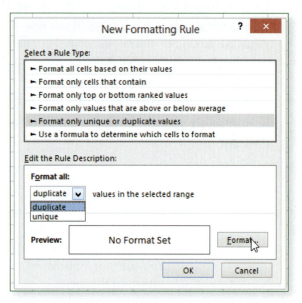

1. Select the cell range to be formatted.
2. Click the **Conditional Formatting** button [*Home* tab, *Styles* group].
3. Click **New Rule** to open the *New Formatting Rule* dialog box (Figure 4-67).
4. Select a rule type from the *Select a Rule Type* list.
5. In the *Edit the Rule Description* area, make choices to build the new rule.
   - The options that are available depend on the type of rule.
   - Click **Format** (when available) to set the format in the *Format Cells* dialog box.
   - Click **OK** to close the *Format Cells* dialog box.
6. Click **OK** to close the *New Formatting Rule* dialog box.

4-67 New Formatting Rule dialog box

Data Bars, Color Scales, and Icon Sets

Excel's data visualization *Conditional Formatting* commands format cells with icons, cell shading, or shaded bars to distinguish the values. They generally highlight the low, middle, or top values or compare the values to each other.

You can access the *Conditional Formatting* button in the *Styles* group on the *Home* tab, or the *Quick Analysis* tool. When you use the *Quick Analysis* tool, a default data bar (or other format) is applied. You can edit it by choosing a different color or style from the *Conditional Formatting* button menu.

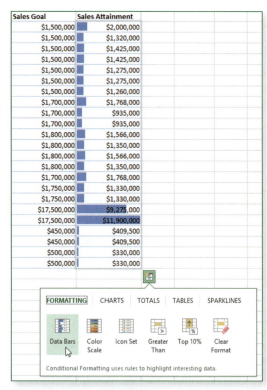

HOW TO: Format Data with Data Bars

1. Select the cell range you want to format.
2. Click the **Quick Analysis** button.
3. Click **Formatting** and choose **Data Bars** (Figure 4-68).
   - A default data bar style and color are applied.
   - The length of the data bars compares the value in each cell to the other values in the selected cell range.
   - *Color Scales* use a variation of two or three colors to indicate low, middle, and high values.
   - *Icon Sets* inserts icons that represent the upper, middle, or lower values of the cell range.

4-68 Conditional Formatting: Data Bars

Manage Conditional Formatting Rules

To edit, delete, or review any *Conditional Formatting* rule, use the **Manage Rules** command. You can update the range to be formatted, edit the actual format, or change the rule.

In the *Conditional Formatting Rules Manager* dialog box, you can choose to display all the rules in the worksheet or rules from other sheets in the workbook. If you choose a cell range before you give the command, the rule for the *Current Selection* is shown (Figure 4-69).

When you click **Edit Rule**, the *Edit Formatting Rule* dialog box opens. This dialog box is very similar to the *New Formatting Rule* dialog box, and you make your changes in the same way.

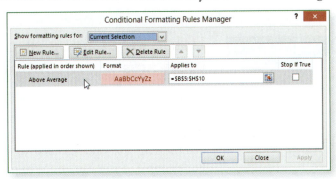

4-69 *Conditional Formatting Rules Manager* dialog box

HOW TO: Manage Conditional Formatting Rules

1. Click the **Conditional Formatting** button [*Home* tab, *Styles* group].
2. Choose **Manage Rules**.
3. In the *Show formatting rules for* list, make a choice.
   - If you selected a cell range, the option is *Current Selection*.
   - Choose **This Worksheet** if you did not select a range or want to see all rules in the worksheet.
4. Select the rule to edit.
5. Click **Edit Rule**.
6. In the *Select a Rule Type* list, choose another type if needed.
7. In the *Edit the Rule Description* area, make choices to change the rule.
   - The choices depend on the rule type (Figure 4-70).
   - Click **Format** when it is an option and make changes in the *Format Cells* dialog box.
8. Click **OK** to close the *Edit Formatting Rule* dialog box.
9. Click **OK** to close the *Conditional Formatting Rules Manager* dialog box and apply the change.

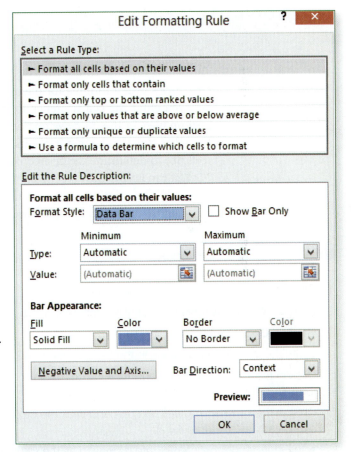

4-70 *Edit Formatting Rule* dialog box for data bars

Clear Conditional Formatting Rules

You can clear rules from a selected cell range or from an entire sheet. Access the **Clear Rules** option by clicking the *Conditional Formatting* button in the *Styles* group on the *Home* tab. For a selected range, you can click the **Quick Analysis** button and choose **Clear Format**.

HOW TO: Clear All Rules

1. Click the **Conditional Formatting** button [*Home* tab, *Styles* group].
2. Choose **Clear Rules**.
3. Click **Clear Rules from Entire Sheet** (Figure 4-71).

4-71 *Clear Rules* options

SLO 4.7

Using Goal Seek and Worksheet Protection

Goal Seek is one type of what-if analysis. It allows you to test values in a cell to "backsolve" a formula. *Backsolving* means knowing the desired results and determining the value needed to reach those results. For example, if you can afford to pay $500 per month for a new car, you can use *Goal Seek* to determine how much you can borrow and end up with a $500 per month car payment.

Worksheet protection allows you to set which cells can be edited in a worksheet. When you share work with others, worksheet protection can safeguard your work from accidental changes by others.

Use Goal Seek

Goal Seek solves a formula for one cell (one argument) in the formula. In the *Goal Seek* dialog box, you enter the cell reference for the formula in the *Set cell* text box. You type a target or goal number in the *To value* text box. For example, in Figure 4-72, an organization is solving the *PMT* function so that it results in a payment of $2,200. *Goal Seek* adjusts the interest rate (cell B6) to determine the desired payment.

You can access *Goal Seek* from the *What-if Analysis* button in the *Data Tools* group on the *Data* tab. The solution appears in the *Goal Seek Status* dialog box. You can click **OK** to accept the solution or keep the original value by clicking **Cancel**.

HOW TO: Use Goal Seek

1. Click the cell with the formula to be solved.
2. Click the **What-if Analysis** button [*Data* tab, *Data Tools* group].
3. Choose **Goal Seek**.
4. Verify the formula cell address in the *Set cell* text box.
5. Click in the *To value* text box and type in your desired formula result.
6. Click in the *By changing cell* text box and click the cell that can be adjusted (Figure 4-72).
   - In Figure 4-72, the interest rate is chosen as the value that can be adjusted.
   - *Goal Seek* can change only one cell.
   - You can key the cell reference instead of selecting the cell.
7. Click **OK**.
   - The solution is shown in the *Goal Seek Status* dialog box (Figure 4-73).
   - The solution is displayed in the cell in the worksheet.

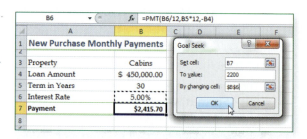

4-72 *Goal Seek* dialog box

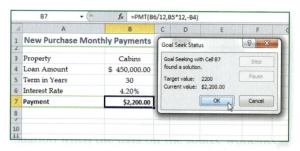

4-73 *Goak Seek Status* dialog box

8. Click **OK** to accept the solution.
   - You can press **Enter** to accept the solution.
   - Choose **Cancel** to ignore the solution.

Worksheet Protection

Worksheet protection is a good way to prohibit changes to your work. It employs the *Locked* cell property. This property is active for all cells in a worksheet by default. However, it has no effect until you set worksheet protection. If you set worksheet protection, no editing is possible in the sheet. When you protect a worksheet, you need to select the cells that can still be edited and disable the *Locked* property. Typically, you do this before protecting the sheet.

Unlock Worksheet Cells

When you protect a sheet, you or others may still want to edit some cells in the worksheet. In an inventory worksheet, for example, you need to update item counts, but you don't need to change the product name or code. In a protected inventory worksheet, you can unlock the item-count cells so that their values can be changed while the other values and codes cannot be edited.

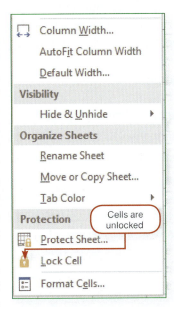 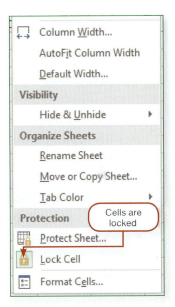

The *Locked* property is on the *Protection* tab in the *Format Cells* dialog box. Open the dialog box from the *Format* button

4-74 *Locked* property off and on

on the *Home* tab [*Cells* group] or by pressing **Ctrl+1**. Alternatively, you can toggle the *Locked* property on and off from the *Format* button menu. When a cell is locked, the command in the menu shows an outline; when a cell is unlocked, there is no outline (Figure 4-74).

HOW TO: Unlock Cells for Editing

1. Select the cell(s) that you still want to be able to edit.
2. Right-click a selected cell.
3. Choose **Format Cells**.
4. Click the **Protection** tab.
5. Click the **Locked** check box to remove the check mark (Figure 4-75).
6. Click **OK**.

4-75 *Format Cells* dialog box; *Protection* tab

Protect a Worksheet

The *Protect Worksheet* command includes a list of editing options that you can allow for locked cells. For example, you can allow users to select cells, but they will not be able to edit them. Or you can give users permission to format cells or to insert or delete rows or columns.

As you set worksheet protection, you can also set a password. Once this added security is enforced, all users must enter the password before they can edit anything in the worksheet. Once the password is entered, the protection is removed.

The *Protect Sheet* button is in the *Changes* group on the *Review* tab. This button is a toggle; when a worksheet is protected, it becomes the *Unprotect Sheet* button. You can also protect a worksheet from the *Format* button [*Home* tab, *Cells* group] (see Figure 4-74).

HOW TO: Protect a Worksheet

1. Unlock the cells that you want to still be able to edit.
2. Click the **Protect Sheet** button [*Review* tab, *Changes* group].
3. Check the commands that should still be available after protection is set.
4. Type a password if desired.
   - You see a placeholder as you type a password (Figure 4-76).
   - A second message box requires that you rekey the password.
   - Passwords are case sensitive.
5. Click **OK**.

4-76 *Protect Sheet* dialog box

Unprotect a Worksheet

If you try to edit a cell in a protected sheet, a message box tells you that the sheet is protected (Figure 4-77). When a worksheet is protected, it cannot be edited until the protection is removed. If there is no password, you just need to click the **Unprotect Sheet** button.

4-77 **Message window for a protected sheet**

When a password has been set, you need to enter the password to remove the protection.

The *Unprotect Sheet* button is in the *Changes* group on the *Review* tab. If a password has been used, a message box for entering the password appears (Figure 4-78).

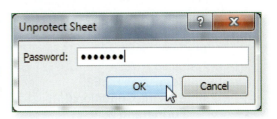

HOW TO: Unprotect a Worksheet

1. Click the **Unprotect Sheet** button [*Review* tab, *Changes* group].
2. Type the password if necessary and click **OK**.

PAUSE & PRACTICE: EXCEL 4-4

For this project, you set conditional formatting using data bars in Paradise Lakes Resort's workbook. You use *Goal Seek* to calculate a possible sales amount for one of the representatives so that average sales can reach a particular goal. Finally, you protect the worksheet but allow editing to the attainment figures.

File Needed: *[your initials] PP E 4-3.xlsx*
Completed Project File Name: *[your initials] PP E4-4.xlsx*

1. Open the *[your initials] PP E4-3* workbook. Enable editing.
2. Save the workbook as *[your initials] PP E4-4*.
3. Click the **Sales Quota Data** sheet tab.
4. Click the **Filter** button [*Data* tab, *Sort & Filter* group] to remove the filter.
5. Apply *Conditional Formatting* using *Highlight Cells Rules*.
   a. Select cells **D3:D25**.
   b. Click the **Quick Analysis** button and choose **Formatting**.
   c. Choose **Greater Than**.
   d. Type 2000000.
   e. Select **Green Fill with Dark Green Text** from the *with* drop-down list.
   f. Click **OK**.
   g. Select cells **B3:B25**.
   h. Click the **Quick Analysis** button and choose **Formatting**.
   i. Choose **Text Contains**.
   j. Type sales trainee.
   k. Select **Light Red Fill with Dark Red Text**.
   l. Click **OK**.
6. Apply *Conditional Formatting* using *Data Bars*.
   a. Select cells **E3:E25**.
   b. Click the **Quick Analysis** button and choose **Formatting**.
   c. Choose **Data Bars**.

7. Manage *Conditional Formatting* rules.
   a. Select cells **E3:E25**.
   b. Click the **Conditional Formatting** button [*Home* tab, *Styles* group].
   c. Choose **Manage Rules**.
   d. Click **Edit Rule**.
   e. Click the **Fill** arrow and choose **Gradient Fill** (Figure 4-79).
   f. Click the **Color** arrow; choose **Gold**, **Accent 3**.
   g. Click **OK** to close the *Edit Formatting Rule* dialog box.
   h. Click **OK** to close the *Conditional Formatting Rules Manager*.

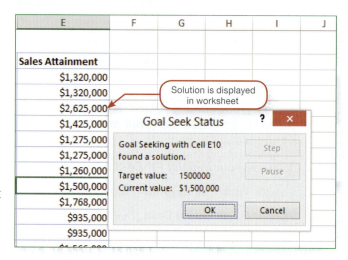

4-79 Edited rule for data bars

8. Click the **Subtotals** sheet tab.

9. Use Goal Seek.
   a. Click cell **E10**.
   b. Click the **What-if Analysis** button [*Data* tab, *Data Tools* group].
   c. Select **Goal Seek**.
   d. Type 1500000 in the *To value* box.
   e. Click in the *By changing cell* box and click cell **E5**. This finds a value for Sharon Wyatte's sales that would result in average sales of $1,500,000.
   f. Click **OK** to run *Goal Seek* (Figure 4-80). Sharon's new sales would have to reach $2,625,000.
   g. Click **OK** to accept the solution.

	E
	Sales Attainment
	$1,320,000
	$1,320,000
	$2,625,000
	$1,425,000
	$1,275,000
	$1,275,000
	$1,260,000
	$1,500,000
	$1,768,000
	$935,000
	$935,000

Solution is displayed in worksheet

Goal Seek Status

Goal Seeking with Cell E10 found a solution.

Target value: 1500000
Current value: $1,500,000

Step   Pause   OK   Cancel

4-80 *Goal Seek* solution

10. Click the **Sales Quota Data** sheet tab.

11. Protect a worksheet with a password.
    a. Select cells **E3:E25**.
    b. Right-click a selected cell.
    c. Choose **Format Cells** from the menu.
    d. Click the **Protection** tab.
    e. Click to remove the check mark for **Locked**.
    f. Click **OK**.
    g. Click the **Protect Sheet** button [*Review* tab, *Changes* group].
    h. Show check marks for **Select locked cells** and **Select unlocked cells**.
    i. Type the password 123 and click **OK**.
    j. Retype the password and click **OK**.

12. Save and close the workbook (Figure 4-81).

	A	B	C	D	E
1			**Sales Table**		
2	**Name**	**Title**	**MN Location**	**Sales Goal**	**Sales Attainment**
3	BJ Francine	Sales Representative	Baudette	$1,700,000	$1,768,000
4	Alec Mikayla	Sales Representative	Baudette	$1,700,000	$935,000
5	Mikayla Anderson	Sales Representative	Baudette	$1,700,000	$935,000
6	Ella Jamison	Sales Manager	Baudette	$1,500,000	$1,320,000
7	David Gazik	Sales Manager	Baudette	$1,500,000	$1,320,000
8	Natasha Ari	Sales Trainee	Baudette	$450,000	$409,500
9	Ari Aronson	Sales Trainee	Baudette	$450,000	$409,500
10	Dennis Frankie	Sales Representative	Breezy Point	$1,800,000	$1,566,000
11	Kendal Shaedon	Sales Representative	Breezy Point	$1,800,000	$1,350,000
12	Frankie Dennis	Sales Representative	Breezy Point	$1,800,000	$1,566,000
13	Kendra Shelton	Sales Representative	Breezy Point	$1,800,000	$1,350,000
14	DJ Bushman	Sales Representative	Breezy Point	$1,700,000	$1,768,000
15	Sharon Wyatte	Sales Manager	Breezy Point	$1,500,000	$1,425,000
16	Suzanne Ouimet	Sales Manager	Breezy Point	$1,500,000	$1,425,000
17	Chad Mei	Sales Representative	Cass Lake	$1,750,000	$1,330,000
18	Mae Gomez	Sales Representative	Cass Lake	$1,750,000	$1,330,000
19	Christopher Bowman	Sales Manager	Cass Lake	$1,500,000	$1,275,000
20	Jeffery Dalton	Sales Manager	Cass Lake	$1,500,000	$1,275,000
21	Corey Daniels	Sales Trainee	Cass Lake	$500,000	$330,000
22	Randy Josephson	Sales Trainee	Cass Lake	$500,000	$330,000
23	Tammy Christine	Sales Representative	Walker	$17,500,000	$9,275,000
24	Josie Daddiline	Sales Representative	Walker	$17,500,000	$11,900,000
25	Nikolai Jalowiec	Sales Manager	Walker	$1,500,000	$1,260,000

4-81 Completed PP E4-4 worksheet

4.1 Import data into Excel from a text file, database file, or web site and use *Flash Fill* and data connections (p. E4-187).

- You can **import** text files in Excel including *.txt* (text) documents, *.csv* (comma separated values) files, and *.prn* (printer) files.
- The *From Text* button is in the *Get External Data* group on the *Data* tab.
- The **Text Import Wizard** guides you through the steps of importing the data.
- You can import data from a Word document and tables and queries in a Microsoft Access database into a worksheet.
- You can import table-formatted data on a web site into a worksheet using the *From Web* button on the *Data* tab.
- Imported data establishes a data connection in the workbook.
- The **Flash Fill** command copies your typing actions from nearby cells.

4.2 Create and format an Excel table and a *PivotTable*, and export data for use in other programs (p. E4-194).

- There are several methods for sorting, filtering, and calculating rows of data in Excel **tables**.
- Data that is set up like a list with a header row and the same type of data in each column can be formatted as a table.
- Create a table by clicking the **Format as Table** button in the *Styles* group on the *Home* tab or by clicking the **Quick Analysis** tool and choosing **Tables**.
- An **AutoFilter** button accompanies each label in the header row of an Excel table.
- When any cell in a table is selected, the *Table Tools Design* tab is available.
- Apply a table style by clicking the **More** button in the *Table Styles* group on the *Table Tools Design* tab.
- Save a customized table style with the *New Table Style* button in the *Table Styles* gallery in the *Table Styles* group on the *Table Tools Design* tab.
- **Table Tools** include commands to remove duplicate rows and to convert a table to a normal cell range. The *Tools* group is on the *Table Tools Design* tab.

- An Excel table is named and uses structured references (names) for each column and other predefined parts.
- A **PivotTable** is a summary report based on a cell range in the worksheet.
- For a selected cell range, use the *Recommended PivotTables* button on the *Insert* tab in the *Tables* group.
- In a *PivotTable*, fields can be repositioned to display different views of the data.
- Use the *PivotTable Fields* pane to reposition fields in a *PivotTable* report.
- Use the **Export** command in the *Backstage* view to save data in a different format.

4.3 Sort data by text, number, color, or icon (p. E4-205).

- List-type data can be sorted alphabetically or by value by one or more columns.
- Sorts can be in **ascending** order (A to Z) or **descending** (Z to A).
- Values can be sorted from smallest to largest (A to Z) or largest to smallest (Z to A).
- To sort a single column, use the *Sort A to Z* or *Sort Z to A* button in the *Sort & Filter* group on the *Data* tab.
- To sort by multiple columns, open the *Sort* dialog box by clicking the **Sort** button on the *Data* tab.
- In the *Sort* dialog box, you can choose to sort by font color, cell color, or cell icon when this type of formatting is used in the data.

4.4 Apply an *AutoFilter* or an *Advanced Filter* to data (p. E4-209).

- The **AutoFilter** command displays an *AutoFilter* button arrow in each column heading.
- Click the **AutoFilter** button to select which records are shown or hidden.
- You can build a custom *AutoFilter* using operators such as *Equals*. There are different operators for text, number, and date filters.
- An **Advanced Filter** provides sophisticated filter options such as using a formula in the filter definition.
- An *Advanced Filter* requires a criteria range in the same workbook to define the criteria.
- An *Advanced Filter* can show the filtered results separate from the actual data.
- The *Advanced* button is in the *Sort & Filter* group on the *Data* tab.

E4-227

4.5 Use the *Subtotal* command and create groups and outlines (p. E4-212).

- The **Subtotal** command inserts summary rows using a function such as *SUM*, *AVERAGE*, *MAX*, or *MIN* in a normal cell range.
- The *Subtotal* command requires that the data be sorted by at least one column.
- The *Subtotal* command formats the results as an **outline**. An outline groups records so that they can be displayed or hidden.
- The *Subtotal* button is in the *Outline* group on the *Data* tab.
- The **Auto Outline** command creates groups based on formulas that are located in a consistent pattern in the data.
- The *Auto Outline* command is available from the *Group* button in the *Outline* group on the *Data* tab.
- You can manually define groups by sorting the data and using the *Group* button in the *Outline* group on the *Data* tab.

4.6 Apply and manage *Conditional Formatting* using cell rules, *Color Scales*, *Icon Sets*, and *Data Bars* (p. E4-218).

- **Conditional Formatting** formats only cells that meet specified criteria.
- Cells rules formatting uses relational or comparison operators such as *Greater Than* or *Equals*.
- In the rule dialog box, you define the rule and choose the format.
- You can create your own conditional formatting rule as well as edit existing rules with the **Manage Rules** command.

- Conditional formatting commands include *Icon Sets*, *Color Scales*, and *Data Bars*.
- An icon, color, or data bar represents a value in relation to other values in the range.
- You can **Clear Rules** from a selected cell range or from an entire sheet.

4.7 Use *Goal Seek* and protect a worksheet (p. E4-222).

- **Goal Seek** is a command that finds a solution for one of the arguments in a formula.
- In a *Goal Seek* command, you set the desired result for the formula to a value and find out how to arrive at that result by changing one cell.
- The *Goal Seek* command is part of the **What-If Analysis** button options on the *Data* tab.
- Worksheet protection is a first step in prohibiting unwanted changes to your work.
- The *Protect Sheet* button is in the *Changes* group in the *Review* tab; it is the *Unprotect Sheet* button when the worksheet is protected.
- To allow cell editing in a protected worksheet, you must disable or remove the *Locked* property for the cells you want to be able to edit.
- The *Locked* property is toggled off and on in the *Format Cells* dialog box on the *Protection* tab.
- Worksheet protection can be set with or without a password.
- Worksheet protection must be removed or turned off before the worksheet can be edited.

Check for Understanding

On the **Online Learning Center** for this text (www.mhhe.com/office2013inpractice), there are a variety of resources that can be used to review the concepts covered in this chapter.

The following Online Learning Resources are available on the Online Learning Center:

- Multiple choice questions
- Short answer questions
- Matching exercises

Guided Project 4-1

For this project you import supplier data in a text file into the inventory worksheet for Wear-Ever Shoes. You use *Flash Fill* to enter product codes and sort the data by supplier and code. You use *AutoFilter* for several tasks, use the *Subtotal* command, and work with *Goal Seek*. Finally, you protect one of the sheets in the workbook.
[Student Learning Outcomes 4.1, 4.3, 4.4, 4.5, 4.7]

Files Needed: *WearEverInventory-04*.xlsx and *Suppliers-04.txt*
Completed Project File Name: *[your initials] Excel 4-1.xlsx*

Skills Covered in This Project

- Import a text file.
- Use *Flash Fill*.
- Sort data.
- Use an *AutoFilter*.
- Create and copy a formula.

- Insert columns.
- Use the *Subtotal* command.
- Use *Goal Seek*.
- Copy and move a worksheet.
- Protect a worksheet without a password.

---

1. Open the **WearEverInventory-04** workbook from your student data files folder. Click the **Enable Editing** button.

2. Save the workbook as **[your initials] Excel 4-1**.

3. Import a text file.
   a. Select cell **J4**.
   b. Click the **From Text** button [*Data* tab, *Get External Data* group].
   c. Find and select the **Suppliers-04.txt** file in the *Import Text File* window.
   d. Click **Import**.
   e. Select the **Delimited** button in the first *Wizard* window. Excel recognizes that this file separates the data into columns with a tab character.
   f. Click **Next**.
   g. Click to place a check mark for **Tab** if necessary.
   h. Click **Next**.
   i. Click **Finish**.
   j. Click **OK**.
   k. Use the **Format Painter** button to copy formatting from **I4** to **J4:K4**.
   l. *AutoFit* columns **J:K**.

4. Use *Flash Fill* to insert a product code.
   a. Insert a column between columns **B** and **C**.
   b. Type Code in cell **C4**.
   c. Type RHB in cell **C5**.
   d. Type r and press **Enter** in cell **C6**.

e. Type r and press **Enter** in cell **C7**. *AutoFill* completes the entries based on what is already in the column. The *Flash Fill* suggestion list does not appear because you did not type a second item to identify the pattern.
f. Click the **Fill** button [*Home* tab, *Editing* group].
g. Choose **Flash Fill**.
h. *AutoFit* column **C**.

5. Sort data in multiple columns.
   a. Click any cell in cells **A5:L40**.
   b. Click the **Sort** button [*Data* tab, *Sort & Filter* group].
   c. Click the **My data has headers** check box if necessary.
   d. Click the **Sort by** arrow and choose **Supplier**.
   e. Check that **Sort On** is **Values** and **Order** is **A to Z**.
   f. Click **Add Level**.
   g. Click the **Then by** arrow and choose **Code**.
   h. Check that **Sort On** is **Values** and **Order** is **A to Z**.
   i. Click **OK** (Figure 4-82).

Wear-Ever Shoes

Current Stock

	A	B	C	D	E	F	G	H	I	J	K	L
4	Product ID	Product	Code	Color	Size	Quantity	Men's or Women's	Cost	Retail	Reorder	Supplier	Phone Number
5	WE009	Comfy Walking Shoes	CWS	Brown	8.5	4	M	$47.50	$65.00	N	Jennifer's Closet	289-433-1555
6	WE010	Comfy Walking Shoes	CWS	Black	9	1	M	$47.50	$65.00	Y	Jennifer's Closet	289-433-1555
7	WE011	Comfy Walking Shoes	CWS	Navy	7.5	4	W	$47.50	$65.00	N	Jennifer's Closet	289-433-1555
8	WE012	Comfy Walking Shoes	CWS	Black	8	1	W	$47.50	$65.00	Y	Jennifer's Closet	289-433-1555
9	WE013	Comfy Walking Shoes	CWS	Taupe	7.5	2	W	$47.50	$65.00	N	Jennifer's Closet	289-433-1555
10	WE014	Comfy Walking Shoes	CWS	Brown	8	3	W	$47.50	$65.00	Y	Jennifer's Closet	289-433-1555
11	WE025	Seriously Tall Boots	STB	Black	6	0	W	$42.50	$80.00	Y	Jennifer's Closet	289-433-1555
12	WE026	Seriously Tall Boots	STB	Black	6.5	0	W	$42.50	$80.00	Y	Jennifer's Closet	289-433-1555
13	WE027	Seriously Tall Boots	STB	Black	7	1	W	$42.50	$80.00	Y	Jennifer's Closet	289-433-1555
14	WE028	Seriously Tall Boots	STB	Black	7.5	0	W	$42.50	$80.00	Y	Jennifer's Closet	289-433-1555
15	WE029	Seriously Tall Boots	STB	Black	8	2	W	$42.50	$80.00	Y	Jennifer's Closet	289-433-1555
16	WE030	Seriously Tall Boots	STB	Black	8.5	1	W	$42.50	$80.00	Y	Jennifer's Closet	289-433-1555
17	WE001	Rugged Hiking Boots	RHB	Brown	8	5	M	$46.50	$90.00	N	Outdoor Inc.	292-555-2334
18	WE002	Rugged Hiking Boots	RHB	Brown	10	3	M	$46.50	$90.00	Y	Outdoor Inc.	292-555-2334
19	WE003	Rugged Hiking Boots	RHB	Black	9.5	6	M	$46.50	$90.00	N	Outdoor Inc.	292-555-2334
20	WE004	Rugged Hiking Boots	RHB	Black	10.5	4	M	$46.50	$90.00	N	Outdoor Inc.	292-555-2334
21	WE005	Rugged Hiking Boots	RHB	Black	7.5	4	W	$53.50	$98.00	N	Outdoor Inc.	292-555-2334
22	WE006	Rugged Hiking Boots	RHB	Black	8	2	W	$53.50	$98.00	Y	Outdoor Inc.	292-555-2334
23	WE007	Rugged Hiking Boots	RHB	Brown	9	3	W	$53.50	$98.00	N	Outdoor Inc.	292-555-2334
24	WE008	Rugged Hiking Boots	RHB	Brown	8.5	2	W	$53.50	$98.00	Y	Outdoor Inc.	292-555-2334
25	WE031	Glide Running Shoes	GRS	White	8	6	M	$48.00	$75.00	N	Sport it!	255-463-7896
26	WE032	Glide Running Shoes	GRS	White	9	6	M	$48.00	$75.00	N	Sport it!	255-463-7896
27	WE033	Glide Running Shoes	GRS	White	10	6	M	$48.00	$75.00	N	Sport it!	255-463-7896
28	WE034	Glide Running Shoes	GRS	Black	8	2	M	$48.00	$75.00	N	Sport it!	255-463-7896
29	WE035	Glide Running Shoes	GRS	Black	9	3	M	$48.00	$75.00	N	Sport it!	255-463-7896
30	WE036	Glide Running Shoes	GRS	Black	10	1	M	$48.00	$75.00	Y	Sport it!	255-463-7896
31	WE015	Lazy Flip-Flops	LFF	Pink	6	4	W	$7.50	$14.00	N	Sport it!	255-463-7896
32	WE016	Lazy Flip-Flops	LFF	Pink	7	0	W	$7.50	$14.00	N	Sport it!	255-463-7896
33	WE017	Lazy Flip-Flops	LFF	Pink	8	2	W	$7.50	$14.00	Y	Sport it!	255-463-7896
34	WE018	Lazy Flip-Flops	LFF	White	6	3	W	$7.50	$14.00	N	Sport it!	255-463-7896
35	WE019	Lazy Flip-Flops	LFF	White	7	1	W	$7.50	$14.00	N	Sport it!	255-463-7896
36	WE020	Lazy Flip-Flops	LFF	White	8	2	W	$7.50	$14.00	Y	Sport it!	255-463-7896
37	WE021	Lazy Flip-Flops	LFF	Brown	8	2	M	$7.50	$14.00	Y	Sport it!	255-463-7896
38	WE022	Lazy Flip-Flops	LFF	Brown	9	4	M	$7.50	$14.00	N	Sport it!	255-463-7896
39	WE023	Lazy Flip-Flops	LFF	Brown	10	2	M	$7.50	$14.00	Y	Sport it!	255-463-7896
40	WE024	Lazy Flip-Flops	LFF	Brown	11	2	M	$7.50	$14.00	Y	Sport it!	255-463-7896

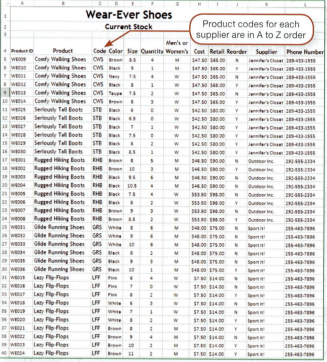

4-82 Data sorted by "Supplier" and "Code"

6. Use an *AutoFilter*.
   a. Click any cell in cells **A5:L40**.
   b. Click the **Filter** button [*Data* tab, *Sort & Filter* group].
   c. Click the **AutoFilter** button for **Supplier** column.
   d. Click **(Select All)** to remove all the check marks.
   e. Click **Jennifer's Closet** to place a check mark for only that supplier.
   f. Click **OK**. The data is filtered to show only records from one supplier.

7. Copy the *Northern Warehouse* worksheet.
   a. Name the copied sheet Subtotals.
   b. Move the *Subtotals* sheet to the right of the *Northern Warehouse* sheet.

8. Use the *Subtotal* command.
   a. Click cell **K5** in the *Subtotals* sheet.
   b. Click the **Filter** button [*Data* tab, *Sort & Filter* group] to remove the filter.
   c. Click the **Subtotal** button [*Data* tab, *Outline* group].
   d. Click the **At each change in** arrow and choose **Supplier**.
   e. Click the **Use function** arrow and choose **Count**.
   f. Check the **Supplier** box in the *Add subtotal to* area and remove check marks for all other fields (Figure 4-83).
   g. Click **OK**. A subtotal row is inserted at the bottom of each group and shows how many products are available from each supplier.
   h. Format the label in cell **J17** as **right-aligned**.
   i. **Right-align** the remaining subtotal labels in column **J** (Figure 4-84).

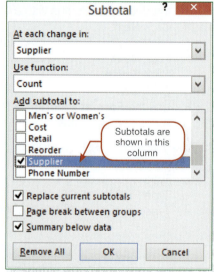

4-83 *Subtotal* dialog box to count the number of products by supplier

9. Copy the **Subtotals** sheet, name it Goal Seek, and move it to the right of the *Subtotals* sheet.

10. Prepare a *Goal Seek* worksheet.
    a. Click cell **K5** in the **Goal Seek** sheet.
    b. Click the **Subtotals** button [*Data* tab, *Outline* group].
    c. Click **Remove All** in the *Subtotal* dialog box.
    d. Insert a column between columns **I** and **J**. Type Margin in cell **J4**. Increase the width of column **J** to **7.43**.
    e. Type the profit margin formula in cell **J5** =(I5-H5)/H5 and press **Enter**. The profit margin subtracts the unit cost from the retail price and divides those results by the cost.
    f. Since the result is a percentage, format the results in cell **J5** as **Percent Style** with no decimals.
    g. Copy the formula in cell **J5** to cells **J6:J40**.
    h. Click the **Filter** button [*Data* tab, *Sort & Filter* group].
    i. Click the **AutoFilter** button for the **Margin** column.
    j. Click **(Select All)** to remove all the check marks.
    k. Click **37%** to place a check mark for that profit margin.
    l. Click **OK**. The data is filtered to show only the rows with the lowest profit margin.

11. Use *Goal Seek*.
    a. Type New Retail Price to Reach 55% Margin in cell **N6** and make it **bold**.
    b. Click cell **J5**.
    c. Click the **What-If Analysis** button [*Data* tab, *Data Tools* group] and choose **Goal Seek**.
    d. In the *To value* box, type **55%**.
    e. In the *By changing cell* box, click cell **I5** (Figure 4-85).
    f. Click **OK** to view the solution in cell **I5**.
    g. Make a note of the results and click **Cancel**.
    h. Click cell **O7** and type $73.63.

12. Protect a worksheet without a password.
    a. Click the **Subtotals** sheet tab.
    b. Click the **Protect Sheet** button [*Review* tab, *Changes* group].
    c. Verify that there are check marks for **Select locked cells** and **Select unlocked cells**.
    d. Click **OK**.

4-84 Subtotals inserted for each group

4-85 *Goal Seek* to find new retail price

13. Save and close the workbook (Figure 4-86).

The following tables are shown in the figure:

	Product		Co⋯	Col⋯	Siz⋯	Quanti⋯	Men's or Women⋯	Cos⋯	Reta⋯	Marg⋯	Reord⋯	Supplier	Phone Numb⋯			
5	Comfy Walking Shoes		CWS	Brown	8.5	4	M	$47.50	$65.00	37%	N	Jennifer's Closet	289-433-1555			
6	Comfy Walking Shoes		CWS	Black	9	1	M	$47.50	$65.00	37%	Y	Jennifer's Closet	289-433-1555		New Retail Price to Reach 55% Margin	
7	Comfy Walking Shoes		CWS	Navy	7.5	4	W	$47.50	$65.00	37%	N	Jennifer's Closet	289-433-1555		$73.63	
8	Comfy Walking Shoes		CWS	Black	8	1	W	$47.50	$65.00	37%	Y	Jennifer's Closet	289-433-1555			
9	Comfy Walking Shoes		CWS	Taupe	7.5	2	W	$47.50	$65.00	37%	N	Jennifer's Closet	289-433-1555			
10	Comfy Walking Shoes		CWS	Brown	8	3	W	$47.50	$65.00	37%	Y	Jennifer's Closet	289-433-1555			

Wear-Ever Shoes — **Current Stock**

	Product⋯	Product	Co⋯	Col⋯	Siz⋯	Quanti⋯	Men's or Women⋯	Cos⋯	Reta⋯	Reord⋯	Supplier	Phone Numb⋯
5	WE009	Comfy Walking Shoes	CWS	Brown	8.5	4	M	$47.50	$65.00	N	Jennifer's Closet	289-433-1555
6	WE010	Comfy Walking Shoes	CWS	Black	9	1	M	$47.50	$65.00	Y	Jennifer's Closet	289-433-1555
7	WE011	Comfy Walking Shoes	CWS	Navy	7.5	4	W	$47.50	$65.00	N	Jennifer's Closet	289-433-1555
8	WE012	Comfy Walking Shoes	CWS	Black	8	1	W	$47.50	$65.00	Y	Jennifer's Closet	289-433-1555
9	WE013	Comfy Walking Shoes	CWS	Taupe	7.5	2	W	$47.50	$65.00	N	Jennifer's Closet	289-433-1555
10	WE014	Comfy Walking Shoes	CWS	Brown	8	3	W	$47.50	$65.00	Y	Jennifer's Closet	289-433-1555
11	WE025	Seriously Tall Boots	STB	Black	6	0	W	$42.50	$80.00	Y	Jennifer's Closet	289-433-1555
12	WE026	Seriously Tall Boots	STB	Black	6.5	0	W	$42.50	$80.00	Y	Jennifer's Closet	289-433-1555
13	WE027	Seriously Tall Boots	STB	Black	7	1	W	$42.50	$80.00	Y	Jennifer's Closet	289-433-1555
14	WE028	Seriously Tall Boots	STB	Black	7.5	0	W	$42.50	$80.00	Y	Jennifer's Closet	289-433-1555
15	WE029	Seriously Tall Boots	STB	Black	8	2	W	$42.50	$80.00	Y	Jennifer's Closet	289-433-1555
16	WE030	Seriously Tall Boots	STB	Black	8.5	1	W	$42.50	$80.00	Y	Jennifer's Closet	289-433-1555

4-86 Excel 4-1 completed worksheets

Guided Project 4-2

Classic Gardens and Landscapes is building a workbook with data about sales revenue and recent promotion campaigns. You copy some data from Word and import other data from an Access database. You also use *Conditional Formatting* and create tables.
[Student Learning Outcomes 4.1, 4.2, 4.4, 4.5, 4.6]

Files Needed: ***ClassicGardensRevenue-04.xlsx***, ***SalesDatabase-04.accdb***, and ***ClassicGardensWord-04.docx***
Completed Project File Name: *[your initials] Excel 4-2.xlsx*

Skills Covered in This Project

- Copy data from Word.
- Apply *Conditional Formatting* using an icon set.
- Import a table from a database file.
- Apply a table style.
- Insert a total row in a table.
- Use the *SUM* function.
- Insert a column.
- Copy a formula.
- Create an *Auto Outline*.
- Create a *PivotTable*.
- Set a report filter in a *PivotTable*.
- Move fields in a *PivotTable*.

---

1. Open the **ClassicGardensRevenue-04** workbook from your student data files folder. Click the **Enable Editing** button.

2. Save the workbook as **[your initials] Excel 4-2**.

3. Click the **Quarterly** sheet tab.

4. Insert six columns between columns **G** and **H**.

5. Copy data from Word.
   a. Open the Word document **ClassicGardensWord-04** from your student data files folder. Click the **Enable Editing** button.
   b. Select all the data in Word and copy it.
   c. Return to the Excel workbook.
   d. Click cell **H4**.
   e. Click the **Paste** button arrow [*Home* tab, *Clipboard* group] and choose **Match Destination Formatting**.
   f. Select cells **N5:N10** and click the *AutoSum* button [*Home* tab, *Editing* group].
   g. Select cells **B10:M10** and sum the columns.

6. Apply *Conditional Formatting*.
   a. Select cells **J5:J9**.
   b. Click the **Quick Analysis** button.
   c. Click **Formatting**.
   d. Choose **Icon Set** (Figure 4-87). The cells display an icon to represent the upper, middle, or lower values of the range.

Classic Gardens and Landscapes (CGL)
Revenue by Quarter

Mar	Apr	May	June	July	Aug	Sep	Oct
$7,886.48	$7,650.23	$7,683.30	$8,094.38	$7,660.13	$7,741.13	$7,886.48	$7,650.23
$12,043.13	$11,803.28	$11,879.78	$12,226.28	$11,819.93	$11,909.48	$12,043.13	$11,803.28
$12,957.30	$13,039.88	$15,318.23	$16,876.13	$15,192.23	$13,070.48	$12,957.30	$13,039.88
$4,475.25	$5,153.63	$5,514.53	$7,919.55	$4,478.18	$4,708.13	$4,475.25	$5,153.63
$631.13	$563.18	$584.78	$698.40	$579.38	$585.23	$631.13	$563.18
$37,993.28	$38,210.18	$40,980.60	$45,814.73	$39,729.85	$38,014.45	$37,993.29	$38,210.20

4-87 Icon set conditional formatting

7. *AutoFit* the columns and make sure all data is visible.

8. Click the **AutoOutline** sheet tab.

9. Enter *SUM* functions.
   a. Enter the *SUM* function in cells **E5:E18**, **I5:I18**, **M5:M18**, and **Q5:Q18**.
   b. Enter the *SUM* function in cells **R5:R18** to add the four quarter totals.
   c. Enter the *SUM* function in cells **B19:R19**.
   d. Do the same to show sums for the remaining sections on the sheet. You can hold down the **Ctrl** key, select multiple nonadjacent ranges, and click the **AutoSum** button.

10. In cell **B35**, type the formula =B19+B26+B34 and press **Enter**.

11. Copy the formula in cell **B35** to cells **C35:R35**. *Autofit* the columns.

12. Create an *Auto Outline*.
    a. Click cell **B5**.
    b. Click the **Group** button arrow [*Data* tab, *Outline* group] and choose **Auto Outline** (Figure 4-88). The *Auto Outline* command uses the column and row formulas to group the data.
    c. Click the **Level 2** column outline button (above the column headings). Only the quarter totals are displayed (Figure 4-89).

13. Import a table from an Access database.
    a. Click the **Table** sheet tab.
    b. Click cell **A4**.
    c. Click the **From Access** button [*Data* tab, *Get External Data* group].
    d. Select **SalesDatabase-04.accdb** in the *Select Data Source* window.
    e. Click **Open**.
    f. Click **tblMailings** in the *Select Table* dialog box.
    g. Click **OK**.
    h. Select **Table** and **Existing worksheet** if necessary.
    i. Click **OK**.

14. Apply a table style and show a total row.
    a. Click any cell within the table.
    b. Click the **Table Styles** More button [*Table Tools Design* tab, *Table Styles* group].
    c. Choose **Table Style Medium 15**.
    d. Click to place a check mark for **Total Row** [*Table Tools Design* tab, *Table Style Options* group].
    e. Click each cell in the range **C30:M30** and choose **SUM**.

15. Merge and center the title across **A1:N1**, and the subtitle across **A2:N2**. Set the font size of the labels to **18 pt.** (Figure 4-90).

16. Click the **PivotTable** sheet tab.

17. Create a *PivotTable*.
    a. Select cells **A3:D28**.
    b. Click the **PivotTable** button [*Insert* tab, *Tables* group]. Depending on how data is arranged, Excel cannot always recommend *PivotTable* layouts. Select the correct cell range if you did not do so before clicking the **PivotTable** button.

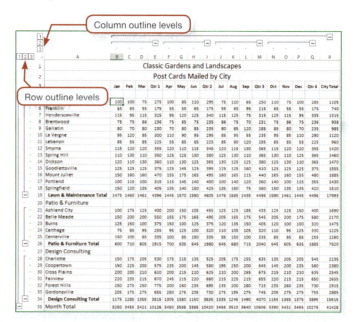

4-88 AutoOutline with three row levels and three column levels

	Jan	Feb	Mar	Qtr 1	Apr	May	Jun	Qtr 2	Jul	Aug	Sep	Qtr 3	Oct	Nov	Dec	Qtr 4	City Total
5	100	100	75	275	100	85	110	295	75	110	65	250	110	75	100	285	1105
6 Franklin	55	65	55	175	55	55	65	175	55	65	95	215	65	55	55	175	740
7 Hendersonville	115	95	115	325	95	120	125	340	115	125	75	315	125	115	95	335	1315
8 Brentwood	75	75	86	236	75	85	75	235	86	75	70	231	75	86	75	236	938
9 Gallatin	80	70	80	230	70	80	85	235	80	85	120	285	85	80	70	235	985
10 La Vergne	95	120	85	300	110	90	95	295	85	95	55	235	95	85	110	290	1120
11 Lebanon	85	55	85	225	55	85	85	225	80	120	85	285	85	85	55	225	960
12 Smyrna	115	120	120	355	125	110	115	345	120	115	130	365	115	120	120	355	1420
13 Spring Hill	110	130	110	350	125	125	130	380	120	130	110	365	130	110	125	365	1460
14 Dickson	120	110	130	360	110	130	125	365	130	125	125	380	125	130	110	365	1470
15 Goodlettsville	125	125	125	375	125	145	125	395	125	125	160	410	125	125	125	375	1555
16 Mount Juliet	150	160	160	470	155	175	165	495	160	165	115	440	165	160	155	480	1885
17 Portland	100	115	100	315	115	145	140	400	140	120	100	360	140	100	115	355	1430
18 Springfield	150	120	135	405	135	140	130	425	135	150	75	360	150	135	135	420	1610
19 **Lawn & Maintenance Total**	1475	1460	1461	4396	1570	1590	1445	4605	1476	1585	1635	4496	1590	1461	1445	4496	17993
20 Patio & Furniture																	
21 Ashland City	100	175	125	400	200	150	105	455	125	125	185	435	125	150	150	400	1690
22 Belle Meade	150	200	200	550	155	175	165	495	205	165	175	545	205	200	175	580	2170
23 Burns	125	150	100	375	150	100	125	375	120	135	150	405	120	100	100	320	1475
24 Carthage	75	85	95	255	95	125	100	320	110	105	105	320	110	95	125	330	1225
25 Centerville	150	100	85	335	100	85	150	335	85	150	100	335	85	85	85	255	1260
26 **Patio & Furniture Total**	600	710	605	1915	700	635	645	1980	645	680	715	2040	645	605	635	1885	7820
27 Design Consulting																	
28 Charlotte	150	175	205	530	175	215	135	525	205	175	255	635	135	205	205	545	2235
29 Coopertown	150	225	200	575	235	200	145	580	195	250	200	645	145	200	235	580	2380
30 Cross Plains	200	200	210	610	200	215	210	625	210	200	265	675	215	210	210	635	2545
31 Fairview	220	235	215	670	245	215	220	680	215	225	215	655	220	215	215	650	2655
32 Forest Hills	250	275	250	775	200	260	235	695	235	200	280	715	235	260	235	730	2915
33 Gordonsville	205	175	275	655	250	275	205	730	275	195	275	745	205	275	275	755	2885
34 **Design Consulting Total**	1175	1285	1355	3815	1305	1380	1150	3835	1335	1245	1490	4070	1155	1365	1375	3895	15615
35 Month Total	3250	3455	3421	10126	3450	3585	3385	10420	3456	3510	3640	10606	3390	3431	3455	10276	41428

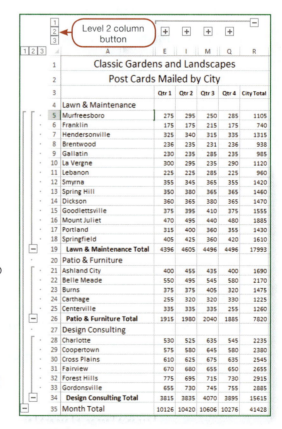

4-89 Outline collapsed at Level 2 column group

	A	Qtr 1	Qtr 2	Qtr 3	Qtr 4	City Total
1	Classic Gardens and Landscapes					
2	Post Cards Mailed by City					
3		Qtr 1	Qtr 2	Qtr 3	Qtr 4	City Total
4	Lawn & Maintenance					
5	Murfreesboro	275	295	250	285	1105
6	Franklin	175	175	215	175	740
7	Hendersonville	325	340	315	335	1315
8	Brentwood	236	235	231	236	938
9	Gallatin	230	235	285	235	985
10	La Vergne	300	295	235	290	1120
11	Lebanon	225	225	285	225	960
12	Smyrna	355	345	365	355	1420
13	Spring Hill	350	380	365	365	1460
14	Dickson	360	365	380	365	1470
15	Goodlettsville	375	395	410	375	1555
16	Mount Juliet	470	495	440	480	1885
17	Portland	315	400	360	355	1430
18	Springfield	405	425	360	420	1610
19	**Lawn & Maintenance Total**	4396	4605	4496	4496	17993
20	Patio & Furniture					
21	Ashland City	400	455	435	400	1690
22	Belle Meade	550	495	545	580	2170
23	Burns	375	375	405	320	1475
24	Carthage	255	320	320	330	1225
25	Centerville	335	335	335	255	1260
26	**Patio & Furniture Total**	1915	1980	2040	1885	7820
27	Design Consulting					
28	Charlotte	530	525	635	545	2235
29	Coopertown	575	580	645	580	2380
30	Cross Plains	610	625	635	635	2545
31	Fairview	670	680	655	650	2655
32	Forest Hills	775	695	715	730	2915
33	Gordonsville	655	730	745	755	2885
34	**Design Consulting Total**	3815	3835	4070	3895	15615
35	Month Total	10126	10420	10606	10276	41428

c. Select **New Worksheet** if necessary.
d. Click **OK**.
e. In the *Choose fields to add to report* area in the *PivotTable Fields* pane, click to place a check for **City**, **# Mailed**, and **# Responses**. These fields are shown in the report layout and in the *Row* and *Values* areas in the pane. The *Columns* area in the pane indicates that the numbers in the columns are summed or totaled in the *Grand Total* row (Figure 4-91).
f. Drag the **Department** field from the *Choose fields to add to report* area to the *Filters* area in the *PivotTable Fields* pane.
g. Click the filter arrow for the **Department** field in cell **B1**.
h. Click to place a check mark for **Select Multiple Items**.
i. Click to remove the check mark for **All**.
j. Click to place a check mark for **Landscape Design** and click **OK**.
k. Format cells **A1:B1** as bold.
l. Close the *PivotTable Fields* pane (Figure 4-92).

18. Save and close the workbook.

ID	City	Jan	Feb	Mar	Apr	May	Jun	Jul	Aug	Sep	Oct	Nov	Dec
1	Murfreesboro	100	100	75	100	85	110	75	110	65	110	75	100
2	Franklin	55	65	55	55	55	65	55	65	95	65	55	55
3	Hendersonville	115	95	115	95	120	125	115	125	75	125	115	95
4	Brentwood	75	75	86	75	85	75	86	75	70	75	86	75
5	Gallatin	80	70	80	70	80	85	80	85	120	85	80	70
6	La Vergne	95	120	85	110	90	95	85	95	55	95	85	110
7	Lebanon	85	55	85	55	85	85	85	80	120	85	85	55
8	Smyrna	115	120	120	120	110	115	120	115	130	115	120	120
9	Spring Hill	110	130	110	125	125	130	125	130	110	130	110	125
10	Dickson	120	110	130	110	130	125	130	125	125	125	130	110
11	Goodlettsville	125	125	125	125	145	125	125	125	160	125	125	125
12	Mount Juliet	150	160	160	155	175	165	160	165	115	165	160	155
13	Portland	100	115	100	115	145	140	100	140	120	140	100	115
14	Springfield	150	120	135	135	140	150	135	150	75	150	135	135
15	Ashland City	100	175	125	200	150	105	125	125	185	125	125	150
16	Belle Meade	150	200	200	155	175	165	205	165	175	205	200	175
17	Burns	125	150	100	150	100	125	120	135	150	120	100	100
18	Carthage	75	85	95	95	125	100	110	105	105	110	95	125
19	Centerville	150	100	85	100	85	150	85	150	100	85	85	85
20	Charlotte	150	175	205	175	215	135	205	175	255	135	205	205
21	Coopertown	150	225	200	235	200	145	195	250	200	145	200	235
22	Cross Plains	200	200	210	200	215	210	210	200	265	215	210	210
23	Fairview	220	235	215	245	215	220	215	225	215	220	215	215
24	Forest Hills	250	275	250	200	260	235	235	200	280	235	260	235
25	Gordonsville	205	175	275	250	275	205	275	195	275	205	275	275
Total		3250	3455	3421	3450	3585	3385	3456	3510	3640	3390	3431	3455

4-90 Imported data formatted as a table

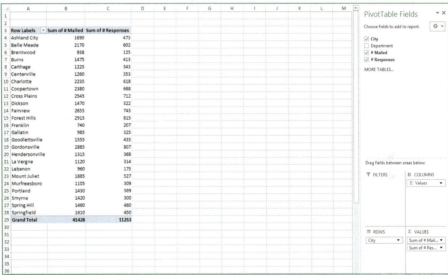

4-91 *PivotTable* layout

Department	Landscape Design 🔽		Report Filter button
Row Labels 🔽	Sum of # Mailed	Sum of # Responses	
Centerville	1260	353	
Charlotte	2235	618	
Forest Hills	2915	815	
Gallatin	985	325	
La Vergne	1120	314	
Portland	1430	389	
Springfield	1610	450	
Grand Total	11555	3264	

4-92 *PivotTable* with report filter

Guided Project 4-3

Clemenson Imaging wants to analyze expense reports from field representatives as well as its patient data and image data. To complete the necessary worksheets, you import a comma-separated text file (.csv), use the *Subtotal* command, and run *Goal Seek*. You also format data as a table and build an advanced filter. Finally, you display data in a *PivotTable*.
[Student Learning Outcomes 4.1, 4.2, 4.3, 4.4, 4.5, 4.6, 4.7]

Files Needed: ***ClemensonForecasts-04.xlsx*** and ***ClemensonExpenseData-04.csv***
Completed Project File Name: *[your initials] Excel 4-3.xlsx*

Skills Covered in This Project

- Create an Excel table.
- Apply a table style.
- Create an *Advanced Filter*.
- Apply *Conditional Formatting*.
- Copy, move, and name a worksheet.
- Insert a row and set column widths.
- Import a comma-separated values text file.
- Sort data.

- Use the *Subtotal* command.
- Expand and collapse groups in an outline.
- Use *Goal Seek*.
- Create a *PivotTable*.
- Create a *PivotChart*.
- Unlock cells.
- Protect a worksheet with a password.

---

1. Open the ***ClemensonForecasts-04*** workbook from your student data files folder. Click the **Enable Editing** button.

2. Save the workbook as *[your initials] Excel 4-3*.

3. Copy the **Past&Projected** sheet and name the copied sheet Adv Filter. Move the **Adv Filter** sheet to the right of the *Past&Projected* sheet.

4. Create and format an Excel table.
   a. Select cells **A4:E60** on the *Adv Filter* sheet.
   b. Click the **Quick Analysis** tool and choose **Tables**.
   c. Click **Table**.

5. Apply a table style.
   a. Click a cell within the table.
   b. Click the **More** button [*Table Tools Design* tab, *Table Styles* group].
   c. Select **Table Style Medium 15**.

6. Create a criteria range for an *Advanced Filter*.
   a. Select cells **A4:E4** and copy and paste them to cell **G4**.
   b. Type Criteria Range in cell **G3** and set the font to **Cambria 16 pt**.
   c. Adjust column **K** width to show the complete label.
   d. Type Extract Range in cell **G8** and set the same font and size.
   e. Copy the labels from cells **G4:K4** to cell **G9**.

7. Create an *Advanced Filter*.
   a. In cell **G5**, type >12/31/16.
   b. In cell **H5**, type mri.

c. In cell **H6**, type ct scan. These criteria will find records dated 2017 or later for MRIs **and** records for CT scans from any year (Figure 4-93).

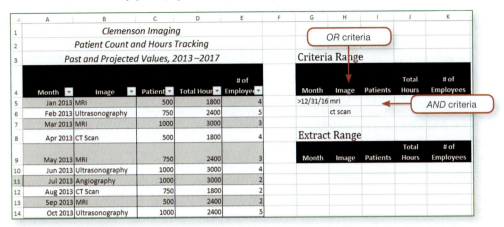

4-93 **Criteria range and extract range**

d. Click a cell in the table.
e. Click the **Advanced** button [*Data* tab, *Sort & Filter* group].
f. Select the **Copy to another location** radio button.
g. Verify that the **List range** is cells **A4:E60**. If the range is incorrect, click and drag to select the range. The list range includes the header row.
h. Click in the **Criteria range** box and select cells **G4:K6**.
i. Click in the **Copy to** box and select cells **G9:K9**.
j. Click **OK** (Figure 4-94). The CT scan records are from all years; the MRI records are only those from 2017 and later.

8. Apply *Conditional Formatting*.
   a. Select cells **I10:I25**.
   b. Click the **Conditional Formatting** button [*Home* tab, *Styles* group].
   c. Choose **Highlight Cells Rules** and **Greater Than**.
   d. Type 751 and choose **Green Fill with Dark Green Text**.
   e. Click **OK**.

9. Import a comma-separated values text file.
   a. Click the **Expense Info** sheet tab.
   b. Select cell **A3**.
   c. Click the **From Text** button [*Data* tab, *Get External Data* group].
   d. Find and select the **ClemensonExpenseData-04.csv** file in the *Import Text File* window.
   e. Click **Import**.
   f. Select the **Delimited** button in the first *Wizard* window. Excel recognizes that this file separates the data into columns with a comma.
   g. Click **Next**.
   h. Click to remove the check mark for **Tab** and click to place a check mark for **Comma**.
   i. Click **Finish** and click **OK**.
   j. Insert two rows at row **3**.
   k. Type Representative in cell **A4**, Date in cell **B4**, and Amount in cell **C4**.
   l. *AutoFit* column **C**.

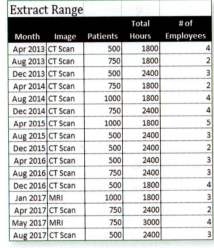

| Extract Range | | | | |
Month	Image	Patients	Total Hours	# of Employees
Apr 2013	CT Scan	500	1800	4
Aug 2013	CT Scan	750	1800	2
Dec 2013	CT Scan	500	2400	3
Apr 2014	CT Scan	750	1800	2
Aug 2014	CT Scan	1000	1800	4
Dec 2014	CT Scan	750	2400	4
Apr 2015	CT Scan	1000	1800	5
Aug 2015	CT Scan	500	2400	3
Dec 2015	CT Scan	500	2400	2
Apr 2016	CT Scan	500	2400	3
Aug 2016	CT Scan	750	2400	3
Dec 2016	CT Scan	500	1800	4
Jan 2017	MRI	1000	1800	3
Apr 2017	CT Scan	750	2400	2
May 2017	MRI	750	3000	4
Aug 2017	CT Scan	500	2400	3

4-94 *Advanced Filter* results

10. Sort data.
    a. Click cell **A5**.
    b. Click the **Sort & Filter** button [*Home* tab, *Editing* group].
    c. Choose **Sort A to Z**.

11. Use the *Subtotal* command.
    a. Click cell **A5**.
    b. Click the **Subtotal** button [*Data* tab, *Outline* group].
    c. Click the **At each change in** arrow and choose **Representative**.
    d. Click the **Use function** arrow and choose **Average**.
    e. Check the **Amount** box in the *Add subtotal to* area.
    f. Click **OK**.
    g. Format the values in column **C** as **Currency** with no decimal places.

12. Use *Goal Seek*.
    a. Type Target March Expense in cell **E4**.
    b. Click cell **C8**.
    c. Click the **What-If Analysis** button [*Data* tab, *Data Tools* group] and choose **Goal Seek**.
    d. In the *To value* box, type 600. This value sets a lower expense for Mary Jo.
    e. In the *By changing cell* box, click cell **C7**.
    f. Click **OK**.
    g. Note the target expense and click **Cancel**.
    h. Type $600 in cell **F5**.

13. Collapse outline groups.
    a. Click the collapse symbol (-) for row **12**.
    b. Click the collapse symbol (-) for each of these rows: **16**, **20**, and **24** (Figure 4-95).

14. Create a *PivotTable*.
    a. Click the **Past&Projected** sheet tab.
    b. Select cells **A4:E60**. You must select the range to display the *Quick Analysis* tool.
    c. Click the **Quick Analysis** tool and choose **Tables**.
    d. Point at several *PivotTable* options to see the *Live Preview*.
    e. Choose the option that shows a sum of each field (Figure 4-96).
    f. Rename the sheet PivotTable.

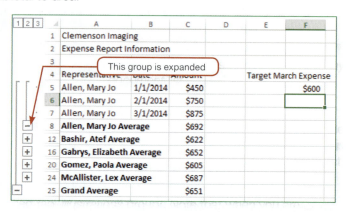

4-95 Expanded and collapsed groups after the Subtotal Command

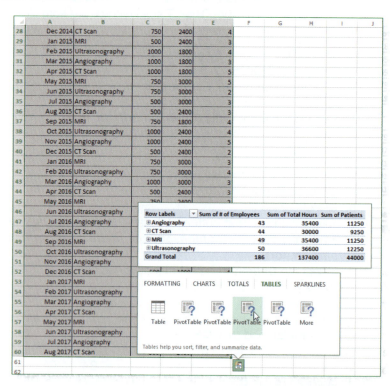

4-96 Suggested *PivotTable* choices from the *Quick Analysis* tool

15. Add a *PivotChart* to the *PivotTable* worksheet.
    a. Click a cell within the *PivotTable*.
    b. Click the **PivotChart** button [*PivotTable Tool Analyze* tab, *Tools* group].
    c. Click **Line** in the type list, and choose **Line with Markers** *PivotChart*.
    d. Click **OK**.
    e. Position the chart to the right of the *PivotTable*.
    f. In the *PivotChart Fields* pane, click to remove the check mark for **# of Employees** (Figure 4-97). The *PivotTable* and *PivotChart* are linked so that field is removed from the table and the chart. The task pane toggles between the *PivotTable* and *PivotChart* fields panes based on which element is active.

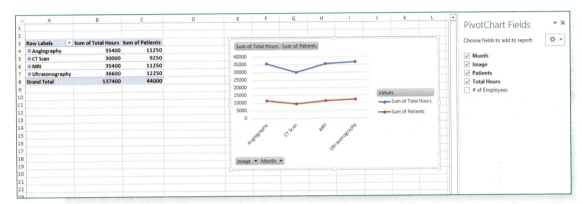

4-97 *PivotChart* and its *PivotTable*

16. Remove the *Locked* property.
    a. Click the **Past&Projected** sheet tab.
    b. Select cells **C5:E60** and right-click any cell in the range.
    c. Select **Format Cells** from the menu.
    d. Click the **Protection** tab.
    e. Clear the check mark for **Locked**.
    f. Click **OK**.

17. Protect a worksheet with a password.
    a. Click the **Protect Sheet** button [*Review* tab, *Changes* group].
    b. Click to place check marks for **Select locked cells** and **Select unlocked cells** if necessary.
    c. Type the password: 321.
    d. Click **OK**.
    e. Retype the password: 321.
    f. Click **OK**. The cells for which the *Locked* property was disabled can be edited.

18. Save and close the workbook.

E4-239

Independent Project 4-4

Eller Software Services has received updated client information with sales numbers. You import the data into the worksheet, sort and filter it, and apply conditional formatting. You also format the data as an Excel table and create a *PivotTable*.
[Student Learning Outcomes 4.1, 4.2, 4.3, 4.4, 4.5, 4.6, 4.7]

Files Needed: *EllerSales-04.xlsx* and *ClientInfo-04.txt*
Completed Project File Name: *[your initials] Excel 4-4.xlsx*

Skills Covered in This Project

- Import a text file.
- Sort data.
- Use an *AutoFilter*.
- Filter data by cell color.
- Copy, name, and move a worksheet.
- Use the *Subtotal* command.

- Apply *Conditional Formatting*.
- Clear filters and conditional formatting.
- Create an Excel table.
- Create a *PivotTable*.
- Protect a worksheet with a password.

1. Open the **EllerSales-04** workbook from your student data files folder.

2. Save the workbook as **[your initials] Excel 4-4**.

3. Import the **ClientInfo-04.txt** file in cell **A4**. The text file is tab-delimited.

4. Unhide row **10**. Fix the phone number in cell C12.

5. Set *Conditional Formatting* to show cells **I5:I13** with **Yellow Fill with Dark Yellow Text** for values that are less than **1500**.

6. Sort the data first by **Product/Service** in **A to Z** order and next by **Client Name** in **A to Z** order (Figure 4-98).

	A	B	C	D	E	F	G	H	I
1				**Eller Software Services**					
2				Adam White Client Information					
3									
4	Client Name	Address	Phone Number	City	State	Zip	Product/Service	Date	Gross Sales
5	Shelly Vicko	402 2nd Ave SE	218-342-2456	Deer River	MN	56636	Accounting Software	9/15/2014	$4,500.00
6	Wade Whitworth	1822 Highway 2	218-556-4211	Cass Lake	MN	56633	Accounting Software	9/21/2014	$5,200.00
7	Charlie Lindberg	345 Lyndale Ave	612-543-2156	Minneapolis	MN	55401	ERP: Enterprise Resource Planning	9/1/2014	$42,000.00
8	Jeremie Midboe	Pilot Knob Rd	651-333-2789	Eagan	MN	55121	POS: Point of Sale Software	11/1/2014	$7,500.00
9	Terri Olander	459 10th Avenue	218-667-8977	Brainerd	MN	56401	POS: Point of Sale Software	10/15/2014	$6,525.00
10	Craig Brand	554 2nd Street	320-751-4433	Saint Cloud	MN	56301	Technical Support	10/1/2014	$1,056.15
11	Mike Gunderson	304 Irvine Ave	218-278-9021	Bemidji	MN	56601	Technical Support	10/28/2014	$990.45
12	Heather Guyan	124 East Street	218-333-2313	Bemidji	MN	56601	Training	10/7/2014	$1,567.04
13	Hilary Marschke	245 West 3rd Ave	320-355-5443	Saint Cloud	MN	56301	Training	11/15/2014	$750.00

4-98 Rows sorted by "Product/Service" and then by "Client Name"

7. Display the *AutoFilter* buttons and filter the **Gross Sales** data by color to show only those cells with yellow fill.

8. Copy the **MN Clients** sheet, name the copied sheet Subtotals, and move it to the right of the *MN Clients* sheet.

9. Clear the filter and the conditional formatting on the **Subtotals** sheet.

10. Sort by **City** in **A to Z** order if necesssary.

11. Use the *Subtotal* command to show a **SUM** function in the **Gross Sales** column at each change in **City** (Figure 4-99).

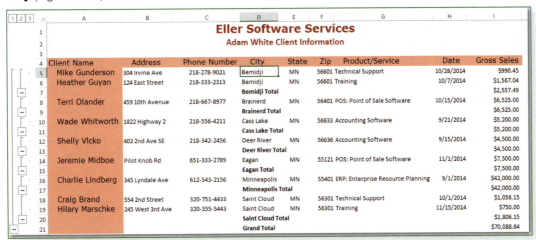

4-99 Subtotal results for gross sales at each change in city

12. Copy the **Subtotals** worksheet, name the copied sheet Table Data, and move it to the right of the *Subtotals* sheet.

13. Remove all subtotals on the **Table Data** sheet.

14. Format cells **A4:I13** as an Excel table with **Table Style Medium 9**. The external connection is from the imported data; click **Yes** in the message box.

15. Display a **Total Row** in the table (Figure 4-100).

4-100 Table with total row

16. Create a *PivotTable* based on cells **A4:I13** in the **Table Data** sheet on its own sheet named PivotTable.

17. Arrange the fields in the *PivotTable* like this: **City** (*FILTERS* area), **Product/Service** (*ROWS* area), and **Gross Sales** (*VALUES* area).

18. Filter the report to display only the data for **Bemidji** and **Brainerd**.

19. Apply **Currency** style to **B4:B7**.

20. Insert a **Clustered Column PivotChart** on the *PivotTable* sheet.

21. Delete the legend from the *PivotChart* and insert the following chart title: Bemidji & Brainerd Gross Sales (Figure 4-101).

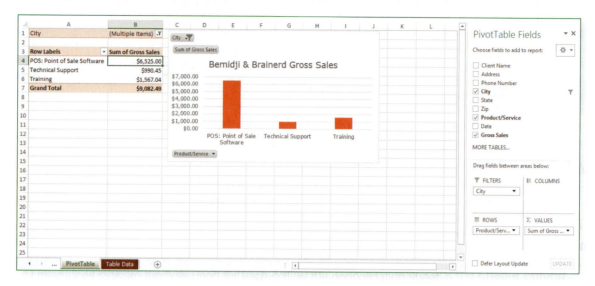

4-101 *PivotTable* with *PivotChart* results

22. Protect the **Table Data** sheet with the password **PasswordC**.

23. Save and close the workbook.

Independent Project 4-5

Boyd Air has received flight data for recent flights. After importing the data, you format it as a table and use a number filter to display the afternoon flights. Display subtotals by city of origin and use a *PivotTable* to illustrate the average capacity of the flights.
[Student Learning Outcomes 4.1, 4.2, 4.3, 4.4, 4.5]

File Needed: *FlightData-04.txt*
Completed Project File Name: *[your initials] Excel 4-5.xlsx*

Skills Covered in This Project

- Import a text file.
- Create an Excel table.
- Filter data.
- Convert a table to a normal range.
- Sort data.

- Use the *Subtotal* command.
- Copy, name, and move a worksheet.
- Create a *PivotTable*.
- Create a *PivotChart*.

1. Open a new workbook and save it as **[your initials] Excel 4-5**.

2. Import the **FlightData-04.txt** text file starting at cell **A3**. The text file is tab-delimited.

3. Click a cell within the data range and format the range as an Excel table using **Table Style Medium 21**.

4. Use the **AutoFilter** button and **Number Filters** to filter the table to display only those flights with a Departure Time after 12 PM (Figure 4-102).

5. Type Boyd Air in cell **A1**. Type Flight Statistics in cell **A2**. Set the font size to **20 pt.** for both labels.

6. Center the labels in cells **A1:A2** across the table data.

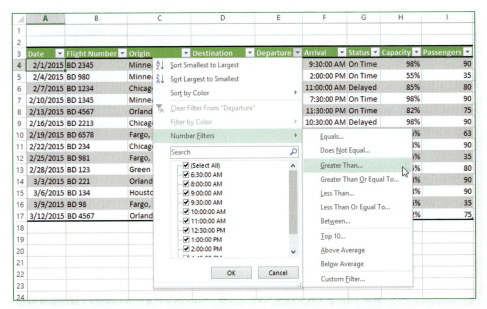

4-102 Number filter for departure time field

7. Name the worksheet Afternoon Flights.

8. Copy the **Afternoon Flights** worksheet, name the copy Subtotals, and move the **Subtotals** sheet to the right of the *Afternoon Flights* sheet.

9. On the **Subtotals** sheet, clear the filter.

10. On the **Subtotals** sheet, sort the data by **Origin** in **A to Z** order.

11. Convert the table on the **Subtotals** sheet to a normal range.

12. Select cells **A3:I17** and use the **Subtotal** command to display a sum for the **Passengers** field at each change in **Origin** (Figure 4-103). You must select the cells for the *Subtotal* command, because the main labels are not separated from the data range by a blank row.

4-103 Subtotals for Passenger field at each change in Origin field

13. Copy the **Afternoon Flights** worksheet, name the copy PivotTable Source, and move the **PivotTable Source** sheet to the right of the *Subtotals* sheet.

14. On the **PivotTable Source** sheet, clear the filter.

15. Select cells **A3:I17** and use the **Quick Analysis** tool to create a *PivotTable* to display average of capacity by origin (Figure 4-104).

4-104 *PivotTable* suggestions from the *Quick Analysis* tool

16. Click cell **B3** in the *PivotTable*. On the *PivotTable Tools Analyze* tab, click **Field Settings** and set a **Number Format** of **Percentage** with 2 decimal places.

17. In the *PivotTable Fields* pane, place a check mark to add the **Passengers** field to the *PivotTable VALUES* area showing a sum.

18. Add a **3-D Pie PivotChart** to the sheet and position the chart to the right of the *PivotTable*.

19. Rename the worksheet PivotTable&Chart and close the task pane (Figure 4-105).

20. Save and close the workbook.

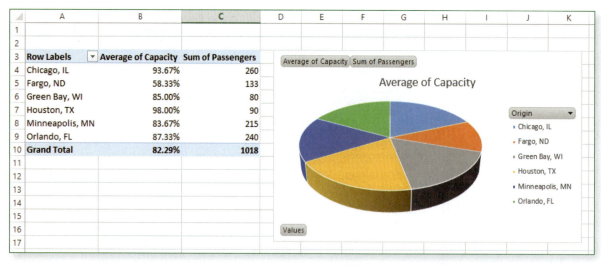

4-105 Excel 4-5 completed *PivotTable* and *PivotChart*

Independent Project 4-6

Life's Animal Shelter maintains its supplier list in a worksheet. You need to copy this data to a Word document for use by a coworker. You also need to define groups so that you can display and hide rows by supplier name.
[Student Learning Outcomes 4.1, 4.3, 4.5, 4.6, 4.7]

File Needed: ***LASSuppliers-04.xlsx***
Completed Project File Name: ***[your initials] Excel 4-6.xlsx***

Skills Covered in This Project

- Copy Excel data to Word.
- Sort data.
- Use *Flash Fill*.
- Insert and delete a column.
- Define a group.
- Collapse a group.
- Apply conditional formatting.
- Protect a worksheet.

1. Open the ***LASSuppliers-04*** workbook from your student data files folder.

2. Save the workbook as ***[your initials] Excel 4-6***.

3. Select cells **A4:D18** and copy them to the *Clipboard*.

4. Open Word and create a new document. Save the document as ***[your initials] Excel 4-6***. Note that because Word and Excel use different file name extensions, you can use the same file name.

5. Paste the data into Word.

6. Save and close the Word document (Figure 4-106).

7. Return to the worksheet and press **Esc** to remove the selection marquee if necessary.

8. In cell **E5**, type (651) 555-6788. In cell **E6**, start to type the number that is in cell **D6** and press **Enter** when the *Flash Fill* suggestion appears.

9. Type Phone in cell **E4**.

10. Delete column **D**.

4-106 Excel data copied to Word

11. Unmerge cell **A1** and then **Merge & Center** it across cells **A1:D1**. Repeat for cell **A2** (Figure 4-107).

12. Copy the worksheet, name the copy Groups and move the copy to the right of the *LAS Suppliers* sheet.

	A	B	C	D
1	**Life's Animal Shelter**			
2	Supplier List			
3				
4	Product Name	Supplier	City	Phone
5	Water bowl, large	American Pets	Minneapolis, MN	(651) 555-6788
6	Water bowl, small	American Pets	Minneapolis, MN	(651) 555-6788
7	Leather collar, small	Animals Inc.	Houston, TX	(713) 334-6577
8	Leather collar, medium	Animals Inc.	Houston, TX	(713) 334-6577
9	Leather collar, large	Animals Inc.	Houston, TX	(713) 334-6577
10	Wipe-Ups	HeatCo, Inc.	Bemidji, MN	(218) 755-2234
11	Plastic bags, 500	HeatCo, Inc.	Bemidji, MN	(218) 755-2234
12	Kitty litter, 50 lbs.	Animals Inc.	Houston, TX	(713) 334-6577
13	Doggie shovel, 12	Beltrami ManCap	Park Rapids, MN	(218) 443-9007
14	Greenlife cage, small	Beltrami ManCap	Park Rapids, MN	(218) 443-9007
15	Greenlife cage, medium	Beltrami ManCap	Park Rapids, MN	(218) 443-9007
16	Greenlife cage, large	Beltrami ManCap	Park Rapids, MN	(218) 443-9007
17	Kitty Kibbles, 50 lbs.	American Pets	Minneapolis, MN	(651) 555-6788
18	Doggie Dots, 50 lbs.	American Pets	Minneapolis, MN	(651) 555-6788

4-107 Phone numbers completed with *Flash Fill*; title recentered

13. On the *Groups* sheet, select and format the labels in row **4** as **bold** and **centered**. You need to distinguish the labels in the header row from the other rows.

14. Select cells **A5:D18** and open the *Sort* dialog box. Sort by **Supplier** in **A to Z** order and then by **Product Name** in **A to Z** order.

15. Insert a blank row at row **5** and type Minneapolis in cell **A5**. Left-align the label.

16. Insert a row at row **10** and type Houston in cell **A10**. **Bold** the label.

17. Repeat step 16 for Park Rapids and Bemidji.

18. Select cells **A6:A9**. Group this data by **Rows**. Do not include the city label in the group.

	A	B	C	D
1	**Life's Animal Shelter**			
2	Supplier List			
3				
4	**Product Name**	**Supplier**	**City**	**Phone**
5	**Minneapolis**			
6	Doggie Dots, 50 lbs.	American Pets	Minneapolis, MN	(651) 555-6788
7	Kitty Kibbles, 50 lbs.	American Pets	Minneapolis, MN	(651) 555-6788
8	Water bowl, large	American Pets	Minneapolis, MN	(651) 555-6788
9	Water bowl, small	American Pets	Minneapolis, MN	(651) 555-6788
10	**Houston**			
11	Kitty litter, 50 lbs.	Animals Inc.	Houston, TX	(713) 334-6577
12	Leather collar, large	Animals Inc.	Houston, TX	(713) 334-6577
13	Leather collar, medium	Animals Inc.	Houston, TX	(713) 334-6577
14	Leather collar, small	Animals Inc.	Houston, TX	(713) 334-6577
15	**Park Rapids**			
20	**Bemidji**	Group can be expanded		
21	Plastic bags, 500	HeatCo, Inc.	Bemidji, MN	(218) 755-2234
22	Wipe-Ups	HeatCo, Inc.	Bemidji, MN	(218) 755-2234
23				

4-108 Data manually defined in groups; Park Rapids group collapsed

19. Repeat the command to group the selected data for each supplier.

20. Collapse the *Park Rapids* group (Figure 4-108).

21. Click the **LAS Suppliers** sheet tab.

22. Apply conditional formatting to show the *American Pets* supplier name with **Green Fill with Dark Green Text** (Figure 4-109).

23. Do not remove the *Locked* property for any cells, but protect the *LAS Suppliers* sheet without a password.

24. Save and close the workbook.

	A	B	C	D
1	**Life's Animal Shelter**			
2	**Supplier List**			
3				
4	Product Name	Supplier	City	Phone
5	Water bowl, large	American Pets	Minneapolis, MN	(651) 555-6788
6	Water bowl, small	American Pets	Minneapolis, MN	(651) 555-6788
7	Leather collar, small	Animals Inc.	Houston, TX	(713) 334-6577
8	Leather collar, medium	Animals Inc.	Houston, TX	(713) 334-6577
9	Leather collar, large	Animals Inc.	Houston, TX	(713) 334-6577
10	Wipe-Ups	HeatCo, Inc.	Bemidji, MN	(218) 755-2234
11	Plastic bags, 500	HeatCo, Inc.	Bemidji, MN	(218) 755-2234
12	Kitty litter, 50 lbs.	Animals Inc.	Houston, TX	(713) 334-6577
13	Doggie shovel, 12	Beltrami ManCap	Park Rapids, MN	(218) 443-9007
14	Greenlife cage, small	Beltrami ManCap	Park Rapids, MN	(218) 443-9007
15	Greenlife cage, medium	Beltrami ManCap	Park Rapids, MN	(218) 443-9007
16	Greenlife cage, large	Beltrami ManCap	Park Rapids, MN	(218) 443-9007
17	Kitty Kibbles, 50 lbs.	American Pets	Minneapolis, MN	(651) 555-6788
18	Doggie Dots, 50 lbs.	American Pets	Minneapolis, MN	(651) 555-6788

4-109 Excel 4-6 completed worksheet

Improve It Project 4-7

Eller Software Services has created a software release workbook, but the sheets contain several errors. For this project, you edit the workbook and correct sorting, filtering, and *PivotTable* problems. [Student Learning Outcomes 4.2, 4.3, 4.4, 4.5]

File Needed: *SoftwareRelease-04*
Completed Project File Name: *[your initials] Excel 4-7.xlsx*

Skills Covered in This Project

- Sort data.
- Remove subtotals.
- Use the *Subtotal* command.
- Edit fields in a *PivotTable*.
- Create a *PivotChart*.
- Edit chart elements.

1. Open the **SoftwareRelease-04** workbook from your student data files folder.

2. Save the workbook as *[your initials] Excel 4-7*.

3. On **Phase 1 Release Dates** sheet, click the **Name Box** arrow and select **Data** to select cells **A5:F19** by its range name. Sort the data by **Platform** in **A to Z** order and then by **Release Date** in **Oldest to Newest** order.

4. On the *Subtotals* sheet, remove the subtotals. Sort the data by **Platform** in **A to Z** order.

5. Use the **Subtotal** command to count the number of projects by platform, showing the count in the **Software Project** column.

6. On the *PivotTable* sheet, click to place check marks for **Software Project**, **Price**, and **Release Date** in the *Choose fields to add to report* area. Remove other check marks.

7. Drag the **Release Date** field into the *Filters* area in the *PivotTable Fields* task pane.

8. Use the **Report** filter to show only the projects that will be released in 2015.

9. Place the **Software Project** field in the *Values* area in the *PivotTable Fields* task pane. This field is in both the *Row* and the *Values* areas.

10. Add a **3-D Pie PivotChart** to the *PivotTable* worksheet. Place the chart to the right of the *PivotTable*.

11. Change the chart title to: Revenue by Project.

12. Click the **Field Buttons** button on the *PivotChart Tools Analyze* tab to hide the pivot buttons in the chart.

13. Close the task pane.

14. Save and close the workbook (Figure 4-110).

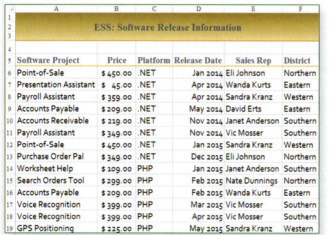

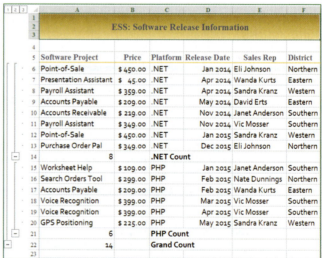

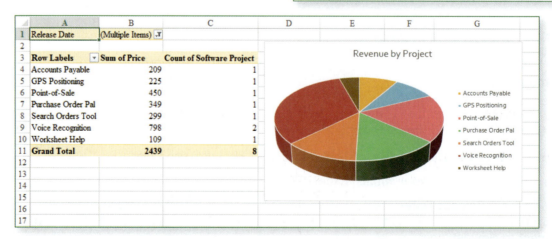

4-110 Excel 4-7 completed worksheets

Challenge Project 4-8

For this project, you import your debit or checkbook account records into an Excel workbook. You format the data as a table and sort and filter the data. Finally, you protect your data with a password.
[Student Learning Outcomes 4.1, 4.2, 4.3, 4.6, 4.7]

File Needed: None
Completed Project File Name: *[your initials] Excel 4-8.xlsx*

Create a new workbook and save it as *[your initials] Excel 4-8*. Modify your workbook according to the following guidelines:

- Import several months of your account activity from your bank's web site into the worksheet.
- If each month is a separate file on the web site, import each month separately so that the data follows one another in the sheet.
- If column headings are not included in the imported data, add headings such "Date", "Transaction", and "Balance" where appropriate.
- Format the data as an Excel table or change the style if you imported it as a table. If you have multiple tables, select all the rows and convert the tables to a normal range. Then format the entire range as a single table.
- If the records are sorted in ascending order by date, reverse the sort order.
- Review your data and apply conditional formatting to a transaction name that appears more than once or to a transaction type that you want to highlight.
- Filter the data by the color used in your conditional formatting command.
- Password protect the sheet without unlocking any cells.

Challenge Project 4-9

For this project, you build a worksheet that will allow you to analyze costs of a decorating or remodeling project in your home or apartment.
[Student Learning Outcomes 4.6, 4.7]

File Needed: None
Completed Project File Name: *[your initials] Excel 4-9.xlsx*

Create a new workbook and save it as *[your initials] Excel 4-9*. Modify your workbook according to the following guidelines:

- Type labels for at least five tasks in a decorating or remodeling project, such as "Purchase paint", "Consult with contractor", etc.
- Type an estimated cost for each task and use a *SUM* formula to show an estimated total.

- Determine a slightly lower total cost than your original estimate and use *Goal Seek* to adjust one of the tasks so that you can reach this preferred lower cost.
- Review your data and apply conditional formatting to display the two most expensive tasks in a different color.
- Add a main title to your worksheet and use different font sizes and borders to effectively display your information.

Challenge Project 4-10

For this project, you create a worksheet that lists names, birth dates, and hair color for 12 people. You format the list as a table and build a *PivotTable*.
[Student Learning Outcomes 4.2, 4.3, 4.4, 4.5]

File Needed: None
Completed Project File Name: *[your initials] Excel 4-10.xlsx*

Create a new workbook and save it as *[your initials] Excel 4-10*. Modify your workbook according to the following guidelines:

- Type your first name, your last name, your birthdate, and your hair color in four columns in a row.
- Type the same information for 11 more people, using real or fictitious data. Use birthdates that are the same year as yours as well as two other years, so that your data has only three birth years. Use only three hair colors for all your people, such as brown, blond, and red.
- Format the data as a table and apply a table style.
- Sort the date by birthdate with the youngest people listed first. Then filter the data to show only those records from the first year listed in the data.
- Make a copy of the table sheet and convert the table to normal range. Use the *Subtotal* command to count the number of persons with each hair color.
- Copy the table again for use as a *PivotTable* source. Create a *PivotTable* that displays something of interest about your list.

Working with Multiple Worksheets and Workbooks

CHAPTER OVERVIEW

As you learned in Chapter 2, you can use a 3D cell reference in a formula to include data from multiple sheets in your workbooks. When several worksheets use an identical layout but include data from different organization locations or different time periods, Excel has a faster method you can use to summarize data from several sheets: the *Consolidate* command. The *Consolidate* command permits you to quickly apply various mathematical and statistical functions that include multiple cell ranges in identical locations on several sheets.

In this chapter, you will learn how to consolidate data from multiple worksheets and how to format consolidated data for consistency. In addition to learning about consolidation and linking worksheets, you will learn key skills that include inserting *SmartArt* graphics and screenshots as well as hyperlinks in your worksheets.

STUDENT LEARNING OUTCOMES (SLOs)

After completing this chapter, you will be able to:

SLO 5.1 Create a static consolidation of data from multiple worksheets (p. E5-252).

SLO 5.2 Create a dynamic consolidation of data from multiple worksheets (p. E5-254).

SLO 5.3 Link workbooks to consolidate data among worksheets (p. E5-261).

SLO 5.4 Insert *SmartArt*, hyperlinks, and screenshots in a worksheet (p. E5-267).

SLO 5.5 Group worksheets and edit and format grouped worksheets (p. E5-273).

CASE STUDY

For the Pause & Practice projects in this chapter, you build consolidated Excel worksheets for the northern Minnesota resort business Paradise Lakes Resort (PLR) to summarize sales activity from each of its four locations.

Pause & Practice 5-1: Create static and dynamic data consolidations.

Pause & Practice 5-2: Link workbooks.

Pause & Practice 5-3: Insert *SmartArt*, hyperlinks, and screenshots in a workbook and edit grouped sheets.

Creating a Static Data Consolidation

A *consolidated worksheet* summarizes data from more than one worksheet using a mathematical or statistical Excel function. In Excel, when data is consolidated among worksheets, we refer to it as being summarized. The *Consolidate* command, located on the *Data* tab, quickly calculates totals, averages, or other functions of related data from several worksheets.

Data Consolidation by Position

In order to use the *Consolidate* command, you must be working with worksheets that have common data located in the same position on each worksheet. This is known as consolidation *by position*, because all data is located in the same rows or columns on each worksheet.

For example, each of the locations for Paradise Lakes Resorts uses the same worksheet layout for its net income data. The only differences are the actual values from each resort. Figure 5-1 shows the worksheets for two locations. Notice that each of the sales category items are in the same cells on both worksheets, cells B5:D8. When all sheets follow the same pattern, as they do in this example, the *Consolidate* command can gather the data from each sheet to calculate a total, an average, or other common functions.

	A	B	C	D	E
1		Cass Lake, PLR			
2		Net Income To Date			
3			Quarter 1		
4	Sales Categories	January	February	March	Total
5	Room and Cabin Rentals	$ 25,760	$35,145	$ 61,101	$122,006
6	Excursions	15,350	27,455	41,320	84,125
7	Spa Services	6,750	7,884	12,010	26,644
8	Shop Purchases	5,500	8,235	7,580	21,315
9	Total Sales	$ 53,360	$78,719	$122,011	$254,090
10					
11	Expense Categories				
12	Salaries and Wages	$ 13,340	$19,680	$ 30,503	$ 63,523
13	Administrative	8,004	11,808	18,302	38,114
14	Marketing	5,336	7,872	12,201	25,409
15	Operations and Maintenance	14,941	22,041	34,163	71,145
16	Total Expenses	$ 41,621	$61,401	$ 95,169	$198,190
17					
18	Net Income		$ 11,739	$17,318	$ 26,842	$ 55,900

	A	B	C	D	E
1		Baudette, PLR			
2		Net Income To Date			
3			Quarter 1		
4	Sales Categories	January	February	March	Total
5	Room and Cabin Rentals	$ 21,030	$15,455	$ 54,030	$ 90,515
6	Excursions	14,320	23,455	34,075	71,850
7	Spa Services	6,750	7,884	12,010	26,644
8	Shop Purchases	5,500	8,235	7,580	21,315
9	Total Sales	$ 47,600	$55,029	$107,695	$210,324
10					
11	Expense Categories				
12	Salaries and Wages	$ 11,900	$13,757	$ 26,924	$ 52,581
13	Administrative	7,140	8,254	16,154	31,549
14	Marketing	4,760	5,503	10,770	21,032
15	Operations and Maintenance	13,328	15,408	30,155	58,891
16	Total Expenses	$ 37,128	$42,923	$ 84,002	$164,053
17					
18	Net Income	$ 10,472	$12,106	$ 23,693	$ 46,271

5-1 Worksheets that can be consolidated

A *consolidation worksheet* is a separate summary worksheet in the same workbook. You create a consolidation sheet by creating a copy of one of the source worksheets so that all of the labels and data are in the same positions. A *source worksheet* is an existing worksheet that contains a range that will be included in the consolidation worksheet. On the copied sheet, which will become the consolidation sheet, you delete the contents of the cells that will be consolidated. In Figure 5-1, for example, the contents of cells B5:D8 would be deleted on the consolidation sheet.

Static Data Consolidation

A *static consolidation* summarizes the data and displays a result that does not update on the consolidated sheet. The result is a calculated value that does not change if one of the values on the source worksheets is edited. In Figure 5-1, for example, a static consolidation of the two sheets would display 11,000 as the sum for cells B8 from both of the sheets. If cell B8 were changed on the *Cass Lake* sheet after the consolidation command was given, however, cell B8 on the consolidation sheet would not be recalculated. When you know that the source data is final and will not be edited, you can use a static consolidation.

You must create the consolidation worksheet prior to applying consolidation functions to your data.

HOW TO: Create a Consolidation worksheet

1. Click and hold your pointer over the sheet tab you want to copy.
2. Press and hold the **Ctrl** key.
   - A small black plus sign appears above your pointer indicating a copy process.
3. Drag the sheet tab to the right of the original tab location.
   - A small black downward pointing arrow appears to the right of the original sheet tab.
4. Release pointer first, then the **Ctrl** key.
5. Format the copied worksheet.
6. Rename the copied worksheet.
7. Move the copied worksheet so it is positioned as the first or last sheet tab in the workbook.
8. Delete the contents of the cells to be summarized from the new sheet (e.g., B5:D8 in Figure 5-2).
   - You may leave the existing formulas if they will be useful.

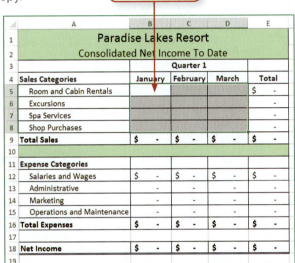

5-2 Consolidation worksheet

Once your consolidation worksheet is ready, you can calculate static data consolidation results.

HOW TO: Create a Static Data Consolidation

1. Select the range of cells to be summarized on the consolidation worksheet (Figure 5-3).
   - You can click the first cell for the consolidation range rather than selecting the entire range.
2. Click the **Consolidate** button [*Data* tab, *Data Tools* group]. The *Consolidate* dialog box opens.
   - If recently used reference ranges are shown in the *All references* list box, select each one and delete it.

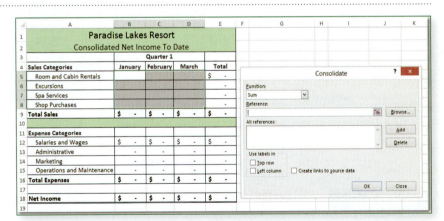

5-3 Consolidation range selected and cleared

3. In the *Consolidate* dialog box, click the **Function** arrow and choose the desired function (Figure 5-3).
4. Click in the *Reference* box. Then click the first sheet tab name with data to be consolidated.
   - Move the *Consolidate* dialog box if necessary to select cells.

5. Select the cells for consolidation on the first sheet (Figure 5-4).

   • When you release the pointer, the cell reference appears in the *Reference* box.

6. Click **Add**.

   • The range information appears in the *All references* list.

7. Click the second sheet tab name.

   • The same range is selected on the next worksheet.

8. Click **Add**.

   • The range information is added to the *All references* list.

9. Repeat steps 7 and 8 for each worksheet you want to include in the consolidation (Figure 5-5).

10. Click **OK**.

   • The data is summarized using the selected function.

   • The consolidated sheet displays a summarized value result in each cell (Figure 5-6).

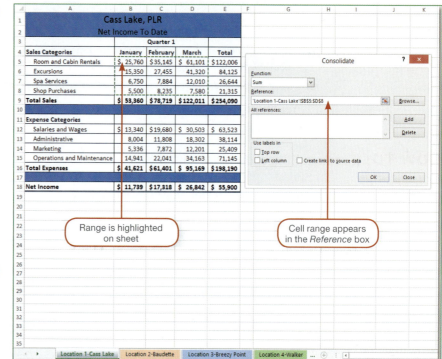

5-4 Consolidation range selected on first sheet

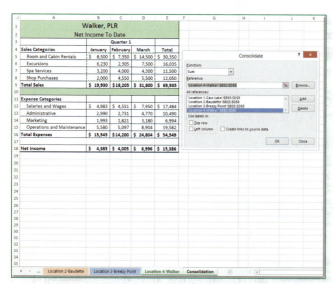

5-5 Data to be consolidated by *Sum* from four worksheets

Paradise Lakes Resort
Consolidated Net Income To Date

	Quarter 1			
Sales Categories	**January**	**February**	**March**	**Total**
Room and Cabin Rentals	$ 70,315	$ 76,305	$171,711	$318,331
Excursions	50,220	74,265	110,970	235,455
Spa Services	24,050	26,268	39,365	89,683
Shop Purchases	18,500	29,255	28,240	75,995
Total Sales	**$163,085**	**$206,093**	**$350,286**	**$719,464**
Expense Categories				
Salaries and Wages	$ 40,771	$ 51,523	$ 87,572	$179,866
Administrative	24,463	30,914	52,543	107,920
Marketing	16,309	20,609	35,029	71,946
Operations and Maintenance	45,664	57,706	98,080	201,450
Total Expenses	**$127,206**	**$160,753**	**$273,223**	**$561,182**
Net Income	**$ 35,879**	**$ 45,340**	**$ 77,063**	**$158,282**

5-6 Consolidated results

SLO 5.2 ## Creating a Dynamic Data Consolidation

A **dynamic consolidation** places formulas on your consolidated sheet and formats that sheet as an outline. If any data on the supporting worksheets is edited once you have created the dynamic consolidation, the formula recalculates and displays updated results on the consolidation sheet. You should use dynamic consolidation when the data on the source worksheets might be edited after you have created your consolidation worksheet.

E5-254

After you create a dynamic consolidation, you can expand each outline item to display the individual values that are summarized. In the *Formula bar*, you can see the formula as well (Figure 5-7).

Dynamic Data Consolidation

You build a dynamic consolidation sheet the same way that you build a static consolidation sheet. Make a copy of one of the source worksheets and delete the contents of the cells that are to be summarized. In the *Consolidate* dialog box, choose the option to create links to the source data. You still need to select each worksheet tab as well as the corresponding range of cells.

5-7 Consolidated results in an outline with 3D reference formulas

The resulting outline in the consolidation worksheet uses 3D reference formulas. These formulas identify the sheet name and individual cell reference used for consolidation.

HOW TO: Create a Dynamic Data Consolidation

1. On the consolidation sheet, delete the contents of the cells to be summarized.
2. Select the range of cells to be summarized.
   - You can click the first cell for the consolidation rather than selecting the entire range.
3. Click the **Consolidate** button [*Data* tab, *Data Tools* group]. The *Consolidate* dialog box appears.
   - If the *All references* list box shows the correct sheets and cell ranges, you don't need to select each tab and cell range again.
4. In the *Consolidate* dialog box, click the **Function** arrow and choose the desired function.
5. Click in the *Reference* box and click the first sheet tab name.
   - You may need to scroll tab names to see all of the options.
6. Select the cells for consolidation on the first sheet.

7. Click **Add**.
   - The range information appears in the *All references* list.
8. Click the second sheet tab name and click **Add**.
   - The range information appears in the *All references* list.
9. Repeat steps 8 and 9 for each worksheet to be consolidated.
10. Click to place a check mark for **Create links to source data** (Figure 5-8).

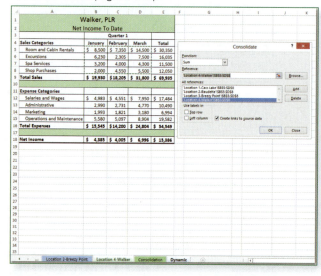

5-8 Data to be consolidated by *Sum* with links to data on four worksheets

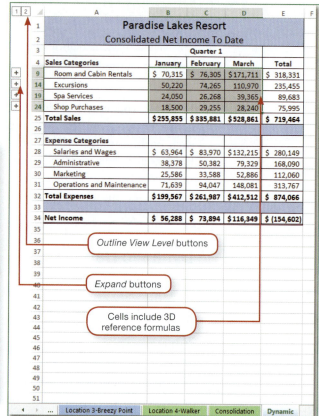

Outline View Level buttons

Expand buttons

Cells include 3D reference formulas

5-9 Dynamic data consolidation results

11. Click **OK** (Figure 5-9).
    - The data is consolidated in outline format using the selected function.
    - Each item is collapsed.
    - The consolidated sheet lists the formula in each cell in the range that is used for consolidation.

Data Consolidation by Category

Data consolidation by position is relatively easy because everything is in the same location on all the worksheets. There may be times, however, when this is not the case. Some source worksheets may have the same row and column labels but the data might be arranged differently. You can build a consolidated worksheet from this type of data as long as the labels are exactly the same. This is consolidation *by category*. Category refers to the row or column labels.

Figure 5-10 shows two worksheets that have the same type of data; they both include data for January, February, and March. The month names are not arranged in the same way, but they are spelled exactly alike on both sheets.

To consolidate data by category, begin with a copy of one of the source worksheets. On the copied sheet that you use to create the consolidation worksheet, delete the data cells to be consolidated including the labels. For example, in Figure 5-10, you would delete cells B4:D8 and the corresponding row labels on the consolidation sheet. When you select the cell range on each supporting worksheet, you select that same range (B4:D8), including the top row labels. In the *Consolidate* dialog box, you activate the option to use the top row or left column labels or both.

Consolidation by category can be static or dynamic; the example we provide in this chapter is dynamic.

Cass Lake, PLR
Net Income To Date

	Quarter 1			
Sales Categories	March	February	January	Total
Room and Cabin Rentals	$ 61,101	$35,145	$ 25,760	$ 25,760
Excursions	41,320	27,455	15,350	15,350
Spa Services	12,010	7,884	6,750	6,750
Shop Purchases	7,580	8,235	5,500	5,500
Total Sales	$122,011	$78,719	$ 53,360	$ 53,360
Expense Categories				
Salaries and Wages	$ 30,503	$19,680	$ 13,340	$ 13,340
Administrative	18,302	11,808	8,004	8,004
Marketing	12,201	7,872	5,336	5,336
Operations and Maintenance	34,163	22,041	14,941	14,941
Total Expenses	$ 95,169	$61,401	$ 41,621	$ 41,621
Net Income	$ 26,842	$17,318	$ 11,739	$ 11,739

Breezy Point, PLR
Net Income To Date

	Quarter 1			
Sales Categories	January	February	March	Total
Room and Cabin Rentals	$ 15,025	$18,355	$ 42,080	$ 75,460
Excursions	14,320	21,050	28,075	63,445
Spa Services	7,350	6,500	11,045	24,895
Shop Purchases	5,500	8,235	7,580	21,315
Total Sales	$ 42,195	$54,140	$ 88,780	$185,115
Expense Categories				
Salaries and Wages	$ 10,549	$13,535	$ 22,195	$ 46,279
Administrative	6,329	8,121	13,317	27,767
Marketing	4,220	5,414	8,878	18,512
Operations and Maintenance	11,815	15,159	24,858	51,832
Total Expenses	$ 32,912	$42,229	$ 69,248	$144,390
Net Income	$ 9,283	$11,911	$ 19,532	$ 40,725

5-10 Data has same labels, different order

HOW TO: Create a Dynamic Data Consolidation by Category

1. On the consolidation sheet, delete the contents of the cells to be summarized and the related labels.

2. Select the range of cells to be summarized, including where the labels will be placed (Figure 5-11).

3. Click the **Consolidate** button [*Data* tab, *Data Tools* group]. The *Consolidation* dialog box opens.

   - The *All references* list box shows recently used cell ranges. Select each one and click **Delete**.

4. Click the **Function** arrow and choose the function.

5. Click in the *Reference* box and click the first sheet tab name.

6. Select the cells and related labels for consolidation on the first sheet (Figure 5-12).

7. Click **Add**.

8. Click the second sheet tab name and click **Add**.

   - By default, the same range is selected on each sheet.

9. Repeat step 8 for each worksheet to be consolidated.

10. Check the box for **Top row** in the *Use labels in* group.

11. Check the box for **Create links to source data** (Figure 5-13).

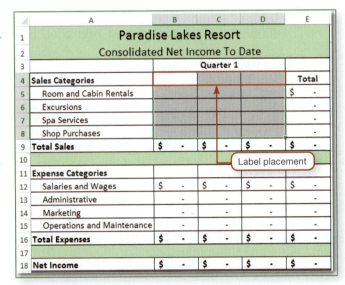

5-11 Consolidation sheet with labels and data deleted

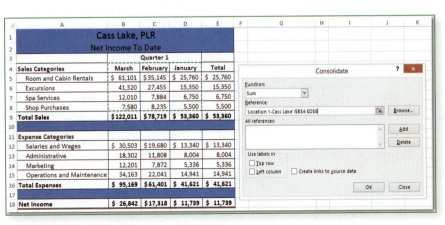

5-12 Labels in row 4 are included in the selection

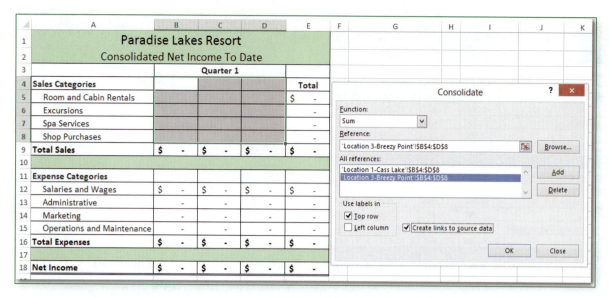

5-13 *Consolidate* dialog box choices for consolidation by category

12. Click **OK** (Figure 5-14).

- Labels are inserted in the consolidated worksheet in the order used in the first sheet listed in the *Consolidate* dialog box.
- The 3D references indicate the cells used for each cell on the consolidation sheet.

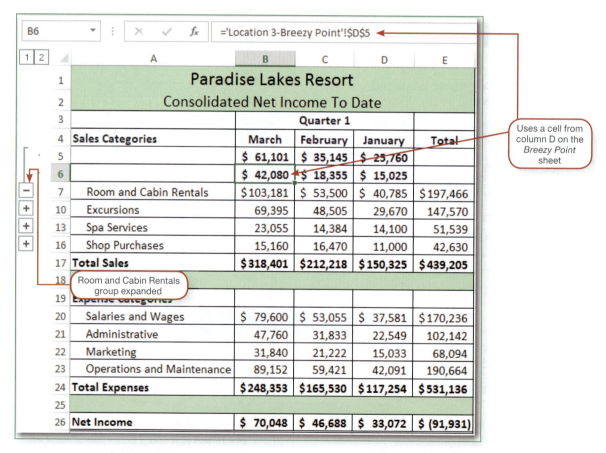

5-14 Labels inserted and 3D reference formulas used in consolidation sheet

For this project, you create a static data consolidation for two locations for Paradise Lakes Resort to sum the income data. You also create a dynamic data consolidation for two locations to average the income data.

File Needed: ***NetIncomePLR-05.xlsx***
Completed Project File Name: ***[your initials] PP E5-1.xlsx***

1. Open the ***NetIncomePLR-05*** workbook.

2. Click the **Enable Editing** button if necessary.

3. Save the workbook as ***[your initials] PP E5-1***.

4. Make a copy of the **Location 1-Cass Lake** worksheet and move to the right of the *Location 4-Walker* worksheet. Name the copied sheet Static.

5. Apply **Green, Accent 6, Lighter 60%** to the **Static** sheet tab.

6. Edit the *Static* sheet tab.
   a. Apply **Green, Accent 6, Lighter 60%** fill color to the following cell ranges: **A2**, **A10:E10**, and **A17:E17**.
   b. Apply a gradient fill effect to **A1** using **White, Background 1** for color 1 and **Green, Accent 6, Lighter 60%** for color 2. Choose the top left corner variant. *Hint: open the Format Cells dialog box and choose Fill Effects to apply the gradient fill.*

7. Change the label in cell **A1** to Paradise Lakes Resorts.

8. Change the label in **A2** to Cass Lake and Baudette Net Income to Date.

9. Select and delete cells **B5:D8** on the **Static** sheet.

10. Create a static data consolidation.
    a. Select cells **B5:D8** on the **Static** sheet if necessary.
    b. Click the **Consolidate** button [*Data* tab, *Data Tools* group]. The *Consolidate* dialog box opens.
    c. Choose the **Sum** function.
    d. If there are any previous references in the *All references* box, select each one and click **Delete**.
    e. Click the *Reference* box and click the **Location 1-Cass Lake** worksheet tab.
    f. Select cells **B5:D8** and release the pointer button.
    g. Click **Add** in the *Consolidate* dialog box.
    h. Click the **Location 2-Baudette** worksheet tab. Verify that the same cell range (**B5:D8**) is selected.
    i. Click **Add** (Figure 5-15).
    j. Click **OK**.

11. Widen columns as needed and click cell **A1**.

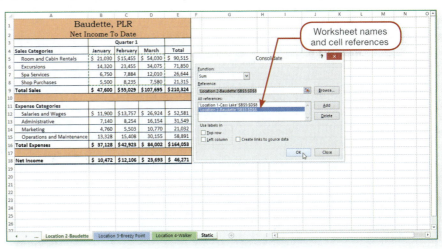

5-15 *Consolidate* dialog box for two worksheets in a static consolidation

12. Make a copy of the **Static** worksheet. Move the copied sheet to the right of the *Static* tab. Name the copied sheet Dynamic.

13. Apply **Blue, Accent 1, Lighter 60%** to the **Dynamic** sheet tab.

14. Format cells in the *Dynamic* sheet tab.
    a. Apply **Blue, Accent 1, Lighter 60%** to the following cell ranges: **A2**, **A10:E10**, and **A17:E17**.
    b. Apply a gradient fill effect to **A1** using **White, Background 1** for color 1 and **Blue, Accent 1, Lighter 60%** for color 2. Choose the top left corner variant. *Hint: open the Format Cells dialog box and choose Fill Effects to apply the gradient fill.*

15. Change the label in **A2** to Breezy Point and Walker Average Income to Date.

16. Select and delete cells **B5:D8** on the **Dynamic** sheet.

17. Create a dynamic data consolidation.
    a. Select cells **B5:D8** on the **Dynamic** sheet if necessary.
    b. Click the **Consolidate** button [*Data* tab, *Data Tools* group].
    c. Choose the **Average** function.
    d. Click the first reference in the *All references* box and click **Delete**.
    e. Delete the second reference in the *All references* box.
    f. Click the *Reference* box and click the **Location 3-Breezy Point** worksheet tab.
    g. Select cells **B5:D8** and release the pointer button.
    h. Click **Add** in the *Consolidate* dialog box.
    i. Click the **Location 4-Walker** worksheet tab and click **Add**. Verify that the same cell range is selected as in step g (e.g., **B5:D8**).
    j. Click to place a check mark for **Create links to source data** (Figure 5-16).
    k. Click **OK**.

18. Save and close the workbook (Figure 5-17).

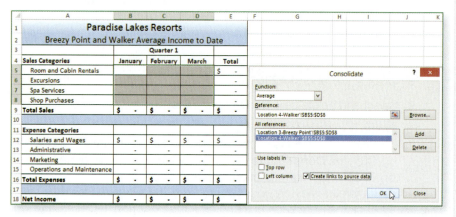

5-16 *Consolidate* dialog box for a dynamic consolidation

	A	B	C	D	E
1	**Paradise Lakes Resorts**				
2	Cass Lake and Baudette Net Income to Date				
3			Quarter 1		
4	**Sales Categories**	January	February	March	Total
5	Room and Cabin Rentals	$ 46,790	$ 50,600	$115,131	$212,521
6	Excursions	29,670	50,910	75,395	155,975
7	Spa Services	13,500	15,768	24,020	53,288
8	Shop Purchases	11,000	16,470	15,160	42,630
9	**Total Sales**	$100,960	$133,748	$229,706	$464,414
10					
11	**Expense Categories**				
12	Salaries and Wages	$ 25,240	$ 33,437	$ 57,427	$116,104
13	Administrative	15,144	20,062	34,456	69,662
14	Marketing	10,096	13,375	22,971	46,441
15	Operations and Maintenance	28,269	37,449	64,318	130,036
16	**Total Expenses**	$ 78,749	$104,323	$179,171	$362,243
17					
18	**Net Income**	$ 22,211	$ 29,425	$ 50,535	$102,171

	A	B	C	D	E
1	**Paradise Lakes Resorts**				
2	Breezy Point and Walker Average Income to Date				
3			Quarter 1		
4	**Sales Categories**	January	February	March	Total
7	Room and Cabin Rentals	$ 11,763	$ 12,853	$ 28,290	$ 52,905
10	Excursions	10,275	11,678	17,788	39,740
13	Spa Services	5,275	5,250	7,673	18,198
16	Shop Purchases	3,750	6,393	6,540	16,683
17	**Total Sales**	$ 69,663	$ 82,813	$124,290	$127,525
18					
19	**Expense Categories**				
20	Salaries and Wages	$ 17,416	$ 20,703	$ 31,073	$ 69,191
21	Administrative	10,449	12,422	18,644	41,515
22	Marketing	6,966	8,281	12,429	27,677
23	Operations and Maintenance	19,506	23,188	34,801	77,494
24	**Total Expenses**	$ 54,337	$ 64,594	$ 96,946	$215,877
25					
26	**Net Income**	$ 15,326	$ 18,219	$ 27,344	$ (88,352)

5-17 **Completed worksheets for PP E5-1**

Linking Workbooks

Like data consolidation, linking workbooks is a common business tool. Linked workbooks are referred to as *dependent* and *source workbooks*. A dependent workbook is a workbook that includes data from another workbook. It may simply display this data or it may reference it in a formula. A source workbook includes data that is referenced in a dependent workbook. For workbooks to be linked, they must all be accessible over a network, on the same computer, or in the cloud.

Paradise Lakes Resorts, for example, maintains a consolidated income workbook (a dependent workbook) at the main office, and each individual resort builds its own similar workbook (sources workbooks). The main workbook has established links to each of the individual resort files so that the consolidated workbook always has up-to-the-minute data.

You can link workbooks using the *Consolidate* command or you can build your own formulas that refer to cells in other workbooks. Whether the reference is entered in the *Consolidate* dialog box or through a formula that you create, it is as an *external reference* formula. An external reference is a formula that refers to cells in another workbook.

Use the Consolidate Command to Link Workbooks

For multiple workbooks, you can build a dynamic consolidation following the same steps and guidelines you use when working with multiple sheets in the same workbook. All workbooks must be open when you use the *Consolidate* command.

> **MORE INFO**
>
> You can also create a static consolidation for multiple workbooks.

The external references include the name of the workbook in square brackets, the sheet name, and the cell address(es), as well as *identifiers*. An identifier is a character such as an exclamation point that marks or signifies a component of the reference. The complete syntax for an external reference with all its identifiers is:

='[WorkbookName]WorksheetName'!CellRange

In the resulting consolidated outline, expand and collapse buttons display for each group. A reference to each cell that is used in the formula displays when that group is expanded.

HOW TO: Link Workbooks with a Dynamic Data Consolidation

1. Open the workbook that includes the consolidation worksheet.
   - This is the dependent workbook.
2. Delete the contents of the cells to be consolidated if necessary.
3. Open the source workbook.
   - If there are multiple source workbooks, open each of them.
4. Return to the dependent workbook and select the range of cells to be summarized from the consolidation worksheet.
5. Click the **Consolidate** button [*Data* tab, *Data Tools* group]. The *Consolidate* dialog box opens.
6. In the *Consolidate* dialog box, click the **Function** arrow and choose the desired function.
   - Select and delete previous references in the *All references* list box.

7. Click in the *Reference* box and click the icon for the first source workbook on the Windows *Taskbar* (Figure 5-18).

   • Press **Ctrl+F6** to switch to the next open workbook rather than using the *Taskbar*.

8. Select the first sheet tab for data consolidation.

9. Select the cell range and click **Add**.

10. Click the next sheet tab name and click **Add** (Figure 5-19).

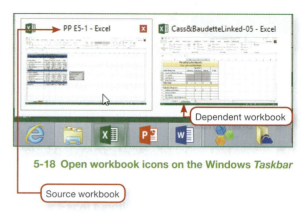

5-18 Open workbook icons on the Windows *Taskbar*

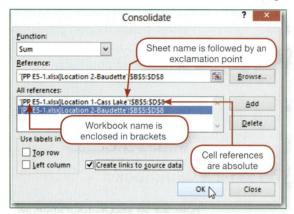

5-19 References with identifiers to another workbook

   • Repeat step 10 for each sheet in the source workbook that you want to be included in the consolidation.
   • If multiple source workbooks are used, click in the *Reference* box and click the icon for the next source workbook on the Windows *Taskbar*.
   • Repeat the steps to select data in each source workbook as needed.

11. Check the box for **Create links to source data**.

12. Click **OK** (Figure 5-20).

   • The external reference formulas include the name of the workbook, the sheet name, and the cell address or range.
   • The outline format is initially collapsed.

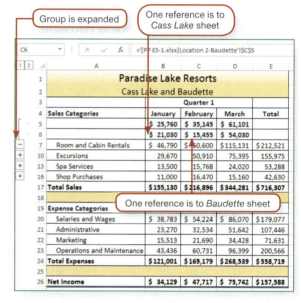

5-20 Dynamic data consolidation with another workbook

Link Workbooks Using a Formula

Recall from *SLO 5.1: Creating a Static Consolidation* that the *Consolidate* command includes a limited list of mathematical and statistical functions. It also requires that the same cell range be used in all references. Those limitations don't apply when you build your own external reference or linking formulas.

> ▶ **MORE INFO**
>
> You can use most Excel functions in an external reference formula.

An external reference formula creates a link to the source workbook. If the source is accessible, this link can be automatically updated each time you open the dependent workbook. If it is not automatically updated, you will see a security warning about updating links as the workbook is opened. You can manage workbook links from the Trust Center Settings (Excel Options) and from the *Edit Links* dialog box [**Edit Links** button, *Data* tab, *Connections* group]. Both dialog boxes are shown in Figure 5-21.

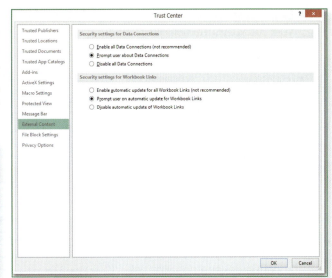

> **ANOTHER WAY**
>
> The source workbook need not be open to build an external reference formula. However, when the source workbook is not open, you must type the entire external reference, including all identifiers and the complete path to locate the file.

You use the same syntax to build an external reference formula that you use in a reference in the *Consolidate* command. Place the external reference in the dependent workbook with absolute references. You can edit those references to make them relative when you want to copy a formula.

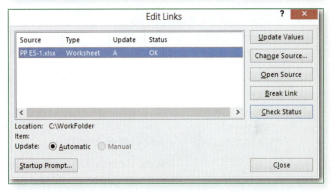

5-21 Trust Center Settings and *Edit Links* dialog boxes for managing workbook links

HOW TO: Link Workbooks with an Addition Formula

1. Open the dependent workbook.
   - This is the workbook that will include the formula with references to another workbook.
2. Open all source workbooks.
3. Return to the dependent workbook and click the cell where you want to place the first formula.
4. Type = to start the formula.
5. Click the icon for the first source workbook on the Windows *Taskbar*.
6. Click the sheet tab and click the cell for the first argument.
7. Type + to add the value in the next cell.
8. Click the next sheet tab, click the cell for the next argument, and type + to add the next cell (Figure 5-22).

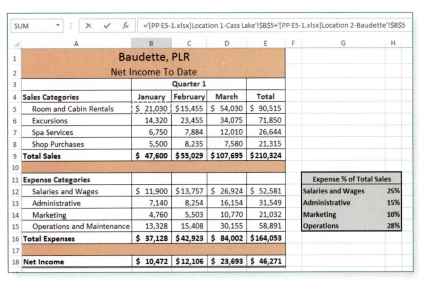

5-22 An external reference formula in the source workbook

- Depending on the data and your formulas, the cells on different sheets need not be in the same location.
- You can use any mathematical operators in a formula.

9. Repeat these steps as needed to insert additional cells and operators into the formula.

10. Press **Enter** (Figure 5-23).
- The dependent workbook is displayed with the formula result.
- The reference includes the name of the workbook, the sheet name, and absolute cell references.
- You can click the **Enter** button in the *Formula bar* to complete the formula and return to the dependent workbook.

Formula bar: B5 = '[PP E5-1.xlsx]Location 1-Cass Lake'!$B$5+'[PP E5-1.xlsx]Location 2-Baudette'!$B$5

Callout: Absolute references can be edited for copying the formula

	A	B	C	D	E	F	G	H	I
1		Paradise Lake Resorts							
2		Cass Lake and Baudette							
3			Quarter 1						
4	Sales Categories	January	February	March	Total				
5	Room and Cabin Rentals	$ 46,790			$ 46,790				
6	Excursions				-				
7	Spa Services				-				
8	Shop Purchases				-				
9	Total Sales	$ 46,790	$ -	$ -	$ 46,790				
10									
11	Expense Categories								
12	Salaries and Wages	$ 11,698	$ -	$ -	$ 11,698				
13	Administrative	7,019	-	-	7,019				
14	Marketing	4,679	-	-	4,679				
15	Operations and Maintenance	13,101	-	-	13,101				
16	Total Expenses	$ 36,496	$ -	$ -	$ 36,496				
17									
18	Net Income	$ 10,294	$ -	$ -	$ 10,294				

5-23 Dependent workbook with external reference formula

▶ ANOTHER WAY

You can arrange open workbooks side by side or horizontally tiled using the **Arrange All** button [*View* tab *Windows* group] and switch between them by pointing and clicking.

▶ ANOTHER WAY

You can use functions when linking workbooks to save time.

PAUSE & PRACTICE: EXCEL 5-2

For this project, you use a dynamic data consolidation with links to data in another workbook. You also create an external reference in a formula.

Files Needed: *[your initials] PP E5-1.xlsx* and **FirstQtrLinkedPLR-05.xlsx**
Completed Project File Name: *[your initials] PP E5-2.xlsx*

1. Open the **FirstQtrLinked-05** workbook. Click the **Enable Editing** button if needed.

2. Save the workbook as *[your initials] PP E5-2*.

3. Open the *[your initials] PP E5-1* workbook. This will be the source workbook.

4. Use the *Consolidate* command to link workbooks.
   a. Click the **CL&Baudette** worksheet tab in the **[your initials] PP E5-2** workbook.
   b. Select cells **B5:D8**.
   c. Click the **Consolidate** button [*Data* tab, *Data Tools* group] to open the *Consolidate* dialog box. If there are references in the *All references* list, select each one and click **Delete**.
   d. Choose **Sum** as the function.
   e. Click in the *Reference* box and click the icon for **[your initials] PP E5-1** on the Windows *Taskbar*. If the name of the file doesn't appear in the path listed in the *Reference* box, then select the title bar of the **[your initials] PP E5-1** file. The file path should appear after selecting cells in step g.
   f. Click the **Location 1-Cass Lake** worksheet tab.
   g. Select cells **B5:D8** and click **Add**.
   h. Click the **Location 2-Baudette** worksheet tab.
   i. Select cells **B5:D8**, if not selected, and click **Add**.
   j. Check the box to **Create links to source data** (Figure 5-24).

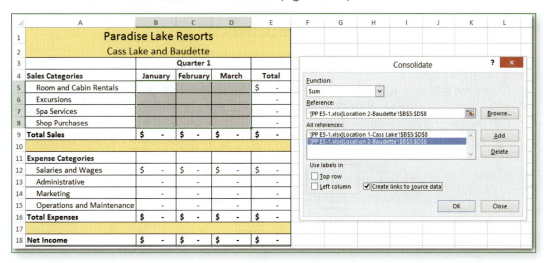

5-24 Links to source workbook in the *Consolidate* dialog box

   k. Click **OK**.

5. In the **[your initials] PP E5-2** workbook, widen columns to display the data (Figure 5-25).

6. Link workbooks using a formula.
   a. Click the **BP&Walker** worksheet tab in **[your initials] PP E5-2**.
   b. Click cell **B5**.
   c. Type **=** to start the formula.
   d. Click the icon for **[your initials] PP E5-1** on the Windows *Taskbar* or press **Ctrl+F6**.
   e. Click the **Location 3-Breezy Point** worksheet tab.
   f. Select cell **B5** and type **+** for an addition formula.
   g. Click the **Location 4-Walker** worksheet tab.
   h. Select cell **B5** and press **Enter** (Figure 5-26).

	A	B	C	D	E
1		Paradise Lake Resorts			
2		Cass Lake and Baudette			
3		Quarter 1			
4	Sales Categories	January	February	March	Total
7	Room and Cabin Rentals	$ 46,790	$ 50,600	$115,131	$212,521
10	Excursions	29,670	50,910	75,395	155,975
13	Spa Services	13,500	15,768	24,020	53,288
16	Shop Purchases	11,000	16,470	15,160	42,630
17	Total Sales	$155,130	$216,896	$344,281	$716,307
18					
19	Expense Categories				
20	Salaries and Wages	$ 38,783	$ 54,224	$ 86,070	$179,077
21	Administrative	23,270	32,534	51,642	107,446
22	Marketing	15,513	21,690	34,428	71,631
23	Operations and Maintenance	43,436	60,731	96,399	200,566
24	Total Expenses	$121,001	$169,179	$268,539	$558,719
25					
26	Net Income	$ 34,129	$ 47,717	$ 75,742	$157,588

5-25 Completed worksheet for PP E5-2 with *Consolidate* command

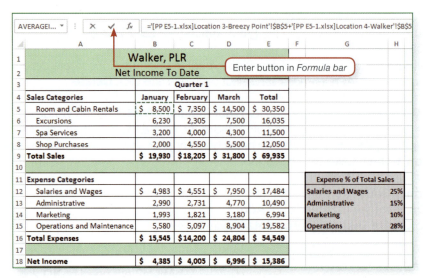

5-26 A linking formula to add cells from PP E5-1

7. Copy the linked formula.
   a. Select cell **B5** in the **BP&Walker** sheet in **[your initials] PP E5-2** and click in the *Formula bar*.
   b. Edit the first cell reference **$B$5** to delete the dollar signs and create a relative reference **B5**.
   c. Edit the second cell reference **$B$5** to create a relative reference **B5** (Figure 5-27).

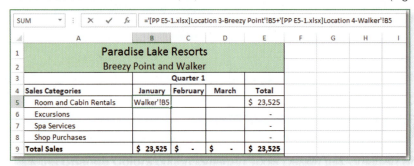

5-27 Linking formula edited to use relative references

   d. Press **Enter**.
   e. Copy the formula in cell **B5** to cells **B6:B8** without fill formatting.
   f. Copy the formulas in cells **B5:B8** to cells **C5:D8**.
   g. Apply formats of **C6** to cells **B6:B8** if needed.

8. Save and close the workbook (Figure 5-28).

9. Close the **[your initials] PP E5-1** workbook without saving it.

	A	B	C	D	E	F	G	H
1		Paradise Lake Resorts						
2		Breezy Point and Walker						
3				Quarter 1				
4	Sales Categories	January	February	March	Total			
5	Room and Cabin Rentals	$ 23,525	$25,705	$ 56,580	$105,810			
6	Excursions	20,550	23,355	35,575	79,480			
7	Spa Services	10,550	10,500	15,345	36,395			
8	Shop Purchases	7,500	12,785	13,080	33,365			
9	Total Sales	$ 62,125	$72,345	$120,580	$255,050			
10								
11	Expense Categories							
12	Salaries and Wages	$ 15,531	$18,086	$ 30,145	$ 63,763			
13	Administrative	9,319	10,852	18,087	38,258			
14	Marketing	6,213	7,235	12,058	25,505			
15	Operations and Maintenance	17,395	20,257	33,762	71,414			
16	Total Expenses	$ 48,458	$56,429	$ 94,052	$198,939			
17								
18	Net Income	$ 13,668	$15,916	$ 26,528	$ 56,111			

5-28 Completed worksheet for PP E5-2 with formula

Inserting SmartArt, Hyperlinks, and Screenshots

In many workbooks, you may find it helpful to include other types of objects that help users understand and navigate through data. For example, you can include an object that directs the people who use your worksheets to navigate between worksheets. Or you might include an image of folder contents to help a coworker learn how to locate a file. You can even include a drawing that illustrates the processes for consolidating quarterly income.

SmartArt Graphics

A **SmartArt** graphic is a high-quality illustration, which often includes text that you can place in Office documents, including Excel worksheets. Examples of *SmartArt* include organization charts, matrices, pyramids, bulleted lists, and other similar diagrams. *SmartArt* graphics are typically text-focused although there are several that can incorporate pictures with text. Figure 5-29 is a *SmartArt* graphic with four pictures.

You can customize the text in a *SmartArt* graphic. A *SmartArt* graphic has a text pane for entering text, but you can also type directly inside the component shapes. The text pane appears on either the left or right side of the

5-29 *SmartArt* graphic with four shapes and pictures

graphic depending on where the graphic is on your worksheet. There is a control for showing or hiding the pane that looks like a left- or right-pointing arrow. As you type an entry, the text and its shape are sized to fit.

A *SmartArt* graphic is not linked to worksheet data.

HOW TO: Insert a SmartArt Graphic

1. Insert a new worksheet or click the worksheet tab where you want to display the *SmartArt*.
2. Click the **Insert a SmartArt Graphic** button [*Insert* tab, *Illustrations* group] to open the *Choose a SmartArt Graphic* dialog box (Figure 5-30).
3. Choose the category from the list in the left pane.
   - The **All** category displays all available *SmartArt* designs.
   - Click a thumbnail image to see a preview and a description in the right pane.
4. Click again to select the *SmartArt* graphic you prefer.
5. Click **OK** (Figure 5-31).
   - A default object is placed at a default size in the worksheet.

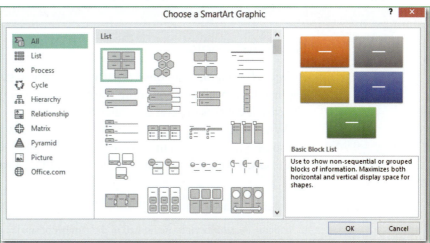

5-30 *Choose a SmartArt Graphic* dialog box

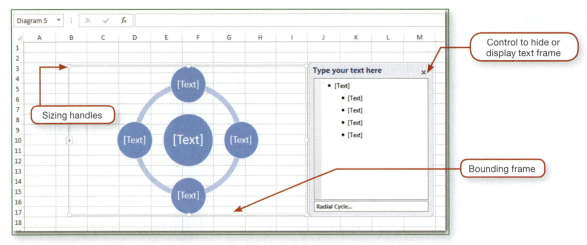

5-31 *SmartArt* graphic with text frame

- The name box displays *Diagram N*, where "N" is a number.
- The text pane may or may not be displayed; you can turn it off and on by clicking the control at the left or right edge of the graphic frame.

6. Click in each shape and type the text (Figure 5-32).

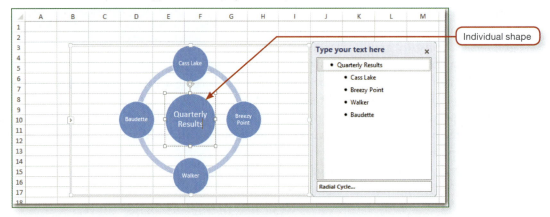

5-32 Text entered in *SmartArt* graphic

- The entry appears in the shape and in the text pane.
- The label is sized to fit the shape as you type.
- You can edit text within the shape or the text frame.
- Each shape has its own selection handles and frame.

SmartArt Tools

A *SmartArt* graphic is an object that you can select, size, and format. It has selection and sizing handles as well as a bounding frame, similar to a chart object. A *SmartArt* graphic is one object that consists of several smaller shapes.

When you first insert a *SmartArt* image, it is placed with the default number of shapes. For some *SmartArt* diagrams, you can add additional shapes as needed. Each individual shape in a *SmartArt* object has its own selection handles, a rotation handle, and a bounding frame.

> **MORE INFO**
>
> Some *SmartArt* shapes are limited in the number of smaller shapes they can contain because of the basic layout and purpose of the diagram.

When a *SmartArt* object is selected, the *SmartArt Tools* tabs are available, including a *Design* tab and a *Format* tab. Using these tabs, you can change to a different shape, choose a style, add a shape, reposition shapes, and add fill, outline, and effects.

A *SmartArt* graphic rests on an invisible, transparent layer in the worksheet. You can only activate a worksheet cell that appears within the frame of the *SmartArt* by using the name box.

HOW TO: Format a SmartArt Graphic

1. Click to select the *SmartArt* graphic.
   - Click near one of the shapes to select the *SmartArt* diagram.
   - The bounding frame is a rectangle that surrounds the graphic.
2. Click the **More** button [*SmartArt Tools Design* tab, *SmartArt Styles* group] to display the gallery of styles.
3. Click a style to select it.
4. Click the **Change Colors** button [*SmartArt Tools Design* tab, *SmartArt Styles* group] to open the color gallery.
5. Click to choose a color scheme.
6. Click an individual shape in the graphic.
7. Click the arrow with the **Shape Fill** button [*SmartArt Tools Format* tab, *Shape Styles* group] and choose a color (Figure 5-33).
8. Point to a corner sizing handle on the *SmartArt* frame to display a resize arrow. Drag the sizing handle to make the graphic larger or smaller.
9. Point to the *SmartArt* frame to display a move arrow. Drag the graphic to the desired location on the worksheet.
10. Click a worksheet cell to deselect the *SmartArt* graphic.

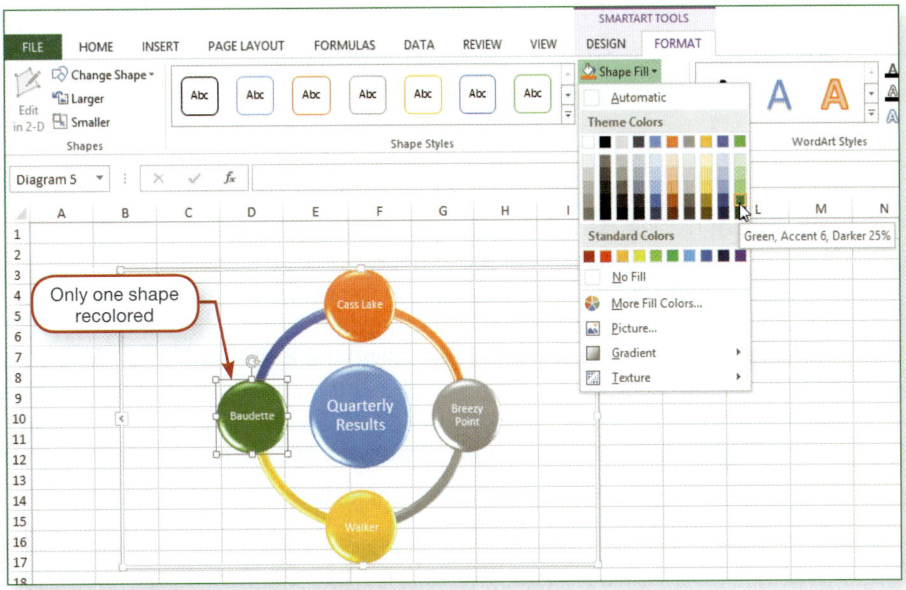

5-33 *Shape Fill* color gallery for a *SmartArt* shape

Hyperlinks

A *hyperlink* is a clickable string of text or object; when it is clicked on, it displays another worksheet, opens another workbook, opens another program, or displays a web page. It is a shortcut or jump term that you create. For example, in a workbook with external references, you might create a hyperlink that opens the source workbook. Similarly, in a workbook with a *SmartArt* graphic, you can create a hyperlink to or from the graphic object.

A hyperlink is usually created in a worksheet cell. It appears as underlined text in the color set in the document theme for hyperlinks. This color is not labeled separately in the color galleries. However, you can edit it from the *Colors* command on the *Page Layout* tab. You can change the color of hyperlink text, and you can change the font name or size.

The *Hyperlink* button is located on the *Insert* tab. You can also insert a hyperlink from the shortcut menu for a cell. From the *Insert Hyperlink* dialog box, you can browse to find another document or navigate to a web site.

HOW TO: Create a Hyperlink to a Location in the Workbook

1. Click the cell where you want to display the hyperlink.
   - You can also select some objects and assign hyperlinks to them as well.
2. Click the **Hyperlink** button [*Insert* tab, *Links* group].
3. In the *Insert Hyperlink* dialog box, click the **Place in This Document** button.
   - Worksheet names, each followed by an exclamation point, appear at the top of the list in the *Text to display* box and the *Cell Reference* group in the *Or select a place in this document* list.
   - *Defined Names* are named cell ranges in the worksheets.
   - These two groups have expand and collapse buttons.
   - You can open another workbook by clicking the **Existing File or Web Page** option and choosing the folder and file name. Alternatively, from the same menu, you can click the **Browse the Web** button and navigate to a web site. The *Browse the web site* button is available only when the *Existing File or Web Page* option is active. The web site address is entered into the *Insert Hyperlink* dialog box when you return to the workbook.
4. In the *Or select a place in this document* list, select a worksheet name.
   - The hyperlink jumps to cell **A1** on the selected sheet by default.
   - Click in the *Type the cell reference* box and type a cell reference other than cell A1, if desired.
5. In the *Text to display* box, select and delete the default label.
6. Type the label you want to appear in the cell.
7. Click the **ScreenTip** button to enter a custom ScreenTip for the hyperlink (Figure 5-34).

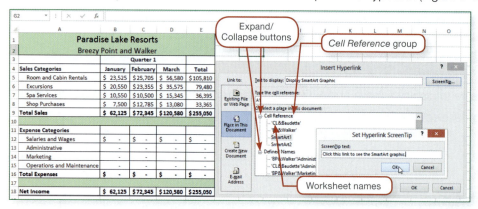

5-34 *Insert Hyperlink* and *Set Hyperlink ScreenTip* dialog boxes

8. Click **OK** in the *Set Hyperlink ScreenTip* dialog box.
9. Click **OK** in the *Insert Hyperlink* dialog box.
   - The hyperlink text appears in the cell.
   - To edit or delete a hyperlink, right-click the hyperlink text and select **Edit Hyperlink** or **Remove Hyperlink** from the context-sensitive menu.
10. Click the hyperlink text to navigate to the location (Figure 5-35).

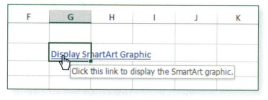

5-35 Hyperlink text and its ScreenTip

Screenshots

A **screenshot** is a picture of something that appeared on-screen, that you insert as an object in a worksheet. You can capture an image of any open window, such as a portion of a Word document or text from a web site. When capturing screenshots of web sites or other file types, be sure you have permission from the author so you do not infringe on any copyright laws.

The *Take a Screenshot* button is located on the *Insert* tab in the *Illustrations* group. When you click the button, you see a gallery of available open windows (Figure 5-36). If you select one of the thumbnail windows, a capture of the full screen is placed in your worksheet. To select part of the window or screen for a screenshot, you can select *Screen Clipping* from the gallery.

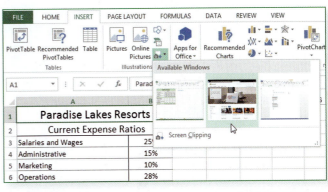

Once you place a screenshot in the worksheet, it is a picture object. When selected, you can format, position, and size it like any object.

5-36 Screenshot gallery with three available windows

> **MORE INFO**
>
> Arrange open windows side by side for ease in taking screenshots.

HOW TO: Insert a Screenshot in a Worksheet

1. Click the worksheet tab where you want to include the screenshot.
2. Open the file that contains the screenshot you want to capture.
   - If the screenshot is from a web site, open the web page and navigate so that the content is visible.
3. Arrange the windows side by side or tile horizontally (Figure 5-37).

5-37 Two workbook windows arranged side by side

- Click the **Arrange All** button on the *View* tab [*Window* group] to arrange two Excel workbooks.
- Right-click the Windows *Taskbar* and choose an option to arrange an Excel window with a window from another application.

4. Click a cell in the worksheet.

5. Click the **Take a Screenshot** button [*Insert* tab, *Illustrations* group].

6. From the gallery, choose **Screen Clipping**.

   • The entire screen dims in a few seconds, and the focus switches to the next available window.

7. With the crosshair pointer, draw a rectangle around the content you want to capture as a screenshot (Figure 5-38).

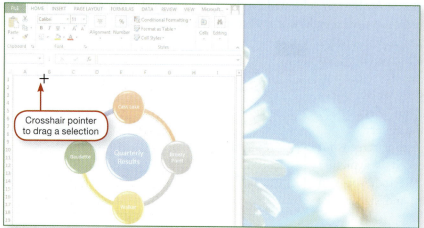

5-38 Dimmed screen for screenshot

8. Release the pointer button (Figure 5-39).

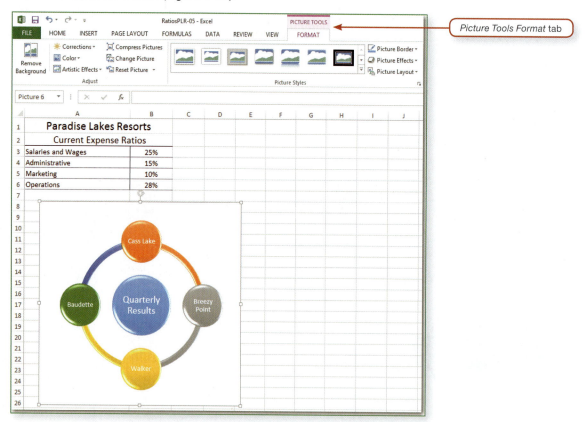

5-39 Screenshot image placed in worksheet

   • The focus returns to the worksheet, and the screenshot is placed at a default size and position.

   • Select the picture object and drag the selection handles with the resize pointer, use the context menu or *Ribbon* to format, and click and drag the object with your move pointer to relocate.

Grouping and Formatting Worksheets

When you have a number of worksheets that have identical layouts, you can group them and edit them with a single command. For example, the Paradise Lakes Resort consolidation workbook you have worked with in this chapter can be formatted so that all sheets are the same fill color after the consolidation. You can also group the sheets and change a font, edit a particular common cell, or enter a new formula for all sheets with a single command.

There are some commands that do not work for grouped worksheets. You cannot insert a graphic on grouped sheets, nor can you apply conditional formatting. When sheets are grouped and a command is not available, the button or option for that command is grayed out.

Group Worksheets

To group worksheets, you select multiple tab names. Use the **Ctrl** or **Shift** keys to do this, as you do in other Windows applications. Alternatively, you can select all worksheets in a workbook from the context-sensitive menu for any tab.

When worksheets are grouped, the title bar reads *[Group]*. The tab names for the sheets that are included in the group are primarily lighter in color with a narrow white band around the tab. When you expect to group worksheets, it is a good idea to set different tab colors for your sheets so that it is easy to identify grouped sheets.

To ungroup sheets, click any tab name that is not part of the group. Alternatively, you can right-click any tab name in the group and choose *Ungroup Sheets*.

HOW TO: Group Worksheets

1. Click the first sheet tab to be included in the group.

   - Complete step 2 for adjacent sheets, step 3 for nonadjacent sheets, or step 4 for all sheets.

2. To select adjacent sheets, press and hold the **Shift** key while clicking the last tab name in the desired group.

3. To select nonadjacent sheets, press and hold the **Ctrl** key while clicking each nonadjacent tab name (Figure 5-40).

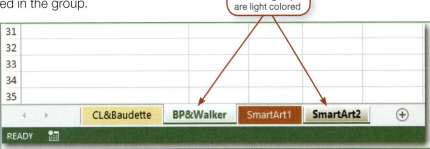

Tabs in group are light colored

5-40 Nonadjacent grouped worksheets

4. To select all the sheets in a workbook, right-click any sheet tab and choose **Select All Sheets**.

> **MORE INFO**
>
> If you save a workbook while sheets are grouped, it opens with grouped sheets the next time you open the file.

Edit and Format Grouped Worksheets

When you group sheets, most editing and formatting commands that you perform affect every sheet in the group. It is important, therefore, that you carefully plan your commands for grouped worksheets. In general, the worksheets should be identical or nearly so. If they are not, you run the risk of making changes on one sheet that are not appropriate for every sheet in the group.

One command that you *can* give for grouped sheets that are not identical is the header or footer command. If you group sheets and use the *Page Setup* dialog box, the same header or footer is inserted on every worksheet in the group. It also is not a problem to change page orientation for multiple sheets that are not identical.

HOW TO: Edit and Format Grouped Sheets

1. Group the worksheets as desired.

2. Click a cell that is available for editing on all sheets and edit.
   - Edit data by typing a new value or label and pressing **Enter**. The change is made on all sheets.

3. Select cells and apply formats.
   - Select the same cell range for all sheets and make formatting changes such as applying bold, changing a font, or setting a fill color.

4. Ungroup the sheets.
   - It is recommended that you ungroup your sheets once you complete your grouped changes. This prevents you from making unwanted changes to a group of sheets in the future.

PAUSE & PRACTICE: EXCEL 5-3

For this project, you insert a *SmartArt* graphic that illustrates how sales results are consolidated for Paradise Lakes Resort. You also insert a hyperlink to the *SmartArt* and include a screenshot. You also edit and format grouped worksheets.

File Needed: *[your initials] PP E5-2.xlsx*
Completed Project File Name: *[your initials] PP E5-3.xlsx*

1. Open the *[your initials] PP E5-2* workbook. Because the workbook has links, you will see a security warning or a message box, depending on your computer (Figure 5-41).

2. Click **Enable Content** or **Update** as necessary.

3. Save the workbook as *[your initials] PP E5-3*.

4. Insert a *SmartArt* graphic.
   a. Click the **New sheet** button on the status bar. Name the new sheet SmartArt and if necessary, move the new sheet to be the last sheet in the workbook.
   b. Click the **Insert a SmartArt Graphic** button [*Insert* tab, *Illustrations* group].
   c. Click **Cycle** in the list on the left.

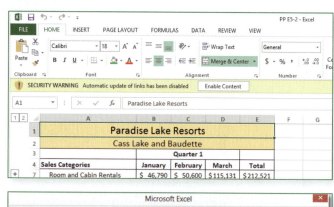

5-41 Security messages for workbook with links

d. Locate and click **Radial Venn** in the gallery of graphics.

e. Click **OK** to insert the *SmartArt* graphic. If the text pane is open, close it.

f. Click the top circle shape and type Room and Cabin Rentals. Do not press *Enter*. Note that the text is sized to fit as you type.

g. Click the leftmost circle shape and type Excursions. If you make an error, click again in the shape and make the correction.

h. In the bottom circle shape, type Spa Purchases. In the rightmost circle shape, type Shop Purchases.

i. In the center shape, type Total Sales (Figure 5-42).

5. Format, position, and size a *SmartArt* graphic.

a. Click the frame of the *SmartArt* graphic to select it.

b. Click the **More** button [*SmartArt Tools Design* tab, *SmartArt Styles* group].

c. In the *3-D* group, click **Inset**.

d. Click the **Change Colors** button [*SmartArt Tools Design* tab, *SmartArt Styles* group].

e. Choose **Colorful – Accent Colors**.

f. Point at the *SmartArt* frame to display a move pointer.

g. Drag the graphic to position the top-left selection handle in cell **A1**. When a *SmartArt* graphic is selected, you can use any of the directional arrow keys to nudge it into position since borderlines disappear when moving.

h. Point at the bottom right selection handle to display a resize pointer.

i. Drag the frame to reach cell **I22** (Figure 5-43).

j. Click cell **K1** to deselect the *SmartArt*.

6. Insert a hyperlink.

a. Click the **BP&Walker** sheet tab.

b. Click cell **G2**.

c. Click the **Hyperlink** button [*Insert* tab, *Links* group].

d. In the *Insert Hyperlink* dialog box, click **Place in This Document** on the left.

e. In the *Or select a place in this document* list, click the sheet name **SmartArt**.

f. In the *Text to display* box, select the default text and type View Illustration.

g. Click the **ScreenTip** button and type Click this link to view the graphic. (Figure 5-44).

5-42 Text entered in shapes in *SmartArt* graphic

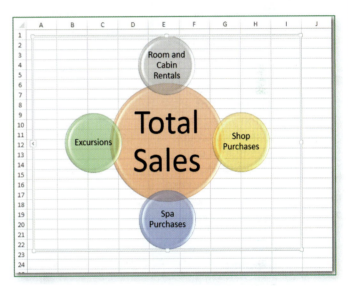

5-43 Styled and positioned *SmartArt*

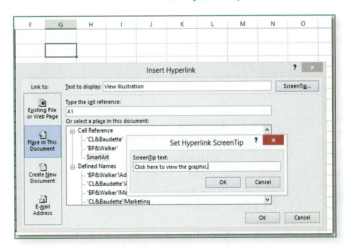

5-44 Hyperlink text and ScreenTip

h. Click **OK** in the *Set Hyperlink ScreenTip* dialog box.

i. Click **OK** in the *Insert Hyperlink* dialog box.

j. Click the link to test it.

7. Insert a screenshot.

a. Click the **CL&Baudette** worksheet tab.

b. Click the **New Window** button [*View* tab, *Window* group] to open a second window for the workbook.

c. Click the **Arrange All** button [*View* tab, *Window* group].

d. Choose **Vertical** and click **OK**. The windows are labeled with **1** and **2** in the title bar. However, it is still one workbook; you are seeing two views. If you see the same window on each side, click one of the sides and select the tab you are missing. You can work in either window, and it does not matter which window is on the left (Figure 5-45).

e. Click the **SmartArt** sheet tab pane.

f. Click to remove the check mark for **Gridlines** [*View* tab, *Show* group].

g. Click cell **A28** in the *CL&Baudette* sheet pane.

h. Click the **Take a Screenshot** button [*Insert* tab, *Illustrations* group]. Note that when you are taking the screenshot, it works best if you close all open programs except Excel.

i. Choose **Screen Clipping**.

j. Drag to draw a rectangle around the *SmartArt* graphic in the dimmed screen (Figure 5-46).

k. Release the pointer button to place the screenshot in the **CL&Baudette** worksheet.

l. Close the **SmartArt** worksheet pane and maximize the **CL&Baudette** pane.

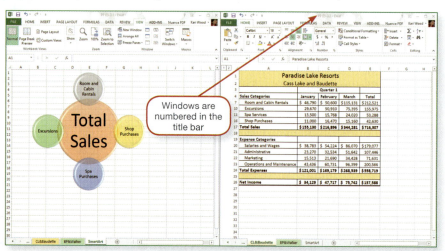

5-45 Same workbook arranged in two vertical windows

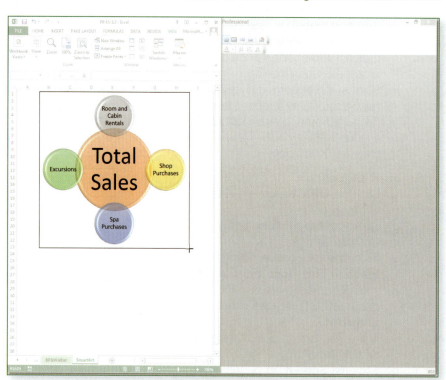

5-46 Screenshot rectangle drawn in dimmed screen

8. Edit and format grouped worksheets.
   a. Click the **CL&Baudette** worksheet tab if necessary and click cell **A1**.
   b. Hold down **Ctrl** and click the **BP&Walker** tab. The *SmartArt* sheet is not part of the group.
   c. Select cells **A1:A2**.
   d. Change the font to **Cambria** and the font size to **16 pt**.
   e. Add a thick dashed border around **A1:A2**.
   f. Click cell **G1** and type your first and last name.
   g. Click the **SmartArt** sheet tab to ungroup the sheets. Click each sheet tab to view the changes.

9. Save and close the workbook (Figure 5-47).

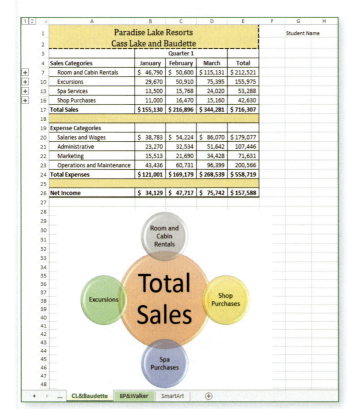

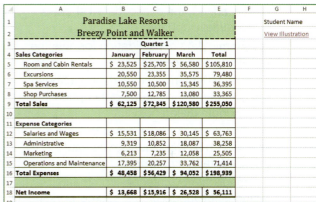

5-47 Completed worksheets for PP E5-3

Chapter Summary

5.1 Create a static consolidation of data from multiple worksheets (p. E5-252).

- A **consolidated worksheet** combines data from multiple worksheets using a mathematical or statistical function.
- When labels and values are in the same position on all worksheets, the consolidation is **by position**.
- A **static consolidation** places a non-changing result in the consolidation sheet, not a formula. If the source data is edited, the consolidated sheet is not updated.
- The **Consolidate** button is located on the *Data* tab in the *Data Tools* group.

5.2 Create a dynamic consolidation of data from multiple worksheets (p. E5-254).

- A **dynamic consolidation** places formulas in the consolidation worksheet. If the source data is edited, the consolidated sheet is automatically updated.
- A dynamic data consolidation formats the results as an Excel outline.
- To build a dynamic consolidation, choose the *Create links to source data* option in the *Consolidate* dialog box.
- If labels and values are not in the same position on all worksheets, you can consolidate **by category**.
- A consolidate by category command includes the labels on the source worksheets and also shows labels on the consolidated worksheet.

5.3 Link workbooks to consolidate data among worksheets (p. E5-261).

- A **dependent workbook** is a workbook that contains data cells from another workbook.
- A **source workbook** is a workbook that supplies data to another workbook.
- An **external reference formula** is a formula in a dependent workbook that refers to cells in a source workbook.
- An external reference formula establishes a link to a source workbook by identifying it in the syntax of the formula.
- When workbooks are linked, you can set *Trust Center Settings* options to automatically update links or to alert you when a workbook with links is opened.

- Source workbooks must be accessible in order for links to be updated.
- You can use the *Consolidate* command to link workbooks by navigating to the source workbook in the *Reference* box in the *Consolidate* dialog box.
- You can build your own formulas and use other Excel functions to link workbooks by switching and pointing between the dependent and the source workbooks.

5.4 Insert *SmartArt*, hyperlinks, and screenshots in a worksheet (p. E5-267).

- A **SmartArt** graphic is an illustration such as a matrix, a cycle diagram, an organization chart, or a process chart.
- *SmartArt* graphics are not linked to worksheet data; they contain descriptive text.
- A *SmartArt* graphic is a selectable object that you can size, position, and style.
- When a *SmartArt* graphic is selected, the *SmartArt Tools Design* and *Format* tabs are available.
- A *SmartArt* graphic consists of several smaller shapes; you can format each individual shape separately.
- A **hyperlink** is a clickable line of text or object that is a shortcut to another location in the workbook, on the computer, or in the cloud.
- Hyperlink text is underlined and formatted in the color determined by the document theme.
- The **Hyperlink** button is located in the *Links* group on the *Insert* tab.
- A **screenshot** is an image of data on the screen that is inserted as a picture in a worksheet.
- The **Take a Screenshot** button displays thumbnails of open windows that you can capture as images.
- You can take a **Screen Clipping** by drawing a rectangle around the desired area in an available window.

5.5 Group worksheets and edit and format grouped worksheets (p. E5-273).

- Grouping worksheets allows you to apply the same formats, enter the same formulas, or type the same data in multiple sheets with one command.
- Group nonadjacent sheets by holding down the **Ctrl** key while clicking the tab name.

- Hold down the **Shift** key to select all sheets between the first tab name that you click and the final tab you select.
- You can group all worksheets in a workbook by right-clicking any tab name and choosing **Select All Sheets**.

- If a command is unavailable for grouped sheets, it is grayed out.

Check for Understanding

In the **Online Learning Center** for this text (www.mhhe.com/office2013inpractice), there are a variety of resources that can be used to review the concepts covered in this chapter.

The following Online Learning Resources are available on the Online Learning Center:

- Multiple choice questions
- Short answer questions
- Matching exercises

Guided Project 5-1

Blue Lake Sports has maintained sales data about three specialty departments throughout the year in quarterly worksheets. For this project, you reformat the quarterly worksheets as a group, insert the *Sum* function, build static and dynamic consolidation sheets, insert a *SmartArt* graphic, and create a hyperlink. **[Student Learning Outcomes 5.1, 5.2, 5.4, 5.5]**

File Needed: ***BlueLakeSales-05.xlsx***
Completed Project File Name: ***[your initials] Excel 5-1.xlsx***

Skills Covered in This Project

- Group and format worksheets.
- Edit grouped worksheets.
- Use *AutoSum* in grouped worksheets.
- Copy, name, and position worksheets.
- Create a static data consolidation.

- Create a dynamic consolidation.
- Insert *SmartArt*.
- Use *SmartArt* tools to format a graphic.
- Insert a hyperlink.

1. Open the ***BlueLakeSales-05*** workbook from your student data files folder. Click the **Enable Editing** button.

2. Save the workbook as ***[your initials] Excel 5-1***.

3. Group and format the worksheets.
   a. Right-click any sheet tab name and choose **Select All Sheets**.
   b. Click cell **A2** and change the font to **Calibri**.
   c. Select cells **A4:E8** and apply **All Borders**.
   d. Select cells **A8:E8** and apply a **Top and Double Bottom Border**.
   e. Select cells **B5:E8** and click the **Decrease Decimal** button twice [*Home* tab, *Number* group].
   f. Select cells **B5:E5** and cells **B8:E8**.
   g. Click the **Accounting Number Format** button [*Home* tab, *Number* group] and then click the **Decrease Decimal** button twice [*Home* tab, *Number* group].

4. Edit grouped worksheets.
   a. Select cells **E5:E8** and delete the contents.
   b. While cells **E5:E8** are selected, click the **AutoSum** button [*Home* tab, *Editing* group].
   c. Click cell **A32** and type your first and last name. *AutoFit* column widths as needed.
   d. Click cell **A1** (Figure 5-48).
   e. Right-click any sheet tab and choose **Ungroup Sheets**.

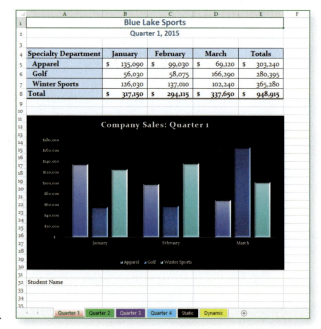

5-48 Completed *Quarter 1* worksheet; other quarter sheets are formatted the same

5. Click the **Quarter 4** worksheet tab. Hold down the **Ctrl** key and drag a copy of the **Quarter 4** worksheet tab to the right.

6. Name the copied sheet Static and change the tab sheet color to **Black, Text 1**.

7. Type Month 1 in cell **B4** and use the *Fill Handle* to extend the labels to cell **D4**.

8. Edit cell **A2** to display Quarter Summaries by First, Second, and Third Month.

9. Create a static data consolidation.
   a. Select cells **B5:D7** on the **Static** sheet and delete the contents.
   b. Click the **Consolidate** button [*Data* tab, *Data Tools* group].
   c. Choose the **Sum** function.
   d. If there are references in the *All references* box, select each one and click **Delete**.
   e. Click the *Reference* box and click the **Quarter 1** worksheet tab.
   f. Select cells **B5:D7** and release the pointer button.
   g. Click **Add** in the *Consolidate* dialog box.
   h. Click the **Quarter 2** worksheet tab. Verify that cells B5:D7 are selected. The chart may not be visible as you move from sheet to sheet.
   i. Click **Add** in the *Consolidate* dialog box.
   j. Add the cell range **B5:D7** from the **Quarter 3** and **Quarter 4** worksheets to the *All references* list in the *Consolidate* dialog box.
   k. Click **OK**.

10. Click the chart title element and edit it to read Results by First, Second, and Third Month.

11. Click cell **A1** (Figure 5-49).

	A	B	C	D	E
1		Blue Lake Sports			
2		Quarter Summaries by First, Second, and Third Month			
3					
4	Specialty Department	Month 1	Month 2	Month 3	Totals
5	Apparel	$ 693,829	$ 676,485	$ 812,593	$ 2,182,906
6	Golf	527,647	550,877	790,943	1,869,467
7	Winter Sports	322,560	421,525	340,623	1,084,708
8	Total	$ 1,544,036	$ 1,648,887	$ 1,944,159	$ 5,137,081

Results by First, Second, and Third Month

(chart with Month 1, Month 2, Month 3; legend: Apparel, Golf, Winter Sports)

Student Name

5-49 Consolidated sheet with edited chart title

12. Click the **Quarter 4** worksheet tab, hold down the **Ctrl** key, and drag a copy to the right of the **Static** sheet. Name the copied sheet Dynamic and change the tab sheet color to **Yellow**.

13. Select and delete the chart. Select and delete columns **B:D**. You will see an error message in the totals column. Edit cell **A2** to read Year Summary (Figure 5-50).

14. Create a dynamic data consolidation.
   a. Delete the contents of cells **B5:B8** on the **Dynamic** sheet. Leave cells **B5:B8** selected.
   b. Click the **Consolidate** button [*Data* tab, *Data Tools* group].
   c. Choose the **Sum** function.
   d. Select each incorrect reference in the *All references* box and click **Delete**.

	A	B
1	Blue Lake Sports	
2	Year Summary	
3		
4	Specialty Department	Totals
5	Apparel	#REF!
6	Golf	#REF!
7	Winter Sports	#REF!
8	Total	#REF!

5-50 Error message before consolidation; label edited

e. Click the *Reference* box and click the **Quarter 1** worksheet tab.

f. Select cells **E5:E8** and release the pointer button.

g. Click **Add** in the *Consolidate* dialog box.

h. Add the cell range **E5:E8** from the **Quarter 2**, **Quarter 3**, and **Quarter 4** worksheets to the *All references* list in the *Consolidate* dialog box.

i. Click to place a check mark for *Create links to source data*.

j. Click **OK**. *AutoFit* column widths as needed in each sheet.

15. Insert a *SmartArt* graphic.

a. Click cell **D2** on the **Dynamic** sheet.

b. Click the **Insert a SmartArt Graphic** button [*Insert* tab, *Illustrations* group].

c. Click **Process** in the list on the left.

d. Find and click **Vertical Equation** in the gallery of graphics.

e. Click **OK** to insert the *SmartArt* graphic. Close the text pane if necessary.

f. Click the top left circle shape and type Apparel. Do not press *Enter*.

g. Click the shape below *Apparel* and type Golf.

h. Click the **Add Shape** button [*SmartArt Tools Design* tab, *Create Graphic* group] (Figure 5-51).

i. In the bottom shape, type Winter Sports.

j. In the large circle shape on the right, type Specialty Departments.

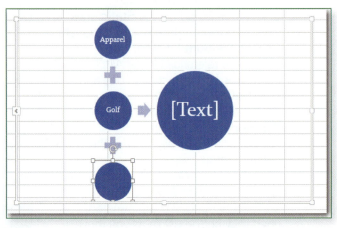

5-51 Shape added to *SmartArt* graphic

16. Format, position, and size a *SmartArt* graphic.

a. Click the frame of the *SmartArt* graphic to select it.

b. Click the **More** button [*SmartArt Tools Design* tab, *SmartArt Styles* group].

c. In the *3-D* group, choose **Polished**.

d. Click the **Change Colors** button [*SmartArt Tools Design* tab, *SmartArt Styles* group].

e. In the *Accent 1* group, choose **Colored Fill – Accent 1**.

f. Point at the *SmartArt* frame to display a move pointer. Drag the graphic to position the top left selection handle in cell **C1**. While the graphic is selected, press the up or left directional arrow to fine tune the position of the graphic.

g. Point at the bottom right selection handle to display a resize pointer. Drag the pointer to reach cell **J35**.

h. While the *SmartArt* frame is selected, click the **Shape Fill** button [*SmartArt Tools Format* tab, *Shapes Styles* group].

i. Choose **White, Background 1, Darker 15%**.

j. Click the **Shape Outline** button [*SmartArt Tools Format* tab, *Shapes Styles* group].

k. Choose **Weight** and **½pt**.

l. Click the **Shape Outline** button again and choose **Blue, Accent 1**.

17. Click cell **A1** to deselect the *SmartArt* (Figure 5-52).

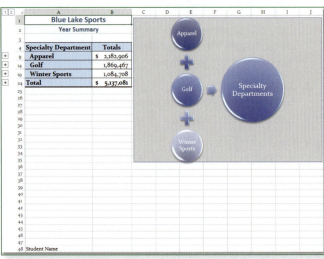

5-52 Dynamic consolidation and completed *SmartArt* graphic

18. Insert a hyperlink.
    a. Click the **Static** sheet tab and select cell **F9**.
    b. Click the **Hyperlink** button [*Insert* tab, *Links* group]. You can right-click the cell and choose **Hyperlink** from the context-sensitive menu.
    c. Click **Place in This Document** in the *Insert Hyperlink* dialog box.
    d. In the *Or select a place in this document* list, click to select **Dynamic**. Sheet names are at the top of the list in the *Cell Reference* group.
    e. Select the default text in the *Text to display* box, and type See the graphic. You will use the default ScreenTip.
    f. Click **OK** in the *Insert Hyperlink* dialog box.
    g. Test the hyperlink.

19. Save and close the workbook (Figure 5-53).

5-53 Completed static consolidation sheet with hyperlink for Excel 5-1

Guided Project 5-2

Sierra Pacific Community College has monitored tuition revenue for three years and recorded it in a workbook. These sheets need to be cleaned up a bit before they can serve as the source workbook for a master dependent workbook. You format the grouped worksheets to save time. After the workbooks are linked, you insert a screenshot in the source workbook and create a hyperlink in the dependent workbook.
[Student Learning Outcomes 5.3, 5.4, 5.5]

File Needed: **SierraPacificCC-05.xlsx**
Completed Project File Names: **[your initials] Excel 5-2.xlsx** and **[your initials] Excel 5-2A.xlsx**

Skills Covered in This Project

- Group and format worksheets.
- Delete a column in grouped sheets.
- Use AutoSum in grouped worksheets.
- Copy, name, and position worksheets.
- Arrange multiple open workbook windows.

- Link workbooks with an external reference formula.
- Edit and copy an external reference formula.
- Insert a screenshot in a worksheet.
- View and break a workbook link.
- Insert a hyperlink.

---

1. Open the **SierrraPacificCC-05** workbook from your student data files folder. Click the **Enable Editing** button if necessary.

2. Save the workbook as **[your initials] Excel 5-2**.

3. Group and format the worksheets.
   a. Click the **2013–14** worksheet tab.
   b. Hold down the **Shift** key and click the **2015–16** worksheet tab to select all the sheets.
   c. Right-click the column **F** heading and choose **Delete**.
   d. Select cells **B8:F8** and click the **AutoSum** button [*Home* tab, *Editing* group].
   e. Select cells **A1:F2** and apply **Outside Borders**.
   f. Click cell **A1**.
   g. Right-click the **2013–14** worksheet tab and choose **Ungroup Sheets**. Save the workbook.

4. Create a new, blank workbook and save it as **[your initials] Excel 5-2A**.

5. Click the **Arrange All** button [*View* tab, *Window* group]. Choose **Vertical** and click **OK**.

6. Copy a worksheet to another workbook.
   a. Right-click the **2013–14** worksheet tab in **[your initials] Excel 5-2**.
   b. Choose **Move or Copy**.
   c. In the *To book* list, click the arrow and choose as **[your initials] Excel 5-2A**.
   d. Click to place a check mark for *Create a copy* (Figure 5-54).
   e. Click **OK**. A copy of the worksheet is placed in the new workbook.

7. Prepare the dependent workbook.
   a. In **[your initials] Excel 5-2A**, edit the label in cell **A2** to read Academic Years 2013–2016.
   b. Select and delete the contents of cells **B4:E7**.
   c. Rename the **2013–2014** tab in **[your initials] Excel 5-2A** as 2013–2016.
   d. Delete **Sheet1**.
   e. Apply **Dark Red** fill to cells **A3:F3** and **A4:A7**.

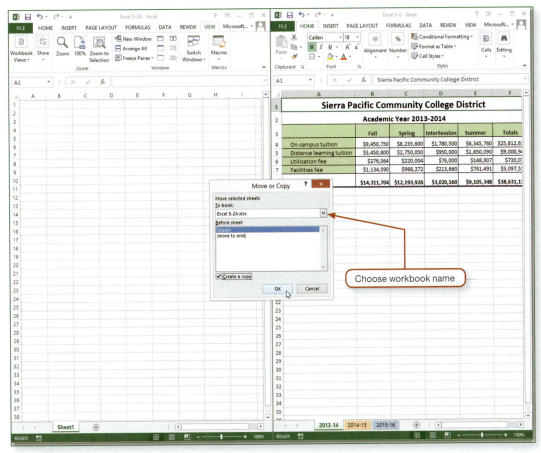

5-54 *Move and Copy* dialog box to copy worksheet to another workbook

8. Build an external reference formula in the dependent workbook.
   a. Click in cell **B4** in the **[your initials] Excel 5-2A** workbook and type = to start the formula.
   b. Click cell **B4** on the **2013-14** sheet tab in **[your initials] Excel 5-2**.
   c. Type + to add the next cell.
   d. Click cell **B4** on the **2014-15** sheet tab in **[your initials] Excel 5-2**.
   e. Type +, and click cell **B4** on the **2015-16** sheet tab in **[your initials] Excel 5-2** (Figure 5-55).

5-55 External reference formula with absolute references

   f. Press **Enter**. The formula is placed in the **[your initials] Excel 5-2A** workbook with absolute references.
   g. Maximize the **[your initials] Excel 5-2A** workbook and click cell **B4**.

9. Edit and copy an external reference formula in the dependent workbook.
   a. Click in the *Formula bar* for cell **B4** in the dependent workbook, *[your initials] Excel 5-2A*.
   b. Delete the **$** symbols in the first occurrence of **$B$4** to change the absolute reference to a relative reference.
   c. Delete the **$** symbols in each occurrence of **$B$4** in the formula (Figure 5-56).
   d. Press **Enter**.
   e. Copy the formula in cell **B4** to cells **B5:B7** without fill formatting. Copy the formula to cells **C4:E7**.
   f. Select the *[your initials] Excel 5-2* workbook. Group worksheets **2013–14**, **2014–15**, and **2015–16**. Select **B5:F7** and apply **Comma** formatting without decimal places. **Ungroup** the sheets.
   g. Switch to *[your initials] Excel 5-2A*. Click cell **B4**.

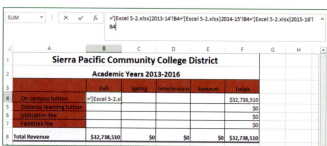

5-56 External reference formula edited to use relative references

10. Insert a screenshot in a workbook.
    a. Click the **Show Formulas** button on the *Formulas* tab [*Formula Auditing* group]. You will take a screenshot of the formulas for placement in the source workbook. *AutoFit* the columns as needed.
    b. From the Windows *Taskbar*, switch to *[your initials] Excel 5-2*. Maximize the window.
    c. Insert a new worksheet and name it Screenshot. Place the sheet at the end of the tab names.
    d. Click the **Take a Screenshot** button [*Insert* tab, *Illustrations* group]. Note that when you are taking the screenshot, it works best if you close all open programs except Excel.
    e. From the gallery of thumbnails, click the thumbnail for *[your initials] Excel 5-2A*. The screenshot is placed on the new worksheet (Figure 5-57).

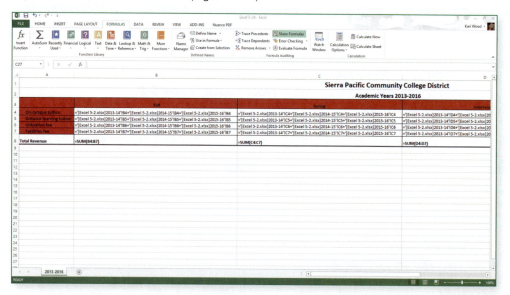

5-57 Screenshot placed in worksheet

    f. Click the dialog box launcher for the *Size* group on the *Picture Tools Format* tab.
    g. Set the **Height** of the screenshot to **5** and press **Enter**. The width is automatically reset to maintain the image's proportion.
    h. Close the *Format Picture* task pane.
    i. Click cell **A26** to deselect the screenshot.

11. Save and close **[your initials] Excel 5-2**.
12. View and break links in the dependent workbook.
    a. Maximize the **[your initials] Excel 5-2A** window if necessary.
    b. Click the **Show Formulas** button on the *Formulas* tab [*Formula Auditing* group] to hide the formulas. *AutoFit* columns as needed.
    c. Click cell **B4** if necessary.
    d. Click the **Edit Links** button [*Data* tab, *Connections* group].
    e. Click **Break Link**. When you break a link, the formulas are replaced with values and this command cannot be undone (Figure 5-58).

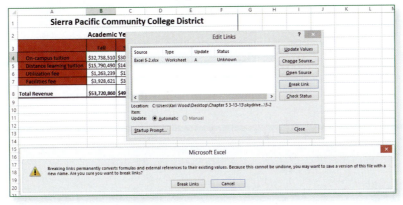

5-58 *Edit Links* dialog box and *Break Links* message box

    f. Click **Break Links**. All formulas are removed, but the cells display the values. Click **Close**.
    g. Select **B5:F7** and apply **Comma** formatting without decimal places.
13. Insert a hyperlink.
    a. Right-click cell **A10** on the **2013–2016** sheet tab.
    b. Choose **Hyperlink** from the context-sensitive menu.
    c. Click **Existing File or Web Page** in the *Insert Hyperlink* dialog box.
    d. In the *Look in* list, select **[your initials] Excel 5-2**. Navigate to the appropriate folder if necessary by clicking the drop-down arrow and choosing the folder name.
    e. Select the default text in the *Text to display* box, and type Open the source workbook. You will use the default ScreenTip (Figure 5-59).

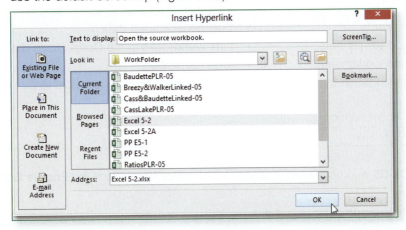

5-59 Hyperlink to open another workbook

    f. Click **OK** in the *Insert Hyperlink* dialog box.
    g. Click the hyperlink text to open the source workbook.

E5-287

14. Close *[your initials] Excel 5-2*. Save and close *[your initials] Excel 5-2A* (Figure 5-60).

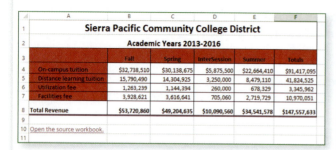
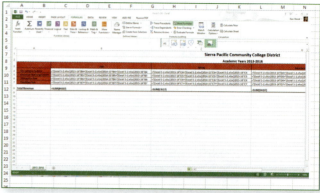

5-60 Completed worksheets for Excel 5-2

Guided Project 5-3

The Hamilton Civic Center tracks the number of participants enrolled in one-time classes and seminars offered at the facility. The first quarter data is kept in a workbook that will be consolidated and used as the source for a dependent workbook. Because the labels are not in the same order on the quarterly sheets, you need to do some work to prepare the worksheets for consolidation.
[Student Learning Outcomes 5.1, 5.2, 5.3, 5.4, 5.5]

Files Needed: *HamiltonCC1-05.xlsx* and *HamiltonCC2-05.xlsx*
Completed Project File Names: *[your initials] Excel 5-3.xlsx* and *[your initials] Excel 5-3A.xlsx*

Skills Covered in This Project

- Group and format worksheets.
- Use *AutoSum* in grouped worksheets.
- Copy, name, and position worksheets.
- Create a static data consolidation by category.
- Create a dynamic data consolidation.

- Sort consolidated data.
- Link workbooks in the *Consolidate* dialog box.
- Insert *SmartArt*.
- Use *SmartArt* tools to format and position a *SmartArt* graphic.

1. Open the **HamiltonCC1-05** workbook from your student data files folder. Click the **Enable Editing button** if needed.

2. Save the workbook as *[your initials] Excel 5-3*.

3. Group the quarterly worksheets.
   a. Click the **January** worksheet tab.
   b. Hold down the **Shift** key and click the **March** tab.

4. Format the grouped worksheets.
   a. Select cells **A5:F12**.
   b. Click the arrow with the **Borders** button [*Home* tab, *Font* group] and select **More Borders**. In the *Format Cells* dialog box, you can build a custom border.
   c. Click the **Color** arrow and choose **Black, Text 1**.
   d. Click the thin solid line **Style** (the bottom choice in the first column of line styles).
   e. Click in the **vertical middle** of the preview box to place a middle vertical border. If you place a border in the wrong location, click it again in the preview to remove it.
   f. Click the second line **Style** in the first column (two below **None**).
   g. Click in the **horizontal middle** of the preview box to place a middle horizontal border. This border will appear between rows.
   h. Click the bottom line **Style** in the second column (a double border).
   i. Click in the **bottom** of the preview box to place a bottom horizontal border (Figure 5-61).
   j. Click **OK**.

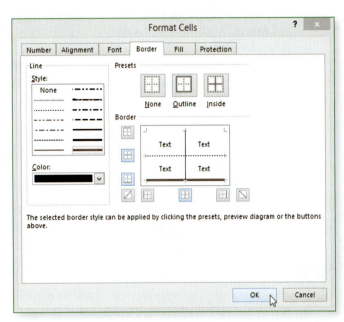

5-61 *Border* tab in *Format Cells* dialog box

5. Use *AutoSum* in grouped worksheets.
   a. Select cells **F6:F11**.
   b. Click the **AutoSum** button [*Home* tab, *Editing* group].
   c. Select cells **B12:F12** and apply **SUM** formulas to them.
   d. Click cell **A1**.
   e. Right-click any selected sheet tab and choose **Ungroup Sheets**.

6. Make a copy of the **March** sheet and place it at the end of the tab names.

7. Name the copied sheet Quarter 1 and change the tab sheet color to **Black, Text 1**.

8. Change the color of all the borders to **Blue** (e.g., top, bottom, and inside lines).

9. Change the fill color gradient in **A1** to **Blue** for *color 2*. *Hint: open the Format Cells dialog box and choose Fill Effects to apply the gradient fill.*

10. Edit cell **A3** to read First Quarter Enrollment in Special Classes.

11. Create a static data consolidation.
    a. Delete the contents of cells **A6:E11** on the **Quarter 1** sheet. Because the labels in column **A** are not all in the same order in the quarterly sheets, you must include them in the consolidation ranges.
    b. Click the **Consolidate** button [*Data* tab, *Data Tools* group].
    c. Choose the **Sum** function.
    d. If there are references in the *All references* box, select each one and click **Delete**.
    e. Click the *Reference* box and click the **January** worksheet tab.
    f. Select cells **A6:E11** and release the pointer button.

g. Click **Add** in the *Consolidate* dialog box.

h. Click the **February** worksheet tab, verify that cells **A6:E11** are selected, and click **Add**.

i. Add the cell range **A6:E11** from the **March** worksheet to the *All references* list.

j. Check the **Left column** box in the *Use labels in* group (Figure 5-62).

k. Click **OK**.

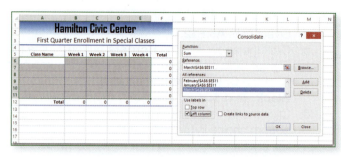

5-62 *Consolidate* dialog box to consolidate by category

12. Sort the consolidated data.
    a. Select cells **A6:E11** on the **Quarter 1** sheet.
    b. Click the **Sort & Filter** button [*Home* tab, *Editing* group].
    c. Choose **Sort A to Z**.
    d. Click cell **A1**.

13. Save the **[your initials] Excel 5-3** workbook and leave it open.

14. Open the **HamiltonCC2-05** workbook from your student data files folder. Click the **Enable Editing** button if needed.

15. Save the workbook as **[your initials] Excel 5-3A**.

16. Create a dynamic data consolidation to link workbooks.
    a. Select cells **D7:D12** on the **FirstQuarter** sheet.
    b. Click the **Consolidate** button [*Data* tab, *Data Tools* group].
    c. Choose the **Sum** function.
    d. Select each reference in the *All references* box and click **Delete** if necessary.
    e. Click the *Reference* box and press **Ctrl+F6** to switch to the **[your initials] Excel 5-3** workbook.
    f. Click the **Quarter 1** sheet tab if necessary.
    g. Select cells **F6:F11** and release the pointer button. When there is only one reference, you don't need to click **Add**.
    h. Check the *Create links to source data* box (Figure 5-63).

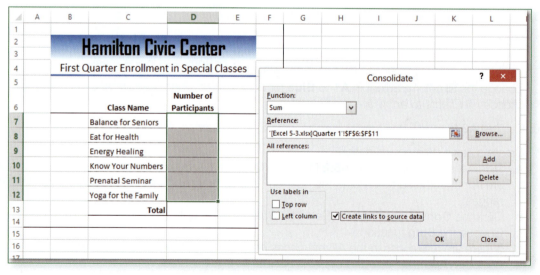

5-63 *Consolidate* dialog box to link workbooks

i. Click **OK**.
   j. Click cell **D19** on *[your initials] Excel 5-3A* and click the **AutoSum** button [*Home* tab, *Editing* group].
   k. Press **Enter**.

17. Insert a *SmartArt* graphic.
   a. Click cell **G2** on the **FirstQuarter** sheet.
   b. Click the **Insert a SmartArt Graphic** button [*Insert* tab, *Illustrations* group].
   c. Click **Process** in the list. Find and click **Basic Chevron Process** in the gallery.
   d. Click **OK**. Close the text pane if necessary.
   e. Click the leftmost shape and type Monthly sheets. Do not press *Enter*.
   f. Click the middle shape and type Quarter workbook.
   g. Click the rightmost shape and type E-mail distribution.

18. Format and position a *SmartArt* graphic.
   a. Click the frame of the *SmartArt* graphic to select it.
   b. Click the **More** button [*SmartArt Tools Design* tab, *SmartArt Styles* group].
   c. In the *3-D* group, choose **Bird's Eye Scene**.
   d. Click the **Change Colors** button [*SmartArt Tools Design* tab, *SmartArt Styles* group].
   e. In the *Colorful* group, choose **Colorful Range – Accent Colors 4 to 5**.
   f. Point at the *SmartArt* frame to display a four-pointed arrow. Drag the graphic to position the top-left selection handle in cell **A21**. Nudge the graphic with the up or left directional arrow.
   g. Click cell **A1**.

19. Save and close the *[your initials] Excel 5-3A* workbook. Save and close the *[your initials] Excel 5-3* workbook (Figure 5-64).

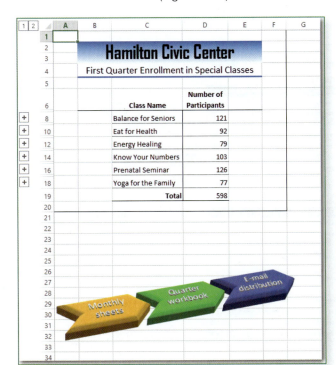

5-64 Completed worksheets for Excel 5-3

Independent Project 5-4

Wilson Home Entertainment Systems tracks cash flow at each of their main locations. The numbers for each location are maintained separately but they are all consolidated at the end of the quarter. The static consolidations must be completed for several nonadjacent cell ranges on the sheets. After the summary is complete, you insert hyperlinks to each of the supporting worksheets.
[Student Learning Outcomes 5.1, 5.4, 5.5]

File Needed: *WilsonHome-05.xlsx*
Completed Project File Name: *Excel 5-4.xlsx*

Skills Covered in This Project

- Group and format worksheets.
- Edit data in grouped worksheets.
- Create a static data consolidation with *Sum*.
- Copy, name, and position worksheets.
- Create a static data consolidation with *Average*.
- Insert a hyperlink.
- Copy a hyperlink.
- Edit a hyperlink.

1. Open the **WilsonHome-05** workbook from your student data files folder.

2. Save the workbook as **[your initials] Excel 5-4**.

3. Group all four worksheets.

4. Edit and format grouped sheets.
   a. In cell **A28**, type First Quarter, 2015 and make it bold.
   b. Merge and center the contents of cells **A1** across cells **A1:B1**. Merge and center cells **A2:B2**.
   c. Edit the contents of cell **A10** to read Cash paid for marketing.
   d. Click cell **A1** and ungroup the sheets.

5. Click the **CashFlow** sheet tab.

6. Consolidate the cash received amounts in the *Cash flow from operations* section.
   a. Select cells **B4:B6**.
   b. Use **Sum** to consolidate the static data from the three location sheets without links to the source data (Figure 5-65).

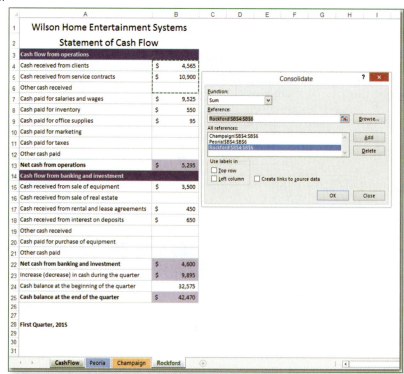

5-65 Consolidate dialog box for location sheets

7. Consolidate the cash paid amounts in the *Cash flow from operations* section.
   a. Select cells **B7:B12**.
   b. Use **Sum** to consolidate the static cash paid amounts on the **Cash Flow** sheet.

8. In the *Cash flow from banking and investment* section on the **CashFlow** sheet, use **Sum** to consolidate the static cash received amounts in cells **B15:B19** without links to the source data.

9. Consolidate the cash paid amounts for the *Cash flow from banking and investment* section on the **CashFlow** sheet.
   a. Use cells **B20:B21** for the static consolidation.
   b. In the message that no data was consolidated, click **OK** (Figure 5-66).

5-66 Message box when selected cells are empty

10. Use **Sum** to consolidate the *cash balance at the beginning of the quarter* amounts in **B24** on the **Cash Flow** sheet.

11. Make a copy of the **CashFlow** sheet, move it to the end of the tab names, and name the sheet Averages.

12. Edit the label in cell **A2** to read Statement of Average Cash Flow.

13. Consolidate the *cash balance at the beginning of the quarter* amounts in the **Averages** sheet.
    a. Select cell **B24**.
    b. Use **Average** to consolidate the data from the three location sheets without links to the source data (Figure 5-67).

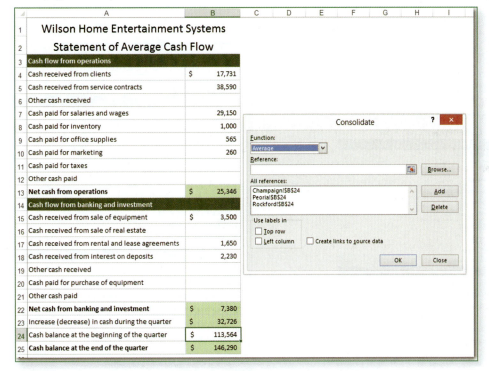

5-67 *Consolidate* dialog box with *Average* function

14. Consolidate the cash received amounts in the *Cash flow from operations* section.
    a. Select cells **B4:B6** and open the *Consolidate* dialog box.
    b. Use **Average** to consolidate the data without links.

E5-293

15. Use **Average** to consolidate cells **B7:B12** and then cells **B15:B19** without links.

16. Insert a hyperlink on the **CashFlow** worksheet.
    a. Click cell **D3** on the **CashFlow** worksheet.
    b. Create a hyperlink that displays Peoria Data and switches to the **Peoria** worksheet.

17. Copy and edit a hyperlink.
    a. Right-click the hyperlink in cell **D3** and choose **Copy** from the menu.
    b. Paste the hyperlink in cell **D5**.
    c. Right-click cell **D5** and choose **Edit Hyperlink** from the menu (Figure 5-68).
    d. Edit the hyperlink to read Champaign Data and to switch to the **Champaign** worksheet.
    e. Right-click the **Champaign** hyperlink and choose **Orange, Accent 6, Darker 25%** as the **Font Color** from the mini toolbar.
    f. Copy either hyperlink to create a third hyperlink for the **Rockford** sheet in cell **D7**. Use **Purple, Accent 4, Darker 25%** as the font color.
    g. Test the hyperlinks.

18. Save and close the workbook (Figure 5-69).

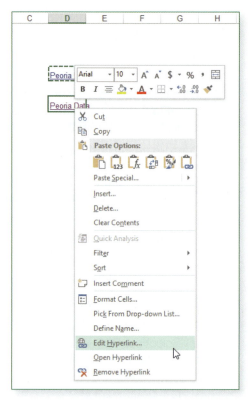

5-68 Context menu for hyperlink

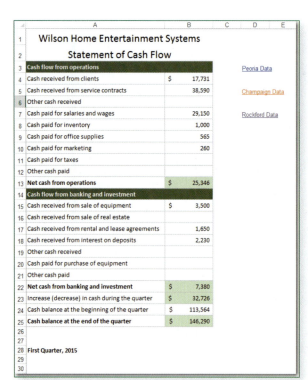

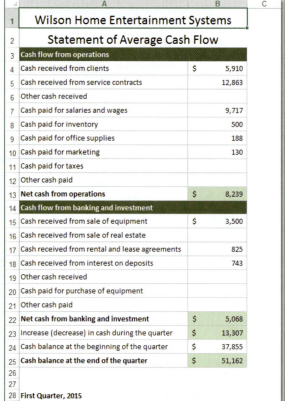

5-69 Completed worksheets for Excel 5-4

Independent Project 5-5

The grade sheet for an instructor's Office class at Sierra Pacific Community College records the data from each class on a separate worksheet. To calculate total points for the course, the data is consolidated on another worksheet. For this project, you edit the segment sheets and calculate the total points for each student.
[Student Learning Outcomes 5.1, 5.4, 5.5]

File Needed: **SierraPacificGrades-05.xlsx**
Completed Project File Name: **[your initials] Excel 5-5.xlsx**

Skills Covered in This Project

- Group and format worksheets.
- Edit data in grouped worksheets.
- Create a static data consolidation.
- Create an addition formula.
- Copy formats and merge and unmerge cells.
- Insert *SmartArt*.
- Use *SmartArt* tools to format a graphic.

1. Open the **SierraPacificGrades-05** workbook from your student data files folder.

2. Save the workbook as **[your initials] Excel 5-5**.

3. Group all five worksheets.

4. Edit grouped sheets.
   a. Select and delete column **C**.
   b. In cell **A28**, type Fall Semester, 2015, and make it **bold**.
   c. Edit the contents of cell **C3** to display Assignment 1.
   d. Edit cell **D3** to display Assignment 2.
   e. *AutoFit* column widths of **B:D**.
   f. Select cells **A1:F25** and apply **Black, Text 1** colored **Outside Borders**. This will reset the outside border to a thin black outline on all sheets.
   g. Click cell **A1** and ungroup the sheets.

5. Click the **Total** sheet tab. Select and delete columns **C:D**.

6. Consolidate the *Assignment Total* data.
   a. Select cells **C4:C25** and open the *Consolidate* dialog box.
   b. Use **Sum** to consolidate cells **E4:E25** from each of the application sheets without links (Figure 5-70).

7. Consolidate using **Sum** the *Exam* static data in **F4:F25** from each of the applications sheets in cells **D4:D25** on the **Total** sheet.

5-70 *Consolidate* dialog box for application sheets

8. Type Total Points in cell **E3**. Set column **E** to a width to **13.00**.

9. Prepare the *Total Points* column.
   a. Use an addition formula in cell **E4** to add the contents of cells **C4** and **D4**.
   b. Copy the format from cell **D4** to cell **E4**.
   c. Copy cell **E4** to cells **E5:E25**.

10. Format the data.
    a. Apply **Wrap Text** to cell **C3** and set the width of column **C** to **13.00**.
    b. Select cells **A3:E3** and apply **Bottom Align** and **Center**.
    c. Merge and center cell **A1:E2**. *(Hint: You may need to click the button twice, once to unmerge and a second time to re-merge.)*
    d. Select cells **A1:E2**. Apply a **Black, Text 1 Outline Border**.

11. Insert and format a *SmartArt* graphic.
    a. Insert a **Radial Cluster** graphic from the **Cycle** category on the **Total** sheet.
    b. Position the *SmartArt* graphic with its top left selection handle in cell **F4**. Size the graphic so that its bottom right selection handle is in cell **O24**.
    c. In the top text box, type Assignment 1. Do not press *Enter* after typing the label.
    d. In the lower left box, type Assignment 2. In the lower right box, type Exam. Type Total Points in the middle box.
    e. Apply the **Flat Scene SmartArt Style** from the **3-D** group.
    f. Change the color to **Colorful Range – Accent Colors 3 to 4**.

12. Change the page orientation to **Landscape**. Scale the contents to fit on a single page.

13. Save and close the workbook (Figure 5-71).

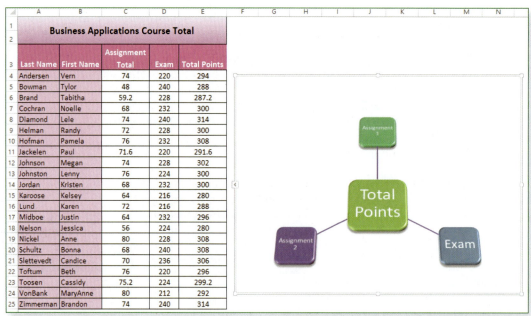

5-71 Completed worksheet for Excel 5-5

Independent Project 5-6

Wear-Ever Shoes is ready to link a new workbook to the workbook that tracks best-seller data for four geographic areas. You are building this new workbook in preparation for the sales review meeting.
[Student Learning Outcomes 5.3, 5.4]

File Needed: *WearEver-05.xlsx*
Completed Project File Name: *[your initials] Excel 5-6.xlsx*

Skills Covered in This Project

- Copy a worksheet to a new workbook.
- Arrange multiple open workbook windows.
- Link workbooks with an addition formula.

- Edit and copy an external reference formula.
- Insert a hyperlink.

1. Open the *WearEver-05* workbook from your student data files folder.

2. Create a new workbook and save it as *[your initials] Excel 5-6*.

3. Arrange the two workbooks to be vertically tiled.

4. Copy the **North** worksheet from the *WearEver-05* file to *[your initials] Excel 5-6*. Rename the sheet Totals. Delete **Sheet1**.

5. Prepare the linked workbook.
   a. In *[your initials] Excel 5-6*, delete the contents of cells **B6:B16**.
   b. Select and delete columns **C:D**.
   c. Edit the label in cell **A3** to show Best Sellers All Sectors.
   d. Change the sheet tab color to **Orange, Accent 2**, and the **Fill Color** for cells **A1:F4** to **Orange, Accent 2**.

6. Link workbooks with an addition formula.
   a. Click cell **B6** in *[your initials] Excel 5-6* and type = to start the formula.
   b. Add the contents of cell **B6** on each of the sheets in the *WearEver-05* workbook in the formula (Figure 5-72).

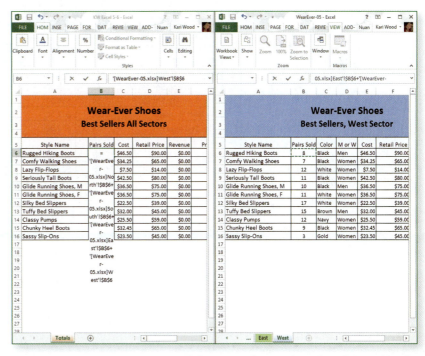

5-72 External reference formula to link workbooks

7. Close the **WearEver-05** workbook without saving and maximize your workbook window.

8. Edit and copy an external reference formula.
   a. Click cell **B6** in *[your initials] Excel 5-6*.
   b. Edit the formula to change each absolute reference to a relative reference.
   c. Copy the formula to complete the *Pairs Sold* column (Figure 5-73).

	Style Name	Pairs Sold	Cost	Retail Price	Revenue	Profit
	Wear-Ever Shoes					
	Best Sellers All Sectors					
6	Rugged Hiking Boots	39	$46.50	$90.00	$3,510.00	$1,696.50
7	Comfy Walking Shoes	41	$34.25	$65.00	$2,665.00	$1,260.75
8	Lazy Flip-Flops	53	$7.50	$14.00	$742.00	$344.50
9	Seriously Tall Boots	43	$42.50	$80.00	$3,440.00	$1,612.50
10	Glide Running Shoes, M	63	$36.50	$75.00	$4,725.00	$2,425.50
11	Glide Running Shoes, F	54	$36.50	$75.00	$4,050.00	$2,079.00
12	Silky Bed Slippers	84	$22.50	$39.00	$3,276.00	$1,386.00
13	Tuffy Bed Slippers	59	$32.00	$45.00	$2,655.00	$767.00
14	Classy Pumps	50	$25.50	$59.00	$2,950.00	$1,675.00
15	Chunky Heel Boots	47	$32.45	$65.00	$3,055.00	$1,529.85
16	Sassy Slip-Ons	19	$23.50	$45.00	$855.00	$408.50

5-73 Relative references copied

9. Insert a hyperlink to open the source workbook **WearEver-05**.
   a. Click cell **G3**.
   b. Create the hyperlink and edit the display text to read Open source data..
   c. Color the hyperlink **Orange, Accent 2**.
   d. Test the hyperlink and close the source workbook.

10. Save and close the workbook (Figure 5-74).

5-74 Completed worksheet for Excel 5-6

Improve It Project 5-7

American River Cycling has created four worksheets and a consolidated sheet that details, by date, the number of participants for recent races. Although it was originally created as a static consolidation, it should have been dynamic so that the data can be updated. For this project, you redo the consolidation and improve the formatting for source worksheets.
[Student Learning Outcomes 5.1, 5.2, 5.5]

File Needed: **AmRiverCycling-05.xlsx**
Completed Project File Name: **[your initials] Excel 5-7.xlsx**

Skills Covered in This Project

- Remove a static data consolidation.
- Create a dynamic data consolidation.
- Group and format worksheets.
- Edit source data.

---

1. Open the **AmRiverCycling-05** workbook from your student data files folder.
2. Save the workbook as **[your initials] Excel 5-7**.
3. Remove the static consolidation data by deleting the contents of cells **B4:D12** on the **Dynamic** sheet tab.
4. Create a **Sum** dynamic data consolidation in cells **B4:D12** on the **Dynamic** sheet. Use cells **E4:G12** on each of the supporting worksheets with links to the source data.
5. Select the dates in column **A** and format them to use mm/dd/yy format (Figure 5-75).
6. Group and format worksheets.
   a. Group all the sheets that have a state as the sheet tab name.
   b. In the grouped sheets, delete columns **C:D**.
   c. In cell **A1** on the grouped sheets, type American River Cycling. Set the font size to **20 pt. Merge and center** the label across cells **A1:E1**.
   d. In cell **A2**, type April-June Race Participation and set the font size to **18 pt. Merge and center** the label across cells **A2:E2**.
   e. *AutoFit* columns **B:C**.
   f. Make the labels in row 3 **bold** and **centered**.
   g. Apply **All Borders** to cells **A3:E12**. Apply **Outside Borders** to cells **A1:E2**.
   h. Set the **Height** of rows **3:12** to **21.00**.
   i. Select the dates in column **A** and format them with mm/dd/yy format.
   j. Apply **Blue, Accent 1** fill color to **A3:E3**.
   k. Click cell **A1** and ungroup the sheets.

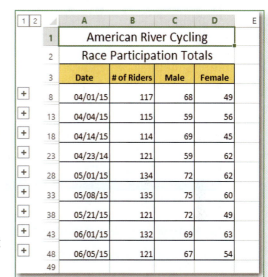

5-75 Dynamic data consolidation and reformatted dates

7. Edit source data.
    a. Open a second window for the workbook and arrange the windows vertically.
    b. Display the **Dynamic** sheet in one window and the **Massachusetts** sheet in the other window.
    c. Edit the **Everett** values in the *Massachusetts* sheet to **45** riders, **25** male, and **20** female (Figure 5-76).

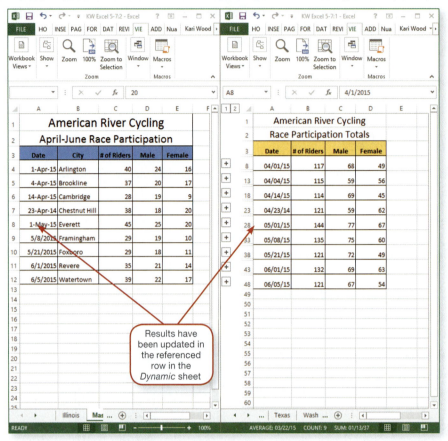

5-76 Edited values in a supporting worksheet

    d. Close either window and maximize the other.

8. Save and close the workbook (Figure 5-77).

	A	B	C	D	E
1	American River Cycling				
2	April-June Race Participation				
3	Date	City	# of Riders	Male	Female
4	1-Apr-15	Arlington	40	24	16
5	4-Apr-15	Brookline	37	20	17
6	14-Apr-15	Cambridge	28	19	9
7	23-Apr-14	Chestnut Hill	38	18	20
8	1-May-15	Everett	45	25	20
9	5/8/2015	Framingham	29	19	10
10	5/21/2015	Foxboro	29	18	11
11	6/1/2015	Revere	35	21	14
12	6/5/2015	Watertown	39	22	17

	A	B	C	D
1	American River Cycling			
2	Race Participation Totals			
3	Date	# of Riders	Male	Female
8	04/01/15	117	68	49
13	04/04/15	115	59	56
18	04/14/15	114	69	45
23	04/23/14	121	59	62
28	05/01/15	144	77	67
33	05/08/15	135	75	60
38	05/21/15	121	72	49
43	06/01/15	132	69	63
48	06/05/15	121	67	54

5-77 Completed *Massachusetts* and *Dynamic* worksheets for Excel 5-7

Challenge Project 5-8

For this project, you work with a classmate (or on your own) to develop a source and a dependent workbook. The source workbook includes details about the amount of time you spend each weekday on each of five activities for four weeks. The dependent workbook uses external reference formulas to summarize the week's activities.
[Student Learning Outcomes 5.3, 5.4, 5.5]

File Needed: None
Completed Project File Names: *[your initials] Excel 5-8.xlsx* and *[your initials] Excel 5-8A.xlsx*

Create a new source workbook and save it as *[your initials] Excel 5-8*. Modify your workbook according to the following guidelines:

- Use the names of the five weekdays as column labels and the names of five activities as row labels. Choose activities such as "Prepare meals," "Work on class assignments," "Exercise or workout," "Watch videos or television," "Attend meetings," "Travel to work," and other similar daily tasks.
- Name the sheet *Week 1* and enter the number of minutes spent each day on each task or activity. Copy the sheet to create separate sheets for weeks 2–4.
- Group the sheets and enter main labels to describe the data. Use a formula to total each activity for the week.
- Format the grouped sheets in an attractive, easy-to-view style.
- Ungroup the sheets and edit several of the values for weeks 2–4.
- Create a second workbook named *[your initials] Excel 5-8A*. Copy one of the sheets from *[your initials] Excel 5-8* into this new workbook and name it *Month*.
- Create an external reference formula to add the first task minutes for Monday using *[your initials] Excel 5-8* as the source workbook. Edit and copy the formula.
- Insert a hyperlink in the dependent workbook to open the source workbook.

Challenge Project 5-9

For this project, you build worksheets in separate workbooks with data about an activity or concept from your neighborhood or your workplace. After the workbooks are prepared, group and edit the worksheets, and insert a *SmartArt* graphic that illustrates the concept. Finally, use a hyperlink on the worksheet to show the *SmartArt*.
[Student Learning Outcomes 5.2, 5.4, 5.5]

File Needed: None
Completed Project File Names: *[your initials] Excel 5-9.xlsx* and *Excel 5-9A.xlsx*

- Create a new source workbook and save it as *[your initials] Excel 5-9*. Modify your workbook according to the following guidelines:

- Type labels and values to illustrate an activity or concept. For example, you might build a worksheet to track the average number of automobiles owned, by street, in your community. You might create a worksheet that details number of workers by department and their commuting time or distance to work. Or, build a worksheet that lists names of family members, their cities of residence, and some of their physical or personality traits.
- Copy the sheet and input data for a different neighborhood, department, or family.
- Group the sheets and apply formatting that suits both sheets.
- Review the *SmartArt* categories and insert a graphic to illustrate a concept related to your data. Place the *SmartArt* on its own sheet. If necessary, explore how to add or remove shapes from the graphic.
- Format the *SmartArt* graphic with a style, change the colors, or add a fill or a border. Size and position the graphic. Save the file.
- On your worksheet, insert a hyperlink that displays the *SmartArt* graphic.
- Create a new workbook and save it as *[your initials] Excel 5-9A*.
- Copy a sheet from the *[your initials] Excel 5-9* workbook to the *[your initials] Excel 5-9A* workbook.
- Use the new copied sheet in the new workbook as the consolidation worksheet.
- Reformat the consolidation sheet and delete the necessary cells.
- Dynamically consolidate the data from both sheets in the *[your initials] Excel 5-9* workbook.

Challenge Project 5-10

For this project, you create a timesheet workbook for five employees. After four weeks, you consolidate their hours to create a worksheet that shows hours worked per month by employee.
[Student Learning Outcomes 5.1, 5.2, 5.4, 5.5]

File Needed: None
Completed Project File Name: *[your initials] Excel 5-10.xlsx*

Create a new workbook and save it as *[your initials] Excel 5-10*. Modify your workbook according to the following guidelines:

- Insert worksheets so that you have five worksheets in the workbook. Name the sheets *Week 1, Week 2, Week 3, Week 4*, and *This Month*.
- Group all the sheets and type the names of five employees in a column as row labels. Use a five- or seven-day workweek, typing the day names as column headings.
- Add a main title. Enter the number of hours worked for each employee for each day worked. If a certain employee did not work on a specific day, type a zero (0) in the cell.
- Total weekly hours by employee and show the total hours worked by day.
- Ungroup the sheets and prepare the *This Month* sheet for consolidation using *Sum* without links.
- Copy one of the sheets to create an *Averages* sheet. Use *Average* to consolidate work hours for all employees with links to the source data.
- Arrange the windows so that you can place a screenshot of the *Averages* worksheet in the *This Month* sheet. Size and position the screenshot to the right of the data. Crop the screenshot, if you can, to remove the unnecessary part of the screenshot.

Using Advanced Functions

CHAPTER OVERVIEW

You have already used basic Excel functions such as *SUM*, *AVERAGE*, *NOW*, and *TODAY*. In addition to these, there are many additional functions that perform more complex and sophisticated calculations for use in business, science, and research. In this chapter, you will become familiar with functions in categories such as database, logical, lookup and reference, financial, and text. In addition to these types of functions, this chapter introduces you to nested functions and statistical calculations.

STUDENT LEARNING OUTCOMES (SLOs)

After completing this chapter, you will be able to:

SLO 6.1 Use database functions such as *DSUM*, *DAVERAGE*, and *DCOUNT* (p. E6-304).

SLO 6.2 Build *AND*, *OR*, and other logical functions and use nested functions (p. E6-307).

SLO 6.3 Use *Lookup & Reference* functions such as *INDEX* and *MATCH* (p. E6-319).

SLO 6.4 Build statistical calculations such as *MAD*, *MSE*, and *STDEV.S* (p. E6-323).

SLO 6.5 Use financial functions such as *PV*, *FV*, and *NPV* (p. E6-328).

SLO 6.6 Use text functions such as *CONCATENATE*, *EXACT*, and *REPLACE* (p. E6-333).

SLO 6.7 Use multiple criteria in functions such as *SUMIFS*, *AVERAGEIFS*, and *COUNTIFS* (p. E6-338).

SLO 6.8 Use the *Watch Window* and *Find and Replace* (p. E6-342).

CASE STUDY

In the *Pause & Practice* projects in this chapter, you continue to work with Excel workbooks for Paradise Lakes Resort (PLR), the northern Minnesota resort company. You create and use advanced functions to enhance the company's forecasting and analysis.

Pause & Practice 6-1: Use database and logical functions.

Pause & Practice 6-2: Create statistical calculations and use reference functions.

Pause & Practice 6-3: Build financial and text functions.

Pause & Practice 6-4: Use statistical functions, the *Watch Window*, and *Find and Replace*.

Using Database Functions

A **database function** performs a mathematical or statistical calculation only if data meets certain criteria. For example, the database function *DSUM* includes in its sum only those cells that match a specified condition or requirement. In a worksheet with sales data for the four locations of Paradise Lakes Resort, for instance, you might use *DSUM* to total only the results for the Cass Lake location.

Common Database Functions

There are terms you will commonly use when working with the *Database* function category. **Database** refers to the entire range of cells, including all rows of data with labels for each column. Each row in a database includes related information and is known as a **record**. The piece of data in a single column is a **field**. When you use database functions, you build a *criteria range* separate from the actual data and type the criteria within that range.

Recall that a *criteria range* was used with *Advanced Filters* in *SLO 4.4: Filtering Data*. The criteria range must be at least two rows. The first row must use column names from the worksheet data but need not use all of them (e.g., Figure 6-1 uses only C2:C3). You type the actual criteria in the second row. You can create a criteria range in empty rows anywhere on the worksheet or on another sheet. In Figure 6-1, the full criteria range is A2:K3 and the database range is A6:K19 (also named *List*). This database function is totaling the *Goal* amounts, located in the *Cass Lake* area from the *List* database range.

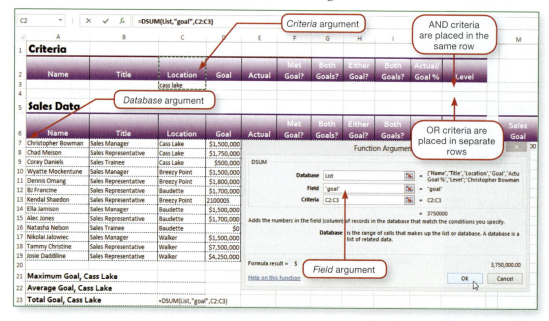

6-1 Database function arguments

You can use multiple rows after the header row in the criteria range to set *AND* or *OR* conditions. If you enter criteria on the same row, they are treated as *AND* conditions. This means both criteria must be met for the record to be displayed.

Database functions all follow the same syntax and have three arguments. The basic syntax is:

FunctionName (database, field, criteria)

The three terms in parentheses—database, field, and criteria—are **arguments**. Recall from *SLO 2.4: Using Functions* that arguments are the pieces of information within parentheses in functions that determine what value a function returns. The first argument, *database,* is the range of cells to be analyzed. This can be a named range of cells or cell references for the range.

The second argument, *field*, refers to the column to be used in the calculation. You can type the column label; you must enclose the label in quotation marks. You can also type the position number of the column in the database. The first column is 1, the second is 2, and so on.

The third argument is *criteria*. This is a cell range in which you have typed the criteria. The criteria argument is not case-sensitive. The criteria range includes the column label in one row and the actual criteria just below it. You can specify *AND* criteria in the same row and *OR* criteria in separate rows. While you are building the function, you can select the criteria range in the worksheet, or you can use its defined name.

The following table shows several database functions and their results:

Database Function	Explanation
DAVERAGE	Averages the values of the cells in the field that meet the criteria
DCOUNT	Counts the cells with values in the field that meet the criteria
DCOUNTA	Counts the cells in the field that are not empty that meet the criteria
DMAX	Displays the largest value in the field that meets the criteria
DMIN	Displays the smallest value in the field that meets the criteria
DSUM	Sums the values of the cells in the field that meet the criteria

You can access database functions from the *Insert Function* dialog box; there is no database button on the *Formulas* tab (Figure 6-2). Alternatively, you can type the name of a database function after an equals sign (=), or you can choose it from the *Formula AutoComplete* list.

HOW TO: Build a Database Function Using the Insert Function Dialog Box

1. Create the criteria range and type the criteria in the appropriate field.
2. Click the cell where you want the result to appear.
3. Click the **Insert Function** button [*Formulas* tab, *Function Library* group].
4. Select the **Or select a category** arrow button and choose **Database** (Figure 6-2).
   - A description of the selected function displays with its syntax in the bottom of the dialog box.
5. Select the database function (e.g., **DSUM**) and click **OK**.
6. In the *Function Arguments* dialog box, click in the **Database** argument text box and select the cell range in the worksheet.
   - When selecting a range, include all data rows and the header row.
   - To display a list of named ranges, press **F3** to open the *Paste Name* dialog box. Choose the name and click **OK**.
7. Click in the **Field** argument text box and type the field name enclosed in quotation marks.
   - Type a number to indicate the field's position in the database instead of typing the label.

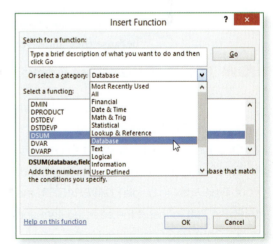

6-2 *Insert Function* dialog box and the Database category

8. Click in the **Criteria** box and select the criteria range in the worksheet (Figure 6-3).

   • You can type the range address.

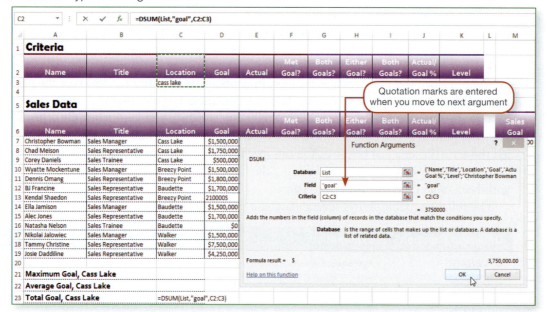

6-3 *Function Arguments* dialog box for *DSUM*

9. Click **OK**.

   • You can press **Enter** to close the dialog box.
   • The *DSUM* function in Figure 6-3 totals the three sales goal values for Cass Lake.

Range Names and Formula AutoComplete

When you are first learning how to build complex functions, the *Function Arguments* dialog box can serve as a useful guide. After you have experience with a particular function, however, you may find it quicker to type the function on your own.

Recall that *Formula AutoComplete* is another way that Excel helps you follow proper syntax while using a function. Capitalizing the function name is unnecessary when you type a formula since *AutoComplete* applies the proper formatting. Defined range names help too, because they allow you to display the list, select the name, and move on.

HOW TO: Build a Database Function Using Formula AutoComplete and Range Names

1. Create the criteria range and type the criteria in the appropriate field.

   • Criteria is not case-sensitive.

2. Click the cell where you want the result to appear.

3. Type = and the beginning letters of the database function name.

   • Type =dav to display *DAVERAGE* in the list of functions.

4. Press **Tab** to insert the selected item and start the function.

   • =DAVERAGE(is entered in the cell.
   • Press **Tab** to insert the selected item and to start the function.

5. Press **F3** to open the *Paste Name* dialog box. Select the range name for the database and click **OK**.

   • You can type the range name to display an *AutoComplete* list and choose it from there.

6. Type a comma (,) to separate the arguments.

   • The next argument **field** is bold in the ScreenTip.

7. Type the field name enclosed in quotation marks.
   - Argument entry is not case-sensitive.
   - If you type a number to indicate the field's position, do not include quotation marks.
8. Type a comma (,) to go to the next argument.
   - The *criteria* argument is bold in the ScreenTip.
9. Select the criteria range in the worksheet (Figure 6-4).
   - You can type the range address.
10. Press **Enter**.
   - The closing parenthesis is automatically entered.
   - Alternatively, you can click the **Enter** button in the *Formula bar*.
   - The *DAVERAGE* function in Figure 6-4 averages the three sales goal values for Cass Lake.

> **ANOTHER WAY**
>
> You can place the criteria range on a different sheet in the workbook.

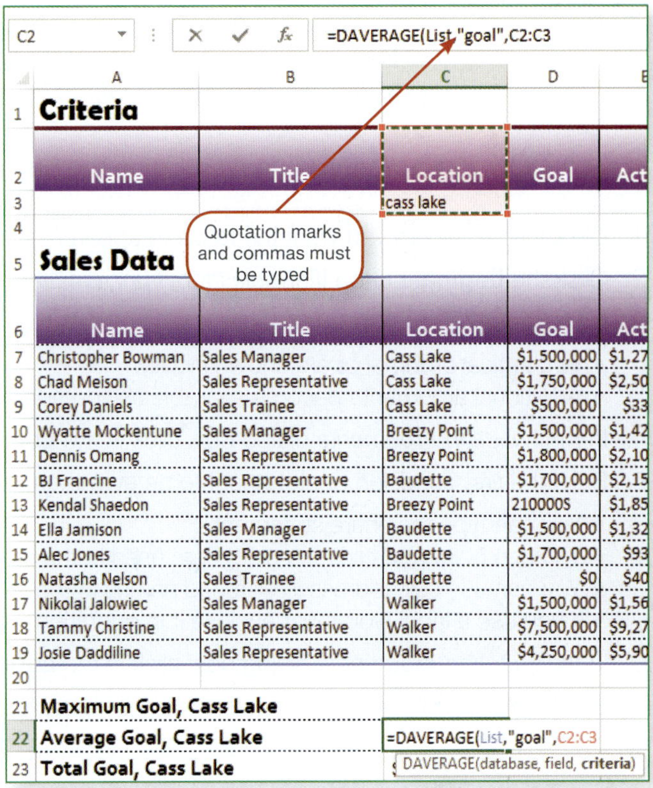

6-4 *DAVERAGE* function typed in worksheet

Building AND, OR, and Nested Functions

In *SLO 2.5: Working with Common Functions*, you learned about the *IF* function, probably the most commonly used logical function. **Logical functions** determine whether or not something is true or if more than one condition exists. The *IF* function can display text or calculate a result. Most logical functions, however, display only TRUE or FALSE as their result.

The AND Function

The *AND* function is used to define more than one condition that must be met for a TRUE result. For example, Paradise Lakes Resort sets individual goals for each employee, but the organization also sets an overall goal that is an additional incentive for everyone. The company can use an *AND* function to display if a given employee meets both goals.

The syntax for an *AND* function is:

=AND(LogicalN)

The *AND* and *OR* functions have one argument named *LogicalN. N* is a number; there can be arguments named *Logical1, Logical2, Logical3*, all the way to *Logical255*. These are the criteria or conditions that must be met for the result to be TRUE in an *AND* condition.

> **MORE INFO**
>
> *AND* functions can be very restrictive or limiting when many conditions must be met.

If you set five arguments in an *AND* formula, every one must be met for the result to be *TRUE*. If any of those five conditions are not true, the result will be *FALSE*.

In each *LogicalN* argument, you build a simple statement that indicates what must be true. For example, an argument might be that "**E7<D7**", indicating that the value in cell E7 must be less than the value in cell D7 for the function to be true.

HOW TO: Build an AND Function Using the Function Arguments Dialog Box

1. Click the cell where you want the result to appear.
2. Click the **Logical** button [*Formulas* tab, *Function Library* group].
3. Choose **AND**.
   - Two logical arguments are shown initially.
   - Additional arguments become available as you add them in the *Function Arguments* dialog box.
4. In the *Function Arguments* dialog box, click in the **Logical1** argument box.
5. Build the first condition or statement to be evaluated.
   - You can type the entire statement.
   - You can point and click to select cells used in the statement.
   - You can use cell addresses or range names in the statement.
   - If you use a label, you must enclose it in quotation marks.
6. In the *Function Arguments* dialog box, click in the **Logical2** box. A third argument box opens.
7. Build the second condition or statement to be evaluated (Figure 6-5).

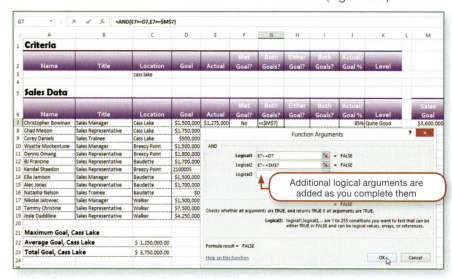

6-5 *AND* function in the *Function Arguments* dialog box

8. Build additional conditions or statements as needed.
9. Click **OK** or press **Enter** (Figure 6-6).
   - If both or all conditions are met, the word *TRUE* appears in the cell.
   - If any one of the conditions is not met, the word *FALSE* appears in the cell.

6-6 *AND* function results

The OR Function

An *OR* function is much less restrictive than an *AND* statement. In an *OR* function, if any one of the arguments is true, the result is *TRUE*. All arguments have to be false for *FALSE* to be the result.

The syntax for an *OR* function is:

=OR(LogicalN)

> **MORE INFO**
>
> Decide whether to use absolute or relative cell references in *AND* or *OR* functions by determining how copying will be done.

OR functions use the same *LogicalN* argument as *AND* functions. You can use as many as are required, up to 255.

HOW TO: Build an OR Function

1. Click the cell where you want the result to appear.
2. Type **=or** and press **Tab**.
   - *=OR(* is entered in the cell.
   - The first argument *logical1* is bold in the ScreenTip.
3. Build the first condition or statement to be evaluated.
   - You can type the statement.
   - You can point and click to select cells.
   - You can use addresses or range names.
   - If you use a label, you must enclose it in quotation marks.
4. Type a comma (,) to separate the arguments (Figure 6-7).
   - The next argument *logical2* is bold in the ScreenTip.
5. Build the second condition or statement to be evaluated (Figure 6-7).

6-7 *OR* function with two arguments

6. If necessary, type a comma (,) to go to the next argument.
   - The *logicaln* argument is bold in the ScreenTip.
7. Build additional conditions or statements as needed.
8. Press **Enter**.
   - If any condition is met, the word *TRUE* appears in the cell.
   - If none of the conditions are met, the word *FALSE* appears in the cell.

The IF Function with AND and OR

A *nested function* is a function within a function. Logical functions are commonly nested. For example, you can use *AND* and *OR* with an *IF* function to build a statement that checks for more than one requirement. In a simple *IF* formula, you can check one logical test and set one value if it is true and another value if it is false. When *AND* or *OR* is nested within an *IF* function, however, you can use multiple tests. And you can display a result other than *TRUE* or *FALSE*, because the *IF* function controls that part of the result.

The following table illustrates examples of nesting *AND* or *OR* within an *IF* function. In the examples shown in the table, assume that the *IF* function is located in cell D4.

Function	Arguments	Explanation
=IF(C4>150000, 5000,0)	Logical_test = C4>150000 Value_if_true = 5000 Value_if_false = 0	If the value in cell C4 is greater than 150,000, cell D4 will display 5,000. If the value in cell C4 is less than or equal to 150,000, it will display 0.
=IF(AND (C4>150000,C7>125000), 5000,0)	Logical_test = C4>150000 and C7>125000 Value_if_true = 5000 Value_if_false = 0	If the value in cell C4 is greater than 150,000 **and** if the value in cell C7 is greater than 125,000, cell D4 will display 5,000. If either of these conditions is false, cell D4 will display 0.
=IF(OR (C4>150000,C7>125000), 5000,0)	Logical_test = C4>150000 or C7>125000 Value_if_true = 5000 Value_if_false = 0	If the value in cell C4 is greater than 150,000 **or** if the value in cell C7 is greater than 125,000, cell D4 will display 5,000. Cell D4 will display 0 when the value in cell C4 is equal to or less than 150,000 **or** the value in cell C7 is equal to or less than 125,000.

> **MORE INFO**
>
> Do not include commas as thousand separators in formula syntax or Excel will mistake the comma for a new argument.

You can type a nested function. However, when you do so, you must know the syntax of the function and be sure to use parentheses as needed. You can also use the *Function Arguments* dialog box to build a nested function. When you use the dialog box, it updates to show the current function and supplies the appropriate parentheses.

> **MORE INFO**
>
> You need to use opening and closing parentheses in pairs in nested functions.

HOW TO: Nest AND and IF Functions

1. Click the cell where you want the result to appear.
2. Type =if(to open the ScreenTip.
   - The *logical_test* argument is bold; the *logical_test* argument is the *AND* function.

3. Type **and** and press **Tab**.

   - The ScreenTip displays arguments for the *AND* function.

4. Enter the first test and type a comma (,) (Figure 6-8).

   - You can click to select a cell rather than typing the reference.
   - Use absolute or relative references as required.

	C	D	E	F	G	H	I	J	K	L	M
	Location	Goal	Actual	Met Goal?	Both Goals?	Either Goal?	Both Goals?	Actual/ Goal %	Level		Sales Goal
6											
7	Cass Lake	$1,500,000	$1,275,000	No	FALSE		=if(AND(E7>=D7,		Quite Good		$3,600,000
8	Cass Lake	$1,750,000	$2,500,000	Yes			AND(logical1, **[logical2]**, [logical3], ...)				

6-8 *AND* function is the *logical_test* argument

5. Enter each argument, followed by a comma.

6. After the last argument for the *AND* condition, type a closing parenthesis and a comma), (Figure 6-9).

   - The focus returns to the *IF* function.

	C	D	E	F	G	H	I	J	K	L	M
	Location	Goal	Actual	Met Goal?	Both Goals?	Either Goal?	Both Goals?	Actual/ Goal %	Level		Sales Goal
6											
7	Cass Lake	$1,500,000	$1,275,000	No	FALSE		=if(AND(E7>=D7,E7>=$M$7),		Quite Good		$3,600,000
8	Cass Lake	$1,750,000	$2,500,000	Yes			IF(logical_test, **[value_if_true]**, [value_if_false])				

6-9 Closing parenthesis returns focus to *IF* function

7. Enter the *value_if_true* argument.

   - If the argument is text, enclose it in quotation marks.
   - Click a cell reference or type its address.
   - Use absolute or relative references as required.

8. Type a comma (,) to move to the next argument.

9. Enter the *value_if_false* argument.

10. Type the closing parenthesis) (Figure 6-10).

> Parentheses pairs are color-matched

	C	D	E	F	G	H	I	J	K	L	M
	Location	Goal	Actual	Met Goal?	Both Goals?	Either Goal?	Both Goals?	Actual/ Goal %	Level		Sales Goal
6											
7	Cass Lake	$1,500,000	$1,275,000	No		=IF(AND(E7>=D7,E7>=$M$7),"Met both","No")					$3,600,000
8	Cass Lake	$1,750,000	$2,500,000	Yes							

6-10 *AND* function nested within *IF*

11. Press **Enter**.

   - You can click the **Enter** button on the *Formula bar*.
   - The result of the formula in Figure 6-10 for the two Cass Lake locations is *No* for the first cell, and *Met both* for the second.

Nested IF Functions

Nested *IF* functions are fairly common. Your course grades, for example, might be calculated with a nested *IF* function. If you receive 92 or more points, you receive an A grade. If you receive 84 up to 91 points, you receive a B. And if you receive 76 up to 83 points, you will earn a C grade. The function for this calculation is as follows:

$$=IF(D2>=92,\text{"A"}, IF(D2>=84,\text{"B"}, IF(D2>=76,\text{"C"},\text{"D"})))$$

In a nested *IF* function, another *IF* function is the *value_if_true* or *value_if_false* argument. In this example, the first logical test is if the value in cell D2 is 92 or higher. If that is true, the result is *A*. If that is false, the next *IF* condition is tested. The second *IF* tests if the value in cell D2 is 84 or higher. If it is, the result is *B*. If that's not true, the third *IF* statement runs and checks if the value is 76 or higher. If it is, a *C* displays. For anything else, any value below 76 displays a *D*.

Most nested *IF* functions can be tested from the higher value to the lower or vice versa. With experience, you will learn how to build the shortest function, but when you are first starting out, it is often less difficult to start at the high value.

Whether you use the dialog box to build a nested function or if you type it, the parentheses are color-coded, which can help you follow the logic of your formula. For many functions, Excel enters the closing parenthesis for you. When a parenthesis is missing, however, Excel displays a message box with a suggested fix.

While working with nested functions from the dialog box, you can switch between functions by clicking anywhere within the function name in the *Formula bar*. When you do this, the *Function Arguments* dialog box displays the arguments for that function.

HOW TO: Create a Nested IF Function Using the Function Arguments Dialog Box

1. Click the cell where you want the result to appear.
2. Click the **Logical** button [*Formulas* tab, *Function Library* group].
3. Choose **IF**.

    • The *Function Arguments* dialog box enters parentheses and quotation marks for you.

4. Enter the *logical_test* argument.
5. Enter the *value_if_true* result.

    • If the conditions in the *logical_test* argument are true, this result will appear.
    • You do not need to use quotation marks for text entries in the *Function Arguments* dialog box.
    • Use uppercase and lowercase as preferred for results.

6. Click in the **value_if_false** box.

    • If the *logical_test* is not true, the next *IF* statement will run.

7. Click **IF** in the *Name* box (Figure 6-11).

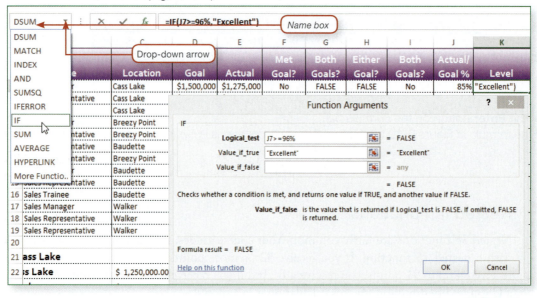

6-11 *Name box* with *IF* function

• When *IF* does not appear in the *Name* box, click the **Name box** arrow and choose **IF** from the list or choose **More Functions** to locate *IF*.
• A new *Function Arguments* dialog box opens for the second *IF* function.
• The *Formula bar* shows the function to this point.

8. Enter the *logical_test* argument for the second *IF* condition.

9. Enter the *value_if_true* result for the second *IF* condition.

   - If the conditions in the *logical_test* argument are true, this result will appear.

10. Click in the **value_if_false** box.

    - If there are no more *logical_tests*, enter the final *value_if_false* entry (Figure 6-12).
    - If the *logical_test* in the second *IF* function is not true, and there is another condition to be tested, add another *IF* function, repeating steps 7–10.

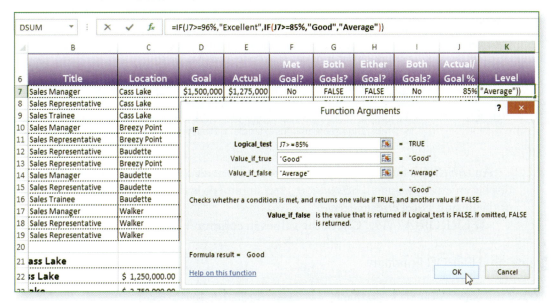

6-12 Nested *IF* functions in the *Function Arguments* dialog box

11. Click **OK**. The result for the function for K7 in Figure 6-12 is *Good*.

The IFERROR Function

Some formula errors show an Excel error value message. These messages hint at what is wrong, but may not always help you or others to solve the problem. There are two error value messages shown in Figure 6-13. When you build a worksheet in which you can clearly identify a common error that you or someone else might make, you can use the *IFERROR* function to display your own custom error message.

A common error, for example, might be typing the letter "o" instead of a zero (0). Excel would display #VALUE! in the cell, and a user may not immediately see what is wrong. To prevent this, you could create your own custom error message to read, "Check that all entries are numbers."

The *IFERROR* function works only for formulas that could return one of these messages. If a formula is just poor mathematics or the wrong reference, it results

	F	G	H	I	J	K
6	Met Goal?	Both Goals?	Either Goal?	Both Goals?	Actual/ Goal %	Level
7	No	FALSE	FALSE	No	85%	Good
8	Yes	FALSE	TRUE	No	143%	Excellent
9	No	FALSE	FALSE	No	66%	Average
10	No	FALSE	FALSE	No	95%	Good
11	Yes	FALSE	TRUE	No	117%	Excellent
12	Yes	FALSE	TRUE	No	126%	Excellent
13	No	FALSE	FALSE	No	#VALUE!	#VALUE!
14	No	FALSE	FALSE	No	88%	Good
15	No	FALSE	FALSE	No	55%	Average
16	Yes	FALSE	TRUE	No	#DIV/0!	#DIV/0!
17	Yes	FALSE	TRUE	No	104%	Excellent
18	Yes	TRUE	TRUE	Met both	124%	Excellent
19	Yes	TRUE	TRUE	Met both	139%	Excellent

6-13 Standard, default error messages

in an error triangle and a suggested fix; an *IFERROR* function is not relevant and does not display its message. The following table lists error values and their descriptions:

Error Value	Description
#N/A	A value or an argument is missing.
#VALUE!	An incorrect data type is used (for example, a label is used instead of a value).
#REF!	A cell reference is empty, usually because cells were deleted.
#DIV/0!	The formula divides by zero (0) or an empty cell.
#NUM!	The formula uses an invalid numeric entry (for example, it could be a wrong data type or a negative number instead of a required positive value).
#NAME?	The formula uses unrecognized text such as a misspelled function, sheet, or range name.
#NULL!	The formula refers to an intersection of two cell ranges that do not intersect, or uses an incorrect range separator (for example, a semicolon or comma instead of a colon).

An *IFERROR* function has two arguments. The **value** argument is the formula that might display an error message. The *value_if_error* argument is the text that should appear in place of the default Excel error message.

=IFERROR(A7/A9, "Check the values in column A.")

HOW TO: Create an IFERROR Function

1. Click the cell where you want the result to appear.
   - This is the cell that may display an error message.
   - Delete the cell contents, if any.
2. Click the **Logical** button [*Formulas* tab, *Function Library* group].
3. Choose **IFERROR**.
4. Enter the *Value* argument.
   - You can type the formula using lowercase letters, or you can select cells in the worksheet.
   - You don't need to type the equals sign when you use the *Function Arguments* dialog box.
5. Enter the *Value_if_error* argument (Figure 6-14).
   - Use uppercase, lowercase, and punctuation as you want it to appear in your message.
   - You don't need to type quotation marks when you use the *Function Arguments* dialog box.
6. Click **OK**.
   - The error message appears only when necessary (Figure 6-15).

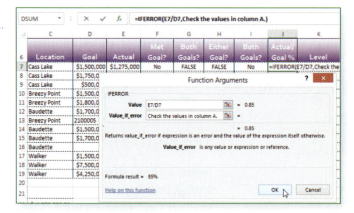

6-14 *IFERROR* with both arguments complete

6-15 Custom error message appears in place of Excel default message

For this project you complete several calculations on the Sales Quota Data worksheet for Paradise Lakes Resort. You use three database functions to calculate values about the Cass Lake location. You also use several logical functions to calculate data about various sales persons' accomplishments.

File Needed: *PLRFinancials-06.xlsx*
Completed Project File Name: ***[your initials] PP E6-1.xlsx***

1. Open the ***PLRFinancials-06.xlsx*** workbook. Click the **Enable Editing** button if prompted.

2. Save the workbook as ***[your initials] PP E6-1***.

3. Build a *DSUM* function using the *Function Arguments* dialog box.
   a. Click the **Sales Quota Data** sheet tab.
   b. In cell **C3**, type cass lake. Criteria is not case-sensitive.
   c. Click cell **C23** and click the **Insert Function** button [*Formulas* tab, *Function Library* group].
   d. Select the **Or select a category** arrow button, and then choose **Database**.
   e. Select **DSUM** and click **OK**.
   f. In the *Database* argument text box, press **F3** to open the *Paste Name* dialog box. The list includes all defined names in the workbook.
   g. Choose **List** and click **OK**.
   h. In the *Field* argument box, type goal. Argument entries are not case sensitive, and quotation marks are entered automatically.
   i. Click in the **Criteria** argument box and select cells **C2:C3** (Figure 6-16).

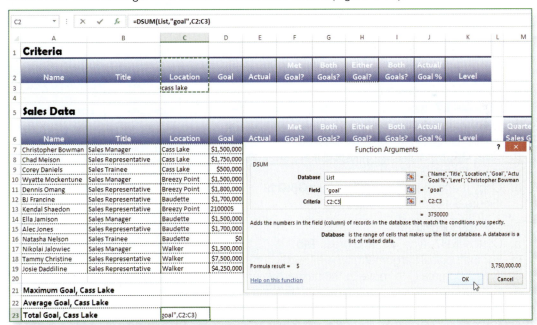

6-16 *DSUM* and its arguments

   j. Click **OK**. The total for Cass Lake is $3,750,000.00

4. Type a *DAVERAGE* function.
   a. Click cell **C22**.
   b. Type =dav to display the *Formula AutoComplete* list and press **Tab** to choose *DAVERAGE*.

c. For the *Database* argument, select cells **A6:K19**. Excel supplies the range name automatically.

d. Type a comma (,) to move to the next argument.

e. For the *Field* argument, type "goal" (include the quotation marks).

f. Type a comma (,) to move to the last argument.

g. For the *Criteria* argument, select cells **C2:C3** (Figure 6-17).

h. Press **Enter**. The closing parenthesis is automatically supplied. The average for Cass Lake is $1,250,000.00.

5. Use the *Function Arguments* dialog box or type to create a *DMAX* function in cell **C21**.

a. Use the same argument ranges listed in step 4.

b. The maximum value for Cass Lake is $1,750,000.00.

6. Use the *Function Arguments* dialog box to build an *AND* function.

a. Click cell **G7** and click the **Logical** button [*Formulas* tab, *Function Library* group].

b. Choose **AND**.

c. In the *Function Arguments* dialog box, click in the **Logical1** argument box.

d. Click cell **E7**, type >=, and click cell **D7**. The first condition is that the value in cell E7 be greater than or equal to the goal in cell D7.

e. Click in the **Logical2** box.

f. Click cell **E7**, type >=, click cell **M7**, and press **F4**. In order to copy the formula down the column, the reference to cell M7 must be absolute.

g. Click **OK**. Because not all logical tests are true, the result for cell G7 is *FALSE*.

h. Copy the formula in cell **G7** to cells **G8:G19** (Figure 6-18).

7. Type an *OR* function.

a. Click cell **H7**, type =or, and press **Tab**.

b. For the *Logical1* argument, type e7>=d7.

c. Type a comma (,) to move to the next argument.

d. For the *Logical2* argument, type e7>=m7 and press **F4** (Figure 6-19).

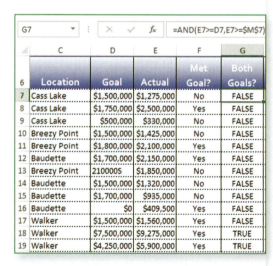

6-17 DAVERAGE and its arguments

G7 fx =AND(E7>=D7,E7>=$M$7)

	C	D	E	F	G
6	Location	Goal	Actual	Met Goal?	Both Goals?
7	Cass Lake	$1,500,000	$1,275,000	No	FALSE
8	Cass Lake	$1,750,000	$2,500,000	Yes	FALSE
9	Cass Lake	$500,000	$330,000	No	FALSE
10	Breezy Point	$1,500,000	$1,425,000	No	FALSE
11	Breezy Point	$1,800,000	$2,100,000	Yes	FALSE
12	Baudette	$1,700,000	$2,150,000	Yes	FALSE
13	Breezy Point	2100005	$1,850,000	No	FALSE
14	Baudette	$1,500,000	$1,320,000	No	FALSE
15	Baudette	$1,700,000	$935,000	No	FALSE
16	Baudette	$0	$409,500	Yes	FALSE
17	Walker	$1,500,000	$1,560,000	Yes	FALSE
18	Walker	$7,500,000	$9,275,000	Yes	TRUE
19	Walker	$4,250,000	$5,900,000	Yes	TRUE

6-18 AND function copied in the worksheet

	D	E	F	G	H	I	J	K	L	M
6	Goal	Actual	Met Goal?	Both Goals?	Either Goal?	Both Goals?	Actual/Goal %	Level		Quarterly Sales Goal
7	$1,500,000	$1,275,000	No		=OR(e7>=d7,e7>=$M$7)		85%			$3,600,000
8	$1,750,000	$2,500,000	Yes		FALS OR(logical1, [logical2], [logical3], ...)		143%			

6-19 OR function typed in the worksheet

e. Type a closing parenthesis).

f. Press **Enter**. Because neither logical test is true, the result for cell H7 is *FALSE*.

g. Copy the formula in cell **H7** to cells **H8:H19**. *OR* functions are less restrictive, so there are more *TRUE* results (Figure 6-20).

8. Nest an *AND* and *IF* function.

   a. Click cell **I7**.

   b. Type **=if(an** and press **Tab** (Figure 6-21). The focus is now on the *AND* formula.

   c. For the *Logical1* argument, type **e7>=d7**.

   d. Type a comma (,) to move to the *Logical2* argument.

   e. For the *Logical2* argument, type **e7>=m7** and press **F4**.

   f. Type a closing parenthesis). The focus within the formula returns to the *IF* function.

   g. Type a comma (,) to complete the *logical_test* argument.

   h. For the *value_if_true* argument, type **"Met both"** including the quotation marks.

   i. Type a comma (,)to move to the *value_if_false* argument.

   j. Type **"No"** (Figure 6-22).

	H7		× ✓ *fx*	=OR(E7>=D7,E7>=$M$7)		
	C	D	E	F	G	H
				Met	Both	Either
6	Location	Goal	Actual	Goal?	Goals?	Goal?
7	Cass Lake	$1,500,000	$1,275,000	No	FALSE	FALSE
8	Cass Lake	$1,750,000	$2,500,000	Yes	FALSE	TRUE
9	Cass Lake	$500,000	$330,000	No	FALSE	FALSE
10	Breezy Point	$1,500,000	$1,425,000	No	FALSE	FALSE
11	Breezy Point	$1,800,000	$2,100,000	Yes	FALSE	TRUE
12	Baudette	$1,700,000	$2,150,000	Yes	FALSE	TRUE
13	Breezy Point	210000S	$1,850,000	No	FALSE	FALSE
14	Baudette	$1,500,000	$1,320,000	No	FALSE	FALSE
15	Baudette	$1,700,000	$935,000	No	FALSE	FALSE
16	Baudette	$0	$409,500	Yes	FALSE	TRUE
17	Walker	$1,500,000	$1,560,000	Yes	FALSE	TRUE
18	Walker	$7,500,000	$9,275,000	Yes	TRUE	TRUE
19	Walker	$4,250,000	$5,900,000	Yes	TRUE	TRUE

6-20 *OR* function results in column H

	G	H	I	J	K
	Both	Either	Both	Actual/	
6	Goals?	Goal?	Goals?	Goal %	Level
7	FALSE	FALSE	=if(AND(	85%	
8	FALSE	TRUE	AND(logical1, [logical2], ...)		

6-21 *AND* function as logical test for *IF* function

	DSUM		× ✓ *fx*	=if(AND(e7>=d7,e7>=$M$7),"Met both", "No"				
	D	E	F	IF(logical_test, [value_if_true], [value_if_false])		K	L	M
			Met	Both	Either	Both	Actual/			Quarterly
6	Goal	Actual	Goal?	Goals?	Goal?	Goals?	Goal %	Level	Sales Goal
7	$1,500,000	$1,275,000	No	=if(AND(e7>=d7,e7>=$M$7),"Met both", "No"					$3,600,000

6-22 Arguments for the *IF* function

k. Type a closing parenthesis) and press **Enter**. Cell I7 displays "No".

l. Copy the formula in cell **I7** to cells **I8:I19**. Widen the column to show the results, if necessary (Figure 6-23).

9. Create a nested *IF* function.

   a. Click the cell **K7**.

   b. Click the **Logical** button [*Formulas* tab, *Function Library* group] and choose **IF**.

	D	E	F	G	H	I	J	K	L	M
			Met	Both	Either	Both	Actual/			Quarterly
6	Goal	Actual	Goal?	Goals?	Goal?	Goals?	Goal %	Level		Sales Goal
7	$1,500,000	$1,275,000	No	FALSE	FALSE	No	85%			$3,600,000
8	$1,750,000	$2,500,000	Yes	FALSE	TRUE	No	143%			
9	$500,000	$330,000	No	FALSE	FALSE	No	66%			
10	$1,500,000	$1,425,000	No	FALSE	FALSE	No	95%			
11	$1,800,000	$2,100,000	Yes	FALSE	TRUE	No	117%			
12	$1,700,000	$2,150,000	Yes	FALSE	TRUE	No	126%			
13	210000S	$1,850,000	No	FALSE	FALSE	No	#VALUE!			
14	$1,500,000	$1,320,000	No	FALSE	FALSE	No	88%			
15	$1,700,000	$935,000	No	FALSE	FALSE	No	55%			
16	$0	$409,500	Yes	FALSE	TRUE	No	#DIV/0!			
17	$1,500,000	$1,560,000	Yes	FALSE	TRUE	No	104%			
18	$7,500,000	$9,275,000	Yes	TRUE	TRUE	Met both	124%			
19	$4,250,000	$5,900,000	Yes	TRUE	TRUE	Met both	139%			

6-23 Results for nested function in column I

c. In the *Logical_test* box, click cell **J7** and type >=96%.

d. Click in the **Value_if_true** box and type Excellent. Quotation marks are not necessary when you use the *Function Arguments* dialog box. If the percentage in cell J7 is 96% or higher, the formula shows *Excellent*.

e. Click in the **Value_if_false** box. If the first *Logical_test* is not true, the nested *IF* statement runs.

f. Click **IF** in the *Name* box. You can choose *IF* from the list in the *Name* box, or choose **More Functions** from the list and find and select **IF**.

g. In the *Logical_test* box for the second *IF* condition, click cell **J7** and type >=85%. If the percentage in cell J7 is not 96% or higher, it is checked to see if it is 85% or higher.

h. Click in the **Value_if_true** box and type Good. If the value in cell J7 is greater than 85%, this text is shown.

i. Click in the **Value_if_false** box.

j. Type Average. If the percentage in cell J7 is not 96% or higher and is not 85% or higher, this result appears in the cell (Figure 6-24).

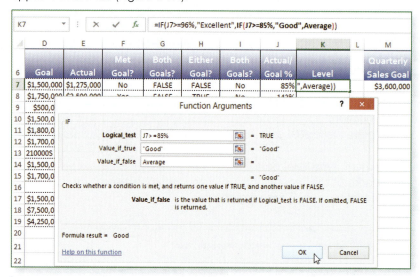

6-24 Completed nested *IF* is visible in the *Formula bar*

k. Click **OK**.

l. Copy the formula in cell **K7** to cells **K8:K19**. Widen the column to show the results, if necessary, and complete the borders to match the rest of the data (Figure 6-25).

	E	F	G	H	I	J	K	L	M
K7				fx		=IF(J7>=96%,"Excellent",IF(J7>=85%,"Good","Average"))			
6	Actual	Met Goal?	Both Goals?	Either Goal?	Both Goals?	Actual/ Goal %	Level		Quarterly Sales Goal
7	$1,275,000	No	FALSE	FALSE	No	85%	Good		$3,600,000
8	$2,500,000	Yes	FALSE	TRUE	No	143%	Excellent		
9	$330,000	No	FALSE	FALSE	No	66%	Average		
10	$1,425,000	No	FALSE	FALSE	No	95%	Good		
11	$2,100,000	Yes	FALSE	TRUE	No	117%	Excellent		
12	$2,150,000	Yes	FALSE	TRUE	No	126%	Excellent		
13	$1,850,000	No	FALSE	FALSE	No	#VALUE!	#VALUE!		
14	$1,320,000	No	FALSE	FALSE	No	88%	Good		
15	$935,000	No	FALSE	FALSE	No	55%	Average		
16	$409,500	Yes	FALSE	TRUE	No	#DIV/0!	#DIV/0!		
17	$1,560,000	Yes	FALSE	TRUE	No	104%	Excellent		
18	$9,275,000	Yes	TRUE	TRUE	Met both	124%	Excellent		
19	$5,900,000	Yes	TRUE	TRUE	Met both	139%	Excellent		

6-25 Nested *IF* function results in column K

10. Create an *IFERROR* function.
    a. Click the cell **J7**. Delete the contents of this cell.
    b. Click the **Logical** button [*Formulas* tab, *Function Library* group] and choose **IFERROR**.
    c. In the *Value* argument box, click cell **E7**, type /, and click cell **D7**. If the formula that determines the percentage results in an error, your message is displayed instead of a standard error value message.
    d. Click in the **Value_if_error** box.
    e. Type Check values in columns E and D. including the period.
    f. Click **OK**.
    g. Copy the formula in cell **J7** to cells **J8:J19**. Widen the columns as needed.

11. Save and close the workbook (Figure 6-26).

	Name	Title	Location	Goal	Actual	Met Goal?	Both Goals?	Either Goal?	Both Goals?	Actual/ Goal %	Level			Quarterly Sales Goal
Criteria														
	Name	Title	Location	Goal	Actual	Met Goal?	Both Goals?	Either Goal?	Both Goals?	Actual/ Goal %	Level			
			cass lake											
Sales Data														
	Name	Title	Location	Goal	Actual	Met Goal?	Both Goals?	Either Goal?	Both Goals?	Actual/ Goal %	Level			$3,600,000
7 Christopher Bowman	Sales Manager	Cass Lake	$1,500,000	$1,275,000	No	FALSE	FALSE	No		85%	Good			
8 Chad Meison	Sales Representative	Cass Lake	$1,750,000	$2,500,000	Yes	FALSE	TRUE	No		143%	Excellent			
9 Corey Daniels	Sales Trainee	Cass Lake	$500,000	$330,000	No	FALSE	FALSE	No		66%	Average			
10 Wyatte Mockentune	Sales Manager	Breezy Point	$1,500,000	$1,425,000	No	FALSE	FALSE	No		95%	Good			
11 Dennis Omang	Sales Representative	Breezy Point	$1,800,000	$2,100,000	Yes	FALSE	TRUE	No		117%	Excellent			
12 BJ Francine	Sales Representative	Baudette	$1,700,000	$2,150,000	Yes	FALSE	TRUE	No		126%	Excellent			
13 Kendal Shaedon	Sales Representative	Breezy Point	2100005	$1,850,000	No	FALSE	FALSE	No	Check values in columns E and D.		Excellent			
14 Ella Jamison	Sales Manager	Baudette	$1,500,000	$1,320,000	No	FALSE	FALSE	No		88%	Good			
15 Alec Jones	Sales Representative	Baudette	$1,700,000	$935,000	No	FALSE	FALSE	No		55%	Average			
16 Natasha Nelson	Sales Trainee	Baudette	$0	$409,500	Yes	FALSE	TRUE	No	Check values in columns E and D.		Excellent			
17 Nikolai Jalowiec	Sales Manager	Walker	$1,500,000	$1,560,000	Yes	FALSE	TRUE	No		104%	Excellent			
18 Tammy Christine	Sales Representative	Walker	$7,500,000	$9,275,000	Yes	TRUE	TRUE	Met both		124%	Excellent			
19 Josie Daddiline	Sales Representative	Walker	$4,250,000	$5,900,000	Yes	TRUE	TRUE	Met both		139%	Excellent			
21 **Maximum Goal, Cass Lake**			$1,750,000.00											
22 **Average Goal, Cass Lake**			$1,250,000.00											
23 **Total Goal, Cass Lake**			$3,750,000.00											

Sales Quota Data | Inventory | Forecasts | Financial Planner | Employee Data | Marketing

6-26 Completed PP E6-1 worksheet

Using Reference Functions

In *SLO 2.5: Working with Common Functions*, you used the *LOOKUP* functions to find matching data in a worksheet. You can also use Excel's *Lookup & Reference* functions, such as *INDEX* or *MATCH*, to locate data in a list. These functions are well suited to large worksheets with many rows of data in which it would be time-consuming to find a specific piece of information.

The INDEX Function

The *INDEX* function displays the contents of the cell at the intersection of an identified column and row. In a large inventory sheet that is sorted by various fields, for example, you could use this to determine what product description is in a list based on a row and column intersection with the current sort order.

The *INDEX* function has two possible arguments lists. When you use the *Function Arguments* dialog box to build this function, you choose which list to use. The first argument list includes an array or range of cells, the row number, and the column number.

The syntax for an *INDEX* function (type one) is:

=INDEX(array, row_num, column_num)

SLO 6.3 Using Reference Functions   E6-319

The syntax for an *INDEX* function (type two) is:
=INDEX(reference, row_num, [column_num], [area_num])

> ### MORE INFO
> The second argument list includes *reference, row_num, column_num, area_num*. With this list, you can refer to multiple numbered arrays.

The first argument, *array*, is the cell range to be searched. This can be a range you select in the worksheet or a range name. The *row_num* argument is the row number in the array. The *column_num* argument is optional. If the array is only one column of cells, you do not need to specify a column number.

HOW TO: Create an INDEX Function

1. Click the cell for the result.
2. Click the **Lookup & Reference** button [*Formulas* tab, *Function Library* group].
3. Choose **INDEX**.
   - The *Select Arguments* dialog box shows the two arguments lists for this function (Figure 6-27).
4. Select the first argument list **array, row_num, column_num** and click **OK**.
5. For the *Array* argument, select the cell range in the worksheet.
   - Alternatively, you can press **F3** and paste the range name.
6. For the *Row_num* argument, type the row number.
7. For the *Column_num* argument, type the column number (Figure 6-28).
8. Click **OK**.
   - The result displays the contents of the cell indicated in the function. Figure 6-28 returns *T-Shirt* as the result of the intersection of row one and column two.

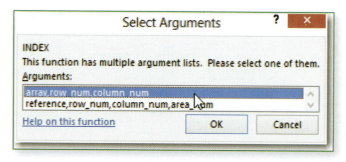

6-27 *Select Arguments* dialog box for *INDEX*

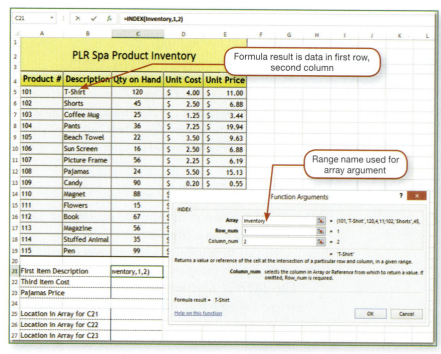

6-28 *Function Arguments* dialog box for *INDEX*

The MATCH Function

The *MATCH* function looks for data that you specify and returns the relative location of the data that matches the search. The *MATCH* function has three arguments: *lookup_value*, *lookup_array*, and *match_type*.

The syntax for a *MATCH* function is:

=MATCH(lookup_value, lookup_array, [match_type])

The *lookup_value* argument is the text or value that you want to locate. You can use a cell reference for this argument or enter it directly. *Lookup_array* is the cell range, either a single row or a single column. You can select the range or use a defined name. These two arguments are required.

The *match_type* argument establishes how the *lookup_value* is compared to the values in the *lookup_array*. The *match_type* argument is optional but it can have an unexpected effect. The following table explains how this argument is used:

Match_type Argument	Result
1 or omitted	The function finds the largest value that is less than or equal to the lookup_value. The lookup_array must be sorted in ascending order.
0	The function finds the first value that exactly matches the lookup_value. The lookup_array can be in any order.
–1	The function finds the smallest value that is greater than or equal to the lookup_value. The lookup_array must be sorted in descending order.

> ### ANOTHER WAY
>
> Click the **Recently Used** button in the *Function Library* group in the *Formulas* tab to choose a function that you have been using.

HOW TO: Create a MATCH Function

1. Click the cell where you want the result to appear.
2. Click the **Lookup & Reference** button [*Formulas* tab, *Function Library* group].
3. Choose **MATCH**.
4. For the *Lookup_value* argument, select the cell with data to be matched.
   - You can type a text entry; quotation marks are entered automatically.
5. For the *Lookup_array* argument, select the cell range in the worksheet.
   - If the range has been named, press **F3** to paste the name.
6. Enter the *Match_type* argument if necessary (Figure 6-29).
   - Type 0 to find an exact match.
   - Type 1 or leave the text box empty when the cell range is sorted in ascending order and you want to find the closest match that is greater than the lookup value.
7. Click **OK**. Figure 6-29 returns *1* as the result of the position of *T-Shirt* in the specified array.

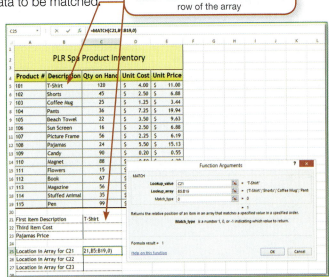

6-29 Function Arguments dialog box for MATCH

You can nest *INDEX* and *MATCH* functions so that they work similarly to *VLOOKUP*. For example, the following syntax =**INDEX(A4:E19, MATCH("T–Shirt", B4:B19,0), MATCH ("Unit Cost", A4:E4,0))** will return *$4.00* for the cost of a T-Shirt in Figure 6-29.

HOW TO: Nest a MATCH Function in an INDEX Function

1. Click the cell where you want the result to appear.
2. Type =in and press **Tab** to start the *INDEX* function.
   - For the *array* argument, press **F3**. Choose the range name and click **OK**.
   - Type a comma (,) to move to the *row_num* argument.
3. Type m and press **Tab** to nest the *MATCH* function.
   - For the *lookup_value* argument, type "The Item Name", (e.g., "pajamas",) including the quotation marks and a comma to move to the next argument.
   - For the *lookup_array* argument, select the cells range and type a comma (,).
   - For the *match_type* argument, click **0** in the AutoComplete list and press **Tab** to select it (Figure 6-30).
   - Type a closing parenthesis) to return to the *INDEX* function.

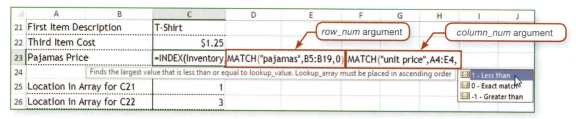

6-30 Choose the *match_type* argument from the list

4. Type a comma (,) to move to the *Column_num* argument, type m and press **Tab** to start a second nested *MATCH* function.
   - For the *lookup_value*, type "The Item Name", (e.g., "pajamas",) with the comma.
   - For the *lookup_array*, select the cells range and type a comma (,) (Figure 6-31).

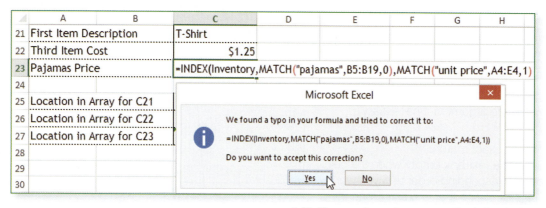

6-31 *MATCH* functions nested as *INDEX* arguments

   - For the *match_type* argument, type 0 and a closing parenthesis).
   - Press **Enter** and choose **Yes** to insert the missing closing parenthesis (Figure 6-32). The result of the function in Figure 6-32 is *$15.13*.

	A	B	C	D	E	F	G	H
21	First Item Description		T-Shirt					
22	Third Item Cost		$1.25					
23	Pajamas Price		=INDEX(Inventory,MATCH("pajamas",B5:B19,0),MATCH("unit price",A4:E4,1)					
24								
25	Location in Array for C21							
26	Location in Array for C22							
27	Location in Array for C23							
28								
29								
30								

Microsoft Excel

We found a typo in your formula and tried to correct it to:

=INDEX(Inventory,MATCH("pajamas",B5:B19,0),MATCH("unit price",A4:E4,1))

Do you want to accept this correction?

Yes   No

6-32 Message box when a parenthesis is missing

Building Statistical Calculations

With its many function categories, Excel has several relatively simple ways for you to build common statistical forecasts and calculations. For companies and other users who depend on market research, concepts such as a mean absolute deviation or a standard deviation are important numbers. When you know the mathematics behind and the purpose of a calculation, you will find it straightforward to build an Excel formula to accomplish your goal.

MAD Calculation

A *mean absolute deviation* (*MAD*) formula illustrates an accurate, statistical analysis of forecasting errors. *Forecast error* is the difference between actual values and predicted values. For example, by comparing *MAD* values for revenue or sales, Paradise Lakes Resort can identify forecast values that need work (large forecast error) as well as those that are accurate (small forecast error).

A mean absolute deviation uses two Excel functions, *ABS* (absolute value function) and *AVERAGE*. The deviation is the difference between the actual and the predicted, a simple subtraction formula. Results are negative numbers when the actual amount is less than the forecast amount. The *ABS* function shows the numeric value of a number—the real value without any sign.

> ### ANOTHER WAY
> The *AVEDEV* function in the *Statistical* category calculates the average deviation of the absolute values in a range without using the *ABS* function.

A *MAD* formula calculates the absolute difference for each cell and averages those cells.

HOW TO: Build a MAD Calculation

1. Click the cell for the first absolute result.
2. Type =ab and press **Tab**.
   - The ScreenTip shows the *number* argument.
3. Type the formula or choose the value (Figure 6-33).
   - You can type the formula or select the cells to build the formula.
4. Press **Enter** or click **Enter** in the *Formula bar.*
5. Copy the formula to the range.
6. Click the cell for the *MAD* formula.
7. Type =aver and press **Tab**.
8. Select the cell range with absolute values.
9. Press **Enter**. The result of the *MAD* for the three cells in Figure 6-33 is *9.333* (the average of 4+22+2).

6-33 *ABS* function's formula argument and MAD result.

MSE Calculation

The *mean square error (MSE)* is a popular measure of accuracy for forecasting. In this calculation, the error values are squared, so larger errors carry more influence. To calculate an *MSE,* you use **SUMSQ** from the *Math & Trig* category to sum the squares of the values. Then you divide this result by the number of values in the range.

The *SUMSQ* function has one required argument, *number1*. *Number1* is the value of the cell (or cells) you wish to square and sum.

HOW TO: Build an MSE Calculation

1. Click the cell where you want the result.

2. Click the **Math & Trig** button [*Formulas* tab, *Function Library* group].

3. Find and choose **SUMSQ**.

4. In the *Number1* argument text box, select the cells with values to be squared.

5. Click **OK**.

   - Each cell in the range is squared and those results are summed.

6. Click in the **Formula bar** and position the cursor after the closing parenthesis.

7. Type / for division.

8. Type cou and press **Tab** to select COUNT.

9. Select the cells to be counted (Figure 6-34).

   - The *COUNT* function returns the number of values in the range.
   - The sum of the squared values is divided by the number of cells in the range to calculate an average or mean square error.

10. Type the closing parenthesis).

11. Press **Enter**. The result of the *MSE* in Figure 6-34 is *134.067*.

Formula is edited in the *Formula bar*

| E4 | | ✕ ✓ *fx* | =SUMSQ(E4:E18)/COUNT(E4:E18 | | |

PLR Spa Products Sales and Forecast

Product #	Description	Sold	Forecast	Forecast Error
101	T-Shirt	120	124	4
102	Shorts	45	23	22
103	Coffee Mug	25	27	2
104	Pants	36	44	8
105	Beach Towel	22	22	0
106	Sun Screen	16	30	14
107	Picture Frame	56	32	24
108	Pajamas	24	23	1
109	Candy	90	88	2
110	Magnet	88	76	12
111	Flowers	15	12	3
112	Book	67	65	2
113	Magazine	56	54	2
114	Stuffed Animal	35	54	19
115	Pen	99	87	12
MAD			8.466666667	
MSE			JNT(E4:E18	
Standard Deviation				

6-34 Sum of the squares divided by a count of cells in the range

Standard Deviation

A ***standard deviation*** measures how broadly values deviate from the mean or average value in the range. This is another statistical tool that can be helpful when analyzing data.

There are several functions in the *Statistical* category that calculate standard deviation. The **STDEV.S** function applies to sample populations and ignores text and logical values that might be part of the argument range.

> ### MORE INFO
>
> To calculate the standard deviation from an entire population instead of a sample, use the function *STDEV.P*.

The syntax for a *STDEV.S* function is:
=STDEV.S(number1,[number2],...)

A *STDEV.S* function has one required argument, *number1*. *Number1* is the first value or cell reference. If the cells or values to be calculated are not adjacent, you can use additional number arguments. When the cells to be calculated are in an array, you can specify the range as the *Number1* argument.

HOW TO: Use the STDEV.S Function

1. Click the cell where you want the result to appear.
2. Type **=stdev.s(**.
   - The *Number1* argument is bold in the ScreenTip.
3. Select the range or type the range address (Figure 6-35).
   - You can select the cell array on the worksheet.
   - You can type individual values or select individual cells, separated by commas.
4. Press **Enter**.
   - The closing parenthesis is supplied. The result of the function in Figure 6-35 is *8.175*.

6-35 Standard deviation function

For this project, you use the *INDEX* and *MATCH* functions to locate and display information from an inventory worksheet for Paradise Lakes Resort. You also calculate statistical data with forecast errors.

File Needed: *[your initials] PP E6-1.xlsx*
Completed Project File Name: *[your initials] PP E6-2.xlsx*

1. Open the *[your initials] PP E6-1* workbook.
2. Save the workbook as: *[your initials] PP E6-2*.
3. Click the **Inventory** worksheet tab.
4. Use the *INDEX* function with one column of data.
   a. Click cell **C21**.
   b. Click the **Lookup & Reference** button [*Formulas* tab, *Function Library* group].
   c. Choose **INDEX**.
   d. Select the first argument list **array, row_num, column_num** and click **OK**.

e. For the *Array* argument, select cells **B5:B19**.

f. For the *Row_num* argument, type 1 to show the data from the first row in the selected range. When using a single column as the array, there is no *Column_num* argument (Figure 6-36).

g. Click **OK**. *T-Shirt* is the description.

5. Use the *INDEX* function with a range name.

a. Click cell **C22**.

b. Click the **Recently Used** button [*Formulas* tab, *Function Library* group] and choose **INDEX**.

c. Select the first argument list and click **OK**.

d. For the *Array* argument, press **F3** to open the *Paste Name* dialog box.

e. Choose **Inventory** and click **OK**.

f. Click in the **Row_num** argument box and type 3 to show data from the third row in the range.

g. Click in the **Column_num** box and type 4 to display data from the fourth column (Figure 6-37).

h. Click **OK**. The cost of the third item (coffee mug) is *1.25*.

6. Use the *MATCH* function.

a. Click cell **C25**.

b. Click the **Lookup & Reference** button [*Formulas* tab, *Function Library* group] and choose **MATCH**.

c. For the *Lookup_value* argument, click cell **C21**.

d. For the *Look_up array*, select cells **B5:B19**.

e. For the *Match_type* argument, type 0 to look for an exact match (Figure 6-38).

f. Click **OK**. The data in cell C21 is located in the first row of the array.

g. Click cell **C26**, type =m, and press **Tab**.

h. Click cell **C22** and type a comma (,) to move to the array argument.

i. For the *look_up array*, select cells **D5:D19** and type a comma (,).

j. Type 0 to locate an exact match.

k. Press **Enter**. The data referenced in cell C22 is located in the third row.

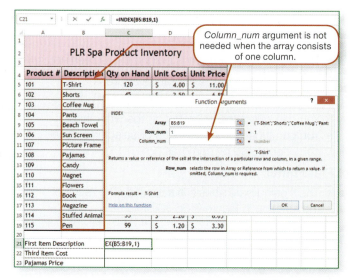

6-36 *INDEX* function to show data from first row

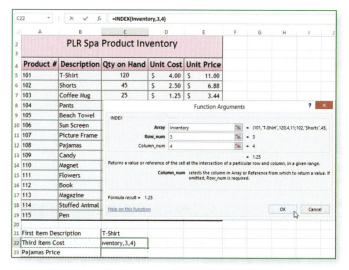

6-37 *INDEX* function to show data from third row, fourth column

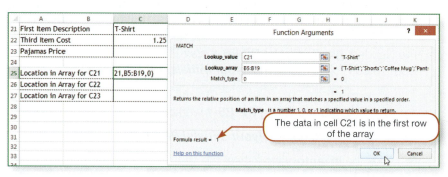

6-38 *MATCH* function for an exact match

7. Nest *INDEX* and *MATCH* functions.
   a. Click cell **C23**.
   b. Type =in and press **Tab** to start the *INDEX* function.
   c. For the *array* argument, press **F3**. Choose **Inventory** and click **OK**.
   d. Type a comma (,) to move to the *row_num* argument.
   e. Type m and press **Tab** to nest the *MATCH* function.
   f. For the *lookup_value* argument, type "pajamas", including the quotation marks and a comma to move to the next argument.
   g. For the *lookup_array* argument, select cells **B5:B19** and type a comma (,).
   h. For the *match_type* argument, click **0** in the *AutoComplete* list and press **Tab** to select it (Figure 6-39).
   i. Type a closing parenthesis) to return to the *INDEX* function.
   j. Type a comma (,) to move to the *Column_num* argument, type m, and press **Tab** to start a second nested *MATCH* function.
   k. For the *lookup_value*, type "unit price", with the comma.
   l. For the *lookup_array*, select cells **A4:E4** and type a comma (,).
   m. For the *match_type* argument, type 0 and two closing parentheses)) (Figure 6-40). Press **Enter**.
   n. Apply **Currency** formatting to **C22:C23**. The result is *$15.13*.

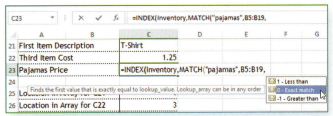

6-39 Choose the *match_type* argument from the list

8. Complete a *MATCH* function in cell **C27**.
   a. Use step 6 as a guide.
   b. For the *Lookup_value* argument, click cell **C23**.
   c. For the *Look_up array*, select cells **E5:E19**.
   d. For the *Match_type* argument, type 0 to look for an exact match. The correct result is *8*.

6-40 Nested *MATCH* and *INDEX* function syntax

9. Calculate the mean absolute deviation (*MAD*) for forecast errors.
   a. Click the **Forecasts** sheet tab and click cell **E4**.
   b. Type =ab and press **Tab**.
   c. Type d4-c4 and press **Enter**.
   d. Copy the formula in cell **E4** to cells **E5:E18**. Absolute values do not show any negative signs.
   e. Click cell **D20**.
   f. Use the *AVERAGE* function to calculate the mean for cells **E4:E18**.

10. Calculate the mean square error (*MSE*) for forecast errors.
    a. Click the cell **D21**.
    b. Click the **Math & Trig** button [*Formulas* tab, *Function Library* group]. Find and choose **SUMSQ**.
    c. In the *Number1* argument text box, select cells **E4:E18**.
    d. Click **OK**.
    e. Click in the **Formula bar** and position the cursor after the closing parenthesis.
    f. Type /cou and press **Tab** to select **COUNT**.
    g. Select cells **E4:E18** (Figure 6-41).
    h. Type a closing parenthesis) and press **Enter**.

E4 | =SUMSQ(E4:E18)/COUNT(E4:E18

COUNT(value1, [value2], ...)

PLR Spa Products Sales and Forecast

Product #	Description	Sold	Forecast	Forecast Error
101	T-Shirt	120	124	4
102	Shorts	45	23	22
103	Coffee Mug	25	27	2
104	Pants	36	44	8
105	Beach Towel	22	22	0
106	Sun Screen	16	30	14
107	Picture Frame	56	32	24
108	Pajamas	24	23	1
109	Candy	90	88	2
110	Magnet	88	76	12
111	Flowers	15	12	3
112	Book	67	65	2
113	Magazine	56	54	2
114	Stuffed Animal	35	54	19
115	Pen	99	87	12
	MAD		8.466666667	
	MSE		NT(E4:E18	
	Standard Deviation			

6-41 *COUNT* and *SUMSQ* are nested to calculate MSE

11. Calculate a standard deviation for forecast errors.
    a. Click cell **D22**.
    b. Type =std, select **STDEV.S** from the list, and press **Tab**.
    c. Select cells **E4:E18**.
    d. Press **Enter**.

12. Save and close the workbook (Figure 6-42).

	A	B	C	D	E
1		**PLR Spa Product Inventory**			
2					
3					
4	**Product #**	**Description**	**Qty on Hand**	**Unit Cost**	**Unit Price**
5	101	T-Shirt	120	$ 4.00	$ 11.00
6	102	Shorts	45	$ 2.50	$ 6.88
7	103	Coffee Mug	25	$ 1.25	$ 3.44
8	104	Pants	36	$ 7.25	$ 19.94
9	105	Beach Towel	22	$ 3.50	$ 9.63
10	106	Sun Screen	16	$ 2.50	$ 6.88
11	107	Picture Frame	56	$ 2.25	$ 6.19
12	108	Pajamas	24	$ 5.50	$ 15.13
13	109	Candy	90	$ 0.20	$ 0.55
14	110	Magnet	88	$ 0.50	$ 1.38
15	111	Flowers	15	$ 4.50	$ 12.38
16	112	Book	67	$ 3.25	$ 8.94
17	113	Magazine	56	$ 4.35	$ 11.96
18	114	Stuffed Animal	35	$ 2.20	$ 6.05
19	115	Pen	99	$ 1.20	$ 3.30
20					
21	First Item Description		T-Shirt		
22	Third Item Cost		$1.25		
23	Pajamas Price		$15.13		
24					
25	Location in Array for C21		1		
26	Location in Array for C22		3		
27	Location in Array for C23		8		

	A	B	C	D	E
1		**PLR Spa Products Sales and Forecast**			
2					
3	**Product #**	**Description**	**Sold**	**Forecast**	**Forecast Error**
4	101	T-Shirt	120	124	4
5	102	Shorts	45	23	22
6	103	Coffee Mug	25	27	2
7	104	Pants	36	44	8
8	105	Beach Towel	22	22	0
9	106	Sun Screen	16	30	14
10	107	Picture Frame	56	32	24
11	108	Pajamas	24	23	1
12	109	Candy	90	88	2
13	110	Magnet	88	76	12
14	111	Flowers	15	12	3
15	112	Book	67	65	2
16	113	Magazine	56	54	2
17	114	Stuffed Animal	35	54	19
18	115	Pen	99	87	12
19					
20	**MAD**			8.466666667	
21	**MSE**			134.0666667	
22	**Standard Deviation**			8.175456883	

6-42 PP E6-2 completed worksheets

SLO 6.5

Working with Financial Functions

Perhaps the most widely used function group in Excel is the *Financial* category. These functions analyze money transactions such as loans, bond purchases, depreciation, mortgage amortization, and many more.

Many of the financial functions use the same or similar arguments. For example, many functions have a *rate* and an *nper* argument. **Rate** refers to the interest rate for the period. Rate reflects the general principle that money now is worth more than money in the future. Another widely used argument is **nper,** the total number of payments. If you deposit money in a savings account regularly or pay back a loan with regular payments, the *nper* is the total number of deposits or payments you make.

The PV Function

The *PV* function represents the *present value* of a transaction. For example, if you buy a life insurance policy that will pay you $50,000 in 20 years, you can use the *PV* function to determine if all the payments you will make during those 20 years add up to a good investment. A lending institution, on the other hand, can use the *PV* function to calculate what the payments you are going to make to it over the period of the loan are worth today. That is typically the amount of money you can borrow.

Like many *Financial* functions, the *PV* function uses the concept of an **annuity**. An annuity is a series of payments, each the same amount, made at the same time of the month or year, for a specified period of time.

The syntax for a *PV* function is:

=PV(rate,nper,pmt,[fv],[type])

The *rate* argument is required. It is the assumed interest rate per period. The *nper* argument, also required, is the total number of periods or payments. These two arguments must use the same period such as monthly or yearly. So, if you make monthly payments but the interest rate is an annual rate, the rate must be divided by 12. The third required argument is *pmt*, the amount paid each period.

There are two optional arguments for a *PV* function, *fv* and *type*. Any cash balance at the end of the last period is set in the *fv* argument, future value. This is usually zero. In the insurance policy example, an *fv* amount is money that you would allow the insurance company to keep. For lenders, this is an amount that would not need to be paid back.

The *type* argument simply specifies if the payment is made at the beginning or the end of the period. When you are the person making the payments, it is less expensive to make the payment at the beginning of the period because you do not incur the interest charge for the month. If you are the lender, however, you most likely would prefer a payment at the end of the month so that you can earn that interest.

HOW TO: Use the PV Function

1. Click the cell where you want the result to appear.
2. Click the **Financial** button [*Formulas* tab, *Function Library* group].
3. Choose **PV**.
4. Click in the **Rate** argument box and select the cell that contains the interest rate.
   - If the interest rate is an annual rate and the payments are monthly, type /12 after the cell address.
   - If the interest rate is an annual rate and the payments are quarterly, type /4 after the cell address.
   - You can type the interest rate in the entry box as a percent or its decimal equivalent.
5. Click in the **Nper** argument box and select the cell that contains the number of years.
   - If the term is shown in years and the payments are monthly, type *12 after the cell address.
   - If the term is shown in years and the payments are quarterly, type *4 after the cell address.
   - You can type the total number of payments in the entry box.
6. Click in the **Pmt** box and select the cell that contains the payment amount.
7. In the *Fv* box, click the cell containing the cash balance amount.
   - You can type a value in the entry box.
   - You can type a zero (0) or leave the entry blank to indicate no cash balance.

8. In the *Type* box, type 1 if the payment is at the beginning of the period (Figure 6-43).
    *   Type 0 or leave the entry blank to indicate payment at the end of the period.

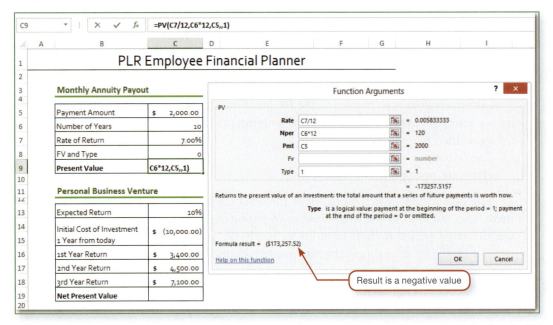

6-43 *Function Arguments* dialog box for *PV*

9. Click **OK**.

> **MORE INFO**
>
> The *PV* function assumes the payments are made *to you* when the payment amount is a positive number. The result is a negative number because that is the amount you pay now.

The FV Function

The *FV* function uses arguments and concepts similar to the *PV* function. However, it determines the *future value* of a series of payments at the same interest rate for a specified period of time. You might, for instance, use this function to calculate the results of an investment or savings plan in which you plan to deposit a specific amount each period.

The syntax for an *FV* function is:

=FV(rate,nper,pmt,[pv],[type])

An *FV* function has the same required arguments as a *PV* function, *rate*, *nper*, and *pmt*. It has two optional arguments, *pv* and *type*.

The *pv* argument is the total amount that all payments are worth now, or a lump sum that is already in the account. It might also be an initial amount that you have to invest in addition to the series of payments. In a savings or investment plan, the *pv* argument is any amount that you start with.

The *type* argument is either 1 or 0 (or omitted) to indicate if the payment is made at the beginning or the end of the period. If you are calculating a savings plan, you would probably want to make your payment at the beginning of the period so that you earn interest for the entire period.

1. Click the cell where you want the result to appear.

2. Click the **Financial** button [*Formulas* tab, *Function Library* group].

3. Choose **FV**.

4. Click in the **Rate** argument box and select the cell that contains the interest rate.

   - If the interest rate is an annual rate and payments are monthly, type /12 after the cell address.
   - If the interest rate is an annual rate and payments are quarterly, type /4 after the cell address.
   - You can type the interest rate in the *Rate* box.

5. Click in the **Nper** argument box and select the cell that contains the number of years.

   - If the term is shown in years and payments are monthly, type *12 after the cell address.
   - If the term is years and payments are quarterly, type *4 after the cell address.
   - You can type the total number of payments in the *Nper* box.

6. Click in the **Pmt** box and select the cell that contains the payment amount.

   - The payment amount is often formatted as a negative value because it is money you pay each period.

7. In the *Pv* box, click the cell with a starting amount.

   - You can type a value in the box.
   - You can type a zero (0) or leave the entry blank to indicate no starting amount.

8. In the *Type* box, type 1 if the payment is at the beginning of the period (Figure 6-44).

   - Type 0 or leave the entry blank to indicate payment at the end of the period.

9. Click **OK**.

6-44 *Function Arguments* dialog box for *FV*

The NPV Function

The *NPV* function calculates the *net present value* of an investment using a discount rate and a series of future payments and receipts. A **discount rate** might be the cost of financing or the rate of return possible with a competing investment. In the *NPV* function, the series of payments and receipts can vary, unlike the payment amounts in *PV* and *FV* functions.

For instance, Paradise Lakes Resort could use the *NPV* function to assess the purchase of another resort property and determine if it would be a good investment. The function would allow management to assign a net present value to the investment by combining cash inflows and outlays and by setting a discount rate.

> **MORE INFO**
>
> The *NPV* function assumes that cash flows occur at the end of each period.

The syntax for an *NPV* function is:
=NPV(rate,value1,value2,...)

The *NPV* function has two required arguments. *Rate* is the discount rate, the cost of financing, or an expected rate of return. The *valueN* arguments are the cash flows, both positive and negative. **Cash flows** are future payments or receipts.

The *value* arguments are listed in the order in which they occur. For example, if you earned $3,400 in the first period, that amount is the *value1* argument. The *value2* argument is the next payment or receipt, and so on. When the initial payment is made at the beginning of the first period (a common situation when investing), that payment is not included as a *value* argument but is added (as a negative amount) to the result of the *NPV* function.

HOW TO: Use the NPV Function

1. Click the cell where you want the result to appear.
2. Click the **Financial** button [*Formulas* tab, *Function Library* group] and choose **NPV**.
3. For the *Rate* argument, click the cell that contains the rate.
   - Use a percentage (10%) or its decimal equivalent (.1).
   - You can type the rate instead of clicking the cell.
4. For the *Value1* argument, click the cell that contains the amount of the cash flow at the end of the first period.
5. For the *Value2* argument, click the cell that contains the amount of the cash flow at the end of the second period.
6. For each additional value argument, click the appropriate cell (Figure 6-45).
   - You can select a cell range with cash flows after pressing tab.
   - Cash flow amounts can be negative or positive.
   - For a year with neither a positive or negative cash flow, type a zero (0) as that *ValueN* argument. Failure to do so will cause the sequence of cash flows to be moved forward one year.

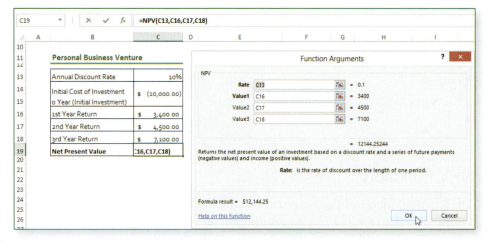

6-45 *Function Arguments* dialog box for *NPV*

7. Click **OK**.
8. To include the initial payment, click the *Formula bar* to edit the formula.
   - The initial payment amount is typically made up front at the beginning of the first period.
9. Place your cursor after the closing parenthesis and type **+**.
10. Click the cell with the initial payment and press **Enter** (Figure 6-46).

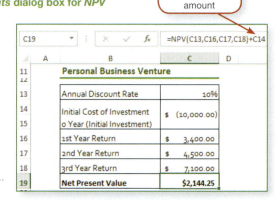

Initial payment amount

6-46 Edited *NPV* function for initial payment made at beginning of the period

Working with Text Functions

Excel has a *Text* function category. You can use these functions to split, join, convert, and otherwise manage labels and values in a worksheet. With a text function, you can format a value as a label. For example, you might do this when using dates or other values in a column with left-aligned labels. You can use other *Text* functions to display labels in uppercase or lowercase letters. Many of the *Text* functions have a basis in programming languages, so if you have programming experience, you may find them straightforward to explore.

The CONCATENATE Function

The *CONCATENATE* function allows you to join or combine up to 255 strings of text, values, or characters. To **concatenate** means to link or join in a chain. A common use of the *CONCATENATE* function is displaying a person's entire name in a single cell by joining two or more cells.

The syntax for a *CONCATENATE* function is:

=CONCATENATE(text1, [text2], . . .)

The *CONCATENATE* function has one argument *TextN*, where *N* is a number. The *Text* argument can be a cell reference or data that you type.

> ► **ANOTHER WAY**
>
> You can concatenate data in a formula using the & operator. The formula **=A1 & B1** will return the same result as **=CONCATENATE(A1,B1)**.

When you concatenate text strings, such as first and last names, you often have to include one or more spaces in the formula to separate the words or values. In addition, concatenated results are usually placed in a separate column or row, preserving the original data. Figure 6-47 shows a *CONCATENATE* function and a formula that accomplishes the same result.

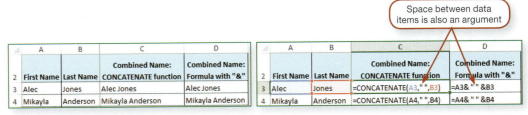

6-47 Both formulas combine the data from the first two columns in a single column

HOW TO: Use the CONCATENATE Function

1. Click the cell where you want the result to appear.
2. Click the **Text** button [*Formulas* tab, *Function Library* group].
3. Choose **CONCATENATE**.
4. For the *Text1* argument, click the cell with the first text string.
   - You can type a text string, space, or punctuation.
   - You do not need to include quotation marks when you use the *Function Arguments* dialog box.
5. Click in the **Text2** argument box and press the **spacebar**.
   - You can type other separators such as a period, a comma, or another character.
   - If you do not need a separator after the first string, click the cell with the second text string. This will cause the arguments to be one continuous text string (e.g., AlecJones).

6. Click in the **Text3** argument box and click the cell with the next text string (Figure 6-48).

   • If you type a space in an argument box, it is enclosed in quotation marks.

7. Complete as many *TextN* argument boxes as needed.

8. Click **OK**.

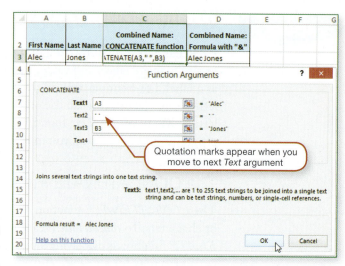

6-48 *Function Arguments* dialog box for *CONCATENATE*

The EXACT Function

The *EXACT* function compares two text strings, values, or characters to determine if they are identical. When you import or update data, you can use this function to ensure accuracy in the data. For example, if you import new email user names from a website listing, you can compare those user names to the current list you have. The *EXACT* function will indicate differences between the imported and original data sets.

The syntax for an *EXACT* function is:

=EXACT(text1, text2)

The *EXACT* function has two required arguments, *Text1* and *Text2*. *Text1* is the first text string and *Text2* is the second text string.

Like a *Logical* function, the result for an *Exact* function is either *TRUE* or *FALSE*. The arguments are case-sensitive but the function does not check formatting.

HOW TO: Use the EXACT Function

1. Click the cell where you want the result to appear.

2. Type =ex and press **Tab**.

   • The *text1* argument is bold in the ScreenTip.

3. Select the cell or type the text string.

   • If you type the text string you want to match, enclose it within quotation marks and use upper- and lowercase as used in the data.

4. Type a comma (,) to move to the *text2* argument.

   • The *text2* argument is bold in the ScreenTip.

5. Select the cell (Figure 6-49).

6. Press **Enter**.

   • The closing parenthesis is supplied.
   • The result is *TRUE* or *FALSE*.

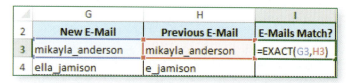

6-49 *EXACT* function has two arguments

The REPLACE Function

The *REPLACE* function allows you to substitute characters for a specified number of characters in existing data. This command is helpful only when data in a column follows a pattern. For example, if all the current products for Paradise Lakes Resort have an ID that starts with *PAR*, you could use the *REPLACE* function to change that part of each ID to *PLR*.

The syntax for a *REPLACE* function is:
=REPLACE(old_text, start_num, num_chars, new_text)

The *REPLACE* function has four required arguments. The *old_text* argument is the cell with data that you want to change. The second argument is *start_num*, which is the position in the cell of the first character to be replaced. For example, if you want to replace the first three characters in a cell, the *start_num* would be 1. However, if you want to replace something in the second word, you need to count each character position, including spaces, to determine the number.

The *num_chars* argument determines how many characters from that position are to be replaced, and the *new_text* argument is the replacement text.

HOW TO: Use the REPLACE Function

1. Click the cell where you want the result to appear.
2. Type =rep and press **Tab**.
   - The *old_text* argument is bold in the ScreenTip.
3. Select the cell with data to be replaced.
4. Type a comma (,) to move to the next argument.
   - The *start_num* argument is bold in the ScreenTip.
   - Count the character positions from the first character on the left.
5. Type a number to indicate the position and type a comma (,) to move to the next argument.
   - The *num_chars* argument is bold in the ScreenTip.
   - Count how many characters are to be replaced.
6. Type the number of replacement characters and type a comma (,).
7. Type the replacement text (Figure 6-50).
   - Enclose the text within quotation marks.
   - Use upper- and lowercase as required.
8. Press **Enter**.
   - The closing parenthesis is supplied.
   - The new text is displayed in the cell. The result in Figure 6-50 is *PLR Representative*.

	D	E
2	**Title**	**Revised Title**
3	Sales Representative	=REPLACE(D3,1,5,"PLR"
4	Sales Manager	REPLACE(old_text, start_num, num_chars, **new_text**)

6-50 *REPLACE* **function has four arguments**

PAUSE & PRACTICE: EXCEL 6-3

For this project, you complete the employee financial planning worksheet so that employees can fill in their own numbers and see their own results. You also update the employee data sheet using text functions.

File Needed: *[your initials] PP E6-2.xlsx*
Completed Project File Name: *[your initials] PP E6-3.xlsx*

1. Open the *[your initials] PP E6-2* workbook.

2. Save the workbook as *[your initials] PP E6-3*.

3. Click the **Financial Planner** sheet tab.

4. Use the *PV* function.
   a. Click cell **C9**.
   b. Click the **Financial** button [*Formulas* tab, *Function Library* group] and choose **PV**.
   c. Click cell **C7** for the *Rate* argument and type */12* after **C7** because the payments are monthly.
   d. Click in the **Nper** argument box and click cell **C6**.
   e. Type **12* after **C6**, because the term is years but payments are monthly.
   f. Click in the **Pmt** box and click cell **C5**.
   g. Press **Tab** two times to skip the *Fv* box and move to the *Type* box.
   h. In the *Type* box, type *1* to indicate payment is at the beginning of the period (Figure 6-51).
   i. Click **OK**. An annuity or insurance policy today would cost over $173,257.52 in order for you to achieve a $2,000 monthly payout over a period of 10 years.

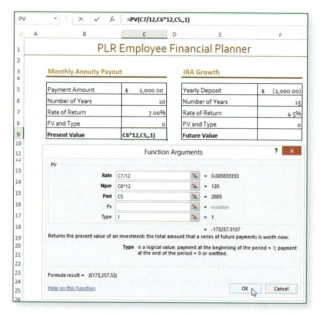

6-51 Payment is made at beginning of period

5. Use the *FV* function.
   a. Click cell **F9**.
   b. Click the **Financial** button [*Formulas* tab, *Function Library* group] and choose **FV**.
   c. Click cell **F7** for the *Rate* argument. The payment is once a year and the rate is per year.
   d. Click in the **Nper** argument box and click cell **F6**. There is only one payment per year.
   e. Click in the **Pmt** box and click cell **F5**. The amount is negative because you must pay it each year.
   f. Press **Tab** two times to skip the *Fv* box and move to the *Type* box. Leave both boxes empty (Figure 6-52).
   g. Click **OK**. If you invest $2,000 a year in an IRA account that earns 4.5% per year, you will have over $41,568.11 at the end of 15 years.

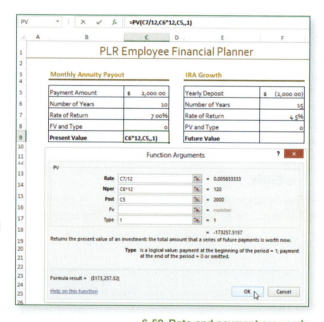

6-52 Rate and payment are yearly

6. Use the *NPV* function.
   a. Click cell **C19**.
   b. Click the **Financial** button [*Formulas* tab, *Function Library* group] and choose **NPV**.
   c. For the *Rate* argument, click cell **C13**.
   d. Click in the **Value1** box and click cell **C16**.
   e. Click in the **Value2** box and click cell **C17**.

f. For the *Value3* argument, click cell **C18** (Figure 6-53).

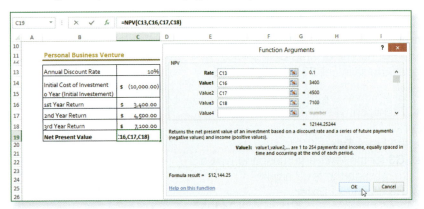

6-53 Initial investment treated as *Value1* argument

g. Click **OK**.
h. Click in the **Formula bar** to edit the formula to include the initial investment payment.
i. Place your cursor after the closing parenthesis and type +.
j. Click cell **C14** and press **Enter** (Figure 6-54). Based on the projected cash flows, this investment is worth $2,144.25 today.

6-54 Edited *NPV* function includes initial investment payment

7. Use the *CONCATENATE* function.
a. Click the **Employee Data** sheet tab and click cell **C3**.
b. Click the **Text** button [*Formulas* tab, *Function Library* group].
c. Choose **CONCATENATE**.
d. For the *Text1* argument, click cell **A3**.
e. Click in the **Text2** argument box and press the **spacebar** to include a space after the first text string.
f. Click in the **Text3** argument box and click cell **B3**. Quotation marks are inserted with the space in the *Text2* box.
g. Click **OK**.
h. Copy the *CONCATENATE* formula in cell **C3** to cells **C4:C25**. Widen the column to display the data (Figure 6-55).

8. Use the *REPLACE* function.
a. Click **E3**.
b. Type =rep and press **Tab**.
c. Select cell **D3** for the *old_text* argument.
d. Type a comma and the number one (,1) to indicate that the *start_num* character is the first character.
e. Type a comma (,) to move to the *num_chars* argument.
f. Type a 5 to indicate that five characters will be replaced.

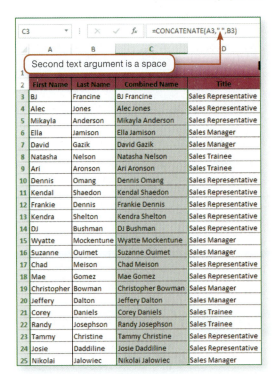

6-55 *CONCATENATE* formula shows results in single cell

g. Type a comma (,) to move to the *new_text* argument.

h. Type "PLR" including the quotation marks.

i. Press **Enter**.

j. Hide column **D**. *AutoFit* column **E**, and copy the *Replace* formula in cell **E3** to cells **E4:E25** (Figure 6-56).

9. Use the *EXACT* function.

a. Click **I3**.

b. Type **=ex** and press **Tab**.

c. Select cell **G3** for the *text1* argument and type a comma (,) to move to the *text2* argument.

d. Select cell **H3** and press **Enter**.

e. Copy the *EXACT* formula in cell **I3** to cells **I4:I25**.

f. Apply a *Highlight Cells* rule to cells **I3:I25** to show *FALSE* values in **Light Red Fill with Dark Red Text**. *Hint: use the Conditional Formatting button [Home tab, Styles group].*

10. Save and close the workbook (Figure 6-57).

6-56 *REPLACE* formula substitutes text

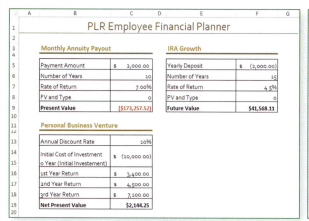

6-57 PP E6-3 completed worksheets

SLO 6.7

Using Multiple Criteria in Functions

You have now used multiple arguments in several functions as well as *AND* and *OR* criteria in various types of filters or formulas. There are three functions that combine several arguments with multiple criteria in one function: *SUMIFS* in the *Math & Trig* category and *AVERAGEIFS* and *COUNTIFS*, both in the *Statistical* category.

The SUMIFS Function

The *SUMIFS* function adds or totals cells only if they meet the specified criteria. For example, in a marketing worksheet, Paradise Lakes Resort can use *SUMIFS* to quickly determine the number of calls made by Breezy Point trainees. In Figure 6-58, for example, *SUMIFS* could be used to sum the cells in column D (*sum_range*) only if the location is Breezy Point (first criteria) and the title is Trainee (second criteria).

	A	B	C	D	E
1	**Marketing Calls and Visits**				
2	Name	Title	Location	Calls	Onsite Visits
3	Christopher Bowman	Manager	Cass Lake	13	22
4	Chad Melson	Representative	Cass Lake	26	7
5	Corey Daniels	Trainee	Cass Lake	18	23
6	Wyatte Mockentune	Manager	Breezy Point	25	19
7	Dennis Omang	Representative	Breezy Point	22	16
8	BJ Francine	Representative	Baudette	32	8
9	Kendal Shaedon	Representative	Breezy Point	5	22
10	Ella Jamison	Manager	Baudette	44	10
11	Alec Jones	Representative	Baudette	26	18
12	Natasha Nelson	Trainee	Baudette	7	23
13	Nikolai Jalowiec	Manager	Walker	26	20
14	Tammy Christine	Representative	Walker	7	41
15	Josie Daddiline	Trainee	Walker	10	21
16	Tara Miller	Trainee	Breezy Point	32	17
17	Robert Andrew	Representative	Walker	15	10
18	Coryn Gomez	Representative	Baudette	35	5
19	Elizabeth Gabrys	Trainee	Cass Lake	43	9
20	Rita Larson	Trainee	Walker	6	36
21	Michael Gentile	Representative	Baudette	38	9

6-58 Criteria from more than one column can be used in SUMIFS, AVERAGEIFS, or COUNTIFS

> **MORE INFO**
>
> The *SUMIFS* function is designed to be used in large list-type worksheets in which it would be cumbersome to calculate these types of results.

The syntax for a *SUMIFS* function is:

=SUMIFS(sum_range, criteria_range1, criteria1, [criteria_range2, criteria2], . . .)

There are three required arguments for a *SUMIFS* calculation: *sum_range, criteria_rangeN,* and *criteriaN. N* represents a number, like the other numbered arguments in this chapter. The *sum_range* is the cell range to be added. The *criteria_rangeN* is the range of cells that holds the criteria; it must have the same number of rows and columns as the *sum_range*. The *criteriaN* argument is a cell or keyed data that must be matched for the cells to be included in the total.

In a *SUMIFS* formula, there is one *sum_range*. There can be up to 127 *criteria_rangeN* arguments, each with a corresponding *criteriaN* argument.

HOW TO: Use SUMIFS

1. Click the cell where you want the result to appear.
2. Click the **Math & Trig** button [*Formulas* tab, *Function Library* group].
3. Choose **SUMIFS**.
4. For the *Sum_range* argument, select the cells with data to be totaled.
   - You can type the cell references.
5. Click in the **Criteria_range1** argument box.
6. Select the range of cells with the first set of criteria.
   - This range must be the same size as the *sum_range* argument.
7. Click in the **Criteria1** argument box.
8. Type the data to be used as a condition.
   - If the criteria is text, enclose it in quotation marks.
   - Text criteria is not case-sensitive.
   - If the criteria is located in a cell on the worksheet, you can select it.
9. Click in the **Criteria_range2** argument box.
10. Select the range of cells with the next set of criteria.
    - This range must be the same size as the *sum_range* argument.

11. Click in the **Criteria2** argument box.

12. Type the second requirement or condition (Figure 6-59).

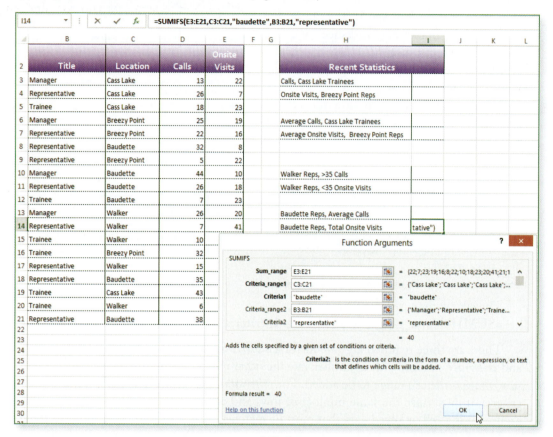

6-59 Data is included in sum only if it meets both criteria

13. Add *Criteria_range* and *Criteria* arguments as needed.

- The size of each *criteria_range* must match the size of the *sum_range*.
- Each *criteria_range* argument must have a corresponding *criteria* argument.

14. Click **OK**.

The AVERAGEIFS and COUNTIFS Functions

AVERAGEIFS and *COUNTIFS* perform their computations only when the data meets multiple criteria, like the *SUMIFS* function. *AVERAGEIFS* and *COUNTIFS* are in the *Statistical* category. In Figure 6-59, for example, you might use *AVERAGEIFS* to calculate the average number of on-site visits made by Walker representatives.

> **ANOTHER WAY**
>
> Many results accomplished by *SUMIFS*, *AVERAGEIFS*, or *COUNTIFS* can also be determined by filtering and sorting data in an Excel table.

The syntax for the *AVERAGEIFS* function is:
=**AVERAGEIFS(average_range, criteria_range1, criteria1, [criteria_range2, criteria2]. . .)**

There are three arguments in an *AVERAGEIFS* calculation: *average_range, criteria_rangeN,* and *criteriaN*. There is one *average_range,* and the *criteria_range* arguments must be the same size as the *average_range.* You can use up to 127 criteria ranges, and each one must have a corresponding criteria.

The syntax for the *COUNTIFS* function is:

=COUNTIFS(criteria_range1, criteria1, [criteria_range2, criteria2]. . .)

The *COUNTIFS* function is similar. It, however, has multiple *criteria_range* arguments, which are the ranges of cells with data to be counted. There is a corresponding *criteria* argument for each *criteria_range* argument, up to 127.

HOW TO: Use AVERAGEIFS

1. Click the cell where you want the result to appear.
2. Click the **More Functions** button [*Formulas* tab, *Function Library* group] and choose **Statistical**.
3. Choose **AVERAGEIFS**.
4. For the *Average_range* argument, select the cells with data to be averaged.
   - You can type cell references.
5. Click in the **Criteria_range1** argument box.
6. Select the range of cells with the first set of criteria.
   - This range must be the same size as the *average_range* argument.
7. Click in the **Criteria1** argument box.
8. Type the data to be used as a condition.
   - If the criteria is text, enclose it in quotation marks.
   - Text criteria is not case-sensitive.
   - If criteria is located in a worksheet cell, you can select it.
9. Click in the **Criteria_range2** argument box.
10. Select the range of cells with the next set of criteria.
    - This range must be the same size as the *average_range* argument.
11. Click in the **Criteria2** argument box.
12. Type the second requirement or condition (Figure 6-60).
13. Add *Criteria_range* and *Criteria* arguments as needed.
    - The size of each *criteria_range* must match the size of the *average_range.*
    - Each *criteria_range* argument must have a corresponding *criteria* argument.
14. Click **OK**.

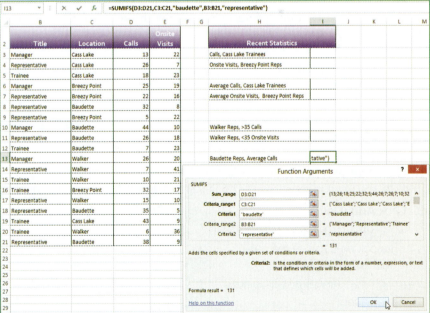

6-60 Data is included in average only if it meets both criteria

Editing Functions

In *SLO 2.1: Creating Basic Formulas,* you learned how to edit a function in the *Formula bar* or within the cell. You may have also used the *Find and Replace* command to change values or labels in a workbook or Word document. Using simple editing techniques with advanced options, such as the *Watch Window,* can save time when troubleshooting formulas or making mass changes. As you work with more complex Excel worksheets, you can use these editing commands in different ways.

Find and Replace

You can use *Find and Replace* to change arguments in a function. For example, in a nested *IF* function that is used in thousands of rows, you could use *Find and Replace* to quickly change a value used as an argument. Or if you mistakenly used *DAVERAGE* many times in a workbook when you should have used *DSUM,* you can easily find and replace those incorrect function names.

> ### ANOTHER WAY
>
> You can use the *Find and Replace* command to replace formats such as font type, fill color, or border style.

The Watch Window

The *Watch Window* is a convenient way to monitor changes in formulas when you work in large worksheets or with multiple sheets. The *Watch Window* enables you to observe the effects of all edits without having to scroll through a large worksheet or switch between numerous sheets in a workbook. For example, if you changed the *value_if_false* argument in a nested *IF* statement, the *Watch Window* can be open in any sheet to see the result of that change. Combining *Find and Replace* with the *Watch Window* can be a powerful editing option.

HOW TO: Replace a Function Argument

1. Click the **Watch Window** button [*Formulas* tab, *Formula Auditing* group].

2. Click **Add Watch** and select the cells you want to monitor.

3. Click **Add** (Figure 6-61).

   • Size the *Watch Window* and its columns to see the data that will be replaced.

4. Select the cell range with data to be replaced.

5. Click the **Find & Select** button [*Home* tab, *Editing* group].

6. Choose **Replace**.

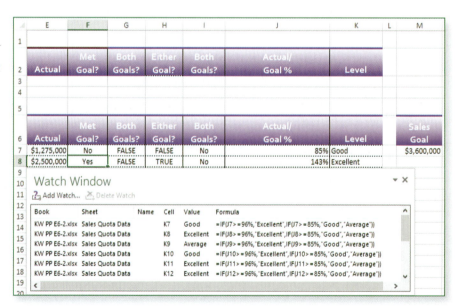

6-61 Resized *Watch Window*

7. Click **Options>>** to expand the *Find and Replace* options.

8. Click in the **Find what** box.
   - Delete existing search strings.
   - If necessary, click the arrow with *Format* and clear the find format.

9. Type the text you want to find.
   - Use uppercase if the case is important to the command.

10. Click in the **Replace with** box and type the replacement text.
    - Use uppercase for characters in the new text as needed.

11. Click to place a check mark for **Match case** if appropriate.

12. Click to place a check mark for **Match entire cell contents** if required.
    - Do not use this choice when looking for a specific part of any cell data.

13. Choose the **Within**, **Search**, and **Look In** options.

14. Click **Find All** (Figure 6-62).
    - Size the *Find and Replace* dialog box to view the results.

15. Click **Replace All**.

16. Click **OK** in the message box.

17. Close the *Find and Replace* dialog box.

18. Select and delete the watches in the *Watch Window*.
    - **Watches** are those cells containing formulas that you added to the *Watch Window*.

19. Close the *Watch Window*.

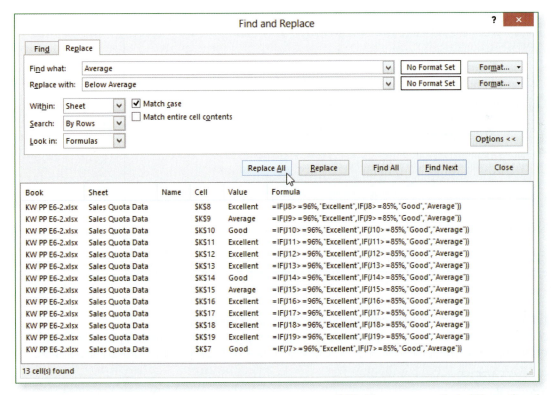

6-62 All occurrences that will be replaced

For this project, you use functions from the *Math & Trig* and *Statistical* categories with multiple criteria ranges to analyze Paradise Lakes Resort marketing data. You also update an argument in a nested *IF* function in the workbook using *Find and Replace*.

File Needed: ***[your initials] PP E6-3.xlsx***
Completed Project File Name: ***[your initials] PP E6-4.xlsx***

1. Open the ***[your initials] PP E6-3*** workbook.

2. Save the workbook as ***[your initials] PP E6-4***.

3. Click the **Marketing** sheet tab.

4. Use the *SUMIFS* function.
   a. Click cell **I3**.
   b. Click the **Math & Trig** button [*Formulas* tab, *Function Library* group] and choose **SUMIFS**.
   c. For the *Sum_range* argument, select cells **D3:D21**.
   d. Click in the **Criteria_range1** box and select cells **C3:C21**, the location column.
   e. Click in the **Criteria1** box and type cass lake to sum only those cells with data for Cass Lake.
   f. Click in the **Criteria_range2** box and select cells **B3:B21**, which is the job title column.
   g. Click in the **Criteria2** box and type trainee to include only those cells with data about trainees (Figure 6-63).

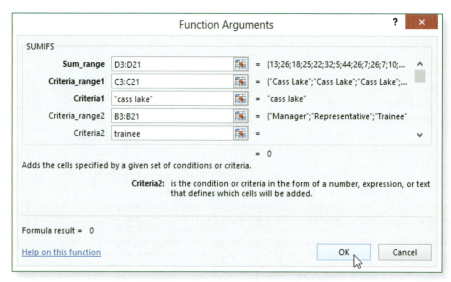

6-63 *SUMIFS* with two criteria ranges

   h. Click **OK**. The total number of calls made by Cass Lake trainees is 61.
   i. In cell **I4**, use the *SUMIFS* function to total the number of *on-site* visits made by *Breezy Point Representatives*. The total number of on-site visits made by Breezy Point representatives is 38.

5. Use the *AVERAGEIFS* function.
   a. Click cell **I6**.
   b. Click the **More Functions** button [*Formulas* tab, *Function Library* group] and choose **Statistical**.
   c. Choose **AVERAGEIFS**.
   d. For the *Average_range* argument, select cells **D3:D21**.

e. Click in the **Criteria_range1** box and select cells **C3:C21** for the location.

f. Click in the **Criteria1** box and type cass lake.

g. Click in the **Criteria_range2** box and select cells **B3:B21** for the job title.

h. Click in the **Criteria2** box and type trainee (Figure 6-64).

i. Click **OK**. The average number of calls made by Cass Lake trainees is 30.5.

j. In cell **I7**, use *AVERAGEIFS* to find the average number of on-site visits made by Breezy Point representatives. The formula result is *19*.

6. Use *COUNTIFS*.

a. Click cell **I10**.

b. Click the **More Functions** button [*Formulas* tab, *Function Library* group] and choose **Statistical**.

c. Choose **COUNTIFS**.

d. For the *Criteria_range1* argument, select cells **C3:C21** for the location.

e. Click in the **Criteria1** box and type walker.

f. Click in the **Criteria_range2** box and select cells **D3:D21**.

g. Click in the **Criteria2** box and type >35 (Figure 6-65). The function counts the number of cells in which the location is Walker and the number of calls is greater than 35.

h. Click **OK**. Cell I10 shows 0. None of the Walker employees made more than 35 calls.

i. In cell **I11**, use *COUNTIFS* to count the number of Walker employees who made fewer than 35 on-site visits. The formula result is *3*.

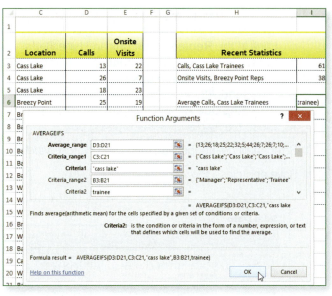

6-64 *AVERAGEIFS* with two criteria ranges

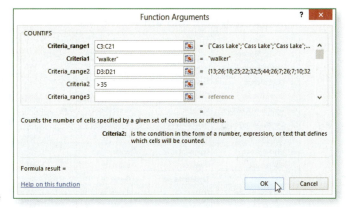

6-65 *COUNTIFS* with two criteria ranges

7. Use *AVERAGEIFS* in cell **I13** and *SUMIFS* in cell **I14** to calculate the value indicated in H13 and H14. The results are *32.75* and *40*, respectively.

8. Prepare the *Watch Window*.

a. Click the **Sales Quota Data** sheet tab.

b. Click the **Watch Window** button [*Formulas* tab, *Formula Auditing* group]. Select and delete any previous watches.

c. Click **Add Watch**, select cells **K7:K19**, and then click **Add**.

d. Size the columns in the *Watch Window* to display the complete formula.

9. Use *Find and Replace*.

a. Select cells **K7:K19** to limit the command to these cells.

b. Click the **Find & Select** button [*Home* tab, *Editing* group] and choose **Replace**.

c. Click the **Options>>** button to expand the *Find and Replace* options. When the dialog box is already expanded, this command appears as *<<Options*.

d. If necessary, click the **Format** arrow button and clear previous find format settings.

e. Click in the **Find what** box and delete previous search strings.

f. Type Average. The *Find what* string is not case-sensitive.

g. Click in the **Replace with** box and type Below Average.

h. Set the *Within* choice to **Sheet**, the *Search* choice to **By Rows**, the *Look In* choice to **Formulas**, and check the **Match case** box.

i. Click **Find All** to review the cells that will be updated. Size the dialog box if needed.

j. Click **Replace All** and click **OK**; 14 replacements are made.

k. Close the *Find and Replace* dialog box.

10. Select and delete the watches in the *Watch Window* and then close the window.

11. Save and close the workbook (Figure 6-66).

Sales Data

Name	Title	Location	Goal	Actual	Met Goal?	Both Goals?	Either Goal?	Both Goals?	Actual/ Goal %	Level
Christopher Bowman	Sales Manager	Cass Lake	$1,500,000	$1,275,000	No	FALSE	FALSE	No		85% Good
Chad Meison	Sales Representative	Cass Lake	$1,750,000	$2,500,000	Yes	FALSE	TRUE	No		143% Excellent
Corey Daniels	Sales Trainee	Cass Lake	$500,000	$330,000	No	FALSE	FALSE	No		66% Below Average
Wyatte Mockentune	Sales Manager	Breezy Point	$1,500,000	$1,425,000	No	FALSE	FALSE	No		95% Good
Dennis Omang	Sales Representative	Breezy Point	$1,800,000	$2,100,000	Yes	FALSE	TRUE	No		117% Excellent
BJ Francine	Sales Representative	Baudette	$1,700,000	$2,150,000	Yes	FALSE	TRUE	No		126% Excellent
Kendal Shaedon	Sales Representative	Breezy Point	2100000S	$1,850,000	No	FALSE	FALSE	No	Check values in columns E and D.	Excellent
Ella Jamison	Sales Manager	Baudette	$1,500,000	$1,320,000	No	FALSE	FALSE	No		88% Good
Alec Jones	Sales Representative	Baudette	$1,700,000	$935,000	No	FALSE	FALSE	No		55% Below Average
Natasha Nelson	Sales Trainee	Baudette	$0	$409,500	Yes	FALSE	TRUE	No	Check values in columns E and D.	Excellent
Nikolai Jalowiec	Sales Manager	Walker	$1,500,000	$1,560,000	Yes	FALSE	TRUE	No		104% Excellent
Tammy Christine	Sales Representative	Walker	$7,500,000	$9,275,000	Yes	TRUE	TRUE	Met both		124% Excellent
Josie Daddiline	Sales Representative	Walker	$4,250,000	$5,900,000	Yes	TRUE	TRUE	Met both		139% Excellent

Marketing Calls and Visits

Name	Title	Location	Calls	Onsite Visits			Recent Statistics	
Christopher Bowman	Manager	Cass Lake	13	22			Calls, Cass Lake Trainees	61
Chad Meison	Representative	Cass Lake	26	7			Onsite Visits, Breezy Point Reps	38
Corey Daniels	Trainee	Cass Lake	18	23				
Wyatte Mockentune	Manager	Breezy Point	25	19			Average Calls, Cass Lake Trainees	30.5
Dennis Omang	Representative	Breezy Point	22	16			Average Onsite Visits, Breezy Point Reps	19
BJ Francine	Representative	Baudette	32	8				
Kendal Shaedon	Representative	Breezy Point	5	22				
Ella Jamison	Manager	Baudette	44	10			Walker Employees, >35 Calls	0
Alec Jones	Representative	Baudette	26	18			Walker Employees, <35 Onsite Visits	3
Natasha Nelson	Trainee	Baudette	7	23				
Nikolai Jalowiec	Manager	Walker	26	20			Baudette Reps, Average Calls	32.75
Tammy Christine	Representative	Walker	7	41			Baudette Reps, Total Onsite Visits	40
Josie Daddiline	Trainee	Walker	10	21				
Tara Miller	Trainee	Breezy Point	32	17				
Robert Andrew	Representative	Walker	15	10				
Coryn Gomez	Representative	Baudette	35	5				
Elizabeth Gabrys	Trainee	Cass Lake	43	9				
Rita Larson	Trainee	Walker	6	36				
Michael Gentile	Representative	Baudette	38	9				

6-66 PP E6-4 completed worksheets

Chapter Summary

6.1 Use database functions such as *DSUM*, *DAVERAGE*, and *DCOUNT* (p. E6-304).

- The functions in the *Database* category perform the calculation only when data meet specified criteria.
- The syntax for a *Database* function is **FunctionName(database, field, criteria)**.
- The **database argument** is the cell range to be analyzed. The **field argument** is the column label or number that is used in the calculation. The **criteria argument** is the range of cells with a column label and the actual criteria just below that label.
- You can use selected cell ranges or named ranges in the arguments for a *Database* function.
- **DAVERAGE** calculates the average of cells that meet the criteria, and **DSUM** totals the values in cells that meet the criteria.

6.2 Build *AND*, *OR*, and other logical functions and use nested functions (p. E6-307).

- **AND** and **OR** functions only return *TRUE* or *FALSE* as a result.
- An *AND* function tests multiple conditions and shows *TRUE* only when all conditions are met.
- An *AND* function has one argument, *logicalN*, but there can be up to 255 *logicalN* arguments or conditions.
- An *OR* function tests multiple conditions and shows *TRUE* if any one of the conditions is met.
- An *OR* function has one argument, *logicalN*, and can have up to 255 *logicalN* arguments.
- A **nested function** is a function within another function.
- *AND* or *OR* can be nested with *IF* to check for multiple tests or conditions. The *AND* or *OR* function becomes the *logical_test* argument for the **IF function**.
- Nested *IF* functions are commonly used to show a result based on several conditions.
- A nested *IF* function uses an *IF* function as the *value_if_true*, or *value_if_false* argument, or both.
- When a formula or function may result in an Excel error message, you can use an **IFERROR function** to override the default message.

- An *IFERROR* function has two arguments, the *value* or formula that might result in an error message and the *value_if_error*, a custom error message.

6.3 Use *Lookup & Reference* functions such as *INDEX* and *MATCH* (p. E6-319).

- The **Lookup & Reference function** category includes many functions that locate data in a worksheet.
- The **INDEX function** returns the contents of the cell at the intersection of the specified column and row.
- Arguments for *INDEX* include *array*, *row_num*, and *column_num*.
- The **MATCH function** returns the relative location of the data that matches the condition.
- Arguments for *MATCH* are *lookup_value*, *lookup_array*, and *match_type*.

6.4 Build statistical calculations such as *MAD*, MSE, and *STDV.S* (p. E6-323).

- You can use Excel functions to build common statistical forecasting calculations.
- **Forecasting error** is the difference between actual values and predicted or forecasted values.
- The **mean absolute deviation** (**MAD**) formula calculates the average of the absolute values of deviation values.
- The **ABS** function from the *Math & Trig* category displays a value without its sign.
- The **mean square error** (**MSE**) sums the squares of a range of values and averages that result.
- To calculate an *MSE*, use **SUMSQ** from the *Math & Trig* category with **COUNT**.
- A **standard deviation** measures how broadly values vary from the mean (average) value.
- To calculate a standard deviation for a sample population, you can use function **STDEV.S** from the *Statistical* category.

6.5 Use financial functions such as *PV*, *FV*, and *NPV* (p. E6-328).

- Financial functions analyze money transactions.
- The **PVfunction** calculates the current value of regular payments at a set interest rate for a specified period of time.

- You can use *PV* to determine the cost effectiveness of buying an annuity now for which you know the future value.
- The **FV function** calculates the total value of regular payments or deposits invested at a constant interest rate for a specified period of time.
- You can use *FV* to evaluate how much money you will accumulate in an investment account over a certain period of time.
- The **NPV function** calculates the net present value of an investment using a discount rate and a series of cash flows.
- You can use *NPV* to assess the financial results of an investment that requires an initial amount of money followed by cash payments and receipts over several years.

6.6 Use text functions such as *CONCATENATE*, *EXACT*, and *REPLACE* (p. E6-333).

- Text functions join, convert, and split labels and value data in a worksheet.
- The **CONCATENATE function** combines up to 255 strings of text, values, or characters in a single cell.
- The *CONCATENATE* function has one argument, *TextN*.
- The **EXACT function** compares two strings of text, values, or characters and displays *TRUE* only if they are identical.
- The **REPLACE function** deletes characters and replaces them with new characters.
- In a *REPLACE* formula, you specify where the replacement starts and how many characters are to be replaced.

6.7 Use multiple criteria in functions such as *SUMIFS*, *AVERAGEIFS*, and *COUNTIFS* (p. E6-338)

- Three functions from the *Math & Trig* and *Statistical* categories enable you to use multiple criteria to calculate a result.
- The *SUMIFS* function sums values for cells that meet up to 127 specified criteria.
- In a *SUMIFS* function, the argument ranges must be the same size, and each criteria range must have its own criteria.
- The *AVERAGEIFS* function averages the values for cells that meet up to 127 specified criteria.
- The *AVERAGEIFS* and *COUNTIFS* functions are in the *Statistical* category.
- *COUNTIFS* counts the number of cells that meet all the criteria specified in the criteria ranges.

6.8 Use the *Watch Window* and *Find and Replace* (p. E6-342)

- The **Find and Replace** command can be used to locate and replace function arguments as well as function names.
- The **Watch Window** enables you to observe the effects of all edits in cells containing formulas without having to scroll through a large worksheet.
- The *Watch Window* can be sized and positioned to show as much data as necessary.

Check for Understanding

On the **Online Learning Center** for this text (www.mhhe.com/office2013inpractice), there are a variety of resources that can be used to review the concepts covered in this chapter.

The following Online Learning Resources are available on the Online Learning Center:

- Multiple choice questions
- Short answer questions
- Matching exercises

Guided Project 6-1

The Boyd Air organization is requesting managers to add advanced formulas to determine bonus options, alerts, and database values. For this project you use *Formula AutoComplete* and nested functions to determine which flights have not met organizational goals and which employees have earned a bonus.
[Student Learning Outcomes 6.1, 6.2, 6.7, 6.8]

File Needed: ***BoydFlights-06.xlsx***
Completed Project File Name: *[your initials] Excel 6-1.xlsx*

Skills Covered in This Project

- Create a *DSUM* function.
- Create a *DAVERAGE* function.
- Create a *DMAX* function.
- Create an *IFERROR* function.

- Create a nested *IF* function.
- Nest *AND* and *IF* functions.
- Create basic formulas.

1. Open the ***BoydFlights-06*** workbook from your student data files folder. Click the **Enable Content** button if prompted.

2. Save the workbook as *[your initials] Excel 6-1*.

3. Create an *IFERROR* function.
   a. Click cell **H9**.
   b. Click the **Logical** button [*Formulas* tab, *Function Library* group] and choose **IFERROR**.
   c. In the *value* argument box, click cell **F9**, type -, and click cell **G9**. If the formula that determines the percentage results in an error, your message is displayed instead of a standard error value message.
   d. Click in the **value_if_error** box.
   e. Type Check Price and Cost columns.
   f. Click **OK**.
   g. Copy the formula in cell **H9** to cells **H10:H18**. Widen the columns as needed (Figure 6-67).

8	H
	Net Income
9	$ 20,992.00
10	$ 23,424.00
11	$ 14,425.60
12	$ 17,274.88
13	$ 14,566.40
14	Check Price and Cost columns
15	$ 25,282.56
16	$ 25,378.90
17	$ 23,424.00
18	$ 18,920.55

6-67 *IFERROR* function results

4. Create a nested *IF* function.
   a. Click cell **I9**.
   b. Click the **Logical** button [*Formulas* tab, *Function Library* group] and choose **IF**.
   c. In the *logical_test* box, type H9<15000.
   d. Click in the **value_if_true** box and type None. Quotation marks are not necessary when you use the *Function Arguments* dialog box. If the value in cell H9 is less than $15,000, the formula shows *None*.
   e. Click in the **value_if_false** box. If the first *logical_test* is not true, the nested *IF* statement runs.
   f. Click **IF** in the *Name* box. You can choose **IF** from the list in the *Name* box, or choose **More Functions** from the list and find and select **IF**.

g. In the *logical_test* box for the second *IF* condition, type H9<23000. If the value in cell H9 is not less than $15,000, it is checked to see if it is less than $23,000 but more than $14,999.99.

h. Click in the **value_if_true** box and type $M$5. If the value in cell H9 is less than $23,000 and more than $14,999.99, this bonus amount is shown. Include absolute value symbols for the future copy process.

i. Click in the **value_if_false** box.

j. Type $M$6. If the value in cell H9 is $23,000 or higher, this bonus result appears in the cell (Figure 6-68).

k. Click **OK**. The result in I9 is *$5,000*.

l. Copy the formula in cell **I9** to cells **I10:I18**. Widen the column to show the results if necessary.

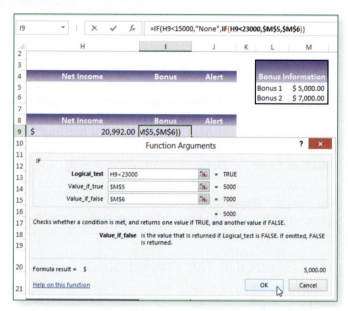

6-68 Complete nested *IF* function is visible in the *Formula bar*

5. Nest *AND* and *IF* functions.

a. Click cell **J9**.

b. Type =if(an and press **Tab**. The focus is now on the *AND* formula.

c. For the *Logical1* argument, type I9="None".

d. Type a comma (,) to move to the **Logical2** argument.

e. For the *Logical2* argument, type D9="Full".

f. Type a closing parenthesis). The focus within the formula returns to the *IF* function.

g. Type a comma (,) to complete the *logical_test* argument.

h. For the *value_if_true* argument, type "Concern" including the quotation marks.

i. Type a comma (,) to move to the *value_if_false* argument.

j. Type "None" (Figure 6-69).

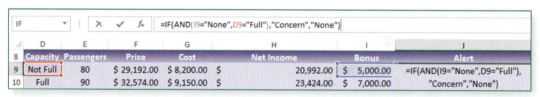

6-69 Arguments for the *IF* function

k. Type a closing parenthesis) and press **Enter**.

l. Copy the formula in cell **J9** to cells **J10:J18**. Widen the column to show the results if necessary. The result in J9 is *None*.

6. Build a *DSUM* function using the *Function Arguments* dialog box.

a. In cell **D5**, type full. Criteria is not case-sensitive.

b. Click cell **C20** and click the **Insert Function** button [*Formulas* tab, *Function Library* group].

c. Click the **Or select a category** drop-down arrow and choose **Database**.

d. Select **DSUM** and click **OK**.

e. In the *Database* argument text box, press **F3** to open the *Paste Name* dialog box. The list includes all defined names in the workbook.

f. Choose **FlightData** and click **OK**.

g. In the *Field* argument box, type net income. Argument entries are not case sensitive, and quotation marks are entered automatically.

h. Click in the **Criteria** argument box and select cells **A4:J5**, or press **F3** to select **Criteria** from the list and **OK** in the *Paste Name* dialog box (Figure 6-70).

i. Click **OK**. Apply **Accounting** formatting to the result. The total net income for full flights is $122,892.39.

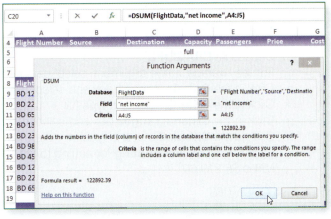

6-70 *DSUM and its arguments*

7. Type a *DAVERAGE* function.

a. Click cell **C21**.

b. Type =dav to display the *Formula AutoComplete* list and press **Tab** to choose *DAVERAGE*.

c. For the *Database* argument, select cells **A8:J18**. Excel supplies the range name automatically.

d. Type a comma (,) to move to the next argument.

e. For the *Field* argument, type "net income".

f. Type a comma (,) to move to the last argument.

g. For the *Criteria* argument, select cells **A4:J5**.

h. Press **Enter**. The closing parenthesis is automatically supplied. Apply **Accounting** formatting to **C21**. The average net income for full flights is *$20,482.07*.

8. Use the *Function Arguments* dialog box or typing to create a *DMAX* function in cell **C22**.

a. Use the same argument ranges listed in step 7.

b. The maximum net income value for full flights is *$25,282.56* (Figure 6-71). Apply **Accounting** format to **C22**.

	A	B	C
20	Total Net Income for Full Flights		$ 122,892.39
21	Average Net Income for Full Flights		$ 20,482.07
22	Maximum Net Income for Full Flights		$ 25,282.56

6-71 **Database function results**

9. Use the *SUMIFS* function.

a. Click cell **I20**.

b. Click the **Math & Trig** button [*Formulas* tab, *Function Library* group] and choose **SUMIFS**.

c. For the *Sum_range* argument, select cells **E9:E18**.

d. Click in the **Criteria_range1** box and select cells **D9:D18**, the location column.

e. Click in the **Criteria1** box and type full to sum only those cells with data for full flights.

f. Click in the **Criteria_range2** box and select cells **B9:B18**, which is the source column.

g. Click in the **Criteria2** box and type Minneapolis, MN to include only those cells with data about Minneapolis (Figure 6-72).

h. Click **OK**. The total number of passengers on full flights from Minneapolis is *180*.

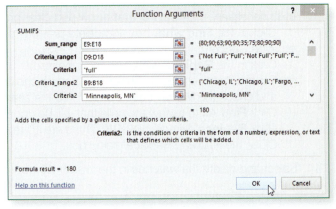

6-72 *SUMIFS with two criteria ranges*

10. Use the *AVERAGEIFS* function.
    a. Click cell **I21**.
    b. Click the **More Functions** button [*Formulas* tab, *Function Library* group] and choose **Statistical**.
    c. Choose **AVERAGEIFS**.
    d. For the *Average_range* argument, select cells **G9:G18**.
    e. Click in the **Criteria_range1** box and select cells **D9:D18** for the capacity.
    f. Click in the **Criteria1** box and type full.
    g. Click in the **Criteria_range2** box and select cells **B9:B18** for the source.
    h. Click in the **Criteria2** box and type Minneapolis, MN.
    i. Click **OK**. Apply **Accounting** formatting to **I21**. The average cost of full flights from Minneapolis, MN is *$6,219.00*.

11. Use *COUNTIFS*.
    a. Click cell **I22**.
    b. Click the **More Functions** button [*Formulas* tab, *Function Library* group] and choose **Statistical**.
    c. Choose **COUNTIFS**.
    d. For the *Criteria_range1* argument, select cells **D9:D18** for the capacity.
    e. Click in the **Criteria1** box and type full.
    f. Click in the **Criteria_range2** box and select cells **C9:C18**.
    g. Click in **Criteria2** box and type Minneapolis, MN. The function counts the number of cells in which the destination is Minneapolis, MN and the flight capacity is full (Figure 6-73).
    h. Click **OK**. One of the flights to Minneapolis was full.

6-73 Multiple criteria results

12. Prepare the *Watch Window*.
    a. Click the **Watch Window** button [*Formulas* tab, *Formula Auditing* group]. Select and delete any previous watches.
    b. Click **Add Watch**, select cells **J9:J18**, and click **Add**.
    c. Size the columns in the *Watch Window* to display the complete formula.

13. Use *Find and Replace*.
    a. Click the **Find & Select** button [*Home* tab, *Editing* group] and choose **Replace**.
    b. Click the **Options>>** button to expand the *Find and Replace* options. When the dialog box is already expanded, this command appears as <<Options.
    c. If necessary, click the **Format** arrow and clear previous find format settings.
    d. Click in the **Find what** box and delete previous search strings.
    e. Type Concern.
    f. Click in the **Replace with** box and type Issue.
    g. Set the *Within* choice to **Sheet**, the *Search* choice to **By Rows**, the *Look In* choice to **Formulas**, and check the **Match case** box to force the search to be case-sensitive.
    h. Click **Find All** to review the cells that will be updated. Size the dialog box if needed.
    i. Click **Replace All** and click **OK**. There are 10 replacements.
    j. Close the *Find and Replace* dialog box.

14. Select and delete the watches in the *Watch Window* and then close the window.

15. Save and close the workbook (Figure 6-74).

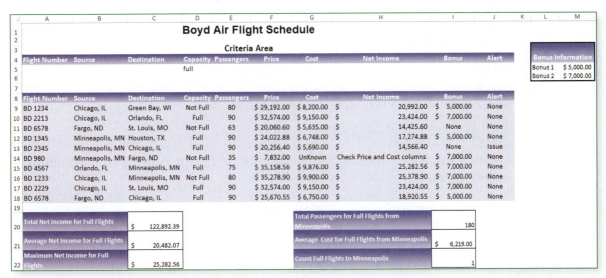

Boyd Air Flight Schedule

Criteria Area

Flight Number	Source	Destination	Capacity	Passengers	Price	Cost	Net Income	Bonus	Alert
			full						

Flight Number	Source	Destination	Capacity	Passengers	Price	Cost	Net Income	Bonus	Alert
BD 1234	Chicago, IL	Green Bay, WI	Not Full	80	$ 29,192.00	$ 8,200.00	$ 20,992.00	$ 5,000.00	None
BD 2213	Chicago, IL	Orlando, FL	Full	90	$ 32,574.00	$ 9,150.00	$ 23,424.00	$ 7,000.00	None
BD 6578	Fargo, ND	St. Louis, MO	Not Full	63	$ 20,060.60	$ 5,635.00	$ 14,425.60	None	None
BD 1345	Minneapolis, MN	Houston, TX	Full	90	$ 24,022.88	$ 6,748.00	$ 17,274.88	$ 5,000.00	None
BD 2345	Minneapolis, MN	Chicago, IL	Full	90	$ 20,256.40	$ 5,690.00	$ 14,566.40	None	Issue
BD 980	Minneapolis, MN	Fargo, ND	Not Full	35	$ 7,832.00	UnKnown	Check Price and Cost columns	$ 7,000.00	None
BD 4567	Orlando, FL	Minneapolis, MN	Full	75	$ 35,158.56	$ 9,876.00	$ 25,282.56	$ 7,000.00	None
BD 1233	Chicago, IL	Minneapolis, MN	Not Full	80	$ 35,278.90	$ 9,900.00	$ 25,378.90	$ 7,000.00	None
BD 2229	Chicago, IL	St. Louis, MO	Full	90	$ 32,574.00	$ 9,150.00	$ 23,424.00	$ 7,000.00	None
BD 6578	Fargo, ND	Chicago, IL	Full	90	$ 25,670.55	$ 6,750.00	$ 18,920.55	$ 5,000.00	None

Bonus Information
Bonus 1 $ 5,000.00
Bonus 2 $ 7,000.00

Total Net Income for Full Flights	$ 122,892.39	Total Passengers for Full Flights from Minneapolis: 180
Average Net Income for Full Flights	$ 20,482.07	Average Cost for Full Flights from Minneapolis: $ 6,219.00
Maximum Net Income for Full Flights	$ 25,282.56	Count Full Flights to Minneapolis: 1

6-74 Excel 6-1 completed

Guided Project 6-2

Eller Software Services wants you to create a reference function to search data for phone numbers. They are also requesting forecasting error calculations to allow for quick review of historical data. For this project you apply *Formula AutoComplete* and reference functions to data to lookup phone numbers and apply statistical functions to forecast error data.
[Student Learning Outcomes 6.1, 6.3, 6.4, 6.6, 6.8]

File Needed: ***ESSClients-06.xlsx***
Completed Project File Name: ***[your initials] Excel 6-2.xlsx***

Skills Covered in This Project

- Use the *ABS* function.
- Create the *MAD* calculation.
- Use the *COUNT* function.
- Create the *MSE* calculation.
- Create basic formulas.
- Use the *STDEV.S* function.

- Apply the *INDEX* function with the *MATCH* function.
- Apply the *CONCATENATE* function.
- Use *Find and Replace*.
- Use the *Watch Window*.

1. Open the **ESSClients** workbook from your student data files folder.

2. Save the workbook as **[your initials] Excel 6-2**.

3. Calculate the mean absolute deviation (*MAD*) for forecast errors.
   a. Click cell **J5**.
   b. Type =ab and press **Tab**.
   c. Type I5-H5 and press **Enter**.
   d. Copy the formula in cell **J5** to cells **J6:J13**. Absolute values do not show any negative signs.
   e. Click cell **B16**.
   f. Use the **AVERAGE** function to calculate the mean for cells **J5:J13**. Apply **Comma** format to **B16**, and increase column widths if necessary. The result is *1,411.46*.

4. Calculate the mean square error (*MSE*) for forecast errors.
   a. Click cell **B18**.
   b. Click the **Math & Trig** button [*Formulas* tab, *Function Library* group]. Find and choose **SUMSQ**.
   c. In the *Number1* argument text box, select cells **J5:J13**.
   d. Click **OK**.
   e. Click in the **Formula bar** and position the cursor after the closing parenthesis.
   f. Type /cou and press **Tab** to select **COUNT**.
   g. Select cells **J5:J13** (Figure 6-75).
   h. Type a closing parenthesis) and press **Enter**. Apply **Comma** format to **B18**.
   i. Increase the width of the column. The result of B18 is *5,335,671.87*.

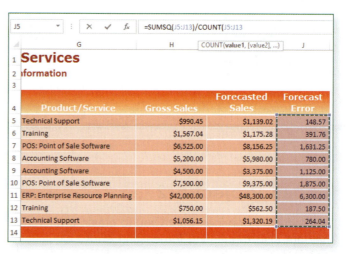

5. Calculate a standard deviation for forecast errors.
   a. Click cell **B20**.
   b. Type =std, select **STDEV.S** from the list, and press **Tab**.
   c. Select cells **J5:J13**.
   d. Press **Enter**. The result of the B20 is *1,939.43*.

6-75 *COUNT* and *SUMSQ* are combined to calculate MSE

6. Nest *INDEX* and *MATCH* functions.
   a. In cell **A23**, enter the text Type Name:, **bold** the label, and increase the font size to **14 pt.**
   b. Enter the name Jeremie Midboe in cell **B23**, **center** the name, increase the font size to **14 pt.**, and **bold** the entry.
   c. Click cell **B22**.
   d. Type =in and press **Tab** to start the *INDEX* function.
   e. For the *array* argument, press **F3**. Choose **List** and click **OK**.
   f. Type a comma (,) to move the *row_num* argument.
   g. Type m and press **Tab** to nest the *MATCH* function.
   h. For the *lookup_value* argument, type B23, including the comma to move to the next argument.
   i. For the *lookup_array* argument, select cells **A4:A13** and type a comma (,).
   j. For the *match_type* argument, click **0** in the *AutoComplete* list and press **Tab** to select it.
   k. Type a closing parenthesis) to return to the *INDEX* function.
   l. Type a comma (,) to move to the *Column_num* argument, type m, and press **Tab** to start a second nested *MATCH* function.
   m. For the *lookup_value*, type "Phone Number", including the quotation marks and comma.
   n. For the *lookup_array*, select cells **A4:J4** and type a comma (,).
   o. For the *match_type* argument, type 0 and two closing parentheses)).

p. The result is *651-333-2789* (Figure 6-76).

q. Click **B23**, type Anne Nickel, and press **Enter**. The number in B22 changes to *218-556-4211*.

7. Use the *CONCATENATE* function.
   a. Insert a column to the right of column **E**.
   b. Click cell **F4** and type City-State.
   c. Click cell **F5**.
   d. Click the **Text** button [*Formulas* tab, *Function Library* group].
   e. Choose **CONCATENATE**.
   f. For the *Text1* argument, click cell **D5**.
   g. Click in the **Text2** argument box and press the **spacebar** to include a space after the first text string.
   h. Click in the **Text3** argument box and click cell **E5**. Quotation marks are inserted with the space in the *Text2* box.
   i. Click **OK**.
   j. Copy the *CONCATENATE* formula in cell **F5** to cells **F6:F13**. Do not include formatting.
   k. Widen the column to display the data. Left align the column. Hide columns **D:E** (Figure 6-77).

8. Prepare the *Watch Window*.
   a. Click the **Watch Window** button [*Formulas* tab, *Formula Auditing* group]. Select and delete any previous watches.
   b. Click **Add Watch**, select cells **F5:F13**, and click **Add**.
   c. Size the columns in the *Watch Window* to display the complete formula.

9. Use *Find and Replace*.
   a. Select cells **F5:F13** to limit the command to these cells.
   b. Click the **Find & Select** button [*Home* tab, *Editing* group] and choose **Replace**.
   c. Click the **Options>>** button to expand the *Find and Replace* options. When the dialog box is already expanded, this command appears as <<*Options*.
   d. If necessary, click the **Format** arrow and clear previous find format settings.
   e. Click in the **Find what** box and delete previous search strings.
   f. Type " ". The *Find what* string is not case-sensitive.
   g. Click in the **Replace with** box and type ",".
   h. Set the *Within* choice to **Sheet**, the *Search* choice to **By Rows**, and the *Look In* choice to **Formulas**.

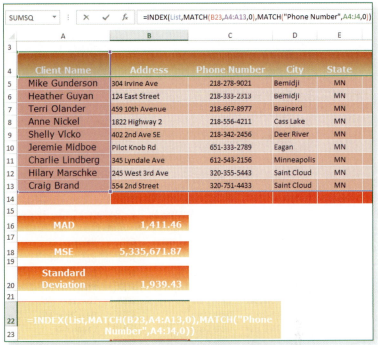

6-76 Nested *MATCH* and *IF* function syntax

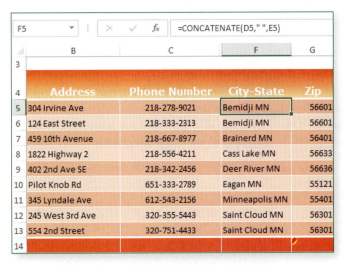

6-77 *CONCATENATE* formula shows results in single cell

i. Click **Find All** to review the cells that will be updated. Size the dialog box if needed (Figure 6-78).

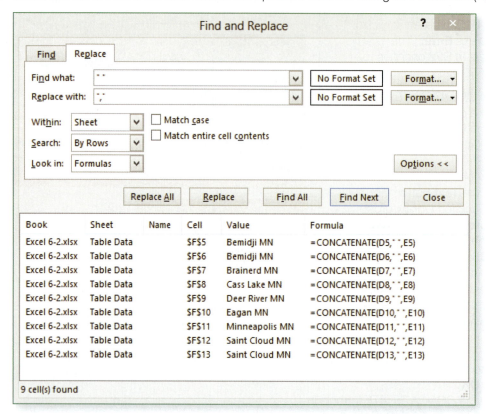

6-78 *Find and Replace* dialog box

j. Click **Replace All** and click **OK**. The city and state are now separated by a comma. There are 9 replacements made.

k. Close the *Find and Replace* dialog box.

l. Select and delete the watches in the *Watch Window*, then close it.

10. Save and close the workbook (Figure 6-79).

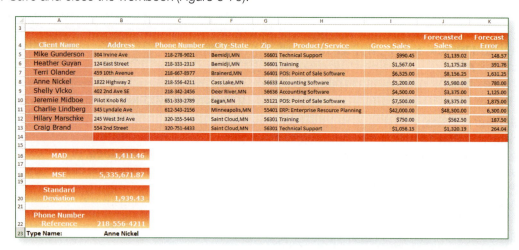

6-79 *Excel 6-2 completed*

Guided Project 6-3

The Wear-Ever Shoes company is requesting that the accounts receivable department create formulas for sales and order data. They are also requesting bonus formulas and a product reference formula to determine a quick way to review on-hand data. Finally, they would like to review some investment options as well.
[Student Learning Outcomes 6.1, 6.2, 6.3, 6.5, 6.6, 6.7, 6.8]

File Needed: ***WEInventory-06.xlsx***
Completed Project File Name: *[your initials] Excel 6-3.xlsx*

Skills Covered in This Project

- Nest an AND function in an *IF* function.
- Apply the *DAVERAGE* function.
- Apply the *DSUM* function.
- Use the *SUMIFS* function.
- Use the *AVERAGEIFS* function.
- Nest the *MATCH* and *INDEX* functions.
- Apply the *PV* function.
- Apply the *FV* function.

- Apply the *NPV* function.
- Create basic formulas.
- Apply order of precedence.
- Create a *DAVERAGE* function.
- Create a *CONCATENATE* function.
- Apply the *REPLACE* function.
- Use the *Watch Window*.
- Use *Find and Replace*.

1. Open the ***WEInventory-06*** workbook from your student data files folder.

2. Save the workbook as *[your initials] Excel 6-3*.

3. Create a formula for net income.
   a. Select the **Northern Warehouse** tab.
   b. Click cell **I5**.
   c. Type =(G5–F5)*H5.
   d. Copy the formula in **I5** to **I6:I13**.
   e. Add the *SUM* function to **I14** to total the net income column. I14 should equal $20,426.15.

4. Nest *AND* and *IF* functions.
   a. Select the **Northern Warehouse** tab.
   b. Click cell **J5**.
   c. Type =if(an and press **Tab**. The focus is now on the *AND* formula.
   d. For the *Logical1* argument, select **I5**, type >=, then select the **Bonus Info** tab, and click **C3**.
   e. Type a comma (,) to move to the *Logical2* argument.
   f. For the *Logical2* argument, select the **Northern Warehouse** tab and then click **I14**. Type >=, select the **Bonus Info** tab, and then click **C4**.
   g. Type a closing parenthesis). The focus within the formula returns to the *IF* function.
   h. Type a comma (,) to complete the *logical_test* argument.
   i. For the *value_if_true* argument, select **D3** from the **Bonus Info** tab, type +, and then select **D4** from the **Bonus Info** tab.
   j. Type a comma (,) to move to the *value_if_false* argument.
   k. Type "None".
   l. Type a closing parenthesis) and press **Enter**.

m. Edit the formula to include absolute symbols to all references except I5 within the formula (Figure 6-80).

6-80 Arguments for the nested *AND* and *IF* functions

n. Copy the formula in cell **J5** to cells **J6:J13**. Widen and right align the column to show the results. The result is *$2,250* in J5.

5. Build a *DSUM* function using the *Function Arguments* dialog box.
   a. Select the **Criteria** tab.
   b. Click cell **E3** and type men. If more text is automatically entered when you type men, then erase the text except for the word men. Criteria is not case-sensitive.
   c. Select the **Northern Warehouse** tab.
   d. Click cell **B16** and click the **Insert Function** button [*Formulas* tab, *Function Library* group].
   e. Click the **Or select a category** arrow button and choose **Database**.
   f. Select **DSUM** and click **OK**.
   g. In the *Database* argument text box, select **A4:J13**.
   h. In the *Field* argument box, type net income. Argument entries are not case sensitive, and quotation marks are entered automatically.
   i. Click in the **Criteria** argument box and select the **Criteria** tab. Select cells **A2:J3** (Figure 6-81).
   j. Click **OK**. Apply **Accounting** formatting to the result. The total net income for men's shoes is *$11,103.25*.

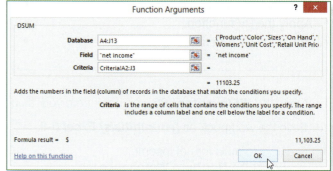

6-81 *DSUM* and its arguments

6. Type a *DAVERAGE* function.
   a. Select the **Northern Warehouse** tab.
   b. Click cell **B17**.
   c. Type =dav to display the *Formula AutoComplete* list and press **Tab** to choose **DAVERAGE**.
   d. For the *Database* argument, select cells **A4:J13**.
   e. Type a comma (,) to move to the next argument.
   f. For the *Field* argument, type "unit cost".
   g. Type a comma (,) to move to the last argument.
   h. For the *Criteria* argument, click the **Criteria** tab and select cells **A2:J3**.
   i. Press **Enter**. The closing parenthesis is automatically supplied. Apply **Accounting** formatting to **B17**. The average unit cost for men's shoes is *$39.08*.

7. Use the *Function Arguments* dialog box or typing to create a *DAVERAGE* function in cell **B18**.
   a. Use the same argument ranges listed in step 6 to determine the average of men's shoes that were actually sold.
   b. The average units sold for men's shoes is *101* (Figure 6-82).

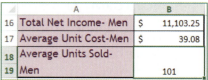

	A	B
16	Total Net Income- Men	$ 11,103.25
17	Average Unit Cost-Men	$ 39.08
18	Average Units Sold-	
19	Men	101

6-82 Database function results

8. Use the *SUMIFS* function.
   a. Select the **Northern Warehouse** tab if needed.
   b. Click cell **G16**.
   c. Click the **Math & Trig** button [*Formulas* tab, *Function Library* group] and choose **SUMIFS**.
   d. For the *Sum_range* argument, select cells **I5:I13**.
   e. Click in the **Criteria_range1** box and select cells **E5:E13**, the "*Mens/Womens*" column.
   f. Click in the **Criteria1** box and type women to sum only those cells with data for women's shoes (Figure 6-83).
   g. Click **OK**. Apply **Accounting** formatting to **G16**. The total net income for women's shoes is *$9,322.90*.

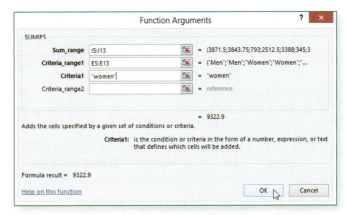

6-83 *SUMIFS* with one criteria range

9. Use the *AVERAGEIFS* function.
   a. Click cell **G18**.
   b. Click the **More Functions** button [*Formulas* tab, *Function Library* group] and choose **Statistical**.
   c. Choose **AVERAGEIFS**.
   d. For the *Average_range* argument, select cells **G5:G13**.
   e. Click in the **Criteria_range1** box and select cells **E5:E13** for women's shoes.
   f. Click in the **Criteria1** box and type women.
   g. Click in the **Criteria_range2** box and select cells **F5:F13** for the unit cost.
   h. Click in the **Criteria2** box and type >30.
   i. Click **OK**. Apply **Accounting** formatting to **G18**. The average retail price for women's shoes that cost greater than $30.00 is $72.50.

10. Nest *INDEX* and *MATCH* functions.
    a. Click the **Northern Warehouse** tab if necessary.
    b. In cell **J18**, enter the text Classy Pumps, increase the font size to **14 pt.**, and **bold** the entry.
    c. Click cell **J17**.
    d. Type =in and press **Tab** to start the *INDEX* function.
    e. For the *array* argument, select **A4:J13**.
    f. Type a comma (,) to move the *row_num* argument.
    g. Type m and press **Tab** to nest the *MATCH* function.
    h. For the *lookup_value* argument, type J18, including the comma to move to the next argument.
    i. For the *lookup_array* argument, select cells **A4:A13** and type a comma (,).
    j. For the *match_type* argument, click **0** in the *AutoComplete* list and press **Tab** to select it.
    k. Type a closing parenthesis) to return to the *INDEX* function.
    l. Type a comma (,) to move to the *Column_num* argument, type m, and press **Tab** to start a second nested *MATCH* function.
    m. For the *lookup_value*, type "On Hand", including the quotation marks and comma. The *lookup_value* is not case-sensitive.
    n. For the *lookup_array*, select cells **A4:J4** and type a comma (,).

o. For the *match_type* argument, type 0 and two closing parentheses)) (Figure 6-84). Press **Enter**.

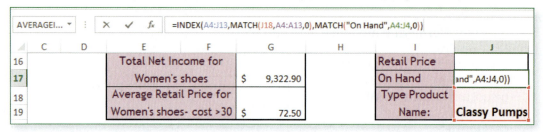

	C	D	E	F	G	H	I	J
16			Total Net Income for				Retail Price	
17			Women's shoes	$	9,322.90		On Hand	and",A4:J4,0))
18			Average Retail Price for				Type Product	
19			Women's shoes- cost >30	$	72.50		Name:	**Classy Pumps**

6-84 Nested *MATCH* and *IF* function syntax

p. The result is *408*.
q. Click **J18** and type Sassy Slip-ons. Apply **wrap text** alignment to **J18**. The number in J17 changes to *25*.

11. Use typing to create another nested *INDEX* and *MATCH* function for the Retail Unit Price.
    a. Click cell **J16** on the **Northern Warehouse** tab.
    b. Use the same argument ranges listed in step 10. For the *lookup_value*, replace *on hand* with *retail unit price*.
    c. Apply **Accounting** formatting to **J16**.
    d. *Hint: Add absolute reference symbols to the original function as required and then copy the formula to J16 for easier editing.* The retail price for sassy slip-ons is *$45.00* (Figure 6-85). The correct syntax is =INDEX($A$4:$J$13,MATCH($J$18,$A$4:$A$13,0),MATCH("Retail Unit Price",$A$4:$J$4,0)).

	I	J
16	Retail Price	$ 45.00
17	On Hand	25
18	Type Product	Sassy Slip-
19	Name:	ons

6-85 Nested *INDEX* and *MATCH* function results

12. Use the *PV* function.
    a. Select the **Investment Options** tab.
    b. Click cell **B7**.
    c. Click the **Financial** button [*Formulas* tab, *Function Library* group] and choose **PV**.
    d. Click cell **B5** for the *Rate* argument and type /12 after **B5**, because the payments are monthly.
    e. Click in the **Nper** argument box and click cell **B4**.
    f. Type *12 after **B4**, because the term is years but payments are monthly.
    g. Click in the **Pmt** box and click cell **B3**.
    h. Press **Tab** two times to skip the *Fv* box and move to the *Type* box.
    i. In the *Type* box, type 1 to indicate payment is at the beginning of the period (Figure 6-86).
    j. Click **OK**. An annuity or insurance policy today would cost $226,309.55 in order for you to achieve a $2,500 monthly payout over a period of 10 years.

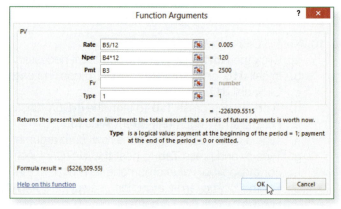

6-86 Payment is made at beginning of period

13. Use the *FV* function.
    a. Select the **Investment Options** tab if necessary.
    b. Click cell **E15**.
    c. Click the **Financial** button [*Formulas* tab, *Function Library* group] and choose **FV**.
    d. Click cell **E13** for the *Rate* argument. The payment is once a year and the rate is annual.
    e. Click in the **Nper** argument box and click cell **E12**. There is only one payment per year.
    f. Click in the **Pmt** box and click cell **E11**. The amount is negative, because you must pay it each year.
    g. Press **Tab** two times to skip the *Fv* box and move to the *Type* box. Leave both boxes empty.
    h. Click **OK**. If you invest $1,200 a year in an IRA account that earns 7% per year, you will have $49,194.59 at the end of 20 years.

14. Use the *NPV* function.
    a. Select the **Investment Options** tab if necessary.
    b. Click cell **B17**.
    c. Click the **Financial** button [*Formulas* tab, *Function Library* group] and choose **NPV**.
    d. For the *Rate* argument, click cell **B11**.
    e. Click in the **Value1** box and click cell **B14**.
    f. Click in the **Value2** box and click cell **B15**.
    g. Click in the **Value3** argument and click cell **B16**.
    h. Click **OK**.
    i. Click in the **Formula bar** to edit the formula to include the initial investment payment.
    j. Place your cursor after the closing parenthesis and type +.
    k. Click cell **B12** and press **Enter** (Figure 6-87). Based on the projected cash flows, this investment is worth $3,407.35 today.

15. Use the *CONCATENATE* function.
    a. Click the **Investment Options** sheet tab and click cell **C22**.
    b. Click the **Text** button [*Formulas* tab, *Function Library* group].
    c. Choose **CONCATENATE**.
    d. For the *Text1* argument, click cell **A22**.
    e. Click in the **Text2** argument box and type . to include a period after the first text string.
    f. Click in the **Text3** argument box and click cell **B22**.
    g. Click in the **Text4** argument box and type @USBanks.com. Quotation marks are inserted with the entries in the *Text2* and *Text4* boxes.
    h. Click **OK**.
    i. Copy the *CONCATENATE* function in cell **C22** to cells **C23:C24**. Widen the column to display the data if necessary (Figure 6-88).

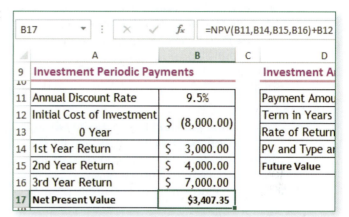

B17	▼	:	×	✓	*fx*	=NPV(B11,B14,B15,B16)+B12

	A	B	C	D
9	**Investment Periodic Payments**			**Investment A**
10				
11	Annual Discount Rate	9.5%		Payment Amou
12	Initial Cost of Investment	$ (8,000.00)		Term in Years
13	0 Year			Rate of Return
14	1st Year Return	$ 3,000.00		PV and Type a
15	2nd Year Return	$ 4,000.00		**Future Value**
16	3rd Year Return	$ 7,000.00		
17	**Net Present Value**	$3,407.35		

6-87 Edited *NPV* function includes initial investment payment

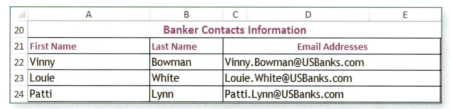

	A	B	C	D	E
20		**Banker Contacts Information**			
21	**First Name**	**Last Name**		**Email Addresses**	
22	Vinny	Bowman		Vinny.Bowman@USBanks.com	
23	Louie	White		Louie.White@USBanks.com	
24	Patti	Lynn		Patti.Lynn@USBanks.com	

6-88 *CONCATENATE* formula shows results in single cell

16. Use the *REPLACE* function.
    a. Select the **Investment Options** tab if necessary.
    b. Click **F22**.
    c. Type =rep and press **Tab**.
    d. Select cell **C22** for the *old_text* argument.
    e. Type a comma and the number one (,1) to indicate that the *start_num* character is the first character.
    f. Type a comma (,) to move to the *num_chars* argument.
    g. Type a 5 to indicate that five characters will be replaced.
    h. Type a comma (,) to move to the *new_text* argument.
    i. Type "V" including the quotation marks.

E6-361

j. Press **Enter**.

k. Repeat this formula in **F23:F24** using each banker's first letter of his/her first name for the *new_text* argument (Figure 6-89).

	C	D	E	F	G	H
21	**Email Addresses**			**Updated Email Address**		
22	=CONCATENATE(A22,".",B22,"@USBanks.com")			=REPLACE(C22,1,5,"V")		
23	=CONCATENATE(A23,".",B23,"@USBanks.com")			=REPLACE(C23,1,5,"L")		
24	=CONCATENATE(A24,".",B24,"@USBanks.com")			=REPLACE(C24,1,5,"P")		

6-89 *REPLACE* and *CONCATENATE* syntax

l. Add the *Today* function to cell **D3** and format it as a **short date**.

17. Prepare the *Watch Window*.

a. Select the **Northern Warehouse** tab.

b. Click the **Watch Window** button [*Formulas* tab, *Formula Auditing* group]. Select and delete any previous watches.

c. Click **Add Watch**, select cells **J5:J13**, and click **Add**.

d. Size the columns in the *Watch Window* to display the complete formula.

18. Use *Find and Replace*.

a. Click the **Find & Select** button [*Home* tab, *Editing* group] and choose **Replace**.

b. Click the **Options>>** button to expand the *Find and Replace* options. When the dialog box is already expanded, this command appears as <<*Options*.

c. If necessary, click the **Format** arrow and clear previous find format settings.

d. Click in the **Find what** box and delete previous search strings.

e. Type "None".

f. Click in the **Replace with** box and delete previous replace text; then type 0.

g. Set the *Within* choice to **Sheet**, the *Search* choice to **By Rows**, the *Look In* choice to **Formulas**, and the check the **Match case** box.

h. Click **Find All** to review the cells that will be updated. Size the dialog box if needed.

i. Click **Replace All** and click **OK**. There were 9 replacements.

j. Close the *Find and Replace* dialog box.

19. Select and delete the watches in the *Watch Window* and then close the window.

20. Save and close the workbook (Figure 6-90).

6-90 Excel 6-3 complete worksheets

Independent Project 6-4

Placer Hills Real Estate (PHRE) is a real estate company with regional offices throughout central California. Real estate agents working for PHRE must create a reference function to search data for listings that meet a criteria. They must also calculate tiered commissions using a nested logical function.
[Student Learning Outcomes 6.2, 6.3, 6.7, 6.8]

File Needed: ***PHREHotSheet-06.xlsx***
Completed Project File Name: ***[your initials] Excel 6-4.xlsx***

Skills Covered in This Project

- Apply a nested *IF* function.
- Use the *COUNTIFS* function.
- Use the *AVERAGEIFS* function.
- Nest the *MATCH* and *INDEX* functions.

- Create basic formulas.
- Apply order of precedence.
- Use the *Watch Window*.

1. Open the ***PHREHotSheet-06*** workbook and save the workbook as ***[your initials] Excel 6-4***.

2. Nest *INDEX* and *MATCH* functions in **N3** on the *Hot Sheet* tab to determine the list price of homes based on the MLS number in **N2**.
   a. Select **N2** and type the number 005.
   b. Click cell **N3** and enter the *INDEX* function.
   c. Select **A3:K15** for the *array* argument.
   d. Use **MATCH(N2,B3:B15,0)** for the *MATCH* function *row_num* argument.
   e. Use **MATCH("List Price",A3:K3,0)** for the *MATCH* function *column_num* argument (Figure 6-91). The result is *$1,800,000.00*.

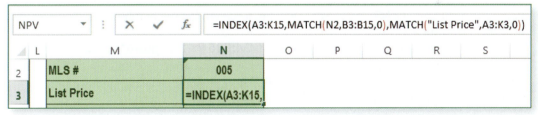

6-91 *MATCH* and *INDEX* function syntax

   f. Click **N2** and type 007. The result changes to *$2,225,000.00*.

3. Use typing to create another nested *INDEX* and *MATCH* function in cell **N4** to determine the square footage based on the MLS number in **N2**.
   a. Use the same argument ranges listed in step 2.
   b. *Hint: Add absolute reference symbols to the original function as required; then copy the formula to N4 for easier editing.*
   c. Apply **Comma** formatting to the result in **N4**. The square footage for MLS number 007 is *3,000*.

4. Nest an *AND* and an *IF* function in **A4** to determine if you show a home based on the number of bedrooms, bathrooms, and list price in **E4**, **F4**, and **I4**, respectively.
    a. Select **A4** on the **Hot Sheet** tab.
    b. Use **E4=N12**, **F4=N13**, and **I4<N14** for the *AND* function arguments.
    c. For the *IF* function, type "Yes" for *value_if_true* argument and "No" for *value_if_false* argument.
    d. Edit the formula to include absolute symbols to all references necessary within the formula.
    e. Copy the formula in cell **A4** to cells **A5:A15** without formats. **Center** align the column to show the results. The result in A4 is *No* (Figure 6-92).

	A4	:	✕	✓	fx	=IF(AND(E4=$N$12,F4=$N$13,I4<$N$14),"Yes","No")

	A	B	C	D	E	F
3	Showing	MLS#	County	Address	Bedrooms	Bathrooms
4	No	001	Alameda	124 Easy Way	4	4
5	No	002	Alameda	901 Whinnie Street	2	1
6	Yes	003	Butte	9023 View Estates	3	2
7	No	004	Butte	455 32nd Avenue	2	2
8	No	005	Humboldt	1610 Sunshine Loop	4	3
9	No	006	Humboldt	7784 Lazy Creek Drive	2	1
10	No	007	Marin	7785 Johnson boulevard	5	4
11	Yes	008	Sacramento	6544 Turtle Lake Turnpike	3	2
12	Yes	009	Sacramento	6102 Turtle Lake Turnpike	3	2
13	No	010	Santa Clara	2533 Affluence Avenue	6	4
14	No	011	Santa Clara	456 North Street	2	1
15	Yes	012	Santa Clara	2098 Irving Avenue	3	2

6-92 Arguments and results for the nested *AND* and *IF* functions

6. Apply the *AVERAGEIFS* function to cell **N7** on the *Hot Sheet* tab to determine the average list price for a home on more than seven-tenths of an acre containing more than two bedrooms.
    a. For the *Average_range* argument, select cells **I4:I15**.
    b. For the *Criteria_range1* box, select cells **K4:K15** for acres.
    c. For the *Criteria1* box, type >.7.
    d. For the *Criteria_range2* box, select cells **E4:E15** for the number of bedrooms.
    e. For the *Criteria2* box, type >2. The result is *$2,181,250.00*.

7. Copy the *AVERAGEIFS* function in cell **N7** to **N9** on the *Hot Sheet* tab to determine the average list price for a home on less than seven-tenths of an acre that has more than two bedrooms.
    a. Apply absolute references as needed in the *AVERAGEIFS* in cell **N7** and copy it to **N9**.
    b. Edit the formula in **N9** so the *Criteria1* is "<.7". The result is *$736,333.33*.

8. Apply *COUNTIFS* to cell **N8** on the *Hot Sheet* tab to determine the number of homes less than seven years old with over 2000 square feet.
    a. For the *Criteria_range1* argument, select cells **G4:G15** for the square footage.
    b. For the *Criteria1* box, type >2000.
    c. For the *Criteria_range2* box, select cells **H4:H15**.
    d. For the Criteria2 box, type <10. The function result is *3.00*.

9. Create a basic formula in **B11** on the *Commissions* tab that multiplies the listing commission by the property sales amount.

10. Create a nested *IF* function to determine realtor commission split.
    a. Select the **Commissions** tab and click the cell **B12**.
    b. Apply a nested *IF* function using the following syntax **=IF(B9<=C4,D4*B11,IF(B9<=C5,B11*D5, IF(B9<=C6,B11*D6,B11*D7)))**. The result is *$181,500*.

11. Create a nested *IF* function to determine fee calculations based on B12 commissions.
    a. Select the **Commissions** tab and click the cell **B13**.
    b. Apply a nested *IF* function using B12 as an example.
    c. *Hint: Use your auditing options to change column D references (commission percentages) to column E (fee percentages) and change all B11 (total commission) references to B12 (realtor commission split). The result in B13 is $22,687.50.*

12. Create a basic formula in **B14** that subtracts the fee calculation from the realtor commission split. The result is $158,812.50.

13. Add cells **B12** and **B13** from the **Commissions** tab to the *Watch Window*.

14. Save and close the workbook (Figure 6-93).

Showing	MLS#	County	Address	Bedrooms	Bathrooms	Sq Ft	Age	List Price	Garage	Acres
			PHRE Hot Sheet Daily Listing Information							
No	001	Alameda	124 Easy Way	4	4	2200	10	$ 1,200,000.00	2	1.00
No	002	Alameda	901 Whinnie Street	2	1	950	12	$ 650,000.00	1	0.50
Yes	003	Butte	9023 View Estates	3	2	1200	7	$ 899,000.00	1	0.70
No	004	Butte	455 32nd Avenue	2	2	1000	10	$ 700,000.00	1	0.55
No	005	Humboldt	1610 Sunshine Loop	4	3	2500	5	$ 1,800,000.00	2	0.75
No	006	Humboldt	7784 Lazy Creek Drive	2	1	900	15	$ 599,000.00	0	0.30
No	007	Marin	7785 Johnson boulevard	5	4	3000	5	$ 2,225,000.00	3	1.50
Yes	008	Sacramento	6544 Turtle Lake Turnpike	3	2	2100	15	$ 675,000.00	1	0.50
Yes	009	Sacramento	6102 Turtle Lake Turnpike	3	2	2000	7	$ 685,000.00	0	0.30
No	010	Santa Clara	2533 Affluence Avenue	6	4	4000	5	$ 3,500,000.00	4	2.00
No	011	Santa Clara	456 North Street	2	1	1250	15	$ 799,000.00	1	0.50
Yes	012	Santa Clara	2098 Irving Avenue	3	2	1500	9	$ 849,000.00	0	0.30

MLS Search Engine

MLS #	007
List Price	$ 2,225,000.00
Square Footage	3,000.00

List Price Information

Avg, >.7 acres, >2 beds	$ 2,181,250.00
Count, >2000 sq ft, <10 yrs	3.00
Avg <.7 acre >2 beds	$ 736,333.33

Enter Home Data for Scheduling Showings

Bedrooms	3
Bathrooms	2
List Price Less Than	$ 1,000,000.00

PHRE COMMISSION INFORMATION

Tier	Minimum Sales	Maximum Sales	Commission Split	Fees
1	$ -	$ 1,499,999.00	25%	9.0%
2	$ 1,500,000.00	$ 5,499,999.00	35%	11.0%
3	$ 5,500,000.00	$ 9,499,999.00	55%	12.5%
4	$ 9,500,000.00	$ 13,499,999.00	75%	13.5%

Property Sale	$ 5,500,000.00
Listing Commission	6%
Total Commission	$ 330,000.00
Realtor Commision Split	$ 181,500.00
Fee Calculation	$ 22,687.50
Net Pay	$ 158,812.50

6-93 Excel 6-4 completed worksheets

Independent Project 6-5

Courtyard Medical Plaza (CMP) is a full-service medical office complex providing customers with a variety of medical services in one plaza location. Your doctor has asked you to create advanced formulas to determine reward options for attaining your workout goals, alerts for diet issues, and database values for average daily calorie intake.
[Student Learning Outcomes 6.1, 6.2, 6.3, 6.6, 6.8]

File Needed: **CMPHealthGoals-06.xlsx**
Completed Project File Name: **[your initials] Excel 6-5.xlsx**

Skills Covered in This Project

- Apply the *DAVERAGE* function.
- Apply the *SUM* function.
- Nest the *MATCH* and *INDEX* functions.
- Nest the *OR* and *IF* functions.

- Apply order of precedence.
- Create a *CONCATENATE* function.
- Use *Find and Replace*.

1. Open the **CMPHealthGoals-06** workbook and save the workbook as **[your initials] Excel 6-5**.

2. Select **C17** on the *Goals* tab and apply the *DSUM* function to total calories burned from the *Fitness Journal* tab when working more than 20 minutes on strength training and 10 minutes on cardio.
   a. Select **A7:H14** in the **Fitness Journal** sheet for the *database* argument.
   b. Use "calories burned" for the *field* argument.
   c. Use the current entries in the criteria range **A3:H4** on the *Fitness Journal* tab for the *criteria* argument. The result is *500*.

3. Select **C18** on the *Goals* tab and apply the *DSUM* function for calorie intake from the *Fitness Journal* tab when working more than 20 minutes on strength training and 10 minutes on cardio.
   a. Select **A7:H14** in the **Fitness Journal** sheet for the *database* argument.
   b. Use "calorie intake" for the *field* argument.
   c. Use the current entries in the criteria range **A3:H4** on the *Fitness Journal* tab for the *criteria* argument. The result is *1800*.

4. Select **F17** on the *Goals* tab and apply the *DAVERAGE* function for weight from the *Fitness Journal* tab when working more than 20 minutes on strength training and 10 minutes on cardio.
   a. Select **A7:H14** in the **Fitness Journal** sheet for the *database* argument.
   b. Use "weight" for the *field* argument.
   c. Use the current entries in the criteria range **A3:H4** on the *Fitness Journal* tab for the *criteria* argument. The result is *145*.

5. Select **F18** on the *Goals* tab and apply the *DAVERAGE* function for cholesterol from the *Fitness Journal* tab when working more than 20 minutes on strength training and 10 minutes on cardio.
   a. Select **A7:H14** for the *database* argument.
   b. Use "cholesterol" for the *field* argument.
   c. Use the current entries in the criteria range **A3:H4** on the *Fitness Journal* tab for the *criteria* argument. The result is *220*.

6. Nest *INDEX* and *MATCH* functions in **I6** on the *Goals* tab to return calorie intake for the date in **I5**.
   a. In cell **I5** enter the date 1/16/2016.
   b. Click cell **I6** and enter the *INDEX* function.
   c. Select **A7:H14** on the *Fitness Journal* tab for the *array* argument.
   d. Use **MATCH(I5,'Fitness Journal'!A8:A14,0)** for the *INDEX* function's *row_num* argument.
   e. Use **MATCH("Calorie Intake",'Fitness Journal'!A7:H7,0)** for the *INDEX* function's *column_num* argument. The result is *2,000*.
   f. Click **I5** and type 1/18/2016. The result is *1,800*.

7. Nest an *INDEX* and *MATCH* function in cell **I7** on the *Goals* tab to return calories burned for the date in **I5**.
   a. Use the same argument ranges listed in step 6.
   b. *Hint: Add absolute reference symbols to the original function as required; then copy the formula to I7 for easier editing*. The total calories burned for 1/18/16 is *500* (Figure 6-94).

6-94 Nested *MATCH* and *INDEX* function syntax with absolute references

8. Create another nested *INDEX* and *MATCH* function in cell **I8** on the *Goals* tab to return weight for the date in **I5**.
   a. Use the same argument ranges listed in step 6 and 7.
   b. *Hint: Add absolute reference symbols to the original function as required; then copy the formula to **I8** for easier editing*. The total weight for 1/18/16 is 145.

9. Nest an *OR* and an *IF* function in cell **I13** on the *Goals* tab to return the reward if one of the daily goals for calorie intake, calories burned, or average weight is met.
   a. Use **I6<=C8**, **I7<=C9**, and **I8<=C14** for the *OR* function arguments.
   b. For the *IF* function, select **C15** for the *value_if_true* argument and enter "No" for the *value_if_false* argument. The result in I13 is *Small Treat* (Figure 6-95).

6-95 Syntax for the nested *OR* and *IF* functions

10. Nest an *OR* and an *IF* function in cell **I14** on the *Goals* tab to return the reward if one of the weekly goals for calorie intake, calories burned, or average weight is met.
    a. Use '**Fitness Journal**'!D15<=Goals!D8, '**Fitness Journal**'!E15<=Goals!D9, and '**Fitness Journal**'!F15<=Goals!D14 for the *OR* function arguments.
    b. For the *IF* function, select **D15** for the *value_if_true* argument and type "No" for the *value_if_false* argument. The result in I14 is *Dine Out*.

11. Nest an *AND* and an *IF* function in cell **I15** on the *Goals* tab to return the reward if both daily and weekly goals are met.
    a. Use **I13<>"No"** and **I14<>"No"** for the *AND* function arguments.
    b. For the *IF* function, type "Yes" for *value_if_true* and "No" for *value_if_false*. The result in I15 is *Yes*.

12. Use the *CONCATENATE* function in cell **E2** on the *Goals* tab to combine the first and last name of the client name and both parts of the client number.
    a. For the *Text1* argument, use cell **C2**.
    b. Click in the **Text2** argument box and type a space (it will be enclosed in quotation marks) to include a space after the first text string.
    c. Click in the **Text3** argument box and click cell **D2**.
    d. Copy the *CONCATENATE* formula (do not include formatting) in cell **E2** to **E3**. Apply **White, Background 1** text format to cells **C2:D3**. This step hides the text that is used in the function.

13. Use *Find and Replace* to replace all occurrences of "No" with "Not Yet" in the formulas in **I13:I15** on the **Goals** tab. Five replacements are made in the functions.

14. Save and close the workbook (Figure 6-96).

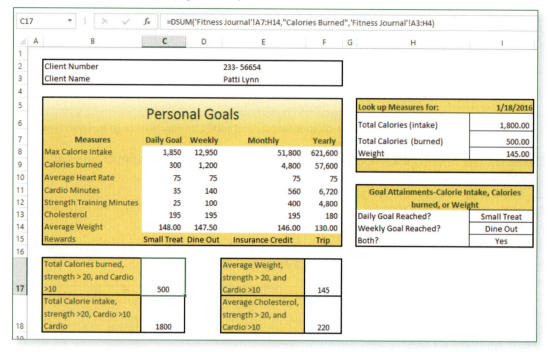

6-96 Excel 6-5 completed worksheet

Independent Project 6-6

Clemenson Imaging LLC is requesting that the accounts receivable department create formulas for order history and order forecasting. They are also asking for bonus formulas and a reference formula to determine a quick way to review types of images. Finally, they would like to review some investment options as well.

[Student Learning Outcomes 6.1, 6.2, 6.3, 6.4, 6.5, 6.6]

File Needed: *TechSchedule-06.xlsx*
Completed Project File Name: *[your initials] Excel 6-6.xlsx*

Skills Covered in This Project

- Use the *ABS* function.
- Use the *SUMSQ* function.
- Use the *COUNT* function.
- Create the *MSE* calculation.
- Apply the *STDEV.S* function.
- Apply the *DAVERAGE* function.

- Apply order of precedence.
- Create a nested *IF* function.
- Nest the *MATCH* and *INDEX* functions.
- Apply the *PV* function.
- Create basic formulas.
- Create a *CONCATENATE* function.

---

1. Open the **TechSchedule-06** workbook and save the workbook as **[your initials] Excel 6-6**.

2. Apply *SUM* formulas to the *Monday* sheet for totals in **D16:E16**. **Center** the results.

3. Select **F9**, apply the *ABS* function to the following formula: **E9–D9**. Copy **F9** to **F10:F15**, and **center** the results.

4. Calculate the mean square error (*MSE*) in **B18** for forecast errors in **F9:F15**. *Hint: see SLO 6.4: Building Statistical Calculations for help*. Apply **Comma** formatting to **B18**. The result is *2.14*.

5. Calculate the standard deviation in **B19** for forecast errors in **F9:F15**. *Hint: see SLO 6.4: Building Statistical Calculations for help*. Apply **Comma** formatting to **F9:F15**. The result is *0.76*.

6. Create a *DAVERAGE* function in **B20** on the *Monday* tab to determine the average number of actual cardiac patients in the database.
   a. Type cardiac in **G3**.
   b. Select **B8:I15** as the *database* argument.
   c. Type "Actual Patients" for the *field* argument.
   d. Select **B2:I3** as the *criteria* argument. Apply **Comma** formatting to **B20**. The result is 5.33.

7. Create a nested *IF* function in **I18** on the *Monday* tab to assign a bonus based on the amount of scans completed.
   a. Input **D16<E19** for the first *logical_test* argument, and 0 for the *value_if_true* argument.
   b. Nest a second *IF* function in the first *IF* function for the *value_if_false* argument using **D16<E20** as the second *logical_test*.
   c. Return **F19** for the second *IF* function's *value_if_true* argument and **F20** for the *value_if_false* argument. The result in I18 is *$350.00*.

8. Nest *INDEX* and *MATCH* functions in **I19** on the *Monday* tab to display the image type that was completed at a hospital entered in **I20**.
   a. In cell **I20** enter the hospital South point, and widen the column to fit the entry.
   b. Click cell **I19**; enter the *INDEX* function.
   c. Select **B8:I15** on the *Monday* tab for the *array* argument.
   d. Use **MATCH(I20,C8:C15,0)** for the *INDEX* function's *row_num* argument.
   e. Use **MATCH("Image Type",B8:I8,0)** for the *INDEX* function's *column_num* argument. The result is *OB*. **Center** the result in **I20**.
   f. Click **I20** and type Haskins. The result changes to *Cardiac*.

9. Use the *PV* function in **B8** on the *Investment Options* tab to determine the present value of an investment if the organization were to invest $2,200.00 per month (at the beginning of the period), for 10 years at a 4.5% rate of return. The result is *negative $213,072.55*.

10. Use the *CONCATENATE* function in **D12** on the *Investment Options* tab to create the new email addresses of the bankers.
    a. The email addresses appear as Firstname.Lastname@USALenders.com.
    b. Copy the *CONCATENATE* formula (do not include formatting) in cell **D12** to **D13:D15**.

11. Add the *Today* function to cell **G4**; format it as a **short date**.

12. Save and close the workbook (Figure 6-97).

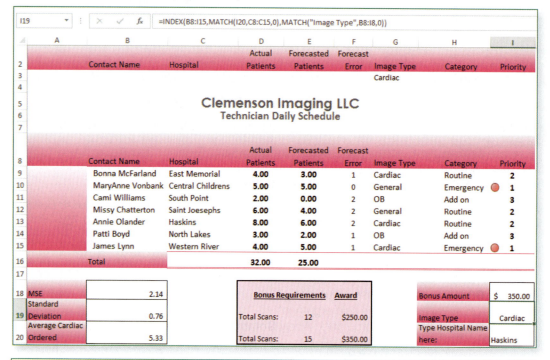

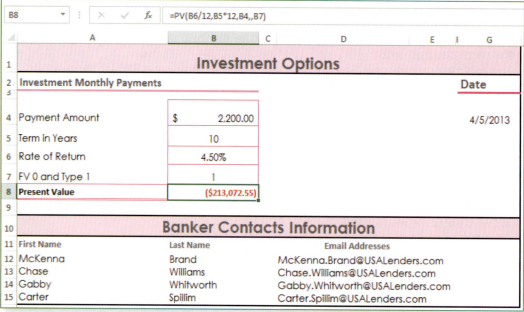

6-97 Excel 6-6 completed worksheets

Improve It Project 6-7

The Livingood Income Tax and Accounting organization is requesting that the accounts receivable department create formulas for payment history and forecasting. They are also requesting penalty formulas and a reference formula to determine a quick way to review types of payments. Finally, they would like to review some investment options as well. You will edit the partially completed worksheet to assure accuracy.

[Student Learning Outcomes 6.1, 6.2, 6.3, 6.4, 6.6, 6.8]

File Needed: *TaxSchedule-06.xlsx*
Completed Project File Name: *[your initials] Excel 6-7.xlsx*

Skills Covered in This Project

- Use the *ABS* function.
- Use the *SUMSQ* function.
- Use the *COUNT* function.
- Create the *MSE* calculation.
- Apply the *STDEV.S* function.
- Apply the *DAVERAGE* function.

- Apply order of precedence.
- Create a nested *IF* function.
- Nest the *MATCH* and *INDEX* functions.
- Create a *CONCATENATE* function.
- Use Find and *REPLACE*.

1. Open the **TaxSchedule-06** workbook and save the workbook as **[your initials] Excel 6-7**.

2. Edit **J9** in the *Payment* worksheet tab to include the *ABS* function.
   a. Apply **Comma** formatting to **J9**.
   b. Copy the correct formula in **J9** to **J10:J15**. The correct value in **J9** is *51.25*.

3. Edit the *MSE* calculation in **C2** on the *Payment* tab to use the forecast error data in column **J** in place of the current arrays. The result is *11,905.41*.

4. Edit the standard deviation calculation in **C3** on the *Payment* tab to use the forecast error data in column **J** in place of the current array. The result is *89.33*.

5. Edit the **DAVERAGE** function in **C4** on the *Payment* tab.
   a. Ensure that everything is spelled correctly in the function.
   b. Apply **Currency** formatting to **C4**. The result is *$801.90*.

6. Edit the nested *IF* function in **K9** on the *Payment* tab.
   a. Indicate a $35.00 (**H3**) penalty if the contact type was a *Letter,* a $75.00 (**H4**) penalty if the contact type was *Collections*, and the word "None" if any other type of contact was made. The result is *None*.
   b. Ensure all absolute reference symbols are included.
   c. Copy this formula from **K9** to **K10:K15**.

7. Edit the nested *INDEX* and *MATCH* formula in **K2** on the *Payment* tab to return **Yes** or **No** if an invoice has been paid that's entered in **K3**. The result is *Yes*.

8. Edit the *PV* function in cell **B8** on the *Investment Options* tab to reflect a monthly payment of $2,000 each month, for 10 years, at a 5.50% rate. The result is negative *$184,287.16*.

9. Edit the *CONCATENATE* function to include a period (**.**) after the first name in **D12**. The result is *Craig.Brand@LendersUS.com*. Copy the formula in **D12** to **D13:D14** without formatting.

10. Save and close the workbook (Figure 6-98).

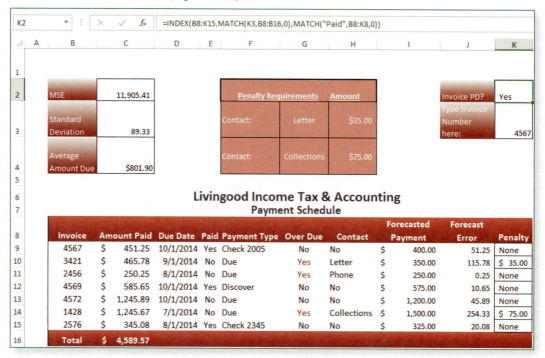

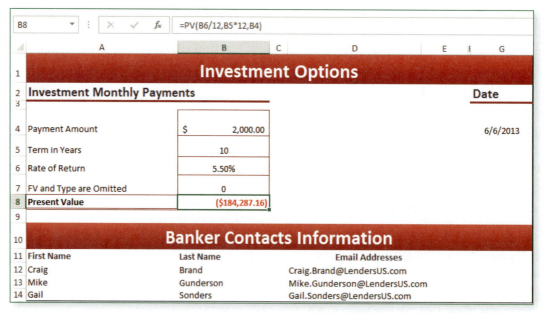

6-98 Excel 6-7 completed worksheets

Challenge Project 6-8

For this project, you will consolidate your monthly bank statements into an Excel workbook. You will apply formatting, advanced functions, and penalty options that are outlined below.
[Student Learning Outcomes 6.2, 6.5, 6.8]

File needed: None
Completed Project File Name: *[your initials] Excel 6-8.xlsx*

Enter all data that you find important from your checking account. Create a new workbook and save it as *[your initials] Excel 6-8*.

- Import or type the website information from your bank for the last month into your Excel workbook.
- When creating your spreadsheets, you may add additional column headings such as "Due Date," "Amount," "Check Number," "Withdrawals," "Deposits," "Overdue," "Paid," "Balance," etc.
- Apply formatting as you see fit.
- Add total formulas to the key columns.
- Create a nested *INDEX* function with a *MATCH* function to find the amount of a check number that was processed.
- Create a nested *IF* function that returns the amount the bank charges for an insufficient funds occurrence for a check or debit transaction. For example, use $25 dollars for a returned check plus $35 dollars for an overdraft on your account.
- Use *Find and Replace* to alter formulas to reflect the accurate overdraft charges after contacting your bank.

Challenge Project 6-9

For this project, you consolidate your professors' contact information and your course information into an Excel workbook. You will combine text strings for email addresses, apply *IFERROR* functions, and use database functions to determine total hours spent in class.
[Student Learning Outcomes 6.1, 6.2, 6.3, 6.6, 6.8]

File Needed: None
Completed Project File Name: *[your initials] Excel 6-9.xlsx*

Enter all data that you find important regarding your class grades and instructor contact information. Create a new workbook and save it as *[your initials] Excel 6-9*.

- Import the website information for this semester from your school's class grades into your Excel workbook.

- When creating your class grading spreadsheet, you may add additional column headings such as "Class Title," "Class Number," "Start Date," "End Date," "Withdraw Deadline," "Location," "Professor," "Email," "Class Days," "Class Times," "Special Notes," "Grades," "Credits," etc.
- Create a criteria range.
- Apply database functions to determine average time spent in a specific classroom or with a specific professor.
- Apply *IF* functions to determine what level of reward you receive if you attain a certain grade.
- Apply *CONCATENATE* functions to your professors' information to create their email addresses.

Challenge Project 6-10

For this project, you create investment options and analyze the results. You apply *PV*, *FV*, and *NPV* functions to three personal financial scenarios. You use nested *IF* functions and nested *INDEX* and *MATCH* functions to look up bank information.
[Student Learning Outcomes 6.2, 6.3, 6.5, 6.6]

File Needed: None
Completed Project File Name: *[your initials] Excel 6-10.xlsx*

Enter all data that you find important regarding three investment options. Create a new workbook and save it as *[your initials] Excel 6-10*.

- For the *NPV* scenario, include items such as annual discount rate, initial cost of investment, first year return, second year return, etc.
- For the *PV* scenario, include payment amount, term in years, and rate of return. Be sure to decide if you are paying monthly or annually.
- For the *FV* scenario (IRA), include the same items as listed above for the *PV* scenario.
- Build a nested *IF* function to determine which investment option is best.
- Create a listing of six local banks in the area and include information such as "Interest Rates," "Contact Name," "Phone Number," and "Website address."
- Add *CONCATENATE* functions where needed to combine contact names and email addresses.
- Create a nested *INDEX* and *MATCH* function to look up a contact name based on the bank name.
- Determine rate of return and discount rate from your local bank.

CHAPTER 7

Setting Validation, Creating Forms, Sharing and Protecting Workbooks

CHAPTER OVERVIEW

There are a number of ways to monitor accuracy in your work. For example, you can use the error-checking features that Excel provides to help you locate formula problems. Another way to increase accuracy in your workbooks is data validation, which checks data as it is entered. Data validation ensures accuracy and consistency in worksheets. Similarly, you can use form controls to streamline data entry. In Excel, templates are available that can also contribute to accuracy as well as consistency. This chapter covers several topics to improve the accuracy of your worksheets and help you manage worksheets when you collaborate and share work with others.

STUDENT LEARNING OUTCOMES (SLOs)

After completing this chapter, you will be able to:

SLO 7.1 Set data validation, input messages, and error alerts (p. E7-376).

SLO 7.2 Create and use a form with form controls and *ActiveX* controls (p. E7-382).

SLO 7.3 Create a workbook from a template and save a new template (p. E7-388).

SLO 7.4 Mark a workbook as final and encrypt a workbook with a password (p. E7-390).

SLO 7.5 Share a workbook, set change tracking options, and compare and merge workbooks (p. E7-397).

SLO 7.6 Inspect a workbook, check compatibility, and define a trusted location (p. E7-402).

Case Study

In the Pause & Practice projects in this chapter, you work with marketing inventory worksheets for Paradise Lakes Resort (PLR). You add data validation for the worksheet to make it easy for each employee to enter data, add form controls, apply protection, and use an Excel template. You also share, compare, and merge workbooks with others.

Pause & Practice 7-1: Add data validation settings to a worksheet.

Pause & Practice 7-2: Use a data form, add form controls, apply workbook protection, and save a template.

Pause & Practice 7-3: Share a workbook, compare and merge workbooks, and prepare a workbook for distribution.

EXCEL

Setting Data Validation

Data validation is a process in which Excel checks data as it is entered to verify that it matches the established requirements. In a marketing worksheet, for example, Paradise Lakes Resort can use data validation to make sure that only certain entries are allowed for locations and job titles. The company might also set a data validation rule that requires an invoice amount to be positive, or require the number of sales calls made to clients to be greater than 5. When entering the amount of sales calls made each day into a spreadsheet, any number less than 5 would cause a pop-up message reminding the data entry person of the error. In its own way, data validation is a type of error checking. It also helps to make your worksheets consistent and easy to use.

When you set data validation, you establish criteria for a range of cells. You can set an optional *error alert message*, a pop-up message that appears after an error is entered. You can also set an optional *input message*, a comment message that appears in an active cell before an entry is made. There are multiple steps involved in setting data validation, so it is primarily used in worksheets that are used repeatedly with routine data entries.

Validation Settings

Validation settings are the rules applied to data as it is entered. You can build a simple condition using relational operators, such as requiring an entry to be a whole number between 1 and 10. You can set date or time limits by specifying a range of dates or times. Or you can limit the length of a text entry as with an abbreviation of a state. It is also possible to use a list or a formula in a data validation setting.

> ### MORE INFO
>
> When any entry is acceptable, the *Data Validation* dialog box allows *Any value*.

When you use an operator, you can specify that a value be greater than, less than, or within a range of values. You can allow or prohibit decimal values, too.

You usually set data validation before any data is entered. You can set it after data is entered but, if you do that, keep in mind that already-entered data that does not meet the rule will not be automatically flagged.

HOW TO: Set Data Validation with an Operator

1. Select the cell or the cell range where you want data validation settings.
2. Click the **Data Validation** button [*Data* tab, *Data Tools* group].
   - The *Data Validation* dialog box opens with three tabs.
3. Click the **Settings** tab.
4. Click the **Allow** drop-down arrow and choose an option.
   - The *Data* options change based on the *Allow* setting.
   - To clear existing validation, choose **Any Value** or click **Clear All**.
   - To set a particular value or range of values, choose **Whole Number** or **Decimal**.
5. Click the **Data** drop-down arrow and choose an operator.
   - Options change based on the operator.

6. Enter a value or select a cell to complete the *Data* settings (Figure 7-1).

7. Click **OK**.

- Cells with data that does not match the criteria are not flagged.

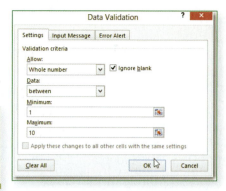

7-1 Data validation settings

> **MORE INFO**
>
> To view examples of formulas used in data validation, search "data validation formula" in your Internet browser.

Validation Lists

In the *Data Validation* dialog box, you can specify that a user select from a specified list. You can type the entries for the list in the dialog box, separating items with commas. Alternatively, you can select a cell range in the workbook that includes the list or use its range name.

When you build a data validation list, the user sees a drop-down arrow when he or she selects the cell on the worksheet as shown in Figure 7-2. The user then selects an entry from the list. If you plan to use a list, it is a good idea to sort the data in alphabetical order or type the entries in some other logical order. This makes it easier for the user to make his or her choice.

7-2 A data validation list

HOW TO: Set a Data Validation List

1. Select the cell or the cell range where you want data validation settings.

2. Click the **Data Validation** button [*Data* tab, *Data Tools* group].

3. Click the **Settings** tab.

4. Click the **Allow** drop-down arrow and choose **List**.

5. Click in the **Source** entry box and perform one of the following options (Figure 7-3):

- Select the range of cells containing the list.
- Press **F3** to display a list of range names, choose the range, and click **OK**.
- Type each entry for the list, followed by a comma.

6. Click **OK**.

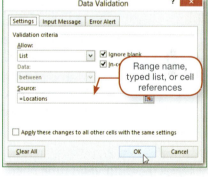

7-3 Validation settings for a list

Circle Invalid Data

It is best to create data validation settings before any data is entered. When that is not the case, though, you can still locate invalid data. ***Invalid data*** is a value or label that does not conform to the validation criteria. Invalid data can occur when data is copied because it is possible to copy such data into a range with validation settings. It might also occur if a formula or an Excel macro calculates an invalid result.

You can highlight invalid data with the *Circle Invalid Data* command. This command places a red ***ellipse*** (an elongated circle) around each cell in which the data does not match the validation criteria.

The *Circle Invalid Data* simply highlights cells with data that does not fit the criteria. It does not edit or correct the data.

HOW TO: Circle Invalid Data

1. Select the cell or the cell range where you want data validation settings.

2. Click the **Data Validation** arrow button [*Data* tab, *Data Tools* group].

3. Select **Circle Invalid Data**.

   - A red circle highlights each cell with invalid data (Figure 7-4).
   - Type or select valid data for each invalid entry.
   - After you enter valid data for a cell, the circle is removed.

4. Click the **Data Validation** arrow button [*Data* tab, *Data Tools* group] and select **Clear Validation Circles** to remove the circles.

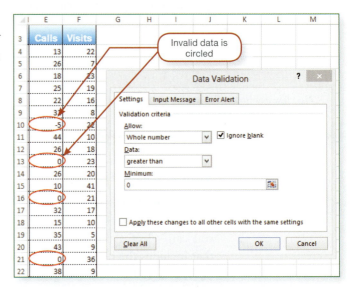

7-4 Validation settings that are violated

Create a Data Validation Input Message

An *input message* is a comment box that appears on screen as soon as a cell with data validation is selected. An input message is a guideline for the person entering the data. For example, it might display "Type a value between 1 and 10" or "Choose a name from this list." Figure 7-5 shows an input message before any data is entered.

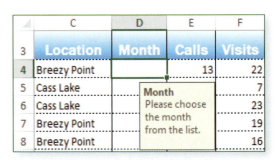

7-5 Input message when the cell is selected

HOW TO: Create an Input Message

1. Select the cell or the range where you want an input message.

   - You can set validation criteria and build an input message at the same time.

2. Click the **Data Validation** button [*Data* tab, *Data Tools* group].

3. Click the **Input Message** tab.

4. Select the **Show input message when cell is selected** check box.

5. Click in the **Title** box and type a name or title for the message box.

   - A title is not required.

6. Click in the **Input message** box and type the message you want to appear on screen (Figure 7-6).

   - Use proper capitalization and punctuation as needed.
   - Be brief so that the input box is not too large.

7. Click **OK**.

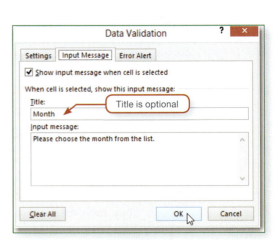

7-6 Input message for data validation

Create a Data Validation Error Alert

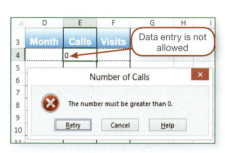

7-7 **Stop style error alert**

An *error alert* is a pop-up message that appears after invalid data is entered, as shown in Figure 7-7. You can set an error alert as well as an input message for each data validation setting in a worksheet.

When you create an error alert, you can specify the type of warning box that appears on screen. This option allows you to prohibit invalid data from being entered or to allow it with a reminder.

With a *Stop* warning, the user is prohibited from making an entry and can either cancel the task or retry. A *Stop* warning displays a white X in a red circle.

If you set a *Warning* box, the message box shows an exclamation point (!) in a yellow triangle. With a *Warning* box the entry is allowed. It can also be edited or canceled. The third warning style is *Information*, which also allows the entry to be made. An information message box features a lowercase i in a blue circle.

After you set the type of warning, you can type a title for the message box as desired. The message you type is the actual message that appears on screen. The message should clearly and briefly explain what the user should do (or not do) to create a valid entry.

HOW TO: Create an Error Alert

1. Click the cell or the range where you want an error alert.
2. Click the **Data Validation** button [*Data* tab, *Data Tools* group].
3. Click the **Error Alert** tab.
4. Click the **Show error alert after invalid data is entered** check box.
5. Click the **Style** arrow and choose a warning type.
   - Use a *Stop* style if the entry should not be allowed.
   - Use a *Warning* or *Information* style if the entry is permissible.
6. Click in the **Title** box and type a label for the message box.
   - A title is optional.
7. Click in the **Error message** box and type the message to appear in the warning box (Figure 7-8).
   - Use proper capitalization and punctuation.
   - Check your spelling and grammar carefully.
8. Click **OK**.

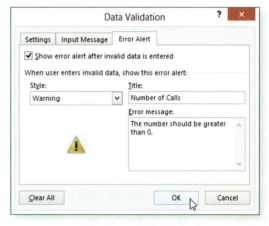

7-8 **Warning style error alert**

For this project, you set several data validation rules to ensure positive values are entered for calls made by sales representatives and accurate titles are inputted for the employees. You also incorporate lists and operators with the validation rules in one of the marketing worksheets for Paradise Lakes Resorts.

File Needed: ***PLRMarketing-07.xlsx***
Completed Project File Name: ***[your initials] PP E7-1.xlsx***

1. Open the ***PLRMarketing-07*** workbook.

2. Save the workbook as ***[your initials] PP E7-1***.

3. Click the **Calls&Visits** worksheet tab.

4. Create data validation settings with an operator.
   a. Select cells **E4:E22**.
   b. Click the **Data Validation** button [*Data* tab, *Data Tools* group].
   c. Click the **Settings** tab.
   d. Click the **Allow** drop-down arrow and choose **Whole Number**.
   e. Click the **Data** drop-down arrow and choose **greater than**.
   f. In the *Minimum* box, type 0.
   g. Do not click *OK*.

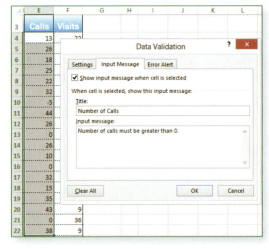

7-9 Selected range with its input message

5. Create an input message for data validation settings.
   a. Click the **Input Message** tab.
   b. Click the **Show input message when cell is selected** check box.
   c. Click in the **Title** box and type Number of Calls.
   d. Click in the **Input message** box and type Number of calls must be greater than 0. (Figure 7-9).
   e. Click **OK**.

6. Circle and delete invalid data.
   a. Click the **Data Validation** arrow button [*Data* tab, *Data Tools* group].
   b. Choose **Circle Invalid Data**. The invalid entries are circled (Figure 7-10).
   c. Click each cell with invalid data and press **Delete**.
   d. Click the **Data Validation** arrow button [*Data* tab, *Data Tools* group] and choose **Clear Validation Circles**.

7. Create data validation settings with a list.
   a. Select cells **D4:D22**.
   b. Click the **Data Validation** button [*Data* tab, *Data Tools* group].
   c. Click the **Settings** tab.
   d. Click the **Allow** drop-down arrow and choose **List**.
   e. Click in the **Source** entry box and click the **Data Lists** worksheet tab.
   f. Select cells **E1:E24**.
   g. Click **OK**.

7-10 Invalid data circled

8. Click cell **D4** and choose **Jan 2014** from the list. The first date appears as a serial value and needs to be formatted (Figure 7-11).

9. Format cell **D4** to show the date in **mm/dd/yy** format. Copy this format to cells **D5:D22**.

	C	D	E	F
3	**Location**	**Month**	**Calls**	**Visits**
4	Cass Lake	41640 ▾	13	22
5	Cass Lake		26	7
6	Cass Lake		18	23

7-11 Unformatted date

10. Click cell **D5** and choose the second date in the validation list. Click each cell in column D and choose the next available date.

11. Create data validation settings with an error alert.
    a. Select cells **B4:B22** and click the **Data Validation** button [*Data* tab, *Data Tools* group].
    b. Click the **Allow** arrow and choose **List**.
    c. Click in the **Source** entry box.
    d. Type Manager, Representative, Trainee with no space after each comma.
    e. Click the **Error Alert** tab.
    f. Click the **Show error alert after invalid data is entered** check box.
    g. Click the **Style** arrow and choose **Warning**. This style will allow an invalid entry to be made.
    h. Click in the **Title** box and type Wait!.
    i. Click in the **Error message** box and type Please choose from the list.
    j. Click **OK**.

12. Click cell **B5**, type Sales Rep, and press **Enter** to display the error alert (Figure 7-12).

13. Choose **Yes** to allow the entry.

14. Save and close the workbook (Figure 7-13).

	A	B	C	D	E	F
3	**Name**	**Title**	**Location**	**Month**	**Calls**	**Visits**
4	Christopher Bowman	Manager	Cass Lake	01/01/14	13	22
5	Chad Meison	Sales Rep	▾ ss Lake	02/01/14	26	7
6	Corey Daniels	Trainee	Cass Lake	03/01/14	18	23
7	Wyatte Mockentune					
8	Dennis Omang					
9	BJ Francine					
10	Kendal Shaedon					
11	Ella Jamison					
12	Alec Jones					
13	Natasha Nelson	Trainee	Baudette	10/01/14		23

Wait! dialog: Please choose from the list. Continue? — Entry can be made — Yes / No / Cancel / Help

7-12 Warning style error alert after invalid entry

	A	B	C	D	E	F
1	**Paradise Lakes Resort**					
2	**Promotional Calls and Visits**					
3	**Name**	**Title**	**Location**	**Month**	**Calls**	**Visits**
4	Christopher Bowman	Manager	Cass Lake	01/01/14	13	22
5	Chad Meison	Sales Rep	Cass Lake	02/01/14	26	7
6	Corey Daniels	Trainee	Cass Lake	03/01/14	18	23
7	Wyatte Mockentune	Manager	Breezy Point	04/01/14	25	19
8	Dennis Omang	Representative	Breezy Point	05/01/14	22	16
9	BJ Francine	Representative	Baudette	06/01/14	32	8
10	Kendal Shaedon	Representative	Breezy Point	07/01/14		22
11	Ella Jamison	Manager	Baudette	08/01/14	44	10
12	Alec Jones	Representative	Baudette	09/01/14	26	18
13	Natasha Nelson	Trainee	Baudette	10/01/14		23
14	Nikolai Jalowiec	Manager	Walker	11/01/14	26	20
15	Tammy Christine	Representative	Walker	12/01/14	10	41
16	Josie Daddiline	Trainee	Walker	01/01/15		21
17	Tara Miller	Trainee	Breezy Point	02/01/15	32	17
18	Robert Andrew	Representative	Walker	03/01/15	15	10
19	Coryn Gomez	Representative	Baudette	04/01/15	35	5
20	Elizabeth Gabrys	Trainee	Cass Lake	05/01/15	43	9
21	Rita Larson	Trainee	Walker	06/01/15		36
22	Michael Gentile	Representative	Baudette	07/01/15	38	9

7-13 PP E7-1 completed worksheet

Creating and Using Forms

A *form* is a worksheet that allows for quick entry, tracking, and organization of data. Excel has a basic data entry form that can be used with list-style data. You can also add *form controls* to a worksheet that can be customized to your own settings or commands. These types of controls can be dynamic or static, allowing you to manage how data is added and edited in a worksheet.

The Developer Tab and the Form Button

The **Insert Controls** button is located on the **Developer** tab on the *Ribbon*. This tab is not displayed by default. Excel's **Form** button, used to create a simple data entry form, is also not shown by default. You can add it to your *Quick Access* toolbar or to another tab on the *Ribbon*.

HOW TO: Display the Developer Tab

1. Click the **Options** button [*File* tab].
   • The *Excel Options* dialog box opens.
2. Click **Customize Ribbon** in the left pane.
3. Click the **Developer** check box in the *Main Tabs* group (Figure 7-14).

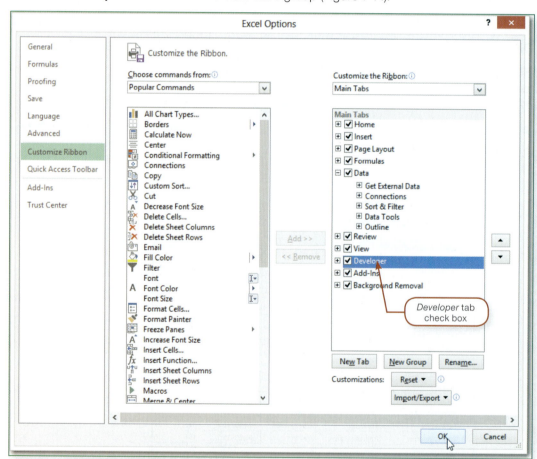

7-14 *Excel Options* dialog box to add *Developer* tab to the Ribbon

4. Click **OK**.
   • The *Developer* tab displays near the right side of the *Ribbon*.

HOW TO: Add the Form Button to the Quick Access Toolbar

1. Click the **Options** button [*File* tab].
2. Click **Quick Access Toolbar** in the left pane.
3. Choose **All Commands** from the drop-down list in the *Choose commands from* box.
4. Choose **Form** from the *Choose commands from* list.
5. Click **Add** to add the command to the *Customize Quick Access Toolbar* list on the right (Figure 7-15).

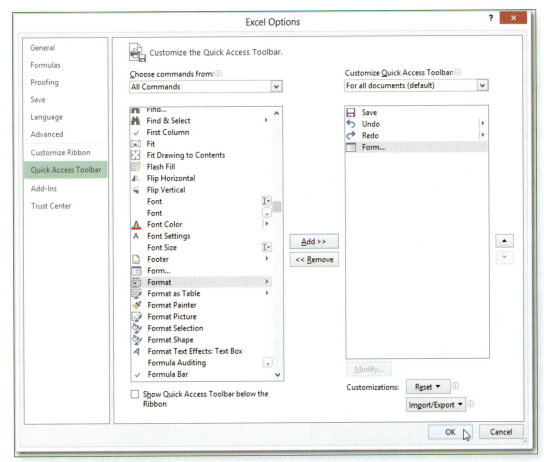

7-15 *Excel Options* dialog box to add *Form* button to the *Quick Access* toolbar

6. Click **OK**.
   • The *Form* button appears on the *Quick Access* toolbar (Figure 7-16).

7-16 Form button and *Developer* tab in the Ribbon

The Data Input Form

Many users find it quicker and easier to enter data in a screen form than in a worksheet row. A ***data input form*** is a window or dialog box that displays labels and entry boxes for data in a top-to-bottom layout. The data input form is a temporary view of worksheet data. As you enter data into it, the worksheet data is updated.

A data input form is automatically created and displayed when you click the *Form* button. This button must be available on the *Ribbon* or the *Quick Access* toolbar.

HOW TO: Create a Data Input Form

1. Select the cell range including column headings you want to include in the form.
2. Click the **Form** button in the *Quick Access* toolbar (Figure 7-17).
   - A data entry form opens and displays the first record in the range.
   - When there are more fields than can be displayed at one time, a scroll bar is available for viewing all fields.
   - Only the first 32 columns are displayed in the data input form.
3. Click **Close** to close the form.

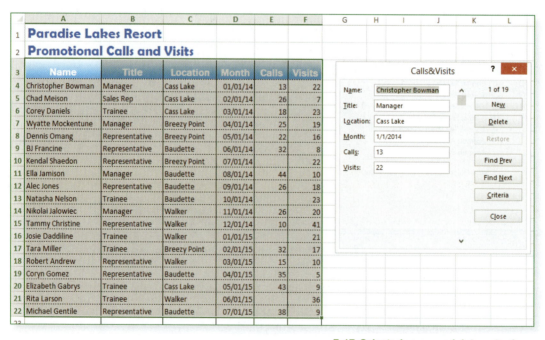

7-17 Selected range and data entry form

From the data input form, you can delete a row or record, add a new record, and filter the records. One record is visible at a time in a data input form. A data input form can display up to 32 fields from the worksheet.

HOW TO: Filter Data in a Form

1. Click a cell included in the form on the spreadsheet.
2. Click the **Form** button on the *Quick Access* toolbar.
   - A data entry form opens and displays the first record in the range.
3. Click **Criteria** to open a blank form (Figure 7-18).
   - Click in the field to be used for filtering data.
   - Type the data to be matched in the entry box in the form.
   - Click **Find Next** to scroll through the records that meet the criteria. The number of records that match the criteria is shown in the data form.
   - Click **Criteria** to return to a blank form.
   - Click **Form** to close the criteria form.
4. Click **Close** to close the data form.

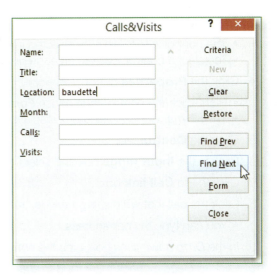

7-18 Data entry criteria form

Insert a Form Control

A *form control* is an object that you can use to execute commands or perform actions in a worksheet. A form control can be static (non-changing) or it can be dynamic (active). Typical static uses include selecting items from a list, adjusting values, and moving data sets in a worksheet. Dynamic uses include linking the form control to a *macro* that performs pre-recorded steps such as opening templates, increasing view size, or automating data entry upon release of the control.

Basic form controls do not require any knowledge of *Visual Basic for Application (VBA)* coding but they do allow you to edit several properties. *VBA* is a programming language that allows you to expand the abilities of Excel. When you select a state abbreviation from a combo box, the form control returns the choice selected in the list as a number. Combining form controls with functions such as *INDEX* can allow more specific results.

> ### MORE INFO
> You can assign a macro to a form control from its context menu. Macros are covered in *SLO 9.1: Creating a Macro.*

A form control has selection handles for sizing and changing its shape. You can use the four-pointed move pointer to move a control, and you can right-click it to open its context menu. From the *Format Control* dialog box, you can alter properties so that the control does not move or change size when the worksheet is adjusted.

Form controls are available from the **Insert Controls** button in the *Controls* group in the *Developer* tab.

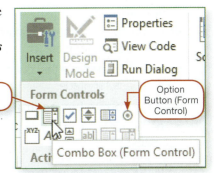

HOW TO: Insert a Combo Box Form Control

1. Click the **Insert Controls** button [*Developer* tab, *Controls* group].
2. Click the **Combo Box** button in the *Forms Controls* group (Figure 7-19).
   - The cursor is a thin cross or plus sign.

7-19 Form controls on the ribbon

3. Click and drag the mouse to draw the control.
   - The control is automatically selected immediately after it is created.
   - To select a control, point to an edge or border and right-click.
4. Click the **Properties** button [*Developer* tab, *Controls* group].
   - Right-click the control and choose **Format Control** to open the *Format Control* dialog box.
   - The *Format Control* dialog box displays tabs specific to the type of control.
5. Click the **Control** tab.
6. Click in the **Input range** box and select the cells with data for the control.
7. Click in the **Cell link** box.
8. Click the cell that will display the index result of the choice made in the combo box.
   - You can type the cell address.
9. In the *Drop down lines* box, type the number of lines to appear in the combo box.
10. Click to place a check mark for 3-D *shading* as desired (Figure 7-20).
    - This applies a 3-D shadow to the control object in the worksheet.

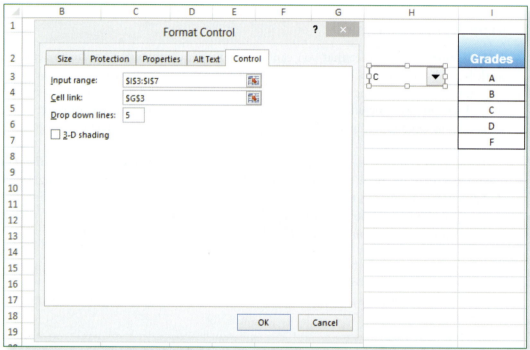

7-20 *Format Control* dialog box

11. Click **OK**.
12. Click the cell for the final result for combo control (e.g., G3 in Figure 7-21).
13. Enter the *INDEX* formula to return information related to the choice selected from the list.
    - Figure 7-21 displays the points awarded in G3 when attaining a C for a letter grade.
14. Click the **combo box control arrow** and make a selection.
    - The *INDEX* location of your choice is displayed in the cell link location.
    - As you change the choice in the combo box, your final results also change (Figure 7-21).

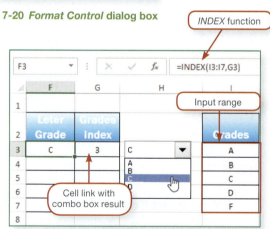

7-21 **Final results and combo box selection**

Excel 2013 Chapter 7 Setting Validation, Creating Forms, Sharing and Protecting Workbooks

Insert an ActiveX Control

An *ActiveX control* is a worksheet object, similar to a form control but more flexible and robust. *Active* X controls can include *events* (sets of actions that occur associated with *VBA* code) depending on the user's choice. For example, you can use a query to populate a combo list box for counties based on the user's selection of a button that lists a specific city. Some cases require knowledge of *VBA* for *ActiveX* controls that perform such advanced options.

Not all *ActiveX* controls can be used on a worksheet; they are available only in **VBA User Forms**.

The *ActiveX* controls are available from the *Insert Controls* button in the *Controls* group on the *Developer* tab as shown in Figure 7-22.

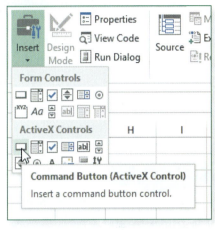

7-22 ActiveX controls

HOW TO: Insert an ActiveX Control

1. Click the **Insert Controls** button [*Developer* tab, *Controls* group].
2. Click the **Command Button** in the *ActiveX Controls* group.
3. Click and drag the mouse to draw the control.
   - The control is selected immediately after it is created.
   - To select a control, point at an edge or border and right-click.
4. Click the **Properties** button [*Developer* tab, *Controls* group] (Figure 7-23).
   - Move and size the *Properties* dialog box as needed.
   - *ActiveX* controls have many editable properties.
5. Click the **Alphabetic** tab and click in the **Caption** line.
6. Type a label for the button.
7. Click the **Design Mode** button [*Developer* tab, *Controls* group] if necessary.
   - The button displays a green/blue background when active.

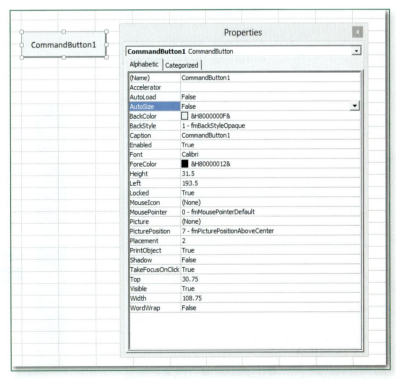

7-23 Properties dialog box for command button

8. Click the **View Code** button [*Developer* tab, *Controls* group] (Figure 7-24).

- This opens the *Visual Basic Editor.*
- You can add or edit *VBA* code for the control.

9. Choose **Close and Return to Microsoft Excel** from the *File* menu.

- When you return to Excel, the worksheet is in *Normal* view.
- You still need to save the workbook when you close it.

10. Close the *Properties* dialog box.

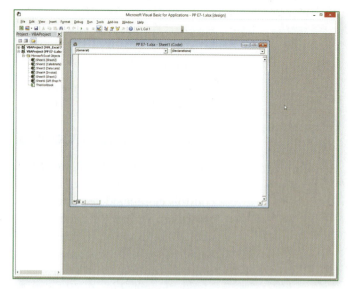

7-24 Visual Basic Editor for an *ActiveX* control

SLO 7.3

Using Excel Templates

A *template* is a model workbook. It can include data, formulas, formatting, charts, images, controls, and more. A template is ideal for routine, repetitive workbooks and makes completion of a new workbook faster and easier. Templates are well suited for work that requires the same layout, the same design, and the same data pattern each time you prepare a workbook.

Create a Workbook from a Template

The *Backstage* view for the *New* command lists the most recently published templates in the *Featured* group. These templates cover many business and personal categories; there are thousands of additional templates available online.

When you create a workbook from a template, a copy of the template opens as an Excel workbook with the same name as the template followed by a number. When you save the workbook that is created from the template, you can save it in your usual file locations.

HOW TO: Create a Workbook from a Template

1. Click the **New** button [*File* tab] (Figure 7-25).

- *Backstage* view for *New* displays an icon and the name for *Featured* templates.
- The *Blank* workbook template creates a new workbook.
- The *Suggested searches* categories search online templates.

2. Click the template icon you want to use.

- To use a template that you created, click **PERSONAL**.
- A preview window describes and rates the template (Figure 7-26).

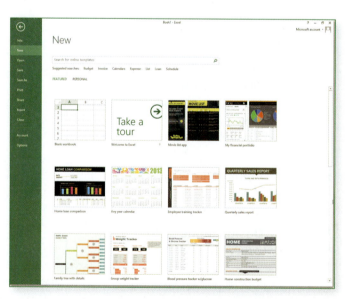

7-25 Backstage view for the *New* command

3. Click **Create**.

- A workbook opens with the same name as the template, followed by a number.
- A template may include sample data and multiple sheets.
- You can save and edit the workbook as usual (Figure 7-27).

7-26 Preview of selected template

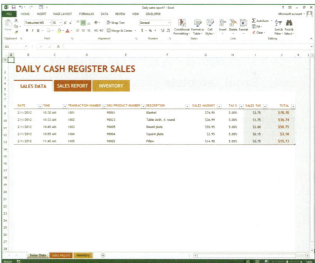

7-27 Workbook created from a template

> **MORE INFO**
>
> Excel templates have an *.xltx* file name extension.

Save a Workbook as a Template

In addition to published and online templates, you can create your own template from any Excel workbook. When you use the same design, formulas, and controls many times in your work, you can create a model, save it as a template, and create new workbooks from this template.

When you choose to save an Excel workbook as a template, it is saved in the *Custom Office Templates* folder in the *My Documents* folder for the current user at your computer. Your saved templates are available in *Backstage* view in the *Personal* category when you click the **New** command [*File* tab].

> **MORE INFO**
>
> You can save a template with a thumbnail preview by setting that option in the *Advanced Properties* dialog box.

You can save templates in any folder but, in that case, their names do not appear in the *Personal* category. You can, however, change the default folder for your personal templates in the *Excel Options* dialog box in the *Save* pane.

HOW TO: Save a Workbook as a Template

1. Click the **Save As** button [*File* tab].
2. Choose **Computer** and any folder.
   - When you select the *Save As* file type, Excel automatically switches to the default template folder.
3. Type the template name in the *File name* box.
4. Select **Excel Template** from the *Save as type* drop-down list (Figure 7-28).
   - Excel selects the default *Custom Office Templates* folder.
5. Click **Save**.
6. Close the template.

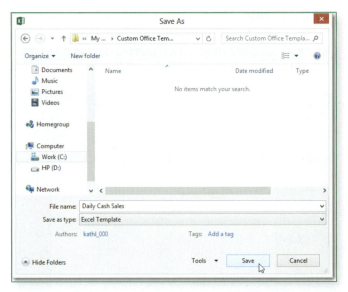

7-28 *Save as type* sets the default templates folder

> **MORE INFO**
>
> You can locate your templates by searching for .xltx extensions in the Windows search pane.

SLO 7.4

Protect a Workbook

Excel allows you to assign various security levels for your work. You can set a simple command to permit a user to view a workbook but not edit it. Or you can prohibit changes to the size and position of workbook windows or not allow the addition of new sheets. And you can assign a password that is required before the workbook can be opened.

Mark a Workbook as Final

You can assign a basic level of protection to an Excel workbook with the ***Mark as Final*** command. This is a read-only file property that alerts the user that the content is final and should not be edited. However, it is still easy for a user to remove the property by clicking the **Edit Anyway** button that appears in the security message bar below the *Ribbon* as shown in Figure 7-29.

In addition to the security bar, there is an icon on the *Status bar* that indicates the security setting as well as the [Read-Only] label in the title bar.

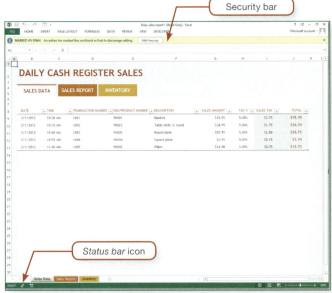

7-29 Workbook that is marked as final

HOW TO: Mark a Workbook as Final

1. Click the **Protect Workbook** button [*File* tab, *Info* area].
   - Protection commands are listed.
2. Select **Mark as Final**.
   - If the workbook has not yet been saved, the *Save As* dialog box opens so that you can set the file location and name.
   - If the workbook has been saved, it is resaved with the same file name.
   - A message box informs you that the file will be marked and saved (Figure 7-30).
3. Click **OK**.
   - A second message box may open and provides details about the *Mark as Final* command.
   - There is a check box in this message to turn off its display (Figure 7-31).
4. Click **OK**.

7-30 **Message box that workbook will be saved and marked as final**

7-31 **Details about the *Mark as Final* property**

Encrypt a Workbook with a Password

A password provides an additional layer of security. This type of password protection is different from assigning a password to protect a sheet. This command requires that the user type the password before the workbook can be opened.

Immediately after you set a password, the *Protect Workbook* button will update to show that the workbook now requires a password as shown in Figure 7-32. You need to save and close the workbook for the password setting to take effect.

To remove a password, you first must open the workbook. You then select the **Encrypt with Password** command, delete the current password leaving the *Password* box empty, and resave the workbook.

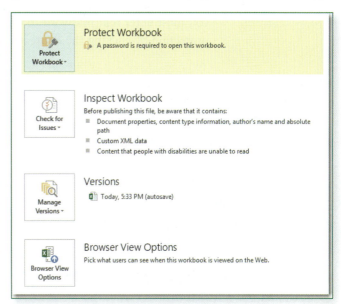

7-32 ***Info* area for a workbook with a password**

HOW TO: Password Protect a Workbook

1. Click the **Protect Workbook** button [*File* tab, *Info* area].
2. Select **Encrypt with Password**.
   - The *Encrypt Document* dialog box opens with a message about remembering your passwords.
3. Type a password in the *Password* box (Figure 7-33).
   - Your password is hidden as you type it.
   - Passwords are case sensitive.
4. Click **OK**.
   - The *Confirm Password* dialog box requires that you retype the password.
5. Retype the password and click **OK**.
6. Click **Save**.
7. Click **Close**.

7-33 Passwords are case-sensitive and are hidden as you type them

Protect Workbook Structure

In *SLO 4.7: Using Goal Seek and Worksheet Protection*, you learned how to protect worksheet data and unlock cells for data entry by setting the command from the *Review* tab. A related command is available on the *Review* tab and is part of the *Protect Workbook* button choices, *Protect Workbook Structure*.

Workbook protection prohibits changes to the structure of the workbook. This means that you can prohibit the insertion or deletion of worksheets as well as the rearranging of the tabs. You can also stop users from hiding or unhiding sheets.

Structure changes can be prohibited in a template or a form. After all the work of preparing the model workbook or form controls, it may be a good idea to ensure that no one accidentally deletes or moves a sheet. You might also want to hide sheets that include combo boxes or lookup lists. When workbook protection is active, the unavailable commands are grayed out or cannot be selected with the pointer.

You can protect workbook structure with or without a password. If you use a password, you must enter that password to remove the protection. You can remove workbook structure protection by clicking the **Protect Workbook** button.

HOW TO: Protect Workbook Structure

1. Click the **Protect Workbook** button [*File* tab, *Info* area].
2. Select **Protect Workbook Structure**.
   - The *Structure* setting is available.
   - The *Windows* setting is disabled by default.
3. Click the **Structure** check box (Figure 7-34).
4. Type a password in the *Password* box and click **OK** as desired.
   - If you include a password, retype it in the *Confirm Password* dialog box and click **OK**.
5. Save and close the file.

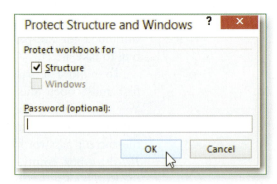

7-34 *Protect Structure and Windows* dialog box

For this project, you create an Excel template with form controls for Paradise Lakes Resort's inventory and invoice worksheets. You create a template from the workbook and add several layers of protection.

File Needed: *[your initials] PP E7-1.xlsx*
Completed Project File Names: *[your initials] PP E7-2.xlsx*, *[your initials] PP E7-2.xltx*, and *[your initials] PP E7-2a.xlsx*

1. Open the *[your initials] PP E7-1* workbook.
2. Save the workbook as *[your initials] PP E7-2*.
3. Click the **Invoice** worksheet tab.
4. Display the *Developer* tab on the *Ribbon* if it is not shown.
   a. Click the **Options** button [*File* tab].
   b. Click **Customize Ribbon** in the left pane.
   c. Click the **Developer** check box in the *Main Tabs* group.
   d. Click **OK**.
5. Display the *Form* button on the *Quick Access* toolbar if it is not shown.
   a. Click the **Options** button [*File* tab].
   b. Click **Quick Access Toolbar** in the left pane.
   c. Choose **All Commands** from the *Choose commands from* drop-down list.
   d. Choose **Form** in the *Choose commands from* list.
   e. Click **Add**.
   f. Click **OK**.
6. Create and use a data input form.
   a. Select cells **B14:D29**.
   b. Click the **Form** button on the *Quick Access* toolbar. If you did not include column headings in the selection, click **OK** in the message box to use the first row as labels when appropriate.
   c. Click **Delete** in the data form to delete the record and click **OK**. The record is deleted from the worksheet.
   d. In the data form, type 2 in the *QTY* box and press **Tab**.
   e. In the *Description* box, type Beach Towel and type 105 in the *ITEM* # box (Figure 7-35).
   f. Click **Close** to add the data to the worksheet and to close the data form. Any errors will be fixed in the next step.

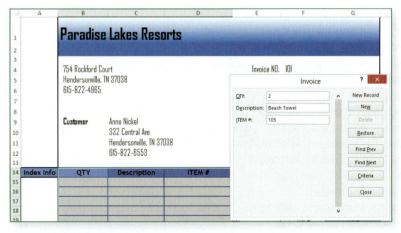

7-35 Record deleted from worksheet and new data entered in data form

7. Edit the "Unit Price" column to include an *IFERROR* formula.
   a. Select cell **F15**. See *SLO 6.2: Building AND, OR, and Nested functions* for review.
   b. Edit (or recreate) the formula to nest the *VLOOKUP* formula as the *Value* argument for an *IFERROR* function so that a zero (0) results instead of an error message (Figure 7-36).
   c. Apply absolute reference symbols to **A3:E18** in cell **F15**. Copy the formula in cell **F15** to cells **F16:F29**. Zeros in this worksheet are formatted to appear as hyphens.

8. In cell **A1**, type 1. In cell **A2**, type 2. Fill this range to reach the number **12** in cell **A12**.

9. Insert a combo box form control.
   a. Click the **Insert Controls** button [*Developer* tab, *Controls* group].
   b. Click the **Combo Box (Form Control)** button.
   c. Click and drag to draw a control directly over cell **B15**.
   d. Click the **Properties** button [*Developer* tab, *Controls* group].
   e. Click the **Control** tab.
   f. In the *Input range* box, select cells **A1:A12**. These values will be selectable in the control.
   g. Click in the **Cell link** box and type B15. The choice made in the combo box will be placed in this cell.
   h. Type 12 as the number of *Drop down lines*.
   i. Check the **3-D shading box** (Figure 7-37).
   j. Click **OK**. Click cell **B17** to deselect the combo box control.
   k. Select **3** from the combo box. The result in cell B15 is the value selected in the combo box.

10. Insert a second combo box.
    a. Click the **Insert Controls** button [*Developer* tab, *Controls* group] and click the **Combo Box** button.
    b. Click and drag to draw a control directly over cell **C15**.
    c. Click the **Properties** button [*Developer* tab, *Controls* group] and the **Control** tab.
    d. Click in the **Input range** box.
    e. Click the **Gift Shop Products** sheet tab and select cells **A4:A18**. These labels are the combo box entries.
    f. Click in the **Cell link** box and type A15.
    g. Type 15 as the number of *Drop down lines* and use **3-D shading**.
    h. Click **OK**. Click cell **C17** to deselect the control.
    i. Select **Beach Towel** from the combo box.
    j. Right-click the combo box control.
    k. Point at any border of the control and click to display the four-pointed arrow. With the move pointer, drag the control down to cell **C18**.

7-36 *LOOKUP* formula nested in *IFERROR* formula

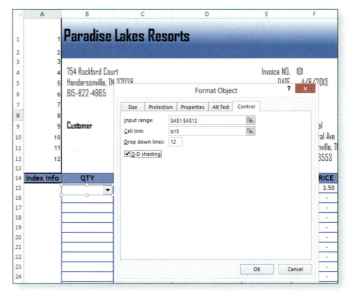

7-37 Combo box control defined in *Format Control* dialog box

l. Select cell **C15** and enter the *INDEX* formula =INDEX('Gift Shop Products' !A4:A18,Invoice!A15) (Figure 7-38). This ensures the correct results for price by returning the *INDEX* result from the list and still allows the user to select from a list.

11. Hide column **A** and delete the contents of cells **C9:C12**, cells **F9:F12**, and cells **F4** and **F6**.

12. Protect the worksheet.
    a. Right-click the combo box control in cell **B15**. With the four-pointed arrow, drag the control down to cell **B18** to move it out of the way temporarily.
    b. Select cells **B15:D28**, cells **C9:D12**, and cells **F9:G12**.
    c. Right-click one of the selected cells and select **Format Cells** from the menu.
    d. Click the **Protection** tab.
    e. Click the **Locked** check box to remove the check mark (Figure 7-39).
    f. Click **OK**.
    g. Move the combo box controls back to their locations in row 15.
    h. Click the **Protect Sheet** button [*Review* tab, *Changes* group].
    i. Allow only the options to select locked and unlocked cells.
    j. Click **OK**.
    k. Save the workbook. Click **No** if a message box appears

13. Save the workbook as a template.
    a. Click the **Save As** button [*File* tab].
    b. Type the file name [your initials] PP E7-2 for the template in the *File name* box. Since a template uses a different file name extension, you can use the same name as your original workbook for this project.
    c. Choose **Excel Template** from the *Save as type* drop-down box. The file will save automatically to the default template location when this option is chosen.
    d. Click **Save**.
    e. Close the template.

14. Create a workbook from a template.
    a. Click the **New** button [*File* tab].
    b. Click **Personal** near the top of the gallery.

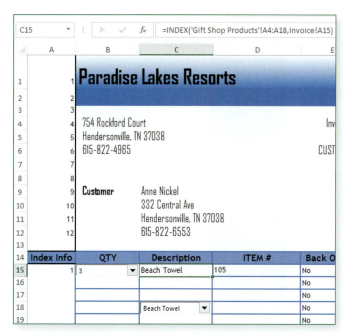

7-38 Combo box control moved away and *INDEX* formula in cell C15

7-39 Cells for data entry unlocked for worksheet protection

c. Click the **icon** for your template (Figure 7-40). A new workbook based on the template is created. If you saved your template elsewhere, double-click the file in its current location.

d. Save the workbook as **[your initials] PP E7-2a** in your usual location for saving workbooks.

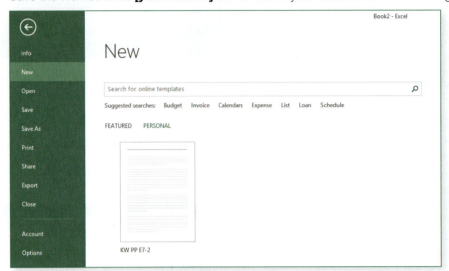

7-40 User-created template in the *Personal* category

15. Protect the workbook structure with a password.
    a. Click the **Protect Workbook** button [*File* tab, *Info* area].
    b. Select **Protect Workbook Structure**.
    c. Verify that there is a check mark for **Structure**.
    d. Type Pass1 in the *Password* box and click **OK**.
    e. Retype the password in the *Confirm Password* dialog box and click **OK**.

16. Encrypt the workbook with a password.
    a. Click the **Protect Workbook** button [*File* tab, *Info* area].
    b. Select **Encrypt with Password**.
    c. Type Pass2 in the *Password* box and click **OK**.
    d. Retype the password in the *Confirm Password* dialog box and click **OK**.

17. Click **Save** and then click **Close**.

18. Review protections in the workbook.
    a. Open the workbook **[your initials] PP E7-2a**.
    b. Type Pass2 in the *Password* box and click **OK**.
    c. Click the *Info* area on the *File* tab (Figure 7-41).
    d. Click **Unprotect** to remove sheet protection from the *Invoice* sheet.
    e. Return to the worksheet.
    f. Right-click the **Invoice** sheet tab. You cannot insert, delete, move, or copy sheets when the workbook structure is protected.
    g. Click the **Protect Workbook** button [*Review* tab, *Changes* group].

7-41 Levels of protection in the Backstage view

h. Type Pass1 in the *Password* box and click **OK**.
i. Right-click the **Invoice** sheet tab. Structure commands are now available.
j. Save and close the workbook (Figure 7-42).

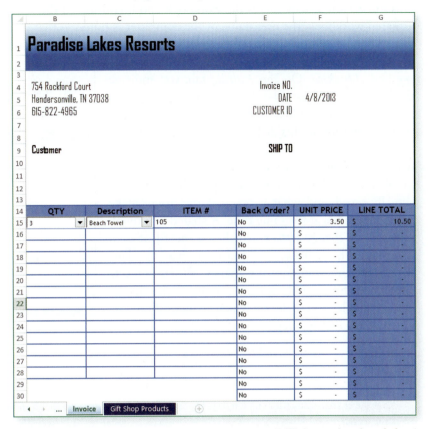

7-42 PP E7-2 completed worksheet

Sharing and Merging Workbooks

Sharing work among multiple users is common in the business environment. A **shared workbook** is one that more than one user edits, either simultaneously or at different times. When a shared workbook is maintained on a network and all users have access to it, each person can work on it as needed. In other instances, a shared workbook can be copied so that each user has his or her own copy. After all members of the work group have completed their part of the work, all of the versions are combined into a final workbook.

Any company that has employees who work away from the office or in different offices can benefit from using shared workbooks. Paradise Lakes Resort, for example, might use a shared workbook for inventory or sales call worksheets. As representatives work from various locations, they record their own data. At some point, all copies are merged to create one report of the latest data.

There are some commands that are not available in a shared workbook. These include deleting sheets, merging cells, inserting or editing charts, setting conditional formatting or data validation, setting worksheet protection, using passwords, and a few more. Most of these tasks, however, can be completed before the workbook is shared.

Share a Workbook

When a workbook is shared, changes are permissible by any user who has access to the work-book. Most shared workbooks are stored on a network, so that editing is live. However, when that is not possible, each person in the work group simply makes a copy of the workbook.

One person usually shares the workbook and is considered the "owner." When you create a shared workbook, the user name of the computer is noted so that changes are identified by user. After a workbook is shared, the word *[Shared]* appears after the file name in the title bar.

The *Share Workbook* dialog box has two tabs, *Editing* and *Advanced*. On the *Editing* tab, you indicate that the workbook is to be shared. If multiple persons are working on the file at the same time, you can view that information in this dialog box (Figure 7-43).

The *Advanced* tab includes several settings that determine how changes are tracked. You can set the number of days that edits are kept, when edits are actually saved, and what happens if two users make conflicting edits at the same time. A shared workbook maintains a ***change history***, which is a record of each edit made. This includes the name of the user, the date, and a brief description of the change. When multiple copies of a shared workbook are combined, the change history enables you to decide which changes should be accepted for the final report.

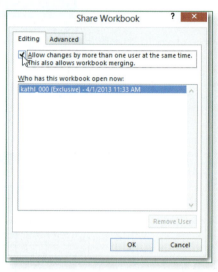

7-43 *Editing* tab in the *Share Workbook* dialog box

> ### MORE INFO
>
> Set the change history for enough days to ensure enough time for all users to complete their part of the work.

HOW TO: Share a Workbook

1. Click the **Share Workbook** button [*Review* tab, *Changes* group].
2. On the *Editing* tab in the *Share Workbook* window, check the box for **Allow changes by more than one user at the same time**.
   - The current user name is shown as the person who has the workbook open.
3. Click the **Advanced** tab (Figure 7-44).
   - In the *Track changes* group, set the number of days to keep the change history. You can also indicate if the change history should not be kept.
   - In the *Update changes* group, choose when the file is to be saved. If you set an automatic save at a specific time interval, you can further choose how to manage others' changes.
   - In the *Conflicting changes between users* group, choose if you will decide which edits to accept or if only those you save will be kept.
   - The *Include in personal view* group allows you to determine if each user can save his or her print and filter choices.
4. Click **OK**.
   - The message box notes that the workbook will be saved, using the same file name.

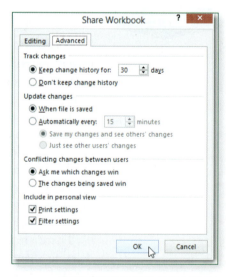

7-44 *Advanced* tab in the *Share Workbook* dialog box

5. Click **OK**.
    - The file name in the title bar includes *[Shared]*.
    - If a shared workbook includes features that are not editable, a pop-up window may alert you.

Protect a Shared Workbook

When you protect a shared workbook, no user can delete the change history. If the number of days set in the *Advanced* tab of the *Share Workbook* window has been reached and you have not added this protection, you will not be able to combine individual copies of the workbook into a final report, because there is no longer a current change history.

When a shared workbook is protected, the option to not keep the change history is not available in the *Advanced* tab of the *Share Workbook* window.

The *Protect Shared Workbook* button is on the *Review* tab in the *Changes* group. It is a toggle that shows *Unprotect Shared Workbook* when protection is active.

> **MORE INFO**
>
> Password protecting a workbook prior to sharing is wise when the workbook is located in a shared server environment.

HOW TO: Protect a Shared Workbook

1. Click the **Protect Shared Workbook** button [*Review* tab, *Changes* group].
    - The *Protect Shared Workbook* window opens.
2. Check the **Sharing with track changes** check box (Figure 7-45).
    - You can encrypt a workbook with a password before sharing it.
3. Click **OK**.

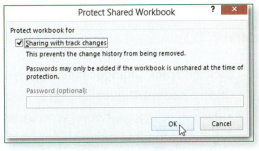

7-45 *Protect Shared Workbook* dialog box

Highlight Changes

After you have shared a workbook, you can highlight changes to decide which edits are acceptable and which should be rejected. Each user's edits are highlighted with a colored border for the cell and a small triangle in the upper left corner. The color of the triangle is matched to the color used for that user name. There is a comment box added automatically for each change which identifies the user name and the edit. To see the comment, click the highlighted cell.

In the *Highlight Changes* dialog box, you can specify which changes should be highlighted. The *When* setting provides four options that include seeing all edits or only those made after a particular date. The *Who* option can be set to show changes by everyone, by everyone else, or by a specific user. There is also a *Where* setting which is used to select a range of cells rather than the entire worksheet. You can choose one or all of these options for identifying which changes should be highlighted.

In the *Highlight Changes* dialog box, you can choose to see the changes on screen or in a printed change history sheet. This history sheet is a generated sheet that is automatically deleted when the workbook is saved.

HOW TO: Highlight Changes in a Shared Workbook

1. Click the **Track Changes** button [*Review* tab, *Changes* group].
2. Choose **Highlight Changes** (Figure 7-46).
   - As desired, select the **When** check box. Click the **When** arrow for its options and make a selection.
   - As desired, select the **Who** check box. Click the **Who** arrow and make a selection.
   - As desired, select the **Where** check *box.* Select the cell range in the worksheet.
3. Click **OK**.
   - If there are no edits that match the settings you specified in the *Highlight Changes* dialog box, a message box appears (Figure 7-47). Click **OK** to close the message box.
4. Point at a cell with a revision triangle to see a description of each edit.

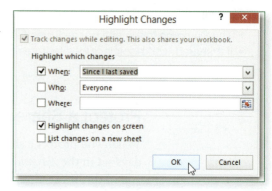

7-46 *Highlight Changes* dialog box

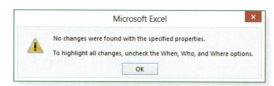

7-47 **No changes found message box**

Accept or Reject Changes

When you highlight changes, you can see which edits were made and by whom. When you want to keep or reject those changes, however, use the ***Accept or Reject Changes*** command.

The *Accept or Reject Changes* command opens a dialog box for each change. After review, you choose to accept the edit or reject it. If you reject a change, the data is reset to what it was before the edit was made.

HOW TO: Accept or Reject Changes in a Shared Workbook

1. Click the **Track Changes** button [*Review* tab, *Changes* group].
2. Choose **Accept/Reject Changes**.
   - If the workbook has not yet been saved, you must save it.
   - The *Select Changes to Accept or Reject* dialog box is similar to the *Highlight Changes* dialog box.
3. Select the **When** check box (Figure 7-48).
4. Click the **When** arrow and choose **Not yet reviewed**.
   - As desired, select the **Who** check box. Click the **Who** arrow and make a selection.
   - As desired, select the **Where** check box. Select the cell range in the worksheet.
5. Click **OK**.
   - The first change is detailed in the *Accept or Reject Changes* dialog box (Figure 7-49).
6. Click **Accept** to accept the edit and move to the next edit.
   - Click **Accept All** to accept all changes in the workbook.
7. Click **Reject** to reject the edit and move to the next edit.
   - Click **Reject All** to reject all changes in the workbook.
   - The dialog box closes after all edits have been accepted or rejected.
8. Save the workbook with the accepted changes.

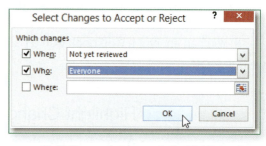

7-48 **Types of changes to be highlighted are confirmed in the dialog box**

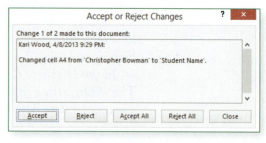

7-49 **Each edit is shown in the *Accept or Reject Changes* dialog box**

Insert Comments

A **comment** is a pop-up text box attached to a cell (Figure 7-50). A basic comment is automatically inserted in a shared workbook when any change is made. You can insert your own comments, too, for additional clarification or discussion in a shared workbook. For example, comments are useful when you or a member of your team wants to add an explanation about a proposed edit or ask a question unrelated to any edits.

7-50 A comment is attached for each edit in a shared workbook

Comments are inserted from the *Review* tab or a cell's context menu. After you add a comment to a cell, a small red triangle (called an **indicator**) appears in the upper-right corner of the cell. To view the comment box, hover the pointer over a cell with an indicator.

> ▶ **ANOTHER WAY**
>
> You can display all comments at once by clicking the **Show All Comments** button on the *Review* tab.

The default setting hides all comments until you point at the cell. You can change this option in *Excel Options* on the *Advanced* tab. You can also temporarily set how comments are displayed or hidden from the *Review* tab.

> ▶ **MORE INFO**
>
> When you print a worksheet, its comments do not print unless you choose the option to print them on the *Sheet* tab in the *Page Setup* dialog box.

After a comment is created, you can edit or delete it by selecting the cell and the appropriate command on the *Review* tab. You can also execute comment-related commands by right-clicking the comment cell and choosing from the menu that displays.

HOW TO: Insert a Comment

1. Select the cell where you want to add a comment.
2. Click the **New Comment** button [*Review* tab, *Comments* group].
   - A *Comment box* appears with the default user name.
   - You can delete or replace the user name.
3. Type the text of your comment (Figure 7-51).
4. Click any cell away from the comment cell.
   - A small red triangle is visible in the upper-right corner of the cell with the comment.
   - View the comment by hovering the pointer over the cell.

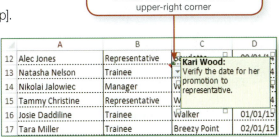

7-51 Comment text for a user-defined comment

Compare and Merge Workbooks

When users make their own copies of shared workbooks, those copies must be combined to assemble a final report. This is accomplished with the ***Compare and Merge Workbooks*** command. The first step is adding the *Compare and Merge Workbooks* button to the *Quick Access* toolbar. You can add this button to custom groups on the *Ribbon* as well.

There are several requirements for workbooks to be merged:

- The original shared workbook must have the change history active.
- Each copy must have been made from the original shared workbook.
- Each copy must have a different file name and cannot have any passwords.

HOW TO: Compare and Merge Workbooks

1. Click the **Options** button [*File* tab] and click **Quick Access Toolbar** in the left pane.
2. Choose **All Commands** from the drop-down list for the *Choose commands from* box.
3. Choose **Compare and Merge Workbooks** from the commands list.
4. Click **Add** to add the command to the *Customize Quick Access Toolbar* list.
5. Click **OK**.
   - The *Compare and Merge Workbooks* button appears on the right of the *Quick Access* toolbar (Figure 7-52).
6. Open the original shared workbook.
7. Click the **Compare and Merge Workbooks** button.
8. Click **OK** to save the workbook.
   - The *Select Files to Merge into Current Workbook* dialog box opens.
9. Navigate to the folder that contains the first file to be merged and click to select the file name (Figure 7-53).
   - Select multiple files from the same folder using the **Ctrl** key.
10. Click **Open**.
    - If a workbook has no changes, you will see a message noting that.
11. Highlight, accept, or reject changes as necessary.

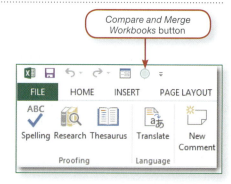

7-52 *Compare and Merge Workbooks* button in the *Quick Access* toolbar

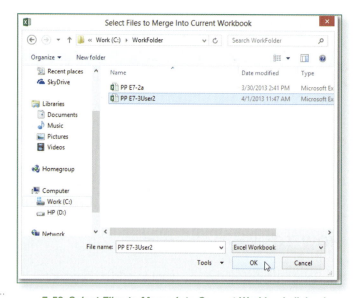

7-53 *Select Files to Merge Into Current Workbook* dialog box

---

SLO 7.6

Prepare a Workbook for Distribution

As you prepare a workbook to distribute to employees, clients, and others, there are several properties that you can check to ensure that the workbook is ready. These include removing properties that you do not want others to see and checking if the workbook is compatible with other Excel versions. There is also a command to check if your work is accessible for persons who have visual disabilities.

Inspect a Workbook

Inspect Document is a command that looks for metadata and personal information stored in a workbook. *Metadata* are properties that are embedded in the file such as the user name at time of creation, the original file location, the date and time, user comments, and more. It is possible to remove some metadata so that others who view the document do not have access to your private data. For example, if you have inserted comments for your team members while working on a shared workbook, you will want those messages to be deleted before a customer sees the workbook. The ***Document Inspector*** can do this quickly and easily.

The *Document Inspector* is the dialog box that lists the properties and data that can be removed from a workbook. You select which properties and types of data should be searched. After the workbook is inspected for these elements, you can choose to remove some or all of them.

HOW TO: Inspect a Workbook

1. Click the **Check for Issues** button [*File* tab, *Info* area].
2. Choose **Inspect Document** from the list of commands.
3. Click **Yes** to save the workbook.

   - The *Document Inspector* lists several categories of content that can be searched (Figure 7-54).
   - All categories are checked by default.
   - Uncheck the box next to any category that should not be searched.

4. Click **Inspect**.

   - The *Document Inspector* identifies what is included in the workbook.
   - Not all metadata can be removed.

5. Click **Remove All** for each category of content to be cleared (Figure 7-55).

   - You can close the dialog box to review content that needs further investigation.
   - You can run the *Document Inspector* again when needed.

6. Click **Close**.

7-54 *Document Inspector* dialog box   7-55 *Document Inspector* dialog box after inspection

Check Compatibility

Check Compatibility opens the *Compatibility Checker* option that looks for commands, features, and objects that are not supported in earlier versions of Excel. When you save a workbook in Excel 97-2003 format, the *Compatibility Checker* automatically runs to alert you to potential issues. You can run the command, however, for any workbook at any time. For instance, early versions of Excel did not have *SmartArt* graphics, so those objects appear as images in early versions, not as a *SmartArt* object that can be edited. This is just one example of a feature that is incompatible. There are functions that do not work in early versions of Excel and they display an error message as well. There are even some formatting features that are not compatible.

The *Compatibility Checker* gives you an opportunity to edit any incompatible data or objects before you save the workbook in a different format. Some problems may be significant and others may be minor.

HOW TO: Check Compatibility

1. Click the **Check for Issues** button [*File* tab, *Info* area].
2. Choose **Check Compatibility** from the list of commands.
   - The *Compatibility Checker* describes each feature that might not work in an earlier version of Excel (Figure 7-56).
   - You can click **Select versions to show** to choose a particular Excel version.
   - The dialog box can be sized or scrolled to view all issues.
3. Click **Copy to New Sheet** to create a sheet that details the issues as desired.
   - A new sheet named *Compatibility Report* is inserted and provides documentation.
   - This command is unavailable in a shared workbook.
4. Click **OK**.
   - The features are unchanged and you can save the workbook in the desired format.
   - You can run the *Compatibility Checker* again when needed.

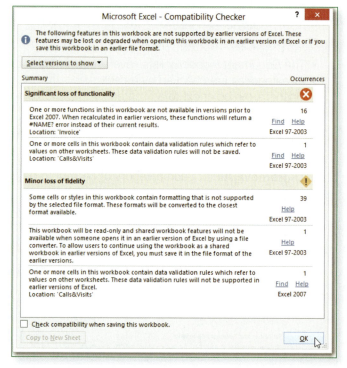

7-56 The *Compatibility Checker* locates incompatible features

---

Define a Trusted Location

Workbooks that might contain data from a questionable source open in **Protected View** so that you can confirm that you trust the document and its source. Workbooks from the web open in *Protected View* as do workbooks with macros and *ActiveX* controls.

A **Trusted Location** is a folder that is identified as one that stores workbooks that are considered safe. When you open a workbook from a trusted location, it will not open in *Protected View*. If you are working with a workbook that includes macros or controls, you can store it in a trusted location and avoid the protected view message.

Trusted locations are part of the *Trust Center* in the *Excel Options* dialog box. You can add and remove folders as needed.

HOW TO: Define a Trusted Location

1. Choose the **Options** command [*File* tab].
2. Choose **Trust Center** in the left pane.
   - The initial dialog box explains several Microsoft security features.
   - The left pane lists categories for each type of security concern.
3. Click **Trust Center Settings**.
4. Click **Trusted Locations** in the left pane (Figure 7-57).
   - Existing trusted folders for your computer are listed.
6. Click **Add new location** in the left pane.
7. Click **Browse**.
   - Browse to find the folder to be trusted, select it, and click **OK**.
   - You can type the path if you prefer.
8. Click in the **Description** box.
   - Type an optional description for the folder (Figure 7-58).
9. Click **OK** to add the folder to the list of trusted locations.
10. Click **OK** to close the *Trust Center*.
11. Click **OK** to close the *Excel Options* dialog box.

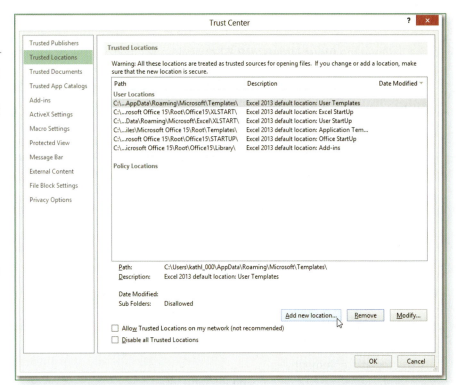

7-57 *Trust Center* options

7-58 **Trusted folder definition**

PAUSE & PRACTICE: EXCEL 7-3

For this project, you share a Paradise Lakes Resort workbook and track changes made to it. You insert comments and merge copies of the workbook. Finally, you inspect the document and check it for compatibility.

File Needed: *[your initials] PP E7-2.xlsx*
Completed Project File Names: *[your initials] PP E7-3.xlsx* and *[your initials] PP E7-3User2.xlsx*

1. Open the *[your initials] PP E7-2* workbook.

2. Save the workbook as *[your initials] PP E7-3*.

3. Unprotect the **Invoice** worksheet.

4. Share the workbook.
   a. Click the **Share Workbook** button [*Review* tab, *Changes* group].
   b. Click the **Allow changes by more than one user at the same time** check box.
   c. Click the **Advanced** tab.
   d. Set the *Keep change history for* option to **25** days.
   e. Click **OK** to close the *Share Workbook* dialog box.
   f. Click **OK** to resave the shared workbook (Figure 7-59). Look for *[Shared]* at the end of the file name in the title bar.

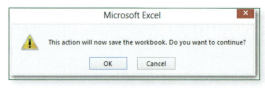

7-59 Shared workbook must be resaved

5. Protect the shared workbook.
   a. Click the **Protect Shared Workbook** button [*Review* tab, *Changes* group].
   b. Click the **Sharing with track changes** check box.
   c. Click **OK**. The option *Don't keep change history* on the *Advanced* tab of the *Share Workbook* dialog box is no longer available.

6. Insert a comment.
   a. Click cell **F12** on the **Calls&Visits** tab.
   b. Click the **New Comment** button [*Review* tab, *Comments* group]. You can select and delete the user name, or replace it with another name.
   c. Type Please confirm that this is the correct number. (Figure 7-60).
   d. Click cell **F13** to finalize the comment.

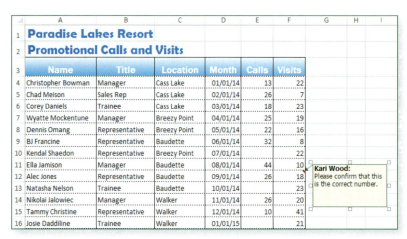

7-60 Typed comment

7. Make a copy of the shared workbook in the same folder.
   a. Click the *File* tab and choose **Save As**.
   b. Save the workbook as *[your initials] PP E7-3User2*.

8. Edit *[your initials] PP E7-3User2*.
   a. Click cell **A4** and type your first and last name.
   b. Right-click cell **B6** and choose **Insert Comment**.
   c. Type Check the date for his promotion to representative.
   d. Click cell **B7** to finalize the comment.
   e. Type 15 in cell **E15**.
   f. Set the width of column **A** to **18.00**.
   g. Save and close the file.

9. Add the *Compare and Merge Workbooks* command to the *Quick Access* toolbar.
   a. Open Excel if necessary.
   b. Click the **Options** command [*File* tab].

c. Click **Quick Access Toolbar** in the left pane.
d. Choose **All Commands** from the *Choose commands from* list.
e. Click **Compare and Merge Workbooks** in the commands list.
f. Click **Add** to add the command to the *Customize Quick Access Toolbar* list.
g. Click **OK**.

10. Merge copies of the shared workbook.
    a. Open the original shared workbook *[your initials] PP E7-3*.
    b. Click the **Compare and Merge Workbooks** button on the *Quick Access* toolbar.
    c. Click **OK** to save the workbook before merging.
    d. In the *Select Files to Merge Into Current Workbook* dialog box, navigate to the folder with the copied workbook named *[your initials] PP E7-3User2* (Figure 7-61).
    e. Click the file name **[your initials] PP E7-3User2** and click **OK**. The copied workbook is merged into the workbook on screen.

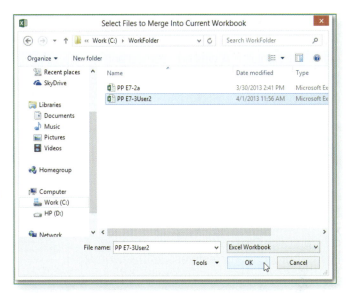

7-61 Choose file and folder for workbook to be merged

11. Highlight changes.
    a. Click the **Track Changes** button [*Review* tab, *Changes* group].
    b. Choose **Highlight Changes**.
    c. Click the **When** arrow and choose **Not yet reviewed**.
    d. Click the **Who** check box, click the **Who** arrow, and choose **Everyone**.
    e. Click **OK**. The highlighted changes (blue triangles in upper-left of cell) are those from the copied workbook. The comments inserted manually are indicated by a red triangle in the upper-right corner of the cell (Figure 7-62).

12. Accept or reject changes.
    a. Click the **Track Changes** button [*Review* tab, *Changes* group].
    b. Choose **Accept/Reject Changes**.
    c. In the *When* box, choose **Not yet reviewed**.
    d. In the *Who* box, choose **Everyone**.

	A	B	C	D	E	F
1	**Paradise Lakes Resort**					
2	**Promotional Calls and Visits**					
3	**Name**	**Title**	**Location**	**Month**	**Calls**	**Visits**
4	Student Name	Manager	Cass Lake	01/01/14	13	22
5	Chad Meison	Sales Rep	Cass Lake	02/01/14	26	7
6	Corey Daniels	Trainee	Cass Lake	03/01/14	18	23
7	Wyatte Mockentune	Manager	Breezy Point	04/01/14	25	19
8	Dennis Omang	Representative	Breezy Point	05/01/14	22	16
9	BJ Francine	Representative	Baudette	06/01/14	32	8
10	Kendal Shaedon	Representative	Breezy Point	07/01/14		22
11	Ella Jamison	Manager	Baudette	08/01/14	44	10
12	Alec Jones	Representative	Baudette	09/01/14	26	18
13	Natasha Nelson	Trainee	Baudette	10/01/14		23
14	Nikolai Jalowiec	Manager	Walker	11/01/14	26	20
15	Tammy Christine	Representative	Walker	12/01/14	15	41
16	Josie Daddiline	Trainee	Walker	01/01/15		21
17	Tara Miller	Trainee	Breezy Point	02/01/15	32	17
18	Robert Andrew	Representative	Walker	03/01/15	15	10
19	Coryn Gomez	Representative	Baudette	04/01/15	35	5
20	Elizabeth Gabrys	Trainee	Cass Lake	05/01/15	43	9
21	Rita Larson	Trainee	Walker	06/01/15		36
22	Michael Gentile	Representative	Baudette	07/01/15	38	9

7-62 Revision triangles are visible for merged data and typed comments

e. Click **OK**. The first edit made in cell **A4** is presented in the *Accept or Reject* dialog box (Figure 7-63).

f. Click **Accept** to accept your name. The edit made in cell E15 is noted.

g. Click **Reject**. The data reverts to the original. Format commands are not tracked so the column width change for column **A** was not merged and is not identified as an edit.

13. Inspect the workbook.
   a. Click the **Check for Issues** button [*File* tab, *Info* option].
   b. Choose **Inspect Document**.
   c. Choose **Yes** to save the document before inspection.
   d. Click **Inspect**. There are several features that cannot be removed in a shared workbook.
   e. Click **Close** without removing any properties or features.

14. Check compatibility.
   a. Click the **Check for Issues** button [*File* tab, *Info* option].
   b. Choose **Check Compatibility**. The option to print a compatibility report is not available for a shared workbook.
   c. Review the issues in the *Compatibility Checker* dialog box. If necessary, you can edit features before saving the workbook in another format (Figure 7-64).
   d. Click **OK**.

15. Save and close the workbook.

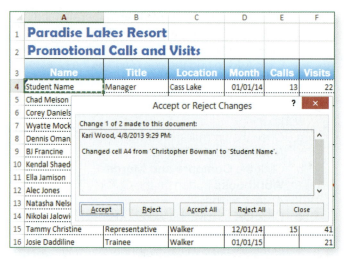

7-63 Each edit can be accepted or rejected

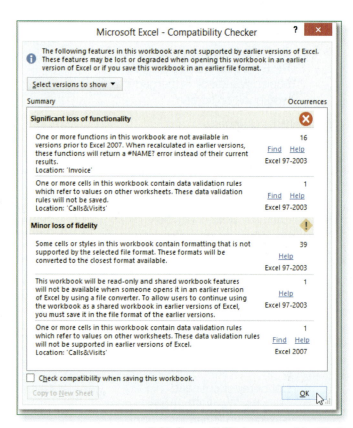

7-64 Compatibility issues are identified

Chapter Summary

7.1 Set data validation, input messages, and error alerts (p. 376).

- **Data validation** is a process of verifying data as it is entered.
- Validation settings are rules that data must meet in order to be accepted or permitted.
- **Data validation settings** can be conditions built with relational operators, choices made from lists, limits set on dates or times, or a formula.
- A data validation list can refer to a range of cells, or the entries that can be typed in the *Data Validation* dialog box.
- An **input message** is a guideline for the person entering data that appears as soon as a cell is selected.
- An **error alert** appears when invalid data is entered in a cell.
- An error alert can be defined to prohibit the invalid entry or to allow it with a warning or reminder.
- Invalid data may occur when data is copied into a cell with data validation, when a formula calculates an invalid result, or when a macro creates or inputs invalid data.
- The command to *Circle Invalid Data* highlights cells with entries that do not match data validation settings.
- These circles only identify cells with problem data; you must correct the entries.

7.2 Create and use a form with form controls and *ActiveX* controls (p. 382).

- A **form** is a worksheet designed for easy entry, tracking, and organizing of data.
- To use form-related commands or controls, you need to display the commands on the *Ribbon* or on the *Quick Access* toolbar.
- Many commands related to forms are available on the **Developer** tab on the *Ribbon*.
- The *Ribbon* and the *Quick Access* toolbar are customized from the *Excel Options* dialog box.
- The **Form** button creates a default data input form.
- You can edit, delete, add, and filter worksheet data in a data entry form.
- A **form control** is a worksheet object that carries out a command or an action.

- An **ActiveX control** also carries out a command or controls events in a worksheet.
- *ActiveX* controls are more complex than basic controls; for optimum use of *ActiveX* controls, it is good to have some knowledge of *Visual Basic for Applications* (*VBA*).

7.3 Create a workbook from a template and save a new template (p. 388).

- A **template** is a model workbook that may include formatting, images, controls, data, formulas, and more.
- The **New** area in *Backstage* view lists the current group of featured templates. You can also search online for professionally designed templates.
- When you create a workbook from a template, a new workbook opens that is a copy of the template. You can save this workbook using a new file name in any folder.
- You can save any Excel workbook as a template.
- Excel templates are saved in a custom folder, identified in the *Save* pane in the *Excel Options* dialog box.
- If you save your own templates in this folder, they appear in the *Personal* category in *Backstage* view for the *New* command.

7.4 Mark a workbook as final and encrypt a workbook with a password (p. 390).

- Within Excel you can set basic levels of security for a workbook.
- The **Mark As Final** command sets the read-only property for a workbook. With this property, the workbook can be viewed but not edited.
- The *Mark as Final* command is located on the **Protect Workbook** button in *Backstage* view on the *Info* area.
- For a higher level of security, you can encrypt a workbook with a password. The password must be entered before the workbook can be opened.
- The **Encrypt with Password** command is located on the *Protect Workbook* button in *Backstage* view on the *Info* area.
- The **Protect Workbook Structure** command is located on the *Protect Workbook* button in *Backstage* view on the Info area and on the *Review* tab in the *Changes* group.

- With workbook structure protection, you can edit cell contents but cannot move, copy, delete, or insert worksheets. You also cannot hide or unhide sheets.
- Workbook structure protection can be set with or without a password.

7.5 Share a workbook, set change tracking options, and compare and merge workbooks (p. 397).

- A *shared workbook* is edited by multiple users, either at the same time on a network or separately in individual copies of the workbook.
- The *Share Workbook* command is on the *Review* tab in the *Changes* group.
- When you share a workbook, you can set how long changes are tracked, when changes are saved, and how conflicts are resolved.
- The *Share Workbook* command maintains a change history for each user.
- In a shared workbook, you can highlight, accept, or reject changes as you are working and after copies are combined.
- When users have individual copies of the shared workbook, the copies are merged into a final workbook.
- The *Compare and Merge Workbooks* command is a button that can be displayed on the *Quick Access* toolbar.
- To be merged, each copy must have its own name and have been made from the original shared workbook.
- In the merged workbook, you can review changes made by all users and accept or reject each.
- You can insert a *comment* to explain data or convey messages to other persons who see your work.

7.6 Inspect a workbook, check compatibility, and define a trusted location (p. 402).

- Before making a workbook available to others, you can set several properties to preserve security.
- The *Inspect Document* command locates features and data that might include personal information.
- The *Inspect Document* command is on the *Check for Issues* button on the *Info* area in *Backstage* view.
- After document inspection, you can remove elements that should not be available to others.
- When you work with others who have earlier versions of Excel, you can check the compatibility of your workbook.
- The *Check Compatibility* command is included on the *Check for Issues* button on the *Info* area in *Backstage* view.
- When you run the *Compatibility Checker*, features, commands, and objects that might not work properly in an earlier version of Excel are noted.
- You can edit these features to improve compatibility as desired.
- A *trusted location* is a folder that contains secure, safe workbooks.
- You can define a folder as a trusted location in the *Trust Center* from the *Excel Options* dialog box.
- When a workbook from a trusted location is opened, it is not opened in protected view.

Check for Understanding

On the *Online Learning Center* for this text (www.mhhe.com/office2013inpractice), there are a variety of resources that can be used to review the concepts covered in this chapter.

The following Online Learning Resources are available on the Online Learning Center:

- Multiple choice questions
- Short answer questions
- Matching exercises

Guided Project 7-1

The Sierra Pacific Community College District (SPCCD) organization is requesting instructors to add validation criteria, and input and error messages to a workbook. Share and merge any shared workbooks for a collaborative editing effort and check for compatibility.
[Student Learning Outcomes 7.1, 7.5, 7.6]

File Needed: ***Grades-07.xlsx***
Completed Project File Names: ***[your initials] Excel 7-1.xlsx*** and ***[your initials] Excel 7-1User2.xlsx***

Skills Covered in This Project

- Set validation criteria.
- Create an input message.
- Create an error message.
- Circle invalid data.
- Set data validation for lists.
- Share a workbook.
- Protect a shared workbook.
- Apply edit options.
- Merge workbooks.
- Highlight changes.
- Accept or reject edits.
- Inspect a workbook.
- Check compatibility.

1. Open the ***Grades-07*** workbook from your student data files folder.

2. Save the workbook as ***[your initials] Excel 7-1***.

3. Set data validation to a range of cells.
   a. Click the **Final Grades** tab.
   b. Select the cell range **C4:C25**.
   c. Click the **Data Validation** button [*Data* tab, *Data Tools* group].
   d. The *Data Validation* dialog box opens.
   e. Select the **Settings** tab.
   f. Click the **Allow** drop-down arrow and choose **Decimal**.
   g. Click the **Data** drop-down arrow and choose the range **between**.
   h. Enter the value .1 into the *Minimum* box and 20 in the *Maximum* box (Figure 7-65).
   i. Do not click *OK*.

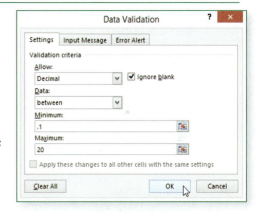

7-65 Validation criteria settings

4. Create an input message for data validation settings.
   a. Click the **Input Message** tab.
   b. Click the **Show input message when cell is selected** check box.
   c. Click in the **Title** box and type Grade Entry.
   d. Click in the **Input message** box and type Please enter any number between 0.1 and 20. (Figure 7-66).
   e. Do not click *OK*.

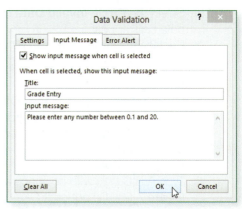

7-66 Input title and message

5. Create an error alert.
   a. Click the **Error Alert** tab.
   b. Click the **Show error alert after invalid data is entered** check box.
   c. Click the **Style** drop-down arrow and choose **Warning**. This style will allow an invalid entry to be made.
   d. Click in the **Title** box and type Grade Entry Error.
   e. Click in the **Error message** box and type Incorrect entry! Please enter any number between 0.1 and 20.
   f. Click **OK**.
   g. Click cell **C4**, type 21, and press **Enter** to display the error alert (Figure 7-67).
   h. Choose **Cancel** to allow the entry to revert back to 19.

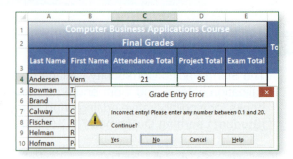

7-67 Warning style error alert after invalid entry

6. Repeat steps 3, 4, and 5 for the "Project Total" grading column.
   a. Select **D4:D25** and then set validation criteria that allow **Decimal** data **between 0.1** and **100**; use step 3 as a guide.
   b. Type Project Grade Entry as the title of the input message, and enter Please enter any number between 0.1 and 100. in the *Input message* box; use step 4 as a guide.
   c. Select the **Warning** style error alert. Click in the **Error Alert Title** box and type Grade Entry Error as the title of the error. Click in the **Error message** box and type Incorrect entry! Please enter any number between 0.1 and 100.; use step 5 as a guide.

7. Repeat steps 3, 4, and 5 for the *Exam Total* column.
   a. Select **E4:E25** and then set validation criteria that allow **Decimal** data **between 0.1** and **300**; use step 3 as a guide.
   b. Type Exam Grade Entry as the title of the input message and enter Please enter any number between 0.1 and 300. in the *Input message* box; use step 4 as a guide.
   c. Select the **Warning** style error alert. Click in the **Error Alert Title** box and type Exam Entry Error as the title of the error. Click in the **Error message** box and type Incorrect entry! Please enter any number between 0.1 and 300.; use step 5 as a guide.

8. Enter in the exam grades data.
   a. Copy the range **A2:A23** from the *Exam Scores* sheet tab.
   b. Paste the range into **E4:E25** in the *Final Grades* tab.

9. Circle invalid data.
   a. Click the **Data Validation** arrow button [*Data* tab, *Data Tools* group].
   b. Select the **Circle Invalid Data** option. Two invalid data cells appear.
   c. Replace the invalid entries in **E7** and **E24** with 300.

10. Set data validation to a range of cells to allow the user to choose only from a list.
   a. Select **H4:H25** and click the **Data Validation** button [*Data* tab, *Data Tools* group].
   b. Click the **Allow** arrow on the *Settings* tab and choose **List**.
   c. Click in the **Source** box.
   d. Type A,B,C,D,F,I with no space after each comma (Figure 7-68). Do not click *OK*.

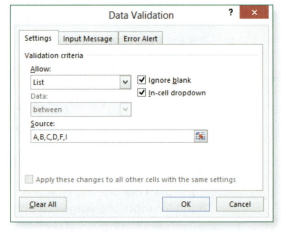

7-68 Validation settings for a list

e. Click the **Error Alert** tab.
f. Click the **Show error alert after invalid data is entered** check box.
g. Click the **Style** arrow and choose **Warning**. This style will allow an invalid entry to be made.
h. Click in the **Title** box and type Wait!.
i. Click in the **Error message** box and type Please choose from the list.
j. Click **OK**. A drop-down arrow will appear in each cell that is in H4:H25 when it's selected (Figure 7-69).
k. Using the drop-down arrow, enter a letter grade for each student; 90% and above is an A, 80–89% is a B, 70–79% is a C, 60–69% is a D, and 59% and lower is an F.
l. **Center** the results.

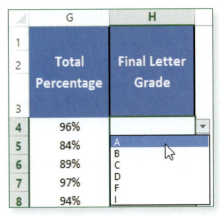

7-69 List result

11. Share the workbook.
    a. Click the **Share Workbook** button [*Review* tab, *Changes* group].
    b. Click to select the **Allow changes by more than one user at the same time** check box.
    c. Click the **Advanced** tab.
    d. Set the *Keep change history for* option to **25** days.
    e. Click **OK** to close the *Share Workbook* dialog box.
    f. Click **OK** to resave the shared workbook. Look for *[Shared]* at the end of the file name in the title bar.

12. Protect the shared workbook.
    a. Click the **Protect Shared Workbook** button [*Review* tab, *Changes* group].
    b. Click the **Sharing with track changes** check box.
    c. Click **OK**. The option *Don't keep change history* on the *Advanced* tab of the *Share Workbook* dialog box is no longer available.

13. Insert a comment.
    a. Click cell **C9** on the **Final Grades** tab.
    b. Click the **New Comment** button [*Review* tab, *Comments* group]. You can select and delete the user name, or replace it with another name.
    c. Type Please confirm that this is the correct grade.
    d. Click cell **B9** to finalize the comment.

14. Make a copy of the shared workbook in the same folder.
    a. Click the **File** tab and choose **Save As**.
    b. Save the workbook as *[your initials] Excel 7-1User2*.

15. Edit *[your initials] Excel 7-1User2*.
    a. Click cell **A5** and type Boyd.
    b. Right-click cell **D5** and choose **Insert Comment**.
    c. Type Check her grade on each project. Her name changed when she got married and it may have been overlooked.
    d. Click cell **D16** to finalize the comment.
    e. Type 80.
    f. Set the width of column **A** to **15.00**.
    g. Save and close the file.

16. Add the *Compare and Merge Workbooks* command to the *Quick Access* toolbar if not shown.
    a. Open *[your initials] Excel 7-1* if necessary.
    b. Click the **Options** command [*File* tab].
    c. Click the **Quick Access Toolbar** in the left pane.

d. Choose **All Commands** from the *Choose commands from* list.

e. Click **Compare and Merge Workbooks** in the commands list.

f. Click **Add** to add the command to the *Customize Quick Access Toolbar* list.

g. Click **OK**.

17. Merge copies of the shared workbook.

a. Click the **Compare and Merge Workbooks** button on the *Quick Access* toolbar.

b. Click **OK** to save the workbook before merging if necessary.

c. In the *Select Files to Merge Into Current Workbook* dialog box, navigate to the folder with the copied workbook.

d. Click the **[your initials] Excel 7-1User2** file name and click **OK**. The copied workbook is merged into the workbook on screen.

18. Highlight changes.

a. Click the **Track Changes** button [*Review* tab, *Changes* group].

b. Choose **Highlight Changes**.

c. In the *When* box, click the **arrow** and choose **Not yet reviewed**.

d. Select the **Who** check box, click the **arrow**, and choose **Everyone**.

e. Click **OK**. The highlighted changes are indicated by blue triangles (upper-left of cell) and are those from the copied workbook. The comments inserted manually are indicated by a red triangle in the upper-right corner of the cell (Figure 7-70).

	A	B	C	D	E	F	G
2			Final Grades			Total Points	Total Percentage
3	Last Name	First Name	Attendance Total	Project Total	Exam Total		
4	Andersen	Vern	19	95	290	404.00	96%
5	Boyd	Tanja	15.5	80	257.5	353.00	84%
6	Brand	Tabitha	17.8	85	269	371.80	89%
7	Calway	Carl	18	90	300	408.00	97%
8	Fischer	Rhonda	19	90	285	394.00	94%
9	Helman	Randy	19	95	270	384.00	91%
10	Hofman	Pamela	18.5	100	292.5	411.00	98%
11	Jenson	Nathan	17.9	100	289.5	407.40	97%
12	Johnson	Megan	19	95	285	399.00	95%
13	Johnston	Lenny	20	95	295	410.00	98%
14	Jordan	Kristen	17.5	95	282.5	395.00	94%
15	Karoose	Kelsey	18	90	270	378.00	90%
16	Lund	Karen	19	80	285	384.00	91%

7-70 Revision triangles are visible for merged data and typed comments

19. Accept or reject changes.

a. Click the **Track Changes** button [*Review* tab, *Changes* group].

b. Choose **Accept/Reject Changes**.

c. In the *When* box, choose **Not yet reviewed**.

d. In the *Who* box, choose **Everyone**.

e. Click **OK**. The first edit made in cell **A5** is presented in the *Accept or Reject* dialog box (Figure 7-71).

f. Click **Accept** to accept the change. The edit made in cell D16 is noted.

g. Click **Reject**. The data reverts to the original. Format commands are not tracked so the column width change for column *A* was not merged and is not identified as an edit.

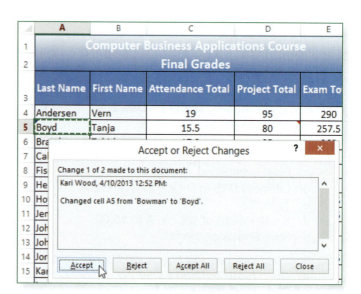

7-71 First edit to accept

20. Inspect the workbook.
    a. Click the **Check for Issues** button [*File* tab, *Info* option].
    b. Choose **Inspect Document**.
    c. Choose **Yes** to save the document before inspection if prompted.
    d. Click **Inspect**. There are several features that cannot be removed in a shared workbook.
    e. Click **Close** without removing any properties or features.

21. Check compatibility.
    a. Click the **Check for Issues** button [*File* tab, *Info* option].
    b. Choose **Check Compatibility**. The option to print a compatibility report is not available for a shared workbook.
    c. Review the issues in the *Compatibility Checker* dialog box. If necessary, you can edit features before saving the workbook in another format.
    d. Click **OK**.

22. Save and close the workbook (Figure 7-72).

	A	B	C	D	E	F	G	H
1	Computer Business Applications Course					Total Points	Total Percentage	Final Letter Grade
2	Final Grades							
3	Last Name	First Name	Attendance Total	Project Total	Exam Total			
4	Andersen	Vern	19	95	290	404.00	96%	A
5	Boyd	Tanja	15.5	80	257.5	353.00	84%	B
6	Brand	Tabitha	17.8	85	269	371.80	89%	B
7	Calway	Cari	18	90	300	408.00	97%	A
8	Fischer	Rhonda	19	90	285	394.00	94%	A
9	Helman	Randy	19	95	270	384.00	91%	A
10	Hofman	Pamela	18.5	100	292.5	411.00	98%	A
11	Jenson	Nathan	17.9	100	289.5	407.40	97%	A
12	Johnson	Megan	19	95	285	399.00	95%	A
13	Johnston	Lenny	20	95	295	410.00	98%	A
14	Jordan	Kristen	17.5	95	282.5	395.00	94%	A
15	Karoose	Kelsey	18	90	270	378.00	90%	A
16	Lund	Karen	19	90	285	394.00	94%	A
17	Midboe	Justin	19	85	280	384.00	91%	A
18	Nelson	Jessica	17	80	250	347.00	83%	B
19	Nickel	Jeremiah	20	100	300	420.00	100%	A
20	Olson	Danya	20	85	260	365.00	87%	B
21	Tisen	Christina	19.5	90	287.5	397.00	95%	A
22	Toftum	Cheryl	19	85	280	384.00	91%	A
23	Toosen	Cassidy	19.8	95	289	403.80	96%	A
24	Zelman	Cassandra	20	100	300	420.00	100%	A
25	Zimmerman	Brandon	19	95	290	404.00	96%	A
26	Fall 2016							
27	Average Scores		18.70	91.59	282.84	392.45		

7-72 Excel 7-1 completed worksheet

Guided Project 7-2

For this project you address the needs of Blue Lake Sports, where employees are to create an order form to allow for quick review of order request data. This form needs protection and should be distributed with editing options.
[Student Learning Outcomes 7.1, 7.2, 7.4, 7.6]

File Needed: **_BLSOrderForm-07.xlsx_**
Completed Project File Name: **_[your initials] Excel 7-2.xlsx_**

Skills Covered in This Project

- Display the *Developer* tab.
- Set validation criteria.
- Create an input message.
- Create an error message.
- Set data validation for lists.

- Insert a form control.
- Insert an option control.
- Unlock cells.
- Protect workbook structures.
- Protect a worksheet.

1. Open the **_BLSOrderForm-07_** workbook from your student data files folder.

2. Save the workbook as **_[your initials] Excel 7-2_**.

3. Set data validation to a range of cells to allow the user to choose only from a list.
   a. Select **D6** and click the **Data Validation** button [*Data* tab, *Data Tools* group].
   b. Click the **Allow** arrow and choose **List**.
   c. Click in the **Source** box.
   d. Type the numbers 1 through 12 separated by commas and without spaces (Figure 7-73).
   e. Click the **Error Alert** tab.
   f. Click the **Show error alert after invalid data is entered** check box.
   g. Click the **Style** arrow and choose **Stop**. This style will not allow an invalid entry to be made.
   h. Click in the **Title** box and type Wait!.
   i. Click in the **Error message** box and type Please choose from the list.
   j. Click **OK** and **Center** the results.

4. Apply data validation to a cell to allow the user to choose only from a list.
   a. Select the cell **G5**.
   b. Click the **Data Validation** button [*Data* tab, *Data Tools* group].
   c. Select the **Settings** tab.
   d. Click the **Allow** arrow and choose **List**.
   e. Click in the **Source** box.

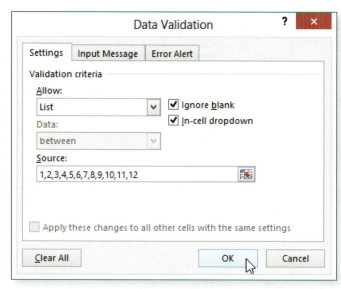

7-73 Validation settings for number of items list

f. Click the **Tables** tab and select the range **D2:D4** (Figure 7-74).

g. Click **OK** and **Center** the results.

5. Apply data validation to other cells to allow the user to choose only from a list; use step 4 as an example.

a. Select the cell **G6**.

b. Select **A2:A5** from the *Tables* tab for the *Source* box.

c. Click **OK** and **Center** the results.

d. Select the cell **G7**.

e. Select **B2:B5** from the *Tables* tab for the *Source* box.

f. Click the **OK** button and **Center** the results.

6. Display the *Developer* tab on the *Ribbon* if it is not shown.

a. Click the **Options** button [*File* tab].

b. Click **Customize Ribbon** in the left pane.

c. Select the **Developer** check box in the *Main Tabs* group.

d. Click **OK**.

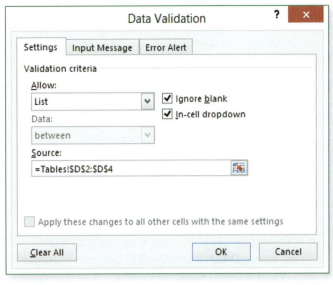

7-74 Validation settings for shipping list

7. Insert a combo box form control.

a. Click the **Insert Controls** button [*Developer* tab, *Controls* group].

b. Click the **Combo Box (Form Control)** button.

c. Click and drag to draw a control directly over cell **D5** in the **Order Form** sheet.

d. Click the **Control Properties** button [*Developer* tab, *Controls* group].

e. Click the **Control** tab.

f. In the *Input range* box, click the **Tables** tab and select cells **C2:C4**. These values will be selectable in the control.

g. Click in the **Cell link** box and click **B13** on the *Tables* tab. The choice made in the combo box will be placed in this cell.

h. Type 3 as the number of *Drop down lines*.

i. Check the **3-D shading** box (Figure 7-75).

j. Click **OK**. Click cell **D7** to deselect the combo box control.

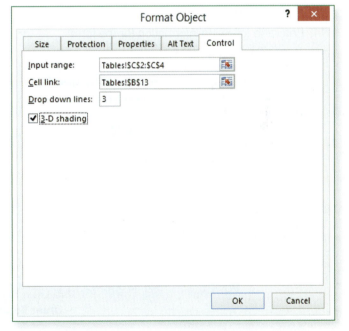

7-75 Combo box control settings

8. Insert an option button control.

a. Click the **Insert** button [*Developer* tab, *Controls* group].

b. Click the **Option Button (Form Control)** button.

c. Click and drag to create the control directly over cell **G10**.

d. Click the **Properties** button [*Developer* tab, *Controls* group].

e. Select the **Control** tab and click the **Unchecked** radio button under *Value*.

f. Do not input anything in the *Cell link* box.

g. Click the **3-D shading** check box (Figure 7-76).

h. Click the **Protection** tab in the *Format Control* dialog box.

i. Clear the **Locked** check box.

j. Click **OK**.

k. Right-click on the **Option Button** and choose **Edit Text**.

l. Delete the text next to the *Options* button and type the following: I Agree.

9. Unlock cells in the worksheet for users to edit.

a. Select **D4:D10** and **G4:G10** and apply **Center** alignment if necessary.

b. Right-click one of the selected cells and select **Format Cells**.

c. Clear the **Locked** checkbox on the *Protection* tab.

d. Click **OK**.

10. Protect the worksheet with a password.

a. Click the **Protect Sheet** button [*Review* tab, *Changes* group].

b. Type the following password: Password1.

c. Retype the password: Password1 in the *Confirm Password* dialog box.

d. Click **OK**.

11. Enter the following information for the form:

a. Name: Gary Livingood

b. Email: GLivingood@yahoo.com

c. Purchase Category: select **Sporting goods**

d. Shipping Method: select **Ground**

e. Number of Items: select **2**

f. Payment Method: select **Credit Card**

g. Address: 1123 Creek Drive

h. CC Type: select **Discover**

i. City: Madison

j. CC Number: 6011-2222-2222-2222

k. State: WI

l. CC Security Code: 111

m. Zip Code: 53704

n. Fill in the *Option* button next to *I Agree* (Figure 7-77).

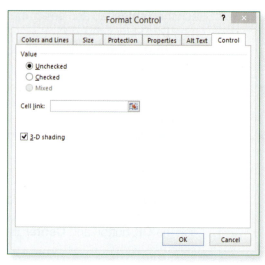

7-76 Option button control settings

7-77 Excel 7-2 completed worksheet

12. Protect the workbook structure with a password.
    a. Click the **Protect Workbook** button [*File* tab, *Info* area].
    b. Select **Protect Workbook Structure**.
    c. Verify that there is a check mark for **Structure**.
    d. Type Password2 in the *Password* box and click **OK**.
    e. Retype the password in the *Confirm Password* dialog box and click **OK**.

13. Save and close the workbook.

Guided Project 7-3

Placer Hills Real Estate (PHRE) is a real estate company with regional offices throughout central California. Real estate agents working for PHRE must create a mortgage calculator template that includes data validation techniques to limit mistakes, applies protection of sheets and workbooks, and allows data entry for a new clients financial data.
[Student Learning Outcomes 7.1, 7.2, 7.3, 7.4, 7.6]

File Needed: ***MortgageCacl-07.xlsx***
Completed Project File Names: ***[your initials] Excel 7-3.xlsx***, ***[your initials] Excel 7-3.xltx***, and ***[your initials] Excel 7-3a.xlsx***

Skills Covered in This Project

- Display the *Developer* tab.
- Apply the *IFERROR* function.
- Create data validation for lists.
- Create an input message.
- Create an alert message.
- Insert a combo box form control.

- Encrypt a workbook.
- Unlock cells for editing.
- Protect workbook structures.
- Save a file as a template.
- Protect a worksheet.

1. Open the ***MortgageCalc-07*** workbook from your student data files folder.

2. Save the workbook as ***[your initials] Excel 7-3***.

3. Apply the *IFERROR* function.
   a. Select **H11**.
   b. Use the current *PMT* function as the *value* argument.
   c. Type 0 for the *value_if_error* argument.
   d. Apply the **Accounting** number format.

4. Apply data validation to a range of cells.
   a. Select cells **C6:C12**, **C14**, **H6**, **H9:H10**, and **H12:H13**.
   b. Click the **Data Validation** button [*Data* tab, *Data Tools* group].

    c. Select the **Settings** tab.

    d. Click the **Allow** drop-down arrow and choose **Decimal**.

    e. Click the **Data** drop-down arrow and choose **greater than or equal to**.

    f. Type 0 in the *Minimum* box (Figure 7-78).

    g. Do not click *OK*.

5. Create an input message for the range of cells that contain validation rules.

    a. Select the **Input Message** tab.

    b. Click in the **Title** box and type Data Entry as the title of the message.

    c. Click in the **Input message** box and type Please type any number greater than or equal to 0.

    d. Do not click the *OK* button.

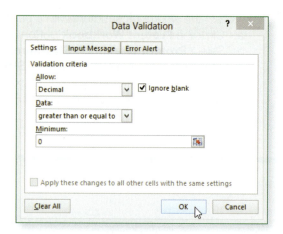

7-78 Validation settings for amount

6. Create an error message for the range of cells that contain validation rules.

    a. Select the **Error Alert** tab.

    b. Click the **Style** drop-down arrow and choose **Stop**.

    c. Click in the **Title** box and type Entry Error! as the title of the error.

    d. Click in the **Error message** box and type Incorrect entry! You must type a number greater than or equal to 0. as the message you want to appear when the cell contents are incorrect (Figure 7-79).

    e. Click **OK**.

7-79 Stop style error alert settings

7. Display the *Developer* tab on the *Ribbon* if it is not shown.

    a. Click the **Options** button [*File* tab].

    b. Click **Customize Ribbon** in the left pane.

    c. Click the **Developer** check box in the *Main Tabs* group.

    d. Click **OK**.

8. Insert a new sheet.

    a. Insert a new sheet. Select **A1:A6**.

    b. Type the following names, pressing **Enter** after each name: Gary Johnson, Shannon Anderson, Sanjeev Phukan, Lucy O'Riley, Dave Smith, Sandra Kranz. Widen the column if needed.

    c. Name the new tab Agents.

9. Insert a combo box form control.

    a. Click the **Purchase Information** tab.

    b. Click the **Insert Controls** button [*Developer* tab, *Controls* group].

    c. Click the **Combo Box (Form Control)** button.

    d. Click and drag to draw a control directly over cell **E24**.

    e. Click the **Control Properties** button [*Developer* tab, *Controls* group].

    f. Click the **Control** tab.

    g. In the *Input range* box, select **A1:A6** on the *Agents* tab. These values will be selectable in the control.

    h. Click in the **Cell link** box and type E24. The choice made in the combo box will be placed in this cell.

    i. Type 6 as the number of *Drop down lines.*

j. Check the **3-D shading** box (Figure 7-80).

k. Click **OK**. Click cell **E25** to deselect the combo box control.

10. Unlock cells in the worksheet for users to edit.

   a. Select cells **C6:C12**, **C14**, **H6**, **H9:H10**, **H12:H13**, **H18**, and **E22:E24** from the **Purchase Information** worksheet.

   b. Right-click one of the selected cells.

   c. Select **Format Cells** from the menu.

   d. Select the **Protection** tab.

   e. Clear the **Locked** check box.

   f. Click **OK**.

11. Protect the worksheet with a password.

   a. Click the **Protect Sheet** button [*Review* tab, *Changes* group].

   b. Allow **Select unlocked cells** only.

   c. Type the following password: Password1.

   d. Retype the password: Password1 in the *Confirm Password* dialog box. Remember that passwords are case sensitive.

   e. Click **OK**. When a user attempts to edit a locked cell in the worksheet, a message will appear informing him or her that the worksheet is protected.

   f. Save the file. If prompted to save the file as a macro-enabled workbook, click **No**.

12. Save the workbook as a template.

   a. Click the **Save As** button [*File* tab].

   b. Type the file name [your initials] Excel 7-3 for the template in the *File name* box. Since a template uses a different file name extension, you can use the same name as your original workbook for this project.

   c. Choose **Excel Template** from the *Save as type* drop-down box.

   d. Click **Save** to place in the default template location.

   e. Close the template.

13. Create a workbook from a template.

   a. Open Excel if needed.

   b. Click the **New** button [*File* tab].

   c. Click **Personal** near the top of the gallery.

   d. Click the icon for your template. A new workbook based on the template is created. If you saved your template elsewhere, double-click the file in its current location.

   e. Save the workbook as **[your initials] Excel 7-3a** in your usual location for saving workbooks.

14. Enter data into the workbook as shown in Figure 7-81.

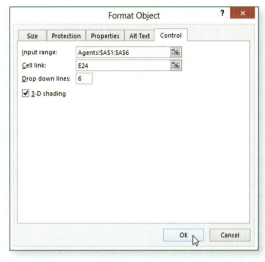

7-80 Combo box control defined in *Format Control* dialog box

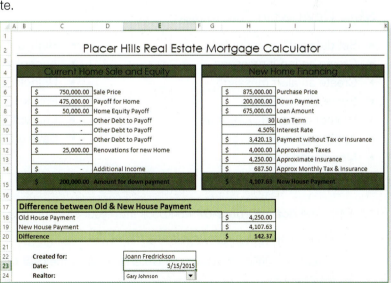

7-81 Excel 7-3 completed worksheet

15. Protect the workbook structure with a password.
    a. Click the **Protect Workbook** button [*File* tab, *Info* area].
    b. Select **Protect Workbook Structure**.
    c. Verify that there is a check mark for **Structure**.
    d. Type PassA in the *Password* box and click **OK**.
    e. Retype the password in the *Confirm Password* dialog box and click **OK**.

16. Encrypt the workbook with a password.
    a. Click the **Protect Workbook** button [*File* tab, *Info* area].
    b. Select **Encrypt with Password**.
    c. Type PassB in the *Password* box and click **OK**.
    d. Retype the password in the *Confirm Password* dialog box and click **OK**.

17. Save and close the workbook.

Independent Project 7-4

Employees at Classic Gardens and Landscapes (CGL) are requesting that management create a password-protected workbook from a template that allows employee access to selected cells to update relevant data. Share the workbook draft to allow multiple employees to edit the file. After merging the changes, save the file as a template and create the new requested encrypted workbook.
[Student Learning Outcomes 7.1, 7.3, 7.4, 7.5]

File Needed: ***ActualOrders-07.xlsx***
Completed Project File Names: *[your initials] Excel 7-4.xlsx*, *[your initials] Excel 7-4.xltx*, *[your initials] Excel 7-4a.xlsx*, and *[your initials] Excel 7-4User2.xlsx*

Skills Covered in This Project

- Set data validation for lists.
- Create an input message.
- Create an alert message.
- Share a workbook.
- Protect a shared workbook.
- Apply edit options.
- Merge workbooks.

- Highlight changes.
- Accept or reject edits.
- Unlock cells for editing.
- Protect a worksheet.
- Encrypt a workbook.
- Save a file as a template.

1. Open the ***ActualOrders-07*** workbook from your student data files folder.

2. Save the workbook as *[your initials] Excel 7-4*.

3. Apply data validation to a range of **G6:G10** to allow the user to choose a bonus of 2000, 5000, or None from a list.

a. Create an input message titled Data Entry that displays Please select 2000, 5000, or None. as the message to appear when you select the cell.

b. Create a *Stop* error message titled Entry Error that displays Incorrect Entry! You must select one of the following options: 2000, 5000, None. as the message to appear when the cell contents is incorrect.

4. Unlock cells **A6:D10** and **G6:G10** in the worksheet for users to edit.

5. Protect the worksheet with PasswordA as the password and allow users to **Select locked cells**, **Select unlocked cells**, and **Edit objects**. Save the file.

6. Share the workbook to **Allow changes by more than one user at the same time** and set the *Keep change history for* option to **25** days.

7. Protect the shared workbook and allow for **Sharing with track changes**.

8. Insert the following comment in cell **A7**: Please confirm that this is the correct category title. and save the file.

9. Make a copy of the shared workbook in the same folder and name the copy *[your initials] Excel 7-4User2*.

10. Edit *[your initials] Excel 7-4User2*.
    a. Click cell **A6** and type Landscape Care.
    b. Insert the following comment in cell **A10**: Can we drop "Design" from this category?
    c. Save and close the file.

11. Add the *Compare and Merge Workbooks* command to the *Quick Access* toolbar.

12. Open *[your initials] Excel 7-4* if necessary.

13. Merge the *[your initials] Excel 7-4User2* copy of the shared workbook.

14. Highlight changes **Not yet reviewed** from **Everyone**.

15. Accept all the changes **Not yet reviewed** by **Everyone** and save the file. Only one change is made.

16. Unshare the workbook and incorporate the comments.
    a. Select the **Unprotect Shared Workbook** button [*Review* tab, *Changes* group].
    b. Click the **Share Workbook** button [*Review* tab, *Changes* group] and clear the check box in the *Editing* tab. Select **OK** in the *Editing* tab and **Yes** in the message box.
    c. Type Trees and Shrubs in **A7** and Consulting in **A10**.
    d. Delete the comments and save the file.

17. Save the file as a template with the name *[your initials] Excel 7-4*.

18. Create a workbook from a template and save the workbook as *[your initials] Excel 7-4a* in your usual location for saving workbooks.

19. Enter data into the workbook as shown in Figure 7-82.

20. Encrypt the workbook with a password PasswordB.

21. Close the workbook.

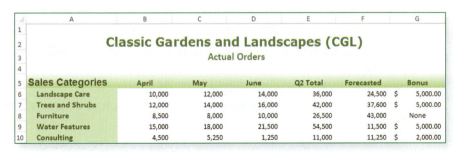

7-82 Excel 7-4 completed worksheet

Independent Project 7-5

You are a student at Sierra Pacific Community College (SPCC). Your advisor would like you to create a GPA calculation form for your MIS degree. She would like you to add controls, validation criteria, input and error messages, and encryption to the workbook you create from the template.
[Student Learning Outcomes 7.1, 7.2, 7.3, 7.4]

File Needed: **GPA-07.xlsx**
Completed Project File Names: **[your initials] Excel 7-5.xlsx**, **[your initials] Excel 7-5.xltx**, and **[your initials] Excel 7-5a.xlsx**

Skills Covered in This Project

- Display the *Developer* tab.
- Set validation criteria.
- Create an input message.
- Create an error message.
- Insert a combo box control.

- Insert a check box control.
- Unlock cells for editing.
- Protect a worksheet.
- Encrypt a workbook.
- Save a file as a template.

---

1. Open the **GPA-07** workbook from your student data files folder.

2. Save the workbook as **[your initials] Excel 7-5**.

3. Apply data validation to **C3:C14**, **C17:C20**, and **C23:C26** that allows the user to choose a grade from a list in **H4:H8**.
   a. Create an input message titled Letter Grade Entry that displays Please select a letter from the list. as the message when you select the cell.
   b. Create a *Warning* error message titled Grade Error that displays Incorrect entry! You should select a letter from the list. as the message when the cell contents are incorrect.

4. Apply data validation to **E3:E14**, **E17:E20**, and **E23:E26** that limits the user to enter whole numbers between 0 and 12.
   a. Create an input message titled Credit Amount that displays Please enter a number between 0 and 12. as the message when you select the cell.
   b. Create a *Stop* error message titled Credit Amount Error that displays Incorrect Entry! You must enter a number between 0 and 12. when the cell contents are incorrect.

5. Add the *Developer* tab.

6. Add two check box form controls to **I23** and **I24** that are **unchecked** and have **3-D shading**. Change the check box names to Check.

7. Unlock cells **C3:C14**, **C17:C20**, **C23:C26**, **E3:E14**, **E17:E20**, **E23:E26**, **B23:B26**, and **I23:I24** in the worksheet for users to edit.

8. Protect the worksheet with Pass1 as the password.
   a. Allow users to **Select locked cells**, **Select unlocked cells**, and **Use AutoFilter**.
   b. Save the file.

9. Save the file as a template with the name **[your initials] Excel 7-5**.

10. Create a workbook from the **[your initials] Excel 7-5** template and save the workbook as **[your initials] Excel 7-5a** in your usual location for saving workbooks.

11. Enter data into the workbook as shown in Figure 7-83.

	I. Required Management Information Systems Courses	Letter Grade	Letter Grade Points	Credits	Calculated Points		Grade Table	
1	**Management Information Systems Major Required Courses**							
3	BuAd 2280 Computer Business Applications	A	4	3	12		A	4
4	BuAd 2381 Structured Application Development	B	3	3	9		B	3
5	BuAd 3281 Decision Support Systems	B	3	3	9		C	2
6	BuAd 3283 E-Commerce Web Development	C	2	3	6		D	1
7	BuAd 3381 Management Information Systems	A	4	3	12		F	0
8	BuAd 3382 Advanced Application System Development	D	1	3	3			
9	BuAd 3383 Data Communications	A	4	3	12			
10	BuAd 3384 Systems Analysis and Design	A	4	3	12			
11	BuAd 3385 User Analysis and Interface Design with C#.NET	B	3	3	9			
12	BuAd 4283 Systems Integration and Web Services	C	2	3	6			
13	BuAd 4385 Data Modeling and Design	B	3	3	9			
14	BuAd 4386 Applied Software Development Project	Not Done	0	0	0			
16	**II. Required Business Environment Courses**							
17	Acct 1101 Principles of Accounting I	B	3	3	9			
18	Acct 1102 Principles of Accounting II	B	3	3	9			
19	BuAd 2231 Business Statistics I	A	4	3	12			
20	BuAd 3520 Business Ethics	Note Done	0	0	0			
22	**III. Required Business Electives** -Any 4 additional Upper-Level BuAd courses with advisor approval						Advisor Approval	
23	BUAD	Not Done	0	0	0		Yes	☐ Check
24	BUAD	Not Done	0	0	0		No	☑ Check
25	BUAD	Not Done	0	0	0			
26	BUAD	Not Done	0	0	0			
27	**Totals**		43	42	129			
29	**Major GPA**	3.07						

7-83 Excel 7-5 completed worksheet

12. Encrypt the workbook with the password Pass2.

13. Save and close the workbook.

Independent Project 7-6

The Hamilton Civic Center is requesting that the accounts receivable department create password-protected payment calculation forms with data validation techniques applied to eliminate errors.
[Student Learning Outcomes 7.1, 7.2, 7.4, 7.6]

File Needed: **HCCAmort-07.xlsx**
Completed Project File Name: **[your initials] Excel 7-6.xlsx**

Skills Covered in This Project

- Apply the *IFERROR* function.
- Set validation criteria.
- Create an input message.
- Create an error message.
- Display the *Developer* tab.
- Insert a label control.

- Insert a check box control.
- Unlock cells for editing.
- Protect a worksheet.
- Encrypt a workbook.
- Check compatibility.

1. Open the **HCCAmort-07** workbook from your student data files folder.

2. Save the workbook as *[your initials] Excel 7-6*.

3. Apply data validation to cells **D5:D6** that allows only decimal numbers between 0 and $750,000.
   a. Create an input message titled Data Entry that displays Please enter any number between 0 and $750,000. as the message when you select the cell.
   b. Create a *Warning* error message titled Data Entry Error as the title of the error that displays Incorrect entry! You should type any number between 0 and $750,000. as the message when the cell contents are incorrect.

4. Apply data validation to **G4** that allows only whole numbers between 1 and 35.
   a. Create an input message titled Number of Years that displays Please enter a whole number between 1 and 35. as the message when you select the cell.
   b. Create a *Stop* error message titled Number of Years Error that displays Incorrect Entry! You must type a whole number between 1 and 35. as the message when the cell contents are incorrect.

5. Apply the *IFERROR* function to the formula in **G5**. Use the existing formula as the *value* argument and 0 as the *value_if_error* argument.

6. Add the *Developer* tab to the *Ribbon* if necessary.

7. Insert a *label* form control over cell **D10** in the spreadsheet. Edit the control text so that it displays: Name of Preparer:.

8. Insert a *label* control button over cell **F10** in the spreadsheet. Edit the control text so that it displays: Management Approved:.

9. Insert a *check box form* control **unchecked**, with **3-D shading** in **F10** beside the label. Delete the default text in the control.

10. Unlock cells **D4:D6**, **D8**, **E10:F10**, and **G4** in the worksheet for users to edit.

11. Protect the worksheet with the password PassA allowing users to **Select unlocked cells** only and to **Format cells**.

12. Protect the workbook structure with the password PassB.

13. Enter the following information in each cell; **D4**: Building, **D5**: 500,000, **D8**: 5%, **E10**: Patti Boyd, **G4**: 15 and in **F10**, click the check box.

14. Check compatibility for any issues with the workbook.

15. Encrypt the workbook with the password PassC.

16. Save and close the workbook (Figure 7-84).

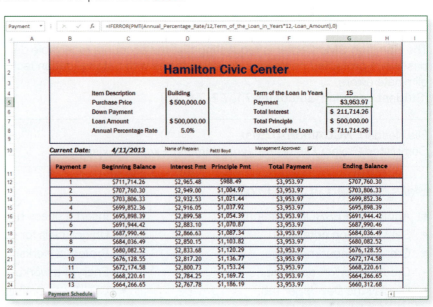

7-84 Excel 7-6 completed worksheet

Improve It Project 7-7

Life's Animal Shelter (LAS) is an animal adoption agency that will not turn any animal away. You must edit the password-protected adoption check-out form to assure accuracy.
[Student Learning Outcomes 7.1, 7.2, 7.4, 7.6]

File Needed: ***Adoption-07.xlsx***
Completed Project File Name: ***[your initials] Excel 7-7.xlsx***

Skills Covered in This Project

- Apply the *VLOOKUP* function.
- Display the *Developer* tab.
- Display the *Form* button.
- Use the data input form.
- Edit a check box control.
- Edit data validation for lists.
- Edit an error message.
- Edit an input message.
- Unlock cells for editing.
- Protect a worksheet.
- Check compatibility.
- Encrypt a workbook.

1. Open the **Adoption-07** workbook from your student data files folder.

2. Save the workbook as ***[your initials] Excel 7-7***.

3. Display the *Form* button on the *Quick Access* toolbar if necessary.

4. Select **A1:F13** on the **Animal Data** tab and edit Riley's age to **10** using the data input form.

5. Unprotect the **Check-Out** worksheet using the password Pass1.

6. Edit cells **C4:E4** on the *Check-Out* tab to include an *IFERROR* function. Use the existing functions in each cell as the *value* argument, and "Not Available" as the *value_if_false* argument.

7. Edit the input message and error alert applied to **F4** so that it is the same as the input message and alert message in **G4**.

8. Add the *Developer* tab to the *Ribbon*.

9. Edit the check box controls so they are **unchecked** and have **3-D shading**. Change the text for the first box to Yes, Please! and the second to No, Thanks!

10. Unlock cells **B4**, **F4:G4**, **A9:G9**, **B11:C11**, and **B15** in the worksheet for users to edit.

11. Protect the *Check-out* sheet with the password Pass1 allowing the users to **Select unlocked cells** only.

12. Check for compatibility issues.

13. Enter data and format the form.
    a. Type 3 in **B4**.
    b. Select **Yes** in **F4** and **G4**.
    c. Type Larry Bowman in **A9**.
    d. Enter 4335 Dunwood as the address in cell **B9**.
    e. Enter Bemidji as the city in cell **C9**.
    f. Enter MN as the address in cell **D9**.
    g. Apply a *VLOOKUP* function to **E9**. Use **C9** as the *lookup_value* argument, **A2:C8** in the **City State** sheet as the *table_array* argument, and 3 as the *col_index_num* argument.

h. Enter $35.00 in **F9** and Lbowman@my.com in **G9**. Apply **Currency** format to **F9**.

i. If necessary, unprotect the sheet and widen column **G**. Apply protection to the sheet again; type Pass1 for the password.

j. Check the **Yes, Please!** box and save the workbook.

14. Apply encryption to the workbook, using Pass2 for the password.

15. Save and close the workbook (Figure 7-85).

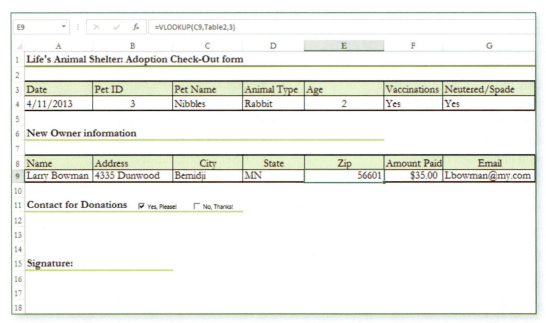

7-85 Excel 7-7 completed worksheet

Challenge Project 7-8

For this project, you create a personal budget template. The template includes data validation, worksheet protection, and workbook encryption.
[Student Learning Outcomes 7.1, 7.3, 7.4, 7.6]

File needed: None
Completed Project File Name: *[your initials] Excel 7-8.xlsx*

Enter all the data from your checking account and monthly expenses that is important to your budgeting (for example, your pay, your rent, your credit card payments). Create a new workbook and save it as *[your initials] Excel 7-8*. Modify your workbook according to the following guidelines:

• Import or type the web site revenue information from your bank for the last month into your Excel workbook.

- Add additional column headings such as "Expenses," "Vacation," Food," "Utilities," "Entertainment," "Savings," etc.
- Apply formatting to make your budget easy to read and use.
- Add total formulas to the key columns.
- Add validation rules, input messages, and error alerts.
- Unlock the cells you would like to access.
- Protect the worksheet with a password of your choice.
- Encrypt the workbook with a password of your choice.

Challenge Project 7-9

For this project, you create a registration worksheet using data validation or controls to select your courses. Save this workbook as a template for future semesters.
[Student Learning Outcomes 7.1, 7.2, 7.3, 7.4]

File needed: None
Completed Project File Name: *[your initials] Excel 7-9.xltx*

Enter all the relevant data regarding your classes and registration information for this semester. Create a new workbook and save it as *[your initials] Excel 7-9*. Modify your document according to the following guidelines:

- Import or review the web site registration information for this semester from your school's registration system.
- Add additional column headings such as "Course Web site," "Class Name," "Class Number," "Start Date," "End Date," "Withdraw Deadline," "Location," "Professor," "Professor Email," "Class Days," "Class Times," "Special Notes," "Grades," "Credits," etc.
- Add a new sheet and name it for the current semester. Add form controls or validation rules to this sheet.
- Add total formulas to the key columns.
- Add validation rules, input messages, and error alerts.
- Add form controls to link to the sheet where all the courses are listed.
- Save the file as a template.

Challenge Project 7-10

For this project, you create investment options and analyze the results. Apply *PV, FV,* and *NPV* to three personal financial scenarios and password-protect the worksheet. Then, you share the workbook, merge the copies, and encrypt the finalized workbook.
[Student Learning Outcomes 7.1, 7.5, 7.6]

File Needed: None
Completed Project File Name: *[your initials] Excel 7-10.xlsx*

Enter all data that you find important regarding three investment options. Create a new workbook and save it as *[your initials] Excel 7-10*.

- For the net present value scenario, include information such as annual discount rate, initial cost of investment, first year return, second year return, etc.
- For the present value scenario, include payment amount, term in years, and rate of return. Be sure to indicate if you are paying monthly or annually.
- For the future value scenario (IRA), include the same items as listed above for the present value scenario.
- Obtain information such as rate of return and discount rate from your local bank.
- Add formulas to the key cells.
- Add validation rules, input messages, and error alerts.
- Unlock the cells you would like to access.
- Share the workbook with your significant other.
- Merge the workbook copies.
- Protect the worksheet with a password of your choice.
- Encrypt the workbook with a password of your choice.

CHAPTER 8

Using Decision-Making Tools and XML

CHAPTER OVERVIEW

In *SLO 4.7: Using Goal Seek and Worksheet Protection*, you learned how to use *Goal Seek*, one of Excel's decision-making tools. In addition to *Goal Seek*, there are other features and commands in Excel designed to help you analyze data in professional or personal work. These include *Solver*, scenarios, and data tables. In this chapter, you explore these additional decision and analysis tools for working with Excel data.

STUDENT LEARNING OUTCOMES (SLOs)

After completing this chapter, you will be able to:

SLO 8.1 Install and use *Solver* to find a solution (p. E8-432).

SLO 8.2 Understand and create *Solver* reports such as the *Answer* report, the *Sensitivity* report, and the *Limits* report (p. E8-435).

SLO 8.3 Create and manage scenarios for worksheet data using *Scenario Manager* (p. E8-437).

SLO 8.4 Customize a *PivotTable* and *PivotChart* by editing value field settings, including a custom calculation; inserting a calculated field; refreshing data; displaying slicers; and formatting (p. E8-442).

SLO 8.5 Build a one-variable data table (p. E8-454).

SLO 8.6 Build a two-variable data table (p. E8-456).

SLO 8.7 Import and work with XML data (p. E8-458).

CASE STUDY

In the *Pause & Practice* projects in this chapter, you continue to edit worksheets for the northern Minnesota business *Paradise Lakes Resort (PLR)*. As you work on these projects, you use the Solver add-in, review Solver *reports, manage scenarios, enhance* PivotTables, *and build data tables.*

Pause & Practice 8-1: Create and display scenarios, enable the *Solver* add-in, and use *Solver* to find a solution.

Pause & Practice 8-2: In a *PivotTable* and *PivotChart,* edit value field settings, insert a calculated field, display slicers, and work with format options.

Pause & Practice 8-3: Build one- and two-variable data tables and import an XML file.

E8-431

SLO 8.1

Using Solver

Solver is an advanced analysis tool that finds the highest, lowest, or specific result for a formula by changing the values in other cells within the limitations that you set. Using *Solver* could be described as solving a problem in reverse, because you start with the desired answer and *Solver* calculates how to reach that answer. For example, you can determine the most profitable product mix or the shortest route to a hospital by using this tool. *Solver* assists with many decision-making scenarios. For example, suppose Paradise Lakes Resort wants to set a sales goal for each employee that would allow the organization to reach combined sales of $75,000,000 in two years. The target is $75,000,000, and *Solver* can determine the best way to reach this target by calculating a goal for each employee.

Solver is a sophisticated analysis tool, but it may not be able to find a solution to every problem. When it cannot do so, the *Solver Results* dialog box informs you that it could not find a solution.

Solver is an Excel **add-in**. An add-in is an enhanced command or feature that is not installed with the initial setup. You can install add-ins from the *Add-Ins* pane in Excel *Options*.

HOW TO: Install Solver

1. Select **Options** [*File* tab].
2. Click **Add-Ins** in the left pane.
   - The *View and manage Microsoft Office Add-ins* pane opens.
   - Applications that are currently active are listed near the top of the window.
3. In the list of *Inactive Application Add-Ins*, click **Solver Add-in** (Figure 8-1).
4. Click **Go** near the bottom of the dialog box to open the *Add-ins* dialog box.
5. Check the box next to *Solver Add-in* (Figure 8-2).
   - You can remove *Solver* by removing the check mark.
6. Click **OK**.
   - The *Solver* button is located in the *Analysis* group on the *Data* tab.

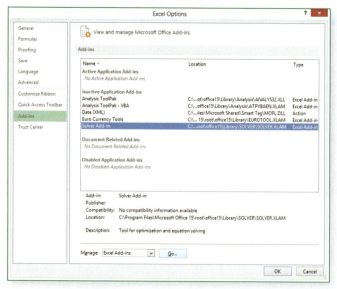

8-1 *Add-Ins* pane in *Excel options*

8-2 *Add-Ins* dialog box

A *Solver* problem has three components, known as **parameters**. A parameter is information used by *Solver* to find a solution. The three parameters are explained in the following sections.

The Objective Cell

The **objective cell** is a cell with a formula that has your desired result. It is sometimes referred to as the **target cell**. You can set the objective cell to a maximum or minimum or to a value. In Figure 8-3, Paradise Lakes wants to increase how much gasoline it saves per week from the use of hybrid vehicles to 450 gallons. The formula in cell D8 is the objective cell.

| D8 | | : | × | ✓ | f_x | =SUM(D4:D7) |

	A	B	C	D
1	**Paradise Lakes Resort**			
2	**Gallons of Gasoline Saved with Hybrids**			
3	Location	Hours Used Per Week	Gallons Saved per Hour	Total Gallons Saved
4	Baudette	30	3.25	97.50
5	Breezy Point	24	2.75	66.00
6	Cass Lake	36	3.15	113.40
7	Walker	18	3.50	63.00
8	Total	108	12.65	339.90

8-3 *Solver* problem for Paradise Lakes

Variable Cells

In order to reach the desired result in the objective cell, *Solver* changes the cells identified as **variable cells**. These cells can also be called **decision cells** or **changing cells**. For example, Paradise Lakes knows that additional use can be made of the hybrid vehicles in Breezy Point and Walker so it must take them into account when working toward its goals. In Figure 8-3, cells B5 and B7 are therefore variable cells that will be changed to reach the target value in cell D8.

Constraints

A **constraint** is a restriction or limitation. It could be a limitation on the formula, a limitation on one or more of the variable cells, or a limitation on other cells that are directly related to the objective cell. For example, in Figure 8-3 a constraint for cell B5, the Breezy Point usage, might be that the usage hours cannot be fewer than 24 or greater than 36. When *Solver* cannot find a solution, it is often because of some issue with the constraints.

> **MORE INFO**
>
> You can use cell references or range names in the *Solver Parameters* dialog box.

To run *Solver*, click the **Solver** button on the *Data* tab in the *Analysis* group. You define each parameter in the *Solver Parameters* dialog box.

HOW TO: Run Solver

1. Click the **Solver** button [*Data* tab, *Analysis* group].
   - The *Solver Parameters* dialog box opens.

2. In the *Set Objective* box, click the cell with the formula to be solved.

   - The objective cell must include a formula.

3. For the *To* parameter, make a selection.

   - You can solve the formula for the minimum or maximum value.
   - You can set a specific value to be shown as the formula result.
   - When you choose *Value Of,* type the target value in the entry box.

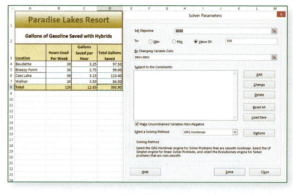

4. Click in the *By Changing Variable Cells* box and select the cells that can be changed (Figure 8-4).

   - You can select the cell range or type the range reference.
   - You can press **F3** and choose a named range.
   - Hold down **Ctrl** to select nonadjacent cells.

8-4 *Solver Parameters* dialog box

5. To add a limitation, click **Add** to the right of *Subject to the Constraints* box.

   - The *Add Constraint* dialog box opens.
   - You can complete more than one constraint for any cell.

6. In the *Cell Reference* box, select the first cell or range that will have a limitation.

7. Click the drop-down arrow and choose an operator.

8. Click in the *Constraint* box and enter the value (Figure 8-5).

   - You can click a cell with a value for the constraint.
   - You can type a value for the constraint.

8-5 *Add Constraint* dialog box

9. To add another constraint, click **Add** in the *Add Constraint* dialog box.

   - If you have clicked **OK** but want to add another constraint, click **Add** to the right of the *Subject to the Constraints* box.

10. When you have identified all constraints, click **OK** in the *Add Constraint* dialog box. The constraints are listed in the *Solver Parameters* dialog box.

11. Check the **Make Unconstrained Variables Non-Negative** box.

    - If you leave this unchecked, a variable cell without a constraint can be set to a negative number.

12. For the *Select a Solving Method,* choose an algorithm from the drop-down menu (Figure 8-6).

    - You can run *Solver* multiple times for a problem, each with a different algorithm dependent upon the formula in the objective cell.
    - *GRG Nonlinear* solves a non-linear problem.
    - *LP Simplex* solves a problem that is linear. This is the most common method.
    - *Evolutionary* solves a non-smooth problem.

13. Click **Solve**.

    - The *Solver Results* dialog box includes an option to keep the solution or to discard it.
    - You can choose to generate a *Solver* report. You will learn more about *Solver* reports in the next section of this chapter, *SLO 8.2: Understanding Solver Reports.*
    - You can save the results as a scenario.

8-6 Completed Solver parameters with constraints

14. Click **OK** to keep the results.

Understanding Solver Reports

As part of the *Solver Results* dialog box, you can choose to generate statistical analysis reports. Each report is placed on a separate sheet. There are three types of reports for a solved problem, *Answer, Sensitivity,* and *Limits*. These reports are straightforward to generate, but you need to have an understanding of statistical concepts and terms to understand and use the reports. The three types of reports are explained in the following material.

> **MORE INFO**
>
> When *Solver* cannot find a solution, *Feasibility* and *Feasibility-Bounds* reports identify constraint issues.

> **MORE INFO**
>
> For an *Evolutionary* method, *Solver* can generate a Population report to provide information on the final population of candidate solutions. There is also a Linearity report that notes linear conditions that were not satisfied.

In the *Solver Results* window, you can choose to generate one report or all three at once. When you click **OK**, the reports are generated and the *Solver Parameter* dialog box reopens. If you have completed your analysis at this point, you can simply close the dialog box.

Answer Report

The *Answer* report identifies and lists each parameter. It includes the original value and the value suggested by *Solver,* as shown in Figure 8-7, as well as statistical values such as slack and integer. The first lines of the report specify the worksheet, the time and date, and the solving method that was used.

The *Answer* report is inserted in your workbook in a worksheet named *Answer Report 1*. If you run *Solver* multiple times, you can generate an answer report each time, and the sheets are named *Answer Report 2, Answer Report 3*, and so on.

Sensitivity Report

The contents of the ***Sensitivity*** report depend on the solving method that is selected when you run *Solver*. This report might include statistical data such as an objective coefficient, a Lagrange

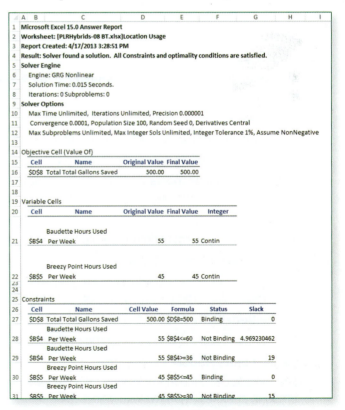

8-7 An *Answer Solver* report

multiplier, and a reduced gradient. Figure 8-8 shows a *Sensitivity* report generated after the Simplex LP solving method was used.

Like an *Answer* report, the first *Sensitivity* report is inserted in a sheet named *Sensitivity Report 1*.

Limits Report

The ***Limits*** report displays data about the lower and upper limits of each variable cell and how those limits impact the objective cell. Figure 8-9 shows a *Limits* report.

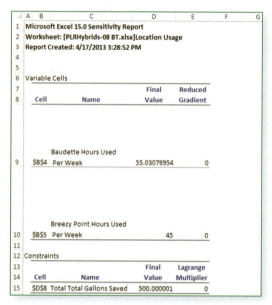

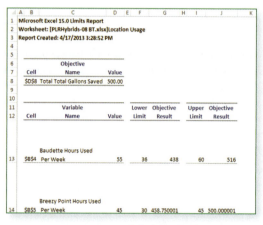

8-9 A *Limits Solver* report

8-8 A *Sensitivity Solver* report

HOW TO: Create Solver Reports

1. Complete the *Solver Parameters* dialog box as needed.
2. Click **Solve**.
3. In the *Solver Results* window, click **Answer** in the *Reports* section to select it.
4. Click **Sensitivity** in the *Reports* section to select it.
5. Click **Limits** in the *Reports* section to select it (Figure 8-10).
   - You can select one, two, or all three reports.
6. Check the **Outline Reports** box if the reports should be formatted as Excel outlines.
7. Click **OK**.
   - Each report is generated on a separate tab.
8. Click the **Answer Report 1** sheet tab.
   - Each parameter might include a cell range name or reference, an original value, a final value, and constraint information.
9. Click the **Sensitivity Report 1** sheet tab.
   - The contents depend upon the solving method.
10. Click the **Limits Report 1** sheet tab.
    - For variable cells, the report includes the range name or reference, the value, the lower limit and objective amount, and the upper limit with objective amount.

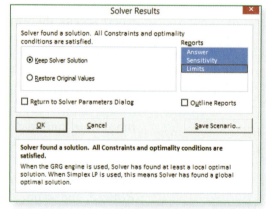

8-10 *Solver Results* window

Creating and Managing Scenarios

A *scenario* is a saved set of values in a worksheet. Scenarios are what-if analysis tools. They enable you to test values in a worksheet and determine potential results.

A worksheet can have multiple scenarios, each one named and saved. For instance, to return to the example we discussed in *SLO 8.1: Using Solver*, in its worksheet for energy results from hybrid vehicles, Paradise Lakes Resort can create many scenarios, each with different usage hours for its four locations. For example, the company can explore low-, average-, and high-usage scenarios as well as a scenario that reflects the actual usage.

> ### MORE INFO
>
> Because each scenario value set must be typed in the *Scenario Values* dialog box, it is time intensive to create numerous scenarios for large sets of values.

You create a scenario by choosing **Scenario Manager** from the **What-If Analysis** button in the *Data Tools* group on the *Data* tab.

Create a Scenario

Before creating a new scenario, save the current data in a worksheet as a scenario so that you can always return to it. After that, you can create another scenario that uses the same cells with different values. The most recently viewed scenario is shown on screen. You can display any scenario whenever you need to, but only one scenario can be displayed at a time in the worksheet.

HOW TO: Create and Show a Scenario

1. Click the **What-if Analysis** button [*Data* tab, *Data Tools* group].
2. Select **Scenario Manager**.
   - The *Scenario Manager* dialog box opens.
   - Existing scenarios, if any, are listed in the dialog box.
3. Click **Add**.
4. In the *Add Scenario* dialog box, type a name for the saved set of values in the *Scenario name* box.
   - Use a descriptive but short name.
   - Use capitalization and spaces as desired.
   - Name your original set of values Original or something similar.
5. Click in the **Changing cells** box and select the cells whose values will be revised.
   - You can use a range name if appropriate.
   - You can select the cell range in the worksheet before starting the *Scenario Manager* command.
6. Click in the **Comment** box to type an optional description or explanation (Figure 8-11).
   - A default comment is inserted for each scenario that includes the user name and date.
7. Click **OK**.
   - The *Scenario Values* dialog box opens.

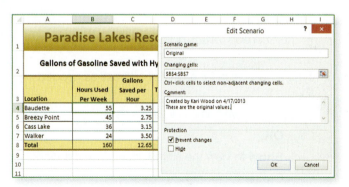

8-11 Scenario setup for the usage hours

- The values currently visible in the worksheet are shown for each cell address.
- Leave the values unchanged when creating a scenario for the original set of values.

8. Type a new value for each cell address (Figure 8-12).

9. Click **OK** in the *Scenario Values* dialog box.
   - The *Scenario Manager* dialog box shows the scenario name.

10. Click **Show**.
   - The values displayed in the worksheet are replaced by the values from the scenario.
   - Select another scenario name and click **Show** if desired.

11. Click **Close** in the *Scenario Manager* dialog box.
   - The values currently displayed remain visible.

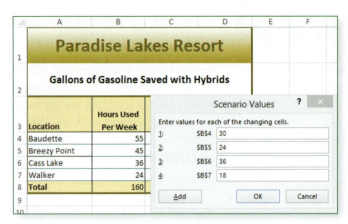

8-12 New values entered in the *Scenario Values* dialog box

Edit a Scenario

When a particular scenario is displayed in a worksheet, you can still make changes to values in any cell. That type of edit is a regular workbook change and the scenario itself is unchanged.

You can also make changes to the values saved in a scenario from the *Scenario Values* dialog box. From the *Edit Scenario* dialog box, you can change a scenario name or reset which cells will be changed.

HOW TO: Edit a Scenario

1. Click the **What-if Analysis** button [*Data* tab, *Data Tools* group].

2. Select **Scenario Manager**.

3. Select the scenario name in the *Scenarios* list.

4. Click **Edit**.
   - The *Edit Scenario* dialog box is the same as the *Add Scenario* dialog box.
   - In the *Edit Scenario* dialog box, you can change the scenario name.
   - You can adjust the cell range if desired.
   - A default comment is inserted each time the scenario is edited.

5. Click **OK**.
   - The *Scenario Values* dialog box shows the current values for the scenario.

6. Type a new value for each cell address as needed (Figure 8-13).
   - You can leave some cell values as is.

7. Click **OK**.

8. Click **Show** to view the edited scenario in the worksheet.

9. Click **Close**.

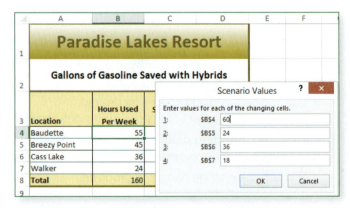

8-13 Not all values must be changed in a scenario

Scenario Summary Reports

A *scenario summary report* is a generated worksheet that describes each scenario in a workbook. It is formatted as an Excel outline with two row outline levels and two column outline levels. In the report, you can hide or display details about the changing cells and the result cells.

If you edit a scenario after creating a summary report, the report is not updated. You can, however, quickly generate another scenario summary report.

For a large worksheet with many scenarios, you can also choose to format a scenario summary report as a *PivotTable*.

HOW TO: Create a Scenario Summary Report

1. Click the **What-if Analysis** button [*Data* tab, *Data Tools* group].
2. Select **Scenario Manager**.
3. Click **Summary**.
   - The *Scenario Summary* dialog box appears.
4. In the *Scenario Summary* dialog box, choose **Scenario summary** as the *Report type*.
5. In the *Result cells* box, select the cell or range (Figure 8-14).
   - This can be the changing cells, or cells that are affected by the changing cells.
6. Click **OK** (Figure 8-15).
   - The report is generated on a sheet named *Scenario Summary.*
   - It is formatted as an outline and in a default style.
   - You can hide or display details.

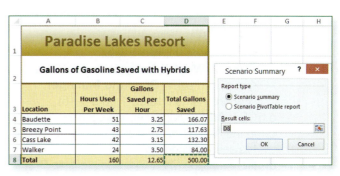

8-14 *Scenario Summary* dialog box

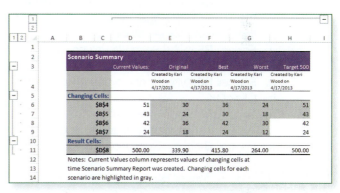

8-15 Scenario summary report

PAUSE & PRACTICE: EXCEL 8-1

For this project, you create three scenarios for hybrid vehicle usage by Paradise Lakes Resort locations and create a scenario summary report. You also enable the *Solver* add-in and use *Solver* to determine what would be required to increase total hybrid vehicle usage to a specified number of hours.

File Needed: **PLRHybrids-08.xlsx**
Completed Project File Name: **[your initials] PP E8-1.xlsx**

1. Open the **PLRHybrids-08** workbook and enable editing if necessary.
2. Save the workbook as **[your initials] PP E8-1**.

3. Click the **Location Usage** worksheet tab.

4. Create a scenario for the original data.
   a. Click the **What-if Analysis** button [*Data* tab, *Data Tools* group].
   b. Select **Scenario Manager**. There are currently no scenarios in the workbook.
   c. Click **Add**.
   d. In the *Add Scenario* dialog box, type Original as the name.
   e. Click in the **Changing cells** box and select cells **B4:B7**.
   f. Click **OK**.
   g. Do not change any values in the *Scenario Values* dialog box and click **OK**.
   h. Click **Close**.

5. Create scenarios with new data.
   a. Click the **What-if Analysis** button [*Data* tab, *Data Tools* group] and select **Scenario Manager**. The *Original* scenario name is listed (Figure 8-16).
   b. Click **Add** to add a second scenario to the workbook.
   c. In the *Add Scenario* dialog box, type Best as the name for the second scenario.
   d. Note that the *Changing cells* are cells **B4:B7** and click **OK**.
   e. For cell **B4** in the *Scenario Values* dialog box, type 36 and press **Tab**. If you accidentally press **Enter** and return to the *Scenario Manager* dialog box, click **Edit** to return to the *Scenario Values* dialog box.
   f. For cell **B5** in the *Scenario Values* dialog box, type 30 and press **Tab**.
   g. For cell **B6**, type 42 and type 24 for cell **B7**.
   h. Click **OK**.
   i. Click **Add** to add a third scenario.
   j. Type Worst as the name and click **OK**.
   k. For cell **B4** in the *Scenario Values* dialog box, type 24 and press **Tab**.
   l. Type 18 for cell **B5**, type 30 for cell **B6**, and type 12 for cell **B7**.
   m. Click **OK** and click **Close**. The original values are still displayed in the workbook.

6. Display a scenario.
   a. Click the **What-If Analysis** button [*Data* tab, *Data Tools* group] and select **Scenario Manager**. The three scenario names are listed (Figure 8-17).
   b. Click **Best** to highlight the name.
   c. Click **Show**. The values for the *Best* scenario are displayed in the worksheet.
   d. Click **Close**.

7. Install the *Solver* add-in.
   a. Select the **Options** command [*File* tab].
   b. Click **Add-Ins** in the left pane.
   c. Click **Solver Add-in** in the *Inactive Application Add-ins* list. If the *Solver Add-in* is in the *Active Application Add-ins* list, click **Cancel** and go on to step 8.
   d. Click **Go** near the bottom of the window.
   e. Select the **Solver Add-in** check box and click **OK**.

8-16 Existing scenario names are listed

8-17 One scenario can be shown in the worksheet

8. Set *Solver* parameters.
   a. Click the **Solver** button [*Data* tab, *Analysis* group] to open the *Solver Parameters* dialog box.
   b. In the *Set Objective* box, click cell **D8**. This cell has a *SUM* formula.
   c. For the *To* parameter, click the **Value Of** radio button and type 500 in the entry box.
   d. Click in the **By Changing Variable Cells** box and select cells **B4:B5**. *Solver* will input new values only for these two locations (Figure 8-18).

9. Add constraints to a *Solver* problem.
   a. Click **Add** to the right of the *Subject to the Constraints* box.
   b. In the *Cell Reference* box, select cell **B4**.
   c. Click the **drop-down arrow** and choose **<=** as the operator.
   d. Click in the **Constraint** box and type 60 (Figure 8-19).
   e. Click **Add** to add another constraint. If you accidentally close the *Add Constraint* dialog box, click **Add** in the *Solver Parameters* dialog box.
   f. In the *Cell Reference* box, select cell **B4** again. Choose **>=** as the operator and type 36 as the constraint. The value in cell B4 must be equal to or less than 60 and equal to or greater than 36.
   g. Add two additional constraints to specify that the value in cell **B5** must be greater than or equal to **30** and less than or equal to **45**.
   h. When all constraints are identified, click **OK** in the *Add Constraint* dialog box (Figure 8-19).
   i. For the *Select a Solving Method,* choose **GRG Nonlinear**.
   j. Check the **Make Unconstrained Variables Non-Negative** box (Figure 8-20).
   k. Click **Solve**. A possible solution to the problem is shown in the worksheet.

10. Manage *Solver* results.
    a. Click **Save Scenario** in the *Solver Results* dialog box.

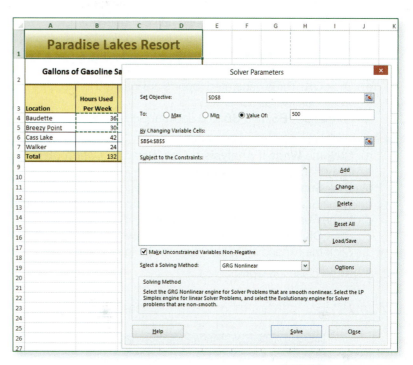

8-18 *Solver* **parameters**

8-19 Constraint for a variable cell

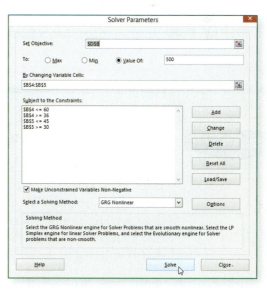

8-20 *Solver* **parameters with constraints**

b. Type Target 500 as the scenario name (Figure 8-21).

c. Click **OK** to return to the *Solver Results* dialog box.

d. Click to select **Answer**, **Sensitivity**, and **Limits** in the *Reports* list.

e. Click **OK**. Three generated reports are inserted in the workbook for the *Solver* reports.

f. Format **B4**, **B5**, and **B8** to **0** decimal places.

11. Create a scenario summary report.

a. Click the **What-If Analysis** button [*Data* tab, *Data Tools* group] and select **Scenario Manager**.

b. Click **Summary**.

c. In the *Scenario Summary* dialog box, choose **Scenario summary** as the *Report type*.

d. In the *Result cells* box, select cell **D8**.

e. Click **OK**. The report is inserted on a new sheet named *Scenario Summary*.

f. Click the expand symbol (**+**) for row **3** (Figure 8-22).

12. Save and close the workbook.

8-21 *Solver* results saved as a scenario

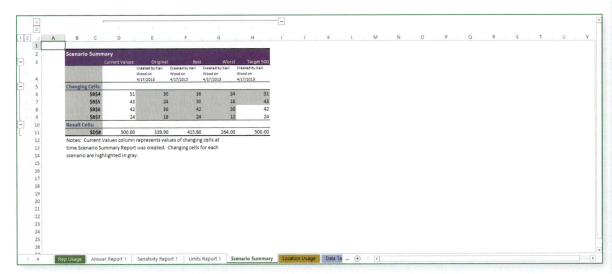

8-22 PP E8-1 Scenario summary report

SLO 8.4

Customizing PivotTables and PivotCharts

You learned in *SLO 4.2: Creating Excel Tables* how to create a *PivotTable* and to rearrange its fields. *PivotTables* and *PivotCharts* have many additional features that allow you to customize what is displayed. You can change the default calculation used for numeric fields, you can display values as different ratios or percentages, and you can even use a calculated field. Recall that a *PivotTable* and its *PivotChart* are linked, so any changes you make in either are immediately reflected in the other.

Value Field Settings

The **Value Field Settings** in a *PivotTable* control how the data is summarized in the table. The default calculation is *Sum*, but you can change this to any one of several other functions such as *Count*, *Average*, *Min*, and *Max*.

From the *Value Field Settings* dialog box, you can edit the label that appears in the *PivotTable*. You can also determine how numbers are formatted. The *Format Cells* dialog box includes the *Number* tab, which features the same choices as those for a cell in a worksheet.

To select a field in a *PivotTable,* click the field name in the *Row Labels* row or any cell in the column. Alternatively, you can select the related field button in the *PivotChart*.

HOW TO: Set Value Field Settings in a PivotTable

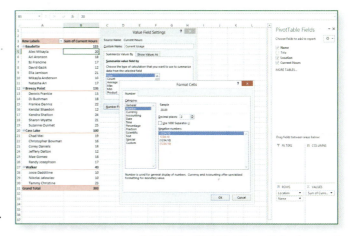

1. Right-click the label in the *Row Labels* row for the field you want to edit.
   - Right-click the field button in the *PivotChart* to open its context-sensitive menu.
2. Select **Value Field Settings** from the menu.
   - The *Value Field Settings* dialog box opens.
   - Click the cell and then click the **Field Settings** button [*PivotTable Tools Analyze* tab, *Active Field* group] to open the *Value Field Settings* dialog box.
3. Click in the **Custom Name** box and type a new label as desired.
   - The label cannot be the same as the field name in the *PivotTable Fields* pane.
4. Click the **Summarize Values By** tab if necessary.
   - Alternatively, you can choose **Summarize Values By** from the context-sensitive menu for a cell in the *PivotTable*.
5. Choose the desired summary function from the *Summarize value field by* list.
6. Click **Number Format**.
7. In the *Format Cells* dialog box, build the preferred number format (Figure 8-23).
   - If you selected a cell in the column, you see a preview of the format. You do not see a format sample if you select the label in the *Row Labels* row.
8. Click **OK** to close the *Format Cells* dialog box.
9. Click **OK** to close the *Value Field Settings* dialog box.
   - The custom label is displayed in the *Row Labels* row.
   - The entire field is reformatted (Figure 8-24).

8-23 *Value Field Settings* dialog box and *Number Format* options

	A	B
1		
2		
3	**Row Labels**	**Current Usage**
4	⊟**Baudette**	**115.00**
5	Alec Mikayla	20.00
6	Ari Aronson	18.00
7	BJ Francine	17.00
8	David Gazik	12.00
9	Ella Jamison	21.00
10	Mikayla Anderson	10.00
11	Natasha Ari	17.00
12	⊟**Breezy Point**	**135.00**
13	Dennis Frankie	13.00
14	DJ Bushman	18.00
15	Frankie Dennis	22.00
16	Kendal Shaedon	12.00
17	Kendra Shelton	24.00
18	Sharon Wyatte	21.00
19	Suzanne Ouimet	25.00
20	⊟**Cass Lake**	**100.00**
21	Chad Mei	19.00
22	Christopher Bowman	16.00
23	Corey Daniels	18.00
24	Jeffery Dalton	12.00
25	Mae Gomez	18.00
26	Randy Josephson	17.00
27	⊟**Walker**	**43.00**
28	Josie Daddiline	10.00
29	Nikolai Jalowiec	10.00
30	Tammy Christine	23.00
31	**Grand Total**	**393.00**
32		

8-24 Value field label edited and number format reset

Custom Calculations

You can display the values in a *PivotTable* with a ***custom calculation***. This type of calculation is a percentage, a ranking, or a ratio. Custom calculations are listed in the *Value Field Settings* dialog box on the *Show Values As* tab. These calculations can be rather complex. You can test them in a *PivotTable* and remove them when they do not illustrate what you want.

If you want to analyze a field in a *PivotTable* as a value and as a ratio or percentage, you can add the field multiple times in the *Values* area. Then, for each occurrence, you can choose a field setting or a custom calculation. In Figure 8-25, for example, the *Current Hours* field is shown twice in the *PivotTable*, once as a value formatted with two decimals (column B), and once as a percentage of the total (column C). The field appears two times in the *Values* area in the *PivotTable Fields* pane.

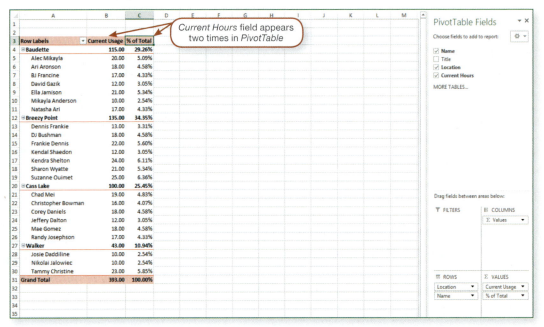

8-25 Value field displayed twice with different calculations

HOW TO: Use a Custom Calculation in a PivotChart

1. Right-click the value field button in the *PivotChart*.
   - These buttons are located in the upper left corner of the chart area.
2. Select **Value Field Settings**.
3. Click the **Show Values As** tab.
4. Click the **Show values as** list drop-down arrow.
5. Choose a calculation (Figure 8-26).
   - To display the value, choose **No Calculation** from the *Show values as* list.

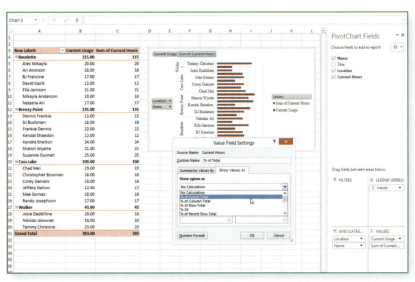

8-26 Value field set to show a custom calculation

6. Click **OK**.
   - The chart is redrawn to show new values.
   - The *PivotTable* displays the custom calculation results (Figure 8-27).

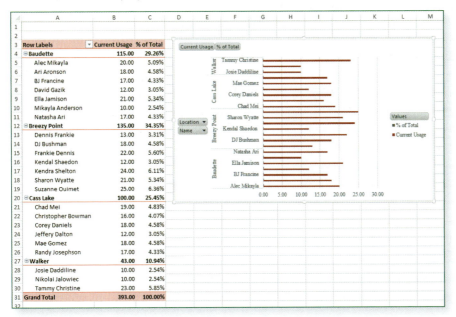

8-27 *PivotChart* and *PivotTable* are updated

Calculated Fields

In a *PivotTable*, a **calculated field** is one that appears in the *PivotTable* but is not a field in the source data. A calculated field uses a value field from the *PivotTable*'s underlying data in a formula.

When you insert a calculated field, it is initially placed as the last field in the *PivotTable*, but you can move it to another location. You can edit the *Value Fields Settings* as well.

HOW TO: Insert a Calculated Field

1. Click a cell in the *PivotTable*.
2. Click the **Fields, Items, & Sets button** [*PivotTable Tools Analyze* tab, *Calculations* group].
3. Select **Calculated Field**.
4. In the *Insert Calculated Field* dialog box, click in the **Name box**.
5. Type a name for the calculated field.
6. Click in the **Formula** box and delete the zero and the space after the equals sign.
7. Enter the formula (Figure 8-28).
   - Double-click a field name in the *Fields* list to insert it in the formula.
   - Field names are inserted with single quotation marks.
   - You can select a field name and click **Insert Field**.

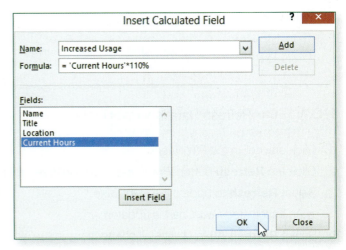

8-28 A calculated field uses a *PivotTable* field in a formula

8. Click **OK**.
   - The calculated field is added at the right in the *PivotTable* (Figure 8-29).
   - The field name is included in the *PivotTable Fields* pane.
   - An associated *PivotChart* is updated to include the new field.

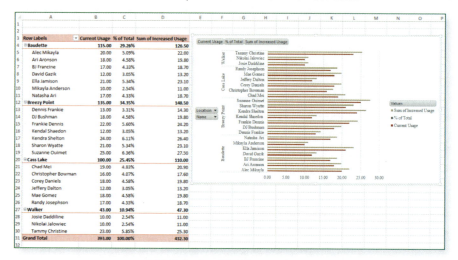

8-29 Calculated field inserted in *PivotTable* and its *PivotChart*

 MORE INFO

To delete a calculated field, click the **Fields, Items, & Sets** button. Choose the field name from the *Name* list and click **Delete**.

Refresh a PivotTable

Changes made in a *PivotTable* or its *PivotChart* are linked. Although the *PivotTable* is based on worksheet data, the *PivotTable* and the chart are not automatically updated if the worksheet data is altered. This is an automatic security measure because a *PivotTable* can be associated with data in a different workbook. However, there is a *PivotTable* option you can use to automatically refresh the data each time the workbook is opened.

When this option is not active, you must refresh the *PivotTable* to update it. To do so, you can use the context-sensitive menu for any cell in the *PivotTable* and choose **Refresh**.

 MORE INFO

View and set *PivotTable* options by clicking the **Options** button [*PivotTable Tools Analyze* tab, *PivotTable* group].

HOW TO: Refresh Data in a PivotTable

1. Click any cell in the *PivotTable*.
2. Click the **Refresh** button [*PivotTable Tools Analyze* tab, *Data* group].
3. Select **Refresh** to update the *PivotTable*.
   - An associated *PivotChart* is updated.
4. Select **Refresh All** to update all connections in the workbook.

The Slicer Tool

The ***Slicer*** tool creates an on-screen window that acts as a filter for a single field in the *PivotTable*. When you are working with a large *PivotTable*, a slicer allows you to display only the data you need at the moment. In the Paradise Lakes worksheet, for example, you can create a slicer that displays one location at a time as shown in Figure 8-30. Because the *PivotTable* and *PivotChart* are linked, when you slice data in the *PivotTable*, the chart (like the table) is redrawn to show only that data as well.

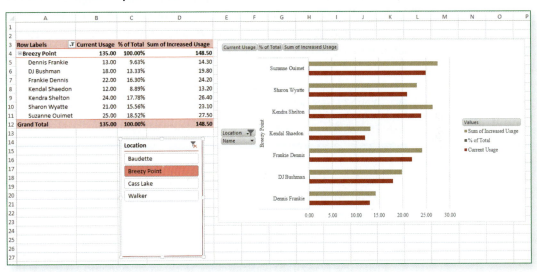

8-30 Location slicer filters data to show only Breezy Point data

You can create slicers by clicking the ***Insert Slicer*** button in the *Filter* group on the *PivotTable Tools Analyze* tab. From the *Insert Slicers* dialog box, select the field you want to display in a slicer. You can choose more than one field, and each field has its own slicer window.

You can save a slicer with the *PivotTable* when you save the workbook. If you no longer need the slicer, select it and press **Delete** to remove it. A slicer is an object that you can size and move just like other Excel objects.

When a slicer window is selected, the *Slicer Tools Options* tab is available. It includes commands to format the slicer, to change its caption, and to size and position the object.

HOW TO: Insert a Slicer in a PivotTable

1. Click a cell in the *PivotTable*.
2. Click the **Insert Slicer** button [*PivotTable Tools Analyze* tab, *Filter* group].
   - The *Insert Slicers* window lists each field displayed in the *PivotTable*.
3. Click to place a check mark for each field to be used for filtering data (Figure 8-31).

8-31 Choose one or more fields to be used in slicers

4. Click **OK**.
   - A slicer window opens for each field.
   - There is no filter applied.
5. In the slicer window, click the item to be used as criteria (Figure 8-32).
   - The *PivotTable* is filtered to display only the data that matches your selection.
   - Select multiple criteria in the slicer by holding down the **Ctrl** key.
   - Remove the filters by clicking the **Clear Filter** button in the top-right corner of the slicer.

8-32 Slicer with filter

Format Options

You can format a *PivotTable* from the *PivotTable Tools Design* tab or from the *Home* tab. The *PivotTable Tools Design* tab includes *PivotTable* styles as well as layout options. *PivotTable* styles are similar to Excel table styles covered in *SLO 4.2: Creating Excel Tables*. You can choose from a gallery to apply fills, alter borders, and change font colors.

> ▶ **ANOTHER WAY**
>
> Select a field in a *PivotTable* and apply format commands from the *Home* tab.

The *Layout* group on the *PivotTable Tools Design* tab lists choices for displaying subtotals and grand totals. The *Report Layout* command provides three choices for the report design and label options. You can also choose whether the row and column headings are emphasized and whether to show banded columns and rows in the *PivotTable Style Options* group. If you use a *PivotTable* style, many of these format choices are addressed in the style.

From the *Home* tab, you can change the font size and style, set the alignment, and more. When you make changes from this tab, the format is applied only to the current cell. Many changes made from the *PivotTable Tools Design* tab affect the entire table.

A *PivotChart* includes the *PivotChart Tools Design* and *Format* tabs. These tabs feature the same style and format commands that are available for Excel charts.

HOW TO: Format a PivotTable

1. Click a cell in the *PivotTable*.
2. Click the **More** button [*PivotTable Tools Design* tab, *PivotTable Styles* group].
   - The style gallery is categorized by light, medium, and dark colors.
   - You can design your own style.
3. Click to select a style (Figure 8-33).
4. Click the **Subtotals** button in the *Layout* group [*PivotTable Tools Design* tab].
   - Select whether and where to display subtotals in the *PivotTable*.
5. Click the **Grand Totals** button in the *Layout* group [*PivotTable Tools Design* tab].
   - You can show grand totals for both columns and rows.
6. Click the **Report Layout** button in the *Layout* group [*PivotTable Tools Design* tab].
   - *Compact* format places row data in one column and occupies the least amount of horizontal space.

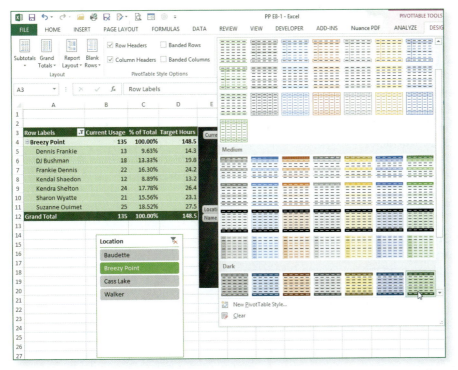

8-33 Choose a predefined *PivotTable* style from the gallery

- *Outline* form places row data in separate columns (Figure 8-34).
- *Tabular* form starts row data in the same row but in separate columns.

7. Click the **Blank Rows** button in the *Layout* group [*PivotTable Tools Design* tab].

  - Make a choice to display a blank row before or after each item.

8-34 Outline form shows row data (*Location* and *Name*) in separate columns

PAUSE & PRACTICE: EXCEL 8-2

For this project, you create a *PivotTable* and *PivotChart* for the hybrid vehicle usage worksheet for Paradise Lakes Resort. You edit the value field settings, insert a calculated field, display slicers, and work with format options.

File Needed: ***PP E8-1.xlsx***
Completed Project File Name: ***[your initials] PP E8-2.xlsx***

1. Open the ***[your initials] PP E8-1*** file.

2. Save the workbook as ***[your initials] PP E8-2***.

3. Create a *PivotTable.*
   a. Click the **Rep Usage** worksheet tab.
   b. Select cells **A3:D26**.
   c. Click the **PivotTable** button [*Insert* tab, *Tables* group] and verify that the *PivotTable* will be on a new worksheet.
   d. Click **OK**.
   e. Name the worksheet tab PivotTable.
   f. In the *PivotTable Fields* pane, check the **Location** box. The field is added to the *Rows* area.
   g. Check the **Name** box and the **Current Hours** box. The numeric field is placed in the *Values* area with the *Sum* calculation.
   h. Click any cell in the *PivotTable.*
   i. Click the **More** button [*PivotTable Tools Design* tab, *PivotTable Styles* group].
   j. Find and click **Pivot Style Light 17** in the gallery.
   k. Point at **Current Hours** in the *Choose fields to add to report* list.
   l. With the four-pointed arrow, drag the field name below the *Sum of Current Hours* field in the *Values* area. A second copy of the field is placed in the *PivotTable* (Figure 8-35).

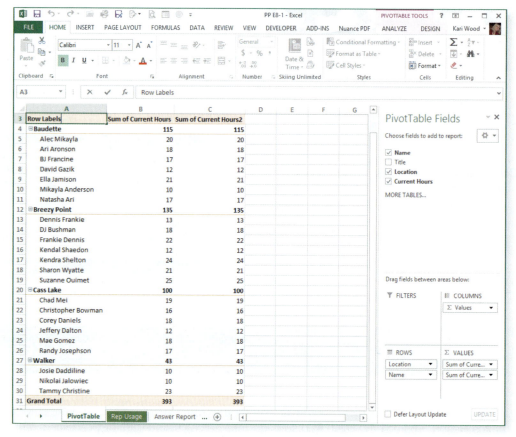

8-35 *Current Hours* field is used two times in the *PivotTable*

4. Edit *Value Field Settings.*
   a. Right-click **Sum of Current Hours** in cell **B3**.
   b. Select **Value Field Settings** from the menu.
   c. On the *Summarize Values By* tab, click in the **Custom Name** box.
   d. Edit the name to Current Usage.
   e. Click **OK** or press **Enter**.
   f. Click cell **C3** and click the **Field Settings** button [*PivotTable Tools Analyze* tab, *Active Field* group].

g. Click in the **Custom Name** box and edit the name to % of Total.
h. Click the **Show Values As** tab.
i. Click the **Show values as** arrow and choose **% of Grand Total** (Figure 8-36).
j. Click the **Number Format** button to ensure there are two decimal places formatted for the percentage. Click **OK**.
k. Click **OK**. The values in column *C* are shown as percentages of the total hours.

5. Create a *PivotChart.*
a. Click any cell in the *PivotTable.*
b. Click the **PivotChart** button [*PivotTable Tools Analyze, Tools* group].
c. Click **Bar** in the list and **Clustered Bar** as the subtype.
d. Click **OK**.

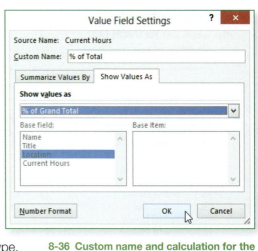

8-36 Custom name and calculation for the *Current Hours* field

e. Click the *PivotChart* background to select the chart.
f. Click the **Change Colors** button [*PivotChart Tools Design* tab, *Chart Styles* group]. Choose the **Color 6** row in the *Monochromatic* list.
g. With the two-pointed arrow, resize the *PivotChart* so that the top-left corner is in cell **D3** and the bottom-right corner is in **K20**. (Figure 8-37).

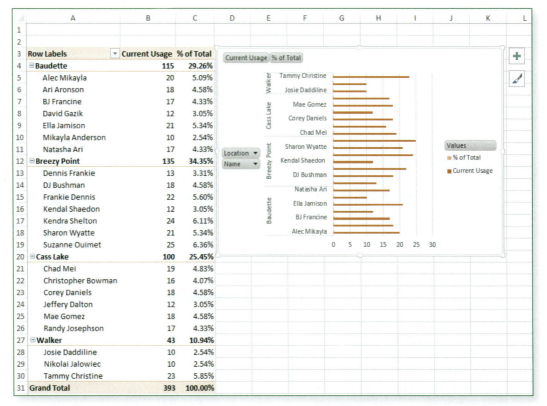

8-37 *PivotTable* and its associated *PivotChart*

6. Refresh the *PivotTable* and *PivotChart.*
a. Click the **Rep Usage** worksheet tab.
b. Select and delete rows **7:10**. Be sure to delete the rows, not just cell contents.

c. Click the **PivotTable** sheet tab. The deleted names are still included in the *PivotTable.*

d. Click the **Refresh** button [*PivotTable Tools Analyze* tab, *Data* group]. The *PivotTable* and *PivotChart* are updated (Figure 8-38).

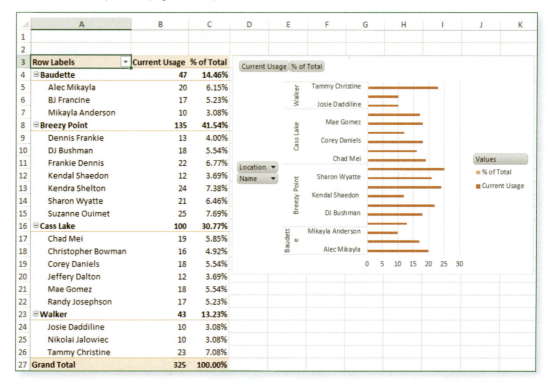

8-38 *PivotTable* and its associated *PivotChart* are both refreshed

7. Insert a calculated field.

   a. Click any cell in the *PivotTable.*

   b. Click the **Fields, Items, & Sets** button [*PivotTable Tools Analyze* tab, *Calculations* group].

   c. Select **Calculated Field**.

   d. In the *Insert Calculated Field* dialog box, click in the **Name** box.

   e. Type Target Use as the name for the calculated field.

   f. Click in the **Formula** box and delete the zero and the space after the equals sign.

   g. Double-click **Current Hours** in the *Fields* list.

   h. Type *110% after =‘Current Hours’ in the *Formula* box (Figure 8-39).

   i. Click **OK**. The new field is inserted in the *PivotTable* and in the *PivotChart.*

   j. Reposition the *PivotChart* to start in column **E**.

   k. Click cell **D3** and click the **Field Settings** button [*PivotTable Tools Analyze* tab, *Active Field* group].

   l. Click in the **Custom Name** box and edit the name to Target Hours.

   m. Click **OK** (Figure 8-40).

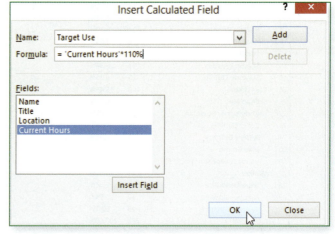

8-39 Formula for a calculated field

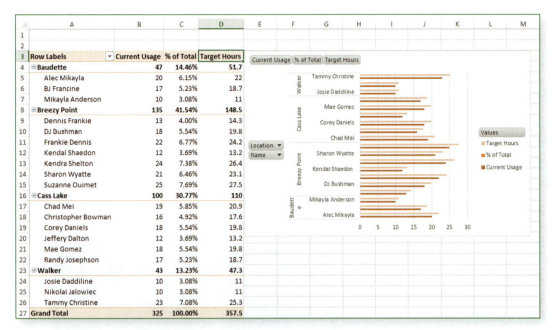

8-40 Calculated field is added to *PivotTable* and *PivotChart*

8. Insert a slicer.
   a. Click any cell in the *PivotTable.*
   b. Click the **Insert Slicer** button [*PivotTable Tools Analyze* tab, *Filter* group].
   c. Check the **Location** box and click **OK**. The *Location* slicer opens.
   d. Click **Baudette** in the slicer. The *PivotTable* and *PivotChart* are filtered to show Baudette data (Figure 8-41).

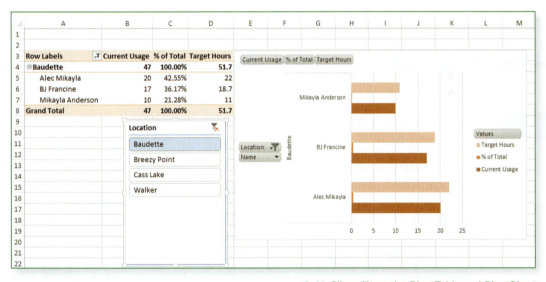

8-41 Slicer filters the *PivotTable* and *PivotChart*

9. Format a *PivotTable,* a *PivotChart,* and a slicer.
   a. Click any cell in the *PivotTable.*
   b. Click the **More** button [*PivotTable Tools Design* tab, *PivotTable Styles* group].
   c. Find and click **Pivot Style Dark 7** in the gallery.
   d. Click the **PivotChart background** to select the chart.

e. Click the **More** button [*PivotChart Tools Design* tab, *Chart Styles* group].

f. Find and click **Style 7** in the gallery.

g. Click the **Change Colors** button [*PivotChart Tools Design* tab, *Chart Styles* group]. Choose the **Color 10** row in the *Monochromatic* list.

h. Click the **slicer background** to select the slicer object.

i. Click the **More** button [*SlicerTools Options* tab, *Slicer Styles* group].

j. Find and click **Slicer Style Dark 6** in the gallery.

k. Position the slicer and the chart as shown (Figure 8-42).

10. Click a worksheet cell.

11. Save and close the workbook.

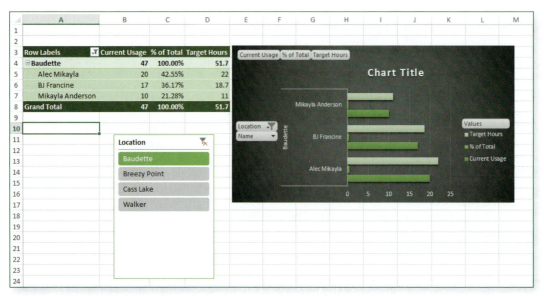

8-42 *PivotTable, PivotChart,* and slicer are formatted

SLO 8.5

Building a One-Variable Data Table

A *data table* is a range of cells that shows calculated results of one or more formulas. *A one-variable data table* substitutes values for one argument in a formula and displays the results when that value is altered. Figure 8-43, for example, shows a data table in which the total sales amount is varied from $100,000 to $200,000 in column *K*. There is a reference to the January formula for total expenses (cell B15) in cell L3 and a reference to the January net income formula (cell B17) in cell M3. The **Data Table** command calculates the results shown in cells L4: M14.

The *Data Table* command looks for an *input value*. An input value is a number from a column or a row. The input values in Figure 8-43 are possible total sales numbers in column *K*. A one-variable data table uses one input value, in either a column or a row. In this example, each input value will be substituted for cell B8; the input values are in a column (*K*).

When the input values are in a column, formulas must start in the column to the right and one row above where the values start. In Figure 8-43, the first formula is in cell L3. It is a reference to cell B15, which is the formula to calculate total expenses for the month. If there are multiple formulas, they must be in the same row. The second formula in the figure is in cell M3; it is a reference to the net income formula in cell B17. Both of these formulas have a relationship to cell B8.

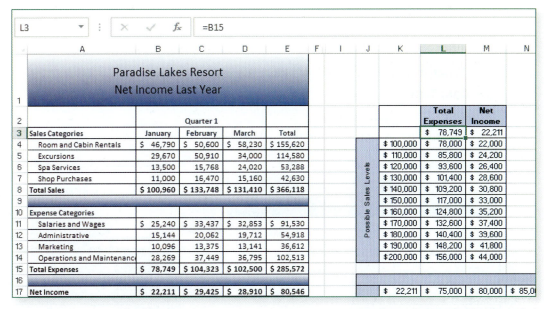

| L3 | ▾ | : | × | ✓ | f_x | =B15 |

	A	B	C	D	E	F	I	J	K	L	M	N
1	Paradise Lakes Resort Net Income Last Year											
2			Quarter 1							Total Expenses	Net Income	
3	Sales Categories	January	February	March	Total					$ 78,749	$ 22,211	
4	Room and Cabin Rentals	$ 46,790	$ 50,600	$ 58,230	$ 155,620				$ 100,000	$ 78,000	$ 22,000	
5	Excursions	29,670	50,910	34,000	114,580				$ 110,000	$ 85,800	$ 24,200	
6	Spa Services	13,500	15,768	24,020	53,288				$ 120,000	$ 93,600	$ 26,400	
7	Shop Purchases	11,000	16,470	15,160	42,630				$ 130,000	$ 101,400	$ 28,600	
8	Total Sales	$ 100,960	$ 133,748	$ 131,410	$ 366,118				$ 140,000	$ 109,200	$ 30,800	
9									$ 150,000	$ 117,000	$ 33,000	
10	Expense Categories								$ 160,000	$ 124,800	$ 35,200	
11	Salaries and Wages	$ 25,240	$ 33,437	$ 32,853	$ 91,530				$ 170,000	$ 132,600	$ 37,400	
12	Administrative	15,144	20,062	19,712	54,918				$ 180,000	$ 140,400	$ 39,600	
13	Marketing	10,096	13,375	13,141	36,612				$ 190,000	$ 148,200	$ 41,800	
14	Operations and Maintenance	28,269	37,449	36,795	102,513				$ 200,000	$ 156,000	$ 44,000	
15	Total Expenses	$ 78,749	$ 104,323	$ 102,500	$ 285,572							
16												
17	Net Income	$ 22,211	$ 29,425	$ 28,910	$ 80,546					$ 22,211	$ 75,000	$ 80,000	$ 85,0(

(Column J, vertical label: Possible Sales Levels)

8-43 Data table shows expense and income numbers when total sales are varied

> ## MORE INFO
> When input values are in a row, the first formula must be one column to the left of the first value and one row below.

Before you apply the *Data Table* command, select the entire data table range. This includes the formulas, the input values, and the empty result cells. In Figure 8-43, the data table range is cells K3:M14.

The *Table* command inserts an **array formula** in each result cell. An array is any group of cells, and an array formula executes a calculation on any number of cells in the group. If you have programming experience, you can use array formulas in Excel to develop sophisticated calculation routines in a worksheet.

The *Data Table* command is an option on the *What-If Analysis* button on the *Data* tab [*Data Tools* group].

HOW TO: Create a One-Variable Data Table

1. Enter the input values in a single column or row on the same sheet as the existing formulas.

   - You can enter a series of values or specific numbers.
   - Excel will substitute these values into the formula you designate in the following steps.

2. Enter the first formula.

   - If the input values are in a column, enter the formula one row above and one column to the right of the first input value.
   - If the input values are in a row, enter the formula one column to the left and one row below the first input value.
   - You can type a reference to the formula in the worksheet.
   - You can type or build the formula with sample data and sample cell references.

3. Enter additional formulas in the same row (Figure 8-44).

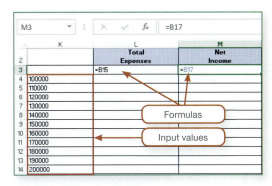

8-44 Input values are in a column; formulas are in the row above, one column to the right

4. Select the data table range.
   - Select all the input values, the formulas, and the empty cells for results.
   - The top-left cell in this range is empty.
5. Click the **What-If Analysis** button [*Data* tab, *Data Tools* group].
6. Choose **Data Table**.
   - The *Data Table* dialog box opens.
7. Enter a column or a row input cell reference (Figure 8-45).

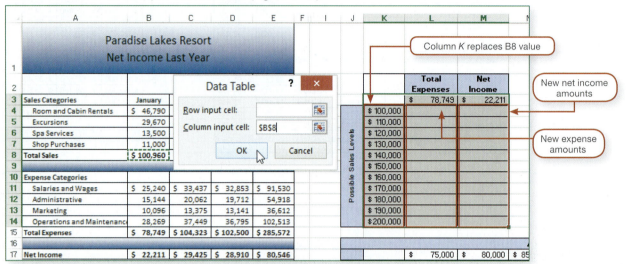

8-45 Values in column *K* will replace the current value in cell B8 in the data table to show new expense and income amounts

   - In a one-variable data table, enter either a row input or a column input reference.
   - You can click the cell in the worksheet for which the input values will be substituted.
8. Click **OK**.
   - The data table cells display potential results for each input value.
   - You can format a data table to add number styles, fill, borders, or explanatory labels.
   - The *TABLE* command is used in an array formula and is entered in each result cell.

SLO 8.6

Building a Two-Variable Data Table

A ***two-variable data table*** looks similar to a one-variable data table (see *SLO 8.5: Building a One-Variable Data Table*). However, it uses two sets of input values instead of one—one in a column, the other in a row. It can use only one formula. Figure 8-46 shows a two-variable data table in which the total sales and the total expenses are varied to calculate net profit. The formula is in cell B17 and is referenced in cell K17. The total sales amounts are column input values (cells K18:K30), and total expenses are row input values (cells L17:S17).

In a two-variable data table, the row input values start one column to the right of the column values. In the figure shown here, the row input values start in cell L17. Row input values must start one row above the starting column input value. Place the formula above the column values and to the left of the row values, cell K17 in this case.

The data table range includes the formula, the input column, the input row, and the empty result cells, cells L18:S30. In Figure 8-46, the column input cell for the *Data Table* command is cell B8; the row input cell is cell B15. Those values are replaced by the column and row inputs to fill in the data table.

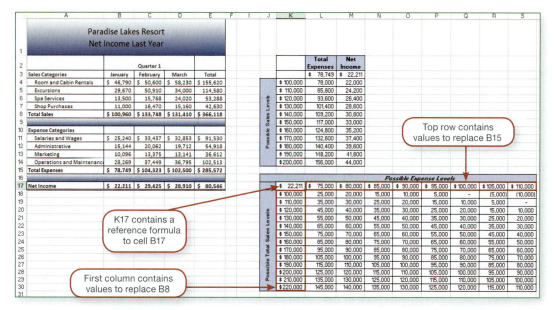

8-46 Two-variable data table

> **MORE INFO**
>
> A data table must be on the same worksheet as its formulas.

> **MORE INFO**
>
> You can use most Excel functions in an array formula by pressing **Ctrl+Shift+Enter** to complete the entry.

A basic feature of an array formula is that it is enclosed in curly braces in the *Formula bar*. Figure 8-47 shows both data tables in formula view. Notice that the array formula is the same for each cell in the data table.

	K	L	M	N	O	P	Q	R	S
2		Total Expenses	Net Income						
3		=B15	=B17						
4	100000	=TABLE(,B8)	=TABLE(,B8)						
5	110000	=TABLE(,B8)	=TABLE(,B8)						
6	120000	=TABLE(,B8)	=TABLE(,B8)						
7	130000	=TABLE(,B8)	=TABLE(,B8)						
8	140000	=TABLE(,B8)	=TABLE(,B8)						
9	150000	=TABLE(,B8)	=TABLE(,B8)						
10	160000	=TABLE(,B8)	=TABLE(,B8)						
11	170000	=TABLE(,B8)	=TABLE(,B8)						
12	180000	=TABLE(,B8)	=TABLE(,B8)						
13	190000	=TABLE(,B8)	=TABLE(,B8)						
14	200000	=TABLE(,B8)	=TABLE(,B8)						
15									
16				*Possible Expense Levels*					
17	=B17	75000	80000	85000	90000	95000	100000	105000	110000
18	100000	=TABLE(B15,B8)	=TABLE(B15,B8)	=TABLE(B15,B8)	=TABLE(B15,B8)	=TABLE(B15,B8)	=TABLE(B15,B8)	=TABLE(B15,B8)	=TABLE(B15,B8)
19	110000	=TABLE(B15,B8)	=TABLE(B15,B8)	=TABLE(B15,B8)	=TABLE(B15,B8)	=TABLE(B15,B8)	=TABLE(B15,B8)	=TABLE(B15,B8)	=TABLE(B15,B8)
20	120000	=TABLE(B15,B8)	=TABLE(B15,B8)	=TABLE(B15,B8)	=TABLE(B15,B8)	=TABLE(B15,B8)	=TABLE(B15,B8)	=TABLE(B15,B8)	=TABLE(B15,B8)
21	130000	=TABLE(B15,B8)	=TABLE(B15,B8)	=TABLE(B15,B8)	=TABLE(B15,B8)	=TABLE(B15,B8)	=TABLE(B15,B8)	=TABLE(B15,B8)	=TABLE(B15,B8)
22	140000	=TABLE(B15,B8)	=TABLE(B15,B8)	=TABLE(B15,B8)	=TABLE(B15,B8)	=TABLE(B15,B8)	=TABLE(B15,B8)	=TABLE(B15,B8)	=TABLE(B15,B8)
23	150000	=TABLE(B15,B8)	=TABLE(B15,B8)	=TABLE(B15,B8)	=TABLE(B15,B8)	=TABLE(B15,B8)	=TABLE(B15,B8)	=TABLE(B15,B8)	=TABLE(B15,B8)
24	160000	=TABLE(B15,B8)	=TABLE(B15,B8)	=TABLE(B15,B8)	=TABLE(B15,B8)	=TABLE(B15,B8)	=TABLE(B15,B8)	=TABLE(B15,B8)	=TABLE(B15,B8)
25	170000	=TABLE(B15,B8)	=TABLE(B15,B8)	=TABLE(B15,B8)	=TABLE(B15,B8)	=TABLE(B15,B8)	=TABLE(B15,B8)	=TABLE(B15,B8)	=TABLE(B15,B8)
26	180000	=TABLE(B15,B8)	=TABLE(B15,B8)	=TABLE(B15,B8)	=TABLE(B15,B8)	=TABLE(B15,B8)	=TABLE(B15,B8)	=TABLE(B15,B8)	=TABLE(B15,B8)
27	190000	=TABLE(B15,B8)	=TABLE(B15,B8)	=TABLE(B15,B8)	=TABLE(B15,B8)	=TABLE(B15,B8)	=TABLE(B15,B8)	=TABLE(B15,B8)	=TABLE(B15,B8)
28	200000	=TABLE(B15,B8)	=TABLE(B15,B8)	=TABLE(B15,B8)	=TABLE(B15,B8)	=TABLE(B15,B8)	=TABLE(B15,B8)	=TABLE(B15,B8)	=TABLE(B15,B8)
29	210000	=TABLE(B15,B8)	=TABLE(B15,B8)	=TABLE(B15,B8)	=TABLE(B15,B8)	=TABLE(B15,B8)	=TABLE(B15,B8)	=TABLE(B15,B8)	=TABLE(B15,B8)
30	220000	=TABLE(B15,B8)	=TABLE(B15,B8)	=TABLE(B15,B8)	=TABLE(B15,B8)	=TABLE(B15,B8)	=TABLE(B15,B8)	=TABLE(B15,B8)	=TABLE(B15,B8)

8-47 *TABLE* command is an array formula

In a data table, you cannot delete the contents of an individual cell, because you cannot "shrink" the array. You can, however, edit a column or row input value. The data table results update automatically.

HOW TO: Create a Two-Variable Data Table

1. Enter column input values in a single column on the same sheet as the existing formulas.

    - Type values or fill a series.
    - You can prepare the row or column input values first.
    - Excel will substitute these values into the formulas you designate in the following steps.

2. Enter row input values in a single row.

    - Start the first row value one row above and to the right of the first column value.
    - Excel will substitute these values into the formula you designate in the following steps.

3. Enter the formula or type a reference to it.

    - It is easier to use a reference to the cell with the formula than to re-enter the formula.
    - Place the formula reference in the cell above the column input values and to the left of the row input values.

4. Select the data table range.

    - Include the column input values, the formula, the row input values, and the result cells.

5. Click the **What-If Analysis** button [*Data* tab, *Data Tools* group].

6. Choose **Data Table**.

7. Enter the row input cell reference.

8. Enter the column input cell reference (Figure 8-48).

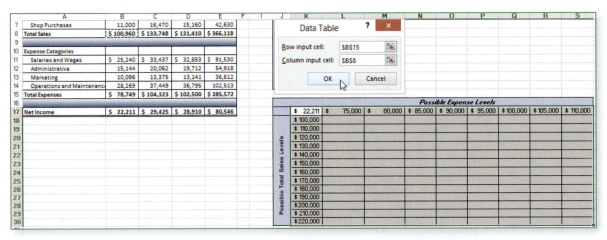

8-48 Two-variable data table setup

9. Click **OK**.

    - The result cells calculate the formula referenced in cell K17.
    - Each result cell substitutes a column and a row input value in the formula.
    - Change any column or row input value to recalculate the data table.

SLO 8.7

Working with XML

XML represents **Extensible Markup Language**, a file format that is designed for exchanging data on the web. An XML file is essentially a text file that can be imported into many applications. An XML data file has an **.xml** file name extension.

In Excel, there are several ways to work with an XML file. You can open an XML file and save it as a workbook, or you can save a workbook as an XML file for use by another program. Also, with the *Web Query* command, you can build a query in a worksheet to get data from an XML web source.

XML Syntax

A properly structured XML file includes tags that describe the data. A ***tag*** is an identifier such as *<Customer>*; a tag is enclosed in chevron braces, which surround the actual piece of data. There is an opening tag and an ending tag for each data field. The ending tag includes a forward slash with the name, for example *</Customer>*.

In addition to individual data tags, in an XML file there are other tags that describe where the file originated and other properties. Figure 8-49 shows an XML file in an Explorer window. The tags become field labels when you import XML data into an Excel worksheet.

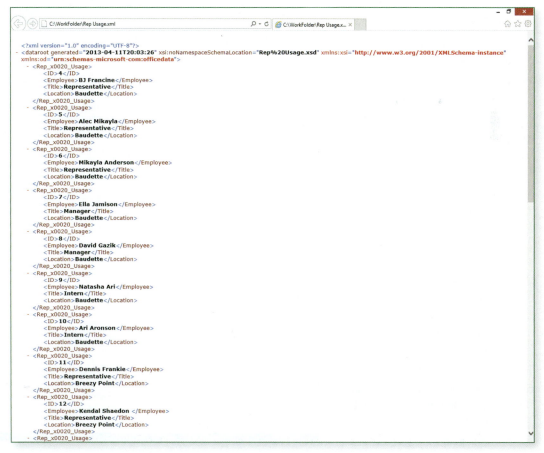

8-49 *XML* **text file in an Explorer window**

Import XML Data

For many XML sources, you can simply open the file in Excel. The *Open XML* dialog box (Figure 8-50) offers an option of opening the file as an XML table. This imports all the data and displays it in an Excel table. Alternatively, from the *Open XML* dialog box, you can choose to import the data as a read-only workbook. This places the data in a tabular layout in a worksheet. In order to edit the data, save the workbook with a different file name.

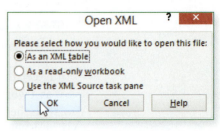

8-50 *Open XML* dialog box

A third option is to use the *XML Source* task pane. This adds a map to the worksheet but no data. An **XML map** is a tree hierarchy of tags and other elements from the source XML file. From the map and the task pane, you can place fields to build a new Excel table. Place a field by dragging it to the cell location, or right-click the field name in the task pane and choose **Map Element**. In the *Map XML Elements* dialog box, click or type the cell reference and click **OK**. After the fields are positioned, refresh the data to finish the import. This establishes a data connection for the workbook.

> ### ANOTHER WAY
> There is an *XML* group located on the *Developer* tab.

HOW TO: Use the XML Source Task Pane

1. Choose **Open** from the *File* tab.
   - You don't need to have a blank workbook open for the XML import results.
2. Navigate to the folder with the XML file.
   - Choose the file with the *.xml* extension to get data.
3. Click **Open**.
   - The *Open XML* dialog box offers three choices for importing the data.
4. Click **Use the XML Source task pane** radio button.
5. Click **OK**.
   - If a blank workbook is open, a second blank workbook is created for the results.
   - The task pane displays available maps in the XML file (Figure 8-51).
   - If an error message box appears, click **OK**.
6. Point at a field name in the *XML Source* task pane and drag it to a cell in the worksheet.
   - The field is mapped, but no data is included.

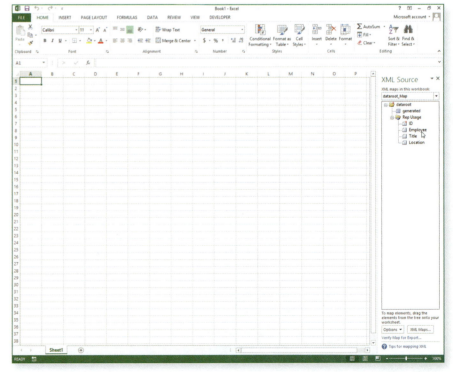

8-51 *XML* file opened using the task pane

- The field name is formatted as the header row in an Excel table.
- Right-click a field name and choose **Map Element**. Enter the cell reference and click **OK**.

7. Drag each field name from the *XML Source* task pane to a cell in the worksheet (Figure 8-52).

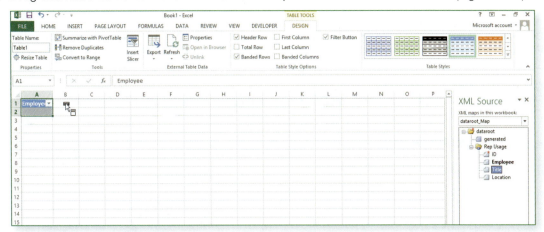

8-52 **Fields are dragged from *XML* task pane to cell location**

8. Click the **Refresh** button [*Table Tools Design* tab, *External Table Data* group].

- Data from the XML file is placed in the worksheet (Figure 8-53).
- You can also click the **Refresh** button on the *Data* tab in the *Connections* group.
- You can apply a table style to the XML data in the worksheet.

9. Save the workbook.

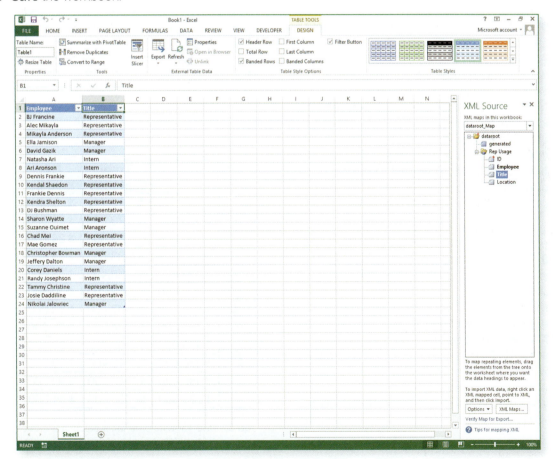

8-53 ***XML* data is updated when you click the *Refresh* button**

For this project, you build a one- and a two-variable data table to determine alternate sales, expenses, and profit levels for Paradise Lakes Resort. You also import an updated employee file from an XML file.

Files Needed: *PP E8-2.xlsx* and *RepUsage-08.xml*
Completed Project File Names: *[your initials] PP E8-3.xlsx* and *[your initials] PP E8-3a.xlsx*

1. Open the *[your initials] PP E8-2* file.
2. Save the workbook as *[your initials] PP E8-3*.
3. Click the **Data Tables** worksheet tab at the end of the tabs.
4. Create a one-variable data table.
   a. Select cells **K4:K5** and use the *Fill Handle* to fill values to reach cell **K14**. These values are the column input values.
   b. Click cell **L3**. This location is one column to the right of the input values and one row above the first value.
   c. Type =, click cell **B15**, and press **Enter** to create a reference to a total expenses formula.
   d. Click cell **M3** and create a reference to cell **B17** for a net income formula (Figure 8-54).
   e. Select cells **K3:M14** as the data table range.
   f. Click the **What-If Analysis** button [*Data* tab, *Data Tools* group] and choose **Data Table**.
   g. In the *Column input cell* entry box, click cell **B8** to indicate that the total sales amount will be replaced by the input values in column *K*.
   h. Click **OK** to create the data table.
   i. Select cells **K4:M14** and format them as **Accounting Number** format with **0** decimal places. *AutoFit* columns **K:M** (Figure 8-55).

5. Create a two-variable data table.
   a. Select cells **K18:K19** and fill values to reach cell **K30**. These values are column input values.
   b. In cell **L17**, type 75000 to replace the existing value.
   c. In cell **M17**, type 80000 to start a new series.
   d. Select cells **L17:M17** and fill values to reach cell **S17**. These values are row input values.
   e. Click cell **K17** to place the formula in one row above the column input values and one column to the left of the row values.
   f. Create a reference to the net income formula in cell **B17**.

		Total Expenses	Net Income
		$ 78,749	=B17
	100000		
	110000		
	120000		
	130000		
Possible Sales Levels	140000		
	150000		
	160000		
	170000		
	180000		
	190000		
	200000		

8-54 Formula references are in same row in a one-variable data table

		Total Expenses	Net Income
		$ 78,749	$ 22,211
	$ 100,000	$ 78,000	$ 22,000
	$ 110,000	$ 85,800	$ 24,200
	$ 120,000	$ 93,600	$ 26,400
	$ 130,000	$ 101,400	$ 28,600
Possible Sales Levels	$ 140,000	$ 109,200	$ 30,800
	$ 150,000	$ 117,000	$ 33,000
	$ 160,000	$ 124,800	$ 35,200
	$ 170,000	$ 132,600	$ 37,400
	$ 180,000	$ 140,400	$ 39,600
	$ 190,000	$ 148,200	$ 41,800
	$ 200,000	$ 156,000	$ 44,000

8-55 One-variable data table calculates both formulas for each column input value

g. Select cells **K17:S30** as the data table range. This range includes the column input values, the formula, the row input values, and the empty result cells (Figure 8-56).

h. Click the **What-If Analysis** button [*Data* tab, *Data Tools* group] and choose **Data Table**.

i. In the *Row input cell* entry box, click cell **B15** to indicate that the expense amounts in row 17 will replace the current value in cell B15.

Possible Expense Levels								
$ 22,211	75000	80000	85000	90000	95000	100000	105000	110000
100000								
110000								
120000								
130000								
140000								
150000								
160000								
170000								
180000								
190000								
200000								
210000								
220000								

8-56 Data table range includes column and row input values, the formula cell, and empty result cells

j. In the *Column input cell* entry box, click cell **B8** to indicate that the sales amounts in column *K* will replace the current value in cell B8 (Figure 8-57).

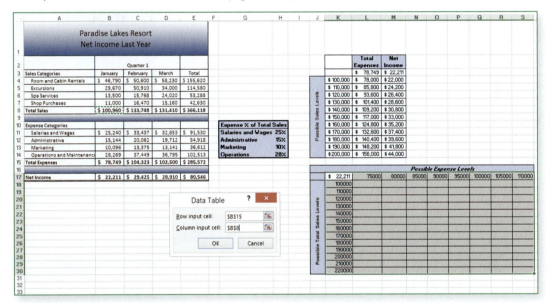

8-57 Two-variable data table uses both input cell references

k. Click **OK** to build the data table.

l. Format all cells in the data table as **Accounting Number** format with **0** decimal places. *AutoFit* columns **K:S**. (Figure 8-58).

Possible Expense Levels								
$ 22,211	$ 75,000	$ 80,000	$ 85,000	$ 90,000	$ 95,000	$ 100,000	$ 105,000	$ 110,000
$ 100,000	$ 25,000	$ 20,000	$ 15,000	$ 10,000	$ 5,000	$ –	$ (5,000)	$ (10,000)
$ 110,000	$ 35,000	$ 30,000	$ 25,000	$ 20,000	$ 15,000	$ 10,000	$ 5,000	$ –
$ 120,000	$ 45,000	$ 40,000	$ 35,000	$ 30,000	$ 25,000	$ 20,000	$ 15,000	$ 10,000
$ 130,000	$ 55,000	$ 50,000	$ 45,000	$ 40,000	$ 35,000	$ 30,000	$ 25,000	$ 20,000
$ 140,000	$ 65,000	$ 60,000	$ 55,000	$ 50,000	$ 45,000	$ 40,000	$ 35,000	$ 30,000
$ 150,000	$ 75,000	$ 70,000	$ 65,000	$ 60,000	$ 55,000	$ 50,000	$ 45,000	$ 40,000
$ 160,000	$ 85,000	$ 80,000	$ 75,000	$ 70,000	$ 65,000	$ 60,000	$ 55,000	$ 50,000
$ 170,000	$ 95,000	$ 90,000	$ 85,000	$ 80,000	$ 75,000	$ 70,000	$ 65,000	$ 60,000
$ 180,000	$ 105,000	$ 100,000	$ 95,000	$ 90,000	$ 85,000	$ 80,000	$ 75,000	$ 70,000
$ 190,000	$ 115,000	$ 110,000	$ 105,000	$ 100,000	$ 95,000	$ 90,000	$ 85,000	$ 80,000
$ 200,000	$ 125,000	$ 120,000	$ 115,000	$ 110,000	$ 105,000	$ 100,000	$ 95,000	$ 90,000
$ 210,000	$ 135,000	$ 130,000	$ 125,000	$ 120,000	$ 115,000	$ 110,000	$ 105,000	$ 100,000
$ 220,000	$ 145,000	$ 140,000	$ 135,000	$ 130,000	$ 125,000	$ 120,000	$ 115,000	$ 110,000

8-58 Completed two-variable data table

6. Save and close the workbook.

7. Import XML data into a worksheet.
   a. Choose **Open** from the *File* tab.
   b. Navigate to the folder with the **RepUsage-08** file in the *Open* dialog box.
   c. Click to select the file name and click **Open** to display the *Open XML* dialog box.
   d. Click the **Use the XML Source task pane** radio button and click **OK**.
   e. If an error message box appears, click **OK**.
   f. Select **Employee** in the *XML Source* task pane; then right-click and choose **Map Element**.
   g. In the *Map XML Elements* dialog box, click cell **A1** (Figure 8-59).
   h. Click **OK**.
   i. Map the **Location** field to cell **B1**.
   j. Click the **Refresh** button [*Table Tools Design* tab, *External Table Data* group].

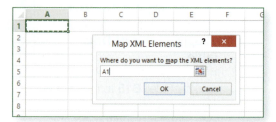

8-59 Mapping an element places it in a cell in the worksheet

8. Format the table with **Table Style Dark 7** (Figure 8-60).

9. Save the workbook as *[your initials] PP E8-3a*.

10. Close the *XML Source* task pane. Close the workbook.

	A	B
1	Employee	Location
2	BJ Francine	Baudette
3	Alec Mikayla	Baudette
4	Mikayla Anderson	Baudette
5	Ella Jamison	Baudette
6	David Gazik	Baudette
7	Natasha Ari	Baudette
8	Ari Aronson	Baudette
9	Dennis Frankie	Breezy Point
10	Kendal Shaedon	Breezy Point
11	Frankie Dennis	Breezy Point
12	Kendra Shelton	Breezy Point
13	DJ Bushman	Breezy Point
14	Sharon Wyatte	Breezy Point
15	Suzanne Ouimet	Breezy Point
16	Chad Mei	Cass Lake
17	Mae Gomez	Cass Lake
18	Christopher Bowman	Cass Lake
19	Jeffery Dalton	Cass Lake
20	Corey Daniels	Cass Lake
21	Randy Josephson	Cass Lake
22	Tammy Christine	Walker
23	Josie Daddiline	Walker
24	Nikolai Jalowiec	Walker

8-60 PP E8-3a worksheet completed

Chapter Summary

8.1 Install and use *Solver* to find a solution (p. E8-432).

- The **Solver** add-in is an analysis tool that solves a problem in reverse.
- You can activate Excel add-ins from the *Add-Ins* pane in the *Excel Options* dialog box.
- The **Solver** button is displayed in the *Analysis* group on the *Data* tab.
- *Solver* evaluates a formula and other parameters to propose how a specified result can be accomplished.
- A *Solver* problem has three components known as **parameters**. *Parameters* are identified and set in the *Solver Parameters* dialog box.
- The **objective cell** is a cell with a formula that will be solved for specific results. It is also called the **target cell**.
- **Variable cells**, also known as **decision cells**, are cells that *Solver* can adjust to reach the objective.
- **Constraints** are restrictions or limitations on variable cells, the formula, or other worksheet cells that are related to the objective cell.
- In the *Solver Parameters* dialog box, you can specify the problem-solving method to be used.
- The *Solver Results* dialog box provides options to keep the solution, to return to the original values, and to save the results as a scenario.

8.2 Understand and create *Solver* reports such as the *Answer* report, the *Sensitivity* report, and the *Limits* report (p. E8-435).

- The *Solver Results* dialog box has a *Reports* section, which lists the types of reports that can be generated for each solution.
- You can generate one or multiple reports for each solution; each *Solver* report is generated on its own worksheet tab in the workbook.
- An **Answer** report lists each parameter with related properties and settings.
- A **Sensitivity** report presents statistical data such as objective coefficient, final value, or Lagrange multiplier. The contents of a *Sensitivity* report depend on the solving method.
- A **Limits** report indicates the lower and upper limits of each variable cell and how those limits impact the objective cell.

8.3 Create and manage scenarios for worksheet data using *Scenario Manager* (p. E8-437).

- A **scenario** is a saved set of values in a workbook.
- A scenario is a what-if analysis tool because it allows you to display and compare multiple data possibilities in a worksheet.
- The **Scenario Manager** command is available from the *What-If Analysis* button in the *Data Tools* group in the *Data* tab.
- In the *Add Scenario* dialog box, you name each scenario and set which cells are to be changed.
- In the *Scenario Values* dialog box, you accept or type new values for each scenario.
- Only one scenario is displayed in the worksheet at a time. You can view scenarios by selecting the name in the *Scenario Manager* dialog box and clicking **Show**.
- From the *Scenario Manager* dialog box, you can create a summary report that displays data about changing and result cells for all scenarios in a workbook.

8.4 Customize a *PivotTable* and *PivotChart* by editing value field settings, including a custom calculation; inserting a calculated field; refreshing data; displaying slicers; and formatting (p. E8-442).

- You can edit a *PivotTable* or its associated *PivotChart* to change the function used for value fields, to show percentages instead of values, or to insert a calculated field.
- The **Value Field Settings** determine how the values are summarized and shown in the *PivotTable* and *PivotChart*.
- The default calculation for a value field is *Sum*, but you can choose from other calculations on the *Summarize Values By* tab in the *Value Field Settings* dialog box.
- From the *Show Values As* tab in the *Value Field Settings* dialog box, you can choose a custom calculation such as a percentage of the total or a ranking.
- A **calculated field** in a *PivotTable* uses a formula with one of the fields in the source data.
- Insert a calculated field from the **Fields, Items, & Sets** button [*PivotTable Tools Analyze* tab, *Calculations* group].

- Values fields can be formatted from the *Value Field Settings* dialog box or from the *Number* group on the *Home* tab.
- Changes made in a *PivotTable* or its *PivotChart* are automatically reflected in the other. Changes made to the source data for a *PivotTable* or *PivotChart* are not automatic.
- You must refresh a *PivotTable* or a *PivotChart* by clicking the **Refresh** button in the *Data* group on the *PivotTable Tools Analyze* tab. You can also right-click any cell in the *PivotTable* and choose **Refresh** from the menu. A **slicer** is a floating filter window for a *PivotTable*. You can insert a slicer for one or more fields in the *PivotTable*.
- In the slicer window, you can select one or more items to filter the *PivotTable* and *PivotChart*.
- The **Insert Slicer** button is in the *Filter* group on the *PivotTable Tools Analyze* tab.
- *PivotTables* and *PivotCharts* are formatted from their respective *Design* tabs with commands similar to Excel worksheet formatting.

8.5 Build a one-variable data table (p. E8-454).

- A **data table** is a range of cells in a worksheet that shows multiple results for one or more formulas.
- A data table is created from the *What-If Analysis* button in the *Data Tools* group on the *Data* tab.
- A **one-variable data table** uses one argument in the formula and varies the value for that argument as its input values.
- **Input values** can be in a row or a column, and the formula must be entered in a specific location.
- The formula or formulas can be re-entered in the data table range, or they can be entered as references to the actual formula in the worksheet.
- In the *Data Table* dialog box, you specify either a row or column input cell, the cell

reference in the worksheet that is replaced with the input values.
- A data table uses the *TABLE* command in an array formula in each result cell.

8.6 Build a two-variable data table (p. E8-456).

- A **two-variable data table** uses two arguments in a single formula and varies values for both arguments.
- Input values are in a row and a column, and the formula must be entered in a specific location.
- The formula can be re-entered in the data table range, or it can be entered as a reference to the formula in the worksheet.
- In the *Data Table* dialog box, you specify both a row and a column input cell. These are the cell references in the worksheet that are replaced with the row and column input values.
- A data table uses the *TABLE* command in an array formula in each result cell. The *TABLE* command in each result cell appears in curly braces and identifies the row and column input cells.

8.7 Import and work with XML data (p. E8-458).

- **XML (Extensible Markup Language)** is a text file format used for exchanging large amounts of data on the web.
- You can save an Excel workbook as an XML file so that the data can be shared across many platforms.
- An XML file uses **tags** to identify each piece of data.
- You can use the **Open** command to import XML data into an Excel workbook.
- From the *Open XML* dialog box, you can choose an Excel table, create a tabular list, or display existing XML maps and create new maps.
- From an XML map, you can place fields in any order to build a table in the worksheet.

Check for Understanding

On the **Online Learning Center** for this text (www.mhhe.com/office2013inpractice), there are a variety of resources that can be used to review the concepts covered in this chapter.

The following Online Learning Resources are available on the Online Learning Center:

- Multiple choice questions
- Short answer questions
- Matching exercises

Guided Project 8-1

The Wear-Ever Shoes organization is requesting that managers use *Solver* for a marketing analysis. Create various scenarios and *Solver* reports to present your recommendation to the CEO
[Student Learning Outcomes 8.1, 8.2, 8.3, 8.4]

File Needed: ***WEMarketing-08.xlsx***
Completed Project File Name: ***[your initials] Excel 8-1.xlsx***

Skills Covered in This Project

- Add the *Solver* button.
- Create *SUMPRODUCT* formulas.
- Set the *Solver* parameters.
- Create *Answer, Sensitivity*, and *Limits* reports.
- Create a scenario.
- Display a scenario.
- Create a scenario summary report.
- Create a scenario *PivotTable* report.

- Create a *PivotTable*.
- Edit value field settings.
- Create a *PivotChart*.
- Insert a slicer.
- Format a *PivotTable*.
- Format a *PivotChart*.
- Format a slicer.

1. Open the ***WEMarketing-08*** workbook from your student data files folder.

2. Save the workbook as ***[your initials] Excel 8-1***.

3. Install the *Solver* add-in.
   a. Select the **Options** command [*File* tab].
   b. Click **Add-Ins** in the left pane.
   c. Click **Solver Add-in** in the *Inactive Application Add-ins* list. If *Solver Add-in* is in the *Active Application Add-ins* list, click **Cancel** and go on to step 4.
   d. Click **Go** near the bottom of the window.
   e. Click the **Solver Add-in** check box and click **OK**.

4. Add the *SUMPRODUCT* formulas.
   a. Select **E7**.
   b. Enter the following formula: =SUMPRODUCT(C7:D7,C13:D13).
   c. Select **E10**.
   d. Enter the following formula: =SUMPRODUCT(C10:D10,C13:D13).
   e. Select **G13**.
   f. Enter the following formula: =SUMPRODUCT(C4:D4,C13:D13).

5. Set *Solver* parameters.
   a. Click the **Solver** button [*Data* tab, *Analysis* group] to open the *Solver Parameters* dialog box.
   b. In the *Set Objective* box, click cell **G13**. This cell has a *SUMPRODUCT* formula.
   c. For the *To* parameter, click the **Max** radio button.
   d. Click in the **By Changing Variable Cells** box and select cells **C13:D13**. *Solver* will input new values only for these two locations.

6. Add constraints to a *Solver* problem.
   a. Click **Add** to the right of the *Subject to the Constraints* box.
   b. In the *Cell Reference* box, select cell **E7**.
   c. Click the **drop-down arrow** and choose **<=** as the operator.
   d. Click in the **Constraint** box and click **G7**.
   e. Click **Add** to add another constraint. If you accidentally close the *Add Constraint* dialog box, click **Add** in the *Solver Parameters* dialog box.
   f. In the *Cell Reference* box, select cell **E10**. Choose **>=** as the operator and click **G10** as the constraint. The value in cell E10 must be greater than or equal to the value in G10.
   g. Add an additional constraint to specify that the value in cell **C13** must be less than or equal to the value in **C15**.
   h. When all constraints are identified, click **OK** in the *Add Constraint* dialog box
   i. For the *Select a Solving Method,* choose **Simplex LP**.
   j. Check the **Make Unconstrained Variables Non-Negative** box (Figure 8-61).
   k. Click **Solve**. The solution 14,550 is shown in G13.

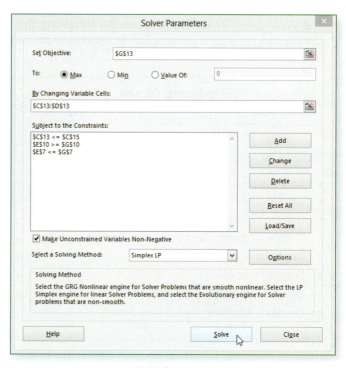

8-61 *Solver* parameters with constraints

7. Manage *Solver* results.
   a. Click **Save Scenario** in the *Solver Results* dialog box.
   b. Type Original Budget as the scenario name.
   c. Click **OK** to return to the *Solver Results* dialog box.
   d. Click to select **Answer**, **Sensitivity**, and **Limits** in the *Reports* list.
   e. Click **OK**. Three generated reports are inserted in the workbook for the *Solver* reports (Figure 8-62).

8. Create scenarios with new data.
   a. Click in cell **G7** and type 4500.
   b. Click cell **G13**.
   c. Click the **Solver** button [*Data* tab, *Analysis* group] to open the *Solver Parameters* dialog box.

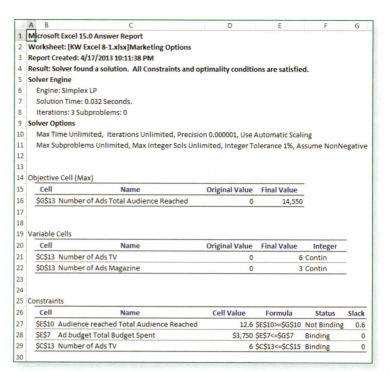

8-62 The *Answer Solver* report

d. Without changing anything, click **Solve**. The new solution 17,100 is shown in B13.

e. Click **Save Scenario** in the *Solver Results* dialog box.

f. Type Max Budget as the scenario name.

g. Click **OK** to return to the *Solver Results* dialog box.

h. Click **OK** in the *Solver Results* dialog box.

9. Display a scenario.

a. Click the **What-if Analysis** button [*Data* tab, *Data Tools* group] and select **Scenario Manager**. The two scenario names are listed.

b. Click **Original Budget** to highlight the name.

c. Click **Show**. The values for the *Original Budget* scenario are displayed in the worksheet.

d. Click **Close**.

10. Create a scenario summary report.

a. Click the **What-if Analysis** button [*Data* tab, *Data Tools* group] and select **Scenario Manager**.

b. Click **Summary**.

c. In the *Scenario Summary* dialog box, choose **Scenario summary** as the *Report type*.

d. In the *Result cells* box, select cell **C13:D13**.

e. Click **OK**. The report is inserted on a new sheet named **Scenario Summary** (Figure 8-63).

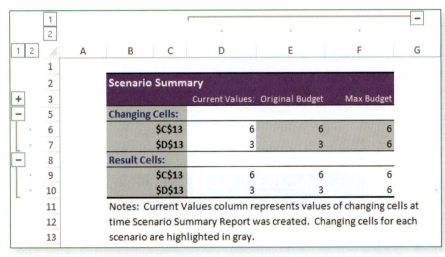

8-63 Scenario summary report for TV and magazine advertisements

11. Create a scenario *PivotTable* report.

a. Select the **Marketing Options** tab.

b. Click the **What-if Analysis** button [*Data* tab, *Data Tools* group] and select **Scenario Manager**.

c. Click **Summary**.

d. In the *Scenario Summary* dialog box, choose **Scenario PivotTable report** as the *Report type*.

e. In the *Result cells* box, select cell **C13:D13** if necessary.

f. Click **OK**. The report is inserted on a new sheet named *Scenario PivotTable*.

g. Drag the **Values** field from the *Columns* area to the *Rows* area in the *PivotChart Fields* pane.

h. Drag the **$C$13:$D$13** field from the *Rows* area to the *Columns* area in the *PivotChart Fields* pane (Figure 8-64).

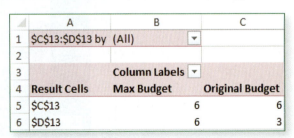

8-64 *Scenario PivotTable* report with swapped fields in Columns and Rows areas

12. Edit *Value Field Settings.*
    a. Right-click **$C$13** in cell **A5**.
    b. Select **Value Field Settings** from the menu.
    c. On the *Summarize Values By* tab, click in the **Custom Name** box.
    d. Edit the name to TV Ads.
    e. Click **OK** or press **Enter**.
    f. Click cell **A6** and click the **Field Settings** button [*PivotTable Tools Analyze* tab, *Active Field* group].
    g. Click in the **Custom Name** box and edit the name to Magazine Ads.
    h. Click **OK** or press **Enter**.

13. Create a *PivotChart.*
    a. Click any cell in the *PivotTable.*
    b. Click the **PivotChart** button [*PivotTable Tools Analyze tab, Tools* group].
    c. Click **Column** in the list and **Clustered Column** as the subtype.
    d. Click **OK**.
    e. Click the **PivotChart background** to select the chart.
    f. With the four-pointed arrow, drag the **PivotChart** so that the top-left corner is in cell **A8**.

14. Format a *PivotTable* and a *PivotChart.*
    a. Click any cell in the *PivotTable.*
    b. Click the **More** button [*PivotTable Tools Design* tab, *PivotTable Styles* group].
    c. Find and click **Pivot Style Medium 17** in the gallery.
    d. Click the **PivotChart background** to select the chart.
    e. Click the **More** button [*PivotChart Tools Design* tab, *Chart Styles* group].
    f. Find and click **Style 8** in the gallery.
    g. Click the **Change Colors** button [*PivotChart Tools Design* tab, *Chart Styles* group]. Choose the **Color 6** row in the *Monochromatic* list (Figure 8-65).

15. Save and close the workbook.

8-65 *PivotTable* and *PivotChart* are formatted

Guided Project 8-2

Sierra Pacific Community College (SPCC) is requesting decision analysis on imported data using a one-variable data table to determine an investment payment if the interest rate changes. Include a *PivotTable* and *PivotChart* to explain the results.
[Student Learning Outcomes 8.3, 8.4, 8.5, 8.6]

File Needed: ***PaymentsSPCC-08.xlsx***
Completed Project File Name: ***[your initials] Excel 8-2.xlsx***

Skills Covered in This Project

- Create a scenario.
- Display a scenario.
- Create a one-variable data table.
- Create a two-variable data table.
- Create a *PivotTable*.
- Edit value field settings.
- Create a *PivotChart*.

- Refresh a *PivotTable*.
- Insert a slicer.
- Insert a calculated field.
- Format a *PivotTable*.
- Format a *PivotChart*.
- Format a slicer.
- Refresh the *PivotTable*.

---

1. Open the ***PaymentsSPCC-08*** workbook from your student data files folder.

2. Save the workbook as ***[your initials] Excel 8-2***.

3. Create a scenario for the original data.
    a. Select the **Payment Schedule** sheet tab.
    b. Click the **What-if Analysis** button [*Data* tab, *Data Tools* group].
    c. Select **Scenario Manager**. There are currently no scenarios in the workbook.
    d. Click **Add**.
    e. In the *Add Scenario* dialog box, type Original Term as the name.
    f. Click in the **Changing cells** box and select cell **G4**.
    g. Click **OK**.
    h. Do not change any values in the *Scenario Values* dialog box and click **OK**.
    i. Click **Close**.

4. Create scenarios with new data.
    a. Click the **What-if Analysis** button [*Data* tab, *Data Tools* group] and select **Scenario Manager**. The *Original* scenario name is listed (Figure 8-66).
    b. Click **Add** to add a second scenario to the workbook.
    c. In the *Add Scenario* dialog box, type Longer Term as the name for the second scenario.
    d. Note that **G4** is listed in the *Changing cells* and click **OK**.
    e. For cell **G4** in the *Scenario Values* dialog box, type 20 and click **OK**.

8-66 *Original Term* scenario name is listed

f. Click **Add** to add a third scenario.

g. Type Shorter Term as the name and click **OK**.

h. For cell **G4** in the *Scenario Values* dialog box, type 7 and press **Enter**.

i. Click **Close**. The original values are still displayed in the workbook.

5. Display a scenario.

a. Click the **What-if Analysis** button [*Data* tab, *Data Tools* group] and select **Scenario Manager**. The three scenario names are listed.

b. Click **Shorter Term** to highlight the name.

c. Click **Show**. The values for the *Shorter Term* scenario are displayed in the worksheet (Figure 8-67).

d. Click **Close**.

6. Create a one-variable data table.

a. Select cells **B14:B15** and use the *Fill Handle* to fill values to reach cell **B22**. These values are the column input values.

b. Click cell **C13**. This location is one column to the right of the input values and one row above the first value.

c. Type =, click cell **G5**, and press **Enter** to create a reference to a payment formula.

d. Select cells **B13:C22** as the data table range.

e. Click the **What-If Analysis** button [*Data* tab, *Data Tools* group] and choose **Data Table**.

f. In the *Column input cell* entry box, click cell **D8** to indicate that the annual percentage rate will be replaced by the input values in column *B*.

g. Click **OK** to create the data table.

h. Select cells **C13:C22**. **Center** and format them as **Currency** format with 2 decimal places (Figure 8-68).

7. Create a two-variable data table.

a. Click cell **E13** to place the formula one row above the column input values and one column to the left of the row values.

b. Create a reference to the total cost of the loan formula in cell **G8**.

c. Select cells **E13:I22** as the data table range. This range includes the column input values, the formula, the row input values, and the empty result cells.

d. Click the **What-If Analysis** button [*Data* tab, *Data Tools* group] and choose **Data Table**.

e. In the *Row input cell* entry box, click cell **G4** to indicate that the term amounts in row 13 will replace the current value in cell G4.

f. In the *Column input cell* entry box, click cell **D8** to indicate that the annual percentage rates in column *E* will replace the current rate in cell D8.

g. Click **OK** to build the data table.

h. **Center** the cells **F14:I22** and apply **Currency** format (Figure 8-69).

8-67 *Shorter Term* **scenario can be shown in the worksheet**

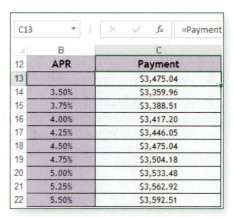

	B	C
12	**APR**	**Payment**
13		$3,475.04
14	3.50%	$3,359.96
15	3.75%	$3,388.51
16	4.00%	$3,417.20
17	4.25%	$3,446.05
18	4.50%	$3,475.04
19	4.75%	$3,504.18
20	5.00%	$3,533.48
21	5.25%	$3,562.92
22	5.50%	$3,592.51

8-68 **One-variable data table calculates the payment formula for the column input value**

	E	F	G	H	I
12		**Total Cost of the Loan**			
13	$291,903.39	15	20	25	30
14	3.50%	$321,697.14	$347,975.83	$375,467.68	$404,140.22
15	3.75%	$327,250.10	$355,732.99	$385,598.40	$416,804.03
16	4.00%	$332,859.57	$363,588.20	$395,877.63	$429,673.77
17	4.25%	$338,525.28	$371,540.68	$406,303.58	$442,745.90
18	4.50%	$344,246.98	$379,589.63	$416,874.36	$456,016.78
19	4.75%	$350,024.36	$387,734.18	$427,588.02	$469,482.60
20	5.00%	$355,857.13	$395,973.44	$438,442.53	$483,139.46
21	5.25%	$361,744.97	$404,306.50	$449,435.79	$496,983.33
22	5.50%	$367,687.55	$412,732.38	$460,565.62	$511,010.10

8-69 **Completed two-variable data table**

8. Create a *PivotTable*.
   a. Click the **CC Location 1** worksheet tab.
   b. Select cells **A4:E7**.
   c. Click the **PivotTable** button [*Insert* tab, *Tables* group] and verify that the *PivotTable* will be on a new worksheet.
   d. Click **OK**.
   e. Name the worksheet tab PivotTable.
   f. In the *PivotTable Fields* pane, check the **Student Tuition Categories** box. The field is added to the *Rows* area.
   g. Check the **Quarter 1**, **Quarter 1**, **Quarter 3**, and **Quarter 4** boxes. The numeric fields are placed in the *Values* area with the *Sum* calculation.
   h. Click any cell in the *PivotTable*.
   i. With the four-pointed arrow, drag the field name **Quarter 4** below the *Sum of Quarter 4* field in the *Values* area. A second copy of the field is placed in the *PivotTable*.

9. Edit *Value Field Settings*.
   a. Right-click **Sum of Quarter 4_2** in cell **F3**.
   b. Select **Value Field Settings** from the menu.
   c. On the *Summarize Values By* tab, click in the **Custom Name** box and edit the name to % of Q4 Total.
   d. Click the **Show Values As** tab.
   e. Click the **Show values as** arrow and choose **% of Grand Total**.
   f. Click **OK**. The values in column *F* are shown as percentages of the total tuition.
   g. Double-click each field in **B3:E3**, click the **Number Format** button, and apply the **Currency** number format. Click **OK** to apply formatting; click **OK** again to close the *Value Field Settings* dialog box.

10. Create a *PivotChart*.
    a. Click any cell in the *PivotTable*.
    b. Click the **PivotChart** button [*PivotTable Tools Analyze, Tools* group].
    c. Click **Bar** in the list and **Clustered Bar** as the subtype.
    d. Click **OK**.
    e. With the two-pointed arrow, resize the **PivotChart** so that the top-left corner is in cell **A9** and the bottom-right corner is in **H26**.

11. Refresh the *PivotTable* and *PivotChart*.
    a. Click the **CC Location 1** worksheet tab.
    b. Select and delete row **7**. Be sure to delete the row, not just cell contents.
    c. Click the **PivotTable** sheet tab. The deleted names are still included in the *PivotTable*.
    d. Select the *PivotTable* and click the **Refresh** button [*PivotTable Tools Analyze* tab, *Data* group]. The *PivotTable* and *PivotChart* are updated (Figure 8-70).

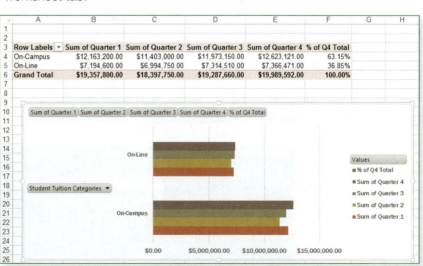

8-70 *PivotTable* and *PivotChart* are both refreshed

12. Insert a calculated field.
    a. Click any cell in the *PivotTable.*
    b. Click the **Fields, Items, & Sets** button [*PivotTable Tools Analyze* tab, *Calculations* group].
    c. Select **Calculated Field**.
    d. In the *Insert Calculated Field* dialog box, click in the **Name** box.
    e. Type Target Use as the name for the calculated field.
    f. Click in the **Formula** box and delete the zero and the space after the equals sign.
    g. Double-click **Quarter 4** in the *Fields* list.
    h. Type *115% after ='Quarter 4' in the *Formula* box.
    i. Click **OK**. The new field is inserted in the *PivotTable* and in the *PivotChart.*
    j. Click cell **G3** and click the **Field Settings** button [*PivotTable Tools Analyze* tab, *Active Field* group].
    k. Click in the **Custom Name** box and edit the name to Q4 Goal.
    l. Click the **Number Format** button, and apply **Currency** formatting. Click **OK**.
    m. Click **OK**.

13. Insert a slicer.
    a. Click any cell in the *PivotTable.*
    b. Click the **Insert Slicer** button [*PivotTable Tools Analyze* tab, *Filter* group].
    c. Check the **Student Tuition Categories** box and click **OK**. The *Student Tuition Categories* slicer opens.
    d. Click **On-Line** in the slicer. The *PivotTable* and *PivotChart* are filtered to show *On-Line* data.
    e. Resize the *PivotChart* so the bottom-right corner is in **J26**.
    f. Position the slicer in row **1**, to the right of the *PivotChart.*

14. Format a *PivotTable,* a *PivotChart*, and a slicer.
    a. Click any cell in the *PivotTable.*
    b. Click the **More** button [*PivotTable Tools Design* tab, *PivotTable Styles* group].
    c. Find and click **Pivot Style Dark 7** in the gallery.
    d. Click the *PivotChart* background to select the chart.
    e. Click the **More** button [*PivotChart Tools Design* tab, *Chart Styles* group].
    f. Find and click **Style 7** in the gallery.
    g. Click the **Change Colors** button [*PivotChart Tools Design* tab, *Chart Styles* group]. Choose the **Color 5** row in the *Monochromatic* list.
    h. Click the **slicer background** to select the slicer object.
    i. Click the **More** button [*Slicer Tools Options* tab, *Slicer Styles* group].
    j. Find and click **Slicer Style Dark 1** in the gallery.
    k. Angle the horizontal axis **Counterclockwise** on the *PivotChart.Hint:* click the **Orientation** button [*Home* tab, *Alignment* group].
    l. Type On-Line Tuition in the *Chart Title* placeholder (Figure 8-71).

15. Save and close the workbook.

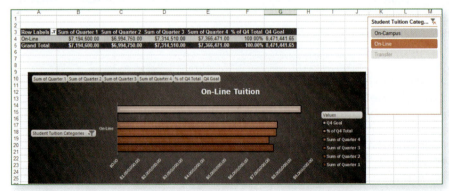

8-71 Excel 8-2 *PivotTable* sheet completed

Guided Project 8-3

Courtyard Medical Plaza is requesting patients to evaluate various workout scenarios to obtain weight loss goals. For this project, you will add several scenarios to determine the highest calorie-burning routine. Include a *PivotTable* and a *PivotChart* to illustrate your findings.
[Student Learning Outcomes 8.1, 8.2, 8.3, 8.4, 8.7]

Files Needed: ***EmployeeList-08.xml*** and ***CalorieBurn-08.xlsx***
Completed Project File Name: *[your initials] Excel 8-3.xlsx*

Skills Covered in This Project

- Import XML data.
- Install the *Solver* add-in.
- Set the *Solver* parameters.
- Create *Answer*, *Sensitivity*, and *Limits* reports.
- Create a scenario.
- Display a scenario.
- Create a scenario summary report.
- Create a one-variable data table.

- Create a *PivotTable*.
- Refresh a *PivotTable*.
- Edit value field settings.
- Create a *PivotChart*.
- Insert a slicer.
- Format a *PivotTable*.
- Format a *PivotChart*.
- Format a slicer.

1. Open the ***CalorieBurn-08*** workbook from your student data files folder.

2. Save the workbook as *[your initials] Excel 8-3*.

3. Import XML data into a worksheet.
   a. Choose **Open** from the *File* tab.
   b. Navigate to the folder with the ***EmployeeList-08*** file in the *Open* dialog box.
   c. Click to select the file name and click **Open** to display the *Open XML* dialog box.
   d. Click the **Use the XML Source task pane** radio button and click **OK**.
   e. If an error message box appears, click **OK**.
   f. Select **Employee** in the *XML Source* task pane; right-click and choose **Map Element**.
   g. In the *Map XML Elements* dialog box, click cell **A1**.
   h. Click **OK**.
   i. Map the **Title** field to cell **B1**.
   j. Click the **Refresh** button [*Table Tools Design* tab, *External Table Data* group].

4. Format the table with **Table Style Medium 3** (Figure 8-72).
   a. Name the sheet Potential Clients.
   b. Move the sheet tab to *[your initials] Excel 8-3* (hint: use the context-sensitive menu). Move the **Potential Clients** tab to the right of the *Food Journal* tab.

	A	B
1	**Employee**	**Title**
2	BJ Francine	Representative
3	Alec Mikayla	Representative
4	Mikayla Anderson	Representative
5	Ella Jamison	Manager
6	David Gazik	Manager
7	Natasha Ari	Intern
8	Ari Aronson	Intern
9	Dennis Frankie	Representative
10	Kendal Shaedon	Representative
11	Frankie Dennis	Representative
12	Kendra Shelton	Representative
13	DJ Bushman	Representative
14	Sharon Wyatte	Manager
15	Suzanne Ouimet	Manager
16	Chad Mei	Representative
17	Mae Gomez	Representative
18	Christopher Bowman	Manager
19	Jeffery Dalton	Manager
20	Corey Daniels	Intern
21	Randy Josephson	Intern
22	Tammy Christine	Representative
23	Josie Daddiline	Representative
24	Nikolai Jalowiec	Manager

8-72 Excel 8-3 *Potential Clients* worksheet completed

5. Install the *Solver* add-in if necessary.
   a. Select the **Options** command [*File* tab].
   b. Click **Add-Ins** in the left pane.
   c. Click **Solver Add-in** in the *Inactive Application Add-ins* list. If *Solver Add-in* is in the *Active Application Add-ins* list, click **Cancel** and go on to step 6.
   d. Click **Go** near the bottom of the window.
   e. Click the **Solver Add-in** check box and click **OK**.

6. Set *Solver* parameters.
   a. Select the **Activities** sheet tab.
   b. Click the **Solver** button [*Data* tab, *Analysis* group] to open the *Solver Parameters* dialog box.
   c. In the *Set Objective* box, click cell **C13**. This cell has a *SUM* formula.
   d. For the *To* parameter, click the **Max** radio button.
   e. Click in the **By Changing Variable Cells** box and select cells **D8:D9**. *Solver* will input new values only for these two activities.

7. Add constraints to a *Solver* problem.
   a. Click **Add** to the right of the *Subject to the Constraints* box.
   b. In the *Cell Reference* box, select cell **E13**.
   c. Click the **drop-down arrow** and choose **>=** as the operator.
   d. Click in the **Constraint** box and click **E14**. The value in cell E13 must be greater than or equal to the value in E14.
   e. Click **Add** to add another constraint. If you accidentally close the *Add Constraint* dialog box, click **Add** in the *Solver Parameters* dialog box.
   f. In the *Cell Reference* box, select cell **D8**. Choose **>=** as the operator and type 1. The value in cell D8 must be greater than or equal to one.
   g. When all constraints are identified, click **OK** in the *Add Constraint* dialog box
   h. For the *Select a Solving Method,* choose **Simplex LP**.
   i. Check the **Make Unconstrained Variables Non-Negative** box (Figure 8-73).
   j. Click **Solve**. A solution to the problem is shown in the worksheet.
   k. Click to select **Answer**, **Sensitivity**, and **Limits** in the *Reports* list.
   l. Click **OK**. Three generated reports are inserted in the workbook for the *Solver* reports (Figure 8-74).

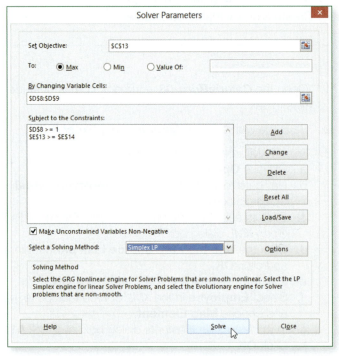

8-73 *Solver* **parameters with constraints**

8. Create a scenario for the original data.
   a. Click the **What-if Analysis** button [*Data* tab, *Data Tools* group].
   b. Select **Scenario Manager**. There are currently no scenarios in the workbook.
   c. Click **Add**.
   d. In the *Add Scenario* dialog box, type Normal Work-Out as the name.
   e. Click in the **Changing cells** box and select cells **D8:D12**.

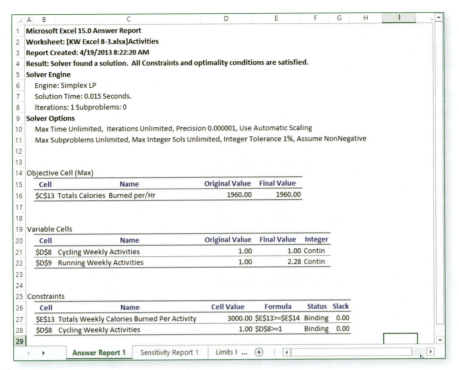

	A	B	C	D	E	F	G	H	I
1	Microsoft Excel 15.0 Answer Report								
2	Worksheet: [KW Excel 8-3.xlsx]Activities								
3	Report Created: 4/19/2013 8:22:20 AM								
4	Result: Solver found a solution. All Constraints and optimality conditions are satisfied.								
5	Solver Engine								
6	Engine: Simplex LP								
7	Solution Time: 0.015 Seconds.								
8	Iterations: 1 Subproblems: 0								
9	Solver Options								
10	Max Time Unlimited, Iterations Unlimited, Precision 0.000001, Use Automatic Scaling								
11	Max Subproblems Unlimited, Max Integer Sols Unlimited, Integer Tolerance 1%, Assume NonNegative								
12									
13									
14	Objective Cell (Max)								
15		Cell	Name		Original Value	Final Value			
16		$C$13	Totals Calories Burned per/Hr		1960.00	1960.00			
17									
18									
19	Variable Cells								
20		Cell	Name		Original Value	Final Value	Integer		
21		$D$8	Cycling Weekly Activities		1.00	1.00	Contin		
22		$D$9	Running Weekly Activities		1.00	2.28	Contin		
23									
24									
25	Constraints								
26		Cell	Name		Cell Value	Formula	Status	Slack	
27		$E$13	Totals Weekly Calories Burned Per Activity		3000.00	$E$13>=$E$14	Binding	0.00	
28		$D$8	Cycling Weekly Activities		1.00	$D$8>=1	Binding	0.00	
29									

Answer Report 1 | Sensitivity Report 1 | Limits I ... ⊕

8-74 Excel 8-3 *Answer Solver* report

   f. Click **OK**.

   g. Change the value in the **$D$9** box to 1; do not change any other values in the *Scenario Values* dialog box, and click **OK**.

   h. Click **Close**.

9. Create scenarios with new data.

   a. Click the **What-if Analysis** button [*Data* tab, *Data Tools* group] and select **Scenario Manager**. The *Normal Work-out* scenario name is listed.

   b. Click **Add** to add a second scenario to the workbook.

   c. In the *Add Scenario* dialog box, type Intense Work-Out as the name for the second scenario.

   d. Verify that the *Changing cells* are cells **D8:D12** and click **OK**.

   e. For cell **$D$8** in the *Scenario Values* dialog box, type 2 and press **Tab**. If you accidentally press **Enter** and return to the *Scenario Manager* dialog box, click **Edit** to return to the *Scenario Values* dialog box.

   f. For cell **$D$9** in the *Scenario Values* dialog box, type 2.5 and press **Tab**.

   g. For cell **$D$10**, type 2.5 and type 2 for cells **$D$11** and **$D$12** (Figure 8-75).

   h. Click **OK**.

   i. Click **Add** to add a third scenario.

   j. Type Light Work-Out as the name and click **OK**.

   k. Adjust the cell values as shown in the *Scenario Values* dialog box in Figure 8-76.

   l. Click **OK** and click **Close**. The original *Solver* values are still displayed in the workbook.

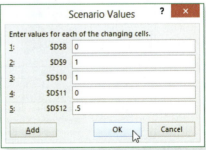

8-75 *Scenario Values* dialog box for intense work-out

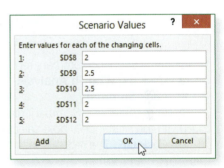

8-76 *Scenario Values* dialog box for light work-out

10. Display a scenario.
    a. Click the **What-If Analysis** button [*Data* tab, *Data Tools* group] and select **Scenario Manager**. The three scenario names are listed.
    b. Click **Normal Work-Out** to highlight the name.
    c. Click **Show**. The values for the *Normal Work-Out* scenario are displayed in the worksheet.
    d. Click **Close** (Figure 8-77).

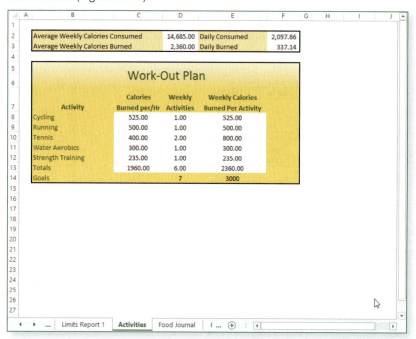

8-77 Normal work-out scenario for calories burned

11. Create a scenario summary report.
    a. Click the **What-If Analysis** button [*Data* tab, *Data Tools* group] and select **Scenario Manager**.
    b. Click **Summary**.
    c. In the *Scenario Summary* dialog box, choose **Scenario summary** as the *Report type*.
    d. In the *Result cells* box, select cell **D13:E13**.
    e. Click **OK**. The report is inserted on a new sheet named **Scenario Summary** (Figure 8-78).

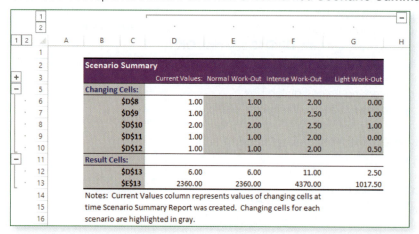

8-78 Scenario summary for calories burned and hours spent on work-outs

12. Create a one-variable data table.
    a. Select the **Food Journal** tab.
    b. Click cell **D14**. This location is one column to the right of the input values and one row above the first value.
    c. Type =, click cell **H10**, and press **Enter** to create a reference to a total calorie formula.
    d. Select cells **C14:D24** as the data table range.
    e. Click the **What-If Analysis** button [*Data* tab, *Data Tools* group] and choose **Data Table**.
    f. In the *Column input cell* entry box, click cell **F10** to indicate that the average calories consumed for dinner will be replaced by the input values in column *C*.
    g. Click **OK** to create the data table.
    h. Select cells **D14:D24** and apply **Comma** format; decrease the decimal places to **0** (Figure 8-79).

D14	▼ : × ✓ *fx*	=H10

	B	C	D
13		Daily Calorie intake	
14			2,098
15		350	1,759
16		400	1,809
17	Number of Calories at Dinner	450	1,859
18		500	1,909
19		550	1,959
20		600	2,009
21		650	2,059
22		700	2,109
23		750	2,159
24		800	2,209

8-79 One-variable data table calculates the formula for the column input value

13. Create a *PivotTable*.
    a. Click the **Food Journal** worksheet tab if necessary.
    b. Select cells **A2:G9**.
    c. Click the **PivotTable** button [*Insert* tab, *Tables* group] and verify that the *PivotTable* will be on a new worksheet.
    d. Click **OK**.
    e. Name the worksheet tab PivotTable.
    f. In the *PivotTable Fields* pane, check the **Date** box. The field is added to the *Rows* area.
    g. Check the **Morning Snack**, **Afternoon Snack**, and **Dessert** boxes. The numeric fields are placed in the *Values* area with the *Sum* calculation.
    h. Click any cell in the *PivotTable*.
    i. With the four-pointed arrow, drag the field name **Dessert** below the *Sum of Dessert* field in the *Values* area. A second copy of the field is placed in the *PivotTable*.

14. Edit *Value Field Settings*.
    a. Right-click **Sum of Dessert2** in cell **E3**.
    b. Select **Value Field Settings** from the menu.
    c. On the *Summarize Values By* tab, click in the **Custom Name** box and edit the name to % of Dessert Weekly Total.
    d. Click the **Show Values As** tab.
    e. Click the **Show values as** arrow and choose **% of Column Total**.
    f. Click **OK**. The values in column *E* are shown as percentages of the total weekly calorie intake for desserts.

15. Create a *PivotChart*.
    a. Click any cell in the *PivotTable*.
    b. Click the **PivotChart** button [*PivotTable Tools Analyze, Tools* group].
    c. Click **Column** in the list and **Clustered Column** as the subtype.
    d. Click **OK**.
    e. With the two-pointed arrow, resize the **PivotChart** so that the top-left corner is in cell **B13** and the bottom-right corner is in **F27**.

16. Refresh the *PivotTable* and *PivotChart*.
    a. Click the **Food Journal** worksheet tab.
    b. Change **G3** to 300.

c. Click the **PivotTable** sheet tab. The old value for G3 is still reflected in D4 in the *PivotTable.*

d. Click the **Refresh** button [*PivotTable Tools Analyze* tab, *Data* group]. The *PivotTable* and *PivotChart* are updated.

17. Insert a slicer.
    a. Click any cell in the *PivotTable.*
    b. Click the **Insert Slicer** button [*PivotTable Tools Analyze* tab, *Filter* group].
    c. Check the **Date** box and click **OK**. The *Date* slicer opens.
    d. Click **1/15/2016** in the slicer, hold **Ctrl**, and click **1/16/2016**. The *PivotTable* and *PivotChart* are filtered to show January 15–16 data.
    e. Position the slicer so the top-left corner is in **A13**. *Hint: repositioning of the PivotChart will occur in the next step.*

18. Format a *PivotTable,* a *PivotChart,* and a slicer.
    a. Click any cell in the *PivotTable.*
    b. Click the **More** button [*PivotTable Tools Design* tab, *PivotTable Styles* group].
    c. Find and click **Pivot Style Dark 5** in the gallery.
    d. Click the **PivotChart background** to select the chart.
    e. Click the **More** button [*PivotChart Tools Design* tab, *Chart Styles* group].
    f. Find and click **Style 4** in the gallery.
    g. Click the **Change Colors** button [*PivotChart Tools Design* tab, *Chart Styles* group]. Choose the **Color 8** row in the *Monochromatic* list.
    h. Click the slicer background to select the slicer object.
    i. Click the **More** button [*SlicerTools Options* tab, *Slicer Styles* group].
    j. Find and click **Slicer Style Dark 4** in the gallery.
    k. Position the slicer and the chart according to Figure 8-80.

19. Save and close the workbook.

8-80 Excel 8-3 *PivotTable* worksheet completed

Independent Project 8-4

Boyd Air is requesting management to use solver for a manufacturing analysis decision between small and large planes. They would like to know how many of each to produce in order to maximize profit. Please include all three reports, a *PivotTable*, and a *PivotChart* to help explain your results.
[Student Learning Outcomes 8.1, 8.2, 8.3, 8.4]

File Needed: ***Planes-08.xlsx***
Completed Project File Name: ***[your initials] Excel 8-4.xlsx***

Skills Covered in This Project

- Install the *Solver* add-in.
- Create *SUMPRODUCT* formulas.
- Set the *Solver* parameters.
- Create *Answer, Sensitivity*, and *Limits* reports.
- Save as *Solver* scenario.
- Create a scenario.
- Display a scenario.
- Create a scenario summary report.

- Create a scenario *PivotTable* report.
- Create a *PivotTable*.
- Edit value field settings.
- Create a *PivotChart*.
- Insert a slicer.
- Format a *PivotTable*.
- Format a *PivotChart*.
- Format a slicer.

---

1. Open the ***Planes-08*** workbook from your student data files folder.

2. Save the workbook as ***[your initials] Excel 8-4***.

3. Install the *Solver* add-in if necessary.

4. Add the *SUMPRODUCT* formulas.
   a. Enter the following formula in **D9**: =SUMPRODUCT(B9:C9,B13:C13).
   b. Enter the following formula in **D10**: =SUMPRODUCT(B10:C10,B13:C13).
   c. Enter the following formula in **F13**: =SUMPRODUCT(B6:C6,B13:C13).

5. Set *Solver* parameters to maximize profit by changing the number of planes produced without using more resources than are available. The number of planes produced must be a whole number.
   a. In the *Set Objective* box, click cell **F13**.
   b. Use the cells **B13:C13** for the *Variable Cells*.
   c. Set **D9:D10 <= F9:F10** for the first constraint and **B13:C13 = int** for the second constraint. *Int* is a selection used to force the values to be integers or whole numbers. *Hint: choose int from the operator drop-down arrow button.*
   d. Choose **Simplex LP** for the *Select a Solving Method* and check **the Make Unconstrained Variables Non-Negative** box.
   e. Click **Solve**. A solution of *10 small planes, 12 large planes*, and *$48,421* in total profit displays (Figure 8-81). Apply **Currency** formatting with **0** decimal places to **F13** if necessary.

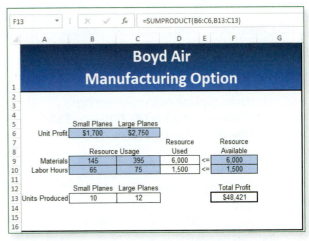

8-81 *Solver* results

6. Save the *Solver* scenario. Click the **Save Scenario** button and Type Original Resources as the scenario name.

7. Create **Answer**, **Sensitivity**, and **Limits** reports for the *Solver* data (Figure 8-82).

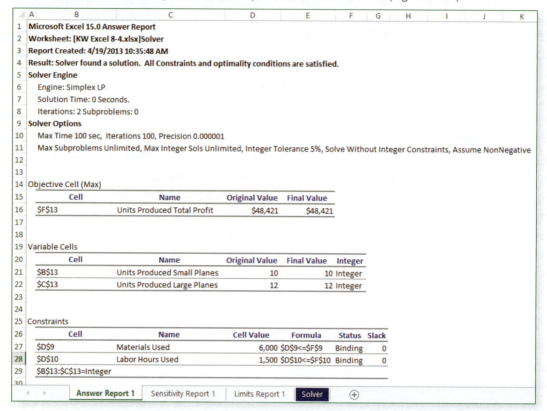

	A	B	C	D	E	F	G	H	I	J	K
1	Microsoft Excel 15.0 Answer Report										
2	Worksheet: [KW Excel 8-4.xlsx]Solver										
3	Report Created: 4/19/2013 10:35:48 AM										
4	Result: Solver found a solution. All Constraints and optimality conditions are satisfied.										
5	Solver Engine										
6	Engine: Simplex LP										
7	Solution Time: 0 Seconds.										
8	Iterations: 2 Subproblems: 0										
9	Solver Options										
10	Max Time 100 sec, Iterations 100, Precision 0.000001										
11	Max Subproblems Unlimited, Max Integer Sols Unlimited, Integer Tolerance 5%, Solve Without Integer Constraints, Assume NonNegative										
12											
13											
14	Objective Cell (Max)										
15		Cell	Name	Original Value	Final Value						
16		$F$13	Units Produced Total Profit	$48,421	$48,421						
17											
18											
19	Variable Cells										
20		Cell	Name	Original Value	Final Value	Integer					
21		$B$13	Units Produced Small Planes	10	10	Integer					
22		$C$13	Units Produced Large Planes	12	12	Integer					
23											
24											
25	Constraints										
26		Cell	Name	Cell Value	Formula	Status	Slack				
27		$D$9	Materials Used	6,000	$D$9<=$F$9	Binding	0				
28		$D$10	Labor Hours Used	1,500	$D$10<=$F$10	Binding	0				
29		$B$13:$C$13=Integer									
30											

| Answer Report 1 | Sensitivity Report 1 | Limits Report 1 | Solver | ⊕ |

8-82 Excel 8-3 *Answer Report 1* sheet completed

8. Create a new *Solver* scenario called **Max Resources** by changing **F9** to 7500 and **F10** to 2000 on the *Solver* tab.
   a. Don't forget to re-solve the problem before saving the scenario.
   b. The results change to 15 small planes, 13 large planes, and $62,829 for profit.

9. Display the *Original Resources* scenario.

10. Create an airplane production scenario summary report using **D9**, **D10**, and **F13** from the *Solver* tab for the result cells (Figure 8-83).

11. Create an airplane production scenario *PivotTable* report using **D9**, **D10**, and **F13** from the *Solver* tab for the result cells.

12. Edit *Value Field Settings* of **B3** in the *Scenario PivotTable* sheet to display Materials, **C4** to display Labor Hours, and **D4** to display Total Profit. Adjust the format of **D3** to display **Currency** formats for values.

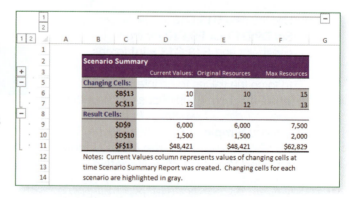

	A	B	C	D	E	F	G
1							
2		Scenario Summary					
3				Current Values:	Original Resources	Max Resources	
5		Changing Cells:					
6			$B$13	10	10	15	
7			$C$13	12	12	13	
8		Result Cells:					
9			$D$9	6,000	6,000	7,500	
10			$D$10	1,500	1,500	2,000	
11			$F$13	$48,421	$48,421	$62,829	
12		Notes: Current Values column represents values of changing cells at					
13		time Scenario Summary Report was created. Changing cells for each					
14		scenario are highlighted in gray.					

8-83 Excel 8-4 *Scenario Summary* worksheet completed

13. Create a **Clustered Bar** *PivotChart* positioned with the top-left corner in **A7** and the bottom-right corner in **G21**.

14. Insert a slicer to the *PivotTable* for **$B$13:$C$13** that displays *Max Resources* for the filter. Position the slicer in row **1** and to the right of the *PivotChart*.

15. Format a *PivotTable* and a *PivotChart*.
    a. Apply **Pivot Style Medium 21** to the *PivotTable*.
    b. Apply **Style 7** to the *PivotChart* and change the colors to **Color 7** in the *Monochromatic* list.
    c. Apply **Slicer Style Dark 3** to the **Slicer** (Figure 8-84).

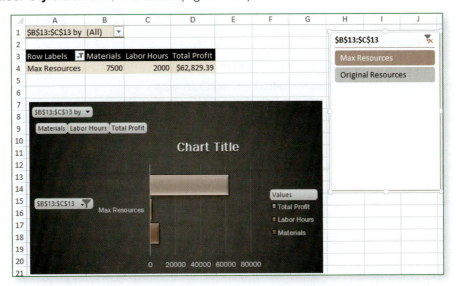

8-84 Excel 8-4 *Scenario PivotTable* **sheet completed**

16. Save and close the workbook.

Independent Project 8-5

Placer Hills Real Estate (PHRE) is a real estate company with regional offices throughout central California. Real estate agents must compare how each commission tier will affect their pay for a sale. Use the scenario manager, a one-variable data table, a two-variable data table, a *PivotTable*, and a *PivotChart* to display the ideal option.
[Student Learning Outcomes 8.3, 8.4, 8.5, 8.6]

File Needed: ***Commission-08.xlsx***
Completed Project File Name: *[your initials] Excel 8-5.xlsx*

Skills Covered in This Project

- Create a scenario.
- Display a scenario.
- Create a one-variable data table.
- Create a two-variable data table.
- Create a *PivotTable*.
- Edit value field settings.
- Create a *PivotChart*.

- Refresh a *PivotTable*.
- Insert a slicer.
- Insert a calculated field.
- Format a *PivotTable*.
- Format a *PivotChart*.
- Format a slicer.
- Refresh the *PivotTable*.

---

1. Open the **Commission-08** workbook from your student data files folder.

2. Save the workbook as *[your initials] Excel 8-5*.

3. Create the following scenarios for **D4:D7** on the *Commissions* tab.
   a. Name the first scenario Original Split. Do not change any of the values.
   b. Create a second scenario called Higher Split that changes the values in **D4**, **D5**, **D6**, and **D7** to 35%, 45%, 65%, and 85%, respectively.
   c. Create a third scenario called Lower Split that changes the values in **D4**, **D5**, **D6**, and **D7** to 20%, 30%, 50%, and 70%, respectively.
   d. Display the *Higher Split* scenario.

4. Create a one-variable data table that displays realtor commission split and net pay when changes in tier 3 commission percentages occur.
   a. Reference **B12** in **I2** and **B14** in **J2**.
   b. Use **D6** as the column input cell.

5. Create a two-variable data table that displays total commission when changes in listing commission percentage and property sales amount occur.
   a. Reference **B11** in **B17**.
   b. Use **B9** as the row input cell and **B10** as the column input cell (Figure 8-85).

8-85 Excel 8-5 *Commissions* worksheet completed

6. Create a *PivotTable* on a new worksheet called PivotTable for **A3:J15** on the *Hot Sheet* tab.
   a. Add the **County** field to the *Rows* area.
   b. Add the following fields to the *Values* area; *Sq Ft, Age, Acres,* and *List Price* boxes.

7. Create a second copy of the *List Price* field so it appears in **F3** in the *PivotTable*.
   a. Change the calculation from Sum to **Average** and edit the name to Average List Price.
   b. Apply **Currency** number format with **0** decimals to fields located in columns **E:F** in the *PivotTable*.

8. Create a *Clustered Column PivotChart* that is positioned with the top-left corner in the center of **C12** and the lower-right corner in **H27**.

9. Edit **B10** on the *Hot Sheet* tab to display Humboldt. Refresh the *PivotTable* and *PivotChart*.

10. Insert a field called Average Offer that calculates an offer by multiplying the *List Price* by 90%. Apply **Currency** number format with **0** decimals.

11. Insert a slicer for counties that displays *Santa Clara, Sacramento,* and *Humboldt*. Place the slicer to the left of the *PivotChart*.

12. Format a *PivotTable, PivotChart,* and slicer.
    a. Apply **Pivot Style Medium 16** to the *PivotTable.*
    b. Apply **Style 12** to the *PivotChart* and change the colors to **Color 9** in the *Monochromatic* list.
    c. Apply **Slicer Style Dark 5** to the slicer and position *PivotChart* and slicer as shown (Figure 8-86).

13. Save and close the workbook.

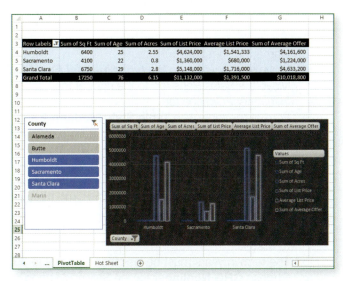

8-86 Excel 8-5 *PivotTable* worksheet completed

Independent Project 8-6

For this project, you are using *Solver* to determine which finance option is the least cost for Wilson Home Entertainment Systems (WHES), an entertainment and security company. Please include an import of the sales reps, all three *Solver* reports, a *PivotTable,* and a *PivotChart* to help explain your results. [Student Learning Outcomes 8.1, 8.2, 8.3, 8.4, 8.7]

Files Needed: ***Investment-08.xlsx*** and ***EmployeeList-08.xml***
Completed Project File Name: ***[your initials] Excel 8-6.xlsx***

Skills Covered in This Project

- Import XML data.
- Install the *Solver* add-in.
- Set the *Solver* parameters.
- Create *Answer, Sensitivity,* and *Limits* reports.
- Create a scenario.
- Display a scenario.
- Create a scenario summary report.
- Create a one-variable data table.

- Create a *PivotTable.*
- Refresh a *PivotTable.*
- Edit value field settings.
- Create a *PivotChart.*
- Insert a slicer.
- Format a *PivotTable.*
- Format a *PivotChart.*
- Format a slicer.

---

1. Open the ***Investment-08*** workbook from your student data files folder.

2. Save the workbook as ***[your initials] Excel 8-6***.

3. Import the ***EmployeeList-08*** XML data into a worksheet using the *XML Source task* pane.
    a. Map all of the *XML Elements* into the worksheet beginning with **ID** in cell **A1**, map **Employee** to **B1**, and so on.
    b. Refresh the data.

c. Name the sheet Sales Reps.

d. Move the sheet tab to the *[your initials] Excel 8-6*. Move the *Sales Reps* tab to the right of the *Investment Options* tab.

e. Format the table with **Table Style Medium 9** and *AutoFit* the contents (Figure 8-87).

4. Install the *Solver* add-in if necessary.

5. Set *Solver* parameters on the *Investment Options* tab to minimize (Min) the payment in **B8** by changing the term in years in **B6** and interest rate in **B7**.

a. The interest rate must be greater than or equal to **3.25%**.

b. The term in years must be less than or equal to **30**.

c. Choose **GRG Nonlinear** for the *Solving Method* and check the **Make Unconstrained Variables Non-Negative** box. Click **Solve**.

d. A solution of *30* years for the term, *3.25%* for the interest rate, and *$1,695.13* for the payment displays (Figure 8-88).

6. Save the *Solver* scenario. Click the **Save Scenario** button and type Minimum Payment as the scenario name.

7. Create **Answer**, **Sensitivity**, and **Limits** reports for the *Solver* data (Figure 8-89).

8. Create a new *Solver* scenario called Minimum Interest Paid by changing the term in years constraint to equal 15 in the *Solver Parameters* dialog box.

a. Don't forget to re-solve the problem before saving the scenario.

b. The results change the payment to *$2,736.89*.

9. Display the *Minimum Payment* scenario.

10. Create a payment scenario summary report using **B8** from the *Investment Options* tab for the result cell (Figure 8-90).

8-87 Excel 8-6 *Sales Reps* worksheet completed

8-88 *Solver* results

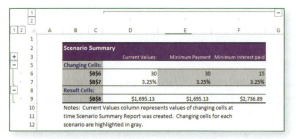

8-90 Excel 8-6 *Scenario Summary* sheet completed

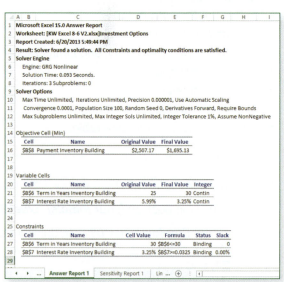

8-89 Excel 8-6 *Answer Report 1* sheet completed

11. Create a *PivotTable* on a new tab named PivotTable using **A4:E7** from the *Annual Forecast* tab.
    a. Add the *Sales Categories* field to the *Rows* area.
    b. Add all four quarter fields to the *Values* area.

12. Create a **Clustered Column** *PivotChart* positioned with the top-left corner in **A9** and the bottom-right corner in **E23**.

13. Apply **Currency** formatting to each field in the *PivotTable.*

14. Add a calculated field called Grand Total that totals all four quarters. Place the calculated field in **F3** and apply **Accounting** formatting to the contents.

15. Insert a slicer to the *PivotTable* for **Sales Categories** that displays *Services* and *Automation (security)* for the filter. Position the slicer to the right of the *PivotChart.*

16. Format a *PivotTable, PivotChart,* and slicer.
    a. Apply **Pivot Style Medium 16** to the *PivotTable.*
    b. Apply **Style 8** to the *PivotChart* and change the colors to **Color 13** in the *Monochromatic* list.
    c. Apply **Slicer Style Dark 1** to the slicer (Figure 8-91).

17. Save and close the workbook.

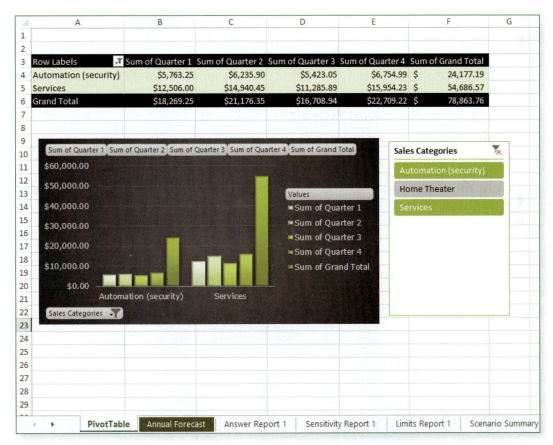

8-91 Excel 8-6 *PivotTable* **sheet completed**

Improve It Project 8-7

Pool and Spa Oasis (PSO) is a licensed contractor for swimming pools, swim spas, and hot tubs for residential customers in middle Tennessee. For this project, you edit the partially completed workbook to assure accuracy for scenarios, the two-variable data table, *PivotTables,* and *PivotCharts.*
[Student Learning Outcomes 8.3, 8.4, 8.5, 8.6]

File Needed: ***Budget-08.xlsx***
Completed Project File Name: ***[your initials] Excel 8-7.xlsx***

Skills Covered in This Project

- Create a scenario.
- Display a scenario.
- Create a one-variable data table.
- Create a two-variable data table.
- Create a *PivotTable.*
- Edit value field settings.
- Create a *PivotChart.*

- Refresh a *PivotTable.*
- Insert a slicer.
- Insert a calculated field.
- Format a *PivotTable.*
- Format a *PivotChart.*
- Format a slicer.
- Refresh the *PivotTable.*

1. Open the **Budget-08** workbook from your student data files folder. Click the **Enable Content** button if necessary.

2. Save the workbook as ***[your initials] Excel 8-7***.

3. Add a scenario called Max Budget that increases each original monthly budget category by 2000.

4. Add a scenario called Min Budget that decreases each original monthly budget category by 2000.

5. Create a scenario summary report using **G5:G9** as the result cells (Figure 8-92). Be sure to display the original scenario before creating the summary report.

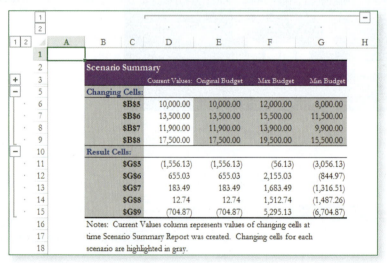

8-92 Excel 8-7 *Scenario Summary* **sheet completed**

6. Edit the one-variable data table on the *Table Data* sheet so that **B5** is the column input cell.

7. Edit the two-variable data table so that **D8** is the row input cell and **C5** is the column input cell (Figure 8-93).

8. Add a calculated field named March % of Grand Total to the *PivotTable* sheet that displays the percentage of grand total by adding a duplicate *March* field in the *values* area to the *PivotTable* and edit accordingly.
   a. Move the *Expense Categories* field to the *Rows* area.
   b. Reposition the *PivotChart* and slicer so the top of each object is in row 8.
   c. Change the calculation of the *Monthly* field headings to *Sum*.

9. Adjust the slicer filter for *Sales Category* on the *PivotChart* to display only *Vehicles* and *Commission*.

10. Apply **Pivot Style Medium 10** to the *PivotTable*, **Chart Style 4** to the *PivotChart*, and **Slicer Style Dark 1** to the slicer (Figure 8-94).

11. Save and close the workbook.

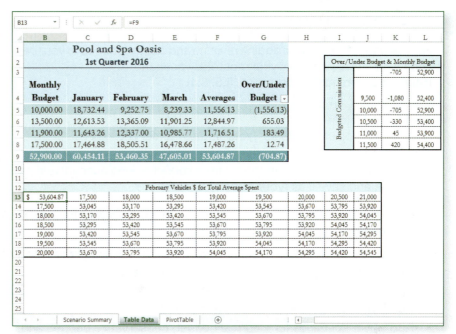

8-93 Excel 8-7 *Table Data* worksheet completed

8-94 Excel 8-7 *PivotTable* sheet completed

Challenge Project 8-8

For this project, you will be adding revenue and cost scenarios to your personal budget. Use *PivotTables* and *PivotCharts* to display your most likely scenario.
[Student Learning Outcomes 8.1, 8.3, 8.4]

File Needed: None
Completed Project File Name: *[your initials] Excel 8-8.xlsx*

Enter all data that you find important from your checking account and monthly expenses. Create a new workbook and save it as *[your initials] Excel 8-8*.

- Import or type the web site revenue information from your bank for the last month into your Excel workbook.
- When creating your spreadsheets, you may add additional column headings such as "Expenses," "Vacation," "Food," "Utilities," "Fun," "Savings," etc.
- Apply formatting as you see fit.
- Add formulas to the key columns as needed.
- Add solver scenarios for a normal budget, conservative budget, and relaxed budget based on minimizing expenses or maximizing overtime revenue.
- Create a summary report for the scenarios.
- Create a *PivotTable* and a *PivotChart* with slicer to display your results.

Challenge Project 8-9

For this project, you will be creating a *Solver* worksheet using data from items you wish to sell in a yard sale.
[Student Learning Outcomes 8.1, 8.2, 8.3]

File Needed: None
Completed Project File Name: *[your initials] Excel 8-9.xlsx*

Enter all data that you find important regarding your yard sale, listing your sales items in categories. Create a new workbook and save it as *[your initials] Excel 8-9*.

- When creating your class spreadsheet, you may want to add column headings such as "Unit Profit," "Resources Used per Unit Produced," "Resources Used," "Resources Available," "Units Produced," and "Total Profit."
- Add *SUMPRODUCT* formulas to the columns "Total Profit" and "Resources Used."
- Add appropriate range names to the worksheet.
- Enter the *Solver* parameters into the *Solver Parameters* dialog box.
- Create an *Answer, Sensitivity*, and *Limits* report.
- Save at least two scenarios, such as best and worst case.

Challenge Project 8-10

For this project, you use *Solver* to determine which location to visit for spring break.
[Student Learning Outcomes 8.3, 8.4, 8.5, 8.6]

File Needed: None
Completed Project File Name: *[your initials] Excel 8-10.xlsx*

Enter all data that you find important regarding a vacation, such as "Cost," "Revenue," "Spending Money," "Location," "Length of Stay," "Hotel Rating," "Amenities," and "Travel Time," on *Sheet1.* Save the workbook as *[your initials] Excel 8-10*.

- Add formulas to the key cells as you see fit.
- Add two scenarios using "Cost" as the changing cell.
- Create a scenario summary report.
- Select the data on *Sheet1* and create a *PivotTable* and a *PivotChart.*
- Change the calculations from *Sum* to *Average* or *Max* in the *PivotTable.*
- Insert a slicer using the "Locations" field. Select your two favorite destinations and compare their costs.
- Create a one-variable data table that uses "Cost" or "Revenue" as a column input cell.
- Create a two-variable data table that uses "Cost" and "Revenue" as input cells to determine the effect on your "Spending Money" while on vacation.

Recording and Editing Macros

CHAPTER OVERVIEW

Once you have become familiar with Excel, many tasks and commands in an Excel workbook become routine. Tasks that involve performing the same steps or entering the same label can often be handled with macros. A **macro** is a series of commands and keystrokes that automatically execute a command. In this chapter, you learn how to run and record a macro, how to edit a macro in the *Visual Basic Editor*, and how to create an Excel macro-enabled template.

STUDENT LEARNING OUTCOMES (SLOs)

After completing this chapter, you will be able to:

SLO 9.1 Enable and disable macros and run an existing macro (p. E9-493).

SLO 9.2 Record a new macro and save an Excel macro-enabled workbook (p. E9-495).

SLO 9.3 Assign a macro to a *Button* form control (p. E9-499).

SLO 9.4 Edit a macro in the Visual Basic Editor (VBE) (p. E9-501).

SLO 9.5 Record a macro with relative references (p. E9-507).

SLO 9.6 Save an Excel macro-enabled template (p. E9-508).

CASE STUDY

In the Pause & Practice projects in this chapter, you continue to work with an Excel workbook for the northern Minnesota resort business Paradise Lakes Resort (PLR). You run and record macros, assign them to buttons, and create macro-enabled templates.

Pause & Practice 9-1: Check macro security, run an existing macro, and record a new macro.

Pause & Practice 9-2: Assign a macro to a button and edit a macro.

Pause & Practice 9-3: Record a macro with relative references and save an Excel macro-enabled template.

Running a Macro

A macro is saved in an Excel macro-enabled workbook which has an *.xlsm* file name extension. When you open an Excel macro-enabled workbook, you will see a security message bar that informs you that macros are disabled. In order to run or edit a macro, you must enable them.

Macro Security

Because macros have become likely targets for viruses, malware (intentionally harmful programs), or malicious code, the default setting in the Excel *Trust Center* is set to disable all macros when a workbook is opened. You should enable macros only when you know they can be trusted.

You can check the macro security settings in the *Trust Center*, which is available from the *Options* command on the *File* tab. Alternatively, the *Developer* tab has a *Macro Security* button that you can use to open the *Macro Settings* pane in the *Trust Center*.

HOW TO: Display the Developer Tab and Check Macro Settings

1. Click the **Options** command [*File* tab].
   - The *Excel Options* window opens.
2. Click **Customize Ribbon** in the left pane.
3. Check the **Developer** box in the *Main Tabs* list.
4. Click **OK**.
5. Click the **Macro Security** button [*Developer* tab, *Code* group].
   - The *Trust Center* window opens to the *Macro Settings* pane (Figure 9-1).
6. If necessary, click to select **Disable all macros with notification**.
   - This setting ensures that you are notified prior to any macro running.
7. Click **OK** to close the *Trust Center*.
   - A workbook with macros opens with a security message bar.
   - The macros are not usable or editable.
   - Click **Enable Content** in the message bar to enable macros for each workbook.

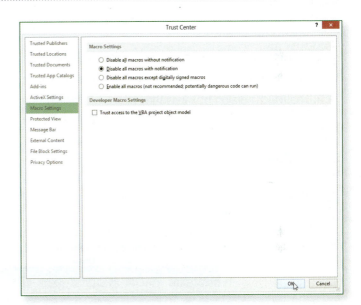

9-1 *Macro Settings* in the Trust Center

> ▶ **MORE INFO**
>
> The security warning bar does not open when you open a workbook with macros if you choose *Enable All Macros* in the *Trust Center*.

Run a Macro

Once macros are enabled, you can run or execute a macro to play out its commands. Common macros can include importing data, formatting cell contents, and applying filtering options.

Execute a macro by selecting the macro name in the *Macro* dialog box and clicking *Run*. Macros can be saved with keyboard shortcuts. If you know the shortcut, you can also run a macro by pressing its shortcut keys.

The *Macro* dialog box lists the names of all macros from all open workbooks. As long as a workbook is open, you can use its macros in any open workbook. In other words, you can execute a macro from *Workbook 2* in *Workbook 1* and vice versa as long as the workbooks are both open.

When a macro runs, it carries out the commands in the current workbook. After the macro is run, you can edit data as usual, if necessary.

Macro-related commands are in the *Code* group on the *Developer* tab. You can also carry out most macro commands from the *Macros* button on the *View* tab.

> ▶ **ANOTHER WAY**
> Click the **Macros** button on the *View* tab to open the *Macro* dialog box.

HOW TO: Run a Macro

1. Open the workbook.
2. Click **Enable Content** in the security bar (Figure 9-2).
3. Click the **Macros** button [*Developer* tab, *Code* group].
   - The *Macro* dialog box lists the names of existing macros.
   - The listed macros are from all open workbooks.
4. Select the macro name in the list (Figure 9-3).
5. Click **Run**.
   - The macro executes its commands in the worksheet.
   - The macro in Figure 9-3, for example, inserts the current date in cell A30 (Figure 9-4).

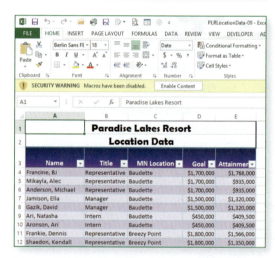

9-2 Security warning bar for a workbook with macros

9-4 The macro inserts the date in cell A30

9-3 *Macro* dialog box

Recording a Macro

Macros are small recorded programs that carry out routine, repetitive tasks. You would not record and save a macro for a one-time task. But if your manager asks you to always save your completed worksheets as PDF files, for example, you could record a macro that performs those steps automatically. Once you have done that, with the click of a button or a keyboard shortcut, you can save any file as a PDF quickly and automatically.

Instead of typing the code or instructions in a macro program, you record it. This means that as you perform all the actual steps in a worksheet, Excel encodes those actions for you. The code behind a macro is written in the programming language *Visual Basic for Applications*, often referred to as *VBA*. However, because you can "record" a macro, you don't need to know VBA to create a macro.

Macros are saved in a workbook. You can save them in your current workbook, in a new workbook, or in a special macros-only workbook such as the *Personal Macro* workbook. Some macros are general purpose macros and should be saved in a macros-only workbook. The *Personal Macro* workbook is this type of workbook. As long as this workbook is open, you can use its macros in any workbook. You must record a practice macro to the *Personal Macro* workbook to activate the file. Then, this file will be loaded in the background when you start Excel.

> ### ▶ MORE INFO
>
> The *Personal Macro* workbook is named *PERSONAL.XLSB* and is saved in the *XLSTART* folder for the current user. When it exists, it opens automatically as a hidden workbook when you start Excel so that its macros are always available.

Record a Macro

Almost any Excel command can be recorded in a macro. Before you begin to record a macro, you should practice what you want to do so that your actual steps while recording are error-free. For example, if you want to record a macro to open a company inventory workbook and insert a new total row, carry out the task you want to record once before you record the macro to be sure you know which folder and file name to select. A macro records every step and every keystroke, and it is very easy to record a macro with errors or unnecessary steps.

Once you know all the steps for your macro, you can start to record. When you record, you actually perform the commands or type the data that will be included in the macro. When you are finished, you click the **Stop Recording** button. To test your macro, delete data or undo the commands that you carried out during recording and run your macro.

By default, a macro is recorded with absolute references. The macro notes the actual cell location for each command or data entry task. There are no positioning commands included in the macro. In other words, if you type the company name in cell A32, the macro records that the company name should be entered in cell A32, no matter where the active cell is when you run that macro.

Macros must be named. The name must begin with a letter and cannot contain spaces or special characters. A macro may include a keyboard shortcut. The first key in a macro shortcut is always **Ctrl**. Many experienced macro writers recommend that you use **Ctrl+Shift+any alphabetic character** for a macro shortcut. They suggest this because if you do not include the **Shift** key as part of the shortcut, you will override common Windows or Excel commands. For example, if you use **Ctrl+P** as a macro shortcut, you override the *Print* command shortcut.

HOW TO: Record a Macro

1. Click the **Record Macro** button [*Developer* tab, *Code* group].

   - The *Record Macro* dialog box opens.
   - A default name displays.

2. In the *Macro name* box, type a name for the macro.

   - Begin the name with a letter.
   - Do not type spaces between words; you can separate words with an underscore.
   - If you use an invalid character in the name, a message box will alert you.

3. In the *Shortcut key* box, hold down **Shift** and type a letter.

   - A shortcut is optional.

4. For the *Store macro in* box, choose **This Workbook**.

   - Choose **Personal Macro Workbook** to create a macros-only workbook for your computer.

5. In the *Description* box, type an optional explanation (Figure 9-5).

   - The description is included as a comment in the VBA code.

6. Click **OK**.

   - Everything that you do is recorded in the macro.
   - The *Record Macro* button toggles to the *Stop Recording* button.

7. Complete each task for the macro.

   - Click a cell and enter data.
   - Select cells and give a command (Figure 9-6).
   - If you make an error, correct it as usual.

8. Click the **Stop Recording** button [*Developer* tab, *Code* group].

   - You can click the **Stop Recording** button in the *Status bar*.
   - The data and commands performed as you recorded the macro are part of the workbook.

9. Delete the data or undo commands that you completed while recording the macro.

10. Test the macro by running the macro.

9-5 Macro name, shortcut, and description

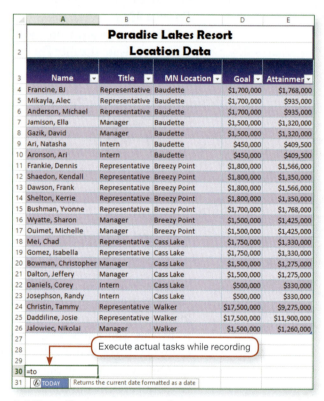

9-6 Recording macro commands to insert the current date in cell A30

> ### ANOTHER WAY
>
> There is a *Record Macro* button in the *Status bar*, next to the mode indicator. This button toggles to a *Stop Recording* button.

> ### MORE INFO
>
> If you need to change the shortcut key or comments in a recorded macro, click the **Options** button in the *Macro* dialog box.

Save an Excel Macro-Enabled Workbook

You can begin the process of recording macros in a regular Excel workbook. To save them, however, you must save the workbook as an Excel macro-enabled workbook. This format allows for the inclusion of the VBA modules where the macros are actually stored. If you try to save a workbook with macros as a regular Excel workbook, a message box, shown in Figure 9-7, reminds you that your VBA work cannot be saved in a regular workbook.

9-7 Macros can only be saved in macro-enabled workbooks

HOW TO: Save an Excel Macro-Enabled Workbook

1. Select **Save As** from the *File* tab.
2. Navigate to the desired folder location.
   - You can save Excel macro-enabled workbooks in any folder. However, Excel automatically saves this file type to a system folder for quick retrieval.
   - Excel automatically saves and stores the *Personal Macro* workbook in the *XLSTART* folder.
3. Type or edit the file name.
4. Click the **Save as type** drop-down arrow and choose **Excel Macro-Enabled Workbook** (Figure 9-8).
5. Click **Save**.

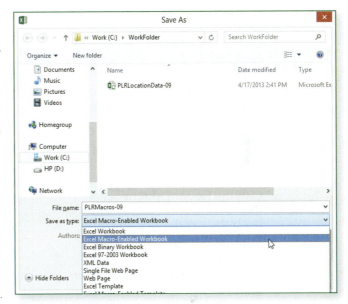

9-8 *Save As* dialog box

> ### MORE INFO
> Use Microsoft Help to learn more about the *PERSONAL.XLSB* workbook if you would like to build a library of macros.

PAUSE & PRACTICE: EXCEL 9-1

For this project, you open an Excel macro-enabled workbook for Paradise Lakes Resort. You enable the macros, run an existing macro to enter the current date, and record a new macro to enter the quarter name in cell A32.

File Needed: ***PLRLocationData-09.xlsm***
Completed Project File Name: ***[your initials] PP E9-1.xlsm***

1. Open the **PLRLocationData-09** workbook.

2. Click the **Enable Editing** button and then the **Enable Content** button in the security bar.

3. Display the *Developer* tab if necessary and check macro security.
   a. Click the **Options** command [*File* tab].
   b. Click **Customize Ribbon** in the left pane.
   c. Select the **Developer** check box in the *Main Tabs* list and click **OK**.
   d. Click the **Macro Security** button [*Developer* tab, *Code* group].
   e. Verify or click to select **Disable all macros with notification**.
   f. Click **OK**.

4. Save the workbook as an Excel macro-enabled workbook named *[your initials] PP E9-1*. Because the original workbook is an Excel macro-enabled workbook, the *Save As* command will suggest the same file type. If it doesn't, choose **Excel Macro-Enabled Workbook** from the *Save as type* list.

5. Run a macro.
   a. Click the **Macros** button [*Developer* tab, *Code* group] to open the *Macro* dialog box.
   b. Select **InsertDate** in the macros list (Figure 9-9). The description for the macro explains what it will do.
   c. Click **Run** to insert the current date in cell A30.

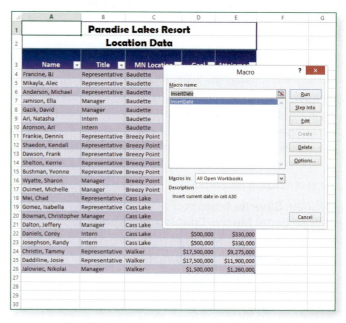

9-9 Select the macro to be run in the *Macro* dialog box

6. Record a macro.
   a. Click the **Record Macro** button [*Developer* tab, *Code* group] to open the *Record Macro* dialog box.
   b. In the *Macro name* box, type FirstQuarter.
   c. In the *Shortcut key* box, hold down **Shift** and type Q. The keyboard shortcut for the macro is **Ctrl+Shift+Q**.
   d. For the *Store macro in* box, choose **This Workbook**.
   e. In the *Description* box, type Display First Quarter in cell A32. (Figure 9-10).
   f. Click **OK** to begin recording.
   g. Click cell **A32**. This is the first step in the macro to make cell A32 active.
   h. In cell A32, type First Quarter and press **Enter**. This macro action enters the label and moves to cell A33 (Figure 9-11).
   i. Click the **Stop Recording** button [*Developer* tab, *Code* group].

7. Run a macro with a shortcut.
   a. Delete the contents of cell **A32** (the label that was entered as you recorded the macro).
   b. Press **Ctrl+Home** to move the cursor to cell **A1**.
   c. Press **Ctrl+Shift+Q** to run the macro. With absolute references, the macro inserts the quarter name in cell A32, because that address was recorded as part of the macro.

9-10 Name the macro and type an optional description in the *Record Macro* dialog box

8. Save and close the workbook (Figure 9-12).

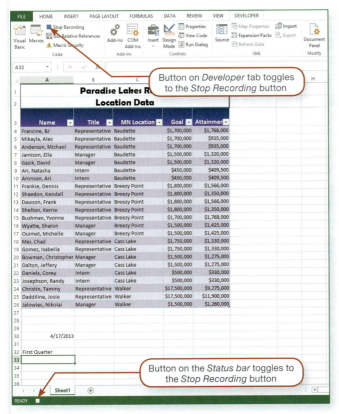

9-11 Type data and perform commands to record a macro

	A	B	C	D	E
1	**Paradise Lakes Resort**				
2	**Location Data**				
3	**Name**	**Title**	**MN Location**	**Goal**	**Attainmer**
4	Francine, BJ	Representative	Baudette	$1,700,000	$1,768,000
5	Mikayla, Alec	Representative	Baudette	$1,700,000	$935,000
6	Anderson, Michael	Representative	Baudette	$1,700,000	$935,000
7	Jamison, Ella	Manager	Baudette	$1,500,000	$1,320,000
8	Gazik, David	Manager	Baudette	$1,500,000	$1,320,000
9	Ari, Natasha	Intern	Baudette	$450,000	$409,500
10	Aronson, Ari	Intern	Baudette	$450,000	$409,500
11	Frankie, Dennis	Representative	Breezy Point	$1,800,000	$1,566,000
12	Shaedon, Kendall	Representative	Breezy Point	$1,800,000	$1,350,000
13	Dawson, Frank	Representative	Breezy Point	$1,800,000	$1,566,000
14	Shelton, Kerrie	Representative	Breezy Point	$1,800,000	$1,350,000
15	Bushman, Yvonne	Representative	Breezy Point	$1,700,000	$1,768,000
16	Wyatte, Sharon	Manager	Breezy Point	$1,500,000	$1,425,000
17	Ouimet, Michelle	Manager	Breezy Point	$1,500,000	$1,425,000
18	Mei, Chad	Representative	Cass Lake	$1,750,000	$1,330,000
19	Gomez, Isabella	Representative	Cass Lake	$1,750,000	$1,330,000
20	Bowman, Christopher	Manager	Cass Lake	$1,500,000	$1,275,000
21	Dalton, Jeffery	Manager	Cass Lake	$1,500,000	$1,275,000
22	Daniels, Corey	Intern	Cass Lake	$500,000	$330,000
23	Josephson, Randy	Intern	Cass Lake	$500,000	$330,000
24	Christin, Tammy	Representative	Walker	$17,500,000	$9,275,000
25	Daddiline, Josie	Representative	Walker	$17,500,000	$11,900,000
26	Jalowiec, Nikolai	Manager	Walker	$1,500,000	$1,260,000
27					
28					
29					
30	4/17/2013				
31					
32	First Quarter				
33					
34					
35					

9-12 PP E9-1 completed worksheet

SLO 9.3

Assigning a Macro to a Button

In *SLO 7.2: Creating and Using Forms*, you worked with form controls to insert a combo box control in a worksheet. The **Button** is a form control that is used to run a macro with a single click. To use a *Button*, you assign a macro to the control.

The *Button* form control is available from the *Insert Controls* button on the *Developer* tab [*Controls* group]. As soon as you draw this control in the worksheet, the *Assign Macro* dialog box opens so that you can select the macro you want to use.

> **ANOTHER WAY**
>
> In a workbook with macros, choose **Quick Access Toolbar** in *Excel Options*. Choose **Macros** from the *Choose commands from* list and add the macro name to the toolbar. Click the icon to run the macro from the toolbar.

HOW TO: Assign a Macro to a Button

1. Click the **Insert Controls** button [*Developer* tab, *Controls* group].
2. Click the **Button (Form Control)** command in the *Form Controls* category (Figure 9-13).

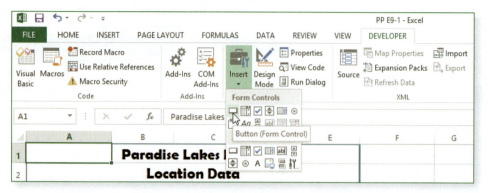

9-13 The *Button* form control is in the *Controls* group

3. Click and drag to draw a button in the worksheet and release the pointer.
   - The *Assign Macro* dialog box opens.
   - You can choose a macro from any open workbook.
4. Select the macro name you want to assign to the control (Figure 9-14).
   - You can draw a *Button* form control without assigning a macro and later assign the macro from its context-sensitive menu.
5. Click **OK**.
   - The button displays the default name *Button N,* where *N* is a number.
   - The button control is selected and displays selection handles.
6. Right-click the button and choose **Edit Text** from the menu. This will display a cursor in the button label text.
7. Delete the default text and type a label for the button.
8. Right-click the button and choose **Exit Edit Text** from the menu (Figure 9-15) or select a worksheet cell.

   - Resize the button by dragging a selection handle.
   - While selection handles are visible, point at a border to display a four-pointed arrow and drag the button to another location.
9. Click a worksheet cell to deselect the *Button* control.

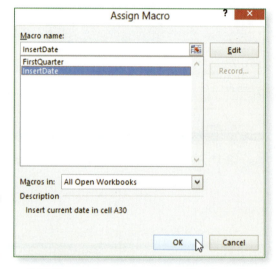

9-14 Macros from any open workbook are listed

9-15 Type a new label for a *Button* form control and exit editing

10. Click the **Button** form control to run the macro.
    - The cursor displays a hand with a pointing finger when it is ready to run the macro.
    - To select the form control without running the macro, right-click the control, and then click a border.
    - To delete a form control, right-click the control, click a border to close the menu, and press **Delete**.

SLO 9.4

Editing a Macro in the Visual Basic Editor (VBE)

Although you do not need to know Visual Basic for Applications (VBA) programming to record a macro, it is helpful when you want to edit a macro. If you have no VBA knowledge, you may find it necessary to delete a macro that isn't working properly and start over. However, with a bit of knowledge and practice, you will find it relatively straightforward to make minor changes in the Visual Basic Editor (VBE).

Visual Basic for Applications (VBA)

Visual Basic for Applications (VBA) is the programming language that underlies Excel macros. As you record a macro, Excel converts your keystrokes into VBA code. *Code* describes the specific programming commands required for an automatic task to run. Program and procedure are other names used for code. VBA is built on the following terms and assumptions.

- *Objects*: An object model is a map of Excel and its abilities. For example, *Application, Workbook, Sheet,* and *PivotChart* are all objects.
- *Properties and Methods*: Adjusting an object's properties or calling its methods allows you to control the object. A property is something that an object contains. For example, a worksheet object contains properties like the worksheet's name, scroll area, and protection. *Calling methods* is a phrase that means the code will cause some action. For example, a workbook contains an open action to view a different workbook. In this example, the workbook is the object and the action of opening another workbook is the method.
- *Collections*: The plural version of an object is a collection. A workbook is an object while workbooks are a collection. Collections are used when you need to apply an action to multiple items. For example, all workbooks must be renamed with PLR as the first three characters.

> **MORE INFO**
>
> To learn more about objects and programming in VBA, review the reference link for VBA at http://msdn.microsoft.com/en-us/library/office/jj236959(v=office.15).

Edit VBA Code

The *Visual Basic Editor (VBE)* is an application that runs in a window separate from Excel. It opens when you choose the command to edit a macro from the *Macro* dialog box or when you click the *Visual Basic* button on the *Developer* tab.

> **ANOTHER WAY**
>
> Open the *VBE* window with the keyboard shortcut **Alt+F11**.

The VBE program has three main panes. They are the *Code* window, the *Project Explorer* pane, and the *Properties* window. Figure 9-16 shows a macro with these three panes visible. These panes are displayed from the *View* menu in the *Visual Basic Editor* program.

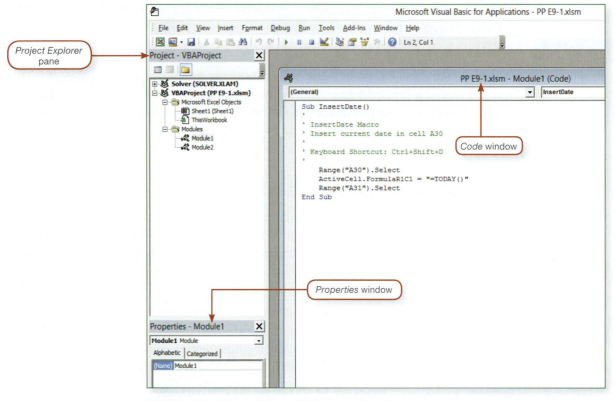

9-16 The Visual Basic Editor with *Code* window, *Project Explorer pane*, and *Properties* window

To edit the actions of your macro, you can make changes in the *Code* window. In Figure 9-16, for example, note that you could change the macro shortcut comment by editing that line in the code window. If you want to insert the data in cell A32 instead of A30, you could edit that line in the code as well as the line that shows where the cursor ends.

While editing code, be careful about punctuation, spacing, and special characters. These may be part of the code. Some errors are identified immediately. When this happens, the line is highlighted in red, as shown in Figure 9-17, and a message box may open. Troubleshooting these types of errors often requires that you know some VBA.

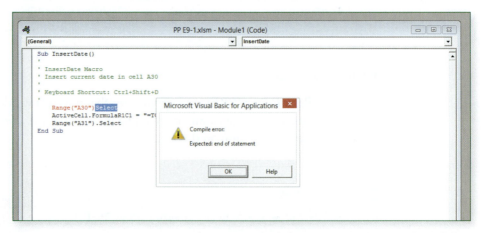

9-17 Coding error in the Visual Basic Editor

Most macros include similar lines and coding so that you can become familiar with them as you analyze lines. For instance, you may see the following in many macros:

- *Sub* means *sub procedure*. A sub procedure macro is one that runs from the workbook or from another macro. The macro name is displayed immediately after *Sub* and the name is followed by a set of parentheses. Sub procedure macros end with *End Sub*.
- Each line preceded by an apostrophe and shown in green is a *comment*. Comment lines are not part of the code. They describe the code, show the shortcut, or separate sections of the macro. The comments in Figures 9-16 and 9-17 were entered automatically as the macro was recorded. If you write a macro in the Visual Basic Editor, you can enter your own comments.
- Lines of text shown in black between *Sub* and *End Sub* are *coding* statements. These are Visual Basic commands and properties that control the macro actions.

A macro is stored in a *module*. In VBA, a module is a list of declarations and procedures. When macros are in the same module, they are separated by a solid border. Macros can also be in separate modules. When you select a macro in the *Macro* window to be edited, the module is automatically selected. Alternatively, you can select a module from the *Project Explorer* pane.

HOW TO: Edit Macro Code in the VBE

1. Click the **Macros** button [*Developer* tab, *Code* group].
   - Macro names are listed in the *Macro* dialog box.
2. Select the name of the macro you want to edit.
3. Click **Edit**.
   - The *Visual Basic Editor* program opens.
   - If the *Code* window is not displayed, choose **Code** from the *View* menu.
   - You can display or hide the *Project Explorer* or the *Properties Window* from the *View* menu.
4. Edit each line as needed (Figure 9-18).
   - You can add or delete code if you know VBA programming commands.
5. Click the **Close** button in the top right corner of the *VBE* window to return to the worksheet.
   - You can also click the **View Microsoft Excel** button at the left of the toolbar. However, this leaves the VBE program open in the background.
   - You can press **Alt+F11** to return to the workbook.
6. Delete the data or undo commands from the recording.
7. Run the macro to test it.
8. Save and close the workbook.
   - The revised macro is saved with the workbook.

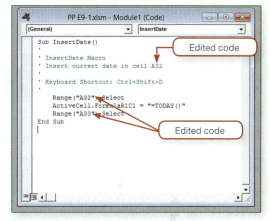

9-18 Edit code lines in the Visual Basic Editor

Macro Issues

In addition to editing a macro, there are some common issues that arise from running or recording a macro. *Syntax errors* are the messages that pop up during a macro that specify code that Visual Basic doesn't recognize. These errors can occur from simple typos in the code or from incorrectly used statements. You can check the VBE to determine the line of code that is causing the issue.

Once you have more experience in VBA, fixing faulty lines of code becomes easier. For additional information on a specific error, select the code in question in the VBE and press **F1**. Review this web site for information regarding specific syntax errors http://msdn.microsoft.com/en-us/library/office/jj692802.aspx. The following table describes common problems that prohibit a macro from running successfully and explains how to correct such issues:

Common Macro Issues and Solutions

Macro Issues	Solutions
Macros are automatically disabled without notification when the workbook is open.	Select **Disable all macros with notification** from the *Macro Security* button [*Developer* tab, *Code* group].
Another macro is currently running.	Stop the current macro before running or recording the next macro.
The worksheet is in *Edit* mode.	Press **Enter** so the cursor disappears, and then run or record a macro.
The worksheet tab is being renamed.	Press **Enter** so the cursor disappears, and then run or record a macro.
The workbook is protected.	Unprotect the workbook before running or recording a macro.
A dialog box is open.	Close the dialog box, and then run or record a macro.

PAUSE & PRACTICE: EXCEL 9-2

For this project, you assign a macro to a button in the worksheet for Paradise Lakes Resort. You edit the *InsertDate* macro from the previous exercise to relocate the date result to a different cell. Finally, you test the macro using the button.

File Needed: *[your initials] PP E9-1.xlsm*
Completed Project File Name: *[your initials] PP E9-2.xlsm*

1. Start Excel and Display the *Developer* tab if necessary.

2. In the *Trust Center,* set macro security to **Disable all macros with notification**.

3. Open the *[your initials] PP E9-1* workbook.

4. Click **Enable Content** in the security bar.

5. Save the workbook as an Excel macro-enabled workbook named *[your initials] PP E9-2*.

6. Assign a macro to a *Button* form control.
   a. Click the **Insert Controls** button [*Developer* tab, *Controls* group].
   b. Click the **Button (Form Control)** command in the *Form Controls* category.
   c. Click and drag to draw a button that covers cells **G2:H2**.
   d. In the *Assign Macro* dialog box, select **InsertDate** and click **OK**. The button is placed as an object in the worksheet (Figure 9-19).
   e. Right-click the button and choose **Edit Text**.
   f. Delete the default text and type Insert Date as the caption or label for the button.

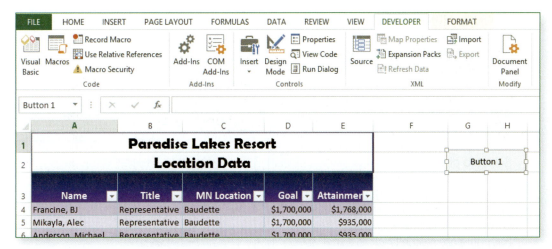

9-19 *Button* form control is inserted as an object

g. Right-click the button and choose **Exit Edit Text** from the menu (Figure 9-20).

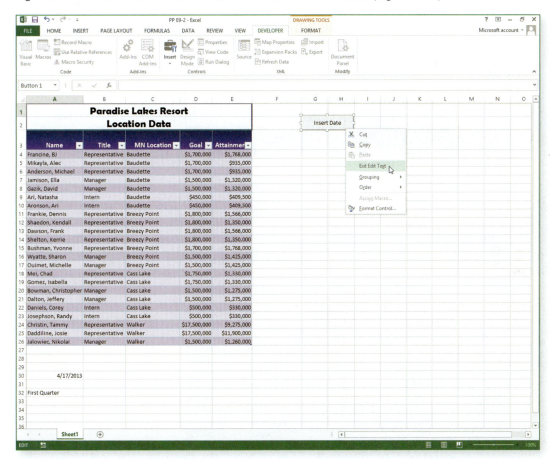

9-20 End editing after new label is typed

h. Click a worksheet cell to deselect the *Button* control.
i. Right-click the **Button** form control and choose **Format Control**.
j. On the *Font* tab, select **Bold Italic** as the *Font style* and click **OK**.
k. Click a worksheet cell to deselect the *Button* control.

7. Edit a macro in the Visual Basic Editor.
   a. Click the **Macros** button [*Developer* tab, *Code* group].
   b. Select **InsertDate** in the list of macro names.
   c. Click **Edit** to open the *Visual Basic Editor* program.
   d. If the *Code* window is not displayed, choose **Code** from the *View* menu.
   e. Click to place an insertion point after **A31** in the comment line "Insert current date in cell A31".
   f. Edit the first code line *Range("A30")*. Select to display A31.
   g. Edit the last line *Range("A31")*. Edit to display A32 (Figure 9-21).
   h. Click the **Close** button in the top-right corner of the VBE window. You automatically switch back to Excel view.

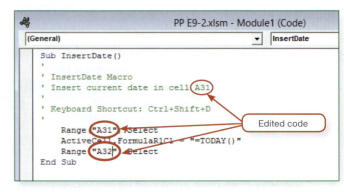

8. Run a macro from a *Button* form control.
   a. Delete the contents of cell **A30** and press **Ctrl+Home**.

9-21 Edit code as needed

   b. Click the **Insert Date** button control. The date is inserted in cell A31 and the active cell is cell A32.

9. Save and close the workbook (Figure 9-22).

9-22 PP E9-2 completed worksheet

Recording a Macro with Relative References

As you record a macro, each step you perform is written as code in the Visual Basic Editor. As you saw in the previous SLO, the code includes cell addresses. When a macro uses absolute references, specific cell references are part of the code. When you run a macro that was recorded with absolute references, your insertion point can be anywhere in the worksheet. The macro will place the data or execute the command at the cell address indicated in the code.

Alternatively, you can record a macro with relative references. In this type of macro, all of your keyboard cursor movement commands are recorded. If you begin by moving the active cell two columns to the right, the macro will include those commands in the code. In Figure 9-23, you can see positioning commands in the code line *ActiveCell.Offset(3,0)*. The syntax is ***ActiveCell.Offset(RowOffset,ColumnOffset)***. This command moves the insertion point down three times in the same column. For example, if you begin with A1 as the active cell, the macro would move the active cell to A4. If you begin with B1 as the active cell, the macro would move to B4, and so on.

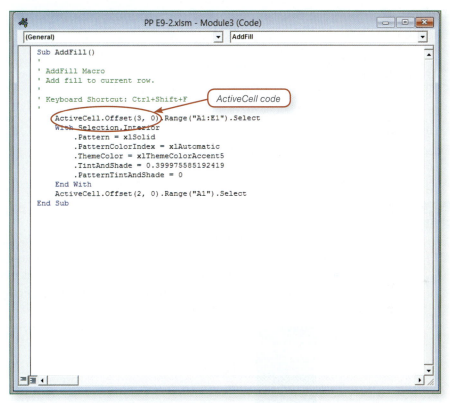

9-23 **Macro recorded with relative references includes positioning commands**

When you run a macro that was recorded with relative references, you must position the active cell at the presumed starting location, because the macro executes its commands relative to that cell.

The ***Use Relative References*** button is located in the *Code* group on the *Developer* tab. It is off or inactive by default.

HOW TO: Record a Macro with Relative References

1. Position the active cell at the beginning location for the commands.
2. Click **Use Relative References** [*Developer* tab, *Code* group].
   - The button displays green shading when it is active (Figure 9-24).
   - The button will remain active until you click to turn it off.

9-24 *Use Relative References* **is enabled**

3. Click the **Record Macro** button [*Developer* tab, *Code* group].

4. In the *Macro name* box, type a name for the macro.
   - Begin the name with a letter and do not use spaces between words.

5. In the *Shortcut key* box, hold down **Shift** and type a letter.
   - A shortcut is optional.

6. For the *Store macro in* box, choose **This Workbook**.
   - Choose **Personal Macro Workbook** to create a macros-only workbook for your computer.

7. In the *Description* box, type an optional explanation.
   - The description appears as a comment in the Visual Basic Editor.

8. Click **OK**.
   - The *Record Macro* button toggles to the *Stop Recording* button.
   - All keyboard positioning commands are recorded.
   - Position the cursor when necessary using keyboard arrow keys or keyboard shortcuts.

9. Complete each task for the macro.
   - Enter and format data.
   - Select cells and give commands.
   - Use the keyboard to position the active cell if necessary.

10. Click the **Stop Recording** button [*Developer* tab, *Code* group].

11. Delete data or undo commands that were entered as the macro was recorded.

12. Save the workbook.
    - Select the starting cell before running the macro.

Saving an Excel Macro-Enabled Template

An ***Excel macro-enabled template*** is an Excel template that includes a macro. An Excel macro-enabled template has an ***.xltm*** file name extension and is automatically saved in the default templates folder for your computer. You can save an Excel macro-enabled template in any folder, but its name will appear in the *Personal* group in *Backstage* view for the *New* command when it is stored in the default folder (Figure 9-25).

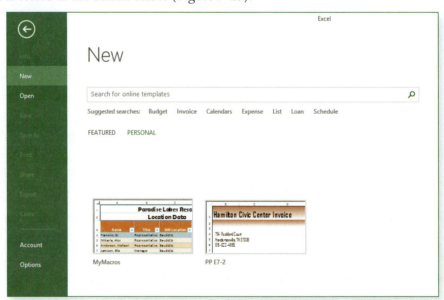

9-25 Excel macro-enabled templates appear in the *Personal* group

Templates, because they are model workbooks, often do include macros. For example, if you create a weekly inventory worksheet from a template, that template might include a macro to copy the sheet in preparation for the following week.

Recording a macro in a template is no different from recording one in a regular workbook. When you create a workbook from an Excel macro-enabled template, you must click **Enable Content** in the *Security Notice* dialog box if it opens. If you have recently used an Excel macro-enabled template, you will see the usual security warning bar and must click **Enable Content** there.

HOW TO: Save an Excel Macro-Enabled Template

1. Enter data and formatting for the template.
   - Include any labels, formatting, and descriptions necessary.
2. Record and test macros.
   - Include any required macros and link them to buttons as desired.
3. Delete data and undo commands that were entered from macros that were recorded.
4. Choose **Save As** from the *File* tab.
5. Navigate to any available folder.
   - The folder will update to the default macros folder for your computer when you choose the file type.
6. Type the file name for the macro-enabled template.
7. Choose **Excel Macro-Enabled Template** from the *Save as type* list (Figure 9-26).
8. Note the default folder location or choose the student file folder.
9. Click **Save**.

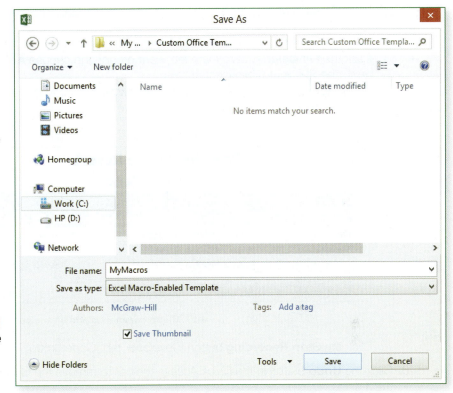

9-26 Excel macro-enabled templates are saved in the default templates folder

PAUSE & PRACTICE: EXCEL 9-3

For this project, you record a macro with relative references to apply customized shading to rows to improve readability in the Paradise Lakes Resort worksheet. You then save the workbook as an Excel macro-enabled template to use on future PLR worksheets.

File Needed: *[your initials] PP E9-2.xlsm*
Completed Project File Names: *[your initials] PP E9-3.xltm* and *[your initials] PP E9-3.xlsm*

1. Open the *[your initials] PP E9-2* workbook.

2. Click **Enable Content** in the security bar.

3. Display the *Developer* tab if necessary.

4. In the *Trust Center*, set macro security to **Disable all macros with notification**.

5. Record a macro with relative references.
   a. Click cell **A4** to activate the cell where the macro will start its commands.
   b. Click **Use Relative References** [*Developer* tab, *Code* group].
   c. Click the **Record Macro** button [*Developer* tab, *Code* group].
   d. In the *Macro name* box, type AddFill.
   e. In the *Shortcut key* box, hold down **Shift** and type F.
   f. For the *Store macro in* box, choose **This Workbook**.
   g. In the *Description* box, type Add fill to row. and click **OK**. All of your keyboard commands will be recorded.
   h. Hold down **Shift** and press the **right arrow** four times to select cells **A4:E4**.
   i. Click the **Fill Color** arrow [*Home* tab, *Font* group] and choose **Aqua, Accent 5, Lighter 80%** to apply the fill color to the selected cells.
   j. Press **Home** and then press the **down arrow** two times to position the cursor in cell **A6**. The cursor is in position to apply fill to another row (Figure 9-27).

9-27 Macro commands add fill and position active cell

    k. Click the **Stop Recording** button [*Developer* tab, *Code* group].

6. Click the **Undo** button in the *Quick Access* toolbar to remove the fill that you applied as you recorded the macro.

7. Click cell **A4** to position the cursor for the start of the macro.

8. Press **Ctrl+Shift+F** to test the macro.

9. Press **Ctrl+Shift+F** to run the macro again in row 6.

10. Select cells **E4:E26** and delete the contents. The template will not include the sales attained by each employee.

11. Press **Ctrl+Home** (Figure 9-28).

12. Save the workbook as an Excel macro-enabled template.
    a. Choose **Save As** from the *File* tab.
    b. Navigate to your student data folder. Excel defaults to a system folder that can be difficult to locate after the save process.

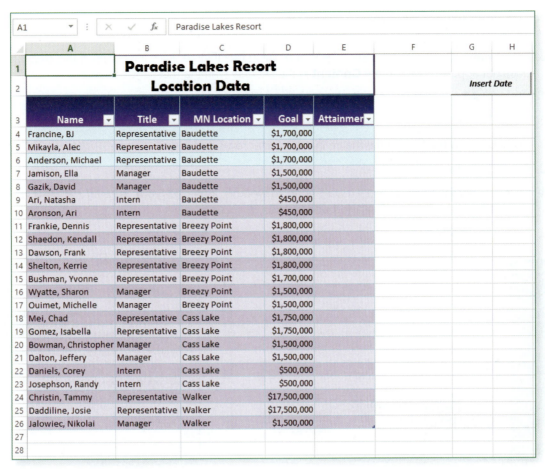

	Paradise Lakes Resort Location Data						Insert Date
Name	Title	MN Location	Goal	Attainmer			
Francine, BJ	Representative	Baudette	$1,700,000				
Mikayla, Alec	Representative	Baudette	$1,700,000				
Anderson, Michael	Representative	Baudette	$1,700,000				
Jamison, Ella	Manager	Baudette	$1,500,000				
Gazik, David	Manager	Baudette	$1,500,000				
Ari, Natasha	Intern	Baudette	$450,000				
Aronson, Ari	Intern	Baudette	$450,000				
Frankie, Dennis	Representative	Breezy Point	$1,800,000				
Shaedon, Kendall	Representative	Breezy Point	$1,800,000				
Dawson, Frank	Representative	Breezy Point	$1,800,000				
Shelton, Kerrie	Representative	Breezy Point	$1,800,000				
Bushman, Yvonne	Representative	Breezy Point	$1,700,000				
Wyatte, Sharon	Manager	Breezy Point	$1,500,000				
Ouimet, Michelle	Manager	Breezy Point	$1,500,000				
Mei, Chad	Representative	Cass Lake	$1,750,000				
Gomez, Isabella	Representative	Cass Lake	$1,750,000				
Bowman, Christopher	Manager	Cass Lake	$1,500,000				
Dalton, Jeffery	Manager	Cass Lake	$1,500,000				
Daniels, Corey	Intern	Cass Lake	$500,000				
Josephson, Randy	Intern	Cass Lake	$500,000				
Christin, Tammy	Representative	Walker	$17,500,000				
Daddiline, Josie	Representative	Walker	$17,500,000				
Jalowiec, Nikolai	Manager	Walker	$1,500,000				

9-28 Template includes data and macros

c. Type *[your initials] PP E9-3* as the file name for the macro-enabled template. This file will have an *.xltm* extension.

d. Choose **Excel Macro-Enabled Template** from the *Save as type* list (Figure 9-29).

e. You may need to navigate back to the student file folder where **[your initials] PP E9-3** is located.

f. Click **Save** to save the template.

13. Close the workbook.

14. Click **New** on the *File* tab and click **Personal**.

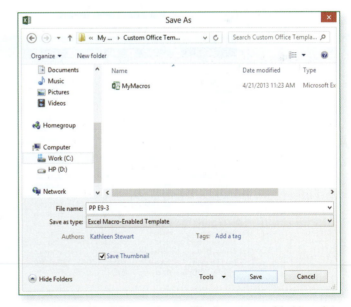

9-29 Workbook is saved as an Excel macro-enabled template

15. Click **[your initials] PP E9-3** in the *Personal* category (Figure 9-30) to create a workbook from the template. If you saved your template elsewhere, double-click the file in its current location.

16. Click **Enable Content** in the *Security Notice* dialog box (Figure 9-31) if it opens. If this dialog box does not appear, click **Enable Content** in the security warning message bar.

17. Click cell **A8** to run the macro.

18. Press **Ctrl+Shift+F**.

19. Press **Ctrl+Shift+F** to run the macro in every other row up to row 26 (Figure 9-32).

20. Press **Ctrl+Home**.

21. Save the workbook as an Excel macro-enabled workbook named **[your initials] PP E9-3** in your student file folder location for saving workbooks.

22. Close the workbook.

9-30 Templates in the default folder are listed in *Personal* category

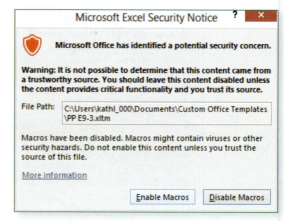

9-31 Macros in a template must be enabled to be used

9-32 PP E9-3 completed workbook

Chapter Summary

9.1 Enable and disable macros and run an existing macro (p. E9-493).

- A **macro** is a series of recorded commands saved in a workbook in **Visual Basic for Applications (VBA)**.
- Macros must be saved in an Excel macro-enabled workbook that has a **.xlsm** file name extension.
- Because macros may hide viruses and troublesome code, you should set the *Trust Center* to disable macros as a workbook is opened.
- When an Excel macro-enabled workbook is opened, the security warning bar includes a command to **Enable Content**. Macros must be enabled to be run.
- From the *Macros* button on the *Developer* tab, you can open the *Macro* dialog box and see the names of existing macros for all open workbooks.
- Select a macro name in the *Macro* dialog box and click **Run** to execute the macro commands.
- When a macro includes a keyboard shortcut, you can run a macro by pressing the appropriate keys.

9.2 Record a new macro and save an Excel macro-enabled workbook (p. E9-495).

- To record a macro, you perform the steps and they are converted to code automatically.
- Click the **Record Macro** button on the *Developer* tab to open the *Record Macro* dialog box.
- Enter a name for the macro and an optional shortcut. You can also type a description.
- Macros are stored in workbooks, and you can choose the current workbook, another open workbook, or the *Personal* macro workbook.
- After you click **OK** in the *Record Macro* dialog box, commands and keystrokes are recorded as part of the macro.
- Click the **Stop Recording** button in the *Developer* tab when you complete the last command or data entry for the macro.
- There is a *Record Macro* button in the *Status bar* which toggles to the *Stop Recording*

button so that you need not display the *Developer* tab to record a macro.
- Macros must be saved in Excel macro-enabled workbooks, selected in the *Save As* dialog box as the *Save as* type.

9.3 Assign a macro to a *Button* form control (p. E9-499).

- The **Button** form control is used to run a macro with a single click.
- The *Button* form control is part of the *Insert Controls* button choices [*Developer* tab, *Form Controls* group].
- Draw the *Button* control as an object in a worksheet.
- The *Assign Macro* dialog box opens as soon as you release the pointer button.
- You can assign a macro from any open workbook.
- To run a macro from a *Button* control, click the button in the worksheet.
- To edit or format a *Button* form control, right-click it and choose a command from the menu.

9.4 Edit a macro in the Visual Basic Editor (VBE) (p. E9-501).

- The **Visual Basic Editor (VBE)** is a separate application. It runs in its own window.
- Open the Visual Basic Editor by clicking the **Visual Basic** button on the *Developer* tab or pressing **Alt+F11**. You can also choose a macro name in the *Macro* dialog box and click **Edit** to open the Visual Basic Editor.
- The Visual Basic Editor has three panes: the *Code* window, the *Project Explorer* pane, and the *Properties* window.
- The *Code* window displays coding statements and properties for each command in the macro.
- The *Code* window may also display comment lines which are preceded by an apostrophe and are shown in green.
- For many simple changes, you can edit the code in the *Code* window. For more complex edits, you may need to know **Visual Basic for Applications (VBA)**.
- After editing the code, return to the Excel workbook. Changes made in the Visual Basic Editor are saved when you save the workbook.

9.5 Record a macro with relative references (p. E9-507).

- By default, a macro is recorded with the cell address (absolute references) for each command.
- The active cell can be positioned anywhere in the worksheet when you run a macro recorded with absolute references.
- You can record a macro with relative references by clicking the **Use Relative References** button in the *Code* group on the *Developer* tab.
- For a macro that was recorded with relative references, you must activate a cell before running the macro.
- In the Visual Basic Editor *Code* window for a macro with relative references, you can view and edit the positioning commands.

9.6 Save an Excel macro-enabled template (p. E9-508).

- An Excel template can include macros.
- A template with macros must be saved as an Excel macro-enabled template with an *.xltm* extension.
- The *Save As* dialog box includes **Excel Macro-Enabled Template** as a file type.
- Macro-enabled templates are saved, by default, in the same folder location as Excel workbook templates.
- Excel macro-enabled templates appear in the *Personal* category for the *New* command in *Backstage* view when they are saved in the default templates folder.

Check for Understanding

In the **Online Learning Center** for this text (www.mhhe.com/office2013inpractice), there are a variety of resources that can be used to review the concepts covered in this chapter.

The following Online Learning Resources are available in the Online Learning Center:

- Multiple choice questions
- Short answer questions
- Matching exercises

Guided Project 9-1

The Boyd Air organization is requesting managers to automate zoom, add *AutoFilter* buttons, and insert a total row using a macro to the following workbook.
[Student Learning Outcomes 9.1, 9.2, 9.3]

File Needed: ***FlightSchedule-09.xlsx***
Completed Project File Name: ***[your initials] Excel 9-1.xlsm***

Skills Covered in This Project

- Display the *Developer* tab.
- Adjust macro security.
- Record a macro.
- Create a *Button* form control.
- Resize the *Button* form control.

- Adjust the *Button* form control properties.
- Assign a macro to a *Button* form control.
- Save the file as an Excel macro-enabled workbook.

1. Open the ***FlightSchedule-09*** workbook from your student data files folder.

2. Click **Enable Content** in the security bar if necessary.

3. Display the *Developer* tab if necessary and check macro security.
   a. Click the **Options** command [*File* tab].
   b. Click **Customize Ribbon** in the left pane.
   c. Select the **Developer** check box in the *Main Tabs* list and click **OK**.
   d. Click the **Macro Security** button [*Developer* tab, *Code* group].
   e. Verify or click to select **Disable all macros with notification**.
   f. Click **OK**.

4. Save the workbook as an Excel macro-enabled workbook named ***[your initials] Excel 9-1***. Choose **Excel Macro-Enabled Workbook** from the *Save as type* list and place in your student file folder.

5. Record a macro.
   a. Verify that the *Use Relative References* option is off [*Developer* tab, *Code* group].
   b. Click the **Record Macro** button [*Developer* tab, *Code* group] to open the *Record Macro* dialog box.
   c. In the *Macro name* box, type Filter_Totals.
   d. In the *Shortcut key* box, hold down **Shift** and type F. The keyboard shortcut for the macro is **Ctrl+Shift+F**.
   e. For the *Store macro in* box, choose **This Workbook**.
   f. In the *Description* box, type Changes the zoom to 115%, adds filter buttons, and inserts a total row to the data. (Figure 9-33).

9-33 *Filter_Totals* macro details

g. Click **OK** to begin recording.

h. Change the viewing magnification to **115%**, add **AutoFilter** buttons to the headings in row 4 by formatting **A4:H11** as **Table Style Medium 6**, and add a **Total Row** option [*Table Tools Design* tab, *Table Style Options* group].

i. Click the **Stop Recording** button [*Developer* tab, *Code* group].

6. Assign a macro to a *Button* form control.

   a. Click the **Insert Controls** button [*Developer* tab, *Controls* group].

   b. Click the **Button (Form Control)** command in the *Form Controls* category.

   c. Click and drag to draw a button that covers cells **A14:A15**.

   d. In the *Assign Macro* dialog box, select **Filter_Totals** and click **OK** (Figure 9-34). The button is placed as an object in the worksheet.

   e. Right-click the button and choose **Edit Text**.

   f. Delete the default text and type Filter and Total as the caption or label for the button.

   g. Click a worksheet cell to deselect the *Button* control.

9-34 *Assign Macro* dialog box

7. Resize and adjust properties of the *Button* form control.

   a. Right-click the button, and click and drag a selection handle if resizing is needed.

   b. Alter the properties of the control so that the control doesn't move or change size when the worksheet is adjusted. *(Hint: Right-click the control, choose* Format control, *and then select the* Don't move or size with cells *radio button on the* Properties *tab.)*

   c. Choose the **OK** button.

8. Run a macro from a *Button* form control.

   a. Decrease the view to **100%**, deselect the **Total Row** *Table Style Option,* convert the table to a normal range, and press **Ctrl+Home**.

   b. Click the **Filter and Total** button control. The view is increased to 115%, *AutoFilter* buttons are added to row 4, and a total row is added to row 12.

9. Save and close the workbook (Figure 9-35).

	A	B	C	D	E	F	G	H
1			**Boyd Air**					
2			**Flight Schedule**					
3								
4	Flight Number ▼	Source ▼	Destination ▼	Arrival Time ▼	Departure Time ▼	Statu ▼	Capacit ▼	Passenger ▼
5	BD 1234	Chicago, IL	Green Bay, WI	10:00:00 AM	12:30:00 PM	Delayed	Not Full	80
6	BD 2213	Chicago, IL	Orlando, FL	6:30:00 AM	7:00:00 AM	Delayed	Full	90
7	BD 6578	Fargo, ND	St. Louis, MO	8:00:00 AM	9:30:00 AM	On Time	Not Full	63
8	BD 1345	Minneapolis, MN	Houston, TX	4:45:00 PM	7:00:00 PM	On Time	Full	90
9	BD 2345	Minneapolis, MN	Chicago, IL	8:00:00 AM	9:30:00 AM	On Time	Full	90
10	BD 980	Minneapolis, MN	Fargo, ND	12:30:00 PM	2:00:00 PM	On Time	Not Full	35
11	BD 4567	Orlando, FL	Minneapolis, MN	9:00:00 PM	10:30:00 PM	On Time	Full	75
12	Total							523
13								
14								
15	Filters and Totals							

9-35 **Excel 8-1 completed worksheet**

Guided Project 9-2

Eller Software Services is requesting management to automate advanced filtering, apply formatting, and clear advanced filtering data with macros in the client information file provided.
[Student Learning Outcomes 9.1, 9.2, 9.3, 9.4, 9.5, 9.6]

File Needed: **Clients-09.xlsx**
Completed Project File Names: **[your initials] Excel 9-2.xlsm** and **[your initials] Excel 9-2.xltm**

Skills Covered in This Project

- Display the *Developer* tab.
- Adjust macro security.
- Record a macro.
- Create a *Button* form control.
- Resize the *Button* form control.
- Adjust the *Button* form control properties.
- Assign a macro to a *Button* form control.

- Save the file as an Excel macro-enabled workbook.
- Record a macro with relative cell references.
- Edit a macro in the Visual Basic Editor (VBE).
- Save the workbook as an Excel macro-enabled template.

1. Open the **Clients-09** workbook from your student data files folder.

2. Save the workbook as an Excel macro-enabled workbook named **[your initials] Excel 9-2**. Choose **Excel Macro-Enabled Workbook** from the *Save as type* list and place in your student file folder.

3. Display the *Developer* tab if necessary and check macro security.
   a. Click the **Options** command [*File* tab].
   b. Click **Customize Ribbon** in the left pane.
   c. Select the **Developer** check box in the *Main Tabs* list and click **OK**.
   d. Click the **Macro Security** button [*Developer* tab, *Code* group].
   e. Verify or click to select **Disable all macros with notification**.
   f. Click **OK**.

4. Record a macro with relative references.
   a. Click cell **A9** to activate the cell where the macro will start its commands.
   b. Click **Use Relative References** [*Developer* tab, *Code* group].
   c. Click the **Record Macro** button [*Developer* tab, *Code* group].
   d. In the *Macro name* box, type AddFill.
   e. In the *Shortcut key* box, hold down **Shift** and type L.
   f. For the *Store macro in* box, choose **This Workbook**.
   g. In the *Description* box, type Add fill to row. and click **OK**. All of your keyboard commands will be recorded.
   h. Hold down **Shift** and press the **right arrow** eight times to select cells **A9:I9**.
   i. Click the **Fill Color** arrow [*Home* tab, *Font* group] and choose **Red, Accent 6, Lighter 80%** to apply the fill color to the selected cells.
   j. Press **Home** and then press the **down arrow** two times to position the active cell in **A11**. The active cell is in position to apply fill to another row (Figure 9-36).
   k. Click the **Stop Recording** button [*Developer* tab, *Code* group].

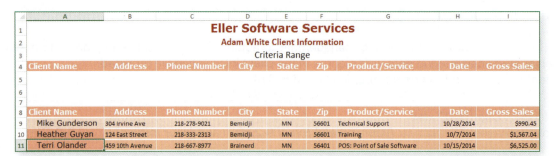

	A	B	C	D	E	F	G	H	I

Eller Software Services
Adam White Client Information
Criteria Range

Client Name	Address	Phone Number	City	State	Zip	Product/Service	Date	Gross Sales
Client Name	Address	Phone Number	City	State	Zip	Product/Service	Date	Gross Sales
Mike Gunderson	304 Irvine Ave	218-278-9021	Bemidji	MN	56601	Technical Support	10/28/2014	$990.45
Heather Guyan	124 East Street	218-333-2313	Bemidji	MN	56601	Training	10/7/2014	$1,567.04
Terri Olander	459 10th Avenue	218-667-8977	Brainerd	MN	56401	POS: Point of Sale Software	10/15/2014	$6,525.00

9-36 Macro commands add fill and position active cell

5. Click the **Undo** button in the *Quick Access* toolbar to remove the fill that you applied as you recorded the macro.

6. Click cell **A9** to position the cursor for the start of the macro.

7. Press **Ctrl+Shift+L** to test the macro.

8. Press **Ctrl+Shift+L** to run the macro again in row **11**. Continue this process through row **17** (Figure 9-37).

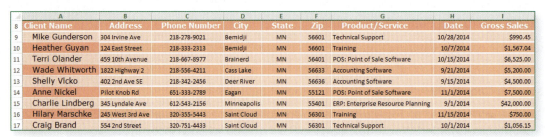

Client Name	Address	Phone Number	City	State	Zip	Product/Service	Date	Gross Sales
Mike Gunderson	304 Irvine Ave	218-278-9021	Bemidji	MN	56601	Technical Support	10/28/2014	$990.45
Heather Guyan	124 East Street	218-333-2313	Bemidji	MN	56601	Training	10/7/2014	$1,567.04
Terri Olander	459 10th Avenue	218-667-8977	Brainerd	MN	56401	POS: Point of Sale Software	10/15/2014	$6,525.00
Wade Whitworth	1822 Highway 2	218-556-4211	Cass Lake	MN	56633	Accounting Software	9/21/2014	$5,200.00
Shelly Vicko	402 2nd Ave SE	218-342-2456	Deer River	MN	56636	Accounting Software	9/15/2014	$4,500.00
Anne Nickel	Pilot Knob Rd	651-333-2789	Eagan	MN	55121	POS: Point of Sale Software	11/1/2014	$7,500.00
Charlie Lindberg	345 Lyndale Ave	612-543-2156	Minneapolis	MN	55401	ERP: Enterprise Resource Planning	9/1/2014	$42,000.00
Hilary Marschke	245 West 3rd Ave	320-355-5443	Saint Cloud	MN	56301	Training	11/15/2014	$750.00
Craig Brand	554 2nd Street	320-751-4433	Saint Cloud	MN	56301	Technical Support	10/1/2014	$1,056.15

9-37 *AddFill* macro results

9. Press **Ctrl+Home**.

10. Record a macro.
    a. Click the **Use Relative Reference** button [*Developer* tab, *Code* group] to ensure it is turned off.
    b. Click the **Record Macro** button [*Developer* tab, *Code* group] to open the *Record Macro* dialog box.
    c. In the *Macro name* box, type CassLakeClients.
    d. In the *Shortcut key* box, hold down **Shift** and type C. The keyboard shortcut for the macro is **Ctrl+Shift+C**.
    e. For the *Store macro in* box, choose **This Workbook**.
    f. In the *Description* box, type Applies advanced filtering for Cass Lake accounting clients. and include the period (Figure 9-38). You may want to test out the following steps before you record the macro.
    g. Click **OK** to begin recording.
    h. Type Cass Lake and Accounting Software in **D5** and **G5** respectively in the *Criteria* range. Apply the **Advanced Filter** option [*Data* tab, *Sort & Filter* group]. Be sure the results are copied to the *Extract* Area, **A20:I20**.
    i. Click the **Stop Recording** button [*Developer* tab, *Code* group]. Wade Whitworth is the only record produced in the "Extract Area."

9-38 *CassLakeClients* macro details

11. Record another macro.
    a. Enter the *Macro Name:* ClearFiltering.
    b. Enter the following *Shortcut key:* **Shift+E**.
    c. Enter the following *Description:* Clears advanced filtering. and include the period (Figure 9-39).
    d. Delete the contents in **A5:I6**, and then delete rows **21:25**. Select **A1**. No results should appear in the "Criteria Area." Deleting extra rows of information ensures that if you edit the macro, extra criteria and results are cleared.
    e. Click the **Stop Recording** button [*Developer* tab, *Code* group].

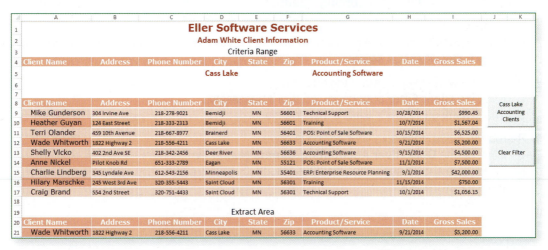

9-39 *ClearFiltering* macro details

12. Assign a macro to a *Button* form control.
    a. Click the **Insert Controls** button [*Developer* tab, *Controls* group].
    b. Click the **Button (Form Control)** command in the *Form Controls* category.
    c. Click and drag to draw a button that covers cells **J8:K10**.
    d. In the *Assign Macro* dialog box, select **CassLakeClients** and click **OK**. The button is placed as an object in the worksheet.
    e. Right-click the button and choose **Edit Text**.
    f. Delete the default text and type Cass Lake Accounting Clients as the caption or label for the button.
    g. Click a worksheet cell to deselect the *Button* control.

13. Assign a macro to a *Button* form control.
    a. Click and drag to draw a button that covers cells **J11:K13**.
    b. Select the **ClearFiltering** macro from the *Assign Macro* dialog box.
    c. Type the name Clear Filter on the macro button.

14. Resize and adjust properties of the *Button* form control.
    a. Right-click each button, and click and drag a selection handle if resizing is needed.
    b. Alter the properties of each control so that the control doesn't move or change size when the worksheet is adjusted. *(Hint: Right-click the control, choose* Format control, *and then select the* Don't move or size with cells *radio button on the Properties tab.)*
    c. Choose the **OK** button.
    d. Test both of the *Button* form controls to make sure your macros work correctly (see Figure 9-40).

9-40 *CassLakeClients* macro results

15. Edit a macro in the Visual Basic Editor.
    a. Click the **Macros** button [*Developer* tab, *Code* group].
    b. Select **CassLakeClients** in the list of macro names.
    c. Click **Edit** to open the *Visual Basic Editor* program.
    d. If the *Code* window is not displayed, choose **Code** from the *View* menu.
    e. Change the two instances of the text **Cass Lake** to Deer River and the two instances of **CassLakeClients** to DeerRiverClients within the *Sub* and *End Sub* entries (Figure 9-41).
    f. Click the **Close** button in the top-right corner of the *VBE* window. You automatically switch back to Excel view.

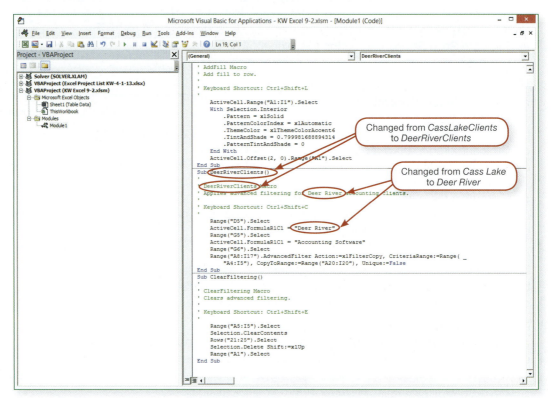

9-41 Edited code for *DeerRiverClients* macro

16. Rename the **Cass Lake Accounting Clients** *Button* form control to Deer River Accounting Clients. (*Hint: You can use the context-sensitive menu and choose* Edit Text.)

17. Assign the *DeerRiverClients* macro to the renamed button. *Hint: You can use the context-sensitive menu and choose Assign Macro.*

18. Prepare the worksheet to re-run the edited macro.
    a. Click the **Clear Filter** button form control if necessary.
    b. The *Criteria* and *Extract* areas should be blank.

19. Re-run the macro to ensure your editing is correct.
    a. Click on the **Deer River Accounting Clients** *Button* form control.
    b. The macro should show the *Deer River* clients (Figure 9-42).
    c. Save the workbook.

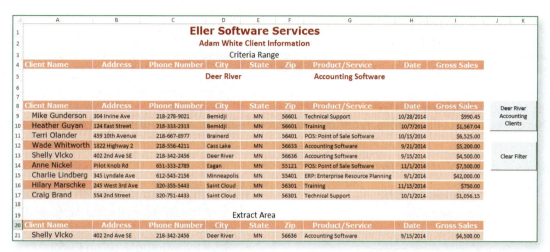

9-42 *DeerRiverClients* macro results

20. Save the workbook as an Excel macro-enabled template.
    a. Run the **ClearFilter** macro.
    b. Select cells **H9:I17** and delete the contents. The template will not include the date or sales attained by each employee (Figure 9-43).
    c. Choose **Save As** from the *File* tab.
    d. Navigate to your student file folder.
    e. Type [your initials] Excel 9-2 as the file name for the Excel macro-enabled template. This file will have an *.xltm* extension.
    f. Choose **Excel Macro-Enabled Template** from the *Save as type* list.
    g. You may need to navigate back to the student file folder where *[your initials] Excel 9-2* is located.
    h. Click **Save** to save the template.

9-43 Excel 9-2 completed template

Guided Project 9-3

Clemenson Imaging LLC is requesting that a macro be created to automate the import process for sales.
[Student Learning Outcomes 9.1, 9.2, 9.3, 9.6]

File Needed: ***Forecast-09.xlsx***
Completed Project File Names: ***[your initials] Excel 9-3.xlsm*** and ***[your initials] Excel 9-3.xltm***

Skills Covered in This Project

- Display the *Developer* tab.
- Adjust macro security.
- Record a macro.
- Create a *Button* form control.
- Resize the *Button* form control.
- Adjust the properties of the *Button* form control properties.

- Assign a macro to a *Button* form control.
- Save the file as an Excel macro-enabled workbook.
- Save the workbook as an Excel macro-enabled template.

---

1. Open the ***Forecast-09*** workbook from your student data files folder.

2. Display the *Developer* tab if necessary and check macro security.
   a. Click the **Options** command [*File* tab].
   b. Click **Customize Ribbon** in the left pane.
   c. Select the **Developer** check box in the *Main Tabs* list and click **OK**.
   d. Click the **Macro Security** button [*Developer* tab, *Code* group].
   e. Verify or click to select **Disable all macros with notification**.
   f. Click **OK**.

3. Save the workbook as an Excel macro-enabled workbook named ***[your initials] Excel 9-3***. Choose **Excel Macro-Enabled Workbook** from the *Save as type* list.

4. Record a macro.
   a. Verify that the *Use Relative References* option is off [*Developer* tab, *Code* group].
   b. Click the **Record Macro** button [*Developer* tab, *Code* group] to open the *Record Macro* dialog box.
   c. In the *Macro name* box, type Import.
   d. In the *Shortcut key* box, hold down **Shift** and type I. The keyboard shortcut for the macro is **Ctrl+Shift+I**.
   e. For the *Store macro in* box, choose **This Workbook**.
   f. In the *Description* box, type Imports the text file containing forecast information. (Figure 9-44).
   g. Click **OK** to begin recording.
   h. Import the text file ***Expenses-09*** into **A4** of the current worksheet. (*Hint: Click the* **From Text**

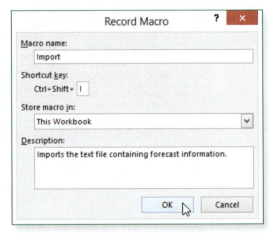

9-44 *Import* macro details

button [*Data tab,* Get External Data *group].*) Accept all defaults in the *Import Wizard.* The data should appear as shown in Figure 9-45.

  i. Click the **Stop Recording** button [*Developer* tab, *Code* group].

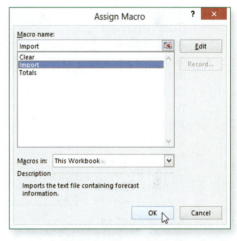

Clemenson Imaging LLC				
Forecast for 1st Quarter 2016				
Expense Categories	**Monthly Budget**	**January**	**February**	**March**
Vehicles	17,500.00	17,464.88	18,505.51	16,478.66
Supplies	11,900.00	11,643.26	12,337.00	10,985.77
Commission	10,000.00	8,732.44	9,252.75	8,239.33
Gas	13,500.00	12,613.53	13,365.09	11,901.25
Totals				

9-45 *Import* macro results

5. Create a second macro.
   a. Enter the *Macro Name:* Totals.
   b. Enter the following *Shortcut key:* **Shift+T**.
   c. Enter the following *Description:* Adds total formulas. and include the period.
   d. Add *SUM* formulas to **B9:E9**. Select **B9** when finished. *Hint: increase the column widths if needed after stopping the macro.*

6. Create a third macro.
   a. Enter the following *Macro Name:* Clear.
   b. Enter the following *Shortcut key:* **Shift+C**.
   c. Enter the following *Description:* Deletes all imported information and the totals. and include the period.
   d. Delete the contents of cells **A4:E8**. Click **Yes** to delete the import query. Then delete the contents of cells **B9:E9**. Select **A1** after you stop recording the macro.

7. Assign a macro to a *Button* form control.
   a. Click the **Insert Controls** button [*Developer* tab, *Controls* group].
   b. Click the **Button (Form Control)** command in the *Form Controls* category.
   c. Click and drag to draw a button that covers cells **A11:A12**.
   d. In the *Assign Macro* dialog box, select **Import** and click **OK** (Figure 9-46). The button is placed as an object in the worksheet.
   e. Right-click the button and choose **Edit Text**.
   f. Delete the default text and type Import as the caption or label for the button.
   g. Click a worksheet cell to deselect the **Button** form control.

9-46 *Assign Macro* dialog box details

8. Assign another macro to a *Button* form control.
   a. Click and drag to draw a button that covers cells **C11:C12**.
   b. Select the **Totals** macro from the *Assign Macro* dialog box.
   c. Type the name Totals on the macro button.

9. Assign another macro to a *Button* form control.
   a. Click and drag to draw a button that covers cells **E11:E12**.
   b. Select the **Clear** macro from the *Assign Macro* dialog box.
   c. Type the name Clear on the macro button.

10. Resize and adjust properties of the *Button* form control.
    a. Right-click each button, and click and drag a selection handle if resizing is needed.
    b. Alter the properties of each control so that the control doesn't move or change size when the worksheet is adjusted. *(Hint: Right-click the control,* choose Format control*, then select the* Don't move or size with cells *radio button on the Properties tab.)*
    c. Choose the **OK** button.

E9-523

11. Test the *Import* macro button to make sure the macro works correctly.
   a. If you get an error, choose the **Debug** button in the *Microsoft Visual Basic* message window (Figure 9-47).
   b. Complete the instructions in the next step to correct the error.

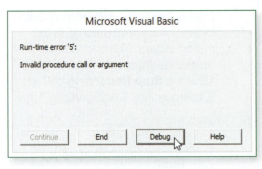

9-47 Visual Basic error message

12. Edit a macro in the Visual Basic Editor.
   a. If the *Code* window is not displayed, choose **Code** from the *View* menu.
   b. Delete the line that the yellow arrow is pointing to (Figure 9-48). It was inserted automatically with the *ActiveSheet. QueryTables. Add* statement which looks for a connection for the dataset. The *CommandType* line therefore doesn't match the *CommandText,* but deleting this line or writing other VBA statements will correct the issue.

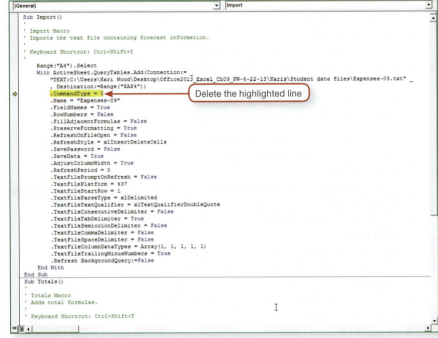

```
(General)                                      Import

Sub Import()
'
' Import Macro
' Imports the text file containing forecast information.
'
' Keyboard Shortcut: Ctrl+Shift+I
'
    Range("A4").Select
    With ActiveSheet.QueryTables.Add(Connection:= _
        "TEXT;C:\Users\Kari Wood\Desktop\Office2013_Excel_Ch09_KW-4-22-13\Karis\Student data files\Expenses-09.txt" _
        , Destination:=Range("$A$4"))
        .CommandType = 0               Delete the highlighted line
        .Name = "Expenses-09"
        .FieldNames = True
        .RowNumbers = False
        .FillAdjacentFormulas = False
        .PreserveFormatting = True
        .RefreshOnFileOpen = False
        .RefreshStyle = xlInsertDeleteCells
        .SavePassword = False
        .SaveData = True
        .AdjustColumnWidth = True
        .RefreshPeriod = 0
        .TextFilePromptOnRefresh = False
        .TextFilePlatform = 437
        .TextFileStartRow = 1
        .TextFileParseType = xlDelimited
        .TextFileTextQualifier = xlTextQualifierDoubleQuote
        .TextFileConsecutiveDelimiter = False
        .TextFileTabDelimiter = True
        .TextFileSemicolonDelimiter = False
        .TextFileCommaDelimiter = False
        .TextFileSpaceDelimiter = False
        .TextFileColumnDataTypes = Array(1, 1, 1, 1, 1)
        .TextFileTrailingMinusNumbers = True
        .Refresh BackgroundQuery:=False
    End With
End Sub
Sub Totals()
'
' Totals Macro
' Adds total formulas.
'
' Keyboard Shortcut: Ctrl+Shift+T
```

9-48 VBE highlights line of incorrect code

   c. Click the **Close** button in the top-right corner of the *VBE* window.
   d. Click **OK** on the *Microsoft Visual Basic for Applications* message window to stop the debugger. You automatically switch back to Excel view.

13. Re-run the edited macro.
   a. Click on the **Import** macro button.
   b. Click the **Totals** macro button. The macro should show the completed worksheet (Figure 9-49). *AutoFit* column widths if necessary.
   c. Save the workbook.

14. Save the workbook as an Excel macro-enabled template.
   a. Click the **Clear** macro button. The template will not include any imported data or totals (Figure 9-50).

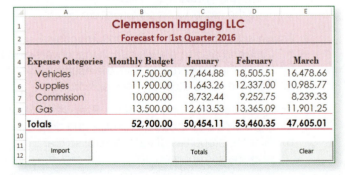

	A	B	C	D	E
1		Clemenson Imaging LLC			
2		Forecast for 1st Quarter 2016			
3					
4	Expense Categories	Monthly Budget	January	February	March
5	Vehicles	17,500.00	17,464.88	18,505.51	16,478.66
6	Supplies	11,900.00	11,643.26	12,337.00	10,985.77
7	Commission	10,000.00	8,732.44	9,252.75	8,239.33
8	Gas	13,500.00	12,613.53	13,365.09	11,901.25
9	Totals	52,900.00	50,454.11	53,460.35	47,605.01
10					
11	Import		Totals		Clear
12					

9-49 Excel 9-3 completed worksheet

b. Choose **Save As** from the *File* tab.

c. Navigate to the student file folder.

d. Type [your initials] Excel 9-3 as the file name for the Excel macro-enabled template. This file will have an *.xltm* extension.

e. Choose **Excel Macro-Enabled Template** from the *Save as type* list.

f. You will need to navigate back to the student file folder where *[your initials] Excel 9-3* is located to save the template.

g. Click **Save** to save the template.

h. Click **No** in the *Microsoft Excel* message window.

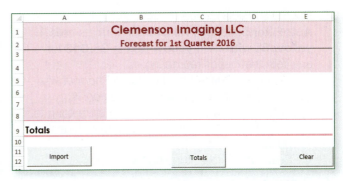

9-50 Excel 9-3 completed template

Independent Project 9-4

Wear-Ever Shoes is requesting managers to add macros that automatically add *AutoFilter* buttons and conditional formatting to items that are low in stock.
[Student Learning Outcomes 9.1, 9.2, 9.3]

File Needed: *Inventory-09.xlsx*
Completed Project File Name: *[your initials] Excel 9-4.xlsm*

Skills Covered in This Project

- Display the *Developer* tab.
- Adjust macro security.
- Record a macro.
- Create a *Button* form control.
- Resize the *Button* form control.

- Adjust the *Button* form control properties.
- Assign a macro to a *Button* form control.
- Save the file as an Excel macro-enabled workbook.

1. Open and enable the **Inventory-09** workbook from your student data files folder.

2. Save the file as an Excel macro-enabled workbook in your student file folder and name it [your initials] Excel 9-4.

3. Display the *Developer* tab.

4. Adjust the macro security in a workbook to **Disable all macros with notification**.

5. Record a macro named Reorder that applies **AutoFilter** buttons to **A4:J13** and formats cells **yellow fill with dark yellow text** in **G5:G13** for any item that needs reordering.
    a. Designate **Shift+R** as the macro *Shortcut key*.
    b. Enter the following macro *Description*: Applies AutoFilter buttons and conditional formatting to items that need to be ordered. and include the period (Figure 9-51).
    c. Select **A1** before stopping the macro.

6. Record a macro named ClearReorder that removes the *AutoFilter* buttons from **A4:J13** and clears the conditional formatting from **G5:G13**.
    a. Enter the following *Shortcut key:* **Shift+D**.
    b. Enter the following *Description*: Clears AutoFilter buttons and conditional formatting. and include the period.
    c. Remove the *AutoFilter* buttons from **A4:J13** and clear the conditional formatting from **G5:G13**.
    d. Select **A1** before stopping the macro.

7. Run each macro to ensure they are all correct.

8. Create a *Button* form control for each macro.
    a. Draw the first *Button* form control within **B15:C16**.
    b. Assign the **Reorder** macro to the first button and name it Reorder Items.
    c. Draw the second *Button* form control within **H15:I16**.
    d. Assign the **ClearReorder** macro the second *Button* form control and name it Clear Reorder.

9. Alter the properties of both the buttons so that the controls don't move or change size when the worksheet is adjusted.

10. Click the **Reorder Items** macro button and then the **Clear Reorder** button to ensure they work properly.

11. Add the **Reorder** macro to the *Quick Access* toolbar.

12. Run the **Reorder** macro button from the *Quick Access* toolbar. Save the macro-enabled workbook and close the file (Figure 9-52).

Record Macro   ? ✕

Macro name:
Reorder

Shortcut key:
Ctrl+Shift+ R

Store macro in:
This Workbook

Description:
Applies AutoFilter buttons and conditional formatting to items that need to be ordered.

OK   Cancel

9-51 *Reorder* macro details

	Product	Color	Size	Mens/Wome	Cos	Retail Pri	Reord	Supplier	Phone Numb	Quanti
5	Chunky Heel Boots	Brown	W 5-11	Women	$32.45	$65.00	Y	Classy Sass	204-565-3290	10
6	Classy Pumps	Navy Blue	R 5-12	Women	$15.45	$30.00	N	Classy Sass	204-565-3290	40
7	Sassy Slip-Ons	Silver	R 5-12	Women	$23.50	$45.00	N	Classy Sass	204-565-3290	25
8	Lazy Flip-Flops	Pink and White	R 5-12	Both	$7.50	$14.00	Y	Jennifer's Closet	289-433-1555	13
9	Seriously Tall Boots	Black	W 5-11	Women	$42.50	$80.00	Y	Jennifer's Closet	289-433-1555	0
10	Silky Bed Slippers	White	R 5-12	Both	$12.50	$20.00	N	Jennifer's Closet	289-433-1555	35
11	Comfy Walking Shoes	Brown and Black	R 5-12	Both	$34.25	$65.00	N	Outdoor Inc.	292-555-2334	52
12	Rugged Hiking Boots	Brown and Black	W 5-11	Men	$46.50	$90.00	N	Outdoor Inc.	292-555-2334	45
13	Glide Running Shoes	Green and Black	R 5-12	Both	$36.50	$75.00	Y	Sport it!	255-463-7896	10

Wear-Ever Shoes

Outlet Product Inventory

Reorder Items   Clear Reorder

9-52 **Excel 9-4 completed worksheet**

Independent Project 9-5

Courtyard Medical Plaza is requesting that management add macros to a worksheet that will automatically generate various interest rate changes for investment options. Then you will edit the macro after reviewing your work.
[Student Learning Outcomes 9.1, 9.2, 9.3, 9.4]

File Needed: **Investments-09.xlsx**
Completed Project File Name: **[your initials] Excel 9-5.xlsm**

Skills Covered in This Project

- Display the *Developer* tab.
- Adjust macro security.
- Record a macro.
- Create a *Button* form control.
- Resize the *Button* form control.

- Adjust the *Button* form control properties.
- Assign a macro to a *Button* form control.
- Save the file as an Excel macro-enabled workbook.
- Edit a macro in the Visual Basic Editor (VBE).

---

1. Open and, if necessary, enable the **Investments-09** workbook from your student data files folder. Click **Don't update** in the message box if prompted.

2. Save the workbook as macro-enabled and name it [your initials] Excel 9-5.

3. Display the *Developer* tab.

4. Adjust the macro security in a workbook to **Disable all macros with notification**.

5. Record a macro named Irate4 that changes the values in **B8** and **E7** to 4%.
   a. Designate **Shift+I** as the macro *Shortcut key*.
   b. Enter the following macro *Description:* Applies 4% to the investment options. and include the period.

6. Record a macro named Irate5 that changes the values in **B8** and **E7** to 5%.
   a. Designate **Shift+F** as the macro *Shortcut key*.
   b. Enter the following macro *Description:* Applies 5% to the investment options. and include the period.

7. Record a macro named Irate6 that changes the values in **B8** and **E7** to 7%.
   a. Designate **Shift+S** as the macro *Shortcut key*.
   b. Enter the following macro *Description:* Applies 6% to the investment options. and include the period. *(Hint: You will edit this macro in a later step.)*

8. Run each macro to ensure no Visual Basic errors appear.

9. Create a *Button* form control for each macro.
   a. Draw the first *Button* form control within **G6:G7**.
   b. Assign the **Irate4** macro to the first button and label the button IR 4%.
   c. Draw the second *Button* form control within **G8:G9**.
   d. Assign the **Irate5** macro to the second button and label the button IR 5%.
   e. Draw the third button form control within **G10:G11**.
   f. Assign the **Irate6** macro to the third button and label the button IR 6%.

10. Test each macro button. Notice that macro *Irate6* has the incorrect percentage.

11. Edit the *IRate6* macro in the *Visual Basic Editor* program to change **7%** entered into **B8** and **E7** to 6% (Figure 9-53). Save the changes and rerun the macro. Test the *IR 6%* button again.

12. Save and close the file (Figure 9-54).

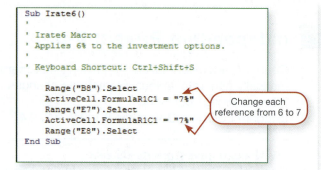

```
Sub Irate6()
'
' Irate6 Macro
' Applies 6% to the investment options.
'
' Keyboard Shortcut: Ctrl+Shift+S
'
    Range("B8").Select
    ActiveCell.FormulaR1C1 = "7%"
    Range("E7").Select
    ActiveCell.FormulaR1C1 = "7%"
    Range("E8").Select
End Sub
```

Change each reference from 6 to 7

9-53 Incorrect *Irate6* macro code in Visual Basic Editor

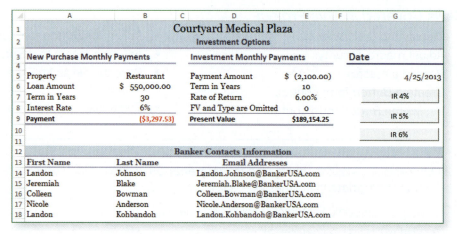

9-54 Excel 9-5 completed worksheet

Independent Project 9-6

Blue Lake Sports is requesting that a macro be created to add shipping charges to their invoices. **[Student Learning Outcomes 9.1, 9.2, 9.3, 9.6]**

File Needed: ***Invoice-09.xlsx***
Completed Project File Names: ***[your initials] Excel 9-6.xlsm*** and ***[your initials] Excel 9-6.xltm***

Skills Covered in This Project

- Display the *Developer* tab.
- Adjust macro security.
- Record a macro.
- Create a *Button* form control.
- Resize the *Button* form control.
- Adjust the properties of the *Button* form control properties.
- Assign a macro to a *Button* form control.
- Save the file as an Excel macro-enabled workbook.

1. Open and enable the *Invoice-09* workbook from your student data files folder. If an update message box appears, click **Don't Update**.

2. Save the workbook as macro-enabled and name it [your initials] Excel 9-6.

3. Display the *Developer* tab.

4. Adjust the macro security in a workbook to **Disable all macros with notification**.

5. Record a macro named Shipping that creates a shipping label and calculation for the invoice.
   a. Enter **Shift+H** for the macro *Shortcut key*.
   b. Enter the following macro *Description*: Inserts a cell for shipping and validation rules for a drop-down box. and include the period.
   c. Insert a row above **33**; then type Shipping in **F33**. Edit the *Total* formula in **G34** to display **=G31+(G31*G32)+G33**. Add validation rules to **G33** that allow a list with the following items; $5.00, $10.00, $20.00. *Hint: click the Data Validation button [Data tab, Data Tools group].* Stop recording the macro.

6. Create a *Button* form control for the macro.
   a. Draw the *Button* form control within **H31:H32**.
   b. Assign the **Shipping** macro to the macro button and label the button Shipping.
   c. Delete row **33** and edit the formula in **G33** to display **=G31+(G31*G32)**.
   d. Run the macro and choose **$5.00** from the shipping list options (Figure 9-55).

7. Alter the properties of the button so that the control doesn't move or change size when the worksheet is adjusted. Save the workbook.

8. Prepare the workbook for template use.
   a. Delete row **33**, and edit the formula in **G33** to display=**G31+(G31*G32)**.
   b. Delete **A15:B17**, **B9:B12**, **E4:E6**, and **E9:E12**.

9. Save the file as a macro-enabled template, place the file in your student file folder, and close the file (Figure 9-56).

9-55 Excel 9-6 completed worksheet

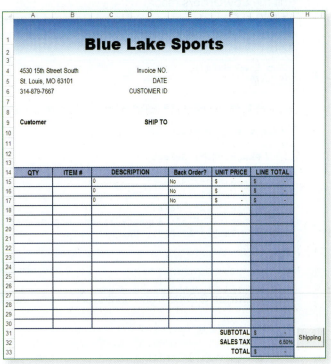

9-56 Excel 9-6 completed template

E9-529

Improve It Project 9-7

The Classic Gardens and Landscapes (CGL) organization is requesting that the sales department edit the following spreadsheet. You will edit the partially completed worksheet to assure accuracy for the two macros that have been recorded.
[Student Learning Outcomes 9.1, 9.2, 9.3, 9.4]

File Needed: **Orders-09.xlsm**
Completed Project File Names: **[your initials] Excel 9-7.xlsm** and **[your initials] Excel 9-7.xltm**

Skills Covered in This Project

- Display the *Developer* tab.
- Adjust macro security.
- Record a macro.
- Create a *Button* form control.
- Resize the *Button* form control.

- Adjust the *Button* form control properties.
- Assign a macro to a *Button* form control.
- Save the file as an Excel macro-enabled workbook.
- Edit a macro in the Visual Basic Editor (VBE).

1. Open and enable the **Orders-09** workbook from your student data files folder.

2. Save the workbook as macro-enabled and name it [your initials] Excel 9-7.

3. Display the *Developer* tab.

4. Adjust the macro security in a workbook to **Disable all macros with notification**.

5. Edit the **LowOrders** macro in the *Visual Basic Editor* program to change *Q2* totals to be less than **11,500** in **E3** and change *Alert* to be **Contact Manager** in **H3** (Figure 9-57). Save the changes and rerun the **LowOrders** macro. Then run the **Clear** macro.

```
Sub LowOrders()
'
' LowOrders Macro
' This macro applies advanced filtering to determine those categories that are less
'
' Keyboard Shortcut: Ctrl+Shift+L
'
    Range("E3").Select
    ActiveCell.FormulaR1C1 = "<11,500"
    Range("H3").Select
    ActiveCell.FormulaR1C1 = "Contact Manager"
    Range("C12").Select
    Range("A9:H15").AdvancedFilter Action:=xlFilterInPlace, CriteriaRange:= _
        Range("A2:H3"), Unique:=False
End Sub
```

9-57 Corrected *LowOrders* macro code in Visual Basic Editor

6. Edit the **Button 2** *Button* form control and assign the **Clear** macro to it. Label the button Clear Criteria.

7. Alter the properties of both buttons so that the controls don't move or change size when the worksheet is adjusted.

8. Click the **Clear Criteria** button first and then the **Low Orders** button.

9. Save the macro-enabled workbook and close the file (Figure 9-58).

9-58 Excel 9-7 completed worksheet

Challenge Project 9-8

For this project, you will be adding macros linked to your personal budget scenarios.
[Student Learning Outcomes 9.1, 9.2, 9.3]

File Needed: None
Completed Project File Name: *[your initials] Excel 9-8.xlsm*

Enter all data that you find important from your checking account and monthly expenses. Create a new workbook and save it as *[your initials] Excel 9-8*.

- Display the *Developer* tab and downgrade macro security for the workbook.
- Import or type the web site revenue information from your bank for the last month into your Excel workbook.

- When creating your spreadsheets, you may add additional column headings such as "Expenses," "Vacation," "Food," "Utilities," "Fun," "Savings," etc.
- Apply formatting as needed.
- Add total formulas to the key columns needed.
- Add a macro to use *Goal Seek* to determine how much savings you would need to take a vacation this year. See *SLO 4.7: Using Goal Seek and Worksheet Protection* for more information.
- Add two more macros that record two scenarios (conservative and aggressive) to determine two paths of saving based on minimizing expenses or maximizing overtime revenue.
- Create *Button* form controls and assign the macros to each button.
- Ensure that the buttons are named, and do not move or size if the worksheet changes.
- Save the file as an Excel macro-enabled workbook.

Challenge Project 9-9

For this project, you will be recording a macro that will import your class schedule into an Excel workbook.
[Student Learning Outcomes 9.1, 9.2, 9.3]

File Needed: None
Completed Project File Name: *[your initials] Excel 9-9.xlsm*

Enter all headings that are useful for your class schedule import process. Create a new workbook and save it as *[your initials] Excel 8-9*.

- When creating your class spreadsheet, you may want to add column headings that match up with the imported file.
- Create a macro while you import your class schedule.
- Create a *Button* form control and assign the macro to the button.
- Change the properties of the button so it doesn't move or size with cells.
- Save the file as an Excel macro-enabled workbook.
- Add additional macros to create formulas that total the credits and courses you have.

Challenge Project 9-10

For this project, you will be creating investment options and analyzing the results. You will be applying either *PV*, *FV*, or *NPV* to a personal financial scenario and recording macros that will change the interest rates or loan amount. Edit the macros in VBE if any mistakes are made during recording.
[Student Learning Outcomes 9.1, 9.2, 9.3, 9.4]

File Needed: None
Completed Project File Name: *[your initials] Excel 9-10.xlsm*

Enter all data that you find important regarding an investment option on *Sheet1* and save the workbook as *[your initials] Excel 9-10*.

- Set up your spreadsheet to include needed information for *PV*, *FV*, or *NPV*.
- For the *PV* scenario, include payment amount, term in years, and rate of return. Be sure to decide if you are paying monthly or annually.
- Determine needed information such as rate of return and discount rate from your local bank.
- Add formulas to the key cells as you see fit.
- Add two macros using the rate of return as the changing cell to increase your *PV* amount. One macro records an increase in the rate of return while the other records a decrease.
- Add two *Button* form controls and assign each macro to a button.
- Change the button properties so that they do not move or size with the cells.
- Save the file as an Excel macro-enabled workbook.

CHAPTER 10

Customizing Excel, Using SkyDrive and Office Web Apps

CHAPTER OVERVIEW

Once you have learned the many features of Excel, you can personalize this software by altering its available settings. Office 2013 also integrates "cloud" technology, which allows you to use your Office files in *SkyDrive*, *SkyDrive* groups, and Office Web Apps. These cloud services let your files and Office settings follow you. With these features, you are not locked into using Office on only one computer, and all files are available as long as the computer you're using has Internet access. This chapter reviews how to alter Excel options and utilize *SkyDrive*, *SkyDrive* groups, and Office Web Apps.

STUDENT LEARNING OUTCOMES (SLOs)

After completing this chapter, students will be able to:

SLO 10.1 Customize Excel options, the *Ribbon*, and the *Quick Access* toolbar to personalize your working environment in Excel (p. E10-535).

SLO 10.2 View and modify Office account settings and add an Office app (p. E10-545).

SLO 10.3 Create a folder, add a file, move and copy a file, and share a file in *SkyDrive* (p. E10-551).

SLO 10.4 Create a group in *SkyDrive*, invite a member, and change group options (p. E10-558).

SLO 10.5 Open, create, edit, print, share, and collaborate on a workbook in Office Web Apps (p. E10-563).

CASE STUDY

For the Pause & Practice projects in this chapter, you customize your Excel settings and use Microsoft cloud services to save, edit, and share files related to the northern Minnesota resort business Paradise Lakes Resort (PLR).

Pause & Practice 10-1: Customize Excel 2013 working environment and Office account settings and add an app.

Pause & Practice 10-2: Use *SkyDrive* and *SkyDrive* groups to save, create, edit, and share files.

Pause & Practice 10-3: Create, save, edit, and share files using Office Web Apps.

SLO 10.1

Customizing Excel 2013

You have learned many customizing options in Excel for a single worksheet or workbook. There are also customization options available that alter Excel settings globally. Once implemented, these options apply to all the workbooks you create and edit in Excel. You can customize these settings in the **Excel Options** dialog box, which you open from the *Backstage* view.

Excel Options

In the *Excel Options* dialog box, the settings are grouped into different option categories. Within each of these categories, you can change many individual settings. In some of the areas, you can open a dialog box to see additional customization settings. The following list includes the different categories in the *Excel Options* dialog box. Each category is discussed further in the sections that follow.

- *General*
- *Formulas*
- *Proofing*
- *Save*
- *Language*
- *Advanced*
- *Customize Ribbon*
- *Quick Access Toolbar*
- *Add-Ins*
- *Trust Center*

HOW TO: Customize Excel Options

1. Click the **File** tab to open the *Backstage* view.
2. Click the **Options** button on the bottom left to open the *Excel Options* dialog box.
3. Click the options category on the left to display the available customization options on the right (Figure 10-1).
4. Change your options using check boxes, text boxes, drop-down lists, or buttons.
   - When you click a button, a dialog box with additional option settings opens.
5. Click **OK** to close the *Excel Options* dialog box and apply the settings.

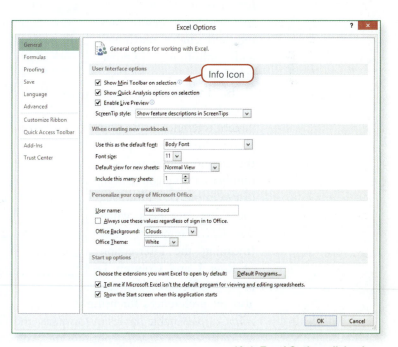

> **MORE INFO**
> Use of Windows 7 with Office 365 may reveal fewer options.

10-1 *Excel Options* dialog box

General

The *General* category includes the following areas: *User Interface options*, *When creating new workbooks*, *Personalize your copy of Microsoft Office*, and *Start up options* (see Figure 10-1).

In the *User Interface options* area, you can show or hide the mini toolbar display, show or hide quick analysis options, and enable or disable live preview. You can also customize the *ScreenTip* style.

> **MORE INFO**
>
> Put your pointer on the *information* icon at the end of a selection to display information about that selection.

In the *When creating new workbooks* area, you can customize the font type, font size, default view of new sheets, and number of sheets within a workbook.

In the *Personalize your copy of Microsoft Office* area, you can change your user name and initials, make it so your Excel settings are imposed for all users on the current computer, and change the Office background and theme.

In the *Start up options* area, you can set Excel as the default program to open files with compatible extensions, and determine whether or not the *Start* screen displays when Excel opens. The *Start* screen displays your recent workbooks and Excel templates.

Formulas

In the *Formulas* options category, you can change options regarding formula calculation, cell reference display, and error handling (Figure 10-2). In the *Calculation options* area, you can set workbook calculations to be automatic or manual, force formulas to recalculate in the workbook before saving, and enable maximum and minimum iterative calculations.

In the *Working with formulas* area, you can set which reference style you prefer. Most users prefer the column name and row number naming convention (for example, *A1*). However, there are instances when the *R1C1* reference style (meaning the intersection of Row 1 and Column 1, or 1A) is desired. You can also set preferences for using

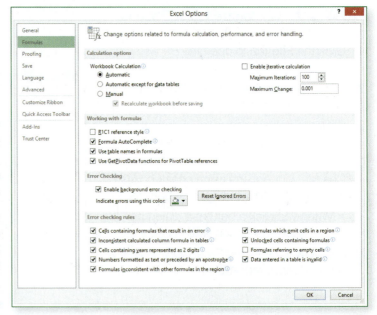

10-2 *Formulas* options in the *Excel Options* dialog box

AutoComplete, table names in formulas, and *GetPivotData* functions for *PivotTable* references.

In the *Error Checking* options area, you can customize if background error checking is on and determine what color the error indicator is.

In the *Error checking rules* area, you are able to set the automated error system to alert you to each selected rule.

Proofing

In the *Proofing* category of the Excel options dialog box, you can change how Excel corrects and formats your text (Figure 10-3). Click the **AutoCorrect Options** button to open the *AutoCorrect* dialog box and change *AutoCorrect*, *AutoFormat As You Type*, *Actions*, and *Math AutoCorrect*.

In the *When correcting spelling in Microsoft Office programs* area, Excel is by default set to ignore words in uppercase, words that contain numbers, and Internet and file addresses. Click the **Custom Dictionaries** button to open the *Custom Dictionaries* dialog box and add, edit, or delete words from the custom dictionary.

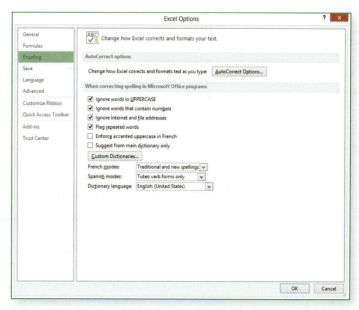

10-3 *Proofing* options in the *Excel Options* dialog box

> **MORE INFO**
>
> Many changes you make in the *Proofing* category are applied in all Office applications and files.

> **MORE INFO**
>
> If any options are grayed out, be sure you have a blank workbook open before going into the *Excel Options* dialog box.

Save

In the *Save* category, you can control how and where workbooks are saved (Figure 10-4). In the *Save workbooks* area, you can set the default file format to save workbooks, establish the frequency that *AutoRecover* saves your open documents, and determine where these files are stored. By default, when you press **Ctrl+O** or **Ctrl+S** to open or save a document, the *Backstage* view is displayed, but you can turn this off. You can also set the default save location for

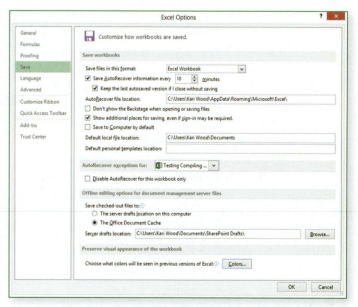

10-4 *Save* options in the *Excel Options* dialog box

files and templates. Click the **Default local file location** text box to enter a different default save location, such as *SkyDrive*.

The *AutoRecover exceptions for* area allows you to disable *AutoRecover* for an individual workbook.

The *Offline editing options for document management server files* area pertains to documents shared in SharePoint. *Preserve visual appearance of the workbook* controls how colors are displayed in earlier versions of Excel. Neither of these customization options is common.

Language

The *Language* category controls the language preferences in Excel and the other Office programs you use (Figure 10-5). In the *Choose Editing Languages* area, you can select the language to use for spelling, grammar, dictionaries, and sorting. You can add a new language, set a language as the default, or remove a language.

In the *Choose Display and Help Languages* area, you can set the language for display tabs, buttons, and *Help*. In the *Choose ScreenTip Language*, you can change the language of the ScreenTips.

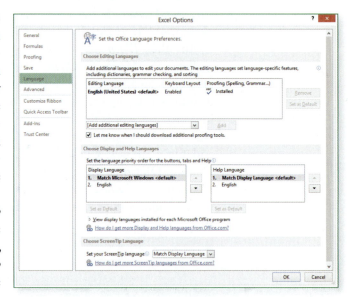

10-5 *Language* options in the *Excel Options* dialog box

> **MORE INFO**
>
> The language settings in Office are determined by the default language you selected when you installed Windows.

Advanced

The *Advanced* category provides you with a variety of customization options (Figure 10-6). The following is a list of the different options in the *Advanced* category. Scroll through each of these areas to familiarize yourself with the different customization options available.

- *Editing options*
- *Cut, copy, and paste*
- *Image Size and Quality*
- *Print*
- *Chart*
- *Display*

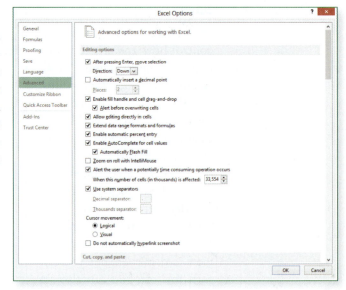

10-6 *Advanced* options in the *Excel Options* dialog box

- *Display options for this workbook*
- *Display options for this worksheet*
- *Formulas*
- *When calculating this workbook*
- *General*
- *Data*
- *Lotus compatibility*
- *Lotus compatibility Settings for*

> **MORE INFO**
>
> The *Customize Ribbon* and *Quick Access Toolbar* options are covered later in this section.

Add-Ins

Add-ins are programs that add functionality to your Office programs. Some programs you install on your computer are recognized by Office as add-in programs such as *Solver* or *Snag-It*.

In the *Add-Ins* category in the *Excel Options* dialog box, you can view the add-in programs that interact with Office (Figure 10-7). You can manage add-ins and make them active or inactive. Click the **Manage** drop-down list to select a category and click **Go**. A dialog box opens and lets you turn on or off specific add-ins.

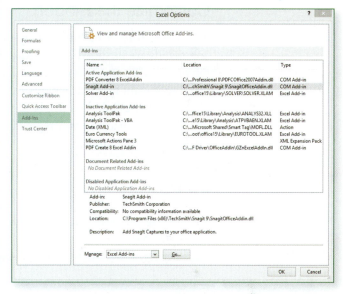

10-7 *Add-Ins* options in the *Excel Options* dialog box

Trust Center

The *Trust Center* was first described in *SLO 9.1: Running a Macro*. This option helps to prevent your files and computer from becoming infected with viruses. There are many different areas that you can customize in the *Trust Center* dialog box. It is generally recommended that you keep the default settings in the *Trust Center* to keep your files and computer safe.

> **MORE INFO**
>
> For more information on macros and the *Trust Center*, see *SLO 9.1: Running a Macro*.

HOW TO: Customize Trust Center Settings

1. Click the **File** tab to open the *Backstage* view.
2. Click the **Options** button on the left to open the *Excel Options* dialog box.
3. Click the **Trust Center** button on the left.

4. Click the **Trust Center Settings** button to open the *Trust Center* dialog box (Figure 10-8).

5. Click the different categories on the left to view the available options. Make changes only as needed.

6. Click **OK** to close the *Trust Center* dialog box.

7. Click **OK** to close the *Excel Options* dialog box.

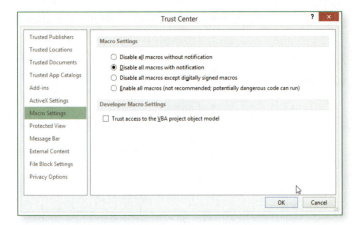

10-8 *Trust Center* dialog box

Customize the Ribbon

The Excel *Ribbon* includes many of the common commands you use, but not all available commands are included on the *Ribbon*. You can customize the *Ribbon* to add a new group to a tab or to add commands you commonly use that are not included on the *Ribbon*. For example, you might want to create a new group on the *Home* tab that includes a button to go back after clicking a hyperlink. You might also want to add a button to add a comment and to turn on *Track Changes* because you regularly use these items. You can also create a custom tab with groups and commands.

> **MORE INFO**
>
> You can add commands to customs groups but cannot add new commands to, or remove existing commands from, existing groups.

HOW TO: Add a Tab, Group, and Commands to the Ribbon

1. Right-click anywhere on the **Ribbon** and select **Customize the Ribbon** from the context menu. The *Excel Options* dialog box opens with *Customize Ribbon* displayed (Figure 10-9).

   - You can also click the **File** tab to open the *Backstage* view, click the **Options** button to open the *Excel Options* dialog box, and select *Customize Ribbon*.
   - The left side lists the different commands and groups available, and the right side lists the existing tabs and groups displayed on the *Ribbon*.
   - The drop-down lists at the top of each of the lists provide you with other commands and tabs to display in these lists.

10-9 *Customize Ribbon* area of the *Excel Options* dialog box

2. On the right, click the tab that will be before the new tab you want to insert.

3. Click the **New Tab** button. A new custom tab and group are inserted.

4. Select the new tab and click **Rename** to open the *Rename* dialog box (Figure 10-10).

5. Type the name of the new tab and click **OK** to close the *Rename* dialog box.

6. Select the new group and click **Rename** to open the *Rename* dialog box (Figure 10-11).

7. Select a symbol (optional), type the new group name in the *Display name* area, and click **OK** to close the *Rename* dialog box.

8. On the right, select the group where you want to add a command.
   - Click the plus or minus sign by a tab or group to expand or collapse it.

9. Click the **Choose commands from** drop-down list on the left side and select **All Commands** to display all the available commands.

10-11 Rename a new group

10-10 Rename a new tab

10. Select the command to add to the group and click the **Add** button between the two lists to add the command to the group (Figure 10-12).

11. Continue to add and rename groups and add commands to groups as desired.

12. Click **OK** to close the *Excel Options* dialog box.
   - The new tab and group display on the *Ribbon* (Figure 10-13).

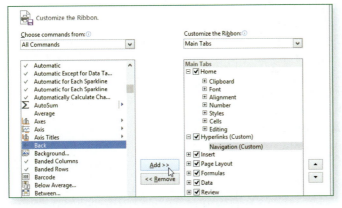

10-12 Add a command to a custom group

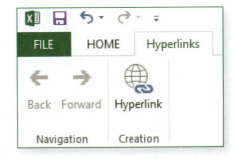

10-13 Custom tab, group, and commands on the *Ribbon*

> **MORE INFO**
>
> You can also rearrange groups on tabs and rearrange tabs on the *Ribbon*. You cannot rearrange existing commands within existing groups, but you can rearrange commands in custom groups.

HOW TO: Rearrange Tabs, Groups, and Commands on the Ribbon

1. Right-click anywhere on the **Ribbon** and select **Customize the Ribbon** from the context menu. The *Excel Options* dialog box opens with *Customize Ribbon* displayed.

2. Select the command, group, or tab you want to rearrange.

3. Click the *Move Up* or *Move Down* button to rearrange the selected item (Figure 10-14).

4. Continue to rearrange commands, groups, and tabs as desired.

5. Click **OK** to close the *Excel Options* dialog box.

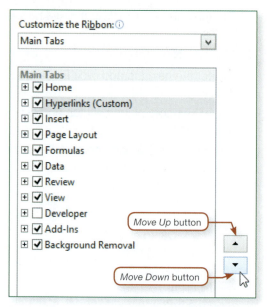

10-14 Rearrange a tab on the *Ribbon*

> **ANOTHER WAY**
>
> In the *Customize Ribbon* area of the *Excel Options* dialog box, right-click an item on the right side and select *Add New Tab, Add New Group, Rename, Remove, Move Up,* or *Move Down* from the context menu

Customize the Quick Access Toolbar

Similar to the way you added *User Form* and *Merge Workbook* buttons to the *Quick Access* toolbar, you can also add commands you frequently use to the *Quick Access* toolbar so you can quickly access them. The *Save, Undo,* and *Redo* commands are by default displayed on the *Quick Access* toolbar. You can add commonly used commands from the *Customize Quick Access Toolbar* drop-down list (Figure 10-15) or you can add other commands in the *Quick Access Toolbar* area in the *Excel Options* dialog box. When customizing the *Quick Access* toolbar, you can choose to customize it for all documents or for the current document only.

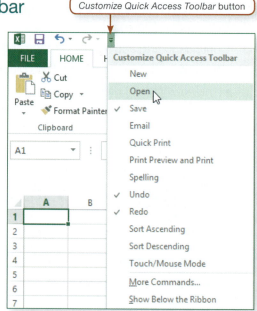

10-15 Add a command to the *Quick Access* toolbar

HOW TO: Customize the Quick Access Toolbar

1. Click the **Customize Quick Access Toolbar** drop-down list on the right edge of the *Quick Access* toolbar (Figure 10-15).

2. Select a command to add to the *Quick Access* toolbar. The command is placed on the *Quick Access* toolbar.

   - Items on the *Customize Quick Access Toolbar* drop-down list with a check mark are commands that are displayed on the *Quick Access* toolbar.

3. To add a command that is not listed on the *Customize Quick Access Toolbar*, click the **Customize Quick Access Toolbar** drop-down list and select **More Commands**. The *Excel Options* dialog box opens with the *Quick Access Toolbar* area displayed (Figure 10-16).

4. Click the **Customize Quick Access Toolbar** drop-down list on the right and select *For all documents* or the current workbook.

   - If you select *For all documents*, the change is made to the *Quick Access* toolbar for all workbooks you open in Excel.
   - If you select the current document, the change is made to the *Quick Access* toolbar in that workbook only.

5. On the left, select the command you want to add.

   - If you can't find the command you're looking for, click the **Choose commands from** drop-down list and select **All Commands**.

6. Click the **Add** button.

7. Add other commands as desired.

8. To rearrange commands on the *Quick Access* toolbar, select the command to move and click the *Move Up* or *Move Down* button.

9. Click **OK** to close the *Excel Options* dialog box.

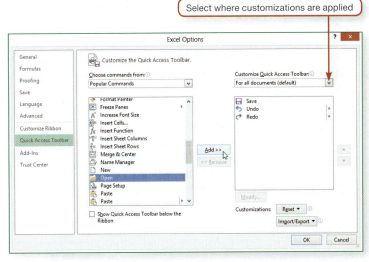

Select where customizations are applied

10-16 Customize the *Quick Access* toolbar

> ### MORE INFO
>
> To display the *Quick Access* toolbar below the *Ribbon*, click the **Customize Quick Access Toolbar** drop-down list and select **Show Below the Ribbon**.

Reset the Ribbon and the Quick Access Toolbar

After you customize your *Ribbon* and your *Quick Access* toolbar, you may want to remove commands, groups, or tabs. There are two different ways to get your *Ribbon* and your *Quick Access* toolbar back to their original settings.

- **Remove:** You can remove commands from the *Quick Access* toolbar or custom groups, and you can remove custom tabs and groups from the *Ribbon*.
- **Reset:** You can reset your *Ribbon* and your *Quick Access* toolbar to their original settings.

HOW TO: Remove Commands from the Quick Access Toolbar

1. Right-click the item you want to remove in the *Quick Access* toolbar.

2. Select **Remove from Quick Access Toolbar** from the context menu.

   - You can also remove commands from the *Quick Access* toolbar in the *Quick Access Toolbar* area of the *Excel Options* dialog box by selecting the command you want to remove and clicking the **Remove** button.

To remove commands, groups, or tabs from the *Ribbon*, use the *Customize Ribbon* area of the *Excel Options* dialog box.

HOW TO: Remove Items from the Ribbon

1. Right-click anywhere on the **Ribbon** and select **Customize the Ribbon** from the context menu. The *Excel Options* dialog box opens with *Customize Ribbon* displayed (Figure 10-17).

   - You can also click the **File** tab to open the *Backstage* view, click the **Options** button to open the *Excel Options* dialog box, and select **Customize Ribbon**.

2. On the right, select the command, group, or tab you want to remove from the *Ribbon*.

   - Click the plus or minus sign to the left of a tab or group to expand or collapse the tab and group.

3. Click the **Remove** button.

4. Click **OK** to close the *Excel Options* dialog box.

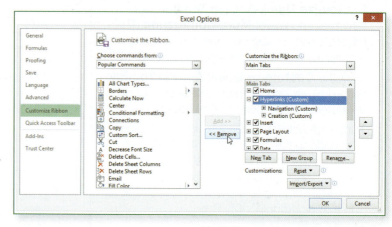

10-17 Remove items from the *Ribbon*

You can also reset the *Ribbon* or the *Quick Access* toolbar to its original settings. When you do this, you reset both the *Quick Access* toolbar and the *Ribbon* in the *Excel Options* dialog box. When resetting the *Ribbon*, you can reset a specific tab or all *Ribbon* customizations.

HOW TO: Reset the Ribbon or the Quick Access Toolbar

1. Open the *Excel Options* dialog box and select either **Customize Ribbon** or **Quick Access Toolbar**.

2. If you are resetting a specific tab, select the tab to reset.

3. At the bottom of the list on the right, click the **Reset** button.

4. Select from the available options (Figures 10-18 and 10-19).

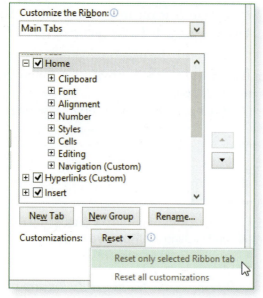

10-18 Reset the *Ribbon*

10-19 Reset the *Quick Access* toolbar

- If you are resetting the *Ribbon*, you can *Reset only selected Ribbon tab* or *Reset all customizations.*
- If you are resetting the *Quick Access* toolbar, you can *Reset only Quick Access Toolbar* or *Reset all customizations.*
- If you select **Reset all customizations** for either the *Ribbon* or *Quick Access* toolbar, Excel resets both the *Ribbon* and the *Quick Access* toolbar.

5. Depending on your selection, a dialog box may open asking you to confirm that you want to reset customizations (Figure 10-20). Click **Yes** to delete the customization.

6. Click **OK** to close the *Excel Options* dialog box.

10-20 Confirm to delete all customizations

Customizing Office Account Options

When you purchase and install Office 2013, you set up your account options. For example, you establish your Microsoft user name and password and choose the Office background. If you upgrade from Office 2010 to Office 2013, many of your settings are automatically transferred for you. You can view and customize your Office account settings in the *Backstage* view.

Microsoft Account Information

One of the features that is new in Office 2013 is the portability of your files and account settings. Your Office settings and files can travel with you, which means that you are not restricted to using just a single computer. For example, you can now log in to Office 2013 on a public computer in a computer lab on your college campus or a public library or on a friend's computer, and your Office 2013 settings are available on that computer.

When you sign in to your computer using Windows 8, you can log in with a Microsoft user name (Live, Hotmail, MSN, Messenger, or other Microsoft service account) and password. Microsoft Office uses this information to transfer your Office 2013 settings to the computer you are using. Your account settings display in the upper right of the Excel window.

Your Microsoft account signs you in not only to Windows and Office but also to other free Microsoft online services, such as *SkyDrive*, *SkyDrive groups*, and *Office Web Apps*. If you don't have a Microsoft account, you can create a free account at www.live.com. For more information on these online Microsoft services, see *SLO 10.3: Using SkyDrive*, *SLO 10.4: Using SkyDrive Groups*, and *SLO 10.5: Using Office Web Apps*.

HOW TO: Use Your Microsoft Account in Office

1. Click your name or the log on area in the upper right of the Excel window (Figure 10-21).

2. Click the **Account settings** link to open the *Account* area on the *Backstage* view (Figure 10-22).
   - You can also click the **File** tab and select **Account** on the left.
   - Your account information is displayed in this area.

3. If you are not logged in to Office 2013, click the **Switch account** link to switch accounts. The *Sign In* dialog box opens.

4. Type in your Microsoft account email address and click **Sign in**. Another *Sign in* dialog box opens (Figure 10-23).

10-21 Microsoft account information

10-22 Office account information and settings

5. Type your password and click **Sign in**.

- If you don't have a Microsoft account, click the **Sign up now** link to take you to a web page where you can create a free Microsoft account.
- You can also use your Microsoft account to log in to *SkyDrive*, where you can create, store, and share files, use Office Web Apps, and create *SkyDrive* groups.

6. Click the **Back** button to return to Excel if needed.

10-23 Sign in to Office using a Microsoft Account

> ▶ **MORE INFO**
>
> If you are using a public computer, be sure to click the **Sign out** link in the *Account* area on the *Backstage view* to log out of your Office account.

Office Background

You can change the Office background in the *General* category in the *Excel Options* dialog box, and you can also change the background in the *Account* area on the *Backstage* view. Click the **Office Background** drop-down list and select a background (Figure 10-24). The background displays in the upper right corner of the Excel window. This background applies to all Office applications you use.

Connected Services

Office 2013 has added many features to allow you to connect to online services. In the *Account* area on the *Backstage* view, add online services you regularly use by clicking the **Add a service** drop-down list and selecting a service

10-24 Change *Office Background* or *Office Theme*

(Figure 10-25). When you add a service, you are usually prompted to enter your user name and password to connect to the online service. The services you are currently connected to are listed in the **Connected Service** area.

All of the connected services in your account travel with you when you log in to Office on another computer. The following services are available in the different service categories listed:

- *Images & Video:* Facebook for Office, Flickr, and YouTube
- *Storage:* Office365 SharePoint and *SkyDrive*
- *Sharing:* Facebook, LinkedIn, and Twitter

10-25 Add an online service to your Office account

Add and Manage Apps for Office

Another feature new to Office 2013 is the ability to add *apps* (applications) to your Office 2013 program. Just like the apps on your smart phone, apps for Office are programs that add functionality to your Office software. For example, you can add a dictionary, an encyclopedia, a news feed, maps, or many other apps.

HOW TO: Add Apps to Office

1. Click the top half of the **Apps for Office** button [*Insert* tab, *Apps* group].
   - The *Apps for Office* button is a split button. Click the bottom half of the button to see your recently used apps or select **See All** to open the *Apps for Office* dialog box (Figure 10-26).
   - You must be signed in to your account to see the apps.

10-26 *Apps for Office* dialog box

- Click **My Apps** to display Office apps you previously installed.
- Click **Featured Apps** to display available apps. Use the search text box to type keywords and search for matching apps.

2. Select an app and click the **Add** link to install that app. The *Apps* pane opens on the right (Figure 10-27)

   - Depending on the app you select, you may be taken to a web site to add the app.

3. If the app does not automatically load in the *Apps* pane, click the **exclamation point** in the upper left of the *Apps* pane to display information about the app, and then click the **Start** button to activate the app. The app is displayed in the *Apps* pane.

   - The app is displayed in the *Apps* pane.
   - You must be online for an app to start and load content.

Apps pane

10-27 Activate the app in the *Apps* pane

> **MORE INFO**
>
> Regularly check the *Apps for Office* dialog box for new and featured apps.

After installing apps in Office, you can manage your apps by clicking the **Manage My Apps** link in the *My Apps* area in *Apps for Office* dialog box. You are taken to the *My Apps for Office and SharePoint* web page where you can view your apps, hide apps, and search for other apps to install (Figure 10-28).

10-28 Manage your apps online

PAUSE & PRACTICE: EXCEL 10-1

For this project, you customize Excel options, add items to the *Ribbon* and the *Quick Access* toolbar, customize your Office account settings, and add an app.

Note: You need a Microsoft account (Live, Hotmail, MSN) to complete this project.

File Needed: **PLRSales-10.xlsx**
Completed Project File Name: **[your initials] PP E10-1.xlsx**

1. Open the **PLRSales-10** workbook.

2. Save the workbook as: **[your initials] PP E10-1**.

3. Log in to Office using your Microsoft account. Skip this step if you are already logged in with your Microsoft account.
   a. In the upper right corner of the Excel window, log in to Office using your Microsoft account.
   b. If you don't have a Microsoft account, go to www.live.com and follow the instructions to create a free Microsoft account.

4. Customize Excel options.
   a. Click the **File** tab to open the *Backstage* view and select **Options** to open the *Excel Options* dialog box.
   b. Select **General** on the left and type your name in the *User name* area if it's not already there.
   c. Uncheck the **Show the Start screen when this application starts** check box.
   d. Select **Save** on the left and check the **Don't show the Backstage when opening or saving files** check box in the *Save workbooks* area.
   e. Select **Advanced** on the left and check the **Show gridlines** check box in the *Display options for this worksheet* area.
   f. Click **OK** to close the *Excel Options* dialog box and apply the changes.

5. Add a tab, group, and commands to the *Ribbon*.
   a. Right-click anywhere on the **Ribbon** and select **Customize the Ribbon** from the context menu to open the *Excel Options* dialog box with the *Customize Ribbon* area displayed.
   b. On the right, click the **Home** tab and then click the **New Tab** button. A new tab and group are inserted below the *Home* tab.
   c. Select **New Tab (Custom)** and click **Rename** to open the *Rename* dialog box.
   d. Type your first name and click **OK** to close the **Rename** dialog box.
   e. Select **New Group (Custom)** and click **Rename** to open the *Rename* dialog box (Figure 10-29).
   f. Select the smiley face symbol, type Common Commands as the group name in the *Display name* area, and click **OK** to close the *Rename* dialog box.

10-29 Rename new custom group

   g. On the right, select the **Common Commands** group.
   h. Click the **Choose commands from** drop-down list on the left side and select **All Commands** to display all the available commands in the list on the left.
   i. Select the **Chart** command and click the **Add** button between the two lists to add the command to the group (Figure 10-30).
   j. Add the **Trace Precedents** and **View Side by Side** commands to the *Common Commands* group.

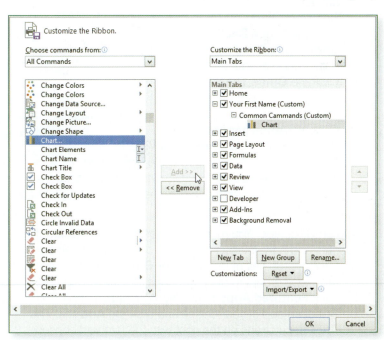

10-30 Add command to custom group

k. Click **OK** to close the *Excel Options* dialog box.

l. Click the **[your first name]** tab on the *Ribbon* (Figure 10-31).

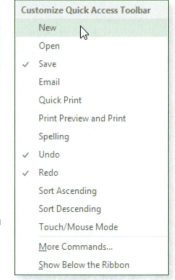

6. Add commands to the *Quick Access* toolbar.

   a. Click the **Customize Quick Access Toolbar** drop-down list and select **New** (Figure 10-32).

   b. Add **Open** and **Quick Print** to the *Quick Access* toolbar if they are not already there.

   c. Click the **Customize Quick Access Toolbar** drop-down list and select **More Commands** to open the *Excel Options* dialog box with the *Quick Access Toolbar* area displayed.

   d. Click the **Choose commands from** drop-down list on the left side and select **All Commands**.

   e. Select **Insert a Comment** and click the **Add** button (Figure 10-33).

   f. Select **Quick Print** on the right and use the **Move Up** button to rearrange it so it appears after *Save* in the *Quick Access* toolbar list of commands.

   g. Click **OK** to close the *Excel Options* dialog box.

10-31 New tab and group

10-32 Add a command to the *Quick Access* toolbar

7. Customize your Office account settings.

   a. Click the **File** tab and select **Account** to display your account information on the *Backstage* view.

   b. Click the **Office Background** drop-down list and select a background of your choice.

   c. Click the **Office Theme** drop-down list and select a theme of your choice.

   d. Click the **Add a service** drop-down list, select **Images & Videos**, and click **YouTube**. YouTube is added in the *Connected Services* area. *Note: depending on your computer specifications, operating system, and browser, these options may not be available.*

8. Add an Office app. You must be logged in to your Microsoft account and have Internet Explorer 9 or later to add an app.

   a. Click the top half of the **Apps for Office** button [*Insert* tab, *Apps* group] to open the *Apps for Office* dialog box.

   b. Click **Featured Apps** to display the featured apps.

   c. Select an app of your choice and click the **Add** link. The *Apps* pane opens on the right with the featured chosen app (Figure 10-34).

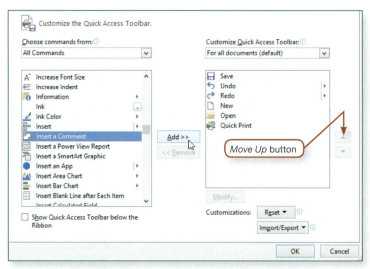

10-33 Add a command to the *Quick Access* toolbar

10-34 *Apps* pane

d. Click the **exclamation point** (if available) in the upper left of the *Apps* pane to display information about the app.

e. Click the **Start** button (if necessary) to activate the app.

f. Close the *Apps* pane.

9. Save and close the workbook (Figure 10-35).

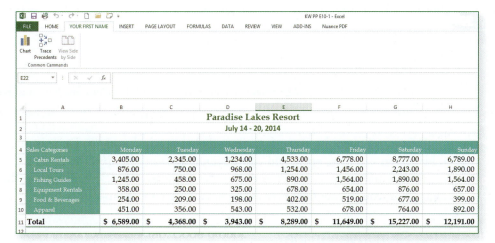

10-35 PP E10-1 completed (customized *Ribbon* and *Quick Access* toolbar displayed)

Using SkyDrive

Microsoft Office 2013 works in conjunction with ***Microsoft SkyDrive*** to provide access to your files from any computer. *SkyDrive* is a "cloud" storage area where you can store files in an online location and access them from any computer. Cloud storage means you don't have to be tied to one computer and you don't have to take your files with you on a portable storage device.

When you have a Microsoft account (Live, Hotmail, MSN, Messenger, or other Microsoft service account), you also have a *SkyDrive* account. Your *SkyDrive* account is a private and secure online location. You can use *SkyDrive* to store files, create folders to organize stored files, share files with others, and create *SkyDrive* groups where you invite people to become members and store and share files. Using Windows 8, you can access your *SkyDrive* files from a Windows folder or you can access *SkyDrive* online from any computer using an Internet browser web page. If you don't have a Microsoft account, you can create a free account at www.live.com.

Use SkyDrive in a Windows Folder

With Windows 8, *SkyDrive* is one of your storage location folders, similar to your *Documents* or *Pictures* folders (Figure 10-36). You can save, open,

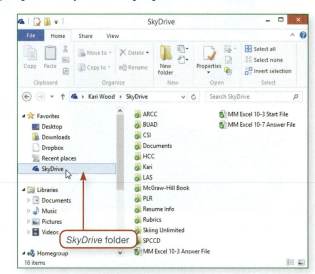

10-36 *SkyDrive* folder displayed in a Windows Explorer folder

and edit your *SkyDrive* files from a Windows folder. Your **SkyDrive folder** looks and functions similar to other Windows folders.

The primary difference between the *SkyDrive* folder and other Windows folders is the physical location where the files are stored. If you save a document in your *Documents* folder, the file is stored on the hard drive on your computer, and you have access to this file only when you are working on your computer. When you save a document in your *SkyDrive* folder, the file is stored on the *SkyDrive* cloud, and you have access to the file from your computer *and* any other computer with Internet access.

> ### MORE INFO
>
> To access your *SkyDrive* folder from Windows, you must be logged into your Microsoft account.

When you open the *Save As* or *Open* dialog box in Excel, *SkyDrive* is one of the available folders. You can save, open, and edit documents from the *SkyDrive* folder. You can also create folders and rename, move, or delete files from your *SkyDrive* folder. In the *Excel Options* dialog box, you can set *SkyDrive* as the default save location.

Use SkyDrive Online

The main benefit of using *SkyDrive* to store your files is the freedom it gives you to access your files from any computer with Internet access. In addition to accessing your *SkyDrive* files from a Windows folder on your computer, you can access your *SkyDrive* files from a web page using an Internet browser. You sign in to the *SkyDrive* web page using your Microsoft account.

HOW TO: Use SkyDrive Online

1. Open an Internet browser Window and go to the *SkyDrive* web site (www.skydrive.com), which takes you to the *SkyDrive* sign in page (Figure 10-37).

10-37 Sign in to *SkyDrive* (www.skydrive.com)

- You can use most Internet browsers to access *SkyDrive* (e.g., Internet Explorer, Google Chrome, or Mozilla Firefox). Check the *SkyDrive* site to see a list of those supported.

2. Type in your Microsoft account email address and password.

- If you are on your own computer, select the **Keep me signed in** check box to stay signed in to *SkyDrive* when you return to the page.

3. Click the **Sign In** button to go to your *SkyDrive* web page (Figure 10-38).

- The different areas of *SkyDrive* are displayed under the *SkyDrive* heading on the left.

4. Click **Files** on the left to display your folders and files in the *Folder* area on the right.

5. Click a file or folder check box on the right to select it.

- Select **List** view in the top right corner if your view doesn't match Figure 10-38.
- At the top, there are buttons and drop-down lists for different actions you can perform on selected files and folders.
- If you click a folder, the folder opens.
- If you click an Office file, the file opens in Office Web Apps (see *SLO 10.5: Using Office Web Apps*).

6. Click the **SkyDrive** drop-down list to navigate between the different areas of your Microsoft Account: *Mail*, *People* (contacts), *Calendar*, and *SkyDrive*.

7. Click your name in the upper right corner and select **Sign out** to sign out of *SkyDrive*.

Click to select other areas of your Microsoft account

10-38 *SkyDrive* online environment

> ### MORE INFO
>
> If you're using a public computer, do not check the *Keep me signed in* check box. You do not want your *SkyDrive* files available to the next person who uses the computer.

Create a Folder

In *SkyDrive*, you can create folders to organize your files in a way that is similar to how you organize Windows folders.

HOW TO: Create SkyDrive Folders

1. Click the **Files** button on the left to display the contents of your SkyDrive folder in the *Folder* area on the right.

2. Click the **Create** button and select **Folder** from the drop-down list. A new folder is created (Figure 10-39).

3. Type the name of the new folder and press **Enter**.

4. Click a folder to open the folder.

- You can create a new folder inside an existing folder, or you can upload files to the folder (see the following *Upload Files* section).
- Click the **[your name] SkyDrive** link above the folder area to return to the main *SkyDrive* folder.

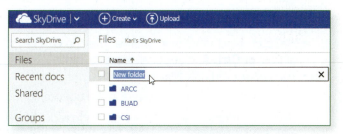

10-39 Add a new *SkyDrive* folder

Upload Files

You can upload files to your *SkyDrive* from a folder on your computer or a portable storage device. When you upload files to your *SkyDrive*, you are not removing the files from the original location but actually copying them to *SkyDrive*.

HOW TO: Upload Files to SkyDrive

1. Click **Files** on the left to display your files and folders in the *Folder* area.
2. Click the **Upload** button (Figure 10-40). The *Choose File to Upload* dialog box opens (Figure 10-41).

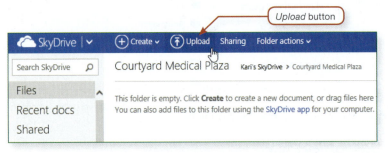

10-40 Upload a file to *SkyDrive*

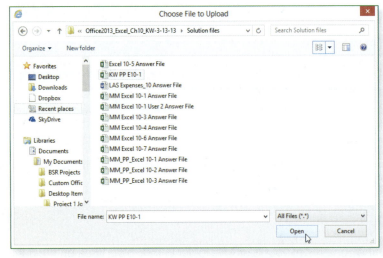

10-41 Select files to upload to *SkyDrive*

3. Select the files you want to upload to your *SkyDrive*.
   - You can select more than one file. Use the **Ctrl** key to select non-adjacent files, the **Shift** key to select a range of files, or **Ctrl+A** to select all files in a folder.
   - You can upload only files, not a folder.
4. An upload status window appears in the bottom right corner when you are uploading files.
   - *SkyDrive* automatically resizes pictures to reduce file size. Deselect the **Resize photos to 2048 px** check box if you don't want photos resized. This option is not visible unless you perform the photo upload.
5. The files you upload appear in the files and folders area of *SkyDrive*.

Move, Copy, and Delete Files and Folders

You can also move, copy, and delete files and folders online in *SkyDrive*. When you move a file or folder, it is removed from its location and placed in the new location you select. When you copy a file or folder, it is copied to the new location you select, and the file or folder also remains in its original location.

HOW TO: Move, Copy, and Delete SkyDrive Files

1. Click the **check box** next to the file or folder you want to move or copy.
   - You can move multiple items by selecting the check boxes of all the items you want to move or copy.
2. Click the **Manage** button at the top and then select **Move to** or **Copy to** from the drop-down list (Figure 10-42). A move or copy window opens (Figure 10-43).

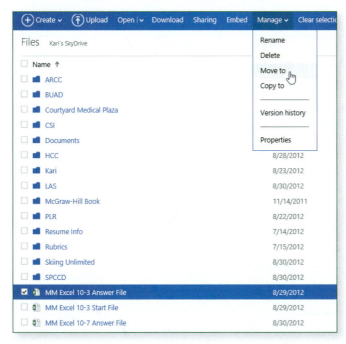

10-42 Move a *SkyDrive* file

10-43 Select folder where you will move or copy selected items

   - You can select and move multiple files at the same time.
   - You can copy only one file at a time.
3. Select the folder where you want to move or copy the selected items.
   - You can place selected items in an existing folder or create a new folder for moved or copied items.
   - Press **Esc** on the keyboard or click away from the move or copy window to cancel the move or copy process and close the window.
4. Click the **Move** or **Copy** button to close the window and move or copy the selected items.
5. To delete a file or folder, click the **check box** to the left of the items to delete.
6. Click the **Manage** button and select **Delete**. A confirmation window opens.

Download a File

If you are working on a computer in a computer lab on your college campus or any other public computer, you can download a file or folder from your *SkyDrive* folder so you can open it in Excel (or other program). After you finish modifying the document, you can upload it to your *SkyDrive* folder so the most recent version of your document is in *SkyDrive*. When you download items from *SkyDrive*, the items are not removed from *SkyDrive*. A copy of the items is downloaded.

HOW TO: Download Files from SkyDrive

1. Click the **check box** to the left of the file or folder you want to download.
   - If you select more than one file or folder to download, a compressed folder downloads with the files and folders you selected.
   - If you select a single file, *SkyDrive* downloads the file.

2. Click the **Download** button at the top. The download window appears at the bottom of your screen.
   - To choose where the file is saved, select the **Save as** option from the **Save** drop-down button in the *Download* window (Figure 10-44).
   - If you select **Save**, your files are saved in the *Downloads* folder on your hard drive.

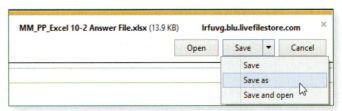

10-44 Download window from *SkyDrive*

3. Select the location where you want to save the downloaded items.

4. If you want to rename the file, type a file name in the *File name* area.

5. Click the **Save** button to close the *Save As* dialog box and download the selected items (Figure 10-45).

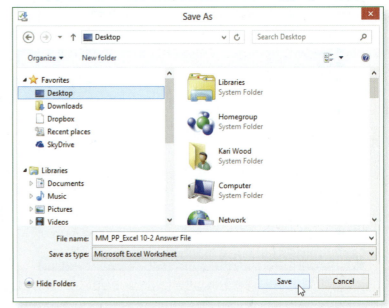

10-45 Save downloaded items from *SkyDrive*

Share Files

SkyDrive allows you to **share files or folders** with others. When you share files or folders with others, you establish the access they have to the items you share. You can choose whether other users can only view files or view and edit files. When you share a file or folder in your *SkyDrive*, you have the option to send an email with a link to the shared item or generate a hyperlink to share with others that gives them access. If your Windows account is connected to LinkedIn, Facebook, or Twitter, you can also post a link to a shared file in one or more of these social networking sites.

HOW TO: Share a SkyDrive File or Folder

1. Select the file or folder you want to share.
   - You can select only one file or folder at a time. You can share as many files or folders as you want, but you have to select and share them one at a time.
   - If you share a folder, shared users have access to all of the files in the folder.

2. Click the **Sharing** button at the top. A sharing window opens with different sharing options (Figure 10-46).

3. To send an email, click **Send email**, type the email address, and then type a brief message.

   - Press **Tab** after typing an email address to add another recipient.
   - You can click **Get a link** to generate a link that you can send to recipients using your own email account, or you can post a link to the shared file on Facebook, Twitter, or LinkedIn.

10-46 Send a sharing email

4. Select the **Recipients can edit** check box if you want the recipient to be able to edit the file.

   - Deselect this check box if you only want recipients to be able to view the file.
   - You can also mandate that recipients sign in to *SkyDrive* in order to view or edit the file by selecting the **Require everyone who accesses this to sign in** check box.

5. Click the **Share** button to send the sharing invitation email.

6. Click **Done** in the confirmation window that opens.

You can change the sharing permission or remove sharing on a file or folder. The **Details pane** on the right displays properties of the selected file or folder.

HOW TO: Change or Remove SkyDrive Sharing

1. Select the shared file or folder.

2. Click the **Details** button in the upper right corner. The *Details* pane opens on the right (Figure 10-47).

   - The *Sharing* area lists those who have permission to view or edit the selected item.

3. Click the **Can view or Can edit link** to open the *Share* window (Figure 10-48).

10-47 Change or remove sharing permission in the *Details* pane

10-48 Change or remove sharing permissions

4. Select or deselect the **Can edit** check box to change this permission (Figure 10-47).

5. Click the **Remove permissions** button to remove all sharing permissions.

6. Click the **Done** button to close the *Share* window.

7. Click the **Details** button again to close the *Details* pane.

Using SkyDrive Groups

If you belong to a team at work or school, or in an organization, you can create a **SkyDrive group** to store and share documents. A *SkyDrive* group is another free Microsoft online service that is connected to your *SkyDrive* account and available from your *SkyDrive* web page. You can invite people to become group members. Members can also access the group from their *SkyDrive* web page.

Create a SkyDrive Group

When you create a *SkyDrive* group, your group has a name, web address, and group email address. After you create a group, you can invite members and establish a role for each member. Members you invite to your group must have a Microsoft account to access the group. Members can store and share files in this group on *SkyDrive*.

HOW TO: Create a SkyDrive Group

1. On your *SkyDrive* web page, click **Groups** on the left to open the area where you create a new group (Figure 10-49).

2. Type the name of the group in the *Group name* text box.

3. Type an email address for the group in the *Group email* text box.
   - SkyDrive group email addresses are limited to 24 characters and can contain only numbers, letters, and hyphens.

4. Click **Create group** to create your group.
   - The new group is listed in the *Groups* area on the left.
   - If the email address is not available, try a different one and click **Create group** again.

5. Click your group in the *Groups* area on the left to select it (Figure 10-50).
   - You can upload files and create folders in your group.

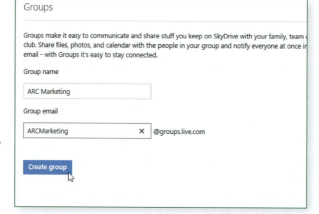

10-49 Create a *SkyDrive* group

10-50 *SkyDrive* group

People you invite as members receive an email that invites them to join the group. When they accept the invitation, they are listed in the *Group membership* area of the group.

> **MORE INFO**
>
> You can upload files to your group the same way you upload files to your *SkyDrive* folder.

Invite and Manage SkyDrive Group Members

After you create your group and invite members, you can add new members, remove members, and change roles of members. You can set members' **roles** as *Owner*, *Co-Owner*, and *Member*.

Roles control the permission level assigned to a group member. **Owners** and **Co-Owners** have full access to create, edit, and delete files and folders in the group, and to customize group options. **Members** can create files and folders, edit them, and view others' files and folders.

HOW TO: Invite and Manage SkyDrive Group Members

1. On your *SkyDrive* web page, select your group.

2. Click the **Group actions** button at the top and select **Invite people** to open an area where you can invite members (Figure 10-51).

3. Type email addresses for those you want to invite to the group.

   - Press **Tab** after typing an email address to enter another one.

4. Click **Invite** to send the group invitation.

   - Invitees receive an email message inviting them to the group.
   - They have to accept the invitation to join the group.
   - When you invite people to become members of a *SkyDrive* group, their role (permission level), by default, is *Member.* You can change members' roles.

5. Click the **Group actions** button and select **View membership** to view group membership, change group members' roles, or remove members. The *Membership* area displays.

6. Select a member, click the **Change role** button, and select a membership role (Figure 10-52).

7. To delete a member, select the **Member** and click the **Remove** button.

10-51 Invite *SkyDrive* group members

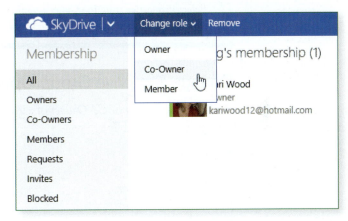

10-52 Change group member's role

Email SkyDrive Group Members

When you create a group, you choose an email address for the group. You can send an email to the group using this SkyDrive group email address. When you send the email, it is sent to each of the group members.

HOW TO: Email SkyDrive Group Members

1. On your *SkyDrive* web page, select your group.

2. Click the **Group Actions** button at the top and select **Send an email message**. A new message opens in your Microsoft account email (Figure 10-53).

   - This window might vary depending on the type of Microsoft email address you have (e.g., Live.com, Hotmail or Outlook.com).
   - The *SkyDrive* group email address is in the *To* area. You can add recipients.

3. Type a subject and a message.

4. Click **Send** to send the email message.

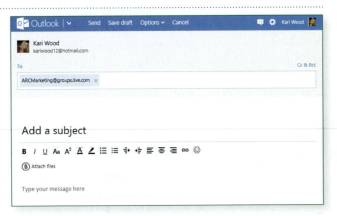

10-53 Send an email to *SkyDrive* group members

You can also create a group email or view email history by clicking on a link in the *Details* pane (Figure 10-54). Click the **Details** button to open the *Details* pane. Click the **group email address** link to create a new group email. Click the **View** link to the right of *Group email history* to view group emails.

10-54 *Details* pane

Change SkyDrive Group Options

If you are the *Owner* or *Co-Owner* of a group, you can customize the group options. The following categories are available:

- *General*
- *Email*
- *Group conversations*
- *Personal*
- *Leave group*
- *Delete group*

Select a group and click the **Group options** button at the top to display the *Options* page (Figure 10-55). Click one of the categories on the left to display the customization options for that category. When you finish making changes, click the **Save** button at the bottom to save and apply the changes. The *Options* area is where you can choose to leave a group or delete a group.

10-55 *SkyDrive* group options

For this project, you upload files to and create folders in your *SkyDrive* folder, move files, share a file, create and modify a SkyDrive group, and invite members.

Note to Students and Instructor:

Students: *For this project, you share SkyDrive files with your instructor and invite your instructor to become a member of your SkyDrive group.*
Instructor: *In order to complete this project, your students need your Microsoft email address. You can create a new Live or Hotmail account for projects in this chapter.*

Files Needed: ***[your initials] PP E10-1.xlsx, SkiingUnlimited-10.docx,*** and ***TrainingGuide-10.docx***
Completed Project File Name: ***[your initials] PP E10-2.xlsx***

1. Open the ***[your initials] PP 10-1*** workbook.

2. Save the workbook as ***[your initials] PP Excel 10-2***.

3. Create a folder in your *SkyDrive* folder and save this workbook in the new folder.
   a. Select **Computer** and click the **Browse** button.
   b. In the *Save As* dialog box select the **SkyDrive** folder on the left (Figure 10-56).
   c. Click the **New Folder** button.
   d. Type your first name and then add -Excel. Press **Enter**.
   e. Double-click **your folder** to open it and click **Save** to save the ***[your initials] PP E10-2*** workbook in your folder in *SkyDrive*.

4. Close the workbook and exit Excel.

5. Log in to *SkyDrive* online, create a new folder, and upload files.
   a. Open an Internet browser window, type www.skydrive.com in the address bar at the top, and press **Enter** to go to the *SkyDrive* log in page.
   b. Type your Microsoft email address and password to log in to *SkyDrive*. The new folder you created is displayed in *SkyDrive* (there might be other folders listed as well). *Hint: if you have Windows 7 installed, download the SkyDrive desktop for Windows to see files and folders in the SkyDrive.*
   c. Click the **Create** button at the top and select **Folder** from the drop-down list (Figure 10-57).

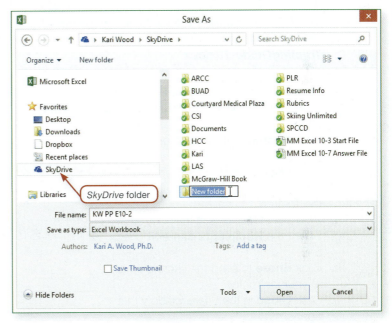

10-56 Create a new folder in your *SkyDrive* folder

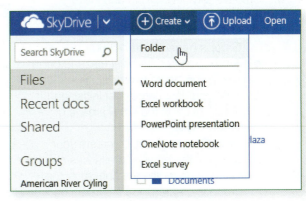

10-57 Create a new folder in *SkyDrive*

d. Type CMP-Excel as the name for the new folder and press **Enter**.

e. Click the **CMP-Excel** folder (not the check box) to open it.

f. Click the **Upload** button at the top to open the *Open* dialog box.

g. Select the *[your initials] PP E10-1.xlsx*, *SkiingUnlimited-10.docx*, and *TrainingGuide-10.docx* files from your student data files and click **Open**. The files are added to the *CMP-Excel* folder.

6. Move a file.

a. Click **Files** on the left to return to your list of folders.

b. Click the *[your first name]-Excel* folder to open it. The *[your initials] PP E10-2* file is in this folder. If it is not, add the file.

c. Select the check box next to the *[your initials] PP E10-2* file to select it.

d. Click the **Manage** button and select **Move to** from the drop-down list. A dialog box opens (Figure 10-58).

e. Select the **CMP-Excel** folder and click **Move**.

f. Click **Files** to return to your list of folders.

g. Click the **CMP-Excel** folder to confirm that the file moved. There should be four files in the CMP-Excel folder: *[your initials] PP E10-1.xlsx*, *[your initials] PP E10-2.xlsx*, *SkiingUnlimited-10.docx*, and *TrainingGuide-10.docx*.

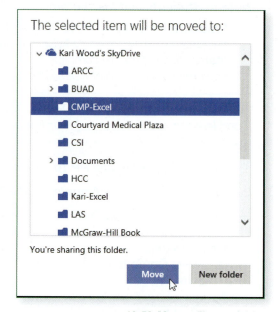

10-58 Move a file to a folder

7. Share a folder.

a. Click **Files** to return to your list of folders.

b. Select the check box to the left of the **CMP-Excel** folder.

c. Click **Sharing** at the top to open the dialog box (Figure 10-59).

d. Select **Send email** on the left.

e. Type your instructor's email address in the *To* area.

f. Type a brief message in the body area.

g. Select the **Recipients can edit** check box.

h. Click **Share** to send the sharing email to your instructor.

i. Click **Close** in the *Share* window that opens.

10-59 Share a folder and send an email

8. Create a *SkyDrive* group and invite a member.

a. Click **Groups** on the left to open the *Groups* page (Figure 10-60).

b. Type Courtyard Medical Plaza-Excel in the *Group name* text box.

c. Type your last name, first initial, and -CMP-Excel in the *email* area (e.g., WoodK-CMP-Excel).

d. Click **Create group** to create your group. If the email address was already taken, type a different one. After the group is created, you are taken back to *SkyDrive* with the *Courtyard Medical Plaza-Excel* group selected.

10-60 Create a *SkyDrive* group

9. Invite a member to your group.
   a. Confirm that the *Courtyard Medical Plaza-Excel* group is selected in the *Groups* area on the left. If it is not, select it.
   b. Click the **Group actions** button at the top and select **Invite people**. An *Invite* window opens.
   c. Type your instructor's email address and click **Invite**.

10. Upload files to your group.
    a. Confirm that the *Courtyard Medical Plaza-Excel* group is selected in the *Groups* area on the left. If it is not, select it.
    b. Click the **Upload** button to open the *Choose File to Upload* dialog box.
    c. Select the ***SkiingUnlimited-10*** and ***TrainingGuide-10*** files from your student data files and click **Open**. The files are added to your group. (*Hint: You may need to refresh your browser window to display the files.*)

11. Change group options.
    a. With your group selected on the left, click the **Group options** button at the top. The *Options* page opens.
    b. Select **Email** on the left if it is not already selected.
    c. In the *Link to group website* area, click the **Only group members can view the group using this link** radio button.
    d. Click the **Save** button. The *Options* page closes and you return to your group.
    e. Click the **Group options** button again to reopen the *Options* page.
    f. Click **Group conversations** on the left.
    g. Click **Turn off group conversations**. The *Options* area closes and you return to your group.
    h. Confirm the two files are in your Courtyard Medical Plaza-Excel group folder (Figure 10-61).

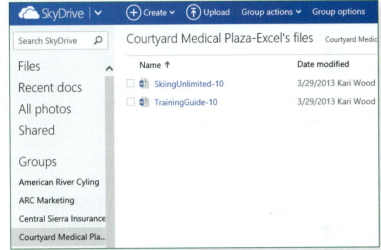

10-61 PP E10-2 completed (*SkyDrive* group displayed)

12. Click **[your name]-Excel** in the upper right corner and select **Sign out** from the *Account* drop-down list.

SLO 10.5

Using Office Web Apps

Office Web Apps is free online software from Microsoft that works in conjunction with your online *SkyDrive* account. With Office Web Apps, you can work with Office files online *without* having Office 2013 installed on the computer you are using, such as when you use a friend's computer that does not have Office 2013 installed.

Office Web Apps is available from your *SkyDrive* web page. Office Web Apps is a scaled-down version of Office 2013 and not as robust in terms of features, but you can use it to create, edit, print, share, and insert comments on files. If you need more advanced features, you can open Office Web Apps files in Office 2013.

Edit Office Web Apps Files

You can use Office Web Apps to open and edit many Office files you have stored in your *SkyDrive* or *SkyDrive* groups. The working environment in Office Web Apps is very similar to Microsoft Office and has the familiar *Ribbon*, tabs, and groups. However, there are not as many tabs and features available in Office Web Apps.

When you initially open a file from either *SkyDrive* or a *SkyDrive* group, it is displayed in **read-only mode** or **edit mode** in the browser window where you view the file. When you edit the file in the browser window, Office Web Apps opens your file in *edit* mode in the appropriate program. Default views are dependent on each web app. For example, Excel files in *SkyDrive* open in *edit* mode in the **Excel Web App** and Word documents open in *read-only* mode in the **Word Web App**.

HOW TO: Edit an Office Web Apps File

1. Log in to your *SkyDrive* account in an Internet browser window.

2. Click an Office file to open from *SkyDrive* or a *SkyDrive* group (Figure 10-62). The file is displayed in *read-only* mode in an Office Web Apps window in some apps (e.g., Word) and in *edit* mode with other apps (e.g., Excel).

   - You cannot edit the file in *read-only* or *reading view* mode.
   - You can also choose a file by selecting its check box, click the **Open** drop-down button, and select **Open in Excel Web App** or **Open in Excel**.

3. The workbook is ready for editing in Office Web Apps.

   - You can also open an Office Web Apps file in Microsoft Office. To do this, you must have Microsoft Office installed on the computer you are using.
   - Click the **Open in Excel** tab in the *Office Web Apps* window to launch Office and open the workbook in the Excel Office application (Figure 10-63).

4. Make desired editing and formatting changes in Office Web Apps (Figure 10-64).

   - The *File*, *Home*, *Insert*, and *View* tabs are on the *Ribbon*.
   - Click **Open in [Office application]** to open the file in Office.

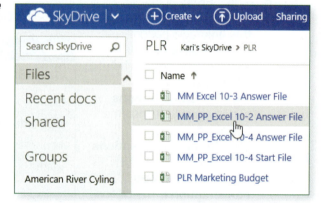

10-62 Open a workbook in Office Web Apps

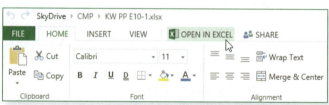

10-63 Open in Excel

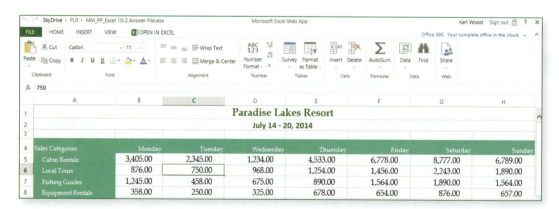

10-64 Edit a workbook in Excel Web Apps

- You can make editing and formatting changes; apply styles; and cut, copy, and paste selected cells.
- When you are using Office Web Apps, some advanced formatting such as text boxes, pictures, charts, and *SmartArt* might not be arranged and aligned as they are when you open the file in Excel 2013.

5. Click the **Save** button or press **Ctrl+S** to save changes to the file.

- Alternatively, click the **SkyDrive** link at the top to return to your *SkyDrive* folders and files.

Create Office Web Apps Files

You are not limited to editing existing documents in Office Web Apps; you can create new Word documents, Excel workbooks, PowerPoint presentations, and OneNote notebooks. When you create an Office Web Apps file, the file is saved in your *SkyDrive* or *SkyDrive* group.

HOW TO: Create an Office Web Apps File

1. In *SkyDrive* or a *SkyDrive* group, select the location where you want to create a new file.
2. Click the **Create** button and select the type of file to create (*Word document, Excel workbook, PowerPoint presentation, OneNote notebook*) (Figure 10-65). The *New* dialog box opens (Figure 10-66).

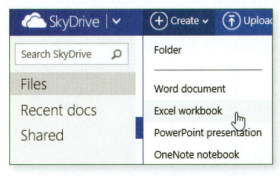

10-65 Create an Excel Web App workbook

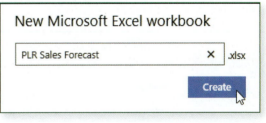

10-66 Create and name a new Excel workbook in Excel Web App

3. Type the name of the file and click the **Create** button. The file opens in the selected Web App in edit mode.
4. Type information in the workbook and apply formatting as desired.
5. Click the **Save** button or press **Ctrl+S** to save changes to the file.
6. Click the **SkyDrive** link at the top to return to your *SkyDrive* folders and files.

Print Office Web Apps Files

You can print files from Office Web Apps similar to how you print files in Office. The difference when printing in Office Web Apps is that the program creates a PDF (portable document format) file when you print a workbook so the file retains its original format. You can print from either *read-only* or *edit* mode.

HOW TO: Print an Office Web Apps File

1. Click a file to open from *SkyDrive* or a *SkyDrive* group.
2. In either *read-only* or *edit* mode, click the **File** tab.
3. Select **Print** on the left and then click the **Print** button (Figure 10-67).
   - The printable PDF file opens in a new window with a preview of the file.
4. Click the **Current Selection** or **Entire Sheet** radio button to determine the print area (Figure 10-68).
5. Click the **Print** button.

10-67 **Print to workbook**

10-68 **Print options**

Share Office Web Apps Files

In addition to sharing a file from *SkyDrive* or a *SkyDrive* group, you can also share a file you are previewing or editing in Office Web Apps. The process for sharing a file in Office Web Apps is similar to sharing a file or folder in *SkyDrive*.

HOW TO: Share an Office Web Apps File

1. Open a file in Office Web Apps.
2. Click the **File** tab and select **Share** at the left. Click **Share with People** to open the *Share* window (Figure 10-69).

10-69 **Share an Office Web Apps file**

3. To send an email, click **Send email**, type the desired recipient's email address, and type a brief message.
   - Press **Tab** after typing an email address to add another recipient.
   - You can also click **Get a link** to generate a link that you can send to recipients.

4. Select the **Recipients can edit** check box if you want the recipient to be able to edit the file.
   - Deselect this check box if you want recipients to be able only to view the file.
   - You can also require recipients to sign in to *SkyDrive* in order to view or edit the file by selecting the **Require everyone who accesses this to sign in** check box.
5. Click the **Share** button.
   - Recipients receive an email containing a link to the shared file or folder.
6. Click **Done** to close the *Share* window and return to the Office Web Apps file.

Collaborate in Office Web Apps

Office Web Apps let you synchronously or asynchronously collaborate on an Office file with others who have access to the shared file. If two or more users are working on the same file in Office Web Apps, collaboration information is displayed in the bottom right corner of the Office Web Apps window (Figure 10-70). You are alerted of available updates and told how many people are editing the file.

10-70 Collaboration information displayed in the *Status* bar

Click **Updates Available** in the *Status bar* to apply updates to your document. Click **People Editing** to view the names of users who are currently editing the file.

PAUSE & PRACTICE: EXCEL 10-3

For this project, you upload a file to your *SkyDrive*, edit a workbook in Excel Web App, share a file, create an Excel Web App workbook, and copy and rename files.

Note to Students and Instructor:

    Students: *For this project, you share a SkyDrive file with your instructor.*
    Instructor: *In order to complete this project, your students need your Microsoft email address. You can create a new Live or Hotmail account for the projects in this chapter.*

File Needed: **CMPRevenue-10.xlsx**
Completed Project File Names: **[your initials] PP E10-3a.xlsx** and **[your initials] EPP 10-3b.xlsx**

1. Open an Internet browser page and log in to your *SkyDrive* account (www.skydrive.com).

2. Upload a file to a folder in your *SkyDrive.*
   a. Click the **CMP-Excel** folder to open it.
   b. Click the **Upload** button to open the *Choose file to Upload* dialog box.
   c. Select **CMPRevenue-10** from your student data files and click **Open** to add this file to the *CMP-Excel* folder.

3. Edit a file in Excel Web App.
   a. Click the **CMPRevenue-10** file in the *CMP-Excel* folder to open it in Excel Web App.
   b. In cell **A2**, change the date to July 21-27, 2014.
   c. Increase the font size of **A5:A8** and **A4:H4** to **14 pt.**
   d. Click the **File** tab and then click the **Save As** button on the left.
   e. Click the **Save As** button to save the workbook.

f. Select the **Over write existing files** check box.

g. Click the **Save** button.

h. Click the **SkyDrive** link at the top to return to your *SkyDrive* folders.

4. Share the workbook with your instructor.

a. Select the **CMP-Excel** folder.

b. Click the **CMPRevenue-10** check box.

c. Click **Sharing** at the top to open the sharing dialog box (Figure 10-71).

d. Select **Send email** on the left.

e. Type your instructor's email address in the *To* area.

f. Type a brief message in the body area.

10-71 Share a workbook

g. Select the **Recipients can edit** check box.

h. Click **Share** to send the sharing email to your instructor. Click the **Close** button.

i. Click the **SkyDrive** link at the top to return to your *SkyDrive* folders.

5. Create a new Excel workbook in Excel Web App.

a. Click the **CMP-Excel** folder to open it.

b. Click the **Create** button and select **Excel workbook**. The *New Microsoft Excel workbook* window opens.

c. Type CMPMarketingBudget as the file name of the new workbook and click **Create**. The new workbook opens in Excel Web App.

d. Type CMP Marketing Budget in **A1** and press **Enter**.

e. *AutoFit* column **A**'s width by double clicking the right column border.

f. Type the following three items in **A3:A5**:

Magazine

Mailings

TV

g. Type the following in **B3:B5**:

35,000

15,000

45,000

h. Apply the **Currency** style to **B3:B5**.

i. The workbook saves automatically to the *SkyDrive* folder **CMP-Excel**. Return to your *SkyDrive* folders.

6. Copy and rename files.

a. Click the **CMP-Excel** folder to open it.

b. Click the **CMPRevenue-10** workbook check box to select it.

c. Click the **Manage** button and select **Copy to** from the drop-down list to open the copy to dialog box (Figure 10-72).

d. Click the **[your first name]-Excel** folder and click **Copy** to close the dialog box and copy the document.

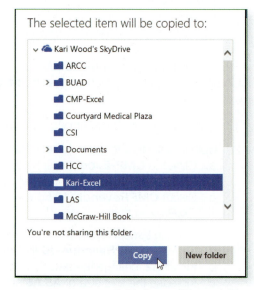

10-72 Copy a file to a folder

e. Copy the **CMPMarketingBudget** workbook to the **[your first name]-Excel** folder.
f. Open the **[your first name]-Excel** folder and click the **CMPRevenue-10** workbook check box to select it.
g. Click the **Manage** button and select **Rename** from the drop-down list.
h. Type [your initials] PP E10-3a and press **Enter** (Figure 10-73).
i. Rename the **CMPMarketingBudget** file as [your initials] PP E10-3b (Figure 10-73).

7. Select **[your name]** in the upper right corner and select **Sign out** from the *Account* drop-down list.

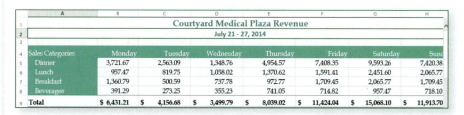

10-73 PP E10-3a and PP E10-3b completed

Chapter Summary

10.1 Customize Excel options, the *Ribbon*, and the *Quick Access* toolbar to personalize your working environment in Excel (p. E10-535).

- The **Excel Options dialog box** allows you to customize global settings in Excel. Some settings apply to all Office programs.
- The *Excel Options* dialog box features the following categories: **General**, **Formulas**, **Proofing**, **Save**, **Language**, **Advanced**, **Customize Ribbon**, **Quick Access Toolbar**, **Add-Ins**, and **Trust Center**.
- Use the *Excel Options* dialog box to customize the **Ribbon**. Create a new tab or group, add commands to custom groups, rearrange existing tabs and groups, and rename existing and custom tabs and groups.
- You can quickly customize and add commands to the **Quick Access** toolbar from the *Customize Quick Access Toolbar* drop-down list, or you can add other commands using the *Excel Options* dialog box.
- Both the *Ribbon* and the *Quick Access* toolbar can be reset to return them to their original settings. You can reset the *Ribbon* or the *Quick Access* toolbar individually or reset all customizations, which resets both the *Ribbon* and the *Quick Access* toolbar.

10.2 View and modify Office account settings and add an Office app (p. E10-545).

- The **Account area** on the *Backstage* view provides you with information and account customization options.
- Your **Office account information and settings** are available whenever you log in to Excel (or any Office application) using your **Microsoft account**. You can obtain your own free Microsoft account through Live, Hotmail, Messenger, or MSN.
- You can change the **Office background** in the *Account* area in *Backstage* view.
- *You can add* **connected services** to your account to access online services for **Images & Videos**, **Storage**, and **Sharing**.
- **Apps** (applications) provide additional functionality to Office. The **Apps for Office** window lists available apps for Office.

10.3 Create folders, upload files, move and copy files, and share files in *SkyDrive* (p. E10-551).

- **SkyDrive** is a **cloud storage** area that provides you with online storage space for your files. If you have a Microsoft account (Live, Hotmail, MSN, Messenger, or other Microsoft service account), you have access to *SkyDrive*.
- You can access your *SkyDrive* files from any computer that has Internet access.
- Log in to *SkyDrive* using your Microsoft account.
- If you use Windows 8, *SkyDrive* is one of your storage options. You can save and edit *SkyDrive* files using a Windows folder or online using an Internet browser.
- In *SkyDrive*, you can upload files, create folders, and move, copy, delete, and download files.
- You can share *SkyDrive* files with others. You determine the access other users have to view and/or edit your *SkyDrive* files.

10.4 Create a *SkyDrive* group in *SkyDrive*, invite a member, and change group options (p. E10-558).

- A **SkyDrive group** is an online workspace you can use to store and share files with other group members.
- *SkyDrive* groups are connected to *SkyDrive*, and you can create groups if you have a Microsoft account.
- You can access groups you create or are a member of from your *SkyDrive* page.
- You can invite a person to join your *SkyDrive* group by becoming a member. You can determine each member's role. A person can be an **owner**, a **co-owner**, or a **member**.
- Each *SkyDrive* group has a **web address** and **group email account**. You can send email to all group members using the group email address.
- You can add and edit files and create folders in groups.

10.5 Open, create, edit, print, share, and collaborate on documents in Office Web Apps. (p. E10-563).

- **Office Web Apps** is free online software that works in conjunction with your *SkyDrive* account and is available from your *SkyDrive* web page.
- Office Web Apps is similar to Microsoft Office 2013 but less robust in available features.

- Office 2013 does not have to be installed on your computer when using Office Web Apps.
- You can edit existing files from your *SkyDrive* account in Office Web Apps and create new Office files using Office Web Apps.
- You can share Office Web Apps files with others.
- More than one user can edit an Office Web Apps files at the same time, which allows real-time collaboration on files.

Check for Understanding

In the **Online Learning Center** for this text (www.mhhe.com/office2013inpractice), there are a variety of resources that can be used to review the concepts covered in this chapter.

The following Online Learning Resources are available in the Online Learning Center:

- Multiple choice questions
- Short answer questions
- Matching exercises

Guided Project 10-1

For this project, you work on a workbook from American River Cycling using *SkyDrive*, Office Web Apps, and *SkyDrive* groups.
[Student Learning Outcomes 10.1, 10.3, 10.4, 10.5]

Note to Students and Instructor:

> **Students:** *For this project, you share a SkyDrive file with your instructor and invite your instructor to a SkyDrive group.*
> **Instructor:** *In order to complete this project, your students need your Microsoft email address.*

Files Needed: ***ARCCCalendar-10.xlsx*** and ***HeartRate-10.docx***
Completed Project File Name: ***[your initials] Excel 10-1.xlsx***

Skills Covered in This Project

- Reset customizations to the *Ribbon* and *Quick Access* toolbar.
- Customize the *Quick Access* toolbar for the current document.
- Log in to *SkyDrive* and create a folder.

- Upload a file to your *SkyDrive* folder.
- Share a *SkyDrive* file.
- Create a *SkyDrive* group and invite a member.
- Upload a file to your group.
- Customize group options.

1. Open the ***ARCCCalendar-10*** workbook.
2. Save the workbook as ***[your initials] Excel 10-1***.
3. Reset the *Ribbon* and *Quick Access* toolbar.
   a. Click the **Customize Quick Access Toolbar** drop-down list and select **More Commands** to open the *Excel Options* dialog box with the *Quick Access Toolbar* area displayed (Figure 10-74).
   b. Click the **Reset** button and select **Reset all customizations**. A confirmation dialog box opens.
   c. Click **Yes** to delete all *Ribbon* and *Quick Access* toolbar customizations.
4. Add commands to the *Quick Access* toolbar for this workbook only.
   a. With the *Excel Options* dialog box still open and the *Quick Access Toolbar* area displayed, click the **Customize Quick Access Toolbar** drop-down list on the right and select **For [your initials] Excel 10-1** (Figure 10-75).
   b. In the list on the left, select **Print Preview and Print** and select **Add**.

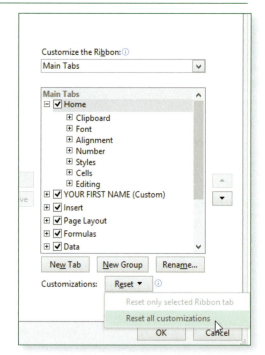

10-74 Reset *Ribbon* **and** *Quick Access* **toolbar customizations**

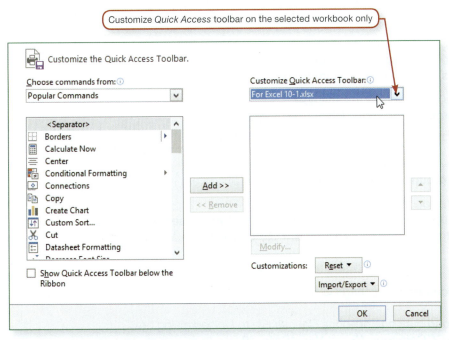

Customize *Quick Access* toolbar on the selected workbook only

10-75 Add commands to the *Quick Access* toolbar on this workbook only

    c. Add **Spelling** and **Open** to the *Quick Access* toolbar.

    d. Click **OK** to close the *Excel Options* dialog box.

5. Save and close the workbook and exit Excel.

6. Open an Internet browser page and log in to your *SkyDrive* account (www.skydrive.com).

7. Create a folder and upload files to your *SkyDrive*.

    a. Click the **Files** button on the left to display your *SkyDrive* folders and files.

    b. Click the **Create** button and select **Folder** from the drop-down list.

    c. Type ARCC-Excel as the name of the new folder and press **Enter**.

    d. Click the **ARCC-Excel** folder to open it.

    e. Click the **Upload** button to open the *Choose File to Upload* dialog box.

    f. Select *[your initials] Excel 10-1* from your solutions files and click **Open** to add this file to the *ARCC-Excel* folder.

    g. Upload the ***HeartRate-10*** file from your student data files to the *ARCC-Excel* folder.

8. Share a file on *SkyDrive* with your instructor.

    a. Click the *[your initials] Excel 10-1* file checkbox in the *ARCC-Excel* folder.

    b. Click **Sharing** at the top to open the *Share* window (Figure 10-76).

    c. Select **Send email** on the left.

    d. Type your instructor's email address in the *To* area.

    e. Type a brief message in the body area.

    f. Check the **Recipients can edit** check box.

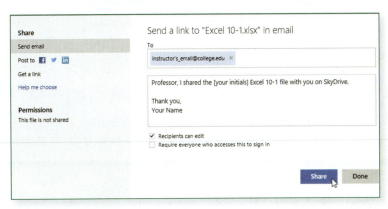

10-76 Share a workbook

g. Click **Share** to send the sharing email to your instructor.

h. Click **Close** to close the *Share* window.

i. Click the **Files** at the top left to return to your *SkyDrive* folders.

9. Create a *SkyDrive* group and invite a member.

a. Click the **Groups** button on the left to open the *Groups* area.

b. Type American River Cycling Club-Excel in the *Group name* text box.

c. Type your last name, first initial, and -ARCC-Excel in the *Group email* text box (e.g., WoodK-ARCC-Excel).

d. Click **Create group** to create your group. If the email address is not available, type a different one.

10. Invite a member to your group.

a. Click the **Group actions** button at the top and select **Invite people**.

b. Type your instructor's email address in the *Invite people to join this group* area.

c. Click **Invite**.

11. Upload files to your group.

a. Select **American River Cycling Club-Excel** in the *Groups* area on the left if it is not already selected.

b. Click the **Upload** button to open the *Choose File to Upload* dialog box.

c. Select the ***ARCCCalendar-10*** and ***HeartRate-10*** files from your student data files and click **Open** to add the files to your group.

12. Change group options.

a. With your group selected, click the **Group options** button at the top. The *Options* page opens.

b. Select **Email** on the left to display email options.

c. In the *Link to group website* area, select the **Only group members can view this group using this link** radio button.

d. Click **Save** at the bottom to save and apply the changes. You are taken back to your *SkyDrive* group. Click the **Group options** button at the top.

e. Select **Group conversations** on the left to display group conversation options.

f. Select **Turn off group conversations**. You are taken back to your *SkyDrive* group.

g. Click **Files** at the top to return to your *SkyDrive* folders and groups.

13. Select **[your name]** in the upper right corner and select **Sign out** from the *Account* drop-down list (Figure 10-77).

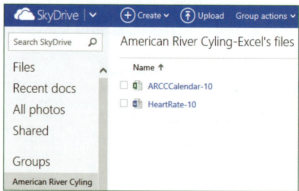

10-77 Excel 10-1 completed (*ARCC-Excel* folder in *SkyDrive* and *American River Cycling Club-Excel* group)

Guided Project 10-2

For this project, you use *SkyDrive* and Excel Web App to customize a workbook for Hamilton Civic Center.
[Student Learning Outcomes 10.1, 10.3, 10.5]

Note to Students and Instructor:

> **Students:** *For this project, you share a SkyDrive folder with your instructor.*
> **Instructor:** *In order to complete this project, your students need your Microsoft email address.*

File Needed: ***HCCYoga-10.xlsx***
Completed Project File Names: ***[your initials] Excel 10-2.xlsx*** and ***[your initials] Excel 10-2 Editable.xlsx***

Skills Covered in This Project

- Create a new group on the *Home* tab.
- Add and arrange commands in the custom group.
- Arrange a group on a tab.
- Save a file to your *SkyDrive* folder.
- Log in to *SkyDrive* and create a folder.
- Copy a file to a *SkyDrive* folder.
- Edit a workbook in Excel Web App.
- Share a *SkyDrive* folder.

1. Open the ***HCCYoga-10*** workbook.

2. Save the workbook as ***[your initials] Excel 10-2***.

3. Customize the *Ribbon* to add a group and commands.
   a. Right-click anywhere on the **Ribbon** and select **Customize the Ribbon** from the context menu. The *Excel Options* dialog box opens with the *Customize Ribbon* area displayed.
   b. On the right, click the **Home** tab in the *Main Tabs* area and click the **New Group** button. A new group is inserted on the *Home* tab.
   c. Select **New Group (Custom)** and click **Rename** to open the *Rename* dialog box.
   d. Select a symbol of your choice, type your first name as the group name in the *Display name* area, and click **OK** to close the *Rename* dialog box.
   e. On the right, select the **[your first name]** group.
   f. Click the **Choose commands from** drop-down list on the left side and select **All Commands** to display all the available commands in the list on the left (Figure 10-78).
   g. Select the **Chart** command and click the **Add** button between the two lists to add the command to the group.
   h. Add the **View Side by Side** and **Trace Precedents** commands to the *[your first name]* group.

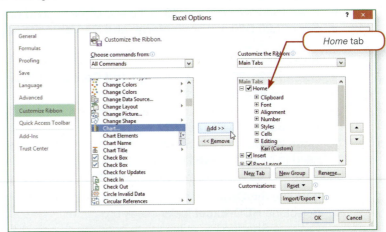

10-78 Add a custom group and commands to the *Home* tab

i. Use the **Move Up** and **Move Down** buttons to arrange the commands in alphabetical order.

j. Select the **[your first name] (Custom)** group and click the **Move Up** button so it appears between the *Styles* and *Cells* groups.

k. Click **OK** to close the *Excel Options* dialog box.

l. Click the **Home** tab to view your custom group (Figure 10-79).

10-79 Custom group displayed on the *Home* tab

4. Save the file to your *SkyDrive* folders.
   a. Open the *Save As* dialog box and select **SkyDrive** on the left.
   b. Double-click the **[your first name]-Excel** folder to open it and click **Save**. If you don't have a *[your first name]* folder in your *SkyDrive*, create it.

5. Close the workbook and exit Excel.

6. Open an Internet browser page and log in to your *SkyDrive* account (www.skydrive.com).

7. Create a folder and copy a file.
   a. Select **Files** on the left if it is not already selected.
   b. Click the **Create** button and select **Folder** from the drop-down list.
   c. Type HCC-Excel as the name of the new folder and press **Enter**.
   d. Click the **[your first name]-Excel** folder to open it.
   e. Click the **[your initials] Excel 10-2** check box to select this file.
   f. Click the **Manage** button and select **Copy to** from the drop-down list to open the copy to dialog box.
   g. Click the **HCC-Excel** folder and click **Copy** to close the dialog box and copy the file to the selected folder.

8. Edit a workbook in Excel Web App.
   a. Click **SkyDrive** at the top to return to your *SkyDrive* folders.
   b. Click the **HCC-Excel** folder to open it.
   c. Click the **[your initials] Excel 10-2** file to open it in Excel Web App.
   d. Click the **continue** button. Various options will not display correctly or at all. Don't try to fix these in Excel Web App. Choose **Save As** from the **File** menu and name the updated file **[your initials] Excel 10-2 - Editable**.
   e. Insert four rows after row **19** at the end of the second body paragraph.
   f. Select **A20:G20** and apply **Merge and Center** to the selected cells.
   g. Click cell **A20**, type Our yoga classes are taught on the following days and times:, and press **Enter** two times.
   h. Select **A22:G22** and apply **Merge and Center** to the selected cells.
   i. Click cell **A22** and type the following line:

      Monday, Wednesday, and Friday at 6 and 8 a.m.
   j. Apply **bold** format to cell **A22**.
   k. Close the workbook in *SkyDrive*. Files will automatically save in *Excel Web App*, so there is no need to click the **Save** button.

9. Share a folder on *SkyDrive* with your instructor.

   a. Click the **SkyDrive** link at the top to return to your *SkyDrive* folders.
   b. Select the **HCC-Excel** folder check box.
   c. Click the **Sharing** link at the top to open the sharing dialog box (Figure 10-80).

d. Select **Send email** on the left.

e. Type your instructor's email address in the *To* area.

f. Type a brief message in the body area.

g. Select the **Recipients can edit** check box.

h. Click **Share** to send the sharing email to your instructor. Click the **Close** button to close the *Share* dialog box.

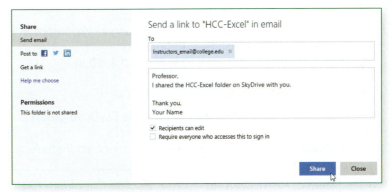

10-80 Share a folder

10. Select **[your name]** in the upper right corner and select **Sign out** from the *Account* drop-down list.

11. Open a workbook in Excel.

a. Open Excel and open the *Open* dialog box.

b. Select **SkyDrive** on the left, double-click the **HCC-Excel** folder to open it, and open the ***[your initials] Excel 10-2 - Editable*** workbook.

12. Save this workbook where you store your completed files and close the workbook (Figure 10-81).

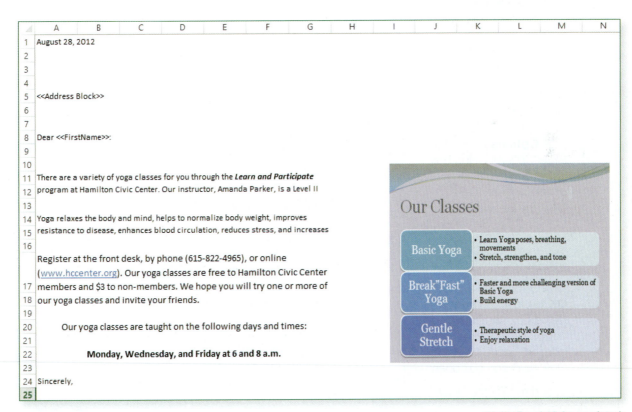

10-81 Excel 10-2 completed

Guided Project 10-3

For this project, you customize your working environment in Excel and create a *SkyDrive* group and modify files for Placer Hills Real Estate.
[Student Learning Outcomes 10.1, 10.3, 10.4, 10.5]

Note to students and instructor:

> **Students:** *For this project, you create a SkyDrive group and invite your instructor to become a member.*
> **Instructor:** *In order to complete this project, your students need your Microsoft email address.*

Files Needed: ***PHREContact-10.xlsx***, ***EscrowChecklist-10.docx***, and ***HomeBuying-10.docx***
Completed Project File Name: *[your initials] Excel 10-3.xlsx*

Skills Covered in This Project

- Change default save location in Excel.
- Reset the *Quick Access* toolbar.
- Add and rearrange commands on the *Quick Access* toolbar.
- Save a file to a *SkyDrive* folder.
- Create a *SkyDrive* group and invite a member.
- Upload a file to your group.
- Create a folder and upload a file in a *SkyDrive* group.
- Edit a document in Excel Web App.
- Rename a *SkyDrive* file.

1. Open the **PHREContact-10** workbook from your student data files.

2. Change default save location.
   a. Click the **File** tab to open the *Backstage* view and click **Options** to open the *Excel Options* dialog box.
   b. Select **Save** to display save options (Figure 10-82).
   c. Click the **Browse** button to the right of *Server drafts location.* The *Browse* dialog box opens.
   d. Select the **SkyDrive** folder on the left and click **OK** to close the *Browse* dialog box and change the default server draft save location. Leave the *Excel Options* dialog box open.

3. Reset and modify the *Quick Access* toolbar.
   a. In the *Excel Options* dialog box, select **Quick Access Toolbar** on the left.

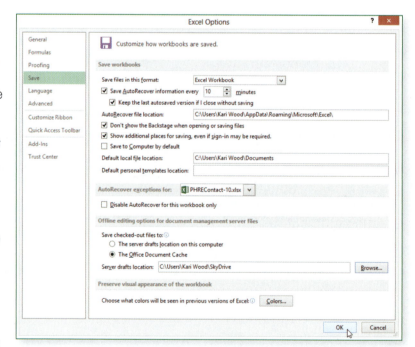

10-82 Change server drafts location

b. Click the **Reset** button and select **Reset only Quick Access Toolbar**. If the option is grayed out, then press the **Esc** key.

c. Click **Yes** in the dialog box that opens to confirm the reset.

d. In the list of commands on the left, select **Email** and click the **Add** button to add it to the *Quick Access* toolbar (Figure 10-83).

e. Add **Name Manager**, **Quick Print**, and **Open** to the *Quick Access* toolbar.

f. Use the **Move Up** button to move *Open* up so it appears after *Save*.

g. Click **OK** to close the *Excel Options* dialog box.

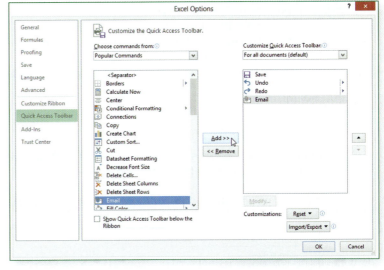

10-83 Add commands to the *Quick Access* toolbar

4. Use the *Save As* dialog box to save this workbook as **PHREContact-10** in the *[your first name]-Excel* folder in the *SkyDrive* folder (don't rename the file).

5. Close the workbook and exit Excel.

6. Create a *SkyDrive* group.
   a. Open an Internet browser page and log in to your *SkyDrive* account (www.skydrive.com).
   b. Click the **Groups** button on the left to open the *Groups* area.
   c. Type Placer Hills Real Estate-Excel in the *Group Name* text box.
   d. Type your last name, first initial, and -PHRE-Excel in the *email* area (e.g., WoodK-PHRE-Excel).
   e. Click **Create group** to create your group. If the email address is not available, type a different one.

7. Invite a member to your group.
   a. Click the **Group actions** button at the top and select **Invite people**.
   b. Type your instructor's email address in the *Invite* area.
   c. Click **Invite**.

8. Upload files to your group.
   a. Select the **Placer Hills Real Estate-Excel** group in the *Groups* area on the left if it is not already selected.
   b. Click the **Upload** button to open the *Choose File to Upload* dialog box.
   c. Select **PHREContact-10** in the *[your first name]-Excel* folder in the *SkyDrive* folder and click **Open** to add the file to your group.
   d. Upload the **EscrowChecklist-10** and **HomeBuying-10** files to your group from your student data files.

9. Create a folder and copy a file.
   a. In the *Placer Hills Real Estate-Excel* group, click the **Create** button and select **Folder** from the drop-down list.
   b. Type Expiration Letters and press **Enter**.
   c. Select the **PHREContact-10** file check box (make sure this is the only selected check box).
   d. Click the **Manage** button and select **Copy to** from the drop-down list to open the copy to dialog box.
   e. Select the **Expiration Letters** folder and click **Copy**.

10. Edit a workbook in Excel Web App.
    a. Click the **Expiration Letters** folder to open it.
    b. Click the **PHREContact-10** file to open it in Excel Web App.
    c. Insert three rows below row **5**.
    d. Enter the following text in each of the corresponding cells:

    A5: Mr. Rick DePonte
    A6: 8364 Marshall Street
    A7: Granite Bay, CA 95863

    e. Replace the *<Salutation>* placeholder text in **A10** with Mr. DePonte (Figure 10-84).
    f. Click the black **x** in the top right-hand corner to close the file (remember, your file is automatically saved).
    g. Click the **SkyDrive** link at the top to return to your *SkyDrive* folders.

10-84 Excel 10-3 completed

11. Rename a file in *SkyDrive*.
    a. Select the **Placer Hills Real Estate-Excel** group on the left and click the **Expiration Letters** folder.
    b. Select the **PHREContact-10** file check box.
    c. Click the **Manage** button and select **Rename** from the drop-down list.
    d. Type [your initials] Excel 10-3 as the file name and press **Enter**.

12. Select **[your name]** in the upper right corner and select **Sign out** from the *Account* drop-down list.

Independent Project 10-4

For this project, you customize the working environment in Excel and use *SkyDrive*, Excel Web App, and a *SkyDrive* group to customize, store, edit, and share files for Sierra Pacific Community College District.
[Student Learning Outcomes 10.1, 10.2, 10.3, 10.4, 10.5]

Note to Students and Instructor:

> **Students:** *For this project, you share a SkyDrive file with your instructor and invite your instructor to become a member of a SkyDrive group.*
> **Instructor:** *In order to complete this project, your students need your Microsoft email address.*

Files Needed: ***LearningPlan-10.xlsx**, **EmergencyProcedures-10.docx**,* and ***WritingTips-10.docx***
Completed Project File Name: *[your initials] Excel 10-4.xlsx*

Skills Covered in This Project

- Create a *SkyDrive* folder.
- Reset the *Ribbon* and the *Quick Access* toolbar.
- Create a new tab and group on the *Ribbon*.
- Add and arrange commands in a custom group.
- Add commands to the *Quick Access* toolbar.
- Log in to *SkyDrive* and upload a file.
- Create a workbook in Excel Web App and apply formatting.
- Share a workbook in Excel Web App.
- Create a *SkyDrive* group and invite a member.
- Upload a file to a group.
- Customize group options.

1. Create a *SkyDrive* folder and open and save a workbook.
   a. Open a Windows folder, open your *SkyDrive* folder, and create a new folder named **SPCCD-Excel**.
   b. Open the **LearningPlan-10** workbook from your student data files.
   c. Save this file as **LearningPlan-10** in the *SPCCD-Excel* folder in your *SkyDrive* folder.

2. Reset and customize the *Ribbon* and the *Quick Access* toolbar.
   a. Reset all *Ribbon* and the *Quick Access* toolbar customizations.
   b. Create a new tab after the *Home* tab.
   c. Rename the new tab **SPCCD**.
   d. Rename the new custom group **Frequent Commands** and select a symbol of your choice.
   e. Add the following commands (in *Popular Commands*) to the *Frequent Commands* group: **Save As**, **Spelling**, **Name Manager**, **Page Setup**, and **Pictures**.
   f. Arrange these commands in alphabetical order.
   g. Add **Open** and **Quick Print** to the *Quick Access* toolbar.

3. Customize Excel options.
   a. Open the *Excel Options* dialog box and select the **General** tab.
   b. Confirm that your *user name* is correct.
   c. Select an *Office Background* of your choice.
   d. Select the **Advanced** category and select the **Quickly access this number of Recent Workbooks** check box in the *Display* content area. Click **OK**.

4. Save the workbook and exit Excel (don't rename the workbook).

5. Upload files to your *SkyDrive* folder.
   a. Open an Internet browser page and log in to your *SkyDrive* account (www.skydrive.com).
   b. Open the **SPCCD-Excel** folder and add **EmergencyProcedures-10** and **WritingTips-10** from your student data files. The **LearningPlan-10** workbook is already in this folder. If it is not, add it.

6. Create a new workbook in Excel Web App.
   a. In the *SPCCD-Excel* folder, create a new **Excel workbook** using Excel Web App and name it *[your initials] Excel 10-4*.
   b. Refer to Figure 10-85 to enter information in the new workbook.
   c. Merge cells **A1:B1**.
   d. Apply **bold** format and standard **Blue** font color to cell **A1**.
   e. Increase the font size to **14 pt** and left align **A1**.
   f. *AutoFit* columns **A:B**.
   g. Return to your *SPCCD-Excel* folder in *SkyDrive* (the file will automatically save).

	A	B
1	SPCCD Fall Semester Important Dates	
2	August 22:	Classes Begin
3	August 30:	Last Day to Register
4	October 1:	Apply for Fall Graduation
5	November 8:	Last Day to Drop
6	December 14-18:	Final Exams

10-85 Data for workbook in Excel Web App

7. Share the file.
   a. Open the *[your initials] Excel 10-4* workbook in Excel Web App.
   b. Share this file with your instructor and allow him or her to edit the file.

8. Create a new group, invite a member, and upload files.
   a. Create a new group named **Sierra Pacific CCD-Excel**.
   b. Type your last name, first initial, and -SPCCD-Excel in the *email* area (e.g., WoodK-SPCCD-Excel).
   c. Use your instructor's email address to invite him or her as a member.
   d. Add the following files from your *SPCCD-Excel* folder in *SkyDrive* to the *Sierra Pacific CCD-Excel* group: *[your initials] Excel 10-4*, **LearningPlan-10**, **EmergencyProcedures-10**, and **WritingTips-10**.

9. Customize the group options.
   a. Verify that group email is turned on.
   b. Change the **Link to group website** so that anyone can view the group without signing in.

10. Sign out of *SkyDrive* (Figure 10-86).

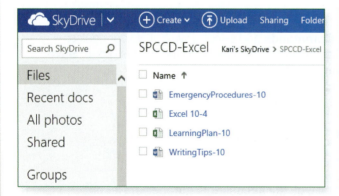
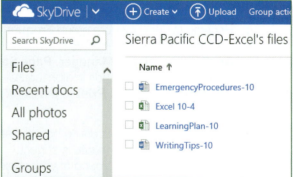

10-86 Excel 10-4 completed (SPCCD-Excel folder in *SkyDrive* and *Sierra Pacific CCD-Excel* group)

Independent Project 10-5

For this project, you use *SkyDrive*, Excel Web App, Word Web App, and a *SkyDrive* group to customize, store, edit, and share files for Life's Animal Shelter.
[Student Learning Outcomes 10.3, 10.4, 10.5]

Note to Students and Instructor:

> **Students:** *For this project, you share a SkyDrive folder with your instructor and invite your instructor to become a member of a SkyDrive group.*
> **Instructor:** *In order to complete this project, your students need your Microsoft email address.*

Files Needed: ***LASExpenses-10.docx*** and ***LASSupportForm-10.docx***
Completed Project File Name: ***[your initials] Excel 10-5.xlsx***

Skills Covered in This Project

- Create a *SkyDrive* folder.
- Upload a file to a *SkyDrive* folder.
- Create a workbook in Excel Web App and apply formatting.
- Edit a workbook in Excel Web App.

- Share a *SkyDrive* folder.
- Create a *SkyDrive* group and invite a member.
- Upload a file to a group.
- Customize group options.

1. Create a *SkyDrive* folder and upload files to the *SkyDrive* folder.
   a. Open an Internet browser page and log in to your *SkyDrive* account (www.skydrive.com).
   b. Create a new folder named **LAS-Excel** in the *Files* area.
   c. Upload the following files from your student data files to the *LAS* folder: ***LASExpenses-10*** and ***LASSupportForm-10***.

2. Create a new workbook in Excel Web App.
   a. In the *LAS-Excel* folder, create a new Excel Web App workbook and name it ***[your initials] Excel 10-5***.
   b. Refer to Figure 10-87 to enter information in the new workbook.
   c. *AutoFit* columns **A:C**.
   d. Select **A2:C5** and click the top half of the **Sort & Filter as Table** button.
   e. Select the **My table has headers** box when prompted.
   f. Apply **14 pt** font size, **bold** format, and the **Merge & Center** option to **A1:C1** (Figure 10-87).
   g. Save the workbook and return to your *LAS-Excel* folder.

10-87 Data for workbook in Excel Web App

3. Share the *LAS-Excel* folder with your instructor, include a brief message, and allow him or her to edit the document.

4. Create a new group, invite a member, and upload files.
   a. Create a new group named **Life's Animal Shelter-Excel**.
   b. Type your last name, first initial, and -LAS-Excel in the email area (e.g., WoodK-LAS-Excel).
   c. Use your instructor's email to invite him or her as a member.
   d. Upload all of the files from your *LAS-Excel* folder in *SkyDrive* to the *Life's Animal Shelter-Excel* group.

5. Customize the group options.
   a. Verify that group email is turned on.
   b. Change the **Link to group website** so that anyone can view the group without signing in to the membership options of your group members.

6. Sign out of *SkyDrive* (Figure 10-88).

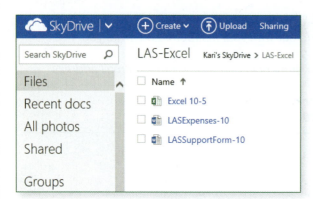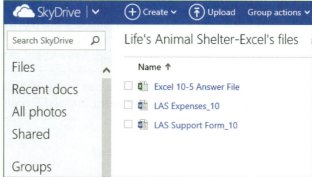

10-88 Excel 10-5 completed (*LAS-Excel* folder in *SkyDrive* and *Life's Animal Shelter-Excel* group)

Independent Project 10-6

For this project, you use *SkyDrive*, Excel Web App, and a *SkyDrive* group to customize, store, edit, and share files for Central Sierra Insurance.
[Student Learning Outcomes 10.1, 10.3, 10.4, 10.5]

Note to Students and Instructor:

> **Students:** *For this project, you share a SkyDrive file with your instructor and invite your instructor to become a member of a SkyDrive group.*
> **Instructor:** *In order to complete this project, your students need your Microsoft email address.*

Files Needed: *CSIRenewal-10.xlsx* and *EmergencyProcedures-10.docx*
Completed Project File Name: *[your initials] Excel 10-6.xlsx*

Skills Covered in This Project

- Reset the *Ribbon* and the *Quick Access* toolbar.
- Edit a workbook and update formulas.
- Log in to *SkyDrive* and create a folder.
- Move a file and upload a file to a *SkyDrive* folder.

- Share a workbook in Excel Web App.
- Create a *SkyDrive* group and invite a member.
- Upload a file to a group.

1. Open the **CSIRenewal-10** workbook from your student data files.

2. Reset and customize the *Ribbon* and *Quick Access* toolbar.
   a. Reset all *Ribbon* and *Quick Access* toolbar customizations.
   b. Add **Open** and **Quick Print** to the *Quick Access* toolbar.
   c. Move **Quick Print** so that it is after *Save*.

3. Save this file as *[your initials] Excel 10-6* in the *[your name]-Excel* folder in your *SkyDrive* folder.

4. Edit information in the table and update formulas.
   a. Select **D23** and change the rate per $1,000 to $19.50.
   b. Increase the decimal places in **D23** to **2**.
   c. Update the formulas in the next three cells to the following:

   E23: =C23/1000*D23.

   F23: =E23*0.15.

   G23: =E23-F23.

   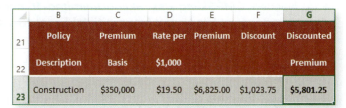

   d. See Figure 10-89 for the new results.

   10-89 Data for Excel 10-6 file

5. Save the workbook and exit Excel.

6. Create a *SkyDrive* folder, move a file, and upload a file to your *SkyDrive.*
   a. Open an Internet browser page and log in to your *SkyDrive* account (www.skydrive.com).
   b. Create a new folder named **CSI-Excel**.
   c. Move the *[your initials] Excel 10-6* from the *[your name]* folder to the *CSI-Excel* folder.
   d. Open the **CSI-Excel** folder and upload the **EmergencyProcedures-10** file from your student data files.

7. Share a workbook.
   a. Open the *[your initials] Excel 10-6* workbook in Excel Web App.
   b. Share this workbook with your instructor, include a brief message, and allow him or her to edit the workbook.

8. Create a new group, invite a member, and upload files.
   a. Create a new group named **Central Sierra Insurance-Excel**.
   b. Type your last name, first initial, and -CSI-Excel in the *email* area (e.g., WoodK-CSI-Excel).
   c. Use your instructor's email address to invite him or her as a member.
   d. Upload both of the files from your *CSI-Excel* folder in *SkyDrive* to the *Central Sierra Insurance-Excel* group.

9. Sign out of *SkyDrive* (Figure 10-90).

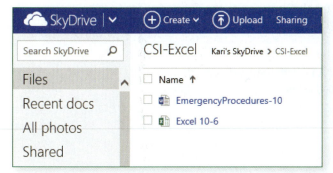
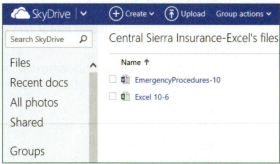

10-90 Excel 10-6 completed (*CSI-Excel* folder in *SkyDrive* and *Central Sierra Insurance-Excel* group)

Improve It Project 10-7

For this project, you customize the working environment in Excel and use *SkyDrive*, Excel Web App, and a *SkyDrive* group to customize, store, edit, and share documents for Skiing Unlimited.
[Student Learning Outcomes 10.1, 10.3, 10.4, 10.5]

Note to Students and Instructor:

> ***Students:*** *For this project, you share a SkyDrive file with your instructor and invite your instructor to become a member of a SkyDrive group.*
> ***Instructor:*** *In order to complete this project, your students need your Microsoft email address.*

Files Needed: ***CMPSkiing.xlsx***, ***SkiingUnlimited-10.docx***, and ***TrainingGuide-10.docx***
Completed Project File Name: ***[your initials] Excel 10-7.xlsx***

Skills Covered in This Project

- Create a *SkyDrive* folder.
- Reset the *Ribbon* and *Quick Access* toolbar.
- Create a new group on an existing tab.
- Add commands to a custom group.
- Arrange a group on a tab.
- Add commands to the *Quick Access* toolbar.

- Log in to *SkyDrive* and upload a file.
- Share a workbook in *SkyDrive*.
- Create a *SkyDrive* group and invite a member.
- Upload a file to a group.
- Customize group options.

---

1. Create a *SkyDrive* folder and save a document.
   a. Open a Windows folder, open your *SkyDrive* folder, and create a new folder named **Skiing Unlimited-Excel**.

2. Open the ***CMPSkiing-10*** workbook from your student data files.

3. Reset and customize the *Ribbon* and the *Quick Access* toolbar.
   a. Reset all *Ribbon* and the *Quick Access* toolbar customizations.
   b. Create a new group on the *Home* tab.
   c. Rename the new custom group **Skiing Unlimited** and select a symbol of your choice.
   d. Add the following commands to the *Skiing Unlimited* group: **Date & Time**, **Page Setup**, **Page Number**, and **Name Manager**. You may have to look in *All Commands* to find the above.
   e. Move this group up so it appears between the *Number* and *Styles* groups.
   f. Add **Open**, **Quick Print**, **Save As**, and **Track Changes** to the *Quick Access* toolbar.

4. Save this file as ***[your initials] Excel 10-7*** in the *Skiing Unlimited-Excel* folder in your *SkyDrive* folder.

5. Edit the workbook.
   a. Replace the *[year]* placeholder text in cell **A17** with the next year (e.g., 2015).
   b. Replace the placeholder text in the bulleted list with the following dates:

   B19: January 18
   B20: January 25
   B21: February 1
   B22: February 8
   B23: February 15

   c. Apply a date format to **B19:B23** if you wish (Figure 10-91).

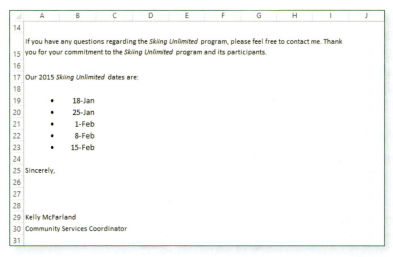

	A	B	C	D	E	F	G	H	I	J
14										
15	If you have any questions regarding the *Skiing Unlimited* program, please feel free to contact me. Thank you for your commitment to the *Skiing Unlimited* program and its participants.									
16										
17	Our 2015 *Skiing Unlimited* dates are:									
18										
19		•	18-Jan							
20		•	25-Jan							
21		•	1-Feb							
22		•	8-Feb							
23		•	15-Feb							
24										
25	Sincerely,									
26										
27										
28										
29	Kelly McFarland									
30	Community Services Coordinator									
31										

10-91 Data for Excel 10-7 file

6. Save the workbook and exit Excel.

7. Upload files to your *SkyDrive*.
   a. Open an Internet browser page and log in to your *SkyDrive* account (www.skydrive.com).
   b. Open the *Skiing Unlimited-Excel* folder and upload the **SkiingUnlimited-10** and **TrainingGuide-10** files from your student data files. The **[your initials] Excel 10-7** workbook is already in this folder. If it is not, add it.

8. Share a file.
   a. Open the **[your initials] Excel 10-7** workbook in Excel Web App.
   b. Share this file with your instructor, include a brief message, and allow him or her to edit the document.

9. Create a new group, invite a member, and upload files.
   a. Create a new group named **Skiing Unlimited-Excel**.
   b. Type your last name, first initial, and -SkiingUnlimited-Excel in the email area (e.g., WoodK-SkiingUnlimited-Excel). If the maximum naming length is reached, just include your last name initial in place of your full last name (e.g., WK-SkiingUnlimited-Excel).
   c. Use your instructor's email address to invite him or her as a member.
   d. Upload the following files from your *Skiing Unlimited-Excel* folder in *SkyDrive* to the *Skiing Unlimited-Excel* group: **[your initials] Excel 10-7**, **SkiingUnlimited-10**, and **TrainingGuide-10**.

10. Customize the group options.
    a. Verify that group email is turned on.
    b. Change the **Link to group website** so that anyone can view the group without signing in Sign out of *SkyDrive* (Figure 10-92).

10-92 Excel 10-7 completed (*Skiing Unlimited-Excel* folder in *SkyDrive* and *Skiing Unlimited-Excel* group)

Challenge Project 10-8

SkyDrive is an excellent place to store and organize your school work. You can create a *SkyDrive* folder and subfolder to store files from all of your classes and share files or folders with your instructors. [Student Learning Outcomes 10.3, 10.5]

Note to Students and Instructor:

> **Students:** *For this project, you share a SkyDrive folder with your instructor.*
> **Instructor:** *In order to complete this project, your students need your Microsoft email address.*

File Needed: None
Completed Project File Name: New *SkyDrive* folder, subfolder, and files

Create a *SkyDrive* folder to store all files for all of your classes. Modify your *SkyDrive* folder according to the following guidelines:

- Create a *SkyDrive* folder and give it your school name.
- Create subfolders for each of your classes and any other folders needed (e.g., Financial Aid, Clubs, Internships, etc.).
- Upload files to each of the folders.
- Share the folder for this class with your instructor.

Challenge Project 10-9

Now that you are familiar with many of the features and working environment in Excel, you can customize the working environment to meet your needs. For this project, you customize the *Ribbon*, the *Quick Access* toolbar, and Excel options to personalize your working environment in Excel. [Student Learning Outcomes 10.1, 10.2]

File Needed: None
Completed Project File Name: ***[your initials] Excel 10-9.xlsx***

Create a new workbook and save it as ***[your initials] Excel 10-9***. List the top 10 new Excel features you have learned in this class and make your *Excel Top 10* list. Customize Excel options, the *Ribbon*, and the *Quick Access* toolbar as desired. Modify your workbook according to the following guidelines:

- Create your *Excel Top 10* list of new features you have learned in this class.
- Apply formatting and design principles you have learned to attractively format and arrange this workbook.
- Modify Excel options to meet your needs.
- Reset the *Ribbon* and the *Quick Access* toolbar.
- Create a new tab and/or group and rename them.

- Add and arrange commands in the group.
- Add commands to your *Quick Access* toolbar.
- Create and name a group in *SkyDrive*.
- Add members who delete extra space appreciate Excel options.
- Upload the *Excel Top 10* list workbook and share it with your group.

Challenge Project 10-10

SkyDrive and *SkyDrive* groups are wonderful tools to store, share, and edit documents when you are collaborating with others. For this project, you create a *SkyDrive* group for a club, organization, work team, or student group and invite members.
[Student Learning Outcomes 10.3, 10.4]

Note to Students and Instructor:

> **Students:** *For this project, you invite your instructor to become a member of a SkyDrive group.*
> **Instructor:** *In order to complete this project, your students need your Microsoft email address.*

File Needed: None
Completed Project Files Name: New *SkyDrive* group, folders, and files

Create a new *SkyDrive* group for a club, organization, work team, or student group. Modify your *SkyDrive* group according to the following guidelines:

- Create a new *SkyDrive* group and invite members (be sure to include your instructor).
- Upload files to the group.
- Create folders in the group.
- Move or copy files as needed.
- Customize group options.
- Customize the roles of members of the group.
- Send a group email to members of the group.

appendices

Common Office 2013 Keyboard Shortcuts

Action	Keyboard Shortcut
Save	Ctrl+S
Copy	Ctrl+C
Cut	Ctrl+X
Paste	Ctrl+V
Select All	Ctrl+A
Bold	Ctrl+B
Italic	Ctrl+I
Underline	Ctrl+U
Close *Start* page or *Backstage* view	Esc
Open *Help* dialog box	F1
Switch windows	Alt+Tab

Excel 2013 Keyboard Shortcuts

Action	Keyboard Shortcut
File Management	
Open a new blank workbook	Ctrl+N
Open an existing workbook from the Backstage view	Ctrl+O
Open an existing workbook from the *Open* dialog box	Ctrl+F12
Close	Ctrl+W
Save	Ctrl+S
Print	Ctrl+P
Move to cell A1	Ctrl+Home
Next worksheet	Ctrl+Page Down
Previous worksheet	Ctrl+Page Up
Switch to an open workbook	Ctrl+F6
Select all files in a folder	Ctrl+A
Editing	
Cut	Ctrl+X
Copy	Ctrl+C
Paste	Ctrl+V
Undo	Ctrl+Z
Redo/Repeat	Ctrl+Y

Action	Keyboard Shortcut
Underline	Ctrl+U
Bold	Ctrl+B
Italics	Ctrl+I
Open *Format Cells* dialog box	Ctrl+1
Edit mode (insertion point appears within the cell)	F2
Manual line break in a cell	Ctrl+Enter
Toggle between formula view and results view	Ctrl+~
Insert a hyperlink	Ctrl+K
Open the VBE window	Alt+F11
Help on VBE error	F1+selected code
Any macro shortcut	Ctrl+Shift+any alphabetic character

Customizing Sheets

Action	Keyboard Shortcut
Hide row	Ctrl+9
Hide column	Ctrl+0
Unhide row	Ctrl+Shift+(
Insert dialog box (cell, row, or column)	Ctrl+Plus sign (+)
Insert worksheet	Shift+F11
Insert chart object	Alt+F1

Formula Creation

Action	Keyboard Shortcut
Open *Insert Function* dialog box	Shift+F3
Insert a plus sign	Shift+=
Insert a multiplication sign	Shift+8
Insert an exponent sign	Shift+6
Insert an open parenthesis	Shift+9
Insert a closed parenthesis	Shift+0
Insert the *SUM* function	Alt+=
Absolute symbol toggle	F4
Complete an array formula	Ctrl+Shift+Enter
Open *Paste Name* dialog box (insert range name)	F3

glossary

.xlsm Excel macro-enabled workbook file name extension that contains macros.

.xltm Excel macro-enabled template file name extension; xltm files are automatically saved in the default templates folder on your computer.

.xml XML data file name extension.

3D cell reference Cell address that is not physically located in the same sheet as the cell containing the reference.

A

absolute cell reference Cell address that contains dollar signs ($), which prevent the specified cell address from being altered during a copy process.

Accept or Reject Changes Command that keeps or rejects changes made to an edited workbook.

Account area Area on the *Backstage* view that displays information and account customization options.

active cell Selected cell in a worksheet; a border around the selected cell and the displayed cell address in the name box indicates the active cell in a worksheet.

ActiveX control Worksheet object that is similar to a form control but more flexible and robust and can include events.

add-in Programs that add functionality to Office programs that are not installed with the initial setup.

Advanced Filter Option that hides rows of data that are unnecessary and exports rows that fit a criteria; allows for more advanced filtering options such as multi-level criteria.

alignment Arrangement of cell contents in relation to the left and right sides of a cell (horizontal) and the top and bottom of a cell (vertical).

annuity Series of equal payments made at the same time of the month or year, for a specified period of time.

Answer report Report that identifies and lists each parameter in the *Solver* problem.

app Short for application; software program or Windows 8 application or accessory.

apps Short for applications; software programs or Windows 8 applications or accessories that add functionality to Office software.

argument Information in a function, which is within parentheses, that determines what value a function returns.

array formula Result inserted in each cell in a data table when using the *Table* command.

array Range of cells such as A1:A4, or series of numbers such as 1, 2, 3, 4, 5.

ascending order Sort order that arranges data from *lowest to highest* in a numeric field or from *A to Z* in a text field.

Auto Outline Option that creates groupings based on pre-existing formulas in your data and displays buttons that collapse or expand groups of data.

AutoCalculate Tool in the status bar that calculates and displays sums, averages, counts, and minimum and maximum values for a selected cell range.

AutoFilter Option in which drop-down arrow buttons appear on column headings that display filter options.

AutoFit Formatting option that automatically adjusts width or height to reveal all the contents within a column or row.

axis title Chart element that names horizontal and vertical axes using placeholders or text boxes.

B

Backstage view Area of an Office application where you perform common actions (such as Save, Open, Print, and Share) and change application options; document properties are displayed here.

blank workbook Pre-built and ready-to-use template with default fonts, font sizes, themes, and margins; all new blank workbooks are based on the blank workbook template.

Button Form control used to run a macro with a single click.

C

calculated field Customized calculation in a *PivotTable* that is not a field in the source data but uses a value field from the *PivotTable*'s underlying data in a formula.

calling methods Phrase that indicates code will cause some action; for example, a workbook may contain an open action to view a different workbook. The code is calling (processing) the open action (method) of a different workbook.

cash flows Future payments or receipts.

category axis (x-axis) Horizontal border in the plot area that measures charted data.

category label Text label in a row or column that describes a data series in a chart.

cell address Letter of the column and number of the row that represent the location of a specific cell; also referred to as a *cell reference.*

cell Intersection of a column and a row.

cell reference Column letter and row number that represent the location of a specific cell; also referred to as a *cell address.*

Cell Style Set of built-in formats, which include a variety of borders, shading, alignment, and other options.

change history Record of each edit made in a shared workbook.

chart area Entire chart including all the elements such as the plot area, labels, legend, and titles.

chart element One of the components that make up a chart, such as chart floor, chart area, data series, chart wall, etc.

chart label Title, legend, or data label used to organize chart data.

chart object Object that represents a chart in a workbook.

chart Object that displays numeric data in the form of a graph to compare data values or display data trends.

Chart Style Tool that allows you to quickly apply a set of built-in formats to alter the look of a chart.

chart title Chart element that names the chart using place-holders or textboxes.

chart type One of several categories of chart, such as column chart, line chart, pie chart, etc.

check box Box that allows you to choose one or more from a group of options.

Check Compatibility Command that opens the *Compatibility Checker*.

circular reference Error that occurs when a formula includes the cell address of the cell where the formula is located.

Clipboard Location where copied items from Office files or other sources such as web pages are stored.

Clipboard pane Pane that displays the contents of the *Clipboard*.

code Specific programming commands required for an automatic task to run; also referred to as program or procedure.

coding Text shown in black between *Sub* and *End Sub*; coding statements are *Visual Basic* commands and properties that control macro actions.

collection Plural of object; for example, a workbook is an object, while workbooks are a collection.

column Vertical grouping of cells in a table or a vertical section of text in a document.

comment Lines that are not part of the code; for example, comments describe code, show a shortcut, or separate sections of a macro.

comment Pop-up text box attached to a cell.

Compare and Merge Workbooks Command that assembles copies of shared workbooks for the final report.

Compatibility Checker Option that searches commands, features, and objects that are not supported in earlier versions of Excel.

concatenate Link or join in a chain.

conditional formatting Formatting automatically applied only to data values that meet a specific condition.

connected services Third-party services users can add to Office application programs, such as Facebook, LinkedIn, and YouTube.

Consolidated worksheet Worksheet that summarizes data from multiple worksheets using a mathematical or statistical Excel function.

constraint Restriction or limitation on a formula, on one or more of the variable cells, or on other cells that are directly related to the objective cell.

context menu Menu of commands that appears when you right-click text or an object.

context sensitive Describes menu options that change depending on what you have selected.

criteria area Range of cells in a spreadsheet designated for customized criteria for Advanced Filter options.

criteria argument Range of cells with a column label and actual criteria just below that label.

custom calculation Complex percentage, ranking, or ratio type of calculation listed in the *Value Field Settings* dialog box on the *Show Values As* tab.

D

data input form Temporary window or dialog box that displays labels and entry boxes for data in a top-to-bottom layout.

data label Label that lists the value, category name, or series name of a component of a chart.

data marker Symbol that represents a single point or value in a charted range of cell information; graphical representation of values shown as columns, bars, slices, or data points.

data point One cell in a data series that is included in a chart.

data series Group of similar data points included in a chart.

data table Chart element which displays the data that creates a chart in table format; table of the values of each data series based on selected source data cells.

data table Range of cells that shows calculated results of one or more formulas.

data validation Process that checks data as it is entered to verify that it matches established requirements.

database Entire range of cells including all rows of data with labels for each column.

default Setting that is automatically applied by an application unless you make specific changes.

delimited Data file type option that ensures that columns are created based on characters in your file instead of specified amount of space between data.

dependent workbook Workbook that includes data from another workbook.

descending order Sort order that arranges data from *highest to lowest* for a numeric field or from *Z to A* for a text field.

destination cell Cell you paste content to after cutting or copying.

Details pane Pane that displays properties of the selected shared file or folder.

dialog box Window that opens and displays additional features.

discount rate Interest rate that demonstrates the cost of financing or the rate of return possible with a competing investment.

Document Inspector Dialog box that lists the properties and data that can be removed from a workbook.

document property Information about a file such as title, author name, subject, etc.

drop-down list List of options that displays when you click a button.

dynamic consolidation Process that places formulas on your consolidated sheet and formats that sheet as an outline; if any data on supporting worksheets is edited after a dynamic consolidation, the formula recalculates and displays updated results on the consolidation sheet.

dynamic Describes results that adjust in real time to data changes.

E

edit mode Office Web Apps view where users can edit and save a file.

effect Formatting feature such as shadow, glow, or soft edges.

ellipse Elongated circle.

Enable Content Security warning bar command that appears when an Excel macro-enabled workbook is opened.

error alert Pop-up message that appears after invalid data is entered.

events Actions associated with *VBA* code.

Excel macro-enabled template Excel template that includes a macro.

Excel Options Dialog box that displays global customization options for Excel settings; once implemented, these options apply to all the workbooks you create and edit in Excel.

Excel Start page Opening area of Excel where you can create a new blank workbook, open a previously saved workbook, or create a new workbook from an Excel template.

Excel Table Group of data with an applied *Table* format, which allows data to be manipulated within the table independently of the data outside the table.

Excel Web App Online Excel application.

Extensible Markup Language (XML) Specifically formatted text file, which can be imported into many applications, and which is designed for exchanging data on the web.

external data Data from an outside source that can be updated whenever a change is made to the original data in its original location.

external reference Formula that refers to cells in another workbook.

extract area Range of cells in a spreadsheet designated for customized results from Advanced Filter application.

extract Create a regular folder from a zipped folder.

F

field Piece of data in a single column.

File Explorer Window where you browse for, open, and manage files and folders (formerly called Windows Explorer).

file name extension A series of letters automatically added to a file name that identifies the type of file.

Fill Handle Small black square that appears in the bottom right corner of a cell and changes to a thin black plus sign pointer that you drag to copy or fill a series.

Find and Replace Command used to locate and replace function arguments as well as function names.

fixed width Data file type option that ensures that columns are determined by a specified amount of space (e.g., every inch).

Flash Fill *Auto Fill* option that recognizes and implements patterns to quickly complete column or row data.

Footer Displays content at the bottom of a document page or object.

Forecast error Difference between actual values and predicted values.

form control Static or dynamic object that you can use to execute commands or perform actions in a worksheet.

form controls Customizable controls that can be dynamic or static, and allow you to manage how data is added and edited in a worksheet

form Worksheet that allows for quick entry, tracking, and organization of data.

Format Painter Tool that duplicates formatting choices such as font, font size, line spacing, indents, bullets, numbering, styles, etc. from one selection to another selection.

Formula Auditing Color-coded editing tool that applies colors to cell ranges and displays lines that point to the cell ranges in a formula's syntax.

Formula bar Area directly below the Ribbon that displays cell contents such as formula syntax, numbers, and letters; you can edit cell contents in the *Formula bar*.

formula Mathematical syntax in a cell that calculates and updates results.

freeze panes View option that allows you to scroll vertically or horizontally while column and row headings remain visible.

function Predefined formula that performs a specific task.

G

gallery Group of options on a tab.

Goal Seek Tool that determines and adjusts the value of a cell until a condition is met in a different cell.

gridlines Lines that visually frame rows and columns.

group Area on a tab that contains related commands and options; option used to organize data in a report so that similar records appear together.

group email account Feature of *SkyDrive* group; each group has a *web address* and group email account that you can use to send email to all group members using the group email address.

Groups Outline option that allows you to apply customized grouping level by row or column.

H

header Displays content at the top of a worksheet.

hyperlink Clickable string of text or objects; when selected, it displays another worksheet, opens another workbook, opens another program, or displays a web page.

I

identifier Character such as an exclamation point that marks or signifies a component in a reference.

Images & Video Online services category.

import Transfer data from another application or browser into Excel.

indent Increase the distance between the cell contents and the left boundary of the cell.

indicator Small red triangle in the upper-right corner of the cell that appears when a comment has been added to a cell.

Information Warning that appears when a user is allowed to make an entry; allows the user to complete, edit, or retry the task. A lowercase i in a blue circle displays in the message box.

input message Comment box that appears on screen as soon as a cell with data validation is selected to serve as a guideline for the person entering the data.

input value Number from a column or a row required for data table calculations.

invalid data Value or label that does not conform to the validation criteria.

K

keyboard shortcut Key or combination of keys that you press to apply a command.

L

label Cell entry that begins with a letter; text in a worksheet that identifies a title and subtitle, row and column headings, and other descriptive information.

legend Descriptive text or key that describes a data series.

Limits report Displays data about the lower and upper limits of each variable cell and how those limits impact the objective cell in the *Solver* problem.

linking workbooks Process of referring to cells from another workbook in the current workbook.

logical function Function that determines whether or not something is true or if more than one condition exists.

M

macro Pre-recorded series of commands and keystrokes that automatically execute a command.

Mark as Final Read-only file property that alerts a user to content that is final and should not be edited.

mathematical order of operations Set of rules which establishes the sequence that operations are performed in multiple-operation expressions and formulas.

maximize Increase the size of the window of an open Office file so it fills the entire computer monitor.

mean absolute deviation (MAD) Formula that illustrates an accurate statistical analysis of forecasting errors.

mean square error (MSE) Popular measure of accuracy for forecasting in which the error values are squared, so larger errors carry more influence.

metadata Properties embedded in a file such as the user name, time of creation, original file location, user comments, and more.

Microsoft account Free account that gives you access to an email account, SkyDrive online storage area, and Office Web Apps.

mini toolbar Toolbar that lists formatting options; appears when you select cells or right-click.

minimize Place an open Office file on the taskbar so it is not displayed on the desktop.

mixed cell reference Cell address that contains one relative cell address component (either the row number or column letter) and one absolute cell address component (the remaining row number or column letter).

module Location where a macro is stored; in VBA, a module is a list of declarations and procedures.

N

Name box Area of the *Formula bar* that displays the cell address of the currently active cell; used to navigate in a worksheet and to name cells.

nested function Function within a function.

normal range Range of cells that does not contain a *Table* format, *AutoFilter* buttons, or an outline and that allows you to apply *Subtotals.*

Nper Argument that refers to the total number of payments.

O

object model Map of Excel and its abilities; *Application*, *Workbook*, *Sheet*, and *PivotChart* are all objects.

objective cell Cell with a formula that has a desired result designated in the *Solver* dialog box; also referred to as the *target cell*.

Office account information and settings Information available whenever you log in to Excel (or any Office application) using your *Microsoft account*.

Office Web Apps Free online Microsoft Office software applications that allow users to create, save, and edit Office files; Office Web Apps are accessed from online *SkyDrive* accounts.

one-variable data table Range of cells that substitutes values for one argument in a formula and displays the results when that value is altered.

operating system Software that makes a computer function and controls the working environment.

outline Border around a selected element.

P

parameter Information *Solver* uses to find a solution.

PDF (portable document format) File format used to convert a file into a static image.

Personal Macro Special macros-only workbook that is loaded in the background of Excel when activated.

PivotChart Charted data that is dynamic (updates in real time) and contains the same movable field buttons and filter options that a *PivotTable* does.

PivotTable List of data that is dynamic and contains movable field buttons and filter options; a user can physically move different components of a *PivotTable* for different analysis options.

pointer Small icon, such as a block plus sign, thin black plus sign, or white arrow, that appears and moves when you move your mouse or touch your touchpad.

print area Range of cells to be printed.

program options Area in each Office application where you can make changes to the program settings.

property Something that an object contains; for example, a worksheet object contains properties such as the worksheet's name, scroll area, and protection.

Protected View Automatic view for workbooks that might contain data from a questionable source; allows you to confirm that you trust the document and its source.

protection Security you can apply to a worksheet that allows various cells to be accessible while others are not.

Q

Quick Access toolbar Area located above the Ribbon with buttons you use to perform commonly used commands.

Quick Analysis Tool that analyzes cell data and provides charts, colors, and formula suggestions.

Quick Layout Tool that allows you to quickly change both the design and labeling elements of a chart instead of changing individual attributes manually.

Quick Style Tool that allows you to quickly apply a combination of color schemes and formats to alter the look of a chart.

R

radio button Round button you click to choose one option from a list.

Range Finder Color-coded editing tool that applies colors to each cell or range included in a formula's syntax.

range Group of cells.

range name Custom name for a cell or range of cells; describes the cell or purpose of a group of cells and makes it easier to interpret a formula.

Rate Argument that refers to the interest rate for the period.

read-only mode Office Web Apps view where users can view and add comments to a file.

record Each row in a database that includes related information.

Recycle Bin Location where deleted files and folders are stored.

relative cell reference Default cell address in Excel; a cell address that changes in the destination cell when copied.

restore down Decrease the size of the window of an open Office file so it does not fill the entire computer monitor.

Ribbon Bar that appears at the top of an Office file window and displays available commands.

roles Settings in SkyDrive groups that control members' ability to view, edit, create, and delete folders and files in the group. *Owners* and *Co-Owners* have full access to create, edit, and delete files and folders in the group, and to customize group options. *Members* can create files and folders, edit them, and view others' files and folders.

row Horizontal grouping of cells.

S

Scenario Manager Command that organizes scenarios; available from the *What-If Analysis* button in the *Data Tools* group in the *Data* tab.

scenario summary report Generated worksheet that describes each scenario in a workbook; formatted as an Excel outline with two row levels and two column levels.

scenario What-if analysis tools that enable you to save a set of values in a worksheet and that test values and determine potential results in a worksheet.

screenshot Picture of something that appeared on a computer screen, that you copy and insert as an object in a worksheet.

ScreenTip Descriptive information about a button, drop-down list, launcher, or gallery selection that appears when you place your pointer on the item.

select method Technique of selecting cell addresses to create a formula.

Sensitivity report Report that includes statistical data such as an objective coefficient, a Lagrange multiplier, and a reduced gradient in the *Solver* problem depending on the solving method that is selected.

shape fill Color that fills a shape or graphic object.

Shape Style Set of built-in formats for shapes; includes borders, fill colors, and effect components.

shared workbook Workbook that more than one user edits, either simultaneously or at different times.

SharePoint web server Web server that runs Microsoft's *SharePoint Services* and allows group members to share information.

Sharing Online sharing category such as Facebook, LinkedIn, and Twitter.

SkyDrive folder Windows folder that displays folders and files stored on a user's SkyDrive account; synchronizes folders and files stored in the SkyDrive folder with SkyDrive cloud storage.

SkyDrive group Free Microsoft online service where folders and files can be stored and users can be invited to become members; group members have access to folders and files stored in the *SkyDrive* group.

SkyDrive Online (cloud) storage area that is a part of your Microsoft account where you can store and access documents from any computer with an Internet connection.

Slicer Pop-up filtering-menu based on the headings in a *table*.

Slicer Tool that creates an on-screen window to act as a filter for a single field in a *PivotTable* or *PivotChart*.

SmartArt graphic High-quality illustration that you can manipulate and format in various ways and place in Office documents.

Solver Advanced analysis tool that finds the highest, lowest, or specific result for a formula by changing the values in other cells within established parameters.

sort Organize data in ascending or descending order.

source cell Original cell that contains content you cut or copy.

Source data Data and label cells that are included in chart creation.

source workbook Workbook that includes data that is referenced in a dependent workbook; for workbooks to be referenced or linked, they must all be accessible over a network, on the same computer, or in the cloud.

source worksheet Existing worksheet which contains a range that will be included in the consolidation worksheet.

Sparklines Miniature chart-like graphics you can add to data in a specified cell.

standard deviation Measurement of how broadly values deviate from the mean or average value in the range.

static consolidation Process that summarizes data and displays a result that does not update on the consolidated sheet if one of the values on the source worksheets is edited.

Stop Warning that appears when a user is prohibited from making an entry; allows the user to cancel the task or retry. An x in a red circle displays in the message box.

Storage Online storage category such as Office365, SharePoint, or *SkyDrive*.

sub procedure (Sub). Describes a macro that runs from the workbook or from another macro. The macro name is displayed immediately after *Sub* and the name is followed by a set of parentheses; sub procedure macros contain coding lines and end with *End Sub*.

subtotals Tool that allows you to group data and quickly apply functions such as *SUM*, *AVERAGE*, *MAX*, or *MIN* to data in a selected cell range.

Syntax error Pop-up message in a macro specifying code that *Visual Basic* doesn't recognize; can result from simple typos in the code or from incorrectly used statements.

syntax Rules that dictate how the various parts of a formula must be written.

T

tab Area on the Ribbon that lists groups of related commands and options.

table style Built-in formats for tables such as border, shading, alignment, and other options.

tag Identifier of data such as *<Customer>* in which a tag is enclosed in chevron braces; the braces surround the actual piece of data in a properly structured XML file.

task pane Area at the left or right of an Office application window where you can perform tasks.

taskbar Horizontal area at the bottom of the Windows desktop where you can launch programs or open folders.

template Model workbook that can include data, formulas, formatting, charts, images, controls, and more.

text box Area where you can type text.

text files Files such as .txt (text) documents, .csv (comma separated values) files, and .prn (printer) files.

theme Collection of fonts, colors, and effects that you can apply to an entire document, workbook, or presentation.

trace dependents Color-coded auditing tool that displays formulas referenced within a selected formula.

trace precedents Color-coded auditing tool that displays the cells within a selected formula.

Trendline Tool that calculates and plots averages and forecasts averages based on previously plotted data and numbers.

trusted location Folder that stores workbooks that are considered safe; when you open a workbook from a trusted location, it does not open in *Protected View*.

two-variable data table Table similar to a one-variable data table but that uses two sets of input values instead of one—one in a column, the other in a row.

U

unlock Format applied to cells prior to applying protection to a worksheet that allows access to specified cells.

Use Relative References Button located in the *Code* group on the *Developer* tab used to designate relative or absolute references while recording macros.

V

validation settings Rules applied to data as it is entered.

value axis (y-axis) Vertical border in the plot area that measures charted data.

Value Field Settings *PivotTable* option that controls how data is summarized and calculated in the table.

value Number that you type in a cell for amounts, currency, dates, and percentages.

variable cells Identified cells *Solver* changes in order to reach the desired result in the objective cell; also referred to as *decision cells* or *changing cells*.

VBA User Forms Special forms that allow use of specific *ActiveX* controls that cannot be used in regular forms.

Visual Basic Editor (VBE) Application that runs in a separate window from Excel; used to edit a macro or the *VBA* of a program.

Visual Basic for Application (VBA) Programming language used in macro creation that allows you to expand the abilities of Excel.

W

Warning Warning that appears when a user is allowed to make an entry; allows the user to complete, edit, or retry the task. An exclamation point (!) in a yellow triangle displays in the message box.

Watch Window Method used to monitor changes in formulas in large worksheets or in multiple sheets.

Windows desktop Working area in Windows.

Windows Start page Opening area of Windows where you select and open programs or apps.

Word Web App Online Word application.

WordArt Graphic object that visually enhances text.

workbook Complete Excel file including all of its worksheets.

worksheet Individual sheet within a workbook—also referred to as a sheet; comparable to a page in a book.

worksheet tab Area near the bottom left of the Excel window that displays the name of the worksheet.

wrap text Formatting tool that enables you to display the contents of a cell on multiple lines.

X

XML map Tree hierarchy of tags and other elements from the source XML file.

Z

zipped (compressed) folder Folder that has a reduced file size and can be attached to an email.

zoom Change file display size.

index

Symbols

- (subtraction) operator, E2-89
/ (division) operator, E2-89
+ (addition) operator, E2-89
= (equal to) operator, E2-101
= (equals sign), E2-79, E2-93, E6-305
! (exclamation point), in Apps pane, E10-548, E10-551
$ (dollar sign), in absolute cell addresses, E2-83
& operator, concatenating data, E6-333
( ) (parentheses). *See* parentheses ( )
* (multiplication) operator, E2-89
^ (caret symbol), for an exponent, E2-90
^ (exponent) operator, E2-89
< (less than) operator, E2-101
<= (less than or equal to) operator, E2-101
<> (not equal to) operator, E2-101
> (greater than) operator, E2-101
>= (greater than or equal to) operator, E2-101, E8-468, E8-476

Numbers

2-D or 3-D pie types, gallery of, E3-157
2-D Pie chart subtype, E3-168
3-D cell references, E2-83, E2-88, E2-92
3-D charts, described, E3-146
3-D pie chart, creating, E3-158
3-D Pie PivotChart, adding, E4-244, E4-248
3-D reference formulas, E5-255
3-D shading box, E7-394, E7-417, E7-418, E7-421
3-D shadow, applying, E7-386

A

A to Z button, E4-205, E4-206
ABS function, E6-323
absolute cell references, E2-83
  adding to an existing formula, E2-98
  copying formulas with, E2-84–E2-85
  creating and copying formulas using, E2-91–E2-92
  in AND or OR functions, E6-309
  macros recorded with, E9-495, E9-507
  nested MATCH and INDEX function syntax with, E6-367
.accdb extension, E4-189
Accept or Reject Changes dialog box, E7-400

Accept or Reject dialog box, E7-408, E7-414
Access
  database files, E4-189–E4-190
  importing a table from, E4-234
Account area, on Backstage view, E10-546
account options, in Office 2013, E10-545
Account settings link, opening Account area on Backstage view, E10-545
Accounting formatting, applying, E6-359
Accounting Number format, E8-462, E8-463
Accounting Number Format button, E1-25
Accounting numeric formatting, applying, E2-121
active cell, E1-6
ActiveX controls, E7-387–E7-388
Add a service drop-down list, E10-546–E10-547, E10-550
Add button, E10-575
Add Chart Element, displaying data labels, E3-145
Add Chart Elements button, E3-142
Add Constraint dialog box, E8-434, E8-441, E8-468, E8-476
Add Scenario dialog box, E8-437, E8-440, E8-471, E8-477
Add Shape button, E5-282
Add subtotal to list box, E4-218
Add to Print Area, E1-51
Add Trendline dialog box, E3-145
add-ins, E8-432, E10-539
addition (+) operator, E2-89
addition formula, E2-89, E2-90
  copying, E2-91
  creating, E2-116
  entering, E2-91
  linking workbooks with, E5-263–E5-264
adjacent cells, selecting, E1-10
adjacent sheets, selecting, E5-273
Advanced button, E4-212, E4-217, E4-237
Advanced category, of Excel Options dialog box, E10-538–E10-539
Advanced Filter, E4-211
  creating, E4-212, E4-236–E4-237
  criteria range for, E4-236
  running, E4-217
Advanced Properties option, E1-43
Advanced tab, of Share Workbook dialog box, E7-398
algorithm, selecting in Solver, E8-434
alignment, of information in a cell, E1-8

B

L

label, defined, E1-6
Label Options button, E3-152, E3-175
Landscape, selecting, E1-45
Landscape radio button, under Orientation, E1-60, E1-63
Language category, of Excel Options dialog box, E10-538
language settings, in Office, E10-538
launcher, opening Format Cells dialog box, E1-21
Layout group, on PivotTable Tools Design tab, E8-448
legend, E3-142, E3-157
Legend Options button, E3-155, E3-157
less than (<) operator, E2-101
Less Than dialog box, E4-219
"Less Than" Highlight Cells Rule, creating, E4-219
less than or equal to (<=) operator, E2-101
Limits report
   selecting, E8-442
   in Solver, E8-436
line and area combination, E3-159
line and column combination, E3-159
line chart sheet, creating, E3-175–E3-176
line chart type, E3-135
Line Sparkline button, E3-177
Line with Markers PivotChart, E4-239
Linearity report, noting linear conditions not satisfied, E8-435
Link to group website area, E10-563, E10-574
linked formula, copying, E5-266
Linked Pictures paste option, E1-14
linking workbooks, E2-88, E5-261–E5-264
List range, E4-237
List range text box, E4-212, E4-217
List view, in SkyDrive, E10-553
Live Preview
   for chart elements, E3-148
   redrawing chart, E3-137
   for shape fill, E3-149
live.com, creating a free account at, E10-545, E10-551
Loan Amortization Schedule, E2-101
loan payment amounts, calculating, E2-99
Location Range box, E3-161, E3-164, E3-170, E3-177
Locked cell property, E4-223
Locked check box, E7-395
Locked property, E4-224, E4-239
Logical button, E6-308, E6-312, E6-316, E6-317, E6-319, E6-349
logical functions, E6-307, E6-310
logical_test argument, E2-101, E2-102
Logical_test argument text box, E2-103
Logical1 argument box, E6-316
LogicalN argument, E6-307

Lookup & Reference button, E6-320, E6-321, E6-325, E6-326
Lookup formula, nesting, E7-394
LOOKUP functions, E2-103–E2-106, E6-319
lookup_array argument, E6-321, E6-327
lookup_value argument, E6-321, E6-327
LP Simplex, solving a linear problem, E8-434

M

macro(s)
   assigning to a Button, E9-499–E9-501
   assigning to a form control, E7-385
   defined, E9-492
   editing in Visual Basic Editor (VBE), E9-501–E9-504, E9-520, E9-524
   enabling, E9-493, E9-512
   executing, E9-494
   including similar lines and coding, E9-503
   issues and solutions, E9-503–E9-504
   library of, E9-497
   linking a form control to, E7-385
   naming, E9-495
   recording, E9-495–E9-497, E9-507–E9-508, E9-510, E9-515–E9-516, E9-517, E9-518–E9-519, E9-522–E9-523
   running, E9-493–E9-494, E9-498, E9-512, E9-518
   security settings for, E9-493
   testing, E9-510, E9-518
macro code, editing in Visual Basic Editor (VBE), E9-503
Macro dialog box, E9-494, E9-503
Macro name box, E9-496, E9-508, E9-510, E9-515, E9-518, E9-522
Macro Security button, E9-493, E9-498, E9-515, E9-517, E9-522
Macro Settings pane, in Trust Center, E9-493
macro-enabled workbooks, saving macros in, E9-497
Macros button, E9-494, E9-498, E9-503, E9-520
macros-only workbook, E9-495, E9-496, E9-508
MAD calculation. *See* mean absolute deviation (MAD)
main chart title, positioning, E3-143
Make Unconstrained Variables Non-Negative box, E8-434, E8-441, E8-468, E8-476
malicious code, macros targets for, E9-493
malware, macros targets for, E9-493
Manage button, E10-568
   Copy to, E10-576
   Delete, E10-555
   Move to selecting, E10-562
   Rename, E10-580
   selecting Copy to, E10-579
Manage My Apps link, E10-548
Manage Rules command, E4-221
manual line break, entering, E1-28
manual page breaks, E1-48, E1-49

editing in Excel Web App, E10-564, E10-576, E10-580

encrypting with passwords, E7-391–E7-392, E7-396, E7-422

entering data into, E1-7

file formats, E1-5

finalizing, E1-41–E1-52

inspecting, E7-403, E7-408, E7-415

linking, E2-88, E5-261–E5-264, E5-265–E5-266, E5-297

marking as final, E7-390–E7-391

opening, E1-5–E1-6, E1-57, E10-564, E10-577

preparing for distribution, E7-402–E7-405

printing, E1-51

protecting, E7-390–E7-392, E7-399

renaming, E1-61

requirements for, E7-402

reviewing protection in, E7-396

saving, E1-3–E1-4

saving and closing, E1-16

saving as templates, E7-390, E7-395, E7-421

saving templates as, E7-389–E7-390

sharing, E7-398–E7-399, E7-406, E7-413, E10-573

sharing and merging, E7-397–E7-402

Working with formulas area, E10-536

worksheet(s), E1-3

  copying, E1-34, E4-230

  copying to another workbook, E5-284

  creating a copy of, E1-35

  customizing, E1-31–E1-34

  customizing printing, E1-49–E1-52

  deleting or inserting multiple, E1-32

  editing and formatting grouped, E5-273–E5-274, E5-277

  formatting, E1-19–E1-23

  grouping and formatting, E5-273–E5-274

  hiding, E1-52

  hiding or unhiding, E1-39–E1-40

  importing an Access table into, E4-190

  importing web data into, E4-191

  inserting and deleting, E1-32

  inserting new, E1-35

  inserting sparklines in, E3-161–E3-162

  moving and copying, E1-33–E1-34

  PivotTables as separate, E4-199

  previewing, E1-51, E1-53, E1-63

  printing, E1-51

  protecting, E4-222, E4-223–E4-225, E7-395

  protecting with passwords, E4-226, E4-239, E7-418, E7-421

  protecting without a password, E4-231

renaming, E1-32–E1-33

selecting, E1-10, E1-34

spell checking, E1-60

splitting into panes, E1-39

unlocking cells for users to edit, E7-418, E7-421

unprotecting, E4-224–E4-225

viewing multiple at the same time, E1-41

worksheet cells

  activating SmartArt graphics, E5-269

  hyperlinks usually created in, E5-269

  unlocking, E4-223–E4-224

worksheet data, editing, E1-16

worksheet tab, E1-31

worksheet title and date, merging and centering, E1-35

Wrap Text, displaying contents of a cell on multiple lines, E1-28

wrap text alignment, applying, E6-360

X

.xls extension, E1-5

.xlsm extension, E1-5, E9-493

.xlsx files, E1-5

.xltm extension, E1-5, E9-508, E9-511, E9-525

.xltx extension, E1-5, E7-390

XML (Extensible Markup Language), E8-458–E8-461

XML data, importing, E8-460–E8-461, E8-464, E8-475

.xml file name extension, E8-458

XML map, described, E8-460

XML Source task pane, E8-460, E8-461, E8-475

XML table, opening a file as, E8-460

.xsd file name extension, E8-459

XY (scatter) chart type, E3-135

Y

YouTube, adding in Connected Services area, E10-550

Z

Z to A button, E4-205, E4-206

zoom, increasing, E1-52

Zoom dialog box, E1-38

zoom level, changing, E1-63

Zoom options, E1-38

Zoom slider, in the Status bar, E1-63

Zoom to Page, adjusting zoom level, E1-51

Zoom to Selection button, E1-38